Rick Steves®

FLORENCE
& TUSCANY

Rick Steves & Gene Openshaw

CONTENTS

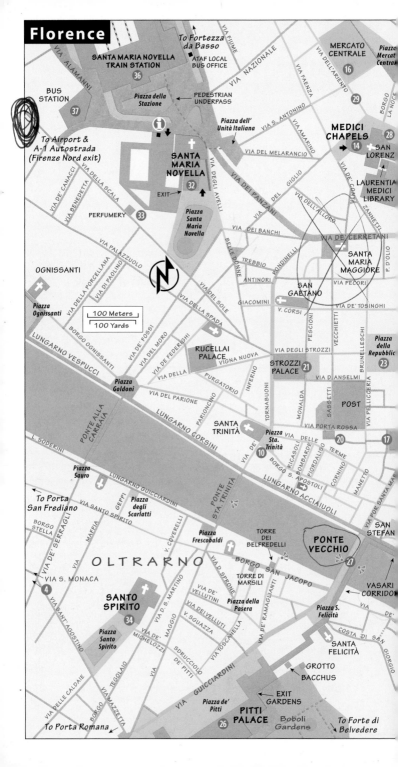

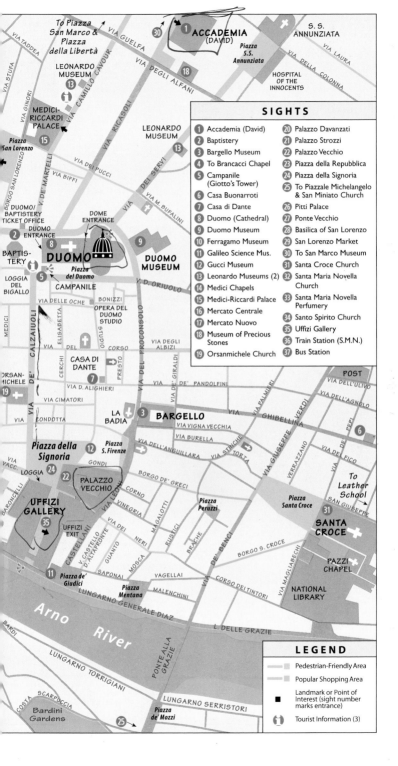

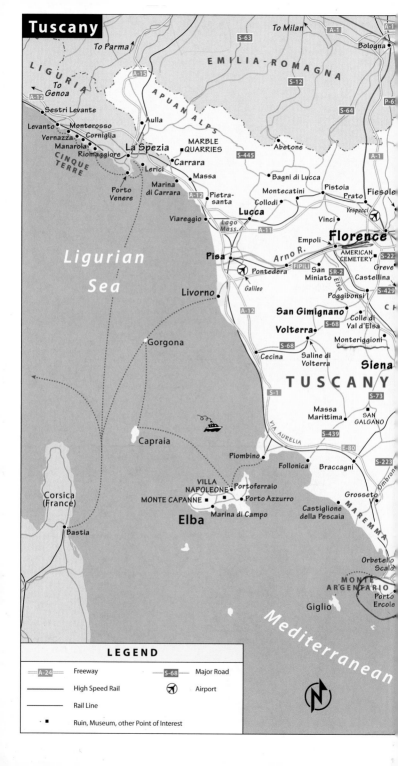

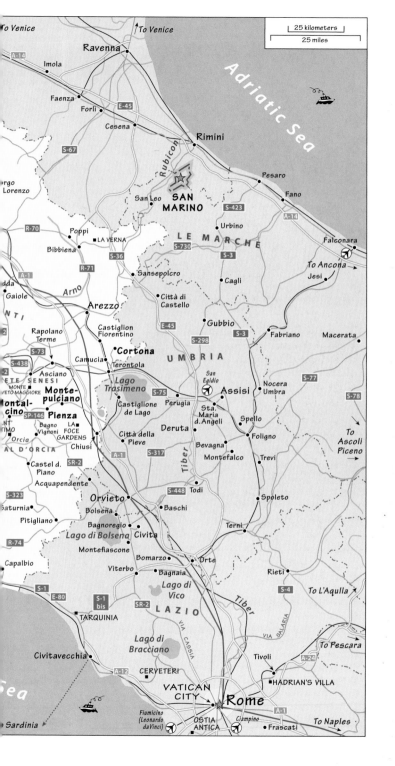

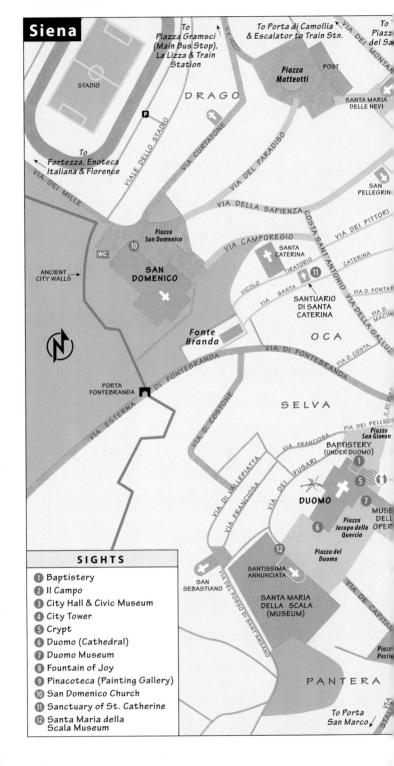

Siena

STADIO

DRAGO

To
Piazza Gramsci
(Main Bus Stop),
La Lizza & Train
Station

To Porta di Camollia
& Escalator to Train Stn.

To
Piazz
del Sa

*Piazza
Matteotti*

POST

SANTA MARIA
DELLE NEVI

VIA DEI MONTAN

VIA DELLO STADIO

VIA CURTATONE

VIA DEL PARADISO

To
Fortezza, Enoteca
Italiana & Florence

VIA DEI MILLE

VIA DELLA SAPIENZA

SAN
PELLEGRIN

VIA DEI PITTORI

VIA CAMPOREGIO

SANTA
CATERINA

COSTA SANT'ANTONIO

CATERINA

*Piazza
San Domenico*

WC

**SAN
DOMENICO**

TIRATORIO

VICOLO

VIA SANTA

VIA DELLA GALLUZ

VIA D. FONTA

VIA D.
MACIN

SANTUARIO
DI SANTA
CATERINA

ANCIENT
CITY WALLS

*Fonte
Branda*

OCA

VIA DI FONTEBRANDA

VIA D. COSTA

VIA D.

PORTA
FONTEBRANDA

DI FONTEBRANDA

VIA ESTERNA

SELVA

VIA D. COSTONE

VIA DEI PELLEG

VIA DI VALLEPIATTA

VIA FRANCIOSA

VIA FRANCIOSA

VIA DEI FUSARI

*Piazza
San Giovan*

BAPTISTERY
(UNDER DUOMO)

DUOMO

*Piazza
Jacopo della
Quercia*

MUSE
DELL
OPER

*Piazza del
Duomo*

SAN
SEBASTIANO

VIA DEI FOSSO DI SANT'ANSANO

SANTISSIMA
ANNUNCIATA

**SANTA MARIA
DELLA SCALA**
(MUSEUM)

VIA DE CAPITAN

Piazz
Postie

PANTERA

STALVIA

To Porta
San Marco

SIGHTS

1. Baptistery
2. Il Campo
3. City Hall & Civic Museum
4. City Tower
5. Crypt
6. Duomo (Cathedral)
7. Duomo Museum
8. Fountain of Joy
9. Pinacoteca (Painting Gallery)
10. San Domenico Church
11. Sanctuary of St. Catherine
12. Santa Maria della
    Scala Museum

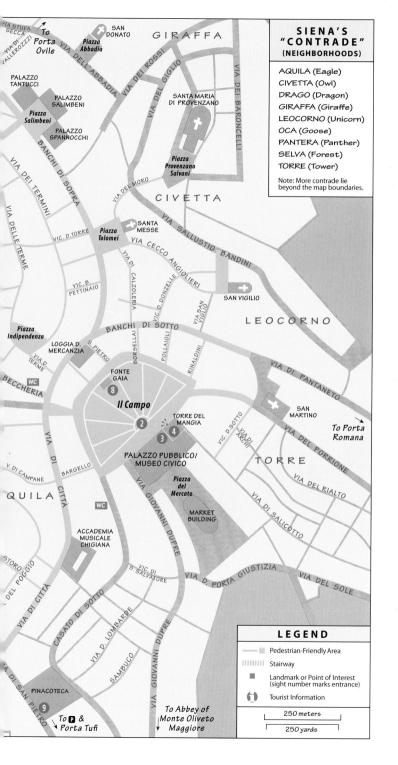

Pisa's Field of Miracles—the Duomo with its leaning Bell Tower

Tuscany—farmhouses, cypress trees, sunshine, and a timeless way of life

Michelangelo's David

Tuscan hill town

Brunelleschi's dome of the Duomo, Florence

Rick Steves®

FLORENCE

& TUSCANY

SANTA MARIA
NOVELLA

MEDICI
CHAPELS

SAN
MARCO

DAVID

BAPTISTERY

CAMPANILE

DUOMO

PALAZZO
VECCHIO

GELATO!

PONTE VECCHIO

BARGELLO

UFFIZI

BRANCACCI
CHAPEL

Arno

PITTI PALACE & GARDENS

Welcome to Rick Steves' Europe

Travel is intensified living—maximum thrills per minute and one of the last great sources of legal adventure. Travel is freedom. It's recess, and we need it.

I discovered a passion for European travel as a teen and have been sharing it ever since—through my tours, public television and radio shows, and travel guidebooks. Over the years, I've taught thousands of travelers how to best enjoy Europe's blockbuster sights—and experience "Back Door" discoveries that most tourists miss.

Written with my talented co-author, Gene Openshaw, this book offers you a balanced mix of Florence's rich cultural heritage and the romantic charm of Tuscany's time-passed villages. And it's selective—rather than listing dozens of hill towns, I recommend only the best ones. My self-guided museum tours and city walks give insight into the region's vibrant history and today's living, breathing culture.

I advocate traveling simply and smartly. Take advantage of my money- and time-saving tips on sightseeing, transportation, and more. Try local, characteristic alternatives to expensive hotels and restaurants. In many ways, spending more money only builds a thicker wall between you and what you traveled so far to see.

We visit Italy to experience it—to become temporary locals. Thoughtful travel engages us with the world, as we learn to appreciate other cultures and new ways to measure quality of life.

Judging from the positive feedback I receive from readers, this book will help you enjoy a fun, affordable, and rewarding vacation—whether it's your first trip or your 10th.

Buon viaggio! Happy travels!

Rich Steves

INTRODUCTION

Florence is Europe's cultural capital. As the home of the Renaissance and the birthplace of the modern world, Florence practiced the art of civilized living back when the rest of Europe was rural and crude. Democracy, science, and literature, as well as painting, sculpture, and architecture, were all championed by the proud and energetic Florentines of the 1400s.

When the Florentine poet Dante first saw the teenaged Beatrice, her beauty so inspired him that he spent the rest of his life writing poems to her. In the same way, the Renaissance opened people's eyes to the physical beauty of the world around them, inspiring them to write, paint, sculpt, and build.

Today, Florence is geographically small and yet it boasts more artistic masterpieces per square mile than anyplace else. In a single day, you can look Michelangelo's *David* in the eyes, fall under the seductive sway of Botticelli's *Birth of Venus*, and climb the modern world's first dome, which still dominates the skyline.

Of course, there's a reality here, too. As the historic center becomes increasingly filled with visitors, rents are rising and locals are fleeing to the suburbs, threatening to make Florence a kind of Renaissance theme park. Sure, Florence is touristy. But where else can you stroll the same pedestrian streets walked by Michelangelo, Leonardo, and Botticelli while savoring the world's best gelato?

To round out your visit, see Florence and then escape to the Tuscan countryside. With its manicured fields, rustic farms, cypress-lined driveways, and towns clinging to nearly every hill, Tuscany is our romantic image of village Italy. Venture beyond the fringes of Florence and you'll find a series of sun- and wine-soaked villages, each with its own appeal. Stretching from the Umbrian border to the Ligurian Sea, the landscape changes from pastoral

(Crete Senesi) to rocky (Chianti) to mountainous (the Montagnola) to flat and brushed with sea breezes (Pisa).

Each of Tuscany's villages seems to have its own claim to fame: Volterra (Etruscan ruins), San Gimignano (towers), Montepulciano (artisans), Montalcino (wine), Pienza (tidy Renaissance-planned streets), and so on. But Tuscany also has a variety of intriguing cities that fully engage even the most restless traveler. Siena huddles around one of Italy's coziest squares and finest cathedrals. Pisa boasts the famous Field of Miracles (with its Leaning Tower, an icon of all Italy) and a gritty working-class-meets-university-town bustle. And Lucca is graced with churches, towers, and a delightful city wall-turned-city park that's ideal for a stroll or pedal.

You'll discover that peaceful Tuscan villages and bustling Florence—with its rough-stone beauty, art-packed museums, children chasing pigeons, students riding Vespas, artisans sipping Chianti, and supermodels wearing Gucci—offer many of the very things you came to Italy to see.

ABOUT THIS BOOK

Rick Steves Florence & Tuscany is a personal tour guide in your pocket. Actually, thanks to my friend and co-author Gene Openshaw, it's two tour guides in your pocket. Since our first "Europe through the gutter" trip together as high school buddies in the 1970s, Gene and I have been exploring the wonders of the Old World. An inquisitive historian and lover of European culture, Gene wrote most of this book's self-guided museum tours and neighborhood walks. Together, Gene and I keep this book up-to-date and accurate (though for simplicity, from this point we've shed our respective egos to become "I").

In this book, you'll find the following chapters:

Orientation to Florence has specifics on public transportation, helpful hints, local tour options, easy-to-read maps, and tourist information. The "Planning Your Time" section suggests a schedule for how to best use your limited time.

Sights in Florence describes the top attractions and includes their cost and hours.

The **Self-Guided Walks & Tours** take you through the core of Renaissance Florence, including Michelangelo's *David*, the artistic wonders of the Uffizi Gallery, the massive Duomo, and the back lanes of the Oltrarno neighborhood. Farther afield, in Tuscany, my tours cover sights from Siena's Duomo to Pisa's Leaning Tower.

Sleeping in Florence describes my favorite hotels, from good-value deals to cushy splurges.

Eating in Florence serves up a buffet of options, from inexpensive cafés to fancy restaurants.

Florence with Children includes my top recommendations for keeping your kids (and you) happy.

Shopping in Florence gives you tips for shopping painlessly and enjoyably, without letting it overwhelm your vacation or ruin your budget.

Nightlife in Florence is your guide to after-dark fun, including concerts, theaters, pubs, and clubs.

Florence Connections lays the groundwork for your smooth arrival and departure, covering transportation by train, bus, car, cruise ship, and plane (with information on Florence's Amerigo Vespucci Airport).

Tuscany introduces you to the countryside destinations beyond Florence.

The **Siena** chapter covers the highlights in this captivating Gothic city, from the stay-awhile central piazza to the 13th-century cathedral.

The **Pisa** chapter takes you beyond the Leaning Tower.

The **Lucca** chapter explores the charms of this little-touristed, well-preserved city.

Three chapters on Tuscan hill towns—**Volterra & San Gimignano, The Heart of Tuscany** (Montepulciano, Pienza, and Montalcino), and **Cortona**—bring you the best of village Italy.

The **Florentine & Tuscan History** chapter takes you on a whirlwind tour through the ages, covering two millennia, from ancient Tuscany to the present.

The **Practicalities** chapter near the end of this book is a traveler's tool kit, with my best advice about money, sightseeing, sleeping, eating, staying connected, and transportation (trains, buses, driving, and flights).

The **appendix** has the nuts-and-bolts: useful phone numbers and websites, a holiday and festival list, recommended books and films, a climate chart, a handy packing checklist, and Italian survival phrases.

Throughout this book, you'll find money- and time-saving tips for sightseeing, transportation, and more. Some businesses—especially hotels and walking-tour companies—offer special discounts to my readers, indicated in their listings.

Browse through this book, choose your favorite destinations, and link them up. Then have a *fantastico* trip! Traveling like a temporary local, you'll get the absolute most out of every mile, minute, and dollar. As you visit places I know and love, I'm happy that you'll be meeting some of my favorite Florentines.

Planning

This section will help you get started planning your trip—with advice on trip costs, when to go, and what you should know before you take off.

TRIP COSTS

Six components make up your total trip cost: airfare to Europe, transportation in Europe, room and board, sightseeing and entertainment, shopping and miscellany, and gelato.

Airfare to Europe: A basic, round-trip flight from the US to Florence can cost about $1,000-2,000 on average, depending on where you fly from and when (cheaper in winter or sometimes if flying into Pisa, Milan, or Rome). If Florence is part of a longer trip, consider saving time and money in Europe by flying into one city and out of another (for instance, into Florence and out of Paris). Overall, Kayak.com is the best place to start searching for international flights.

Transportation in Europe: Most of Florence's sights, clustered in the downtown core, are within easy walking distance of each other. If you'd rather use taxis than walk, allow at least $80-100 over the course of a one-week visit (taxis can be shared by up to four people). Round-trip, second-class train transportation to recommended nearby destinations is affordable (about $11 by train or bus to Pisa, Siena, or San Gimignano). For a one-way trip between Florence's airport and the city center, allow $8 by bus or $30 by taxi. The other cities and villages covered in this book are made for walking. For more on public transportation and car rental, see "Transportation" in Practicalities.

Room and Board: You can thrive in Tuscany on $135 a day per person for room and board. This allows $15 for lunch, $35 for dinner, and $85 for lodging (based on two people splitting the cost of a $170 double room that includes breakfast). Students and tightwads can enjoy Tuscany for as little as $65 a day ($30 for a bed, $35 for meals and snacks).

Sightseeing and Entertainment: Consider the Firenze Card, which covers many sights in the city (see page 30). Otherwise, figure about $20 for major sights (Michelangelo's *David*, Uffizi Gallery), $5-10 for minor ones (museums, palaces), and $35-50 for splurge experiences (such as walking tours and concerts). An overall average of $40 a day works for most people. Don't skimp here. After all, this category is the driving force behind your trip—you came to sightsee, enjoy, and experience Florence.

Shopping and Miscellany: Figure $3 per postcard, coffee, soft drink, or gelato. Shopping can vary in cost from nearly noth-

Tuscany at a Glance

▲▲▲**Florence** Art-packed, bustling city—starring Michelangelo's *David,* Renaissance paintings, and Brunelleschi's dome—with Ponte Vecchio spanning the flood-prone Arno River.

▲▲▲**Siena** Red-brick hilltop city known for its pageantry, Palio horse race, and a stunning traffic-free main square—great anytime but best after dark. It's also a fine home base for exploring the Tuscan countryside with a driving tour of the Crete Senesi.

▲▲▲**Heart of Tuscany** Picturesque, wine-soaked villages of Italy's heartland—including mellow Montepulciano, Renaissance Pienza, and Brunello-fueled Montalcino—and jaw-dropping scenery best seen on a driving tour (I've outlined two: the region's heart and the Brunello wine country).

▲▲**Pisa** A city more famous for its iconic Leaning Tower than for its other equally impressive monuments on the gleaming white Field of Miracles.

▲▲**Lucca** Charming city with a lively (and flat) town center, ringed by intact old walls wide enough for biking and strolling.

▲▲**Volterra** Just far enough off the beaten path, surrounded by thick walls and hilly scenery, with a long Etruscan history and unusually interesting sightseeing for a small town.

▲**San Gimignano** Epitome of a hill town, spiked with medieval towers offering superb views, popular with tourists who crowd the narrow alleys by day.

Cortona Hillside town under the Tuscan sun, with historic churches and museums featuring Etruscan and Renaissance artifacts and art.

ing to a small fortune. Good budget travelers find that this category has little to do with assembling a trip full of lifelong memories.

WHEN TO GO

Tuscany's best travel months (also its busiest and most expensive) are April, May, June, September, and October. These months combine the conveniences of peak season with pleasant weather.

The most grueling thing about travel in Tuscany is the summer heat in July and August, when temperatures hit the high 80s and 90s. Most midrange hotels come with air-conditioning—a

Florence Almanac

Population: Approximately 360,000 people

Currency: Euro

City Layout: Florence is the capital of Tuscany and lies on the Arno River. It's divided into five administrative wards: the Historic Center, Campo di Marte, Gavinana, Isolotto, and Rifredi.

Best Viewpoints: Piazzale Michelangelo (and San Miniato Church, above it) overlooks the city and the Duomo from across the river, as does the top of the Boboli Gardens. For other panoramic views of Florence, climb the Campanile or the Duomo's dome (next to each other) or the tower at the Palazzo Vecchio. If you like your beverage with a view, try a rooftop café (see page 297).

Sweetest Festival: In spring, the city hosts an annual gelato festival, featuring tastings and demonstrations by gelato makers from all over Italy (www.gelatofestival.it).

Tourist Tracks: Tourism in Florence and Tuscany is booming. Each year, nearly two million tourists flock to the Uffizi Gallery to gaze at Botticelli's *Birth of Venus.*

Culture Count: A little over 90 percent of Florence's population is indigenously Italian and Roman Catholic. Immigrant groups are mostly European (3.5 percent) and East Asian (2 percent), with small percentages of North and South Americans and Northern Africans.

Famous Florentines: Florence, birthplace of the Renaissance, bred many great minds, including Michelangelo, Leonardo, Donatello, Brunelleschi, Machiavelli, Dante, and...Florence Nightingale, whose English parents named her after the city in which she was born.

Average Florentine: The average Florentine is 49 years old (7 years older than the average Italian) and will live to be 82.

worthwhile splurge in the summer—but it's often available only from June through September. August is vacation time for Italians, with cities emptying out for a week before and two weeks after the August 15 Ferragosto holiday (marking the Assumption of Mary). City hotels consider this period low season.

In April and October, you'll generally need a sweater or light jacket in the evening. In winter the temperatures can drop to the 40s or 50s (for more specifics, see the climate chart in the appendix). Off-season has none of the sweat and stress of the tourist season, but sights may have shorter hours, lunchtime breaks, and fewer activities. Confirm your sightseeing plans locally, especially when traveling off-season.

Before You Go

You'll have a smoother trip if you tackle a few things ahead of time. For more information on these topics, see the Practicalities chapter (and www.ricksteves.com, which has helpful travel tips and talks).

Make sure your passport is valid. If it's due to expire within six months of your ticketed date of return, you need to renew it. Allow up to six weeks to renew or get a passport (www.travel.state. gov).

Arrange your transportation. Book your international flights. You won't want a car in congested Florence (driving is prohibited in parts of the city center—if you drive in restricted areas, you can be fined without the police ever stopping you). If you'll be touring the countryside, figure out your main form of transportation: train, bus, or rental car. (You can wing it in Europe, but it may cost more.) Drivers: Consider bringing an International Driving Permit (sold at AAA offices in the US, www.aaa.com) along with your license.

Book rooms well in advance, especially if your trip falls during peak season or any major holidays or festivals.

Reserve or buy tickets ahead for major sights, saving you from long ticket-buying lines. Or, **buy a Firenze Card in Florence** to avoid standing in long lines for the Uffizi (Renaissance paintings) and Accademia (Michelangelo's *David*). The Uffizi is often booked up a month or more in advance, while the Accademia is usually full at least a few days out. Also make reservations to climb the dome of the Duomo. Reservations are explained on page 34, and the Firenze Card on page 30.

Consider travel insurance. Compare the cost of the insurance to the cost of your potential loss. Check whether your existing insurance (health, homeowners, or renters) covers you and your possessions overseas.

Call your bank. Alert your bank that you'll be using your debit and credit cards in Europe. Ask about transaction fees, and get the PIN number for your credit card. You don't need to bring euros for your trip; you can withdraw euros from cash machines in Europe.

Use your smartphone smartly. Sign up for an international service plan to reduce your costs, or rely on Wi-Fi in Europe instead. Download any apps you'll want on the road, such as maps, translation, transit schedules, and Rick Steves Audio Europe (see sidebar).

Pack light. You'll walk with your luggage more than you think. I travel for weeks with a single carry-on bag and a daypack. Use the packing checklist in the appendix as a guide.

🎧 Stick This Guidebook in Your Ear! 🎧

My free Rick Steves Audio Europe app makes it easy for you to download my audio tours of many of Europe's top attractions and listen to them offline during your travels. In this book, these include my **Renaissance Walk** and tours of the **Accademia, Uffizi Gallery, Bargello,** and **Museum of San Marco** in Florence, and my **City Walk** in Siena. Sights covered by audio tours are marked in this book with this symbol: 🎧. The app also offers insightful travel interviews from my public radio show with experts from Italy and around the globe. It's all free! You can download the app via Apple's App Store, Google Play, or Amazon's Appstore. For more info, see www.ricksteves.com/audioeurope.

Travel Smart

Many people travel through Italy thinking it's a chaotic mess. They feel that any attempt at efficient travel is futile. This is dead wrong—and expensive. Italy, which seems as orderly as spilled spaghetti, actually functions quite well. If you equip yourself with good information (this book) and expect to travel smart, you will.

Read—and reread—this book. To have an "A" trip, be an "A" student. As you study up on sights, note opening hours, closed days, crowd-beating tips, and whether reservations are required or advisable. Check the latest at www.ricksteves.com/update. Saving Michelangelo's *David* for your trip finale is risky, and impossible on Mondays, when Florence's major sights are closed. If you visit Siena as a short day trip, you'll miss the city's medieval magic at twilight.

Be your own tour guide. As you travel, get up-to-date info on sights, reserve tickets and tours, reconfirm hotels and travel arrangements, and check transit connections. Visit local tourist information offices (TIs). Upon arrival in a new town, lay the groundwork for a smooth departure; confirm the train, bus, or road you'll take when you leave.

Outsmart thieves. Pickpockets abound in crowded places where tourists congregate. Treat commotions as smokescreens for theft. Keep your cash, credit cards, and passport secure in a money belt tucked under your clothes; carry only a day's spending money in your front pocket. Don't set valuable items down on counters or café tabletops, where they can be quickly stolen or easily forgotten.

Minimize potential loss. Keep expensive gear to a minimum.

Bring photocopies or take photos of important documents (passport and cards) to aid in replacement if they're lost or stolen.

Beat the summer heat. If you wilt easily, choose a hotel with air-conditioning, start your day early, take a midday siesta at your hotel, and resume your sightseeing later. Churches offer a cool haven (though dress modestly—no bare shoulders or shorts). Take frequent gelato breaks. Join the *passeggiata*, when locals stroll in the cool of the evening.

Guard your time and energy. Taking a taxi can be a good value if it saves you a long wait for a cheap bus or an exhausting walk across town. To avoid long lines, follow my crowd-beating tips, such as making advance reservations, or sightseeing early or late. Make your itinerary a mix of intense and relaxed stretches. To maximize rootedness in Tuscany, minimize one-night stands. It's worth taking a long drive after dinner to be settled in a town for two nights. Every trip—and every traveler—needs slack time (laundry, picnics, people-watching, and so on). Pace yourself.

Be flexible. Even if you have a well-planned itinerary, expect changes, strikes, closures, sore feet, bad weather, and so on. Your Plan B could turn out to be even better.

Attempt the language. Many Italians—especially in the tourist trade and in cities—speak English, but if you learn some Italian, even just a few phrases, you'll get more smiles and make more friends. Practice the survival phrases near the end of this book, and even better, bring a phrase book.

Connect with the culture. Interacting with locals carbonates your experience. Enjoy the friendliness of the Italian people. Ask questions; most locals are happy to point you in their idea of the right direction. Set up your own quest for the best gelato, piazza, *enoteca* (wine bar), or Renaissance painting or sculpture. Slow down and be open to unexpected experiences. When an opportunity pops up, make it a habit to say "yes."

Italy...here you come!

FLORENCE
Firenze

ORIENTATION TO FLORENCE

The best of Florence lies on the north bank of the Arno River. The main historical sights cluster around the venerable dome of the cathedral (Duomo). Everything is within a 20-minute walk of the train station, cathedral, or Ponte Vecchio (Old Bridge). The less famous but more characteristic Oltrarno area (south bank) is just over the bridge.

Though small, Florence is intense. Prepare for scorching summer heat, crowded narrow lanes and sidewalks, slick pickpockets, few WCs, steep prices, and long lines. Easy tourist money has corrupted some locals, making them greedy and dishonest (check your bill carefully).

FLORENCE: A VERBAL MAP

For a big and touristy city, Florence (pop. 380,000) is remarkably compact and easy to navigate. Most of the attractions lie just north of the Arno River, clustered in distinct zones. Here's a neighborhood-by-neighborhood rundown of the city:

Historic Core: The Duomo—with its iconic, towering dome—is the visual, geographical, and historical center of Florence. A 10-minute walk away is the Palazzo Vecchio (city hall), with its skyscraping medieval spire. Connecting these two landmarks is the north-south pedestrian street called Via de' Calzaiuoli. This central axis—Duomo to the Palazzo Vecchio to the Arno River—is the spine for Florentine sightseeing and the route of my self-guided Renaissance Walk. Via de' Calzaiuoli also links two central piazzas—Piazza della Repubblica and Piazza della Signoria (fronting the Uffizi Gallery). To the west of this axis is a glitzy shopping zone, and to the east is a characteristic web of narrow lanes.

Accademia/San Lorenzo (North of the Duomo): The area

north of the Duomo is less atmospheric but has several crucial sights. From the Duomo, Via Cavour runs north, bisecting the neighborhood. To the east lies the Accademia (Michelangelo's *David*) and the Museum of San Marco. The western part clusters around the Basilica of San Lorenzo, with its Medici Chapels. The area near San Lorenzo teems with tourists: There are the vendor stalls of San Lorenzo Market, the lively Mercato Centrale, and many hotels and trattorias that cater to out-of-towners—convenient, if not fully authentic.

Train Station/Santa Maria Novella (West of the Duomo): The area near the train station and Church of Santa Maria Novella is somewhat urban and dreary, but has inexpensive hotels and characteristic eateries. Closer to the river (near Palazzo Strozzi) is a posh shopping zone, with a more affordable mix of shops lining Via del Parione and Borgo Ognissanti.

Santa Croce (East of the Duomo): A 10-minute walk east from the Palazzo Vecchio leads to the neighborhood's main landmark, the Church of Santa Croce. Along the way is the Bargello sculpture museum. The area stretching north and west from Santa Croce is increasingly authentic and workaday, offering a glimpse at untouristy Florence.

Oltrarno (South of the River): Literally the "Other Side of the Arno River," this neighborhood reveals a Florence from a time before tourism. Many artisans still have workshops here, and open their doors to passing visitors. The Oltrarno starts just across Ponte Vecchio (jammed with tourists and tackiness) and stretches south to the giant Pitti Palace and surrounding gardens (Boboli and Bardini). To the west is the rough-but-bohemian Piazza di Santo Spirito (with its namesake church) and the lavishly frescoed Brancacci Chapel. To the east of Pitti, perched high on the hill, is Piazzale Michelangelo, with Florence's most popular viewpoint. Tucked between there and the river is the funky little San Niccolò neighborhood, with its lively bars and eateries.

Farther Out: Everything mentioned above is within about a 30-minute walk of the Duomo. To venture farther, one popular choice is the adjacent hilltop town of Fiesole, easily reached by public bus or taxi, with its archaeological sites and fine views.

PLANNING YOUR TIME

Set up a good itinerary in advance. Get the latest opening hours from the TI. Use the "Daily Reminder" (see page 22) to plan which sights are open on which days. In general, Sundays and Mondays are not ideal for sightseeing, as many places are either closed or have shorter hours. Sights may also have shorter hours off-season. On the first Sunday of the month, many museums

ORIENTATION

Florence Overview

To
Museum of
San Marco

CAVOUR

RICASOLI

MERCATO
CENTRALE

SAN
LORENZO

ACCADEMIA
(DAVID)

S.M.N.
TRAIN
STN.

CERRETANI

DUOMO
MUSEUM

SANTA MARIA
NOVELLA

DUOMO

VIA DE'
CALZAIUOLI

RITZY
SHOPPING
ZONE

Piazza
della
Repubblica

BARGELLO

PALAZZO
VECCHIO

AREA OF ANCIENT
ROMAN TOWN →

Piazza
della
Signoria

UFFIZI

SANTA
CROCE

PONTE
VECCHIO

LUNGARNO

BRANCACCI
CHAPEL

OLTRARNO

Arno River

GUICCIARDINI

SANTO
SPIRITO

PITTI
PALACE

SAN NICOLO

To
Piazzale
Michelangelo

Not to Scale

Boboli
Gardens

are free (yay!), but unfortunately that can make them impossibly crowded.

Most importantly, use my strategies to avoid wasting hours in long lines. This is especially true for peak season (April-Oct), holidays and weekends, and for the big attractions—the Uffizi Gallery and Accademia (starring Michelangelo's *David*). To avoid these lines, either buy a skip-the-line **Firenze Card** (see page 30) or **make reservations** (see page 34).

The following day plans are jam-packed but doable if you're well-organized. With more time, spread out these priorities to give yourself some breathing room. However you plan your visit, do my Renaissance Walk either in the morning or late afternoon to avoid heat and crowds.

Florence in One Brutal Day

8:15   Uffizi Gallery (finest paintings)—with Firenze Card or a reservation.

10:00   Take Renaissance Walk through town center.

12:00   Bargello (great statues) or Duomo Museum (great bronze work).

13:30   Grab a quick lunch in or near Mercato Centrale.

14:00   Shopping at San Lorenzo Market (or elsewhere).

17:30 Accademia *(David)*—with Firenze Card or a
reservation.

19:30 Cross Ponte Vecchio and take the Oltrarno Walk
(best local color) and have dinner across the river at
21:00.

Florence in Two Days
Day 1

8:30 Accademia *(David)*—with Firenze Card or a
reservation.

10:00 Museum of San Marco (art by Fra Angelico).

12:00 Explore Mercato Centrale and have lunch.

14:00 Medici Chapels (Michelangelo sculptures).

16:00 Visit Duomo interior and/or the Baptistery.

17:30 Renaissance Walk through heart of old town.

20:00 Dinner in the old center or tour the Palazzo Vecchio
(open many evenings until 23:00).

Day 2

9:00 Bargello (great statues). ✗

10:30 Duomo Museum (statues by Donatello and
Michelangelo) or the Galileo Science Museum (if art's
not your thing).

12:30 Lunch, then wander and shop.

14:00 Take a bike or walking tour.

16:30 Uffizi Gallery (finest paintings)—with Firenze Card
or a reservation.

19:00 Cross Ponte Vecchio for the Oltrarno Walk.

21:00 Dinner in Oltrarno.

Florence in Three (or More) Days
Day 1

8:30 Accademia *(David)*—with Firenze Card or a
reservation.

10:00 Museum of San Marco (Fra Angelico).

ORIENTATION

12:00	Explore San Lorenzo Market area, shop, and have lunch in or near Mercato Centrale.
14:00	Medici Chapels (Michelangelo) and Basilica of San Lorenzo.
16:00	Baptistery, Duomo interior, or climb the dome or Campanile.
17:00	Renaissance Walk through heart of old town.
19:00	Explore and shop the Piazza della Signoria/Ponte Vecchio area.
20:00	Dinner in the old center.

Day 2

9:00	Bargello (great statues).
11:00	Duomo Museum or Galileo Science Museum (if you prefer science to art).
13:00	Lunch, then wander and shop.
15:30	Uffizi Gallery (finest paintings)—with Firenze Card or a reservation.
18:00	Cross Ponte Vecchio, take the Oltrarno Walk, and have dinner in Oltrarno.

Day 3

9:00	Whatever you didn't get to yesterday morning (Duomo Museum or Galileo).
13:00	Lunch and time to shop, relax, or get to any sights you haven't seen yet (you could circle back to the daytime Oltrarno sights—Brancacci Chapel and the Pitti Palace—or tour the Church of Santa Maria Novella, near the train station).
16:00	San Miniato Church (Gregorian chants generally at 17:30), Piazzale Michelangelo (city views), walk back into town.

Day 4

Side-trip to Siena (sights open daily; 1.5 hours away by bus), or consider an overnight stay to enjoy the town at twilight.

Overview

TOURIST INFORMATION

The city TI's crowded main branch is across the square from the **train station** (Mon-Sat 9:00-19:00, Sun until 14:00; at the back corner of the Church of Santa Maria Novella at Piazza della Stazione 4; tel. 055-212-245, www.firenzeturismo.it). For help you'll need to take a number from the touch-screen computer by the door. Upstairs, the "Experience Florence" visitors center has big touch screens to virtually explore the city, and a well-produced 3-D movie of the big landmarks (free, 13 minutes, English subtitles).

A smaller branch is centrally located **next to the Duomo,** at the west corner of Via de' Calzaiuoli (inside the Loggia, same hours as train station branch, tel. 055-288-496).

The least crowded and most helpful TI (covering both the city and the greater province of Florence) is a couple of blocks **north of the Duomo,** just past the Medici-Riccardi Palace (Mon-Fri 9:00-13:00, closed Sat-Sun, Via Cavour 1 red, tel. 055-290-832). There's also a TI at the **airport.**

Most TIs sell the **Firenze Card,** an expensive but handy sightseeing pass that allows you to skip the lines at top museums (see page 30).

At any TI, you can pick up a city map and handout with the latest opening hours. For information on goings-on around town, pick up the monthly *Florence & Tuscany News,* and check *The Florentine* newspaper, which has great articles with cultural insights (in English, published monthly and updated online every other Thu at www.theflorentine.net), along with the similar *Florence Is You* (www.florenceisyou.com).

ARRIVAL IN FLORENCE

For a rundown on Florence's train station, bus station, airport, and cruise ship arrival at the Livorno port, see the Florence Connections chapter.

HELPFUL HINTS

Theft Alert: Florence has hardworking gangs of thieves who hang out near the train station, the station's underpass (especially where the tunnel surfaces), and at major sights. American tourists are considered easy targets. Some thieves even dress like tourists to fool you. Any crowded bus likely holds at least one thief.

Also beware of the "slow count": Cashiers may count change back with odd pauses in hopes you'll gather up the money early and say, *"Grazie."*

Medical Help: To reach a doctor who speaks English, call **Medical Service Firenze** (tel. 055-475-411, www.medicalservice. firenze.it); the phone is answered 24/7. You can have a doctor come to your hotel within an hour of your call, or go to the clinic when the doctor's in (Mon-Sat 11:00-12:00 & 13:00-15:00 plus Mon-Fri 17:00-18:00, closed Sun, no appointment necessary, Via Roma 4, between the Duomo and Piazza della Repubblica).

Dr. Stephen Kerr is an English doctor specializing in helping sick tourists (drop-in clinic open Mon-Fri 15:00-

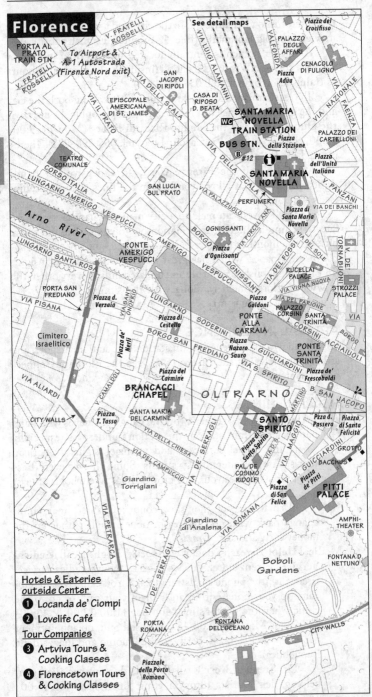

Florence

See detail maps

Piazza del Crocifisso

PORTA AL PRATO TRAIN STN.

V. FRATELLI ROSSELLI

V. FRATELLI ROSSELLI

To Airport & A-1 Autostrada (Firenze Nord exit)

VIA DELLA SCALA

SAN JACOPO DI RIPOLI

V. LUIGI ALAMANNI

V. VALFONDA

PALAZZO DEGLI AFFARI

CENACOLO DI FULIGNO

VIA NAZIONALE

VIA FAENZA

EPISCOPALE AMERICANA DI ST. JAMES

VIA IL PRATO

CASA DI RIPOSO D. BEATA

Piazza Adua

SANTA MARIA NOVELLA TRAIN STATION

WC

Piazza della Stazione

BUS STN.

PALAZZO DEI CARTELLONI

TEATRO COMUNALE

CORSO ITALIA

LUNGARNO AMERIGO VESPUCCI

SAN LUCIA SUL PRATO

VIA DELLA SCALA

VIA PALAZZUOLO

B #12

SANTA MARIA NOVELLA

Piazza dell'Unità Italiana

V. PANZANI

Arno River

LUNGARNO SANTA ROSA

PONTE AMERIGO VESPUCCI

L. AMERIGO

PERFUMERY

OGNISSANTI

BORGO OGNISSANTI

Piazza d'Ognissanti

VIA PORCELLANA

VIA DEI BANCHI

Piazza di Santa Maria Novella

B

VIA DEL SOLE

VIA DEL FOSSI

VIA DEL TORNABUONI

V. DE'

PORTA SAN FREDIANO

VIA PISANA

Piazza d. Verzaia

VIA SANT'ONOFRIO

LUNGARNO SODERINI

VESPUCCI

RUCELLAI PALACE

VIA VIGNA NUOVA

VIA DEL PARIONE

STROZZI PALACE

VIA

Cimitero Israelitico

VIA CAMALDOLI

Piazza di Cestello

BORGO SAN FREDIANO

Piazza Goldoni

PALAZZO CORSINI

L. CORSINI

SANTA TRINITÀ

PONTE ALLA CARRAIA

Piazza Nazare Sauro

L. GUICCIARDINI

VIA S. SPIRITO

PONTE SANTA TRINITÀ

BORGO ACCIAIUOLI

Piazza de' Frescobaldi

VIA ALIARDI

CITY WALLS

Piazza T. Tasso

Piazza de' Nerli

Piazza del Carmine

BRANCACCI CHAPEL

SANTA MARIA DEL CARMINE

VIA DE' SERRAGLI

OLTRARNO

VIA MARTINO

B. SAN JACOPO

VIA DELLA CHIESA

SANTO SPIRITO

Pza d. Passera

Piazza di Santa Felicità

Piazza di Santo Spirito

VIA D. S.

GROTTO

BACCHUS

VIA DEL CAMPUCCIO

Giardino Torrigiani

VIA MAGGIO

VIA D. GUICCIARDINI

PAL. DE COSIMO RIDOLFI

Piazza di San Felice

Piazza de' Pitti

PITTI PALACE

VIA PETRARCA

Giardino di Analena

VIA ROMANA

AMPHITHEATER

Boboli Gardens

FONTANA D. NETTUNO

Hotels & Eateries outside Center

1 Locanda de' Ciompi

2 Lovelife Café

Tour Companies

3 Artviva Tours & Cooking Classes

4 Florencetown Tours & Cooking Classes

PORTA ROMANA

FONTANA DELL'OCEANO

CITY WALLS

Piazzale della Porta Romana

ORIENTATION

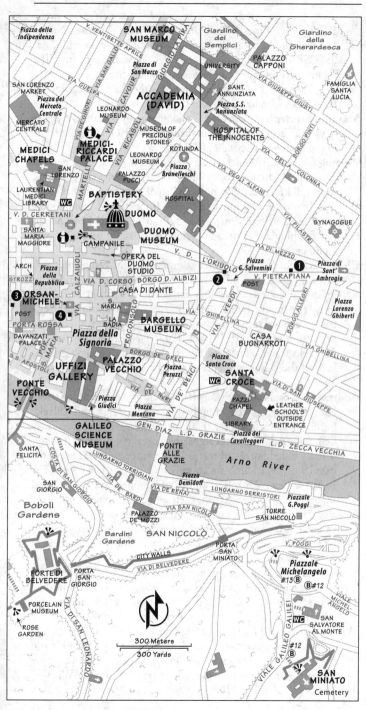

17:00, other times by appointment, Piazza Mercato Nuovo 1, between Piazza della Repubblica and Ponte Vecchio, tel. 055-288-055, mobile 335-836-1682, www.dr-kerr.com). The TI has a list of other English-speaking doctors.

There are 24-hour **pharmacies** at the train station and on Borgo San Lorenzo (near the Baptistery).

Museum Strategies: I can't stress enough the importance of either buying a **Firenze Card** or **making reservations** to avoid waiting in lines (see pages 30 and 34).

Visiting Churches: Modest dress is required in some churches, including the Duomo, Santa Maria Novella, Santa Croce, Santa Maria del Carmine/Brancacci Chapel, and the Medici Chapels (see page 616 for details). Be respectful of worshippers and the paintings; don't use a flash. Many churches, though not the biggies we mention, close from 12:00 or 12:30 until 15:00 or 16:00.

Chill Out: Schedule several breaks into your sightseeing when you can sit, pause, cool off, and refresh yourself with a sandwich, gelato, or coffee. Carry a water bottle to refill at Florence's twist-the-handle public fountains (near the Duomo dome entrance, around the corner from the "Piglet" at Mercato Nuovo, or in front of the Pitti Palace). Try the *fontanello* (dispenser of free cold water, *gassata* or *naturale*) on Piazza della Signoria, behind the statue of Neptune (on the left side of the Palazzo Vecchio).

Addresses: Florence has a ridiculously confusing system for street addresses, with "red" numbers for businesses and "black" numbers for residences, though the red numbers are slowly being phased out. Street signs are indeed red or black (though usually faded and hard to read); in print, addresses are indicated with "r" (as in Via Cavour 2r) or "n" (for black—*nero*, as in Via Cavour 25n). Red and black numbers are interspersed together on the same street; each set goes in roughly consecutive order, but their numbers bear no connection with each other. I'm lazy and don't concern myself with the distinction (if one number's wrong, I look nearby for the other) and easily find my way around.

Pedestrian Safety: Once nightmarish for pedestrians, the city is increasingly delightful on foot, though even in traffic-free zones delivery trucks and nearly silent hybrid taxis nudge their way through crowds with a persistent beep-beep-beep.

Wi-Fi: Virtually all Florence hotels have Wi-Fi free for guests, and many cafés and restaurants will tell you their password if you buy something. The city's free Wi-Fi hotspot network covers all of the main squares (network name is "Firenze WiFi"— click on *"Accedi"*; good for two hours).

Bookstores: For a good selection of brand-name guidebooks (including mine), try these: **Paperback Exchange** has the widest selection of English books, new and used (Mon-Fri 9:00-19:30, Sat from 10:30, closed Sun and a couple of weeks in Aug, just south of the Duomo on Via delle Oche 4 red, tel. 055-293-460). **RED** (stands for "Read, Eat, Dream"), a flagship store for the Feltrinelli chain (the Italian Barnes & Noble) with a café and restaurant inside, has a small selection of English books (daily 9:30-23:00, on Piazza della Repubblica). For locations, see the map on page 316.

WCs: Public restrooms are scarce. Use them when you can, in any café or museum you patronize. Pay public WCs are typically €1. Convenient locations include one at the Baptistery ticket office (near the Duomo), just down the street from Piazza Santa Croce (at Borgo Santa Croce 29 red), up near Piazzale Michelangelo, and inside the train station (near track 5).

Laundry: The **Wash & Dry Lavarapido** chain offers long hours and efficient, self-service launderettes at several locations (generally daily 7:30-23:00). These locations are close to recommended hotels: Via dei Servi 105 red (near *David*), Via del Sole 29 red and Via della Scala 52 red (between train station and river), Via Ghibellina 143 red (Palazzo Vecchio), and Via dei Serragli 87 red (Oltrarno neighborhood).

Bike Rental: The **city of Florence** rents bikes cheaply at the train station (€2/hour, €5/5 hours, €10/day, mobile 346-883-7821; information at any TI). **Florence by Bike** rents two-wheelers of all sizes (€3/hour, €9/5 hours, includes bike lock and helmet, child seat-€3; Mon-Sat 9:00-19:30, Sun until 18:00, closed Sun Nov-March; a 15-minute walk north of the Duomo at Via San Zanobi 54 red, tel. 055-488-992, www.florencebybike.it).

Travel Agencies: While it's easy to buy train tickets to destinations within Italy at machines at the station, travel agencies can be more convenient and helpful for getting both domestic and international tickets (€2 fee), reservations, and supplements. Convenient travel agencies in the town center are **Intertravel Viaggi** (also a DHL package mailing office, Mon-Fri 9:00-18:30, Sat 9:30-12:30, closed Sun, centrally located south of Piazza della Repubblica at Via de Lamberti 39 red, tel. 055-280-706) and **Turishav Travel** (Mon-Fri 9:30-

ORIENTATION

Daily Reminder

Sunday: Mercato Centrale is closed (but food court is open). The Bargello, Palazzo Davanzati, and the Medici Chapels close on the second and fourth Sundays of the month. The Museum of San Marco is closed on the first, third, and fifth Sundays.

The Baptistery's interior closes early, at 14:00. A few sights are open only in the afternoon: the Duomo and its dome (13:30-16:40), Santa Croce Church (14:00-17:30), Basilica of San Lorenzo (13:30-17:30), Brancacci Chapel (13:00-17:00), and Church of Santa Maria Novella (13:00-17:30).

The following sights are free and crowded on the first Sunday of the month, and reservations are not available: Uffizi, Accademia, Pitti Palace, Bargello, and Medici Chapels. While it's best to avoid the Accademia and Uffizi on free Sunday, the lines at the other sights can move quickly.

Monday: The biggies are closed, including the Accademia *(David)* and the Uffizi Gallery, as well as the Pitti Palace's Palatine Gallery, Royal Apartments, and Gallery of Modern Art. The Pitti Palace's Boboli and Bardini Gardens, Argenti/Silverworks Museum, Costume Gallery, and Porcelain Museum close on the first and last Mondays. The Museum of San Marco closes on the second and fourth Mondays. The Bargello, Palazzo Davanzati, and the Medici Chapels are closed on the first, third, and fifth Mondays. San Lorenzo Market is closed on Mondays in winter.

18:00, closed Sat-Sun, Via dei Servi 23 red, a block off the Duomo, tel. 055-292-237).

GETTING AROUND FLORENCE

I organize my sightseeing geographically and do it all on foot. I think of Florence as a Renaissance treadmill—it requires a lot of walking. You likely won't need public transit, except maybe to head up to Piazzale Michelangelo and San Miniato Church for the view, or to Fiesole.

By Bus

The city's full-size buses don't cover the old center well (the whole area around the Duomo is off-limits to motorized traffic). Pick up a map of transit routes at the ATAF windows at the train station; you'll also find routes online (www.ataf.net) and on the app "ATAF 2.0" (free from Apple's App Store and Google Play). Of the many bus lines, I find these to be of most value for seeing outlying sights:

Bus **#12** goes from the train station, over the Carraia bridge to Porta Romana, then up to San Miniato Church and Piazzale Michelangelo. Bus #13 makes the return trip down the hill.

Target these sights on Mondays: the Duomo, Duomo Museum, Campanile, Baptistery, Medici-Riccardi Palace, Brancacci Chapel, Mercato Nuovo, Mercato Centrale, Casa Buonarroti, Galileo Science Museum, the Palazzo Vecchio, and churches (including Santa Croce and Santa Maria Novella). Or take a walking tour.

Tuesday: Casa Buonarroti and the Brancacci Chapel are closed. The Duomo Museum is closed on the first Tuesday of the month. The Galileo Science Museum closes early (13:00).

Wednesday: The Medici-Riccardi Palace is closed.

Thursday: The following sights close early: the Palazzo Vecchio (14:00) and off-season, the Duomo (16:30).

Friday: All sights are open.

Saturday: All sights are open, but the Duomo's dome closes earlier than usual, at 17:40.

Early Closing Warning: Some of Florence's sights close surprisingly early, as early as 13:50 for the following sights—the Bargello (early closure off-season only), Palazzo Davanzati, Medici Chapels (off-season only), and the Museum of San Marco (on weekdays only, open later on Sat and when open on Sun). Mercato Centrale's lower level closes at 14:00 (except on Sat, when it stays open until 17:00).

For all sights, be advised the last entry is usually 30 to 60 minutes before posted closing times.

Bus **#7** goes from Piazza San Marco (near the Accademia and Museum of San Marco) to Fiesole, a small town with big views of Florence.

The train station and Piazza San Marco are two major hubs near the city center; to get between these two, either walk (about 15 minutes) or take bus #1, #6, #14, #17, or #23.

Fun little **minibuses** (many of them electric—*elettrico*) wind through the tangled old center of town and up and down the river—just €1.20 gets you a 1.5-hour joyride. These buses, which run every 10 minutes from 7:00 to 21:00 (less frequent on Sun), are popular with sore-footed sightseers and eccentric local seniors. The minibuses also connect many major parking lots with the historic center (buy tickets from machines at lots).

Bus **#C1** stops behind the Palazzo Vecchio and Piazza Santa Croce, then heads north, passing near San Marco and the Accademia before ending up at Piazza Libertà. On its southbound route, this bus also stops near the train station and the Basilica of San Lorenzo.

Bus **#C2** twists through the congested old center from the train station, passing near Piazza della Repubblica and Piazza della Signoria to Piazza Beccaria.

Bus **#C3** goes up and down the Arno River, with stops near Piazza Santa Croce, Ponte Vecchio, the Carraia bridge to the Oltrarno (including the Pitti Palace), and beyond.

Bus **#D** goes from the train station to Ponte Vecchio, cruises through the Oltrarno (passing the Pitti Palace), and finishes in the San Niccolò neighborhood at Ponte San Niccolò.

Buying Bus Tickets: Buy bus tickets at tobacco shops *(tabacchi)*, newsstands, or the ATAF ticket windows inside the train station (€1.20/90 minutes, €4.70/4 tickets, €5/24 hours, €12/3 days, €18/week, day passes aren't always available in tobacco shops, tel. 800-424-500, www.ataf.net). Be sure to validate your ticket in the machine on board. You can sometimes buy a ticket on board, but you'll pay more (€2; must have exact change), and you still need to validate it in the machine. Follow general bus etiquette: Board at front or rear doors, exit out the center.

By Taxi

The minimum cost for a taxi ride is €5 (€8.30 after 22:00, €7 on Sun); rides in the center of town should be charged as tariff #1. A taxi ride from the train station to the Duomo costs about €8. Taxi fares and supplements (e.g., €2 extra to call a cab rather than hail one) are clearly explained on signs in each taxi. Look for an official, regulated cab (white; marked with *Taxi/Comune di Firenze*, red fleur-de-lis, and one of the official phone numbers: 4390 or 4242). Before getting in a cab at a stand or on the street, ask for an approximate cost (*"Più o meno, quanto costa?"* pew oh MEH-noh, KWAHN-toh KOH-stah). If you can't get a straight answer or the price is outrageous, wait for the next one. It can be hard to find a cab on the street; to call one, dial 055-4390 or 055-4242 (or ask your waiter or hotelier to call for you). Uber does not operate in Florence.

Tours in Florence

For extra insight with a personal touch, consider the tour companies and individual Florentine guides listed here. Hardworking and creative, they offer a worthwhile array of organized sightseeing activities.

∩ To sightsee on your own, download my **free audio tours** that illuminate some of Florence's top sights and neighborhoods (see page 8).

Several tour companies (such as Florencetown or Artviva) offer regularly-scheduled group tours that anyone can sign up for. This is usually the cheapest option for individual travelers. But families

Affordable Tuscany

Here are some ideas to help stretch your travel dollars:

Sightseeing

- Many of Florence's sights are free. There is no entry charge for the Duomo, Orsanmichele Church, Santo Spirito Church, and San Miniato Church. It's free to visit the leather school at Santa Croce Church and the perfumery near the Church of Santa Maria Novella. The three markets (Centrale for produce, San Lorenzo and Nuovo for goods) are fun to browse.
- Free public spaces include the Uffizi, Palazzo Vecchio (with a small exhibit of scenes of old Florence), and Palazzo Strozzi courtyards; the art-filled loggia on Piazza della Signoria; the quintessentially Renaissance square Piazza S.S. Annunziata; and Piazzale Michelangelo, with glorious views over Florence. A walk across the picturesque Ponte Vecchio costs nothing at all, and a stroll anywhere with a gelato in hand is an inexpensive treat.
- In the evening, street musicians often perform on the Piazza della Signoria and Ponte Vecchio.

Hotels

- Contact the hotel directly, rather than on booking websites, and ask for their best price.
- Choose hotels that offer a Rick Steves discount.
- Offer to pay cash to get the lowest rate.

Dining

- Don't order too much at restaurants. Servings are often big—and splittable. While restaurants frown on a couple splitting just one dish, if you order a selection and enjoy them family-style, you can sample several things, save some euros, and still have room for gelato. Pizzerias and cafés are your best bets for a cheap meal.
- Takeaway sandwich shops and food carts abound in Florence's old center, making it easy to grab a €3-4 lunch to enjoy on a picturesque piazza. Or order takeout from delicatessens. Many shops have ready-to-eat entrées and side dishes, and will heat them up and provide plastic cutlery and napkins.
- For a cheap, light dinner, head to an *aperitivo* happy hour. All over town, bars—many of them very elegant with fine views—attract customers with free little buffets of light bites. Buy a drink, and make it a meal—a practice locals call *"apericena"* (combining the word *aperitivo* with *cena*—dinner). For a €10 cocktail or glass of wine, you'll enjoy a light meal for no extra charge.

and small groups can book a private guide for a similar price (since rates are hourly for any size of group).

Some tour companies offer bus excursions that go out to smaller towns in the Tuscan countryside. The most popular day trips are Siena, San Gimignano, Pisa, and into Chianti country for wine tasting. To see Florence itself, it's clearly best on foot.

WALKING (AND BIKING) TOURS

While I've outlined the general offerings for each company, check their websites or pick up their brochures for other tour options and to confirm specific times and prices.

Many also offer food tours and cooking classes, sometimes including a shopping trip to pick up ingredients at a local market. This can be fun, memorable, educational, efficient (combining a meal with a "sightseeing" experience)...and delicious. For more on these options, see page 302.

Artviva

Artviva offers an intriguing variety of tours (guided by native English speakers, 18 people maximum). Popular choices include their overview tours (€29 "Original Florence" 3-hour town walk; €104 "Florence in One Glorious Day" combines town walk and tours of the Uffizi and Accademia, 6 hours total). They also have standalone Uffizi and Accademia tours, cooking classes, art classes, food tours, minibus tours around Tuscany and to the Cinque Terre, and more. They offer a 10 percent discount at www.artviva.com/ricksteves (username "ricksteves," password "reader"). Their office is above Odeon Cinema near Piazza della Repubblica (Mon-Sat 8:00-18:00, Sun 8:30-13:30, Via de' Sassetti 1, second floor, tel. 055-264-5033, www.artviva.com).

Florencetown

This company runs English-language tours on foot or by bike. They offer student rates (10 percent discount) to anyone with this book, with an additional 10 percent off for second tours (if booking online, enter the code "RICKSTEVES"). Their most popular offerings are "Walk and Talk Florence" (basic stops including the Oltrarno, €25, 2.5 hours) and "I Bike Florence" (15-stop blitz of town's top sights, €29 for ages 12 and over, free for kids 5 and under; 2.5 hours on one-speed bike, helmets optional; in bad weather it goes as a walking tour). Their office is at Via de Lamberti 1 (facing Orsanmichele Church; see map on page 18); they also have a "Tourist Point" kiosk on Piazza della Repubblica, under the arches at the corner with Via Pellicceria (also offers cooking classes, tel. 055-281-103, www.florencetown.com).

Florentia
Top-notch private walking tours—geared for thoughtful, well-heeled travelers with longer-than-average attention spans—are led by one of six Florentine scholars. The tours range from introductory city walks and museum visits to in-depth thematic walks, such as the Oltrarno, Jewish Florence, and family-oriented tours (€275 and up, includes planning assistance by email, www.florentia.org, info@florentia.org).

Context Florence
This scholarly group of graduate students and professors leads "walking seminars," such as a 3.5-hour study of Michelangelo's work and influence (€85/person, plus museum admission) and a two-hour evening orientation stroll (€70/person). I enjoyed the fascinating three-hour fresco workshop (€80/person plus materials, take home a fresco you make yourself). See their website for other innovative offerings: Medici walk, family tours, and more (tel. 06-9672-7371, US tel. 800-691-6036, www.contexttravel.com, info@contexttravel.com).

Walks Inside Florence
Two art historians—Paola Barubiani and Marzia Valbonesi—and their partners provide quality guided tours. They offer a daily 2.5-hour introductory tour (€55/person, 8 people maximum; includes *David*) and four-hour private tours (€260, €60/hour for more time, this is a discounted Rick Steves rate and for groups of up to 6 people). Among their tour options are an insightful shopping tour that features select artisans, a guided evening walk, and cruise excursions from the port of Livorno (Paola's mobile 335-526-6496, www.walksinsideflorence.com, paola@walksinsideflorence.it).

LOCAL GUIDES
Alessandra Marchetti, a Florentine who has lived in the US, gives private walking tours of Florence and driving tours of Tuscany. Her passion is teaching about Michelangelo (€60-75/hour, mobile 347-386-9839, www.tuscanydriverguide.com, alessandramarchettitours@gmail.com).

Paola Migliorini and her partners offer museum tours, city walking tours, private cooking classes, wine tours, and Tuscan excursions by van—you can tailor tours as you like (€60/hour without car, €70/hour in a van for up to 8 passengers, mobile 347-657-2611, www.florencetour.com, info@florencetour.com). They also do cruise excursions from the port of Livorno (€580/up to 4 people, €680/up to 6, €780/up to 8).

Elena Fulceri, specializing in art, history, and secret corners, is a delightful and engaging guide. She organizes heartfelt, tailor-made private tours, has good Oltrarno artisan connections, and enjoys family tours (€60/hour, tel. 347-942-2054, www.florencewithflair.com, info@florencewithflair.com).

BUS OR CAR TOURS
Hop-On, Hop-Off Bus Tours

Since the most important sights are buried in the old center where big buses can't go, Florence doesn't really lend itself to this kind of tour bus. Look at the route map before committing. As the name implies, you can hop off when you want and catch the next bus (usually every 30 minutes, less frequent off-season). Tourists on the top deck can listen to brief recorded descriptions of the sights, snap photos, and enjoy a drive-by look at major landmarks (€23/1 calendar day, €28/48 hours, pay as you board, www.firenze.city-sightseeing.it).

Driving Tours

500 Touring Club offers a unique look at Florence: from behind the wheel of one of the most iconic Italian cars, a vintage, restored Fiat 500. After a lesson in *la doppietta* (double-clutching), you'll head off in a guided convoy, following a lead car while listening to Italian oldies, with photo stops at the best viewpoints. Tours depart from a 15th-century villa on the edge of town; the tiny Fiats are restored models from the 1960s and 1970s. Itineraries vary from basic sightseeing to countryside excursions with winemaking and lunch. They also offer tours by Vespa—the equally iconic Italian scooter; see their website for options (classic 2.5-hour tour-€80/person, US tel. 713/570-9025, Italian mobile 346-826-2324, Via Gherardo Silvani 149a, www.500touringclub.com, info@500touringclub.com, David).

TOUR PACKAGES FOR STUDENTS

Andy Steves (Rick's son) runs Weekend Student Adventures (WSA Europe), offering 3-day and 10-day budget travel packages across Europe including accommodations, skip-the-line sightseeing, and unique local experiences. Locally guided and DIY unguided options are available for student and budget travelers in 13 of Europe's most popular cities, including Florence (guided trips from €199, see www.wsaeurope.com for details). Check out Andy's tips, resources, and podcast at www.andysteves.com.

SIGHTS IN FLORENCE

In this chapter, some of Florence's most important sights have the shortest listings and are marked with a 📖. That's because they are covered in much more detail in one of the self-guided walks or tours included in this book. A 🎧 means the walk or tour is available as a free audio tour (via my Rick Steves Audio Europe app—see page 8). Some walks and tours are available in both formats—take your pick.

For general tips on sightseeing, see page 615. Remember to check www.ricksteves.com/update for any significant changes that have occurred since this book was printed.

Opening Hours: Check opening hours carefully and plan your time well. Many museums have erratic hours (for example, closing on alternating Sundays and Mondays), and Florence—more than most cities—has a tendency to change these hours from season to season. Get the most up-to-date info at the TIs or online.

Price Hike Alert: Most of the major museums host special exhibits that boost the base admission price. Even if you only want to see the permanent collection, you'll pay for the special exhibit. Consider yourself lucky if you happen to visit when admission is the normal price.

Free First Sundays: Many museums are free on the first Sunday of each month (no reservations are available). In Florence, this includes the Uffizi, Accademia, Pitti Palace, Bargello, and Medici Chapels. Unfortunately, crowds pack the Uffizi and Accademia—I'd make it a point to avoid those two on the free Sunday. The Pitti Palace, Bargello, and Medici Chapels are also crowded then, but the lines move fairly quickly.

SKIPPING LINES

Florence's two most popular sights (the Uffizi Gallery and the Accademia—with *David*) have notorious lines all year long. Smart travelers save hours in one of two ways.

The **Firenze Card** (€72 per person) is the easiest option. It lets you skip the line at nearly all of the city's main sights. You'd have to sightsee like mad to make the card actually pay for itself, but the savings in time are worth the extra cost for many travelers. Getting the card makes the most sense from April through October, when crowds are worst.

Alternatively, you can make **reservations** for the Accademia and Uffizi. This is cheaper than the Firenze Card, and makes sense if you won't be visiting the many other museums covered by the card.

Here's more information on these two options:

Firenze Card

This three-day sightseeing pass gives you admission to many of Florence's sights, including the Uffizi Gallery and Accademia. It lets you skip the ticket-buying lines without making reservations (except for the Duomo dome climb). With the card, you simply go to the entrance, find the Firenze Card priority line, show the card, and they let you in.

There are a few hitches. Even with the card, security bottlenecks may delay your entry. At some sights, you must first present your card at the ticket booth to get a physical ticket before proceeding to the entrance. For the Duomo sights, this means going to the ticket office across from the Baptistery (at #7), though there's a priority queue for card holders. Note that the Firenze Card does *not* let you skip the line for the Duomo dome climb—you must make a reservation for that—nor does it let you skip the line to enter the (free) Duomo.

Cost and Coverage: The Firenze Card costs €72 and is valid for 72 hours from when you validate it at your first museum (for example, Tue at 15:00 until Fri at 15:00). Validate your card only when you're ready to tackle the covered sights on three consecutive days. Make sure the sights you want to visit will be open (see the "Daily Reminder" on page 22). The Firenze Card covers the regular admission price as well as any special-exhibit surcharges, and is good for one visit per sight. (The €77 Firenze Card+ also includes free public transportation.)

What's Included: Here's a sampling of popular sights and their individual ticket prices:

- Uffizi Gallery (€12.50, or €8 if no special exhibits, plus €4 fee if reserved ahead)
- Accademia (same as Uffizi)
- Palazzo Vecchio (€10 apiece for museum or tower, €18 for combo-ticket that includes museum, tower, and excavations)
- Bargello (€8)
- Medici Chapels (€8)
- Museum of San Marco (€4)
- Duomo sights: Baptistery, Campanile, dome climb (reservation required), Santa Reparata crypt (inside the Duomo), and Duomo Museum (€15)
- Pitti Palace sights: Palatine Gallery and Royal Apartments (€13, or €8.50 if no special exhibits)
- Santa Croce Church (€8)
- Basilica of San Lorenzo (€6)

If you enter all the above sights within three days—an ambitious plan—the Firenze Card will pay for itself. But the big advantage is saving time. Without the card, it's not hard to spend at least €50 on tickets and reservations anyway. With the card, you avoid the hassle of making reservations and scheduling your time around them.

The Firenze Card also covers a long list of minor sights that you might enjoy popping into, but wouldn't otherwise pay for. Of the Florence sights I list, the only one *not* covered by the Firenze Card is the Gucci Museum. For a complete list of included sights, see www.firenzecard.it.

Buying the Firenze Card: Don't bother buying the card in advance online, because you'll still have to exchange your voucher for a card once you arrive in Florence.

In Florence, you can buy the card at most TIs and most participating sights. The least-crowded sales point is the TI at Via Cavour 1 red, north of the Duomo. The Palazzo Strozzi also has short lines and long hours. Other uncrowded, central sights selling the card include the Bargello, the Bardini Museum, and the back ticket desk at the Church of Santa Maria Novella (on Piazza della Stazione, across from the train station). Buying the card at the Uffizi Gallery is surprisingly easy: Just enter door #2, passing to the left of the ticket-buying line.

You can also buy the card at more crowded places like the TI across from the train station and the airport TI, though not from the TI near the Duomo. It's also sold at big sights like the Palazzo Vecchio and Pitti Palace.

The Fine Print: If you plan to climb the Duomo's dome, you must make a reservation in person when you present your Firenze Card at the Duomo ticket office—but in high season the chances of getting a time slot for the same day are slim (you're better off

Florence at a Glance

▲▲▲Accademia Michelangelo's *David* and powerful (unfinished) *Prisoners*. Reserve ahead or get a Firenze Card. **Hours:** Tue-Sun 8:15-18:50, possibly Tue until 22:00 June-Sept, closed Mon. See page 41.

▲▲▲Uffizi Gallery Greatest collection of Italian paintings anywhere. Reserve well in advance or get a Firenze Card. **Hours:** Tue-Sun 8:15-18:50, closed Mon. See page 55.

▲▲▲Bargello Underappreciated sculpture museum (Michelangelo, Donatello, Medici treasures). **Hours:** Tue-Sat 8:15-17:00, until 13:50 Nov-March; also open second and fourth Mon and first, third, and fifth Sun of each month. See page 60.

▲▲▲Duomo Museum Freshly renovated cathedral museum with the finest in Florentine sculpture. **Hours:** Daily 9:00-20:00, closed first Tue of each month. See page 41.

▲▲Duomo Gothic cathedral with colorful facade and the first dome built since ancient Roman times. **Hours:** Mon-Fri 10:00-17:00 (Thu until 16:30), Sat 10:00-16:45, Sun 13:30-16:45. See page 36.

▲▲Museum of San Marco Best collection anywhere of artwork by the early Renaissance master Fra Angelico. **Hours:** Tue-Fri 8:15-13:50, Sat 8:15-16:50; also open 8:15-13:50 on first, third, and fifth Mon and 8:15-16:50 on second and fourth Sun of each month. See page 43.

▲▲Medici Chapels Tombs of Florence's great ruling family, designed and carved by Michelangelo. **Hours:** Tue-Sat 8:15-17:00 except Nov-March until 13:50; also open second and fourth Mon and first, third, and fifth Sun of each month. See page 48.

▲▲Palazzo Vecchio Fortified palace, once the home of the Medici family, wallpapered with history. **Hours:** Museum and excavations open Fri-Wed 9:00-23:00 (Oct-March until 19:00), Thu 9:00-14:00; shorter hours for tower. See page 57.

▲▲Galileo Science Museum Fascinating old clocks, telescopes, maps, and three of Galileo's fingers. **Hours:** Wed-Mon 9:30-18:00, Tue until 13:00. See page 59.

▲▲Santa Croce Church Precious art, tombs of famous Florentines, and Brunelleschi's Pazzi Chapel in 14th-century church. **Hours:** Mon-Sat 9:30-17:30, Sun 14:00-17:30. See page 61.

▲▲Church of Santa Maria Novella Thirteenth-century Dominican church with Masaccio's famous 3-D painting. **Hours:** Mon-Thu

9:00-19:00 (Oct-March until 17:30), Fri 11:00-19:00 (Oct-March until 17:30), Sat 9:00-17:30, Sun 13:00-17:30. See page 62.

▲▲Pitti Palace Several museums in lavish palace plus sprawling Boboli and Bardini Gardens. **Hours:** Palatine Gallery, Royal Apartments, and Gallery of Modern Art open Tue-Sun 8:15-18:50, closed Mon; Boboli and Bardini Gardens, Costume Gallery, Argenti/Silverworks Museum, and Porcelain Museum open daily June-Aug 8:15-19:30, April-May and Sept until 18:30, March and Oct until 17:30, Nov-Feb until 16:30, closed first and last Mon of each month. See page 63.

▲▲Brancacci Chapel Works of Masaccio, early Renaissance master who reinvented perspective. **Hours:** Mon and Wed-Sat 10:00-17:00, Sun 13:00-17:00, closed Tue. Reservations required, though often available on the spot. See page 64.

▲▲San Miniato Church Sumptuous Renaissance chapel and sacristy showing scenes of St. Benedict. **Hours:** Mon-Sat 9:30-13:00 & 15:30-20:00, until 19:00 off-season, Sun 9:30-20:00, closed sporadically for special occasions. See page 67.

▲Climbing the Duomo's Dome Grand view into the cathedral, close-up of dome architecture, and, after 463 steps, a glorious city vista; reservations required. **Hours:** Mon-Fri 8:30-20:00, Sat 8:30-17:40, Sun 13:00-16:00. See page 39.

▲Campanile Bell tower with views similar to Duomo's, 50 fewer steps, and shorter lines. **Hours:** Daily 8:30-20:00. See page 40.

▲Baptistery Bronze doors fit to be the gates of paradise. **Hours:** Doors always viewable; interior open Mon-Sat 8:15-20:00, Sun 8:30-14:00. See page 40.

▲Piazza S.S. Annunziata Lovely square epitomizing Renaissance harmony, with Brunelleschi's Hospital of the Innocents, considered the first Renaissance building. See page 42.

▲Medici-Riccardi Palace Lorenzo the Magnificent's home, with fine art, frescoed ceilings, and Gozzoli's lovely Chapel of the Magi. **Hours:** Thu-Tue 8:30-19:00, closed Wed. See page 50.

▲Ponte Vecchio Famous bridge lined with gold and silver shops. See page 58.

▲Piazzale Michelangelo Hilltop square with stunning view of Duomo and Florence, with San Miniato Church just uphill. See page 66.

SIGHTS

buying a Duomo combo-ticket online well in advance and booking your climb time then).

The Firenze Card is not shareable, and there are no family or senior discounts for Americans or Canadians. Since children under 18 are allowed free into most museums, they can generally skip the line with their Firenze Card-holding parents. However, at the Uffizi and Accademia, children still must (technically) pay the €4 "reservation fee" (which can be paid on the spot—no need to reserve ahead). Don't confuse this card with the Firenze PASSport.

Advance Reservations (Without the Firenze Card)

If you don't get a Firenze Card, it's smart to make reservations at the often-crowded Accademia and Uffizi Gallery. Reservations are mandatory to climb the Duomo's dome. Some other Florence sights—including the Bargello, Medici Chapels, and the Pitti Palace—offer reservations, but they are generally not necessary.

The Brancacci Chapel officially requires a reservation, but it's usually possible to get one on the spot at the chapel or in advance at the Palazzo Vecchio (for details, see the Brancacci Chapel Tour chapter).

Accademia and Uffizi Reservations

Get reservations for these two top sights as soon as you know when you'll be in town. Without a reservation at the Accademia and Uffizi, you can usually enter without significant lines from November through March after 16:00. But from April through October and on weekends, it can be crowded even late in the day. I'd reserve a spot any time of year. Note that reservations are not possible on the first Sunday of the month, when the museums are free and very busy.

There are several ways to make a reservation:

Online: You can book and pay for your Accademia or Uffizi visit via the city's official site (€4/ticket reservation fee, www.firenzemusei.it—click on "B-ticket"). You'll receive an order-confirmation email, which is followed shortly by a voucher email. Bring your voucher to the ticket desk to swap for an actual ticket.

Pricey middleman sites—such as www.uffizi.com and www.tickitaly.com—are reliable and more user-friendly than the official site, but their booking fees run about €10 per ticket. (When ordering from a broker site, don't confuse Florence's Accademia with Venice's gallery of the same name.)

By Phone: From a US phone, dial 011-39-055-294-883, or from an Italian phone call 055-294-883 (€4/ticket reservation fee; booking office open Mon-Fri 8:30-18:30, Sat 8:30-12:30, closed Sun). When you get through, an English-speaking operator walks you through the process—a few minutes later you say *grazie*, having secured an entry time and a confirmation number. You'll present your confirmation number at the museum and pay for your ticket. You pay only for the tickets you pick up (e.g., if you reserved two tickets but only use one, you'll pay for just one ticket).

Through Your Hotel: Some hoteliers will book museum reservations for their guests (ask when you reserve your room); some offer this as a service, while others charge a small booking fee.

Private Tour: Various tour companies—including the ones listed on page 26—sell tours that include a reserved museum admission.

Last-Minute Strategies: If you arrive without a reservation, call the reservation number (see "By Phone," earlier), ask your hotelier for help, or head to a booking window, either at Orsanmichele Church (daily 9:00-16:00, closed Sun, along Via de' Calzaiuoli—see map on page 44) or at the My Accademia Libreria bookstore across from the Accademia's exit (Tue-Sun 8:15-17:30, closed Mon, Via Ricasoli 105 red—see map on page 44). It's also possible to go to the Uffizi's official ticket office (ask the custodian at door #2 and ignore the long ticket-buying line), and ask if they have any short-notice reservations available. Any of these options will cost you the €4 reservation fee. Because the museums are closed on Mondays, the hardest day to snare a last-minute, same-day reservation is Tuesday—get an early start. As a last resort, buy a Firenze Card just for the line-skipping privileges.

SIGHTS

THE DUOMO AND NEARBY SIGHTS

Florence's most distinctive monuments—the Duomo, Baptistery, and Campanile—are gathered between the pedestrian-only Piazza San Giovanni and Piazza del Duomo. The Duomo Museum is just behind the cathedral.

📖 The Renaissance Walk chapter and 🎧 free audio tour connect the Duomo sights.

Ticketing: While the Duomo itself is free to enter, several associated sights are covered by a single €15 **combo-ticket,** valid for 48 hours: the Baptistery, dome, Campanile, Duomo Museum, and Santa Reparata crypt (enter from inside the Duomo).

The only way to climb the dome is to make a reservation. You can buy the €15 combo-ticket in advance online and make a **dome-climb reservation** at www.museumflorence.com. Dome climb time slots can fill up days in advance, so it's smart to reserve well ahead. Otherwise, you can try to reserve a time in person at a Duomo ticket office or at a ticket machine in the Duomo Museum lobby.

The main ticket office faces the Baptistery entrance (at #7 on the square). It has a staffed counter (credit cards or cash) as well as self-service machines (credit cards only, requires PIN). There's another office at the Duomo Museum. You can also buy tickets at the Santa Reparata crypt or at the Campanile, but they don't make reservations for the dome climb.

All of these sights are also covered by the Firenze Card. Before entering any of the Duomo sights, you must present your Firenze Card at the ticket office opposite the Baptistery (look for a priority queue) to obtain a free combo-ticket and (with luck) reserve a time for the dome climb.

Tours: Themed tours (€30 each, includes combo-ticket) include a Duomo visit and access to the north terrace of the church (daily at 10:30), an opportunity to watch contemporary stonemasons at work in the same workshop where Michelangelo carved *David* (Mon, Wed, and Fri at 12:00), and an up-close look at the mosaics of the Baptistery (Mon, Wed, and Fri at 16:30). To book a spot, call 055-230-2885, email info@operaduomo.firenze.it, or stop by the main ticket office.

SIGHTS

▲▲Duomo (Cattedrale di Santa Maria del Fiore)

Florence's Gothic cathedral has the third-longest nave in Christendom. The church's noisy Neo-Gothic facade (from the 1870s) is covered with pink, green, and white Tuscan marble. The cathedral's claim to artistic fame is Brunelleschi's magnificent dome—the first Renaissance dome and the model for domes to follow. While viewing it from the outside is well worth ▲▲, the massive but empty-feeling interior is lucky to rate ▲—it doesn't justify the massive crowds that line up to get inside.

Cost and Hours: Free; Mon-Fri 10:00-17:00 (Thu until 16:30), Sat 10:00-16:45, Sun 13:30-16:45, opening times sometimes change due to religious functions, modest dress code enforced, tel. 055-230-2885, www.museumflorence.com.

Lines: Because the church is free (and therefore not "covered" by the Firenze Card), lines can be long, but they move fast.

Mass: The church is open to all for Mass: English Mass on Sat at 17:00 and old-school Latin Mass with Gregorian chants on Sun at 10:30.

❸ Self-Guided Tour: Enter the Duomo (from Latin *domus*, as it's the "house" of God).

Survey the ❶ **huge nave**—it's 500 feet long and 300 feet wide. The structural elements are unabashedly highlighted by the gray stone and cream-colored filling. In medieval times, engineers weren't accustomed to spanning such distances, so they used iron support bars between the columns to ensure stability. A church has

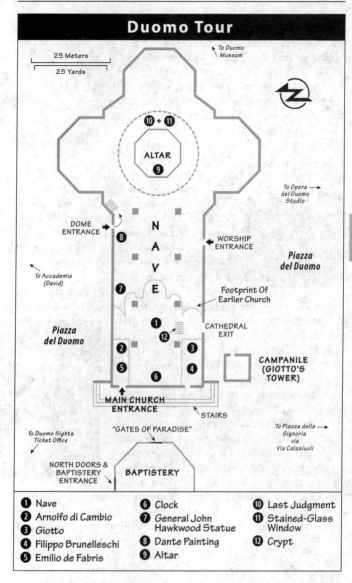

Duomo Tour

To Duomo Museum

25 Meters
25 Yards

⑩ + ⑪

ALTAR

⑨

To Opera del Duomo Studio

DOME ENTRANCE ➤

⑧

N
A
V
E

◀ **WORSHIP ENTRANCE**

Piazza del Duomo

To Accademia (David)

⑦

Footprint Of Earlier Church

① **CATHEDRAL EXIT**

Piazza del Duomo

⑫

② ③

CAMPANILE (GIOTTO'S TOWER)

⑤ ④

⑥

MAIN CHURCH ENTRANCE

STAIRS

To Duomo Sights Ticket Office

"GATES OF PARADISE"

To Piazza della Signoria via Via Calzaiuoli

NORTH DOORS & BAPTISTERY ENTRANCE

BAPTISTERY

① Nave
② Arnolfo di Cambio
③ Giotto
④ Filippo Brunelleschi
⑤ Emilio de Fabris

⑥ Clock
⑦ General John Hawkwood Statue
⑧ Dante Painting
⑨ Altar

⑩ Last Judgment
⑪ Stained-Glass Window
⑫ Crypt

been on this spot since the fall of Rome c. A.D. 500. (You can see part of the earlier church at the end of this tour.)

While there are no tombs here, the church honors its great architects—❷ **Arnolfo di Cambio,** ❸ **Giotto,** ❹ **Filippo Brunelleschi,** and ❺ **Emilio de Fabris**—with four small, round *(tondo)* memorials on either wall near the rear of the nave. In 1296, the present church was begun under Arnolfo (shown here holding the Duomo's blueprint), who also built the Palazzo Vecchio and Santa Croce Church. Giotto started the church's Campanile in 1334.

By 1420, the nave was done, except for a 140-foot-wide hole in the roof over the altar. Brunelleschi covered that with the famous dome that helped define the Renaissance. Finally, in the 19th century, the church was completed with a multicolored facade by Fabris.

Above the main entrance is a ❻ **huge clock,** painted by Paolo Uccello (1443). It still works. It's a 24-hour clock, starting with sunset as the first hour, and turning counterclockwise.

As you stroll down the nave, notice the equestrian portraits on your left. The church, originally financed by the city of Florence, honors great (secular) men, such as ❼ **General John Hawkwood** (on horseback; 1436, it's the second horse picture, colored green). Paolo Uccello wowed Florence by creating this 3-D illusion of an equestrian statue on the flat wall. Farther up the left (north) wall is a painting of Florence's great poet ❽ **Dante,** in a frilly stone frame. He holds his *Divine Comedy,* points toward Hell (Inferno), puts his back to Mount Purgatory (a spiral with souls working their way out of limbo, upward to heaven), and turns toward Paradise—its skyline none other than that of Florence (circa 1465).

Continue all the way up to the very front of the church, beneath the brightly painted dome. The ❾ **altar** area is octagonal, echoing the shape of the Baptistery. At the base of the crucifix is a high-backed wooden chair—the cathedra of Florence's bishop, which makes the Duomo a "cathedral." Looking up, notice how the dome stretches halfway into the transepts—that was one big hole Brunelleschi had to cover. Look up 300 feet, into the dome, to see the expansive (if artistically uninteresting) ❿ *Last Judgment* by Giorgio Vasari and Federico Zuc-

cari. From their graves, the dead rise into a multilevel heaven to be judged by a radiant Christ. Beneath Christ, Mary intercedes. Below them is the pagan god Kronos with the hourglass and a skeleton—symbolizing that mankind's time is up, and they (we) are entering eternity.

Just below that, on the base that supports the dome, is a ⓫ **round stained-glass window** by Donatello, showing the coronation of the Virgin—demonstrating that human beings can eventually be exalted through the Christian faith.

Follow the crowds back toward the exit. Before leaving, if you have a combo-ticket for the Duomo sights (or would like to buy one without a line), consider a quick visit to the ⓬ **crypt,** an archaeological cross-section of 1st- to 14th-century Florence, with the footprint and miscellaneous historical fragments of an earlier church called Santa Reparata. But as there's little to see and it's sparsely explained, it's skippable. Brunelleschi's tomb is tucked unceremoniously (and free to view) in a corner of the crypt's bookstore.

▲Climbing the Duomo's Dome

For a grand view into the cathedral from the base of the dome, a chance to see Brunelleschi's "dome-within-a-dome" construction, and a glorious Florence view from the top, climb 463 steps up the dome. The claustrophobic one-way route takes you up narrow, steep staircases and walkways to the top.

Cost: €15 combo-ticket covers all Duomo sights, covered by Firenze Card; with either, must reserve dome-climb time when obtaining your ticket—best to buy combo-ticket and reserve a time well ahead at www.museumflorence. com.

Hours: Mon-Fri 8:30-20:00, Sat 8:30-17:40, Sun 13:00-16:00, enter from outside church on north side. The dome is closed during rain.

Climbing the Dome: While you line up to enter at your reserved time, spend a few minutes studying the recently restored side-entrance door, called the Porta della Mandorla ("Almond Door"). Just above the delicately carved doorframe is a colorful Annunciation mosaic by Nanni di Banco, and above that, in a sculpted almond-shaped frame, the Madonna is borne up to heaven by angels. If you look up from here you'll see an empty pedestal atop the transept. Michelangelo's *David* was originally destined to adorn one of these.

The climb is long but there are small landings where you can pull over and take a breather. Halfway up, you'll stroll on the walkway high above the altar where you can get a great view of Vasari's ceiling and a vertigo-inducing view of the nave. After a few tight, winding staircases and a steep final climb, you'll pop out of the hatch on the crowded terrace with a grand city view. If possible, visit at sunset for a romantic experience.

If you can't get a reservation, consider ascending the Campanile instead, which rarely has a line and is far less claustrophobic.

📖 For more on the dome, see page 77 of the Renaissance Walk chapter.

▲Campanile (Giotto's Tower)

The 270-foot bell tower has 50-some fewer steps than the Duomo's dome (but that's still 414 steps—no elevator); offers a faster, less-claustrophobic climb (with typically short lines); and has a view of that magnificent dome to boot. On the way up, there are several intermediate levels where you can catch your breath and enjoy ever-higher views. The stairs narrow as you go, creating a mosh-pit bottleneck near the very top—but the views are worth the hassle. While the viewpoints are enclosed by cage-like bars, the gaps are big enough to let you snap great photos.

Cost and Hours: €15 combo-ticket covers all Duomo sights, covered by Firenze Card, daily 8:30-20:00, last entry 40 minutes before closing.

📖 For more on the Campanile, see page 79 of the Renaissance Walk chapter.

▲Baptistery

Michelangelo said the bronze doors of this octagonal building were fit to be the gates of paradise. Check out the gleaming copies of Lorenzo Ghiberti's bronze doors facing the Duomo (the originals are in the Duomo Museum). Making a breakthrough in perspective, Ghiberti used mathematical laws to create the illusion of receding distance on a basically flat surface.

The doors on the north side of the building (around to the right) were designed by Ghiberti when he was young; he'd won the honor and opportunity by beating Brunelleschi in a competition (the rivals' original entries are in the Bargello).

Inside, sit and savor the medieval mosaic

ceiling, where it's always Judgment Day and Jesus is giving the ultimate thumbs-up and thumbs-down.

Cost and Hours: €15 combo-ticket covers all Duomo sights, covered by Firenze Card, interior open Mon-Sat 8:15-20:00, Sun 8:30-14:00. The (facsimile) bronze doors are on the exterior, so they are always "open" and viewable.

☐ For more on the Baptistery, see page 81 of the Renaissance Walk. For more on the famous doors, see page 134 of the Bargello Tour chapter and page 158 of the Duomo Museum Tour chapter.

▲▲▲Duomo Museum (Museo dell'Opera del Duomo)

The recently spiffed-up, often-overlooked cathedral museum is filled with some of the best sculpture of the Renaissance, including a late Michelangelo *Pietà* and statues from the original Baptistery facade. It also holds Brunelleschi's models for his dome, Donatello's anorexic *Mary Magdalene* and playful choir loft, and Ghiberti's original bronze Gates of Paradise panels (the ones on the Baptistery's doors today are copies).

Cost and Hours: €15 combo-ticket covers all Duomo sights, valid 48 hours, covered by Firenze Card; daily 9:00-20:00, closed first Tue of each month, last entry one hour before closing; one of the few museums in Florence always open on Mon; behind the church at Via del Proconsolo 9, tel. 055-230-2885, www.museumflorence.com.

☐ See the Duomo Museum Tour chapter.

NORTH OF THE DUOMO
▲▲▲Accademia (Galleria dell'Accademia)

This museum houses Michelangelo's *David,* the consummate Renaissance statue of the buff, biblical shepherd boy ready to take on the giant. Nearby are some of the master's other works, including his powerful (unfinished) *Prisoners* and *St. Matthew,* as well as a *Pietà* (possibly by one of his disciples). Florentine Michelangelo Buonarroti, who would work tirelessly through the night, believed that the sculptor was a tool of God. He would chip away at the stone to let the intended sculpture emerge. Beyond the magic marble are some mildly interesting pre-Renaissance and Renaissance paintings, including a couple of Botticellis, the plaster model of Giambologna's *Rape of the Sabine Women,* and a musical instrument collection with an early piano.

Cost and Hours: €12.50 (€8 if there's no special exhibit), additional €4 for recommended reservation, free and crowded on first Sun of the month, covered by Firenze Card; Tue-Sun 8:15-18:50, possibly Tue until 22:00 June-Sept, closed Mon; audioguide-€6, Via Ricasoli 60, reservation tel. 055-294-883, www.galleriaaccademiafirenze.beniculturali.it. To avoid long lines in peak season, get the Firenze Card or make reservations (see pages 30 and 34).

📖 See the Accademia Tour chapter or 🎧 download my free audio tour.

▲Piazza S.S. Annunziata

The most Renaissance square in Florence is tucked just a block behind the Accademia. It's like an urban cloister from the 15th centu-

ry, with three fine buildings—a convent church, a hospital, and an orphanage—ringing a fine equestrian statue of Ferdinand, a Medici grand duke. Stand in the center and slowly spin, imagining being here in 1500 as you survey the only Renaissance square in Florence, with the towering Duomo down the street.

Filippo Brunelleschi's **Hospital of the Innocents** (Ospedale degli Innocenti), built in the 1420s, is considered the first Renaissance building. Its graceful arches and columns, with each set of columns forming a square, embody the quintessence of Renaissance harmony and typified the new aesthetic of calm balance and symmetry. It's ornamented with terracotta medallions by Luca della Robbia—each showing a different way to wrap an infant (meant to help babies grow straight, and practiced in Italy until about a century ago). Terra-cotta—made of glazed and painted clay—was a combination of painting and sculpture, but cheaper than either. For three generations, the Della Robbia family guarded the secret recipe and made their name by bringing affordable art to Florence.

With its mission to care for the least among society (parentless or unwanted children), this hospital was also an important symbol of the increasingly humanistic and humanitarian outlook of Renaissance Florence. For four centuries (until 1875), orphans would be left at the "wheel of the innocents" (the small, barred window at the far left of the porch). Today the building houses a **museum**

(Museo degli Innocenti), telling the story of the babies left here, and serving as UNICEF's local headquarters (€7, covered by Firenze Card, daily 10:00-19:00).

I love sleeping on this square (at the recommended Hotel Loggiato dei Serviti) and picnicking here during the day (with the riffraff, who remind me of the persistent gap—today as in Medici times—between those who appreciate fine art and those just looking for some cheap wine).

The 15th-century **Santissima Annunziata church** (with its Bill and Melinda Gates-type patronage attribution to the Pucci brothers: Alexander and Roberto) is also worth a peek. The welcoming cloister has early 16th-century frescoes by Andrea del Sarto, and the church's interior is slathered in Baroque—rare in Florence.

▲▲Museum of San Marco (Museo di San Marco)

Located one block north of the Accademia, this 15th-century monastery houses the greatest collection anywhere of frescoes and

paintings by the early Renaissance master Fra Angelico. The ground floor features the monk's paintings, along with some works by Fra Bartolomeo.

Upstairs are 43 cells decorated by Fra Angelico and his assistants. While the monk/painter was trained in the medieval religious style, he also learned and adopted Renaissance techniques and sensibilities, producing works that blended Christian symbols and Renaissance realism. Don't miss the cell of Savonarola, the charismatic monk who rode in from the Christian right, threw out the Medici, turned Florence into a theocracy, sponsored "bonfires of the vanities" (burning books, paintings, and so on), and was finally burned himself when Florence decided to change channels.

Cost and Hours: €4, covered by Firenze Card, Tue-Fri 8:15-13:50, Sat 8:15-16:50; also open 8:15-13:50 on first, third, and fifth Mon and 8:15-16:50 on second and fourth Sun of each month; reservations possible but unnecessary, on Piazza San Marco, tel. 055-238-8608.

📖 See the Museum of San Marco Tour chapter or 🎧 download my free audio tour.

Museum of Precious Stones
(Museo dell'Opificio delle Pietre Dure)

This unusual gem of a museum features room after room of exquisite mosaics of inlaid marble and other stones. The Medici loved

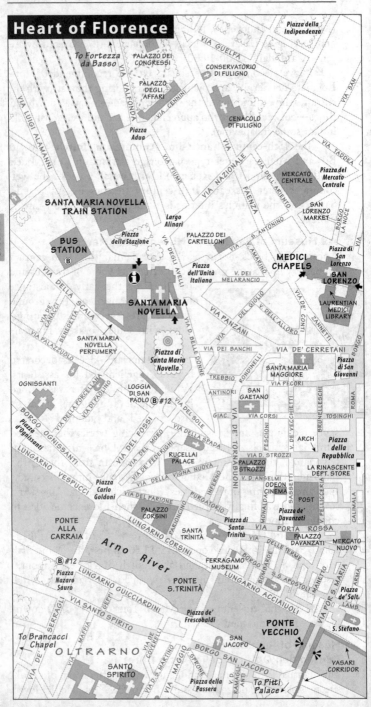

Heart of Florence

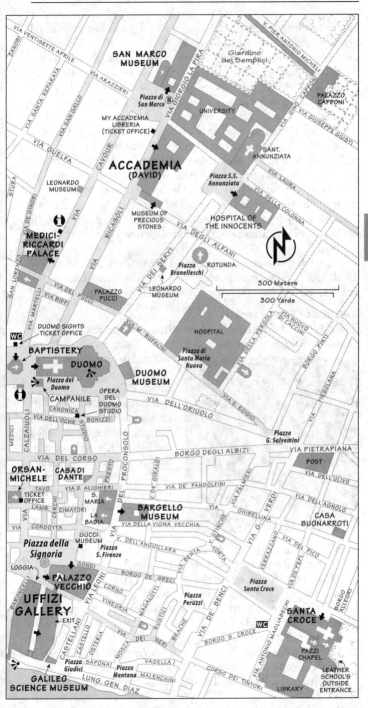

SIGHTS

colorful stone tabletops and floors; you'll even find landscapes and portraits (find Cosimo I in Room I). Upstairs, you'll see tools and examples of the trade, including wooden workbenches from the Medici workshop (1588), complete with foot-powered saws and drills. Rockhounds can browse 500 different stones (lapis lazuli, quartz, agate, marble, and so on) and the tools used to cut and inlay them. Borrow the English descriptions in each room.

Today, Florence is known less for artistic production, but continues its tradition of craftsmanship as a world leader in restoration technique. While not accessible to the public, the rooms off the humble courtyard serve as an active workshop and the center of the city's preservation work. Here Ghiberti's famous bronze doors from the Baptistery were restored, and work continues on Andrea Pisano's south doors. It bears remembering that revenue from sight admission tickets helps preserve Florentine masterpieces for future generations.

Cost and Hours: €4, covered by Firenze Card, Mon-Sat 8:15-14:00, closed Sun, around corner from Accademia at Via degli Alfani 78, tel. 055-265-1357, www.opificiodellepietredure.it.

Basilica of San Lorenzo

The Basilica of San Lorenzo—on the site of the first Christian church in Florence—was built outside the Roman walls and con-

secrated in A.D. 393, then rebuilt in the early 1400s. That's when Filippo Brunelleschi was hired to replace a Romanesque church that stood here. Brunelleschi designed the building, and Donatello worked on the bronze pulpits inside (among other things). Adjacent to the church is a cloister where you can visit the crypt and the library. (The famed Medici Chapels, with Michelangelo's tomb sculptures, are part of the church complex but have a separate ticket; see next listing.)

Cost and Hours: €6 for the church and crypt, buy ticket just inside cloister to the left of the facade, €8.50 combo-ticket also covers the library, covered by Firenze Card; church and crypt open Mon-Sat 10:00-17:30, Sun 13:30-17:30, closed Sun Nov-Feb; library open Mon, Wed, and Fri 8:00-14:00, Tue and Thu 8:00-17:30, closed Sat-Sun; Piazza di San Lorenzo, tel. 055-214-042, www.operamedicealaurenziana.it.

Visiting the Basilica: The exterior of San Lorenzo is rough and exposed brick—unfinished because the Church pulled the plug on the project due to dwindling funds—after Michelangelo had labored on a facade plan for four years, from 1516 to 1520. (Throughout the following decades, the square in front of the church was a literal marble yard with the materials stacked and awaiting construction. That marble was finally sliced up and used to pave the floor of the Duomo.)

Inside though, things are finished and you feel the spirit of Florence in the 1420s, with gray-and-white columns and arches in perfect Renaissance symmetry and simplicity. The simple color scheme seems designed to show off the architectural lines. Brunelleschi designed the interior to receive an even, diffused light. This is a post-Gothic church—with clear rather than stained glass. The Medici coat of arms decorates the ceiling, and everywhere are images of St. Lawrence, one of the Medici patron saints (who was martyred on a grill).

The highlights of the church include two finely sculpted Donatello pulpits overlooking the nave. One, dating from 1466, shows scenes from the Passion. Donatello heightens the drama by compressing the depth.

The high altar features exquisite inlaid stonework. Look closely at this 17th-century *pietre dure* work, uniquely Florentine and a favorite way for the Medici to show off. The round inlaid marble in the floor before the main altar marks where Cosimo the Elder—Lorenzo the Magnificent's grandfather—is buried. His actual tomb is immediately under the altar (viewable in the crypt, described later), where he physically supports the church (like his money supported Florentine culture).

The Martelli Chapel (left wall of the left transept) has Filippo Lippi's *Annunciation,* featuring a graceful angel greeting Mary in a 3-D courtyard. Light shines through the vase in the foreground, like the Holy Spirit entering Mary's womb.

The Old Sacristy (in the far-left corner as you face the front altar), designed by Brunelleschi and decorated by Donatello and Luca della Robbia, was the burial chapel for Giovanni di Bicci, the first Medici who made all the money and the family's patriarch (Cosimo the Elder's father). His tomb is in the center, under what looks like a fancy marble ping-pong table. Overhead, the dome above the altar shows the exact arrangement of the heavens on July 4, 1442, leaving scholars to hypothesize about why that particular date was used.

Cloister, Crypt, and Library: Outside the church, just to the left of the main door, is a cloister with peek-a-boo Duomo views (free entry, just walk past the church ticket line) and two worthwhile sights: the crypt (included with church entry) and library (separate ticket required).

The **crypt** features the tomb of Cosimo the Elder, who died in 1464. A great patron of the arts, he was fabulously wealthy and powerful. The tomb is past the black gate, directly under the church's high altar (again, as if supporting the entire thing). Cosimo's friend Donatello (a cultural soul mate) is buried nearby under a simple tombstone (near where you entered). The adjacent treasury has fine reliquaries, a holy Whitman's Sampler of saintly bones. Outside the treasury stands a white plaster statue of Anna Maria Luisa de' Medici (died 1743). The last of the family line, she willed all Medici art to the city with the legal obligation to keep it here in order to "provoke the interest and curiosity of the foreigners." Without this "family pact," signed in Vienna in 1737, many of the Renaissance treasures of the Medici would have ended up in Habsburg palaces and museums in Vienna and elsewhere. Anna Maria Luisa is particularly appreciated by Florentine guides, whose steady work is due to her visionary will.

The **Laurentian Medici Library,** designed by Michelangelo and finished by others, is worth a look (from the cloister, climb upstairs). It stars Michelangelo's impressive staircase and vestibule. Viewed from the top of the staircase, it almost seems that Michelangelo woke from a stormy architectural dream and threw together a nonsensical warehouse of elements—empty niches, scrolls, oddly tapering pilasters—in a way that was revolutionary in 1520. Enter the Reading Room—a long, rectangular hall with a coffered-wood ceiling—designed to host scholars enjoying the Medici family's collection of manuscripts. It has the feel of a Renaissance church, with its high ceiling, rows of ergonomic "pews," and stained-glass windows. But instead of religious scenes, the windows are filled with Medici heraldic emblems. Knowledge is power, and this was like a public library—but the Medici were firmly in control. Various books were literally chained to the pews as the information was organized by subject (notice the proto-"index cards" at the front of each pew). The library includes special exhibits on historic books (in back room).

Nearby: Around the back end of the church is the entrance to the **Medici Chapels** and the New Sacristy, designed by Michelangelo for a later generation of dead Medici. And the lanes leading to Mercato Centrale (one block north) are clogged with the vendor stalls of **San Lorenzo Market.**

▲▲Medici Chapels
(Cappelle Medicee)

The burial site of the ruling Medici family in the Basilica of San Loren-zo includes the dusky crypt; the big, domed Chapel of Princes; and the

magnificent New Sacristy, featuring architecture, tombs, and statues almost entirely by Michelangelo. The Medici made their money in textiles and banking, and patronized a dream team of Renaissance artists that put Florence on the cultural map. Michelangelo, who spent his teen years living with the Medici, was commissioned to create the family's final tribute.

Cost and Hours: €8, free and crowded on first Sun of the month, covered by Firenze Card; Tue-Sat 8:15-17:00 except Nov-March until 13:50, last entry 40 minutes before closing; also open second and fourth Mon and first, third, and fifth Sun of each month; reservations possible but unnecessary (€3 fee), audioguide-€6, modest dress required, tel. 055-238-8602.

☐ See the Medici Chapels Tour chapter.

▲San Lorenzo Market

Florence's vast open-air market sprawls in the streets just north of the Basilica of San Lorenzo, between the Duomo and the train station (daily 9:00-19:00, closed Mon in winter). You'll find the highest concentration in the streets ringing Mercato Centrale, a block away.

More popular with tourists than locals, it's a hodgepodge of vendors selling T-shirts, scarves, cheap souvenirs, and leather goods of varying quality. Many of the leather stalls are run by Iranians selling South American leather that was tailored in Italy; a few more-established, more-reputable leather shops with permanent addresses are nearby. At stalls or shops, prices are soft—don't be shy about bargaining. (For advice about shopping for leather—including recommendations for specific shops—see page 312.) Every night, in a poignant little parade that feels centuries old, the merchants fold their wares into their wheeled wooden stalls and push them through the city streets to their overnight parking spaces.

▲Mercato Centrale (Central Market)

Florence's giant iron-and-glass-covered central market, a wonderland of picturesque produce, is fun to explore. While the nearby San Lorenzo Market—with its garment and souvenir stalls in the streets—feels only a step up from a haphazard flea market, Mercato Centrale retains a Florentine elegance, particularly now that the upper level has been completely renovated and turned into an upscale food court. Wander around.

Downstairs, you'll see parts of the cow (and bull) you'd never dream of eating (no, that's not a turkey neck), enjoy free samples, watch pasta being made, and have your pick of plenty of fun eateries sloshing out cheap and tasty pasta to locals (Mon-Fri 7:00-14:00, Sat until 17:00, closed Sun).

Upstairs, the meticulously restored glass roof and steel rafters soar over a sleek and modern food court, serving up a bounty of Tuscan cuisine (daily 10:00-24:00). For eating ideas downstairs, upstairs, and around the market, see page 285.

▲Medici-Riccardi Palace
(Palazzo Medici-Riccardi)

Lorenzo the Magnificent's home is worth a look for its art. The tiny Chapel of the Magi contains colorful Renaissance gems such as the *Procession of the Magi* frescoes by Benozzo Gozzoli. The former library has a Baroque ceiling fresco by Luca Giordano, a prolific artist from Naples known as "Fast Luke" *(Luca fa presto)* for his speedy workmanship. While the Medici originally occupied this 1444 house, in the 1700s it became home to the Riccardi family, who added the Baroque flourishes.

Cost and Hours: €10, cash only, covered by Firenze Card, Thu-Tue 8:30-19:00, closed Wed, ticket entrance is north of the gated courtyard, videoguide-€4, Via Cavour 3, tel. 055-276-0340, www.palazzo-medici.it.

▯ See the Medici-Riccardi Palace Tour chapter.

Leonardo Museums

Two different-but-similar entrepreneurial establishments—Le Macchine di Leonardo da Vinci and Museo Leonardo da Vinci—

are several blocks apart and show off reproductions of Leonardo's ingenious inventions. While there are no actual historic artifacts, each museum shows dozens of Leonardo's inventions and experiments made into working models. You might see a full-size armored tank, walk into a chamber of mirrors, operate a rotating crane, or watch experiments in flying. The exhibits are described in English, and you're encouraged to touch and play with many of the models (great for kids). The Macchine has larger scale models; the Museo is more extensive and has better visitor information. Either is fun for anyone who wants to crank the shaft and spin the ball bearings of Leonardo's fertile imagination.

Cost and Hours: Admission to each museum is €7 for adults, €5 for kids 6 and older, free for kids 5 and under (€1-2 discount with this book). **Le Macchine di Leonardo da Vinci**—daily 9:30-19:30, Nov-March 10:30-18:30, last entry one hour before closing; in Galleria Michelangelo at Via Cavour 21; tel. 055-295-264, www.museoleonardodavincifirenze.com. **Museo Leonardo da Vinci**—daily 10:00-19:00, Nov-March until 18:00, last entry 45 minutes before closing, Via dei Servi 66 red, tel. 055-282-966, www.mostredileonardo.com.

BETWEEN THE DUOMO AND PIAZZA DELLA SIGNORIA
Casa di Dante (Dante's House)

Dante Alighieri (1265-1321), the poet who gave us *The Divine Comedy,* is the Shakespeare of Italy, the father of the modern Italian language, and the face on the country's €2 coin. However, most Americans know little of him. Unfortunately, this small museum (in a building near where Dante likely lived) is not the ideal place to start. Even though it has English information, the museum assumes visitors have prior knowledge of the poet. It's not a medieval-

flavored house with period furniture—it's just a small, low-tech museum about Dante. Still, Dante lovers can trace his interesting life and works through pictures, models, and artifacts, and learn about the medieval city Dante lived in.

Cost and Hours: €4, covered by Firenze Card, April-Sept daily 10:00-18:00; Oct-March Tue-Sun 10:00-17:00, closed Mon; near the Bargello at Via Santa Margherita 1, tel. 055-219-416, www.museocasadidante.it.

Visiting the Museum: As you traverse the three floors of this museum, you'll walk through Dante's life—from starry-eyed youth to bitter exile, to the beatific legacy of his poetic genius. Some call Dante the father of the Renaissance. If you're new to the poet, the following information may help the museum seem less Dante-ing.

First Floor: Begin in Room I (straight ahead from the ticket desk). Dante was born into the noble Alighieri family (see his family tree) and baptized in the Baptistery (see old sketch). His plan in life was to be a doctor, symbolized by the glass cases of herbs.

Continue into Room II to see the life-changing moment when Dante first set eyes on Beatrice Portinari, and fell in love with her (look for a starry-sky picture of the event). They ended up marrying other people, but Beatrice remained Dante's muse, inspiring him to give up medicine in favor of writing lofty poetry.

In Room III, a model of Dante's Florence shows it as a walled city of many towers, housing feuding Monatague and Capulet-type clans. Room IV features the decisive Battle of Campaldino (on "San Barnaba Saturday"). Florence's army (including Dante) won, establishing the city's dominance, and elevating Dante to a prominent ambassadorship. Now 35 years old—"midway along the journey" of man's traditional 70-year lifespan—Dante was at his peak. Then it all went bad.

Second Floor: Head upstairs into Room V. Dante became ensnared in the confusing political battles between the pope (Boniface VIII) and the Holy Roman Emperor (Henry VII)—between the Black Guelphs and the White Ghibellines. Dante's side lost. Suddenly, politically incorrect Dante was exiled—see the *Book of the Nail ("Libro del Chiodo")* that condemned him. He would never again see his beloved Florence.

Dante roamed Italy, where he was taken in by sympathetic nobles. On display, you'll see a flattering modern portrait of Dante (hanging high above the book). Opposite the book, inside a reconstruction of a medieval bedroom, there's a more realistic painting of him—in red, forlorn, having received the news of his exile, with his distinctive ear-flap cap, hooked nose, and jutting chin.

In exile, Dante completed his magnum opus, *The Divine Comedy*. In 1321, still forbidden to return to his homeland, he died (see his death mask) and was buried in Ravenna.

Top Floor: Dante's most enduring legacy is *The Divine Comedy*. The entire poem is displayed on the wall along with 14th-century illuminated (illustrated) manuscripts of the masterpiece. Displays bring the poem to life. The *Divine Comedy* tells the story of a lost pilgrim who must journey through Hell (*inferno,* a spiral-shaped hole through the Earth), Purgatory (*purgatorio,* a spiral-shaped mountain), and Paradise (*paradiso,* the concentric orbits of satellites that surround Earth). After his years of wandering, he finally comes home to Paradise, guided by his spiritual muse—Beatrice.

▲Orsanmichele Church

In the ninth century, this loggia (covered courtyard) was a market used for selling grain (stored upstairs). Later, it was enclosed to make a church.

Outside are dynamic, statue-filled niches, some with accom-

SIGHTS

panying symbols from the guilds that sponsored the art. Donatello's *St. Mark* and *St. George* (on the northeast and northwest corners) step out boldly in the new Renaissance style.

The interior has a glorious Gothic tabernacle (1359), which houses the painted wooden panel that depicts *Madonna delle Grazie* (1346). The iron bars spanning the vaults were the Italian Gothic answer to the French Gothic external buttresses. Look for the rectangular holes in the piers—these were once grain chutes that connected to the upper floors. The museum upstairs (free, open Monday only) displays most of the original statues from the niches outside the building, including ones by Ghiberti, Donatello, Brunelleschi, and others.

Cost and Hours: Free, daily 10:00-17:00, free upstairs museum open only Mon 10:00-16:45, niche sculptures always viewable from the outside.

Evening Concerts: You can give the *Madonna delle Grazie* a special thanks if you're in town when the church is hosting an evening concert (sometimes held in museum, tickets sold on day of concert from door facing Via de' Calzaiuoli; also books Uffizi and Accademia tickets, ticket window open Mon-Sat 9:00-16:00, closed Sun).

📖 See page 85 of the Renaissance Walk chapter.

▲Mercato Nuovo (a.k.a. the Straw Market)

This market loggia is how Orsanmichele looked before it became a church. Originally a silk-and-straw market, Mercato Nuovo still functions as a rustic yet touristy market (at the intersection of Via Calimala and Via Porta Rossa; daily 9:00-18:30). Prices are soft, but San Lorenzo Market (listed earlier) is much better for haggling. Notice the circled X in the center, marking the spot where people landed after being hoisted up to the top and dropped as punishment for bankruptcy (easiest to find when the market is closed and the vendors disappear). You'll also find *Il Porcellino* (a statue of a wild boar nicknamed "The Piglet"), which people rub and give coins to ensure their return to Florence. This new copy, while only a few years old, already has a polished snout. At the back corner, a wagon sells tripe (cow innards) sandwiches—a local favorite (for more on this Tuscan taste treat, see page 284).

▲Piazza della Repubblica

Located on the site of the original Roman Forum, this square holds all that survives of Roman Florence: a single column nicknamed the "belly button of Florence." In the 1500s, this historical square served as the center of the city's Jewish quarter (which became a ghetto after Cosimo I walled it up in 1571). The city razed the ghetto and the city walls in the 1860s to make way for Florence's transformation into the grand capital of the newly united nation of

Italy. This square was to be its centerpiece, and the triumphal arch is inscribed accordingly: "The squalor of the ancient city is given a new life."

For more about Piazza della Repubblica, 🕮 see page 84 of the Renaissance Walk chapter.

Nearby: Between here and the river, you'll find characteristic parts of the medieval city that give a sense of what this neighborhood felt like before it was bulldozed. Back in the Middle Ages, writers described Florence as so densely built up that when it rained, pedestrians didn't get wet. Torches were used to light the lanes in midday. The city was prickly with noble families' towers (like San Gimignano) and had Romeo and Juliet-type family feuds. But with the rise of city power (c. 1300), no noble family was allowed to have an architectural ego trip taller than the Palazzo Vecchio, and nearly all other towers were taken down.

Palazzo Strozzi

The former home of the wealthy Strozzi family, great rivals of the Medici, offers a textbook example of a Renaissance palace (built between 1489 and 1538). It feels like an attempt to one-up the Medici-Riccardi Palace just a few blocks away. Step into its grand courtyard and imagine how well-to-do families competed to commission grandiose structures (and artistic masterpieces) to promote their status and wealth. The Strozzi were bankers. And, considering how the family name, Strozzi, gave Italian its words for loan shark *(strozzino)* and strangle *(strozzare)*, their loans (with notoriously high interest rates) must have come with some aggressive banking practices. Today the palace hosts top-notch special exhibitions, which are usually uncrowded and well described in English. The courtyard also hosts a tranquil, shaded café.

Cost and Hours: Free entry to courtyard and café, both open daily 9:00-20:00 and sometimes later; gallery price depends on changing exhibits—typically around €10, covered by Firenze Card, daily 10:00-20:00, Thu until 23:00, last entry one hour before closing; just west of Piazza della Repubblica at Piazza Strozzi, tel. 055-264-5155, www.palazzostrozzi.org.

▲Palazzo Davanzati

This five-story, late-medieval tower house offers a rare look at a noble dwelling built in the 14th century. The ground-floor loggia and first floor are always open to visitors; to see the remaining floors (more living quarters and the kitchen), you must make a timed-entry reser-

vation for an escorted visit (usually at 10:00, 11:00, and 12:00; call ahead to be sure there's space or ask when you arrive). Like other buildings of the age, the exterior is festooned with 14th-century horse-tethering rings made from iron, torch holders, and poles upon which to hang laundry and fly flags. Inside, though the furnishings are pretty sparse, you'll see richly painted walls, a long chute that functioned as a well, plenty of fireplaces, a lace display, and even an indoor "outhouse." You can borrow English descriptions in each room.

Cost and Hours: €6, covered by Firenze Card, Tue-Sat 8:15-13:50; also open first, third, and fifth Sun and second and fourth Mon of each month; Via Porta Rossa 13, tel. 055-238-8610.

ON AND NEAR PIAZZA DELLA SIGNORIA
▲▲▲Uffizi Gallery

This greatest collection of Italian paintings anywhere features works by Giotto, Leonardo, Raphael, Caravaggio, Titian, and

Michelangelo, and a roomful of Botticellis, including the *Birth of Venus*. Start with Giotto's early stabs at Renaissance-style realism, then move on through the 3-D experimentation of the early 1400s to the real thing rendered by the likes of Botticelli and Leonardo. Finish off with Michelangelo and Titian. Because only 600 visitors are allowed inside the building at any one time, there's generally a very long wait. The good news: no Vatican-style mob scenes inside. The museum is nowhere near as big as it is great. Few tourists spend more than two hours inside.

Cost and Hours: €12.50 (€8 if there's no special exhibit), extra €4 for recommended reservation, free and crowded on first Sun of the month, covered by Firenze Card; Tue-Sun 8:15-18:50, closed Mon, last entry 45 minutes before closing; audioguide-€6, reservation tel. 055-294-883, www.uffizi. beniculturali.it. To avoid the long ticket lines, get a Firenze Card (see page 30) or make reservations (see page 34).

📖 See the Uffizi Gallery Tour chapter or 🎧 download my free audio tour.

Uffizi Courtyard: Enjoy the courtyard (free), full of artists and souvenir stalls. (Swing by after dinner when it's crowd-free, and talented street musicians take advantage of the space's superior acoustics.) The surrounding statues honor earthshaking Florentines.

Nearby: The **Loggia dei Lanzi,** across from the Palazzo Vecchio and facing the square, is where Renaissance Florentines once

The Medici in a Minute and a Half

The Medici family—part *Sopranos,* part Kennedys, part John-D-and-Catherine-T art patrons—dominated Florentine politics for 300 years (c. 1434-1737). Originally a hardworking, middle-class family in the cloth, silk, and banking businesses, they used their wealth, blue-collar popularity, and philanthropy to rise into Europe's nobility, producing popes and queens.

1400s: The Princes

Lorenzo the Magnificent (ruled 1469-1492), Cosimo the Elder's grandson, epitomized the Medici ruling style: publicly praising Florence's constitution while privately holding the purse strings. A true Renaissance Man, Lorenzo's personal charisma, public festivals, and support of Leonardo, Botticelli, and teenage Michelangelo made Florence Europe's most enlightened city.

1494-1532: Exile in Rome

After Lorenzo's early death, the family was exiled by the Florentines. The Medici became victims of bank failure, Savonarola's reforms, and the Florentine tradition of democracy. They built a power base in Rome under Lorenzo's son (Pope Leo X, who made forays into Florence) and nephew (Pope Clement VII, who finally invaded Florence and crushed the republic).

1537-1737: The Grand Duchy—Mediocre Medici

Backed by Europe's popes and kings, the "later" Medici—descendants of Cosimo the Elder's brother—ruled Florence and Tuscany as just another duchy. Cosimo I was politically repressive but a generous patron of the arts, leaving his mark on the Palazzo Vecchio, the Uffizi, and the Pitti Palace. Cosimo II supported Galileo. Famous throughout Europe, the Medici married into Europe's royal families (Catherine and Marie de' Medici were queens of France), even while Florence declined as a European power.

debated the issues of the day; a collection of Medici-approved sculptures now stand (or writhe) under its canopy, including Cellini's bronze *Perseus.*

Loggia dei Lanzi and the Uffizi courtyard are covered starting on page 89 of my 📖 Renaissance Walk chapter and in my 🎧 free Renaissance Walk audio tour.

SIGHTS

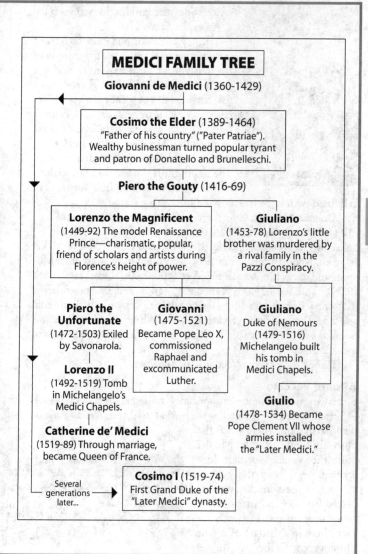

MEDICI FAMILY TREE

Giovanni de Medici (1360-1429)

Cosimo the Elder (1389-1464)
"Father of his country" ("Pater Patriae").
Wealthy businessman turned popular tyrant
and patron of Donatello and Brunelleschi.

Piero the Gouty (1416-69)

Lorenzo the Magnificent
(1449-92) The model Renaissance
Prince—charismatic, popular,
friend of scholars and artists during
Florence's height of power.

Giuliano
(1453-78) Lorenzo's little
brother was murdered by
a rival family in the
Pazzi Conspiracy.

Piero the Unfortunate
(1472-1503) Exiled
by Savonarola.

Giovanni
(1475-1521)
Became Pope Leo X,
commissioned
Raphael and
excommunicated
Luther.

Giuliano
Duke of Nemours
(1479-1516)
Michelangelo built
his tomb in
Medici Chapels.

Lorenzo II
(1492-1519) Tomb
in Michelangelo's
Medici Chapels.

Giulio
(1478-1534) Became
Pope Clement VII whose
armies installed
the "Later Medici."

Catherine de' Medici
(1519-89) Through marriage,
became Queen of France.

Several generations later...

Cosimo I (1519-74)
First Grand Duke of the
"Later Medici" dynasty.

▲▲Palazzo Vecchio

This castle-like fortress with the 300-foot spire dominates Florence's main square. In Renaissance times, it was the Town Hall, where citizens pioneered the once-radical notion of self-rule. Its official name—Palazzo della Signoria—refers to the elected members of the city council. In 1540, the tyrant Cosimo I made the building his personal palace, redecorating the interior in lavish

style. Today the building functions once again as the Town Hall.

Entry to the ground-floor courtyard is free, so even if you don't go upstairs to the museum, you can step inside and feel the essence of the Medici. There's also a fine little exhibit of scenes from old Florence. Paying customers can see Cosimo's (fairly) lavish royal apartments, decorated with (fairly) top-notch paintings and statues by Michelangelo and Donatello. The highlight is the Grand Hall (Salone dei Cinquecento), a 13,000-square-foot hall lined with huge frescoes and interesting statues.

Cost and Hours: Courtyard-free, museum-€10, tower climb-€10 (418 steps), museum plus tower-€14, excavations-€4, combo-ticket for all three-€18, covered by Firenze Card (pick up ticket at ground-floor information desk before entering museum). Museum and excavations open Fri-Wed 9:00-23:00 (Oct-March until 19:00), Thu 9:00-14:00 year-round; tower keeps shorter hours (last entry one hour before closing); last tickets for all sights sold one hour before closing; videoguide-€5, English tours available (see page 171), Piazza della Signoria, tel. 055-276-8224, www.musefirenze.it.

📖 See the Palazzo Vecchio Tour chapter.

▲Ponte Vecchio

Florence's most famous bridge has long been lined with shops. Originally these were butcher shops that used the river as a handy

disposal system. Then, when the powerful and princely Medici built the Vasari Corridor (described next) over the bridge, the stinky meat market was replaced by more elegant gold and silver shops (some of which remain here to this day). A statue of Benvenuto Cellini, the master

goldsmith of the Renaissance, stands in the center, ignored by the flood of tacky tourism.

📖 For more about the bridge, see page 91 of the Renaissance Walk chapter and page 220 of the Oltrarno Walk chapter.

Vasari Corridor

This elevated and enclosed passageway, constructed in 1565, gave the Medici a safe, private commute over Ponte Vecchio from their Pitti Palace home to their Palazzo Vecchio offices. It's open only by special appointment. While enticing to lovers of Florence, the actual tour experience isn't much. Entering from inside the Uffizi Gallery, you walk along a modern-feeling hall (wide enough to carry a Medici on a sedan chair) across Ponte Vecchio, and end in the Pitti Palace. Half the corridor is lined with Europe's best collection of self-portraits, along with other paintings (mostly 17th- and 18th-century) that seem like they didn't make the cut to be hung on the walls of the Uffizi.

Entering the Corridor: As of this printing, the corridor was closed for safety improvements, but may reopen in time for your visit. Check at the TI or on the Uffizi website (www.uffizi.org/the-vasari-corridor/). When it's open, only a very limited number of tourists are allowed in (typically only for a few weeks each spring, requires a reservation and sells out far in advance; tel. 055-294-883).

▲▲Galileo Science Museum
(Museo Galilei e Istituto di Storia della Scienza)

When we think of the Florentine Renaissance, we think of visual arts: painting, mosaics, architecture, and sculpture. But when the visual arts declined in the 1600s (abused and co-opted by political powers), music and science flourished in Florence. The first opera was written here. And Florence hosted many scientific breakthroughs, as you'll see in this fascinating collection of Renaissance and later clocks, telescopes, maps, and ingenious gadgets. Trace the technical innovations as mod-

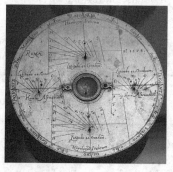

ern science emerges from 1000 to 1900. Some of the most talked about bottles in Florence are the ones here that contain Galileo's fingers. Exhibits include various tools for gauging the world, from a compass and thermometer to Galileo's telescopes. Other displays delve into clocks, pumps, medicine, and chemistry. It's friendly, comfortably cool, never crowded, and just a block east of the Uffizi on the Arno River.

Cost and Hours: €9, covered by Firenze Card, Wed-Mon 9:30-18:00, Tue until 13:00, guided tours available—see page 254, Piazza dei Giudici 1, tel. 055-265-311, www.museogalileo.it.

📖 See the Galileo Science Museum Tour chapter.

▲Fashion Museums

Medici, Michelangelo, meh. Fashionistas who've had enough of 15th-century Florence enjoy delving into the 21st century at one of these fresh, well-presented, and stylish museums.

The **Gucci Museum** (which may be closed) is on Piazza della Signoria and tells the story of famous designer Guccio Gucci, who, in 1921, founded the company that has been synonymous with style for decades. Seven rooms show off carefully curated items from the Gucci archives, while two more feature changing contemporary art exhibits, all watched over by the impeccably attired staff. Your visit begins with a section dedicated to travel, a limited-edition 1979 Gucci Cadillac, and all manner of top-of-the line travel cases. Then you'll head up for temporary exhibits of contemporary art, along with exhibits on the company's unique Flora pattern, handbags from every era, and eveningwear. The top floor shows how the interlocking-clasp "GG" logo has evolved and been incorporated into fashion over time, displays Gucci home decor, and shows off several of the company's iconic bamboo-handle handbags. The suitably stylish café and bookshop are open even to those not visiting the museum (€7, not covered by Firenze Card, daily 10:00-20:00, Fri until 23:00, Piazza della Signoria 10, tel. 055-7592-7010, www.guccimuseo.com).

The **Ferragamo** flagship store has an interesting, nine-room **shoe museum.** The specific exhibit changes each year, but it's typically more fanciful and imaginative than the Gucci Museum (€6, covered by Firenze Card, daily 10:00-19:30, near Santa Trinità bridge at Piazza Santa Trinità 5 red, see map on page 316 for location, tel. 055-356-2846, www.ferragamo.com/museo/en/usa).

EAST OF PIAZZA DELLA SIGNORIA
▲▲▲Bargello (Museo Nazionale del Bargello)

This underappreciated sculpture museum is in a former police station-turned-prison that looks like a mini-Palazzo Vecchio. It

has Donatello's very influential, painfully beautiful *David* (the first male nude to be sculpted in a thousand years), multiple works by Michelangelo, and rooms of Medici treasures. Moody Donatello, who embraced realism with his lifelike statues, set the personal and artistic style for many Renaissance artists to follow. The best pieces are in the ground-floor room at the foot of the outdoor staircase (with fine works by Michelangelo, Cellini, and Giambologna) and in the "Donatello room" directly above (including his two different *David*s, plus Ghiberti and Brunelleschi's revolutionary dueling door panels and yet another *David* by Verrocchio).

Cost and Hours: €8, cash only, free and crowded on first Sun of the month, covered by Firenze Card; Tue-Sat 8:15-17:00 (later for special exhibits), Nov-March until 13:50; also open second and fourth Mon and the first, third, and fifth Sun of each month, last entry 40 minutes before closing; reservations possible but unnecessary, Via del Proconsolo 4, tel. 055-238-8606.

☐ See the Bargello Tour chapter or ♪ download my free audio tour.

▲▲Santa Croce Church

This 14th-century Franciscan church, decorated with centuries of precious art, holds the tombs of great Florentines. The loud 19th-

century Victorian Gothic facade faces a huge square ringed with tempting shops and littered with tired tourists. Escape into the church and admire its sheer height and spaciousness. Your ticket includes the Pazzi Chapel and a small museum; the complex also houses a leather school.

Cost and Hours: €8, covered by Firenze Card, Mon-Sat 9:30-17:30, Sun 14:00-17:30, multimedia guide-€6, modest dress required, 10-minute walk east of the Palazzo Vecchio along Borgo de' Greci, tel. 055-246-6105, www.santacroceopera.it. The **leather school,** at the back of the church, is free and sells church tickets—handy when the church has a long line (daily 10:00-18:00, closed Sun Nov-March, has own entry behind church plus an entry within the church, www.scuoladelcuoio.com).

☐ See the Santa Croce Tour chapter.

▲Casa Buonarroti (Michelangelo's House)

A property once owned by Michelangelo, this house was built after the artist's death by his grand-nephew "Michelangelo the Younger," who turned it into a little museum honoring his famous relative. The highlights—Michelangelo's first sculptures and some sketches—are not must-sees in art-heavy Florence, but are appreciated by Michelangelovers. The place where Michelangelo actually grew up is only a few blocks from here, at 10 Via de' Bentaccordi.

Cost and Hours: €6.50, covered by Firenze Card, Wed-Mon 10:00-17:00, closed Tue, Via Ghibellina 70, tel. 055-241-752, www.casabuonarroti.it.

Visiting the Museum: After browsing the ground floor (of

Michelangelo the Younger's collection of ancient pottery), climb the stairs to the first-floor landing, where you come face-to-face with portraits (by his contemporaries) of 60-year-old Michelangelo, the Buonarroti family walking sticks, and some leather slippers thought to be Michelangelo's.

The room to the left of the landing displays two relief panels, Michelangelo's earliest known sculptures. Teenage Michelangelo carved every inch of the *Battle of the Centaurs* (1490-1492). This squirming tangle of battling nudes shows his fascination with anatomy. He kept this in his personal collection all his life. *The Madonna of the Stairs* (c. 1490) is as contemplative as *Centaurs* is dramatic. Throughout his long career, bipolar Michelangelo veered between these two styles—moving or still, emotional or thoughtful, pagan or Christian.

In an adjoining room is the big wooden model of a project Michelangelo took on but never completed: the facade of the Basilica of San Lorenzo (which remains bare brick to this day). The reclining river god was a model for one of the statues in the Medici Chapels.

Back near the landing, step into the darkened room with Michelangelo's sketches *(disegni)*. This is only a slice of the museum's vast collection. Vasari claimed that Michelangelo wanted to burn his preliminary sketches, lest anyone think him less than perfect.

Another room near the landing displays small clay and wax models—some by Michelangelo, some by pupils—used by the artist to sketch out ideas for his statues.

You'll also visit a series of ornately paneled and frescoed rooms where Michelangelo the Younger lived, carrying on the legacy of his esteemed forebear. Back downstairs, a room often hosts excellent temporary exhibits.

NEAR THE TRAIN STATION
▲▲Church of Santa Maria Novella

This 13th-century Dominican church is rich in art. Along with crucifixes by Giotto and Brunelleschi, it contains the textbook example of the early Renaissance mastery of perspective: *The Trinity* by Masaccio. The exquisite chapels trace art in Florence from medieval times to early Baroque. The

outside of the church features a dash of Romanesque (horizontal stripes), Gothic (pointed arches), Renaissance (geometric shapes), and Baroque (scrolls). Step in and look down the 330-foot nave for a 14th-century optical illusion.

Next to the church are the cloisters and the **museum,** located in the old Dominican convent of Santa Maria Novella. The museum's highlight is the breathtaking Spanish Chapel, with walls covered by a series of frescoes by Andrea di Bonaiuto.

Cost and Hours: Church and museum—€5, covered by Firenze Card; Mon-Thu 9:00-19:00 (Oct-March until 17:30), Fri 11:00-19:00 (Oct-March until 17:30), Sat 9:00-17:30, Sun 13:00-17:30, last entry 45 minutes before closing; multimedia guide—€3, modest dress required, main entrance on Piazza Santa Maria Novella, tel. 055-219-257, www.chiesasantamarianovella.it.

📖 See the Santa Maria Novella Tour chapter.

Nearby: Behind the church you'll find a top-of-the-line *parfumerie,* the **Farmacia di Santa Maria Novella,** which was founded by the Dominicans in 1612 (daily 9:00-20:00, Via della Scala 16). Even nonshoppers enjoy exploring its elegant halls and heaven-scent. For details, see page 318.

THE OLTRARNO (SOUTH OF THE ARNO RIVER)

📖 The Oltrarno Walk chapter connects several of these sights, including the Pitti Palace, Brancacci Chapel, and Santo Spirito Church.

▲▲Pitti Palace

The imposing Pitti Palace, several blocks southwest of Ponte Vecchio, has many separate museums and two gardens. The main

reason to visit is to see the Palatine Gallery, which houses a fine painting collection that picks up where the Uffizi leaves off.

Cost and Hours: The Palatine Gallery, Royal Apartments, and Gallery of Modern Art are covered by **ticket #1**—€13 (€8.50 if no special exhibits)—and are open Tue-Sun 8:15-18:50, closed Mon, last entry 45 minutes before closing. The Boboli and Bardini Gardens, Costume Gallery, Argenti/Silverworks Museum (the Medici treasures), and Porcelain Museum are covered by **ticket #2**—€10 (€7 if no special exhibits)—and are open daily June-Aug 8:15-19:30, April-May and Sept until 18:30, March and Oct until 17:30, Nov-Feb until 16:30, closed first and last Mon of each month, last entry one hour before closing. Reservations are possible

1 Hotel Silla
2 Antico Ristoro Di' Cambi
3 Trattoria Al Tranvai
4 Trattoria Sabatino
5 Antica Mescita San Niccolò

6 Bar Il Baretto del Rifrullo & Il Gelato di Filo
7 Zeb Wine Bar
8 Negroni & Zoe Nightclubs
9 Clet Gallery
10 Legatoria La Carta

but unnecessary. All palace sights are covered by the Firenze Card. The place is free and crowded on the first Sun of the month. The €8 audioguide explains the sprawling palace. Tel. 055-238-8614, www.uffizi.beniculturali.it.

📖 See the Pitti Palace Tour chapter.

▲▲Brancacci Chapel

For the best look at works by Masaccio (one of the early Renaissance pioneers of perspective in painting), see his restored frescoes here. Instead of medieval religious symbols, Masaccio's paintings feature simple, strong human figures with facial expressions that

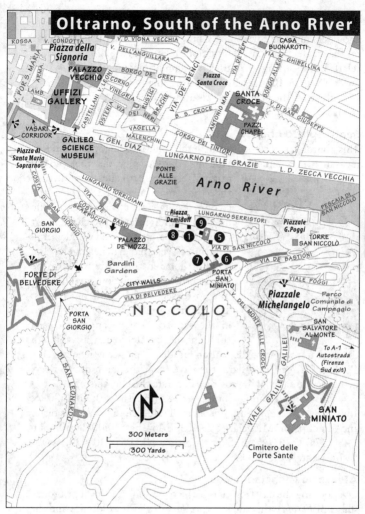

Oltrarno, South of the Arno River

reflect their emotions. The accompanying works of Masolino and Filippino Lippi provide illuminating contrasts.

Cost and Hours: €6, cash only, covered by Firenze Card; free and easy reservations required, though it's usually possible to walk right in on weekdays and any day off-season, especially if you arrive before 15:30; Mon and Wed-Sat 10:00-17:00, Sun 13:00-17:00, closed Tue, last entry 45 min-

utes before closing; free 20-minute film, videoguide—€3, knees and shoulders must be covered, in Church of Santa Maria del Carmine on Piazza del Carmine, reservations tel. 055-276-8224, ticket desk tel. 055-284-361, http://museicivicifiorentini.comune.fi.it.

📖 See the Brancacci Chapel Tour chapter.

Nearby: The neighborhoods around the church are considered the last surviving bits of old Florence.

Santo Spirito Church

This church has a classic Brunelleschi interior—enjoy its pure Renaissance lines (and ignore the later Baroque altar that replaced the

original). Notice Brunelleschi's "dice"—the large stone cubes added above the column capitals that contribute to the nave's playful lightness. The church's art treasure is a painted, carved wooden crucifix by 17-year-old Michelangelo. The sculptor donated this early work to the monastery in appreciation for allowing him to dissect and learn about bodies. The Michelangelo *Crocifisso* is displayed in the sacristy, which can be accessed through the cloister, entering through the door to the left of the church facade. Copies of Michelangelo's *Pietà* and *Risen Christ* flank the nave (near the main door). Beer-drinking, guitar-playing rowdies decorate the church steps.

Cost and Hours: Church—free, Thu-Tue 10:00-12:30 & 16:00-18:00 except Sun opens at 11:30, closed Wed; cloister and crucifix of Michelangelo—€3, Mon-Sat 10:00-18:00, Sun 14:00-17:00; Piazza di Santo Spirito, tel. 055-210-030, www.basilicasantospirito.it.

▲Piazzale Michelangelo

Overlooking the city from across the river (look for the huge bronze statue of *David*), this square has a superb view of Florence and the

stunning dome of the Duomo. It's worth the 25-minute hike, taxi, or bus ride.

An inviting café (open seasonally) with great views is just below the overlook. The best photos are taken from the street immediately below the overlook (go around to the right and

down a few steps). Off the west side of the piazza is a somewhat hidden terrace, an excellent place to retreat from the mobs. After dark, the square is packed with school kids licking ice cream and each other. About 200 yards beyond all the tour groups and teen-agers is the stark, beautiful, crowd-free, Romanesque San Miniato Church (next listing). A WC is located just off the road, halfway between the two sights.

Getting There (and Back): It makes sense to take a taxi or ride the bus up and then enjoy the easy downhill walk back into town. Bus #12 takes you up (departs from train station, near Piazza di Santa Maria Novella, and just over the Ponte alla Carraia bridge on Oltrarno side of river—see map on page 18 for bus stops; takes 20-30 minutes, longer in bad traffic).

The hike down is quick and enjoyable (or take bus #13 back down). Find the steps between the two bars on the San Miniato Church side of the parking lot (Via San Salvatore al Monte). At the first landing (marked #3), peek into the rose garden (Giardino delle Rose). After a few minutes, you'll walk through the old wall (Porta San Miniato) and emerge in the delightful little Oltrarno neighborhood of San Niccolò, with a fun and funky passel of cafés and restaurants (for recommendations, see page 300).

SIGHTS

▲▲San Miniato Church

According to legend, the martyred St. Minias—this church's namesake—was beheaded on the banks of the Arno in A.D. 250.

 He picked up his head and walked here (this was before the #12 bus), where he died and was buried in what became the first Christian cemetery in Florence. In the 11th century, this church was built to house Minias' remains. Imagine this fine church all alone—without any nearby build-ings or fancy stairs—a peaceful ref-uge where white-robed Benedictine monks could pray and work (their motto: *ora et labora*). The evening vesper service with the monks chanting in Latin offers a meditative worship experience—a peaceful way to end your visit.

Cost and Hours: Free, Mon-Sat 9:30-13:00 & 15:30-20:00, until 19:00 off-season, Sun 9:30-20:00, closed sporadically for spe-cial occasions, tel. 055-234-2731, www.sanminiatoalmonte.it.

Getting There: It's about 200 yards above Piazzale Michelan-gelo. From the station, bus #12 takes you right to the San Miniato al Monte stop (hop off and hike up the grand staircase); bus #13 takes you back down the hill.

Gregorian Chants: To experience this mystical medieval space at its full potential, time your visit to coincide with a prayer service of Gregorian chants. In general, these are held each eve-ning at 17:30 and last 30 minutes—but as the schedule is subject to change, double-check with any TI, the church's website, or call ahead.

Visiting the Church: For a thousand years, San Miniato Church—still part of a functioning monastery—has blessed the city that lies at the foot of its hill. Carved into the marble of its threshold on the left door is the Genesis verse *"Haec est Porta Coeli"* ("This is the Gate of Heaven").

The church's green-and-white marble **facade** (12th century) is classic Florentine Romanesque, one of the oldest in town. The perfect symmetry is a reminder of the perfection of God. The central mosaic shows Christ flanked by Mary and St. Minias. Minias, who was King of Armenia before his conversion, offers his secular crown to the heavenly king. The eagle on top, with bags of wool in his talons, reminds all who approach the church who paid for it—the wool guild.

Stepping inside **the nave,** you enter the closest thing to a holy space that medieval Florentines could create. The "carpet of marble" dates from 1207. The wood ceiling is painted as it was originally. The glittering 13th-century golden mosaic that dominates the dome at the front of the nave repeats the scene on the church's facade: St. Minias offering his paltry secular crown to the king in heaven.

The Renaissance tabernacle front and center was commissioned by the Medici. It's a résumé of early Renaissance humanism, with experiments in 3-D paintings (including St. Minias, in red) and a plush canopy of glazed terra-cotta panels by Luca della Robbia.

On the left side of the nave is an exquisite chapel dedicated to Cardinal Jacopo of Portugal. When 26-year-old Jacopo died in Florence (1459), his wealthy family mourned him by adding a chapel to the church (by cutting a hole in the church wall) and hiring the best artists of the day to decorate it. The family could enter their private chapel, take a seat on the throne (on the left), and meditate on the tomb of Jacopo (on the right).

The church is designed like a split-level rambler, with staircases on either side of the altar, leading upstairs and down. Downstairs in the **crypt,** an alabaster window helps create a quiet and mysterious atmosphere. The forest of columns and capitals are all recycled...each from ancient Roman buildings and each different. The floor is paved with the tombstones of long-forgotten big shots. Look through the window in the marble altar to see St. Minias' name, carved on the box that holds his mortal remains.

At the **staircase** to the right of the main altar, notice the sinopia on the wall. A sinopia is a pattern that guides the fresco artist and also gives the patron a peek at what the artist intends to create before it's set in plaster. There's a sinopia behind every surviving fresco in Florence.

Step upstairs and enter the **sacristy** (the room on the right), which is beautifully frescoed with scenes from the life of St. Benedict (circa 1350, by a follower of Giotto). Drop €2 into the electronic panel in the corner to light the room for five minutes. The elegantly bearded patron saint of Europe was the founder of the vast network of monasteries that gave the Continent some cohesiveness in the cultural darkness that followed the collapse of Rome. Benedict is shown as an active force for good, with his arm always outstretched: busy blessing, being kissed, preaching, helping, chasing the devil, bringing a man (crushed by a fallen tower) back to life, reaching out even on his death bed. Notice Benedict on the ramp, scooting up to heaven to be welcomed by an angel. And, overseeing everything, in the starry skies of the ceiling, are the four evangelists—each with his book, pen, and symbolic sidekicks.

Outside the Church: Before leaving, stroll through the cemetery behind the church (go right as you exit the church and head through the passage) to marvel at the showy crypts and headstones of Florentine hotshots from the last two centuries. *Pinocchio* fans take note: Author Carlo Lorenzini (pen name Collodi) was born in Florence and is buried here (from the bell tower, climb the steps to the wall and head right to the relatively nondescript Lorenzini family crypt at #37).

To get to Piazzale Michelangelo, head out and back down the grand staircase, savoring views of Florence along the way. Or for a quieter walk, turn right from the cemetery and pass into the adjacent park; keep veering left and you'll emerge at the viewpoint.

NEAR FLORENCE
Florence American Cemetery and Memorial

The compelling sight of endless rows of white marble crosses and Stars of David recalls the heroism of the young Americans who

fought so valiantly in World War II to free Italy (and ultimately Europe) from the grip of fascism. This cemetery is the final resting place of more than 4,000 Americans who died in the liberation of Italy. Climb the hill past the perfectly manicured lawn lined with grave markers to the memorial, where maps and a history of the Italian campaign detail the Allied advance. A staff member is on duty in the visitors center to answer questions.

Cost and Hours: Free, daily 9:00-17:00, tel. 055-202-0020, www.abmc.gov.

Getting There: The cemetery is 7.5 miles south of Florence, off Via Cassia, which parallels the *superstrada* between Florence and Siena, 2 miles south of the exit signed *Firenze Impruneta* on A-1 autostrada. If you don't have time to visit, you can see the cemetery as you drive by on the SR-2 highway from Florence to Siena (after you get on SR-2 south from the A-1 ring road, the cemetery will be on your right as you leave Florence).

Fiesole

Perched on a hill overlooking the Arno valley, the tidy little town of Fiesole (fee-AY-zoh-lay), just north of Florence, gives weary

travelers a break in the action and—during the heat of summer—a breezy location from which to admire the city below. It's a small town with a main square, a few restaurants and shops, a few minor sights, and a great view. It's fitting that the E. M. Forster novel and the Merchant-Ivory film adaptation *A Room with a View* both have ties here.

The ancient Etruscans knew a good spot when they saw one, and chose to settle here, establishing Fiesole about 400 years before the Romans founded Florence. The Romans—more concerned with water access than with Fiesole's strategic, sky-high position—shifted the region's focus down into the valley, allowing Fiesole to evolve on a more relaxed track than bustling Florence. Wealthy Renaissance families in pre-air-conditioning days chose Fiesole as a preferred vacation spot, building villas in the surrounding hillsides. Later, 19th-century Romantics spent part of the Grand Tour admiring the vistas, much like the hordes of tourists do today. Most come here for the view—the actual sights pale in comparison to those in Florence. Shutterbugs visit in the morning for the best light, while some prefer the evening for sunset.

GETTING TO FIESOLE

It's only a half-hour away by bus or taxi. From Florence's Piazza San Marco, take bus #7—enjoying a peek at gardens, vineyards, orchards, and villas—to the last stop, Piazza Mino (3-4/hour, fewer after 21:00 and on Sun, 30 minutes, €1.20, €2 if bought on bus, validate on board; departs Florence from Piazza San Marco to the right of the museum). As bus tickets can be tricky to buy in Fiesole (the lone tobacco stand that sells them can be unexpectedly closed), bring a return ticket with you from Florence—or be ready to pay extra to buy your ticket on board. Taxis from Florence cost about €25-35 (ride to the view terrace near La Reggia restaurant, then hike up to the Church of San Francesco—which is hard to reach by car—and finally explore downhill).

ORIENTATION TO FIESOLE

From the bus stop on Piazza Mino, face the long side of the church (Duomo). The best view terrace, the Church of San Francesco, and La Reggia restaurant are to the left, up the steep, stone Via San Francesco. The TI and Archaeological Area are behind the Duomo, just to the right of the bell tower. Up the main drag to the right (Via Gramsci), you'll find the Alcedo *pasticceria* and the Co-op supermarket. The small street to the far right (Via Giuseppe Verdi) leads up to a few more panoramic views in a residential neighborhood. And across the piazza is the restaurant Fiesolano.

Tourist Information: The TI is a two-minute walk from the bus stop, inside the ticket office for the Roman Archaeological Area—just head behind the church (Fri-Mon 10:00-13:00 & 14:00-17:00, closed Tue-Thu, open weekends only in Oct, closed Nov-March, Via Portigiani 3, tel. 055-596-1311, www.fiesoleforyou.it).

Market Day: Fiesole weekends often come with markets—produce on Saturday mornings, antiques on the first Sunday of each month, and all-day artisan markets on some Sundays.

SIGHTS IN FIESOLE
On or Near the Main Square
Duomo

While this church has a drab, 19th-century exterior, the interior is worth a look. The cool, clean architecture—with round Romanesque arches and narrow slits for light—is enlivened by some glittering Gothic altarpieces and a wood-beamed ceiling. Over the main door, look for the blue-and-white glazed Giovanni della Robbia statue of St. Romulus (not the founder of Rome, but Fiesole's similarly named patron saint). Then climb up the stairs past the altar and bear right to find the smiling, head-cocked tomb of Bishop Salutati, which was carved by Mino da Fiesole, a talented student of Donatello.

Cost and Hours: Free, generally daily 7:30-12:00 & 15:00-17:30, across Piazza Mino from the bus stop.

Archaeological Area and Museum

Florence has few visible Roman ruins—and archaeological finds are far, far better elsewhere in Italy—but if you're dying to see some local ancient history, Fiesole is probably your best chance.

This overpriced and sparse but well-presented complex features a largely intact Roman theater, some less-intact fragments of other buildings, and a decent museum of local finds. And the valley view and peaceful setting are lovely. If you don't want to spring for the hefty entry fee, you can get a peek of the grounds from the café terrace just to the left of the turnstile.

Cost and Hours: €10, €12 combo-ticket also covers Bandini Museum, includes excellent videoguide, covered by Firenze Card; daily 9:00-19:00, March and Oct 10:00-18:00; Nov-Feb Wed-Mon 10:00-15:00, closed Tue; behind the Duomo at Via Portigiani 1, www.museidifiesole.it.

Visiting the Ruins and Museum: Buy your ticket at the TI/ticket office (a half-block to the right, as you face the entrance). Be sure to borrow the included tablet videoguide, with ample English information and a well-produced virtual tour of the ruins before they were ruined. Then head inside, proceed straight ahead, and belly up to the railing.

At your feet is the area's chief attraction, its **Roman theater.** Occasionally used today for plays and concerts, the well-preserved theater held up to 2,000 people in its heyday. About half of what you see here has been rebuilt. More ruins sprawl nearby: To the right, marked by the three arches, are fragments of a bath complex; and to the left, in the trees, is what's left of a temple. While there's little to see, a pleasant loop walk connects everything.

The **museum,** located in the faux-temple within the Archaeological Area, imparts insight into Fiesole's Etruscan and Roman roots with well-displayed artifacts (borrow the English descriptions that supplement the videoguide). You'll see fragments of tombs (boxy bases and ornately decorated lids, depicting the departed lounging at an eternal banquet), bronze votive statues and tools, and jewelry. Upstairs are Attica-style black-and-red pottery vases. As this look originated in ancient Greece, their existence here is evidence of widely traveled Etruscan traders (who brought this style home with them). You'll also see several *bucchero* vases—a method for turning red clay into shiny black pottery pieces, in order to resemble highly prized bronze.

Bandini Museum

This petite museum displays the wooden panels of lesser-known Gothic and Renaissance painters as well as the glazed terra-cotta figures of Andrea della Robbia.

Cost and Hours: €5, €12 combo-ticket with Archaeological Area and Museum, covered by Firenze Card, Fri-Sun 9:00-19:00, closed Mon-Thu, shorter hours Oct-March, behind Duomo at Via Dupre 1.

Up the Hill, at the Top of Town

To reach these sights, you'll have to huff your way about 10 minutes steeply up from the main square and bus stop. First you'll pass the recommended La Reggia restaurant, then the terrace, and finally (a few more vertical minutes up) the church complex.

▲▲Terrace and Garden with a View

Catch the sunset (and your breath) from the sweeping view terrace just above La Reggia restaurant. Florence stretches out from the Duomo's stately dome, with the Oltrarno and Piazzale Michelangelo in the background. And the hillsides all around are draped with vineyards and speckled with luxury villas of Renaissance bigwigs who knew how to maximize a great city view.

For overachievers in search of similar views—and a peek at residential Fiesole—climb up the opposite side of the square, along the equally steep road hugging the ridgeline.

SIGHTS

Church of San Francesco

For even more hill-climbing, continue up from the view terrace to this charming church. Its small scale and several colorful altar paintings make it arguably more enjoyable than Fiesole's Duomo. Inside, you'll also find a quirky collection of souvenirs from local missionaries' travels.

Cost and Hours: Church—free, daily 7:00-20:00 except closed Fri morning, Nov-March 7:30-19:00, tel. 055-59-175; museum—free but donation suggested, same hours as church; tel. 055-59-175; both at Via San Francesco 13.

Visiting the Church: Before entering the church, poke in the doorway to the right for a look at the tranquil **cloister.** Climbing the nearby stairs, you'll find a hall of monastic cells, where Franciscan monks would meditate on colorful frescoes of bible stories. You'll see similar cells at the San Marco Museum, but these feel more lived-in.

Next head **inside** the church. The simple, clean interior allows the vibrant altar paintings that line the nave to really shine. Walking from the back to the front of this church, notice how the altarpieces evolve from rigid, staged-looking late Gothic to fully flowering, more organic High Renaissance.

Within the church complex (to the left of the altar, find the door into the cloister, then head downstairs) is the eclectic little **Franciscan Ethnographic Missionary Museum** (Museo Missionario Etnografico Francescano). Consisting primarily of items that Franciscan missionaries brought back from exotic lands, it features an Egyptian mummy, ancient coins, and Chinese Buddhas and vases. It all sits upon some very old history: One wall of the museum is actually part of the third-century Etruscan town wall.

EATING IN FIESOLE

The first restaurant is right on Piazza Mino, where the bus from Florence stops; the other is near the view terrace above town.

$$ Fiesolano, a local favorite, serves authentic Tuscan dishes at a fair price. They're particularly well-regarded for their Florentine steaks. Choose between the homey, cluttered interior, the few sidewalk tables facing the main square, or the shady garden terrace (daily 12:30-14:30 & 19:30-23:30, Piazza Mino 9 red, tel. 055-59-143, Leonardo).

$$$ Ristorante La Reggia degli Etruschi has some of the highest prices—and best views—in town, as long as you're willing to make the steep walk up. As you're paying for the panorama, it's essential to reserve a table at a window or on their terrace to fully enjoy the vista (daily 12:00-15:00 & 19:00-22:00, Via San Francesco 18, tel. 055-59-385, www.lareggiadeglietruschi.com).

Picnics: Fiesole is made-to-order for a scenic and breezy picnic. Grab a simple sandwich and a pastry at Fiesole's best *pasticceria,* **$ Alcedo** (head up the main drag from the bus stop to Via Gramsci 39, Tue-Sat 7:00-20:00, Sun 7:00-13:00, closed Mon). Round out your goodies across the street at the **Co-op** supermarket (Mon-Sat 8:00-13:00 & 16:00-20:00, closed Sun) before backtracking to the panoramic terrace. Or, for more convenience and less view, picnic at the shaded park on the way to the view terrace (walk up Via San Francesco about halfway to the terrace, and climb the stairs to the right).

RENAISSANCE WALK

After centuries of labor, Florence gave birth to the Renaissance. We'll start with the soaring church dome that stands as the proud symbol of the Renaissance spirit. Just opposite, you'll find the Baptistery doors that opened the Renaissance. Finally, we'll reach Florence's political center, dotted with monuments of that proud time. As great and rich as this city is, it's easily covered on foot. While these days many of the crowded and commercial streets of Florence have the elegance of an amusement park, you'll still find inspirational sights everywhere you look...assuming you know where to look.

The Duomo, the cathedral with the distinctive red dome, is the center of Florence and the orientation point for this walk. If you ever get lost, home's the dome. We'll start here, see several sights in the area, and then stroll down the city's pedestrian-only main street to the Palazzo Vecchio and the Arno River. Along the way, we'll pass elegant stores, lively eateries, and the parade of people that make up Florence today.

Orientation

Length of This Walk: The walk is less than a mile long. Allow two hours, including visits to the interiors of the Baptistery and Orsanmichele Church (but not the other sights mentioned).

Duomo (Cathedral): Free; Mon-Fri 10:00-17:00 (Thu until 16:30), Sat 10:00-16:45, Sun 13:30-16:45. A modest dress code is enforced.

Campanile (Giotto's Tower): €15 combo-ticket covers all Duomo sights, covered by Firenze Card, daily 8:30-20:00, 414 steps.

Baptistery: €15 combo-ticket covers all Duomo sights, covered by Firenze Card; interior open Mon-Sat 8:15-20:00, Sun 8:30-14:00. The facsimiles of the famous *Gates of Paradise* bronze doors on the exterior are always viewable (and free to see); the original panels are in the Duomo Museum.

Climbing the Dome: Though the €15 combo-ticket covers all Duomo sights, to climb the dome you must make a reservation either at the ticket office or online (www.museumflorence.com). The dome is also covered by the Firenze Card—but you must still make a reservation in person (and hope slots are available) at the ticket office opposite the Baptistery, at #7 (open daily 8:00-18:50).

Dome open Mon-Fri 8:30-20:00, Sat 8:30-17:40, Sun 13:00-16:00, 463 steps. See page 39.

See page 39.

Orsanmichele Church: Free, daily 10:00-17:00, free upstairs museum open only Mon. The replica niche sculptures are always viewable from the outside. The church hosts evening concerts; tickets are sold on the day of the concert from the door facing Via de' Calzaiuoli. At the same ticket window, you can book tickets (often same-day) for the Uffizi and Accademia (€4 reservation fee).

Palazzo Vecchio: Courtyard-free, museum-€10, tower climb-€10, museum plus tower-€14, excavations-€4, combo-ticket that includes all three-€18, covered by Firenze Card; museum open Fri-Wed 9:00-23:00 (Oct-March until 19:00), Thu 9:00-14:00 year-round.

Information: There's a TI right on Piazza del Duomo (just south of Baptistery, at the corner of Via de' Calzaiuoli), and another one on Via Cavour 1 red, a couple of blocks north of the Duomo (immediately beyond the Medici-Riccardi Palace).

Tours: ⋒ Download my free Renaissance Walk audio tour.

Services: Pay WCs are at the ticket office opposite the Baptistery. You can refill your water bottle at public twist-the-handle fountains at the Duomo (left side, by the dome entrance), the Palazzo Vecchio (behind the Neptune fountain), and on Ponte Vecchio.

Eating: You'll find plenty of cafés, self-service cafeterias, bars, and gelato shops along the route, including several recommended eateries (see the Eating in Florence chapter for details): **$ Self-Service Ristorante Leonardo** (near the Duomo), **$$ Cantinetta dei Verrazzano,** a bakery/café with good *focacce* sandwiches, and **$ Club del Gusto** and **$ All'Antico Vinaio** (both on Via dei Neri, behind the Palazzo Vecchio). **La Congrega** is a nice wine and coffee bar near the Duomo (see page 331).

(see page 331).

A fully stocked supermarket called **Sapori & Dintorni** is virtually invisible just 50 yards north of the Duomo at Borgo San Lorenzo 15 red.

Starring: Brunelleschi's dome, Ghiberti's doors, and the city of Florence—old and new.

The Walk Begins

Stroll around the piazza in front of the cathedral (the Duomo), and take in the sights. There's the church itself, with its ornate white, green, and pink facade. The Duomo is topped with a soaring red-and-white dome—though from close up, it's hard to even see the dome because the church itself is so big. To the right of the Duomo rises its skyscraping bell tower (the Campanile). In front of the church is the Baptistery, an octagonal, black-and-white stone building that's bigger than many churches.

The piazza is always buzzing with activity—tourists, horse buggies, and Florentines on their way to somewhere else—as this is one of the main intersections in town. Get a feel for the place, then let's explore.

❶ The Duomo

Florence's massive cathedral is Florence's geographical and spiritual heart. Its dome, visible from all over the city, inspired Floren-

tines to do great things. (Most recently, it inspired the city to make the area around the cathedral delightfully traffic-free.)

The church was begun in the 1296, in the Gothic style. After generations of work, it was still unfinished. The facade was little more than bare brick, and it stood that way until it was completed in 1870 in the "Neo"-Gothic style. Its "retro" look captures the feel of the original medieval facade, with green, white, and pink marble sheets that cover the brick construction. You'll see Gothic (pointed) arches and three stories decorated with mosaics and statues. This over-the-top facade is adored by many, while others call it "the cathedral in pajamas." The Duomo is dedicated to the

RENAISSANCE WALK

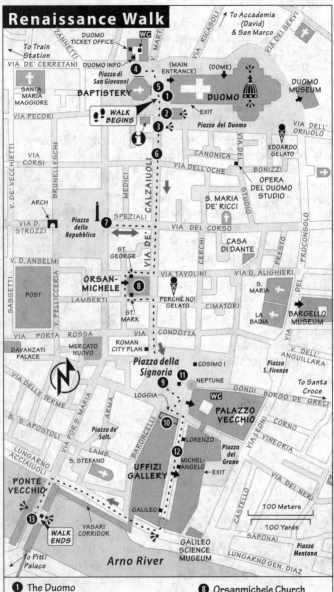

Renaissance Walk

1 The Duomo
2 Campanile
3 View of the Dome
4 Baptistery – North Doors
5 Baptistery – East Doors (Gates of Paradise)
6 Via de' Calzaiuoli
7 Piazza della Repubblica
8 Orsanmichele Church
9 Piazza della Signoria
10 Loggia dei Lanzi
11 Savonarola Plaque
12 Uffizi Courtyard Statues
13 Ponte Vecchio

Virgin Mary. Find her statue right in the center—above the main doorway but below the round window.

We won't go inside the church on this tour. It has a cavernous, bare interior with a few noteworthy sights. Entry is free, but there's often a long wait (lines decrease late in the day). For my brief self-guided tour of the interior, see page 36.

• *Now turn to the church's bell tower, to the right.*

❷ Campanile (Giotto's Tower)

The 270-foot bell tower was begun in the 1300s by the great painter Giotto. As a forerunner of the Renaissance genius, Giotto excelled

in many artistic fields, just as Michelangelo would do two centuries later. In his day, Giotto was called the ugliest man to ever walk the streets of Florence, but he designed what many call the most beautiful bell tower in all of Europe.

The bell tower served as a sculpture gallery for Renaissance artists. Find the four statues of prophets (about a third of the way up) done by the great Early Renaissance sculptor, Donatello. The most striking of them is bald-headed Habbakuk. Closer to ground level are several hexagonal panels that ring the Campanile. These reliefs depict Bible scenes: God Creates Adam, then Eve, and they set to work. Then Jabal learns to till the soil while Jubal blows his horn...and so on. The realism of these groundbreaking works paved the way for Michelangelo and the High Renaissance generations later.

(By the way, these are copies—the originals are at the excellent **Duomo Museum,** just behind the church. There you'll find more statues from the Duomo, plus displays on the dome, Ghiberti's bronze doors, and a late Pietà by Michelangelo. ▢ See the Duomo Museum Tour chapter.)

You can climb the Campanile for great views. It doesn't require a reservation, just a Duomo combo-ticket (see page 40 for information about climbing the tower).

• *Now take in the Duomo's star attraction: the dome. The best viewing spot is just to the right of the facade, from the corner of the pedestrian-only Via de' Calzaiuoli.*

❸ View of the Dome, by Brunelleschi

The dome rises 330 feet from ground level. It's made of red brick, held together with eight white ribs, and capped with a lantern.

Remember, though construction of the church had begun in

The Florentine Renaissance

In the 13th and 14th centuries, Florence was a powerful center of banking, trading, and textile manufacturing. The resulting wealth fertilized the cultural soil. Then came the Black Death in 1348. Nearly half the population died, but the infrastructure remained strong, and the city rebuilt better than ever. Led by Florence's chief family—the art-crazy Medici—and propelled by the naturally aggressive and creative spirit of the Florentines, it's no wonder that the long-awaited Renaissance finally took root here.

The Renaissance—the "rebirth" of Greek and Roman culture that swept across Europe—started around 1400 and lasted about 150 years. In politics, the Renaissance meant democracy; in science, a renewed interest in exploring nature. The general mood was optimistic and "humanistic," with a confidence in the power of the individual.

In medieval times, poverty and ignorance had made life "nasty, brutish, and short" (for lack of a better cliché). The church was the people's opiate, and their lives were only a preparation for a happier time in heaven after leaving this miserable vale of tears.

Medieval art was the church's servant. The noblest art form was architecture—churches themselves—and other arts were considered most worthwhile if they embellished the house of God. Painting and sculpture were narrative and symbolic, de-signed to tell Bible stories to the devout and illiterate masses.

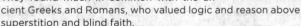
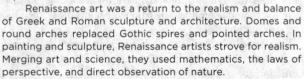

As prosperity rose in Florence, so did people's confidence in life and themselves. Middle-class craftsmen, merchants, and bankers felt they could control their own destinies, rather than be at the whim of nature. They found much in common with the an-cient Greeks and Romans, who valued logic and reason above superstition and blind faith.

Renaissance art was a return to the realism and balance of Greek and Roman sculpture and architecture. Domes and round arches replaced Gothic spires and pointed arches. In painting and sculpture, Renaissance artists strove for realism. Merging art and science, they used mathematics, the laws of perspective, and direct observation of nature.

This was not an anti-Christian movement. Artists saw themselves as an extension of God's creative powers. The church even supported the Renaissance and commissioned many of its greatest works—for instance, Raphael frescoed images of Plato and Aristotle on the walls of the Vatican. But for the first time in Europe since Roman times, there were rich laymen who wanted art simply for art's sake.

After 1,000 years of waiting, the embers of Europe's classical heritage burst into flames right here in Florence.

1296, by the 1400s there still was no suitable roof. They'd intended to top it with a dome, but the technology to span the 140-foot-wide hole had yet to be invented. *Non c'è problema*. The brash Florentines knew that someday someone would come along who could handle the challenge. That man was Filippo Brunelleschi.

Brunelleschi had a plan. He would cap the church's octagonal hole-in-the-roof with a round Roman-style dome. It would be a tall, self-supporting dome as grand as that of the ancient Pantheon—which he had studied.

Brunelleschi used a dome within a dome. What you see is the outer shell, covered in terra-cotta tile. The inner dome is thicker and provides much of the structural support. The grand white skeletal ribs connect at the top, supporting each other in a way similar to a pointed arch. Hidden between them are interlocking bricks, laid in a herringbone pattern. Rather than being stacked horizontally, like traditional brickwork, the alternating vertical bricks act as "bookends." The dome grew upward like an igloo, supporting itself as it proceeded from the base. When the ribs reached the top, Brunelleschi arched them in and fixed them in place with the lantern at the top. His dome, built in only 14 years, was the largest since ancient Rome's Pantheon.

When completed in 1436, Brunelleschi's dome was the wonder of the age. It became the model for many domes to follow, from

St. Peter's to the US Capitol. People gave it the ultimate compliment, saying, "Not even the ancients could have done it." Michelangelo, setting out to construct the dome of St. Peter's, drew inspiration from the dome of Florence. He said, "I'll make its sister...bigger, but not more beautiful."

You can climb the dome for Florence's best views, but it requires a reservation, usually in advance (for details, see page 39).

• *Next up, the Baptistery. Step into the zone between the Duomo and the Baptistery that local tour guides call the "Piazza of Paradise."*

Baptistery and Ghiberti's Bronze Doors

Florence's Baptistery is dear to the soul of the city. Built in the 11th century, atop Roman foundations, it's Florence's oldest surviving building—a thousand years old. In medieval and Renaissance times, the locals—eager to link themselves to the classical past—believed (wrongly) that this was actually an ancient Roman structure. And for a thousand years, most of the city's festivals and parades have either started or ended here.

The Baptistery is known for its doors. The most famous ones are the East Doors, which face the cathedral, but let's start with the North Doors—around to the right, where tourists go in. (Note that the doors on the Baptistery are copies. The originals are in the Duomo Museum and well worth seeing.)

❹ North Doors: The huge doors are made of rectangular panels that feature 28 scenes from the New Testament. For example, the second row from the bottom has the four Evangelists: John (with his eagle), Matthew (inspired by an angel), Luke (just chilling), and Mark.

Some say that these doors actually started the Renaissance. It was the year 1401, and Florence was holding a competition to find the best artist to make some doors for the Baptistery entrance. Florence had a long tradition of strong civic spirit, with different guilds (powerful trade associations) and merchant groups embellishing their city with superb art. All the greats entered the contest, including Donatello and Brunelleschi. The winner was relatively unknown 24-year-old Lorenzo Ghiberti. (Brunelleschi—after losing the Baptistery gig—went to Rome with Donatello, studied the Pantheon, and returned to build the Duomo's dome.)

For the next 25 years, Ghiberti worked on these North Doors, creating such realistic figures that all of Florence was astounded. But that was just the beginning.

• *Now return to the more famous doors facing the church.*

❺ East Doors (Gates of Paradise): When the Baptistery needed another set of doors, this time there was literally no contest. Ghiberti's bronze panels for these doors added a whole new dimension to art—depth. Michelangelo said these doors were fit to be the "Gates of Paradise." Here we see how the Renaissance masters merged art and science. Realism was in, and Renaissance artists used math, illusion, and dissection to create it.

Find the Jacob and Esau panel (just above eye level on the

left). The receding arches, floor tiles, and banisters create a background for a realistic scene. The figures in the foreground stand and move like real people, telling the Bible story with human details. Amazingly, this spacious, 3-D scene is made from bronze only a couple of inches deep.

Find Ghiberti's tiny self-portrait—he's the bald guy in the center of the door's frame, atop the second row of panels. Ghiberti's groundbreaking use of 3-D and the laws of perspective went on to influence the next generation of painters and artists, who would usher in the full bloom of the Renaissance. (For a full description and diagram of the doors, see page 158.)

• *At some point in your visit, you'll want to go inside the Baptistery (which requires a ticket).*

Inside the Baptistery: The interior features a fine example of pre-Renaissance mosaic art (1200s-1300s) in the Byzantine style. Workers from St. Mark's in Venice came here to make the remarkable ceiling mosaics (of Venetian glass) in the late 1200s.

The Last Judgment on the ceiling gives us a glimpse of the medieval worldview. Life was a preparation for the afterlife, when

you would be judged and saved, or judged and damned—with no in-between. Christ, peaceful and reassuring, blessed those at his right hand with heaven (thumbs up) and sent those on his left to hell (the ultimate thumbs-down), to be tortured by demons and gnashed between the teeth of monsters. This hellish scene looks like something out of the *Inferno* by Dante, who was dipped into the baptismal waters right here.

The rest of the ceiling mosaics tell the history of the world, from Adam and Eve (over the north/entrance doors, top row) to Noah and the Flood (over south doors, top row), to the life of Christ (second row, all around) to the life, ministry, and eventual beheading of John the Baptist (bottom row, all around)—all bathed in the golden glow of pre-Renaissance heaven.

• *Now head south, down the busy pedestrian-only street that runs from here toward the Arno River.*

❻ Via de' Calzaiuoli

Via de' Calzaiuoli (kahlts-ay-WOH-lee), the former "street of the stocking makers," is today lined with shops that cater to the mobs of tourists. This street has long been the main axis of the city, and it was part of the ancient Roman grid plan that became Florence.

RENAISSANCE WALK

Around the year 1400, as the Renaissance was blooming, this street connected the religious center (where we are now) with the political center (where we're heading), a five-minute walk away. Back then, the shops sold cheese, flags, and horse bridles. The street bustled with men in colorful Romeo-style tights, with swords in their belts, and caps with a feather in it. The women promenaded by in Juliet-style dresses with poufy sleeves and brocaded patterns, their elaborate braids tucked into hairnets.

Nowadays this historic core is home to tourists in shorts, licking the drips on their gelato cones. Since most vehicles were banned a few years back, this street has been transformed into a pleasant place to stroll, people-watch, window-shop, and wonder why American cities can't become more pedestrian-friendly.

• *Continue down Via de' Calzaiuoli. Two blocks down from the Baptistery, turn right on Via degli Speziali toward the triumphal arch that marks...*

RENAISSANCE WALK

❼ Piazza della Repubblica

This large square sits on the site of the original Roman Forum. Florence was founded 2,000 years ago as a riverside garrison town,

with its main square here at the intersection of the two main roads (Via Corso and Via Roma). The lone column that still stands here—nicknamed the "belly button of Florence"—once marked that intersection. If you look at a map of Florence today, you can make out the ghost of Rome in its streets: a grid-plan city center surrounded by a circular city wall.

By the 1500s, this square was the heart of the Jewish quarter. In 1571, Cosimo I had it walled in and made into a ghetto.

In the 1860s, the square got its magnificent triumphal arch. It celebrated the unification of Italy. In fact, from 1865 to 1870, Florence became the capital of the newly united nation of Italy. To live up to its role, the city was spiffed up: City walls were taken down, grand European-style boulevards were blasted through, and the Jewish ghetto was razed to create this imposing, modern forum surrounded by stately circa-1890 buildings. Notice the proud statement atop the triumphal arch, which proclaims, "The squalor of the ancient city is given a new life."

Venerable cafés and stores line the square. During the 19th century, intellectuals met in cafés here. Gilli, on the northeast corner, is a favorite for its grand atmosphere and tasty sweets (cheap if you stand at the bar, expensive to sit down), while the recommended Paszkowski Café has good lunch options (see page 288).

The department store La Rinascente, facing Piazza della Repubblica, is one of the city's mainstays, and has a bar with a rooftop terrace for great Duomo and city views (see page 297).

• *Return to the main street and continue walking toward the river. A block farther, at the intersection with Via Orsanmichele, is the...*

❽ Orsanmichele Church

The Orsanmichele Church provides an interesting look at Florence's medieval roots. It's a combo church/granary. Originally, this was an open loggia (covered porch) with a huge grain warehouse upstairs. Then, as you can see, the arches of the loggia were artfully filled in (14th century) to make walls, and the building gained a new purpose—as a church. This was prime real estate on what had become the main drag between the church and palace.

The 14 niches in the walls feature remarkable-in-their-day statues paid for by the city's rising middle class of merchants and their 21 guilds. Florence in 1400 was a republic, a government working for the interests not of a king, but of these guilds (much as modern America is controlled by and caters to corporate interests). The guilds commissioned statues as PR gestures, hiring the finest artists of the time. As the statues were done over several decades, they function as a textbook of the evolution of Florentine art.

Orsanmichele Exterior

In earlier Gothic times, statues were set deep into church niches, simply embellishing the house of God. Here at the Orsanmichele Church, we see statues—as restless as man on the verge of the Renaissance—stepping out from the protection of the Church.

• *Circle the church exterior counterclockwise to enjoy the statues. While these are all copies, on Mondays you can see the originals in the museum on the church's top floor. The most famous of the statues* (St. George) *is in the Bargello.*

Starting on the church's right side (along Via Orsanmichele), in the third niche is...

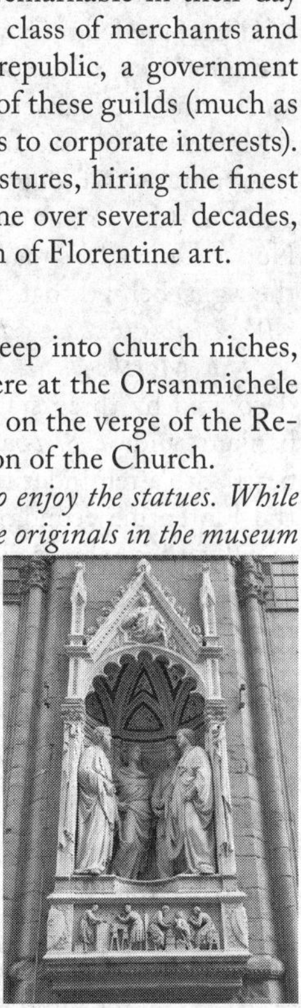

Nanni di Banco's *Quattro Santi Coronati* **(c. 1415-1417):** These four early Christians were sculptors martyred by the Roman emperor Diocletian because they refused to sculpt pagan gods. They seem to be contemplating the consequences of the fatal decision they're

(vertical text in right margin) RENAISSANCE WALK

about to make. Beneath some of the niches, you'll find the symbol of the guilds that paid for the art. Art historians differ here. Some think the work was commissioned by the carpenters' and masons' guild. Others contend it was by the guys who did discount circumcisions.

• *While Banco's saints are deep in the church's niche, the next statue feels ready to step out. Just to the right is...*

Donatello's *St. George*: George is alert, perched on the edge of his niche, scanning the horizon for dragons and announcing the new age with its new outlook. His knitted brow shows there's a drama unfolding. Sure, he's anxious, but he's also self-assured. Comparing this Renaissance-style *St. George* to *Quattro Santi Coronati*, you can psychoanalyze the heady changes underway. This is humanism.

This *St. George* is a copy of the c. 1417 original (now in the Bargello; 📖 see the Bargello Tour chapter).

The predella (small carving below the statue) shows St. George slaying the dragon and saving the damsel, who's in a classic damsel-in-distress pose. It reminds viewers that this statue was brought to you by the sword-and-armor makers' guild. Art historians consider this relief a breakthrough in realism. Notice Donatello's mathematically correct receding colonnade (on the right) behind that delightful little S-shaped figure.

• *Walk across the back side of the church, bypassing the entrance for now.*

St. Matthew, St. Stephen, and St. Eligius: The back side is decorated by three statues worth a look. *St. Matthew*, patron of bankers, and *St. Stephen*, patron of wool merchants (both by Ghiberti), are a reminder that banking and textiles were mainstays of the Florentine economy. Nanni di Banco's *St. Eligius*, patron of metalworkers, shows workers shoeing a horse.

• *Around the corner, the first niche you come to features...*

Donatello's *St. Mark* (1411-1413): The evangelist cradles his gospel in his strong, veined hand and gazes out, resting his weight on the right leg while bending the left. Though subtle, St. Mark's twisting *contrapposto* pose was the first seen since antiquity. Commissioned by the linen sellers' guild, the statue has elaborately detailed robes that drape around the natural contours of his weighty body. When the guild first saw the statue, they

thought the oversized head and torso made it top-heavy. Only after it was lifted into its raised niche did Donatello's cleverly designed proportions look right—and the guild accepted it. Eighty years after young Donatello carved this statue, a teenage Michelangelo Buonarroti stood here and marveled at it.

• *Backtrack to the entrance and go inside.*

Orsanmichele Interior

Step into Florence circa 1350. The church does not have a typical nave because it was adapted from a granary. Look for the pillars (on the left wall) with rectangular **holes** in them about four feet off the ground. These were once used as chutes for delivering grain from the storage rooms upstairs. Look up to see the **rings** hanging from the ceiling, used to anchor pulleys for either lifting grain or hoisting platforms with candles to act as chandeliers. The iron bars spanning the vaults are there for support.

The fanciful **tabernacle** by Andrea Orcagna was designed exactly for this space: Like the biggest Christmas tree possible, it's

capped by an angel whose head touches the ceiling. Take in the Gothic tabernacle's medieval elegance. What it lacks in depth and realism it makes up for in color, with an intricate assemblage of marble, glass, gold, and expensive lapis lazuli. Florence had just survived the terrible bubonic plague of 1348, which killed half the population. The elaborate tabernacle was built to display Bernardo Daddi's *Madonna delle Grazie,* which received plague survivors' grateful prayers of thanks—*grazie.*
While it's great to see art in museums, it's even better to enjoy it in its original setting—"in situ"—where the artist intended it to be seen. When you view similar altarpieces out of context in the Uffizi, think back on the candlelit medieval atmosphere that surrounds this altarpiece.

Upstairs is a free museum (open Mon only) displaying most of the originals of the statues you just saw outside. They represent virtually every big name in pre-Michelangelo Florentine sculpture: Donatello, Ghiberti, Brunelleschi, Giambologna, and more.

The church hosts atmospheric evening concerts, sometimes in the upper level; same-day tickets are sold from the door facing Via de' Calzaiuoli. You can also book tickets here for the Uffizi and Accademia.

• *The Bargello, with Florence's best collection of sculpture, is a few blocks east, down Via dei Tavolini. But let's continue down the mall 50 more yards, to the huge and historic square...*

❾ Piazza della Signoria

What a view! This piazza—the main civic center of Florence—is dominated by the massive stone facade of Palazzo Vecchio, with a tower that reaches for the sky. The square is dotted with statues. The stately Uffizi Gallery is nearby, and the marble greatness of old Florence litters the cobbles. Piazza della Signoria, with the feel of an open-air museum of statuary, still vibrates with the echoes of the city's past—executions, riots, and great celebrations. There's even Roman history: Look for the **chart** showing the ancient city (on a waist-high, freestanding display to your right as you enter the square, in front of Chanel). Today, it's a tourist's world with pigeons, selfie sticks, horse buggies, and tired spouses. If it would make your tired hubby or weary wife come to life, stop in at the recommended but expensive **Rivoire** café to enjoy its fine desserts, pudding-thick hot chocolate, and the best-view seats in town (see page 289).

Before you towers the **Palazzo Vecchio,** the "old palace" and palatial Town Hall of the Medici—a fortress designed to contain riches and survive the many riots that went with local politics. The windows are just be-yond the reach of angry stones, and the tower was a handy lookout post. Justice was doled out sternly on this square. Until 1873, Michelan-gelo's *David* stood where you see the replica today. The original was damaged in a 1527 riot (when a bench thrown from a palace window knocked its left arm off), but it remained here for several centuries, before being moved in-doors for protection.

Step past the fake *David* through the front door into the Palazzo Vecchio's courtyard (free). This palace was Florence's symbol of civic power. You're surrounded by art for art's sake—a cherub frivolously marks the courtyard's center, and ornate stuccoes and frescoes decorate the walls and columns. Such luxury represented a big change 500 years ago.

For a self-guided tour of the palace, including more on this courtyard, see the 📖 Palazzo Vecchio Tour chapter.

• *Back outside, check out the arcade of three arches filled with statues.*

❿ Loggia dei Lanzi (a.k.a. Loggia della Signoria)

The loggia, once a forum for public debate, was perfect for a city that prided itself on its democratic traditions. But later, when the Medici figured that good art was more desirable than free speech, it was turned into an outdoor sculpture gallery. Notice the squirming Florentine themes—conquest, domination, rape, and decapitation. The statues lining the back are Roman originals brought back to Florence by a Medici when his villa in Rome was sold. Two statues in the front deserve a closer look.

At the right end of the loggia, *The Rape of the Sabine Women* (c. 1583)—with its pulse-quickening rhythm of muscles—is from the restless Mannerist period, which followed the stately and confident Renaissance. The sculptor, Giambologna, proved his mastery of the medium by sculpting three entangled bodies from one piece of marble. The composition is best viewed from below and in front. The relief panel below shows a wider view of the terrible scene. (In the Accademia, you can see the original plaster model of this statue that was used to guide Giambologna's workers in helping him create it.)

Benvenuto Cellini's *Perseus* (1545-1553), the loggia's most noteworthy piece, shows the Greek hero who decapitated the snake-headed Medusa. They say Medusa was so ugly she turned humans who looked at her to stone—though one of this book's authors thinks she's kinda cute. Cellini, a notorious braggart, placed his name prominently across the sash on the front and amazingly, included a secret self-portrait on the back of Perseus'

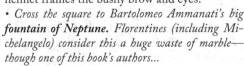

head: his locks form the beard while the helmet frames the bushy brow and eyes.

• *Cross the square to Bartolomeo Ammanati's big* ***fountain of Neptune.*** *Florentines (including Michelangelo) consider this a huge waste of marble—though one of this book's authors...*

Near the Neptune statue is a bronze equestrian statue. The guy on the horse is Cosimo I, the post-Renaissance Medici who commissioned the Uffizi. Find the round marble plaque on the ground 10 steps in front of the fountain.

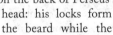

RENAISSANCE WALK

⓫ Savonarola Plaque

The plaque's inscription begins with the word *"Qui"*—"here." It explains that a crucial event in Florentine history happened right on this spot.

In the 1490s (when Michelangelo was a teenager) the Medici family was briefly thrown from power by an austere and charismatic monk named Savonarola, who made Florence a constitutional republic. He organized huge rallies lit by roaring bonfires here on the square where he preached. While children sang hymns, the devout brought their rich "vanities" (such as paintings, musical instruments, and playing cards) and threw them into the flames.

But not everyone wanted a return to the medieval past. Encouraged by the pope, the Florentines fought back and arrested Sa-

vonarola. For two days, they tortured him, trying unsuccessfully to persuade him to see their side of things. Finally, on the very spot where Savonarola's followers had built bonfires of vanities, the monk was burned. The plaque, engraved in Italian *("Qui dove...")*, reads, "Here, Girolamo Savonarola and his Dominican brothers were hanged and burned" in the year "MCCCCXCVIII" (1498), ending

his theocracy. Soon after, the Medici returned to power and the Renaissance picked up where it left off. (For more on Savonarola, see the 📖 Museum of San Marco Tour chapter.)

• *Stay cool, we have 200 yards to go. Follow the gaze of the fake* David *into the courtyard of the two-tone horseshoe-shaped building.*

⓬ Uffizi Courtyard Statues

The top floor of this building, known as the *uffizi* (offices) during Medici days, is filled with the greatest collection of Florentine painting anywhere. It's one of Europe's top four or five art galleries (see the 📖 Uffizi Gallery Tour chapter).

The Uffizi courtyard, filled with merchants and hustling young artists, is watched over by 19th-century statues of the great figures of the Renaissance—all Tuscans. Tourists zero in on the visual accomplishments of the era, but let's pay tribute to the many other accomplishments of the Renaissance as well, as we wander through Florence's Renaissance Hall of Fame.

LORENZO IL MAGNIFICO

• Stroll down the left side of the courtyard from the Palazzo Vecchio to the river, noticing the following greats.

Lorenzo the Magnificent, the Medici ruler, was a great art patron and cunning power broker. Excelling in everything except modesty, he set the tone for the Renaissance. His statue is tucked under the arcade, by an Uffizi doorway.

Giotto, holding the plan to the city's bell tower (which is named for him) was the great pre-Renaissance artist whose paintings foretold the future of Italian art.

Donatello, the sculptor who served as a role model for Michelangelo, holds a hammer and chisel.

Alberti wrote a famous book, *On Painting,* which taught early Renaissance artists the mathematics of perspective.

Leonardo da Vinci was a scientist, sculptor, musician, engineer...and not a bad painter either. This well-roundedness marked the epitome of a Renaissance genius.

Michelangelo ponders the universe and/or stifles a belch.

Dante, with the laurel-leaf crown and lyre of a poet, says, "I am the father of the Italian language." He was the first Italian to write a popular work *(The Divine Comedy)* in the Florentine dialect, which soon became "Italian" throughout the country (until Dante, Latin had been the language of literature).

Petrarch, the poet, wears laurel leaves from Greece, a robe from Rome, and a belt from Walmart.

Boccaccio wrote *The Decameron,* stories told to pass the time during the 1348 Black Death. He helped popularize literature in the people's language rather than Latin.

Machiavelli looks like he's deviously hatching a plot—his book *The Prince* taught that the end justifies the means, paving the way for the slick-and-cunning "Machiavellian" politics of today.

Vespucci (in the corner) was an explorer who gave his first name, Amerigo, to a fledgling New World.

Galileo (in the other corner) holds the humble telescope he used to spot the moons of Jupiter. By the way, Galileo's actual fingers are preserved and on display in the Galileo Science Museum, a block from here (see page 59).

• Pause at the Arno River, overlooking...

NICCOLÒ MACCHIAVELLI

⓭ Ponte Vecchio

The Arno runs east to west. It starts in the Apennine Mountains that form the spine of Italy; 150 miles later, it spills out into the

Mediterranean near Pisa. For centuries, the river was a crucial east-west trade route linking northern Italy. The north-south trade ran along a highway, from northern Europe to Rome, with Florence in between. So, since ancient times, a bridge has stood at this narrow spot in the Arno. When a flood washed away the old wooden bridge, this one was built in 1345, and is now called the Ponte Vecchio (Old Bridge). To get into the exclusive little park below (on the north bank), you'll need to join the Florence rowing club.

• *Finish your walk by hiking to the center of the bridge.*

In times past, these shops were inhabited by butchers and hide-tanners—a natural fit, because they could empty their waste into the river below. In the 1500s, the Medici booted them out and installed gold- and silversmiths who still tempt visitors to this day. Fittingly, a famous goldsmith is honored with a fine bust at the central point of the bridge—the sculptor Cellini. (For more on this bridge, see the start of the □ Oltrarno Walk chapter.)

Look up to notice the windows running across the upper part of the buildings. This is the Vasari Corridor—a protected and elevated passageway, built by the Medici. It led from the Palazzo Vecchio through the Uffizi, across Ponte Vecchio, and up to the immense Pitti Palace, four blocks beyond the bridge.

Looking upstream and down, you have timeless views of the city. The neighborhood across the river, known as the Oltrarno, is more rustic and working-class. The other bridges are all modern replacements. During World War II, the local German commander was instructed to blow up all of Florence's bridges to cover the Nazi retreat. But even some Nazis appreciate history: He blew up the others, and left the Ponte Vecchio impassable but intact.

The Ponte Vecchio is a very romantic spot, especially in the evening. The sun sets behind the hills, and the bridges cast their reflection on the flat water. Street musicians play and lovers hold hands. The city of Florence—born in Roman times, flourishing in the medieval age, and blossoming in the Renaissance—is a vibrant city still, and the cultural capital of Europe.

• *From the Duomo to the Arno, we've taken in sights from Florence's medieval roots and Renaissance greats. After this introduction, several of the finest museums in Europe await your discovery—or perhaps it's time for a nice espresso or gelato. Enjoy.*

ACCADEMIA GALLERY TOUR

Galleria dell'Accademia

One of Europe's great thrills is seeing Michelangelo's *David* in the flesh at the Accademia Gallery. Seventeen feet high, gleaming white, and exalted by a halo-like dome over his head, *David* rarely disappoints, even for those with high expectations. And the Accademia doesn't stop there. With a handful of other Michelangelo statues and a few other interesting sights, it makes for an uplifting visit that isn't overwhelming. *David*, a must-see on any visit to Florence, is always mobbed with visitors. Plan carefully to minimize your time in line.

Orientation

Cost: €12.50 (€8 if there's no special exhibit), additional €4 fee for recommended reservation, free and crowded on the first Sun of the month, covered by Firenze Card.

Hours: Tue-Sun 8:15-18:50, possibly Tue until 22:00 June-Sept, closed Mon.

Information: Reservation tel. 055-294-883, www.galleria accademiafirenze.beniculturali.it.

Avoiding Lines: In peak season (April-Oct), it's smart to buy a Firenze Card or reserve ahead (see pages 30 and 34 for info on both options). Those with reservations or the Firenze Card line up at the entrance labeled *Reserved*. (Note that the *Reserved* entrance is split into two queues—groups to the left and individuals to the right.) If you show up without a reservation or Firenze Card, and there's a long line at the *Not Reserved* entrance, try dropping by the My Accademia Libreria reservation office, just across the street from the exit, to see if they have any times available later that day (€4 fee).

When to Go: From June-Sept, the museum may stay open late Tue evenings—when you'll find it free of crowds. In peak season, the museum is most crowded on Sun, Tue before 18:00, and between about 10:00 and 13:00; in spring and fall, Sat is also quite busy. On busy days, even those with reservations or Firenze Cards may have a 30-minute wait to get through the security-check bottleneck (see below). On off-season weekdays (Nov-March), you can sometimes get in with no reservation and no lines before 8:30 or after 16:00—but it's best to treat it as if reservations are required.

Getting There: It's at Via Ricasoli 60, a 15-minute walk from the train station or a 10-minute walk northeast of the Duomo.

Tours: A €6 audioguide (€10/2 people) is available in the ticket lobby.

🎧 Download my free Accademia audio tour.

Length of This Tour: While *David* and the *Prisoners* can be seen in 30 minutes, allow an hour so you can linger and explore other parts of the museum.

Security: You'll have to pass through a metal detector and put your bag through an X-ray (on crowded days, this can take up to 30 minutes). Leave pocketknives and corkscrews at your hotel. The museum has no bag-check service, and large backpacks are not allowed.

Cuisine Art: My favorite place for a nearby picnic is the picturesque Renaissance Piazza S.S. Annunziata, just a block away; grab a takeout lunch and munch it on the square (see recommendations for takeout and sit-down dining on page 293).

Starring: Michelangelo's *David* and *Prisoners*.

The Tour Begins

• *From the entrance lobby, show your ticket, turn left, and look right down the long hall with* David *at the far end, under an illuminating circular skylight. Yes, you're really here. With* David *presiding at the "altar," the* Prisoners *lining the "nave," and hordes of "pilgrims" crowding in to look, you've arrived at Florence's "cathedral of humanism."*

Start with the ultimate...

❶ David, 1501-1504

When you look into the eyes of Michelangelo's *David*, you're looking into the eyes of Renaissance Man. This six-ton, 17-foot-tall symbol of divine victory over evil represents a new century and a whole new Renaissance outlook. This is the age of Columbus and classicism, Galileo and Gutenberg, Luther and Leonardo—of Florence and the Renaissance.

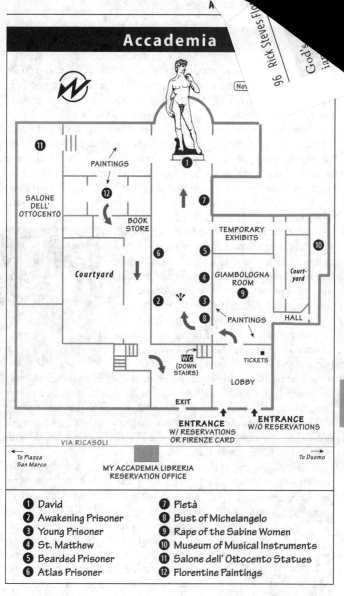

Accademia

PAINTINGS

⑫

SALONE DELL' OTTOCENTO

⑪

BOOK STORE

Courtyard

⑥ ⑤ ② ③ ⑧

Nov

① David

⑦ Pietà

TEMPORARY EXHIBITS

GIAMBOLOGNA ROOM ⑨

Courtyard

⑩

HALL

PAINTINGS

WC (DOWN STAIRS)

TICKETS

LOBBY

EXIT

ENTRANCE W/ RESERVATIONS OR FIRENZE CARD

ENTRANCE W/O RESERVATIONS

VIA RICASOLI

← To Piazza San Marco

MY ACCADEMIA LIBRERIA RESERVATION OFFICE

To Duomo →

① David	⑦ Pietà
② Awakening Prisoner	⑧ Bust of Michelangelo
③ Young Prisoner	⑨ Rape of the Sabine Women
④ St. Matthew	⑩ Museum of Musical Instruments
⑤ Bearded Prisoner	⑪ Salone dell' Ottocento Statues
⑥ Atlas Prisoner	⑫ Florentine Paintings

In 1501, Michelangelo Buonarroti, a 26-year-old Florentine, was commissioned to carve a large-scale work for the Duomo. He was given a block of marble that other sculptors had rejected as too tall, shallow, and flawed to be of any value. But Michelangelo picked up his hammer and chisel, knocked a knot off what became *David*'s heart, and started to work.

The figure comes from an Old Testament story. The Israelites, chosen people, are surrounded by the Philistines, barbarian warriors led by a brutish giant named Goliath. The giant challenges the Israelites to send out someone to fight him. Everyone is afraid except for one young shepherd boy—David. Armed only with a sling, which he's thrown over his shoulder, David gathers five smooth stones from the stream and faces Goliath.

The statue captures David as he's sizing up his enemy. He stands relaxed but alert, leaning on one leg in a classical pose known as *contrapposto*. In his powerful left hand, he fondles the handle of the sling, ready to fling a stone at the giant. His gaze is steady—searching with intense concentration, but also with extreme confidence. Michelangelo has caught the precise moment when David is saying to himself, "I can take this guy."

While some think that he's already slain the giant, the current director of the Accademia believes, as I do, that Michelangelo has portrayed David facing the giant. (Unlike most depictions of David after the kill, this sculpture does not show the giant's severed head.)

David is a symbol of Renaissance optimism. He's no brute. He's a civilized, thinking individual who can grapple with and overcome problems. He needs no armor, only his God-given physical strength and wits. Look at his right hand, with the raised veins and strong, relaxed fingers—many complained that it was too big and overdeveloped. But this is the hand of a man with the strength of God on his side. No mere boy could slay the giant. But David, powered by God, could...and did.

Originally, the statue was commissioned to stand atop the roofline of the Duomo. But during the three years it took to sculpt,

they decided instead to place it guarding the entrance of Town Hall—the Palazzo Vecchio. (If the relationship between *David*'s head and body seems a bit out of proportion, it's because Michelangelo designed it to be seen "correctly" from far below the rooftop of the church.)

The colossus was placed standing up in a cart and dragged across rollers from Michelangelo's workshop (behind the Duomo) to the Palazzo Vecchio, where it replaced a work by Donatello. There *David* stood—naked and outdoors—for 350 years. In the right light, you can see signs of weathering on his shoulders. Also, note the crack in *David*'s left arm where it was

broken off during a 1527 riot near the Palazzo Vecchio. In 1873, to conserve the masterpiece, the statue was moved indoors and today resides under this wonderful Renaissance-style dome designed just for him, while a copy adorns Palazzo Vecchio (see photo on previous page).

Circle *David* and view him from various angles. From the front, he's confident, but a little less so when you gaze directly into his eyes. Around back, see his sling strap, buns of steel, and Renaissance mullet. Up close, you can see the blue-veined Carrara marble and a few cracks and stains. From the sides, Michelangelo's challenge becomes clear: to sculpt a figure from a block of marble other sculptors said was too tall and narrow to accommodate a human figure.

Renaissance Florentines could identify with *David*. Like him, they considered themselves God-blessed underdogs fighting their city-state rivals. In a deeper sense, they were civilized Renaissance people slaying the ugly giant of medieval superstition, pessimism, and oppression.

• *Hang around a while. Eavesdrop on tour guides. The Plexiglas shields at the base of the statue are a reminder of an attack by a frustrated artist, who smashed the statue's feet in 1991.*

Lining the hall leading up to David *are other statues by Michelangelo—his* Prisoners, St. Matthew, *and* Pietà. *Start with the* Awakening Prisoner, *the statue at the end of the nave (farthest from* David*). He's on your left as you face* David.

The Prisoners (Prigioni), c. 1516-1534

These unfinished figures seem to be fighting to free themselves from the stone. Michelangelo believed the sculptor was a tool of God, not creating but simply revealing the powerful and beautiful figures that God had encased in the marble. Michelangelo's job was to chip away the excess, to reveal. He needed to be in tune with God's will, and whenever the spirit came upon him, Michelangelo worked in a frenzy, without sleep, often for days on end.

The *Prisoners* give us a glimpse of this fitful process, showing the restless energy of someone possessed, struggling

against the rock that binds him. Michelangelo himself fought to create the image he saw in his mind's eye. You can still see the grooves from the chisel, and you can picture Michelangelo hacking away in a cloud of dust. Unlike most sculptors, who built a model and then marked up their block of marble to know where to chip, Michelangelo always worked freehand, starting from the front and working back. These figures emerge from the stone (as his colleague Vasari put it) "as though surfacing from a pool of water."

The so-called ❷ *Awakening Prisoner* (the names are given by scholars, not Michelangelo) seems to be stretching after a long nap, still tangled in the "bedsheets" of uncarved rock. He's more block than statue.

On the right, the ❸ *Young Prisoner* is more finished. He buries his face in his forearm, while his other arm is chained behind him.

The *Prisoners* were designed for the never-completed tomb of Pope Julius II (who also commissioned the Sistine Chapel ceiling). Michelangelo may have abandoned them simply because the project itself petered out, or he may have deliberately left them unfinished. Having perhaps satisfied himself that he'd accomplished what he set out to do, and seeing no point in polishing them into their shiny, finished state, he went on to a new project. Two slightly more completed statues from the same series are in the Louvre in Paris, while the much-scaled-down tomb, featuring another of his masterpieces, *Moses,* is in the church of St. Peter-in-Chains in Rome.

ACCADEMIA

Walking up the nave toward *David,* you'll pass by Michelangelo's ❹ *St. Matthew* (1503), on the right. Though not one of the *Prisoners* series, he is also unfinished, perfectly illustrating Vasari's "surfacing" description.

The next statue (also on the right), the ❺ *Bearded Prisoner,* is the most finished of the four, with all four limbs, a bushy face, and even a hint of daylight between his arm and body.

Across the nave on the left, the ❻ *Atlas Prisoner* carries the unfinished marble on his stooped shoulders, his head still encased in the block.

As you study the *Prisoners,* notice Michelangelo's love and understanding of the human body. His greatest days were spent sketching the muscular, tanned, and sweating bodies of the workers in the Carrara marble quarries. The prisoners' heads and faces are the least-developed part—they "speak" with their poses.

Comparing the restless, claustrophobic *Prisoners* with the serene and confident *David* gives an idea of the sheer emotional range in Michelangelo's work.

• *The unfinished threesome closest to* David *is the...*

❼ *Pietà*

The figures struggle to hold up the sagging body of Christ. Michelangelo (or, more likely, one of his followers) emphasizes the

heaviness of Jesus' dead body, driving home the point that this divine being suffered a very human death. Christ's massive arm is almost the size of his bent and broken legs. By stretching his body—if he stood up, he'd be more than seven feet tall—the weight is exaggerated.

• *After getting your fill of Michelangelo, consider taking a spin around the rest of the Accademia. Michelangelo's statues are far and away the highlight here, but the rest of this small museum—housed in a former convent—has a few bonuses. Head back toward the entrance. Near the* Young Prisoner *find a...*

❽ Bust of Michelangelo

The bronze bust depicts a craggy, wrinkled Michelangelo, age 88, by Daniele da Volterra. (Daniele, one of Michelangelo's colleagues and friends, is best known

as the one who painted loincloths on the private parts of Michelangelo's nudes in the Sistine Chapel.) As a teenager, Michelangelo got his nose broken in a fight with a rival artist. Though Michelangelo went on to create great beauty, he was never classically handsome.

• *Enter the room near the museum entrance dominated by a large, squirming statue.*

Giambologna Room

This full-size plaster model of ❾ *Rape of the Sabine Women* (1582) guided Giambologna's assistants in completing the marble version in the Loggia dei Lanzi (on Piazza della Signoria, next to the Palazzo Vecchio, described on page 88). A Roman warrior tramples a fighter from the Sabine tribe and carries off the man's wife. Husband and wife exchange one final, anguished glance. Circle the statue and watch it spiral to life around its axis. Giambologna was clearly influenced (as a

David, David, David, and *David*

Several Italian masters produced iconic sculptures of David—all of them different. Compare and contrast the artists' styles. How many ways can you slay a giant?

Donatello's *David* (1430, Bargello, Florence)

Donatello's *David* is young and graceful, casually gloating over the head of Goliath, almost Gothic in its elegance and smooth lines. While he has a similar weight-on-one-leg *(contrapposto)* stance as Michelangelo's later version, Donatello's *David* seems feminine rather than masculine. (For further description, see page 132 of the Bargello Tour chapter.)

Andrea del Verrocchio's *David* (c. 1470, Bargello, Florence)

Wearing a military skirt and armed with a small sword, Verrocchio's *David* is just a boy. The statue is only four feet tall—dwarfed by Michelangelo's monumental version. (For more, see page 131 of the Bargello Tour chapter.)

Michelangelo's *David* (1501-1504, Accademia, Florence)

Michelangelo's *David* is pure Renaissance:

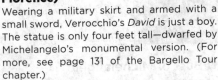

plaque with photo points out) by Michelangelo's groundbreaking *Victory* in the Palazzo Vecchio (1533-1534, described on page 176). Michelangelo's statue of a man triumphing over a fallen enemy introduced both the theme and the spiral-shaped pose that many artists imitated.

Browse the room clockwise (from the entrance) to locate **minor paintings** by artists you'll encounter elsewhere in Florence. Domenico Ghirlandaio's paintings of Renaissance Florence are behind the altar of the Church of Santa Maria Novella (see page 204). Francesco Granacci, a childhood friend of Michelangelo, assisted him on the Sistine Ceiling. Benozzo Gozzoli decorated the personal chapel of the Medici in the Medici-Riccardi Palace (see page 194). Filippino Lippi is known for his frescoes in the Brancacci Chapel

massive, heroic in size, and superhuman in strength and power. The tensed right hand, which grips a stone in readiness to hurl at Goliath, is more powerful than any human hand. It's symbolic of divine strength. A model of perfection, Michelangelo's *David* is far larger and grander than we mere mortals. We know he'll win. Renaissance Man has arrived.

Gian Lorenzo Bernini's *David* (1623, Borghese Museum, Rome)

Flash forward more than a century. In this self-portrait, 25-year-old Bernini is ready to take on the world, slay the pretty-boy Davids of the Renaissance, and invent Baroque. Unlike Michelangelo's rational, cool, restrained *David,* Bernini's is a doer: passionate, engaged, dramatic. While Renaissance *David* is simple and unadorned— carrying only a sling—Baroque Dave is "cluttered" with a braided sling, a hairy pouch, flowing cloth, and discarded armor. Bernini's *David,* with his tousled hair and set mouth, is one of us; the contest is less certain than with the other three Davids.

To sum up: Donatello's *David* represents the first inkling of the Renaissance; Verrocchio's is early Renaissance in miniature; Michelangelo's is textbook Renaissance; and Bernini's is the epitome of Baroque.

(see page 236) and Church of Santa Maria Novella (page 206). And Botticelli's *Birth of Venus* hangs in the Uffizi (see page 114).
• *From the Giambologna Room, head down a short hallway leading to a few rooms containing the...*

⑩ Museum of Musical Instruments

Between 1400 and 1700, Florence was one of Europe's most sophisticated cities, and the Medici rulers were trendsetters. Musicians like Scarlatti and Handel flocked to the court of Prince Ferdinando (1663-1713). You'll see late-Renaissance cellos, dulcimers, violins, woodwinds, and harpsichords. (Listen to some on the computer terminals.)

As you enter, look for the two group paintings that include the prince (he's second from the right in both paintings, with the yellow bowtie) hanging out with his musician friends. The gay prince played a mean harpsichord, and he helped pioneer new variations.

ACCADEMIA

More Michelangelo

If you're a fan of earth's greatest sculptor, you won't leave Florence until there's a check next to each of these:

Bargello: Several Michelangelo sculptures, including the *Bacchus* (pictured here; ☐ see the Bargello Tour chapter).

Duomo Museum: Another moving pietà (see page 162).

Medici Chapels: The *Night* and *Day* statues, plus others done for the Medici tomb, located at the Basilica of San Lorenzo (see the ☐ Medici Chapels Tour chapter).

Laurentian Medici Library: Michelangelo designed the entrance staircase and more, located at the Basilica of San Lorenzo (see page 46).

Palazzo Vecchio: His *Victory* statue (see page 176).

Uffizi Gallery: A rare Michelangelo painting (see page 119).

Casa Buonarroti: Built on property Michelangelo once owned, at Via Ghibellina 70, containing some early works (see page 61).

Santa Croce Church: Michelangelo's tomb (see page 61).

Santo Spirito Church: Wooden crucifix thought to be by Michelangelo (see page 66).

ACCADEMIA

In the adjoining room, you'll see musical instruments from times past—some familiar, some weird and now obsolete.

The highlight is a room of several experimental keyboards, including some by Florence's keyboard pioneer, Bartolomeo Cristofori. As the exhibits point out, the breakthrough in keyboard technology was about how to make the string ring. The harpsichord plucked the string. By 1700, they'd invented the "pianoforte"—the piano, which used a padded hammer that could strike it either soft *(piano)* or hard *(forte)*. The tall piano on display (from 1739) is considered by some to be the world's first upright piano.

• *Head one more time back up the nave to say goodbye to Dave.*

More Sights on the Way to the Exit

To the left of *David*, at the end of the hall, is the **⓫ Salone dell'Ottocento**—a long room crammed with plaster statues and busts. These were the Academy art students' "final exams"—preparatory models for statues, many of which were later executed in marble. The black dots on the statues are sculptors' "points," guiding them on how deep to chisel. The Academy art school has been attached to the museum for centuries, and you may see the next Michelangelo wandering the streets nearby.

Finally, near *David* (in several rooms' adjoining halls) is the museum's pleasant-but-underwhelming **⓬ collection of paintings.** You'll be hard-pressed to find even one by a painter whose name you recognize. As you look at these somber medieval altarpieces, mentally contrast them with the confident optimism of Michelangelo's *David*, done a century later. It's a testament to how far Florence evolved from the depths of medieval despair to the full bloom of the Renaissance.

• *Our tour is finished. To exit, pass through the bookstore and into the open air, for some sun, peace, and quiet...aaaah.*

UFFIZI GALLERY TOUR

Galleria degli Uffizi

In the Renaissance, Florentine artists rediscovered the beauty of the natural world. Medieval art had been symbolic, telling Bible stories. Realism didn't matter. But Renaissance people saw the beauty of God in nature and the human body. They used math and science to capture the natural world on canvas as realistically as possible.

The Uffizi Gallery (oo-FEET-zee) has the greatest overall collection anywhere of Italian painting. We'll trace the rise of realism and savor the optimistic spirit that marked the Renaissance.

My eyes love things that are fair,
and my soul for salvation cries.
But neither will to Heaven rise
unless the sight of Beauty lifts them there.
　　—Michelangelo Buonarroti, sculptor, painter, poet

Orientation

Cost: €12.50 (€8 if there's no special exhibit), additional €4 fee for recommended reservation, free and crowded on the first Sun of the month, covered by Firenze Card.

Hours: Tue-Sun 8:15-18:50, closed Mon, last entry 45 minutes before closing.

Information: Reservation tel. 055-294-883, www.uffizi. beniculturali.it.

Renovation: The gallery is nearing the end of a major, multiyear overhaul. Pieces frequently move, and new rooms open, so expect changes. If you can't find a work, ask a guard, *"Scusi, dov'è...?"* and point to the picture in this book.

Avoiding Lines: To skip the notoriously long ticket-buying lines, either get a Firenze Card or reserve ahead (for details on both, see pages 30 and 34). During summer and on weekends, the Uffizi can be booked up a month or more in advance. Without a Firenze Card or reservation, you can usually enter without major lines off-season after 16:00. But in peak season (April-Oct) and on weekends, the wait can be hours, and it can be crowded even late in the day. The busiest days are Tues, Sat, and Sun. Crowds tend to be lighter at lunchtime (12:00-13:30).

Getting There: It's on the Arno River between the Palazzo Vecchio and Ponte Vecchio, a 15-minute walk from the train station.

Getting In: There are several entrances (see map on next page). Which one you use depends on whether you have a Firenze Card, a reservation, or neither.

Firenze Card holders enter at door #1 (labeled *Reservation Entrance*). Read the signs carefully and get in the line for individuals—not groups—between door #1 and door #2.

People **buying a ticket on the spot** line up with everyone else at door #2, marked *Main Entrance.* An estimated wait time is posted.

To **buy a Firenze Card,** or to see if there are any same-day reservations available (€4 extra), enter door #2 (marked *Booking Service and Today* or *Advance Sale*) to the left of the same-day ticket-buying line. Don't be shy: Ask the attendant to let you pass—and don't get into the long ticket-buying line. The doorway is kept open for same-day reservation buyers.

If you've **already made a reservation** and need to pick up your ticket, go to door #3 (labeled *Reservation Ticket Office,* across the courtyard from doors #1 and #2, under an archway and to the right). Tickets are available for pickup 10 minutes before your appointed time. If you booked online and have already paid, you'll exchange your voucher for a ticket. If you (or your hotelier) booked by phone, give them your confirmation number and pay. Then walk briskly past the looooong ticket-buying line—pondering the IQ of this gang. Get in the right queue: groups to the left of door #1, individuals between doors #1 and #2.

At especially busy times, expect long waits even if with a reservation or Firenze Card. There may be a queue to pick up your reservation at door #3 and another 30-minute wait to enter at door #1.

Just after the doors are metal detectors and X-ray machines—re-

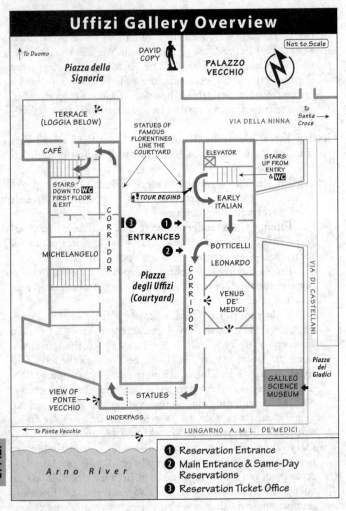

Uffizi Gallery Overview

↑ To Duomo

Piazza della Signoria

DAVID COPY

PALAZZO VECCHIO

Not to Scale

TERRACE (LOGGIA BELOW)

STATUES OF FAMOUS FLORENTINES LINE THE COURTYARD

VIA DELLA NINNA

To Santa Croce →

CAFÉ

ELEVATOR

STAIRS UP FROM ENTRY & **WC**

STAIRS DOWN TO **WC** FIRST FLOOR & EXIT

🚶 TOUR BEGINS

EARLY ITALIAN

CORRIDOR

❸ ❶ ➤ **ENTRANCES** ❷ ➤

MICHELANGELO

Piazza degli Uffizi (Courtyard)

BOTTICELLI

LEONARDO

CORRIDOR

VENUS DE' MEDICI

VIA DI CASTELLANI

Piazza dei Giudici

GALILEO SCIENCE MUSEUM

VIEW OF PONTE VECCHIO →

STATUES

UNDERPASS

← To Ponte Vecchio

LUNGARNO A. M. L. DE'MEDICI

Arno River

❶ Reservation Entrance
❷ Main Entrance & Same-Day Reservations
❸ Reservation Ticket Office

UFFIZI

member to leave pocketknives and corkscrews at your hotel, and expect a slow shuffle through security.

Tours: A 1.5-hour audioguide costs €6 (€10/2 people; must leave ID). ∩ Download my free Uffizi Gallery audio tour.

Length of This Tour: Allow two hours. If you have less time, concentrate on the top floor, especially Botticelli, Leonardo, and Michelangelo.

Services: Baggage check is available in the entrance lobby; all backpacks and large bags must be checked. A WC, post office, and extensive book/gift shop are in the entrance/exit hall on the ground floor. The Uffizi guidebook makes a nice souvenir.

Once in the gallery, there are no WCs until near the end of our tour, on the staircase leading down from the café.

Cuisine Art: The simple café at the top end of the gallery has an outdoor terrace with stunning views of the Palazzo Vecchio and the Duomo's dome. They serve pricey sandwiches, salads, and desserts, but a €5 cappuccino outside, with that view, is one of Europe's great treats. Plenty of handy eateries are nearby and described in the Eating in Florence chapter.

Starring: Botticelli, Venus, Raphael, Giotto, Titian, Leonardo, and Michelangelo.

The Tour Begins

• *Walk up the four long flights of the monumental staircase to the top floor. (Those with limited mobility can take the elevator.) At the top of the stairs, just before the ticket taker, stop for a moment to survey the busts of the Medici family, the great patrons of the arts and in many ways the funders of the Florentine Renaissance. Early, influential members of the family are on the right, while on the left you can see how generations of decadence took their toll. Once you're past the ticket taker, get oriented.*

OVERVIEW

The Uffizi is U-shaped, running around the courtyard. This left wing contains Florentine paintings from medieval to Renaissance times. At the far end, you pass through a short hallway filled with the kind of ancient sculpture that inspired the Renaissance. The right wing (which you can see across the courtyard) has a rare painting by Michelangelo, and a view café terrace, perfect for a break. The visit concludes downstairs with many more rooms of art, showing how the Florentine Renaissance spread to Rome (Raphael) and Venice (Titian), and inspired the Baroque (Caravaggio). We'll concentrate on the Uffizi's forte, the Florentine section, then get a taste of the art that followed.

• *Head up the long hallway, and enter the first door on the left, Room 2. You come face-to-face with a large painting of the Virgin Mary on a throne, by Giotto. It's flanked left and right by two similar works by other artists.*

MEDIEVAL—WHEN ART WAS AS FLAT AS THE WORLD (1200-1400)
Duccio, Cimabue, and Giotto, a Trio of Madonnas with Child

Mary and Baby Jesus sit on a throne in a golden never-never land symbolizing heaven. It's as if medieval Christians couldn't imagine holy people inhabiting our dreary material world. It took Renaissance painters to bring Mary down to earth and give her human realism. For the Florentines, "realism" meant "three-dimensional."

The three similar-looking Madonna-and-Bambinos in this room—all painted within a few decades of each other, in about the year 1300—show baby steps in the march to realism.

❶ **Duccio**'s piece (on the left as you face Giotto) is the most medieval and two-dimensional. There's no background. The angels are just stacked one on top of the other, floating in the golden atmosphere. Mary's throne is crudely drawn—the left side is at a three-quarter angle while the right is practically straight on. Mary herself is a wispy cardboard-cutout figure seemingly floating just above the throne.

On the opposite wall, the work of ❷ **Cimabue**—mixing the iconic Byzantine style with budding Italian realism—is an improvement. The large throne creates an illusion of depth; the angels alongside peek out from behind its massive architecture. Mary's foot actually sticks out over the lip of the throne. Still, the angels are stacked totem-pole-style, serving as heavenly bookends. Cimabue wowed the people of his day with his technique (including his much-loved crucifix for the Church of Santa Croce; see page 216), but he was quickly overshadowed by one of his students—Giotto—who grew to be more talented and famous.

❸ **Giotto** employs realism to make his theological points. He creates a space and fills it. Like a set designer, he builds a three-dimensional "stage"—the canopied throne—then peoples it with real beings. The throne has angels in front, prophets behind, and a canopy over the top, clearly defining its three dimensions. The steps up to the throne lead from our space to Mary's, making the scene an extension of our world. But the real triumph here is Mary herself—big and monumental, like a Roman statue. Beneath her robe, she has a real live body, with knees and breasts that stick out

Duccio: cardboard cutout (left), Cimabue: peekaboo throne (center), Giotto: Madonna in 3-D (right).

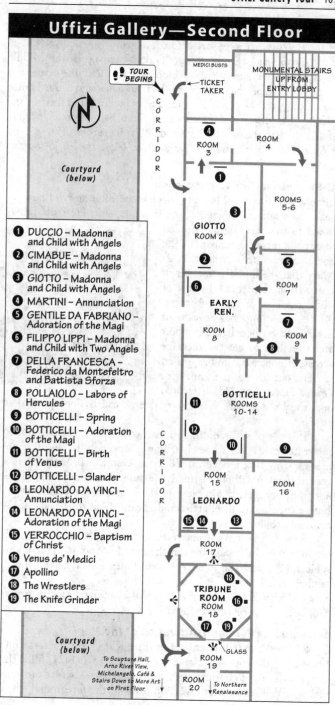

Uffizi Gallery—Second Floor

TOUR BEGINS

MEDICI BUSTS

MONUMENTAL STAIRS UP FROM ENTRY LOBBY

← TICKET TAKER

CORRIDOR

N

Courtyard (below)

4
ROOM 3

ROOM 4

1

ROOMS 5-6

3

GIOTTO ROOM 2

2

5

6

ROOM 7

EARLY REN.

7

ROOM 8

ROOM 9

8

BOTTICELLI ROOMS 10-14

11

12

10

9

CORRIDOR

ROOM 15

ROOM 16

LEONARDO

15 **14**

13

ROOM 17

TRIBUNE ROOM
ROOM 18

18

16

17 **19**

Courtyard (below)

GLASS
ROOM 19

To Scupture Hall, Arno River View, Michelangelo, Café & Stairs Down to More Art on First Floor

ROOM 20

To Northern Renaissance

UFFIZI

1 DUCCIO – Madonna and Child with Angels

2 CIMABUE – Madonna and Child with Angels

3 GIOTTO – Madonna and Child with Angels

4 MARTINI – Annunciation

5 GENTILE DA FABRIANO – Adoration of the Magi

6 FILIPPO LIPPI – Madonna and Child with Two Angels

7 DELLA FRANCESCA – Federico da Montefeltro and Battista Sforza

8 POLLAIOLO – Labors of Hercules

9 BOTTICELLI – Spring

10 BOTTICELLI – Adoration of the Magi

11 BOTTICELLI – Birth of Venus

12 BOTTICELLI – Slander

13 LEONARDO DA VINCI – Annunciation

14 LEONARDO DA VINCI – Adoration of the Magi

15 VERROCCHIO – Baptism of Christ

16 Venus de' Medici

17 Apollino

18 The Wrestlers

19 The Knife Grinder

at us. This three-dimensionality was revolutionary in its day, a taste of the Renaissance a century before it began.

Giotto was one of the first "famous" artists. In the Middle Ages, artists were mostly unglamorous craftsmen, like carpenters or cable-TV repairmen. They cranked out generic art. But Giotto was recognized as a genius, a unique individual. He died in the plague that devastated Florence. If there had been no plague, would the Renaissance have started 100 years earlier?

• *Enter Room 3 featuring art from Siena. It's to the left as you face Giotto.*

❹ Simone Martini, *Annunciation*

Simone Martini (c. 1284-1344) depicts the Bible story of how Jesus's mom got the news that she was pregnant. He boils things

down to the basic figures needed to get the message across: (1) The angel appears to sternly tell (2) Mary that she'll be the mother of Jesus. In the center is (3) a vase of lilies, a symbol of purity. Above is (4) the Holy Spirit as a dove about to descend on her. If the symbols aren't enough to get the message across, Simone Martini has spelled it right out for us in Latin: *"Ave Gratia Plena..."* or, "Hail, favored one, the Lord is with you." Mary doesn't exactly look pleased as punch.

This is not a three-dimensional work. The point was not to re-create reality but to teach religion, especially to the illiterate masses. This isn't a beautiful Mary or even a real Mary. She's a generic woman without distinctive features. We know she's pure—not from her face, but because of the halo and symbolic flowers. Before the Renaissance, artists didn't care about the beauty of individual people.

Simone Martini's *Annunciation* has medieval features you'll see in many of the paintings in the next few rooms: (1) religious subject, (2) gold background, (3) two-dimensionality, and (4) meticulous detail.

• *Pass through Rooms 4-6, full of golden altarpieces. Exiting Rooms 5-6, hang a U-turn left into Room 7.*

❺ Gentile da Fabriano, *Adoration of the Magi*

Look at the incredible detail of the Three Kings' costumes, the fine horses, and the cow in the cave. Fabriano (c. 1370-1427) filled the canvas from top to bottom with realistic details—but it's far from realistic. While the Magi worship Jesus in the foreground, their

return trip home dangles over their heads in the "background."

This is a textbook example of the International Gothic style popular with Europe's aristocrats in the early 1400s: well-dressed, elegant people in a colorful, design-oriented setting. The religious subject is just an excuse to paint secular luxuries such as jewelry and clothes made of silk brocade. And the scene's background and foreground are compressed together to create an overall design that's pleasing to the eye.

Such exquisite detail work raises the question: Was Renaissance three-dimensionality truly an improvement over Gothic, or simply a different style?

EARLY RENAISSANCE (MID-1400s)
• *Enter Room 8. Look straight ahead, to a painting of Mary with her hands folded and baby Jesus being lifted up by playful angel boys.*

❻ Fra Filippo Lippi, *Madonna and Child with Two Angels*
Mentally compare this Mary with the generic female in Simone Martini's *Annunciation*. We don't need the wispy halo over her

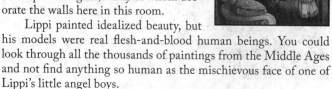

head to tell us she's holy—she radiates sweetness and light from her divine face. Heavenly beauty is expressed by a physically beautiful woman.

Fra (Brother) Lippi (1406-1469), an orphan raised as a monk, lived a less-than-monkish life. He lived with a nun who bore him two children. He spent his entire life searching for the perfect Virgin. Through his studio passed Florence's prettiest girls, many of whom decorate the walls here in this room.

Lippi painted idealized beauty, but his models were real flesh-and-blood human beings. You could look through all the thousands of paintings from the Middle Ages and not find anything so human as the mischievous face of one of Lippi's little angel boys.

• *Nearby—either here in Room 8 or in the following Room 9—find a freestanding double-portrait painting of a man and wife.*

❼ Piero della Francesca, *Federico da Montefeltro and Battista Sforza*
In medieval times, only saints and angels were worthy of being painted. In the humanistic Renaissance, however, even nonreli-

gious folk like this husband and wife by Francesca (c. 1412-1492) had their features preserved for posterity. Usually the man would have appeared on the left, with his wife at the right. But Federico's right side was definitely not his best—he lost his right eye and part of his nose in a tournament. Renaissance artists discovered the beauty in ordinary people and painted them, literally, warts and all.

• *In Room 9, find the glass case with two tiny works by Pollaiolo.*

❽ Antonio del Pollaiolo, *Labors of Hercules*

Hercules gets a workout in two small panels showing the human form at odd angles. The poses are the wildest imaginable, to show how each muscle twists and tightens. While Uccello worked on perspective, Pollaiolo (c. 1431-1498) studied anatomy. In medieval times, dissection of corpses was a sin and a crime (the two were the same then). Dissecting was a desecration of the human body, the temple of God. But Pollaiolo was willing to sell his soul to the devil for artistic knowledge. He dissected.

There's something funny about this room that I can't put my finger on...I've got it—no Madonnas. Not one. (No, that's not a Madonna; she's a Virtue.)

We've seen how Early Renaissance artists worked to conquer reality. Now let's see the fruits of their work, the flowering of Florence's Renaissance.

• *Enter the large space (Rooms 10-14) where works by Botticelli are displayed. Stroll around and take it all in, as you think about the optimistic generation that produced such works of beauty.*

THE RENAISSANCE BLOSSOMS (1450-1500)

Florence in 1450 was in a Firenz-y of activity. There was a can-do spirit of optimism in the air, led by prosperous merchants and bankers and a strong middle class. The government was reasonably democratic, and Florentines saw themselves as citizens of a strong republic—like ancient Rome. Their civic pride showed in the public monuments and artworks they built. Man was leaving the protection of the church to stand on his own two feet.

Lorenzo de' Medici, head of the powerful Medici family, epitomized this new humanistic spirit. Strong, decisive, handsome, poetic, athletic, sensitive, charismatic, intelligent, brave, clean, and reverent, Lorenzo was a true Renaissance Man, deserving of the nickname he went by—the Magnificent. He gathered Florence's best and brightest around him for evening wine and discussions of great ideas. One of this circle was the painter Botticelli.

❾ Sandro Botticelli, *Spring*

It's springtime in a citrus grove. The winds of spring blow in (Mr. Blue, at right), causing the woman on the right to sprout flowers from her lips as she morphs into Flora, or Spring—who walks by, spreading flowers from her dress. At the left are Mercury and the Three Graces, dancing a delicate maypole dance. The Graces may be symbolic of the three forms of love—of beauty, love of people, and sexual love, suggested by the raised intertwined fingers. (They forgot love of peanut butter on toast.) In the center stands Venus, the Greek goddess of love. Above her flies a blindfolded Cupid, happily shooting his arrows of love without worrying about whom they'll hit.

Here is the Renaissance in its first bloom, its "springtime" of innocence. Madonna is out, Venus is in. Adam and Eve hiding their nakedness are out, glorious flesh is in. This is a return to the pre-Christian pagan world of classical Greece, where things of the flesh are not sinful. But this is certainly no orgy—just fresh-faced innocence and playfulness.

Botticelli (1445-1510) emphasizes pristine beauty over gritty realism. The lines of the bodies, especially of the Graces in their see-through nighties, have pleasing, S-like curves. The faces are idealized but have real human features. There's a look of thoughtfulness and even melancholy in the faces—as though everyone knows that the innocence of spring will not last forever.

• *You may (or may not) find the following painting nearby, giving a glimpse into the world of the Medici.*

⑩ Botticelli, *Adoration of the Magi*

Here's the rat pack of confident young Florentines who reveled in the optimistic pagan spirit—even in a religious scene. Botticelli included himself among the adorers, at the far right, looking vain in the yellow robe. Lorenzo is the Magnificent-looking guy at the far left.

• *Now approach the room's most famous painting, thronged by admirers.*

⑪ Botticelli, *Birth of Venus*

According to myth, Venus was born from the foam of a wave. Still only half awake, this fragile, newborn beauty floats ashore on a clam shell, blown by the winds, where her maid waits to dress her. The pose is the same S-curve of classical statues (as we'll soon see). Botticelli's pastel colors make the world itself seem fresh and newly born.

This is the purest expression of Renaissance beauty. Venus' naked body is not sensual, but innocent. Botticelli thought that physical beauty was a way of appreciating God. Remember Michelangelo's poem: Souls will never ascend to heaven "...unless the sight of Beauty lifts them there."

Botticelli finds God in the details—Venus' windblown hair, her translucent skin, the maid's braided hair, the slight ripple of the wind god's abs, and the flowers tumbling in the slowest of slow motions, suspended like musical notes, caught at the peak of their brief life.

Mr. and Mrs. Wind intertwine—notice her hands clasped around his body. Their hair, wings, and robes mingle like the wind. But what happened to those splayed toes?

• *"Venus on the Half-Shell" (as many tourists call this) is one of the masterpieces of Western art. Take some time with it. Then find a small canvas nearby depicting a more turbulent scene.*

UFFIZI

⑫ Botticelli, *Slander*, a.k.a. *Calumny of Apelles*

The spring of Florence's Renaissance had to end. Lorenzo died young. The economy faltered. Into town rode the monk Savonarola, preaching medieval hellfire and damnation for those who embraced the "pagan" Renaissance spirit. "Down, down with all gold and decoration," he roared. "Down where the body is food for the worms." He presided over huge bonfires, where the people threw in their fine clothes, jewelry, pagan books...and paintings.

Slander spells the end of the Florentine Renaissance. The architectural setting is classic Brunelleschi, but look what's taking

place beneath those stately arches. These aren't proud Renaissance men and women but a ragtag, medieval-looking bunch, a Court of Thieves in an abandoned hall of justice. The accusations fly, and everyone is condemned. The naked man pleads for mercy, but the hooded black figure, a symbol of his execution, turns away.

The figure of Truth (naked Truth)—straight out of *The Birth of Venus*—looks up to heaven as if to ask, "What has happened to us?" The classical statues in their niches look on in disbelief.

Botticelli got caught up in the teachings of Savonarola. He burned some of his own paintings and changed his artistic tune. The last works of his life were darker, more somber, and pessimistic about humanity.

The 19th-century German poet Heinrich Heine said, "When they start by burning books, they'll end by burning people." After four short years of power, Savonarola was burned in 1498 on his own bonfire in Piazza della Signoria, but by then the city was in shambles. The first flowering of the Renaissance was over.

• *Enter the next room (#15), and find another Annunciation scene, by one of Florence's brightest lights.*

⓭ Leonardo da Vinci, *Annunciation*

A scientist, architect, engineer, musician, and painter, Leonardo da Vinci (1452-1519) was a true Renaissance Man. He worked at his own pace rather than to please an employer, so he often left works unfinished. The two paintings in this room aren't his best, but even a lesser Leonardo is enough to put a museum on the map, and they're definitely worth a look.

In the *Annunciation,* the angel Gabriel has walked up to Mary, and now kneels on one knee like an ambassador, saluting her. See how relaxed his other hand is, draped over his knee. Mary, who's been reading, looks up with a gesture of surprise and curiosity.

Leonardo constructs a beautifully landscaped "stage" and puts his characters in it. Look at the bricks on the right wall. If you extended lines from them, the lines would all converge at the center of the painting, the distant blue mountain. Same with the edge of the sarcophagus and the railing. This subtle touch creates a subconscious feeling of balance, order, and spaciousness in the viewer.

Think back to Simone Martini's *Annunciation* to realize how much more natural, relaxed, and realistic Leonardo's version is. He's taken a miraculous event—an angel appearing out of the blue—and presented it in a very human way.

⓮ Leonardo da Vinci, *Adoration of the Magi*

Leonardo's human insight is even more apparent here, in this unfinished work (it may be under restoration during your visit). The poor

kings are amazed at the Christ child—even afraid of him. They scurry around like chimps around a fire. This work is as agitated as the *Annunciation* is calm, giving us an idea of Leonardo's range. Leonardo was pioneering a new era of painting, showing not just the outer features but the inner personality.

Nearby hangs the ⓯ *Baptism of Christ* by Andrea del Verrocchio, Leonardo's teacher. Leonardo painted the angel on the far left when he was only a teenager. Legend has it that when Verrocchio saw that some kid had painted an angel better than he ever would... he hung up his brush for good.

Florence saw the first blossoming of the Renaissance. But when the cultural climate turned chilly, artists flew south to warmer climes. The Renaissance shifted to Rome.

• *Proceed past the Leonardo into the small hallway. Straight ahead is a doorway (with a glass barrier) to the Tribuna (a.k.a. Room 18). Gazing inside, you'll see the famous* Venus de' Medici *statue. (If this little hallway is extremely crowded, keep going—there's a viewing doorway in the main hallway, and another around the corner in Room 19.)*

TRIBUNE ROOM

If the Renaissance was the foundation of the modern world, the foundation of the Renaissance was classical sculpture. Sculptors, painters, and poets alike turned for inspiration to these ancient Greek and Roman works as the epitome of balance, 3-D perspective, human anatomy, and beauty. The Tribune Room features several well-known statues. Start with the goddess of love.

⓰ *Venus de' Medici,* first century B.C.

Is this pose familiar? Botticelli's *Birth of Venus* has the same position of the arms, the same S-curved body, and the same lifting of

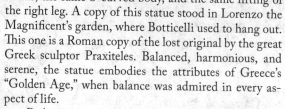

the right leg. A copy of this statue stood in Lorenzo the Magnificent's garden, where Botticelli used to hang out. This one is a Roman copy of the lost original by the great Greek sculptor Praxiteles. Balanced, harmonious, and serene, the statue embodies the attributes of Greece's "Golden Age," when balance was admired in every aspect of life.

Perhaps more than any other work of art, this statue *(Venere dei Medici)* has been the epitome of both ideal beauty and sexuality. In the 18th and 19th centuries, sex was "dirty," so the sex drive of cultured aristocrats was channeled into a love of pure beauty. Wealthy sons and daughters of Europe's aristocrats made the pilgrimage to the Uffizi to complete their classical education...where they swooned in ecstasy before the cold beauty of this goddess of love.

UFFIZI

Louis XIV had a bronze copy made. Napoleon stole her away to Paris for himself. And in Philadelphia in the 1800s, a copy had to be kept under lock and key to prevent the innocent from catching the Venere-al disease. At first, it may be difficult for us to appreciate such passionate love of art, but if any generation knows the power of sex to sell something—be it art or underarm deodorant—it's ours.

The Other Statues, first-second century A.D.

Check out some of the other ancient statues. Facing Venus—leaning on a tree trunk—is Venus' male counterpart, ❼ **Apollino**. Affectionately called "Venus with a Penis," Apollino is also carved by that ancient Greek master of smooth, cool lines: Praxiteles.

These other works are later Greek (Hellenistic), when quiet balance was replaced by violent motion and emotion. ❽ *The Wrestlers,* to the left of Venus, is a study in anatomy and twisted limbs—like Pollaiolo's paintings a thousand years later.

The drama of ❾ *The Knife Grinder* to the right of Venus stems from the offstage action—he's sharpening the knife to flay a man alive.

Now check out the room itself, gazing up into the dazzling dome. This fine room was a showroom, or a "cabinet of wonders," back when this building still functioned as the Medici offices. Filled with family portraits, it's a holistic statement that symbolically links the Medici family with the four basic elements: air (weathervane in the lantern), water (inlaid mother of pearl in the dome), fire (red wall), and earth (inlaid stone floor).

• *Exit into the main hallway. Breathe. Sit. Admire the ceiling. Look out the window. See you in five. Back already? Now continue strolling to the end of the hall, where a standing nude statue welcomes you to the...*

SCULPTURE HALL

A hundred years ago, no one even looked at Botticelli—they came to the Uffizi to see the sculpture collection. And today, these 2,000-year-old Roman copies of 2,500-year-old Greek originals are hardly noticed...but they should be. Only a few are displayed here now.

The most impressive is the male nude, *Doriforo* ("spear carrier"), a Roman copy of the Greek original by Polykleitos, located in the middle of the hallway, where it turns right.

The purple statue in the center of the hall—headless and limbless—is a **female**

wolf (*lupa*, c. A.D. 120) done in porphyry stone. This was the animal that raised Rome's legendary founders and became the city's symbol. Renaissance Florentines marveled at the ancient Romans' ability to create such lifelike, three-dimensional works. They learned to reproduce them in stone...and then learned to paint them on a two-dimensional surface.

• *Gaze out the windows from the hall. At the far end, enjoy the best...*

View of the Arno: This is my favorite view of the river and Ponte Vecchio. You can also see the red-tiled roof of the Vasari Corridor, the "secret" passage connecting the Palazzo Vecchio, Uffizi, Ponte Vecchio, and the Pitti Palace on the other side of the river—a half-mile in all. This was a private walkway, wallpapered in great art, for the Medici family's commute from home to work.

As you appreciate the view, remember that it's this sort of pleasure that Renaissance painters wanted you to get from their paint-

ings. For them, a canvas was a window you looked through to see the wide world. Their paintings re-create natural perspective: Distant objects (such as bridges) are smaller, dimmer, and higher up the "canvas," while closer objects are bigger, clearer, and lower.

We're headed down the home stretch now. If your little U-feetsies are killing you, and it feels like torture, remind yourself that it's a pleasant torture and smile...like the *Marsia Rosso* statue hanging around next to you.

• *Round the bend and start down the far hallway. About 40 yards down, at the fourth doorway, turn left into Room 35 and head for the round painting opposite the entry. (You may have to step around a huge statue of a reclining woman.)*

MICHELANGELO ROOM
Michelangelo Buonarroti, *Holy Family,*
a.k.a. *Doni Tondo*

This is the only completed easel painting by the greatest sculptor in history. Florentine painters were sculptors with brushes; this shows it. Instead of a painting, it's more like three clusters of statues with some clothes painted on.

The main subject is the holy family—Mary, Joseph, and Baby Jesus—and in the background are two groups of nudes looking like classical statues. The background represents the old pagan world, while Jesus in the foreground is the new age of Christianity. The figure of young John the Baptist at right is the link between the two.

This is a "peasant" Mary, with a plain face and sunburned arms. Michelangelo (1475-1564) shows her from a very unflattering angle—we're looking up her nostrils. But Michelangelo himself was an ugly man, and he was among the first artists to recognize the beauty in everyday people.

Michelangelo was a Florentine—in fact, he was like an adopted son of the Medici, who recognized his talent—but much of his greatest work was done in Rome as part of the pope's face-lift of the city. We can see here some of the techniques he used on the Sistine Chapel ceiling that revolutionized painting—monumental figures; dramatic angles (looking up Mary's nose); accentuated, rippling muscles; and bright, clashing colors (all the more apparent since both this work and the Sistine Chapel ceiling have recently been cleaned). These elements added a dramatic tension that was lacking in the graceful work of Leonardo and Botticelli.

Michelangelo painted this for his friend Agnolo Doni for 70 ducats. (Michelangelo designed, but didn't carve, the elaborate frame.) When the painting was delivered, Doni tried to talk Michelangelo down to 40. Proud Michelangelo took the painting away and would not sell it until the man finally agreed to pay double...140 ducats.

Also on display in the room is the hard-to-miss statue of *Sleeping Ariadne.* The third-century work was much copied, and Michelangelo was inspired by it. (Hmm. Does Mary in the *Doni Tondo* have a few touches of Ariadne? The twisting pose, the position of the arms, and the heavily wrinkled robe?)

• *Return to the hallway and continue to the end—past the special exhibits and rooms where masterpieces from closed rooms are temporarily displayed.*

REST OF THE TOP FLOOR
Laocoön (16th-century copy)

At the far end of the hall is a copy of the dramatic ancient Greek statue of *Laocoön* (the original is at the Vatican Museums). It depicts the moment when this priest of Troy is overcome by snakes, and he realizes his people are doomed. ("Snakes? Why did it have to be snakes?") One of the most famous statues of antiquity, it was discovered in 1506—just in time to inspire Renaissance greats like Michelangelo. After seeing *Laocoön*, Michelangelo began creating

UFFIZI

figures with more restless motion and tragic emotion. *Laocoön's* anguished face may exude tragedy, but right now Mr. Laocoön seems to be saying, "Time for a coffee break." Just past him is a fine café and an open-air terrace where you can enjoy a truly aesthetic experience...

Little Capuchin Monk (Cappuccino)

This drinkable art form, born in Italy, is now enjoyed all over the world. It's called the "Little Capuchin Monk" because the coffee's

frothy, light- and dark-brown foam looks like the two-toned cowls of the Capuchin order. Sip it on the terrace in the shadow of the towering Palazzo Vecchio, and be glad we live in an age where you don't need to be a Medici to enjoy all this fine art. *Salute.*

• *When you're ready to move on, go down the staircase near the café, to the first floor. On your way down, you'll pass the WC. Once on the first floor, we'll be making our way through dozens of rooms with a lot more art. Breeze through quickly, making a few key stops along the way.*

FIRST FLOOR—MORE ART ON THE WAY TO THE EXIT

At the bottom of the staircase, turning right, you enter Room 56, a long red-walled room lined with the kind of **ancient statues** that inspired Renaissance painters. Continue through more rooms to Room 65, with **portraits by Bronzino** of Duke Cosimo I de' Medici, his wife, Eleonora, their cute bird-holding son, and their daughters.

• *Stop in Room 66 for...*

Raphael, *Madonna of the Goldfinch*

Raphael (Raffaello Sanzio, 1483-1520) brings Mary and bambino down from heaven and into the real world of trees, water, and sky. He gives Baby Jesus (right) and John the Baptist a realistic, human playfulness. It's a tender scene painted with warm colors and a hazy background that matches the golden skin of the children.

Raphael perfected his craft in Florence, following the graceful style of Leonardo. In typical Leonardo fashion, this group of Mary, John the Baptist,

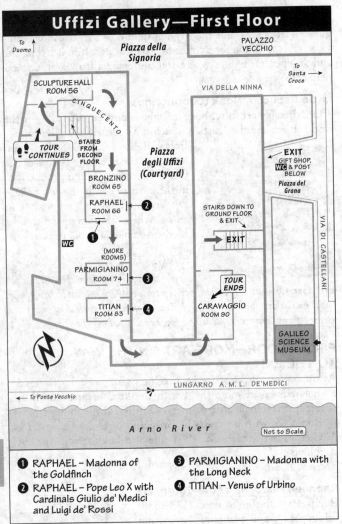

Uffizi Gallery—First Floor

To Duomo

Piazza della Signoria

PALAZZO VECCHIO

To Santa Croce

SCULPTURE HALL ROOM 56

VIA DELLA NINNA

CINQUECENTO

TOUR CONTINUES

STAIRS FROM SECOND FLOOR

Piazza degli Uffizi (Courtyard)

EXIT
GIFT SHOP, **WC** & POST BELOW
Piazza del Grana

BRONZINO ROOM 65

RAPHAEL ROOM 66 ❷

STAIRS DOWN TO GROUND FLOOR & EXIT

VIA DI CASTELLANI

❶

WC

EXIT

(MORE ROOMS)

PARMIGIANINO ROOM 74 ❸

TOUR ENDS

TITIAN ROOM 83 ❹

CARAVAGGIO ROOM 90

GALILEO SCIENCE MUSEUM

LUNGARNO A. M. L. DE'MEDICI

← To Ponte Vecchio

Arno River

Not to Scale

UFFIZI

❶ RAPHAEL – Madonna of the Goldfinch
❷ RAPHAEL – Pope Leo X with Cardinals Giulio de' Medici and Luigi de' Rossi
❸ PARMIGIANINO – Madonna with the Long Neck
❹ TITIAN – Venus of Urbino

and Jesus is arranged in the shape of a pyramid, with Mary's head at the peak.

The two halves of the painting balance perfectly. Draw a line down the middle, through Mary's nose and down through her knee. John the Baptist on the left is balanced by Jesus on the right. Even the trees in the background balance each other, left and right. These things aren't immediately noticeable, but they help create the subconscious feelings of balance and order that reinforce the atmosphere of maternal security in this domestic scene—pure Renaissance.

• *On the wall to the left is...*

Raphael, *Pope Leo X with Cardinals Giulio de' Medici and Luigi de' Rossi*

Raphael was called to Rome at the same time as Michelangelo, working next door in the Vatican apartments while Michelangelo painted the Sistine Chapel ceiling.  Raphael peeked in from time to time, learning from Michelangelo's monumental, dramatic figures, and his later work is grittier and more realistic than the idealized, graceful, and "Leonardoesque" Madonna.

Pope Leo X is big, like a Michelangelo statue. And Raphael captures some of the seamier side of Vatican life in the cardinals' eyes—shrewd, suspicious, and somewhat cynical. With Raphael, the photographic realism pursued by painters since Giotto was finally achieved.

The Florentine Renaissance ended in 1520 with the death of Raphael. Raphael (see his **self-portrait** nearby) is considered both the culmination and conclusion of the Renaissance. The realism, balance, and humanism we associate with the Renaissance are all found in Raphael's work. He combined the grace of Leonardo with the power of Michelangelo. With his death, the High Renaissance ended as well.

• *A few rooms farther along, you reach Room 74, with a tall painting.*

Parmigianino, *Madonna with the Long Neck*

Once Renaissance artists had mastered reality, where could they go next?

Mannerists such as Parmigianino (1503-1540) tried to go beyond realism, exaggerating it for effect. Using brighter colors and twisting poses, they created scenes more elegant and more exciting than real life.

By stretching the neck of his Madonna, Parmigianino (like the cheese) gives her an unnatural, swanlike beauty. She has the same pose and position of hands as Botticelli's *Venus* and the *Venus de' Medici*. Her body forms an arcing S-curve—down her neck as far as her elbow, then back the other way along Jesus' body to her knee, then down to her foot. Baby Jesus seems to be blissfully gliding down this slippery slide of sheer beauty.

UFFIZI

Six Degrees of Leo X

This sophisticated, luxury-loving pope was at the center of an international Renaissance world that spread across Europe. He

crossed paths with many of the Renaissance men of his generation. Based on the theory that any two people are linked by only "six degrees of separation," let's link Leo X with the actor Kevin Bacon:

- Leo X's father was Lorenzo the Magnificent, patron of Botticelli and Leonardo.
- When Leo X was age 13, his family took in 13-year-old Michelangelo.
- Michelangelo inspired Raphael, who was later hired by Leo X.
- Raphael exchanged masterpieces with fellow genius Albrecht Dürer, who was personally converted by Martin Luther (who was friends with Lucas Cranach), who was excommunicated by...Leo X.

- Leo X was portrayed in the movie *The Agony and the Ecstasy,* which starred Charlton Heston, who was in *Two-Minute Warning* with J. A. Preston, who was in *A Few Good Men* with... Kevin Bacon.

• *Continue on to long Room 83, with a number of works by Titian.*

Titian, *Venus of Urbino*

Compare this *Venus* with Botticelli's newly-hatched *Venus,* and you get a good idea of the difference between the Florentine and Venetian Renaissances. Botticelli's was pure, innocent, and otherworldly. Titian's should have a staple in her belly button. This isn't a Venus, it's a centerfold—with no purpose but to please the eye (and other organs). While Botticelli's allegorical *Venus* is a message, this is a massage. The bed is used.

Titian (c. 1490-1576) and his fellow Venetians took the pagan spirit pioneered in Florence and carried it to its logical hedonistic conclusion. Using bright, rich colors, they captured the luxurious life of happy-go-lucky Venice.

While other artists may have balanced their compositions with a figure on the left and one on the right, Titian balances his painting in a different way—with color. The canvas is split down the middle by the curtain. The left half is dark, the right half is

UFFIZI

lighter. The two halves are connected by a diagonal slash of luminous gold—the nude woman. The girl in the background is trying to find her some clothes.

In the Uffizi, we've seen many images of female beauty: from ancient goddesses to medieval Madonnas, from Parmigianino's cheesy slippery-slide to Michelangelo's peasant Mary, from Botticelli's pristine nymphs to Titian's sensuous centerfold. Their physical beauty expresses different aspects of the human spirit.

By the way, visitors from centuries past panted in front of this Venus by Titian. The Romantic poet Byron called it *"the* Venus." With her sensual skin, hey-sailor look, and suggestively placed hand, she must have left them blithering idiots.

• *Our tour is n-n-n-nearly over. Turn left through a long connecting hallway, then left again into still more rooms. It's worth pausing in Room 90, with works by* **Caravaggio**, *including the shocking ultrarealism of* Sacrifice of Isaac *and macabre head of* Medusa, *painted on a ceremonial shield.*

When you're ready to leave, the exit takes you back down to the WCs/bookstore/post office, and the way out to the street. You'll pop out behind the Uffizi, a block up from the river and very near the Galileo Science Museum and the Bargello (sculpture museum). Stepping back into the real world after your Uffizi experience, you may see it with new eyes.

BARGELLO TOUR

The Renaissance began with sculpture. The great Florentine painters were "sculptors with brushes." You can see the birth of this revolution of 3-D in the Bargello (bar-JEL-oh), which boasts the best collection of Florentine sculpture. It's a small, uncrowded museum and a pleasant break from the intensity of the rest of Florence. You'll see 150 years of great statues, spanning the history of Florence's heyday. And it's all set in a rustic palazzo with a medieval atmosphere.

Orientation

Cost: €8, cash only, free and crowded on first Sun of the month, covered by Firenze Card.

Hours: Tue-Sat 8:15-17:00, later for special exhibits, until 13:50 Nov-March; also open these times on the second and fourth Mon and first, third, and fifth Sun of each month, last entry 40 minutes before closing. You can reserve an entrance time, but it's unnecessary. Tel. 055-238-8606.

Getting There: It's located at Via del Proconsolo 4, a three-minute walk northeast of the Uffizi. Facing the Palazzo Vecchio, go behind the Palazzo and turn left. Look for a rustic brick building with a spire that looks like a baby Palazzo Vecchio. If lost ask, *"Dov'è Bargello?"* (doh-VEH bar-JEL-oh).

Getting In: You must pass through a metal detector, and bags go through an X-ray machine before you enter.

Tours: ∩ Download my free Bargello audio tour.

Length of This Tour: Allow one hour. If your time is limited, be sure to see the Michelangelo statues on the ground floor and the Donatello *David* statues on the first.

Cuisine Art: Inexpensive bars and cafés await in the surrounding streets. See recommended eateries on page 289.

Starring: Michelangelo, Donatello, Brunelleschi, Ghiberti, and four different *David*s.

The Tour Begins

COURTYARD

• *Buy your ticket and take a seat in the courtyard.*

The Bargello, built in 1255, was Florence's original Town Hall and also served as a police station *(bargello)*, and later a prison. The heavy

fortifications tell us that keeping the peace in medieval Florence had its occupational hazards. While the stoniness of this building seems to fit its past, it is interesting to note that the independent Duchy of Tuscany abolished torture and capital punishment in the 18th century, when Florence was its capital. They gathered the tools of torture and executions and burned them right here in this courtyard.

This cool and peaceful courtyard is at the center of the three-story rectangular building. The best statues are found in two rooms—one on the ground floor at the foot of the outdoor staircase, and another one flight up, directly above. We'll proceed from Michelangelo to Donatello to Verrocchio.

But first, meander around this courtyard and get a feel for sculpture in general and the medium of stone in particular. Sculpture is a much more robust art form than painting. Think of just the engineering problems of the sculpting process: quarrying and cutting the stone, transporting the block to the artist's studio, all the hours of chiseling away chips, then

the painstaking process of sanding the final product by hand. A sculptor must be strong enough to gouge into the stone, but delicate enough to groove out the smallest details. Think of Michelangelo's approach to sculpting: He wasn't creating a figure—he was liberating it from the rock that surrounded it.

The Renaissance was centered on humanism—and sculpture is the perfect medium in which to ex-

BARGELLO

Bargello—Ground Floor

50 Feet

To Duomo

VIA GHIBELLINA

TOWER

ENTRANCE

TICKETS

EXIT

TEMPORARY EXHIBITS

COURTYARD

WELL

WC & ELEVATOR

VIA PROCONSOLO

COLUMN

STAIRS UP TO DONATELLO ROOM (FIRST FLOOR)

VIA DELLA VIGNA VECCHIA

To Santa Croce →

↓ To Palazzo Vecchio & Uffizi

1 MICHELANGELO – Bacchus
2 MICHELANGELO – Pitti Tondo
3 MICHELANGELO – Brutus
4 MICHELANGELO – David (Apollo)
5 Copies of Michelangelo's Works
6 DANIELE – Bust of Michelangelo
7 CELLINI – Models of Perseus (2)
8 GIAMBOLOGNA – Flying Mercury

press it. It shows the human form, standing alone, independent of church, state, or society, ready to fulfill its potential.

Finally, a viewing tip. Every sculpture has an invisible "frame" around it—the stone block it was cut from. Visualizing this frame helps you find the center of the composition.

GROUND FLOOR

· *Head into the room at the foot of the courtyard's grand staircase, turn left, and be greeted by a tall, marble party animal.*

❶ Michelangelo, *Bacchus,* c. 1497

Bacchus, the god of wine and revelry, raises another cup to his lips, while his little companion goes straight for the grapes.

Maybe Michelangelo had a sense of humor after all. Mentally compare this tipsy Greek god of wine with his sturdy, sober *David,* begun a few years later. Raucous *Bacchus* isn't nearly so muscular, so monumental... or so sure on his feet. Hope he's not driving. The pose, the smooth muscles, the beer belly, and the swaying hips look more like Donatello's boyish *David* (upstairs). The little satyr is considered the first such twisting serpentine figure since ancient times.

This was Michelangelo's first major commission. Check the date it was carved: c.1497. The city of Florence was caught in the grip of the puritanical monk Savonarola. Meanwhile, young Michelangelo had fled to Rome, where he hobnobbed with the festive Medici exiles and created this ultra-pagan Bacchus. Michelangelo often vacillated—showing man either as strong and noble, or as weak and perverse. This isn't the nobility of the classical world, but the decadent side of orgies and indulgence.

• *Behind Bacchus' right cheek is a circular relief.*

❷ Michelangelo, *Madonna and Child with the Young St. John,* a.k.a. *Pitti Tondo,* c. 1505

By 1504, Michelangelo had just finished his monumental, heroic statue *David*. In a complete change of pace, he turned to this quiet, small-scale marble work.

The Virgin Mary sits reading a book, while Baby Jesus and (probably) John the Baptist look on. The round "tondo" format gave Michelangelo a compositional opportunity. He combined the vertical (the upright Madonna) and the horizontal (her forearms and thighs), all enfolded in a warm family circle. Jesus curves lovingly around his mom, casually glancing at her book. Another dimension to the composition is depth: The bench Mary sits on juts outward, and her face rises from the stone in a cameo effect. Finally, Michelangelo added an element of surprise to the standard tondo by letting Mary's head pop out from the top of the frame.

The tondo is unfinished, giving us a chance to look at Michelangelo's work process. He started first with the easy stuff—Mary's robe and the bench, which are nearly finished. Mary's blouse is still in rough form, being chiseled out in Michelangelo's cross-hatch technique. Find the little details beginning to emerge—the small child at left and the tiny face in Mary's diadem. But called away to a bigger project in Rome, Michelangelo abandoned the not-quite-finished tondo. Compare this ultra-sacred sculpture with the ultra-pagan Bacchus. Throughout his life, Michelangelo would veer between these two poles.

• *Farther back in the room, a marble bust against a square column is...*

❸ Michelangelo, *Brutus,* 1540

Another example of the influence of Donatello is this so-ugly-he's-beautiful bust by Michelangelo. His rough intensity gives him the look of a man who has succeeded against all odds, a dignified and heroic quality that would be missing if he were too pretty.

The subject is Brutus, the Roman who, for the love of liberty, murdered his friend and dictator, Julius Caesar *("Et tu...?")*. A Floren-

tine in exile commissioned the bust after the 1537 assassination of a contemporary tyrant—the Medici Duke Alessandro. Michelangelo could understand this man's dilemma. He himself was torn between his love of the democratic tradition of Florence and loyalty to his friends the Medici, who had become dictators.

So he gives us two sides of a political assassin. The right profile (the front view) is heroic. But the hidden side (view from right), with the drooping mouth and squinting eye, makes him more cunning, sneering, and ominous. Michelangelo depicted a complex individual—a man who could bravely defend his Republic...and murder a close friend with a knife.

• *Nearby is...*

❹ Michelangelo, *David*, a.k.a. *Apollo*, 1530-1532

This restless, twisting man is either David or Apollo. (Is he reaching for a sling or a quiver?) Demure (and left unfinished), this statue is light years away from Michelangelo's famous *David* in the Accademia (1501-1504), which is so much larger than life in every way. We'll see three more *David*s upstairs. As you check out each one, compare and contrast the artists' styles.

In the glass cases in the corner are ❺ **small-scale copies** of some of Michelangelo's most famous works. In the center of the room, against a square column, look for a dark-bronze ❻ **bust of Michelangelo.** Made from his death mask by fellow sculptor Daniele da Volterra, the bust captures his broken nose and brooding nature. (You may recognize this bust from the Accademia, which has a copy.)

• *Circling back clockwise toward the entrance, look for small statues in a glass case, by a pillar.*

❼ Cellini, Models of *Perseus,* 1545-1554

The life-size statue of Perseus slaying Medusa, located in the open-air loggia next to the Palazzo Vecchio, is cast bronze. Benvenuto Cellini started with these smaller models (one in wax, one in bronze) to master the difficult process of producing the first bronze statue of its kind in the Renaissance. Next to the statue, note the exquisite pedestal with four fine bronzes—built to support Cellini's statue of Perseus.

• *Take three steps toward the door to find...*

❽ Giambologna, *Flying Mercury,* before 1580

The messenger of the gods, naked from the winged helmet down, speeds off on his errands. The pose was made famous as a logo for

a well-known flower-delivery company. Despite all the bustle and motion, *Mercury* has a solid Renaissance core: the line of balance that runs straight up the center, from toes to hip to fingertip. He's caught in midstride. His top half leans forward, counterbalanced by his right leg in back, while the center of gravity rests firmly at the hipbone. Down at the toes, notice the cupid practicing for the circus.

• *We've seen statues from Florence's Renaissance heyday. Now, to see the roots of Florence's Renaissance, climb the courtyard staircase to the next floor up and turn right into the large Donatello room.*

FIRST FLOOR

• *Entering the room, cross to the middle of the far wall, and check out the first of three Davids in this room (the marble one wearing the long skirt).*

❾ Donatello, *David,* c. 1408

This marble sculpture is young Donatello's first take on the popular subject of David slaying Goliath. His dainty pose makes him a little unsteady on his feet. He's dressed like a medieval knight—fully clothed but showing some leg through the slit skirt. The generic face and blank, vacant eyes give him the look not of a real man but of an anonymous decoration on a church facade. At age 22, Donatello still had one foot in the old Gothic world. *David*'s right leg makes his body sway in the Gothic style, while his left leg is planted in the *contrapposto* Renaissance. To tell the story of David, Donatello plants a huge rock right in the middle of Goliath's forehead. Stepping behind the statue, you see how flat it is—designed to be not freestanding but up against a wall, connected with a hook.

• *Nearby, find a smaller, black-metal statue. It's the same subject, of David, but by a different artist.*

❿ Andrea del Verrocchio, *David,* c. 1466-1469

Verrocchio (1435-1488) is best known as the teacher of Leonardo da Vinci, but he was also the premier sculptor of the generation between Donatello and Michelangelo. Verrocchio's bronze *David* is definitely the shepherd "boy" described in

Donatello
(1386-1466)

Donatello was the first great Renaissance genius, a model for Michelangelo and others. He mastered realism, creating the first truly lifelike statues of people since ancient times. Donatello turned out highly personal work. Unlike the ancient Greeks—but like the ancient Romans—he often sculpted real people, not idealized versions of pretty gods and goddesses. Some of these people are downright ugly. In the true spirit of Renaissance humanism, Donatello appreciated the beauty of flesh-and-blood human beings.

Donatello's personality was also a model for later artists. He was moody and irascible, purposely setting himself apart from others in order to concentrate on his sculpting. He developed the role of the "mad genius" that Michelangelo would later perfect.

the Bible. (Some have speculated that the statue was modeled on Verrocchio's young, handsome, curly-haired apprentice, Leonardo da Vinci.) *David* leans on one leg, not with a firm, commanding stance but a nimble one (especially noticeable from behind). Compare the smug smile of the victor with Goliath's "Oh, have I got a headache" expression.

• *Finally, near the corner, is another shiny black-metal statue...*

⓫ Donatello, *David*, c. 1440

He's naked. Donatello sees David as a teenage boy wearing only a

helmet, boots, and sword. The smooth-skinned warrior sways gracefully, poking his sword playfully at the severed head of the giant Goliath. His *contrapposto* stance is similar to Michelangelo's *David*, resting his weight on one leg in the classical style, but it gives him a feminine rather than masculine look. Gazing into his coy eyes and at his bulging belly is a very different experience from confronting Michelangelo's older and sturdier Renaissance Man.

Circle the statue clockwise. From the side, you see his ramrod-straight right leg. It's echoed by the sword he carries. Around back, glance up at *David*'s neck. On the hair, there are still traces of the original gilding. Check out *David*'s promi-

Bargello—First Floor

50 Feet

To Duomo

VIA GHIBELLINA

TOWER

VIA PROCONSOLO

CHAPEL

⑪ ⑫ ⑬ ⑭

⑩

DONATELLO ROOM

⑨

COURTYARD

STAIRS UP FROM GROUND FLOOR

ELEVATOR

STAIRS UP TO SECOND FLOOR

UPPER LOGGIA

VIA DELLA VIGNA VECCHIA

To Palazzo Vecchio & Uffizi

To Santa Croce

⑨ DONATELLO – David (c.1408)
⑩ VERROCCHIO – David (c.1469)
⑪ DONATELLO – David (c.1440)
⑫ DONATELLO (or Desiderio) – Niccolò da Uzzano
⑬ DONATELLO – St. George
⑭ GHIBERTI & BRUNELLESCHI – The Sacrifice of Isaac (2 versions)

nent buttocks—clearly those of a young man, almost a boy. Now, check out the severed head of Goliath. _David_'s toes curl around it, drawing your attention to it. Notice the huge feather on the giant's helmet. It directs the viewer's eyes sensually up, up, up to _David_'s inviting back side.

This bronze _David_ paved the way for Michelangelo's. Europe hadn't seen a freestanding male nude like this in a thousand years. In the Middle Ages, the human body was considered a dirty thing, a symbol of man's weakness, something to be covered up in shame. The church prohibited exhibitions of nudity like this one and certainly would never decorate a church with it. But in the Renaissance, a new class of rich and powerful merchants appeared, and they bought art for personal enjoyment. Reading Plato's _Symposium_, they saw the ideal of Beauty in the form of a young man. This particular statue stood in the palace of the Medici (today's Medici-Riccardi Palace)...where Michelangelo, practically an adopted son, grew up admiring it.

• _Along the wall behind the last_ David _is..._

⑫ Donatello (or Desiderio da Settignano), *Niccolò da Uzzano,* after 1450

Not an emperor, not a king, not a pope, saint, or prince, this is one of Florence's leading businessmen, in a toga, portrayed in the style of an ancient Roman bust. In the 1400s, when Florence was inventing the Renaissance that all Europe would soon follow, there was an optimistic spirit of democracy that gloried in everyday people. Donatello (or his student) portrayed this man as he was—with wrinkles, a quizzical look, and bags under his eyes.

• *In the niche at the end of the room stands...*

⑬ Donatello, *St. George,* c. 1417

The proud warrior has both feet planted firmly on the ground and stands on the edge of his niche looking out alertly. He tenses his powerful right hand as he prepares to attack.

George, the Christian slayer of dragons, was just the sort of righteous warrior that proud Renaissance Florentines could rally around in their struggles with nearby cities. Nearly a century later, Michelangelo's *David* replaced *George* as the unofficial symbol of Florence, but *David* was clearly inspired by *George*'s relaxed intensity and determination. (This is the original statue; a copy stands in its original niche at Orsanmichele Church—see page 52.)

The relief panel below shows *George* doing what he's been pondering. To his right, the sketchy arches and trees create the illusion of a distant landscape. Donatello, who apprenticed in Ghiberti's studio, is credited with teaching his master how to create 3-D illusions like this.

• *On the wall next to* George, *you'll find some bronze relief panels. Don't look at the labels just yet.*

⑭ Ghiberti and Brunelleschi, Baptistery Door Competition Entries, 1401

Some would say these two different relief panels represent the first works of the Renaissance. These two versions of *The Sacrifice of Isaac* were finalists in a contest held in 1401 to decide who would create the bronze doors of the Baptistery. The contest sparked citywide excitement, which evolved into the Renaissance spirit. Lorenzo Ghiberti won and later did the doors known as the Gates of Paradise. Filippo Brunelleschi lost—fortunately for us—freeing him to design the dome of the cathedral (or Duomo).

Both artists catch the crucial moment when Abraham, obeying God's orders, prepares to slaughter and burn his only son as a sacrifice. At the last moment—after Abraham has passed this test of faith—an angel of God appears to stop the bloodshed.

Let's look at the composition of the two panels: One is integrated and cohesive (yet dynamic), while the other is a balanced knickknack shelf of segments. Human drama: One has bodies and faces that speak. The boy's body is a fine classical nude in itself, so real and vulnerable. Abraham's face is intense and ready to follow God's will. Perspective: An angel zooms in from out of nowhere to save the boy in the nick of time.

Is one panel clearly better than the other? You be the judge. Pictured here are the two finalists for the Baptistery door competition—Ghiberti's and Brunelleschi's. Which do you like best?

It was obviously a tough call, but Ghiberti's was chosen, perhaps because his goldsmith training made him better suited for the technical work. (Ghiberti used the lost wax technique to cast his bronze panels. This was far cheaper than Brunelleschi's panels, which were molded with solid bronze. Economics may have entered into the decision-making process.)

Whatever the reason, Ghiberti got the gig, and that started a historic chain of events: Ghiberti went on to make the famous Baptistery doors, the ones so popular with tourists. Meanwhile, Brunelleschi was free to build his awe-inspiring dome. And Donatello graduated from Ghiberti's workshop to revolutionize sculpture. All three of these artists inspired Michelangelo, who built on their work and spread the Renaissance all across Europe. And it all started with these panels.

Ghiberti's panel, on the left, won.

THE REST OF THE BARGELLO

Our tour is done. But there's much more to see from the dynamic Renaissance. At the other end of this room are painted, glazed porcelains by the masterful Della Robbia family. Elsewhere on this floor, you can browse jewelry, ivories, and traditional Tuscan majolica ceramics. There's even an upper floor, with medallions, armor, colorful terra-cotta, and models of famous statues.

From swords to statues, from *Brutus* to Brunelleschi, from *David* to *David* to *David* to *David*—the Bargello's collection of civilized artifacts makes it clear that Florence was the birthplace of the Renaissance.

MUSEUM OF SAN MARCO TOUR

Museo di San Marco

Two of Florence's brightest lights lived in the San Marco Monastery, a reminder that the Renaissance was not just a secular phenomenon. At the Museum of San Marco, you'll find these two different expressions of 15th-century Christianity—Fra Angelico's radiant paintings, fusing medieval faith with Renaissance realism, and Savonarola's moral reforms, fusing medieval faith with modern politics.

Orientation

Cost: €4, covered by Firenze Card.

Hours: Tue-Fri 8:15-13:50, Sat 8:15-16:50; also open 8:15-13:50 on first, third, and fifth Mon and 8:15-16:50 on second and fourth Sun of each month. You can reserve an entrance time, but it's unnecessary.

Information: Tel. 055-238-8608.

Getting There: It's on Piazza San Marco, a block north of the Accademia, and several long blocks northeast of the Duomo (head up Via Ricasoli or Via Cavour). Piazza San Marco is a hub for many buses.

Visitor Information: Consider picking up the compact, worthwhile, official guide (€10) at the bookstore.

Tours: ∩ Download my free Museum of San Marco audio tour.

Length of This Tour: Allow one hour.

Baggage Check: Large bags are not allowed in the museum, and no baggage check is available (but if you ask nicely, the ticket taker might watch your bag for you).

Cuisine Art: For recommended eateries nearby, see page 293.

Starring: Fra Angelico's paintings and Savonarola's living quarters.

OVERVIEW

In 1439, Cosimo the Elder (the founder of the Medici ruling dynasty and Lorenzo the Magnificent's grandpa) hired the architect Michelozzo to build the monastery, and invited Fra Angelico's Dominican community to move here from Fiesole. (Being a moneylender, Cosimo had a big challenge: to give enough to charity to overcome his sinful occupation in order to earn salvation.) Fra Angelico (c. 1400-1455) turned down an offer to be archbishop of Florence, instead becoming prior (head monk) of this monastery. He quickly began decorating the monastery walls with frescoes.

The ground floor of this museum features the world's best collection of Fra Angelico paintings. The upstairs contains the monks' cells (living quarters), decorated by Fra Angelico, and the cell of the most famous resident, Savonarola.

The Tour Begins

GROUND FLOOR

• *Buy your ticket, and just inside the entrance, stop and take in...*

The Cloister

Feel the spirituality of this place, a respite from the hubbub of modern Florence. A cloister like this is a private area in a monastery for mental and physical exercise. Monasteries often have two cloisters: one, more public and finely decorated, for pilgrims and visitors; the other, more private and deeper in the complex. This was the cloister where the public met the monastery.

Enjoy the calm, rhythmic symmetry of the stately columns and Renaissance arches, framing Gothic cross-vaulting. The proportion and harmony are very Renaissance. It just says 1439. This is an apt introduction to a monastery built during an optimistic time, when Renaissance humanism dovetailed with medieval spirituality.

• *Before hooking right into the first room, look down the corridor straight ahead. On the wall at the far end of the first corridor, in the corner of the cloister, is Fra Angelico's...*

❶ Crucifixion with St. Dominic (San Domenico in Adorazione del Crocifisso)

The fresco shows Dominic, the founder of the order, hugging the bloody cross like a groupie adoring a rock star. Monks who lived here—including Fra Angelico, Savonarola, and Fra Bartolomeo—renounced money, sex, ego, and pop music to follow a simple, regimented life, meditating on Christ's ultimate sacrifice.

SAN MARCO

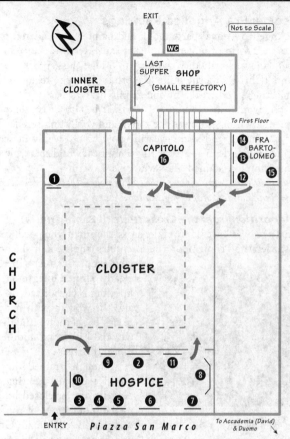

Museum of San Marco— Ground Floor

Not to Scale

EXIT

WC

INNER CLOISTER

LAST SUPPER   SHOP
(SMALL REFECTORY)

To First Floor

CAPITOLO ⓰

⓮ FRA BARTO-LOMEO
⓭
⓬   ⓯

❶

CLOISTER

CHURCH

❾   ❷   ⓫

⓾   HOSPICE   ❽

❸ ❹ ❺   ❻   ❼

ENTRY   *Piazza San Marco*   To Accademia (David) & Duomo

Fra Angelico
❶ Crucifixion with St. Dominic
❷ Deposition from the Cross
❸ Triptych of St. Peter Martyr
❹ Wedding & Funeral of the Virgin
❺ Last Judgment
❻ Door Panels of a Cupboard for Silver
❼ Lamentation
❽ Altarpiece of the Linen-Drapers
❾ Annalena Altarpiece
⓾ San Marco Altarpiece
⓫ Bosco ai Frati Altarpiece

Fra Bartolomeo
⓬ Ecce Homo
⓭ St. Dominic
⓮ St. Thomas Aquinas
⓯ Portrait of Savonarola

More Fra Angelico
⓰ Crucifixion with Saints

SAN MARCO

• *Immediately to the right of the entry, a door leads into the Hospice* (Ospizio).

Hospice: Fra Angelico Paintings

Fra Angelico—equal parts monk and painter—considered painting to be a form of prayer. He fused early-Renaissance technique with medieval spirituality, working to bridge the gap between the infinite (Christ) and the finite (a mortal's ability to relate to God) by injecting an ethereal atmosphere into his frescoes.

His works can be admired for their beauty or contemplated as spiritual visions. Browse the room, and you'll find serene-faced Marys, Christs, and saints wearing gold halos, evenly lit scenes, and meticulous detail—all creating a mystical world apart, glowing from within like stained-glass windows.

• *Start with the large three-peaked altarpiece—showing the* Deposition—*in the middle of the long, windowless wall.*

❷ Deposition from the Cross (Pala di Santa Trinità)

Christ's body is lowered from the cross, mourned by haloed women (on the left) and contemporary Florentines (right, likely the nobles

who paid for this). There's a clearly defined foreground (the kneeling, curly-headed man and the woman with her back to us), background (the distant city and hills), and middle distance (the trees).

Though trained in medieval religious painting, Fra Angelico never closed his eyes to the innovations of the budding Renaissance, using both styles all his life. There are Gothic elements, such as the altarpiece frame, inherited from his former teacher (who painted the pinnacles on top). The holy wear halos, and the stretched-out "body of Christ" is symbolically "displayed" like the communion bread.

But it's truly a Renaissance work. The man in green, lowering Christ, bends forward at a strongly foreshortened (difficult to draw) angle. Christ's toes, kissed by Mary Magdalene, cross the triptych wall, ignoring the frame's traditional three-arch divisions. Fra Angelico was boldly "coloring outside the lines" to create a single, realistic scene.

And the holy scene has been removed from its golden heaven and placed in the first great Renaissance landscape—on a lawn, among flowers, trees, cloud masses, real people, and the hillsides of Fiesole overlooking Florence (far right). Fra Angelico, the ascetic monk, refused to renounce one pleasure—his joy in the natural beauty of God's creation.

• *Turn to your left and head to the corner behind you to find...*

❸ Triptych of St. Peter Martyr
(Trittico di San Pietro Martire)

In this early, more "medieval" work, Fra Angelico sets (big) Mary and Child in a gold background flanked by (small) saints standing obediently in their niches.

When he joined the Dominican community in Fiesole, the artist took the name Giovanni (as he was known in his lifetime), and he wore the same attire as these famous Dominicans (including St. Dominic, far left, and St. Thomas Aquinas, far right)—white robe, black cape, and tonsured haircut.

Peter Martyr (on the right, next to Mary, with bloody head) exemplified the unbending Dominican spirit. Attacked by heretics (see the scene above Peter), he was hacked in the head with a dagger but died still preaching, writing with his own blood: *"Credo in Deum"* ("I believe in God").

• *Move left to look at the two small panels sharing one long frame.*

❹ Wedding and Funeral of the Virgin
(Sposalizio, Funerali della Vergine)

Fra Angelico's teenage training was as a miniaturist, so even these small predella panels (descriptive lower panels of a larger altarpiece) are surprisingly realistic. The folds in the clothes, the gold-brocade hemlines, and the precisely outlined people are as though etched in glass. Notice the Renaissance perspective tricks he was exploring, setting the wedding in front of receding buildings and the funeral (on the right) among candles that get shorter at the back of the scene.

• *Next up is...*

❺ Last Judgment (Giudizio Universale)

Despite the Renaissance, Florence in the 1420s was still a city in the Christian universe described by Dante. Hell (to the right) is a hierarchical barbecue where sinners are burned, boiled, and tortured by a minotaur-like Satan, who rules the bottom of the pit.

The blessed in heaven (left) play ring-around-the-rosy with angels. In the center, a row of open tombs creates a 3-D highway to Hell, stretching ominously to that final Judgment Day. Notice the crowd of big shots—bishops, royals, monks of other orders—being herded to Hell.

• On the other side of the pillar are several panels. Look at the one on the left.

❻ Door Panels of a Cupboard for Silver (Pannelli dell'Armadio degli Argenti)

The first nine scenes in this life of Christ (the big panel on the left end) are by Fra Angelico himself (the rest by assistants). Like storyboards for a movie, these natural, realistic, and straightforward panels "show" through action, they don't just "tell" through symbols. (The Latin inscription beneath each panel is redundant.) The miraculous is presented as an everyday occurrence.

1. The Wheel of Ezekiel prophesies Christ's coming.
2. In the Annunciation, the angel gestures to tell Mary that she'll give birth.
3. Newborn Jesus glows, amazing his parents, while timid shepherds sneak a peek.
4. Precocious Jesus splays himself and says, "Cut me."
5. One of the Magi kneels to kiss the babe's foot.
6. In the temple, the tiny baby is dwarfed by elongated priests and columns.
7. Mary and the baby ride, while Joseph carries the luggage all the way to Egypt.
8. Meanwhile, innocent babies are slaughtered in a jumble of gore, dramatic poses, and agonized faces.
9. The commotion contrasts with the serenity of the child Jesus preaching in the temple.

This work by 50-year-old Fra Angelico—master of many styles, famous in Italy—has the fresh, simple, and spontaneous storytelling of a children's book.

• Near the left end of this wall is...

❼ Lamentation (Compianto sul Cristo morto)

This painting of the executed Christ being mourned silently by loved ones was the last thing many condemned prisoners saw dur-

ing their final hours. It once hung in a church where the soon-to-be executed were incarcerated.

The melancholy mood is understated, suggested by a series of horizontal layers—Christ's body, the line of mourners, the city walls, landscape horizon, layered clouds, and the bar of the cross. It's as though Christ is being welcomed into peaceful rest, a comforting message from Fra Angelico to the condemned.

"Fra Angelico" (Angelic Brother) is a nickname that describes the artist's reputation for sweetness, humility, and compassion. It's said he couldn't paint a Crucifixion without crying. In 1984, he was beatified by Pope John Paul II and made patron of artists.

• *At the end of the room hangs...*

❽ *Altarpiece of the Linen-Drapers* (*Tabernacolo dei Linaioli*)

Check out the impressive size and marble frame (by Ghiberti, of baptistery-door fame), which attest to Fra Angelico's worldly success and collaboration with the Renaissance greats. The monumental Mary and Child, as well as the saints on the doors, are gold-backed and elegant, to please conservative patrons. In the three predella panels below, Fra Angelico gets to display his Renaissance chops, showing haloed saints mingling with well-dressed Florentines amid local cityscapes and realistic landscapes.

• *Find three similar-looking altarpieces (one may be out for restoration). They show how Fra Angelico, exploring Renaissance techniques, developed the theme of "Sacred Conversations"* (*Sacra Conversaziones*) *over his lifetime. These paintings show Mary and Child surrounded by saints "conversing" informally about holy matters, inviting the viewer to join in.*

❾ *Annalena Altarpiece* (*Pala d'Annalena*)

In the *Annalena Altarpiece* (c. 1435)—considered Florence's first true *Sacra Conversazione*—the saints flank Mary in a neat line, backed by medieval gold in the form of a curtain. Everyone is

either facing out or in profile—not the natural poses
of a true crowd. There's little
eye contact, and certainly no
"conversation."

Mary and Jesus direct
our eye to Mary's brooch, the
first in a series of circles ra-
diating out from the center:
brooch, halo, canopy arch,
and the imaginary circle that
enfolds the group of saints.
Set in a square frame, this painting has the circle-in-a-square composition that marks many *Sacra Conversaziones*.

• *Now find (if it has returned from long-term restoration) the next altarpiece.*

⑩ San Marco Altarpiece (Pala di San Marco)

Cosimo the Elder commissioned this painting (c. 1440) as the centerpiece of the new church next door. For the dedication Mass, Fra
Angelico theatrically "opens the curtain," revealing a stage set with
a distant backdrop of trees, kneeling saints in the foreground, and a
crowd gathered around Mary and Child at center stage on a raised,
canopied throne. The carpet makes a chessboard-like pattern to establish 3-D perspective. The altarpiece was like a window onto a
marvelous world where the holy mill about on earth as naturally
as mortals.

To show just how far we've come from Gothic, Fra Angelico
gives us a painting-in-a-painting—a crude, gold-backed Crucifixion.

• *Finally, find the...*

⑪ Bosco ai Frati Altarpiece (Pala di Bosco ai Frati)

This altarpiece (c. 1450) is Fra Angelico's last great work, and he
uses every stylistic arrow in his quiver: the detailed friezes of the

miniaturist; medieval halos and gold
backdrop; monumental, naturally
posed figures in the style of Masaccio (especially St. Francis, on the left,
with his relaxed *contrapposto*); 3-D
perspective established by the floor
tiles; and Renaissance love of natural
beauty (the trees and sky).

Fra Angelico's bright colors are
eye-catching. The gold backdrop sets
off the red-pink handmaidens, which
set off Jesus' pale skin. The deep blue

of Mary's dress, frosted with a precious gold hem, turns out at her feet to show a swath of the green inner lining, suggesting the 3-D body within.

Despite Renaissance realism, Fra Angelico creates an ideal world of his own—perfectly lit, with no moody shadows, dirt, frayed clothing, or imperfections. The faces are certainly realistic, but they express no human emotion. These mortals, through sacrifice and meditation, have risen above the petty passions celebrated by humanist painters to achieve a serenity that lights them from within.

• *Exit through the room, returning to the open-air courtyard. Head for the far right corner, and enter the set of rooms marked* Lavabo e Refettorio. *To your right is the former monks' dining hall—above the door is the Risen Christ, reminding monks that every meal is a communion with God, a reenactment of the Last Supper. Now enter the small room on the left, with paintings by Fra Bartolomeo.*

Room of Fra Bartolomeo Paintings

Fra Bartolomeo (1472-1517) lived and worked in this monastery a generation after the "Angelic" brother.

• *Locate the first small painting on the left.*

⑫ Ecce Homo

This shows the kind of Christ that young, idealistic Dominican monks (like Fra Bartolomeo) adored in their meditations—curly-haired, creamy-faced, dreamy-eyed, bearing the torments of the secular world with humble serenity.

• *The fourth panel to the right of Jesus is...*

⑬ St. Dominic (San Domenico)

St. Dominic holds a finger to his lips—"Shh! We have strict rules in my order." Dominic (c. 1170-1221), a friend of St. Francis of Assisi, formed his rules after seeing the austere *perfetti* (perfect ones) of the heretical Cathar sect of southern France. He figured they could only be converted by someone just as extreme, following Christ's simple, possession-free lifestyle. Nearing 50, Dominic made a 3,400-mile preaching tour—on foot, carrying his luggage—from Rome to Spain to Paris and back. Dominic is often portrayed with the star of revelation over his head.

• *Two more panels to the right is...*

⑭ St. Thomas Aquinas (San Tommaso d'Aquino)

St. Thomas Aquinas (c. 1225-1274, wearing a hood)—the intellectual giant of the U. of Paris—used logic and Aristotelian models to defend and explain Christianity (building the hierarchical belief system known as Scholasticism). He's often shown with a heavy build and the sun of knowledge burning in his chest.

• *As you face the door, to the left you'll see...*

⓯ Portrait of Savonarola
(Ritratto di Fra' Girolamo Savonarola)

This is the famous portrait—in profile, hooded, with big nose and clear eyes, gazing intently into the darkness—of the man reviled as

the evil opponent of Renaissance modernity. Would it surprise you to learn that it was Savonarola who inspired Fra Bartolomeo's art? Bartolomeo was so moved by Savonarola's sermons that he burned his early nude paintings (and back issues of *Penthouse*), became a monk, gave up painting for a few years...then resurfaced to paint the simple, sweet frescoes we see here.

• *Leaving the world of Fra Bartolomeo, return to the cloister, turn right, and continue to the next room.*

Capitolo

This room contains Fra Angelico's ⓰ *Crucifixion with Saints (Crocifissione dell'Angelico)*. Set against a bleak background, this is

one of more than 20 versions of Christ's torture/execution in the monastery. It was in this room that naughty monks were examined and judged.

Among the group of hermits, martyrs, and religious extremists who surround the cross, locate Dominic (kneeling

at the foot of the cross, in Dominican white robe, black cape, and tonsured hair, with star on head), Peter Martyr (kneeling in right corner, with bloody head), and Thomas Aquinas (standing behind Peter, with jowls and sun on chest).

The bell in the room is the original church bell. One night in 1498, this bell rang out, trying to warn Savonarola that a Florentine mob was coming to arrest him. (The mob was so mad at the bell, they whipped it in public and then, for good measure, exiled it for 10 years.) Ah, but we're getting ahead of the story. For that, we need to head upstairs...

• *Return to the cloister, and go through the next door. At the end of the short hall peek into the private, deeper cloister where the public wasn't allowed. This is the domain of the Dominicans, who still run this place 600 years after Fra Angelico. Then head upstairs.*

FIRST FLOOR

• *At the top of the staircase, you'll come face-to-face with Fra Angelico's...*

❶ Annunciation (Annunciazione)

Sway back and forth and watch the angel's wings sparkle (from glitter mixed into the fresco) as he delivers "the good news" to the very humble and accepting Virgin—particularly effective by torchlight and with a 15th-century mindset. Mary is under an arcade that's remarkably similar to the one in the cloister. Fra Angelico brings this scene home to the monks quite literally.

Paintings such as this one made Fra Angelico so famous that the pope called on him to paint the Vatican. Yet this work, like

the other frescoes here, was meant only for the private eyes of humble monks. Monks gathered near this *Annunciation* for common prayers, contemplating Christ's life from beginning *(Annunciation)* to end *(Crucifixion with St. Dominic,* over your left shoulder). The caption reads: Remember to say your prayers.

• *From the* Annunciation, *take a few steps to the left, and look down the (east) corridor lined with...*

The Monks' Living Quarters

This floor is lined with the cells (bedrooms) of those who lived in the monastery: monks, novice monks (farther down), and lay people and support staff (to your right). We'll see Savonarola's quarters in the far corner, later on this tour. Each cell features a fresco by Fra Angelico or his assistants.

After a long day of prayer, meditation, reading, frugal meals, chopping wood, hauling water, translating Greek, attending Mass, and more prayer, a monk retired to one of these small, bare, lamplit rooms. His "late-night TV" was programmed by the prior—Fra Angelico—in the form of a fresco to meditate on before sleep. In monastic life, everything is a form of prayer. Pondering these scenes, monks learned the various aspects of worship: humility, adoration, flagellation, reflection, and so on.

Fra Angelico and his assistants decorated 43 cells in the early 1440s. Many feature a crucifix and St. Dominic, but each shows Dominic in a different physical posture (kneeling, head bowed,

Museum of San Marco—First Floor

Not to Scale

LIBRARY

STAIRS UP FROM GROUND FLOOR

⑮

①

② ③ ④ ⑤ ⑥ ⑦ ⑧ ⑨ ⑩ ⑪

FRA ANGELICO FRESCOES

⑰

⑯

FOR LAY PEOPLE

CLOISTER (BELOW)

CLERICS

SAVONAROLA'S CELLS & POSSESSIONS

NOVICES

⑭ ⑬ ⑫

① Annunciation
② Noli me Tangere
③ Lamentation
④ Annunciation
⑤ Crucifixion
⑥ Birth of Jesus
⑦ Transfiguration
⑧ The Mocking of Christ
⑨ The Empty Tomb
⑩ Mary Crowned
⑪ Presentation in the Temple
⑫ Savonarola's Banner
⑬ Savonarola's Cloak & Crucifix
⑭ Savonarola's Cells
⑮ Library
⑯ Kiss of Judas
⑰ Cosimo the Elder's Cells

SAN MARCO

head raised, hands folded), which the monks copied to attain a more spiritual state.

• *Some of Fra Angelico's best work is found in the 10 cells along the left-hand side. Begin with the first of these cells and check out the entire lineup.*

② *Noli me Tangere:* The resurrected Jesus, appearing as a hoe-carrying gardener, says, "Don't touch me" and gingerly sidesteps Mary Magdalene's grasp.

The flowers and trees represent the blossoming of new life, and

they're about the last we'll see. Most scenes have stark, bare backgrounds, to concentrate the monk's focus on just the essential subject.

❸ *Lamentation:* Christ and mourners are a reverse image of the Lamentation downstairs. Christ levitates, not really supported by the ladies' laps. The colors are muted grays, browns, and pinks. Dominic (star on head) stands contemplating, just as the monk should do, by mentally transporting himself to the scene.

❹ *Annunciation:* The painting's arches echo the room's real arch. (And they, in turn, harmoniously "frame" the "arch" of Mary and the angel bending toward each other to talk.) Peter Martyr (bloody head) looks on.

You can't call these cells a wrap until you've found at least six crosses, three Dominics, three Peters, and a Thomas Aquinas. Ready...go.

❺ *Crucifixion:* That's one cross. And another Dominic.

❻ *Birth of Jesus:* And there's your second Peter.

❼ *Transfiguration:* Forsaking Renaissance realism, Fra Angelico emphasizes the miraculous. In an aura of blinding light, Christ spreads his arms cross-like, dazzling the three witnesses at the bottom of the "mountain." He's joined by disembodied heads of prophets, all spinning in a circle echoed by the room's arch. These rooms, which housed senior monks, have some of the most complex and intellectually demanding symbolism.

❽ *The Mocking of Christ:* From Renaissance realism to Dalí Surrealism. Dominic, while reading the Passion, conjures an image of Christ—the true king, on a throne with a globe and scepter—now blindfolded, spit upon, slapped, and clubbed by...a painting of medieval symbols of torment. This must have been a puzzling riddle from the Master to a fellow monk.

❾ *The Empty Tomb:* The worried

women are reassured by an angel that "he is risen." Jesus, far away in the clouds, seems annoyed that they didn't listen to him.

🔟 *Mary Crowned:* ...triumphantly in heaven, while Dominic, Peter, Aquinas, Francis, and others prepare to celebrate with high-fives.

⓫ *Presentation in the Temple:* Baby Jesus is swaddled like a mummy. And there's your final Peter.

• *Continue around the bend—Savonarola's three rooms are at the far end of the corridor.*

Savonarola's Cells (Celle del Savonarola)

Girolamo Savonarola (1452-1498) occupied the cluster of rooms at the end of the hall. But before you climb the three steps to his cells, stop at the last two rooms along the hall (on the right). Here you'll find a number of his possessions, including ⓬ fragments of a crucifixion **banner** carried during processions (labeled *Crocifissione* or *Lo Stendardo del Savonarola*) and ⓭ his **cloak** and personal **crucifix**. Savonarola's life changed dramatically at 22, when he heard a sermon on repentance. He traded his scholar's robes for the black cloak of a simple Dominican monk. He quickly became known for his asceticism, devotion, and knowledge of the Bible. His followers rallied around this banner, painted with a gruesome Crucifixion scene in the Fra Angelico style. They paraded through the streets reminding all that Christ paid for their worldly Renaissance sins.

• *Now climb three steps and enter* ⓮ *Savonarola's Cells.*

First Room

The **portrait bust** shows the hooded monk, whose personal charisma and prophetic fervor led him from humble scholar to celebrity preacher to prior of San Marco to leader of Florence for four years to controversial martyr. The **relief** under the portrait bust shows Savonarola at his greatest moment. He stands before the Florence city council and pledges allegiance to Florence's constitution, assuming control of the city after the exile of the Medici (1494). Reviled as a fanatical, regressive tyrant and praised as a saint, reformer, and champion of democracy, Savonarola was a complex man in a position of great power during turbulent times.

Various **paintings** depict Savonarola in action, including one by Federico Andreotti, which shows the powerful monk reproaching two troublemakers in his study.

• *The next room is Savonarola's...*

Study (Studiolo)

Seated at this **desk,** in his ecclesiastical folding **chair,** Savonarola scoured his Bible for clues to solve Florence's civic strife.

In 1482 at age 30, the monk had come to San Marco as a lecturer. He was bright, humble...and boring. Then, after experi-

encing divine revelations, he spiced his sermons with prophecies of future events...which started coming true. His sermons on Ezekiel, Amos, Exodus, and the Apocalypse predicted doom for the Medici family. He made brazen references to the pope's embezzling and stable of mistresses, and preached hope for a glorious future after city and church were cleansed.

Packed houses heard him rail against the "prostitute church...the monster of abomination." Witnesses wrote that "the church echoed with weeping and wailing," and afterward "everyone wandered the city streets dazed and speechless." From this humble desk, he corresponded with the worldly pope, the humanist Pico della Mirandola, and fans, such as Lorenzo the Magnificent, who begrudgingly admired his courage.

Lorenzo died, the bankrupt Medici were exiled, and Florence was invaded by France...as Savonarola had prophesied. In the power vacuum, the masses saw Savonarola as a moderate voice who championed a return to Florence's traditional constitution. He was made head of a Christian commonwealth.

• *Finally, step into the...*

Room with Savonarola's Possessions (Le Reliquie del Savonarola)

Savonarola's personal moral authority was unquestioned, as his simple **wool clothes** and **rosary** attest.

At first, his rule was just. He cut taxes, reduced street crime, shifted power from rich Medici to citizens, and even boldly proposed banning Vespas from tourist zones.

However, Savonarola had an uncompromising and fanatical side, as his **hair-shirt girdle** suggests. His government passed strict morality laws against swearing, blasphemy, gambling, and ostentatious clothes, which were enforced by gangs of thuggish teenagers. At the height of the Christian Republic, during Lent of 1497, followers built a huge "bonfire of vanities" on Piazza della Signoria, where they burned wigs, carnival masks, dice, playing cards, musical instruments, and discredited books and paintings.

In 1498, several forces undermined Savonarola's Republic: scheming Medici, crop failure, rival cities, a pissed-off pope threatening excommunication for Savonarola and political isolation for Florence, and a public tiring of puritanism. Gangs of opponents (called *Arrabbiati*, "Rabid Dogs") battled Savonarola's supporters (the "Weepers"). Meanwhile, Savonarola was slowly easing out of public life, refusing to embroil the church in a lengthy trial, retiring to his routine of study, prayer, and personal austerity.

Egged on by city leaders and the pope, a bloodthirsty mob marched on San Marco to arrest Savonarola. *Arrabbiati* fought monks with clubs (imagine it in the **courtyard** out the window), while the church bells clanged and the monks shouted, *"Salvum fac populum tuum, Domine!"* ("Save thy people, Lord!"). The *Arrabbiati* stormed up the stairs to this floor, and Savonarola was handed over to the authorities. He was taken to the Palazzo Vecchio, tortured, tried, and sentenced.

On May 23, 1498 (see the **painting** *Supplizio del Savonarola in Piazza della Signoria*), before a huge crowd in front of the Palazzo Vecchio (where today a memorial plaque is embedded in the pavement of the Piazza della Signoria), Savonarola was publicly defrocked, then publicly forgiven by a papal emissary. Then he was hanged—not Old West-style, in which the neck snaps, but instead slowly strangled, dangling from a rope, while teenage boys hooted and threw rocks.

The crowd looked upon the lifeless body of this man who had once captivated their minds, as they lit a pyre under the scaffold—see the **stick** *(palo)* from the fire. The flames rose up, engulfing the body, when suddenly…his arm shot upward!—like a final blessing or curse—and the terrified crowd stampeded, killing several. Savonarola's ashes were thrown in the Arno.

THE REST OF THE MUSEUM

The corridor to the right of Fra Angelico's *Annunciation* is well worth a look.

⑮ Library: Also designed by Michelozzo, this room contains music and other manuscripts. Music hymnals needed to be large so the entire choir could read from one. Take a close look at the music pages, many made of vellum (sheep skin), gorgeously illuminated (painted), and with fancy leather bindings complete with buckles. Monks would chant, reading the rhythm (according to quarter notes, half notes, and so on), in a pitch relative to a C clef (rather than the G and F clefs that we are most familiar with). The C clef could slide depending on the range needed, marking middle C. A chest at the far end (well-described in English) shows tools and ingredients for making, painting, and binding these fine books.

⓰ *Kiss of Judas* Fresco: In a cell a few steps past the library is Fra Angelico's *Kiss of Judas*. The theme proved prophetic, since it was outside that cell that Savonarola was arrested.

⓱ Cosimo the Elder's Cells: These are at the end of the corridor (right side). As the builder of this monastery, he often retired here for spiritual renewal. Inside, the painting of the Magi includes a kneeling king kissing the baby's little holy toes—a portrait of Cosimo. As at the Medici-Riccardi Palace, the family favored this Biblical scene, since it was one of the few in which it was acceptable to portray themselves as kings to showcase their wealth and power. Even in religious endeavors they constantly reminded people of their stature (you see their familiar coat of arms, with six balls, located over windows and doors throughout this building). After Cosimo financed the building of the complex, the pope granted him absolution for all of his sins.

• *To exit, return to the stairway and descend. Take a right at the bottom into a bookshop decorated with a fine **Ghirlandaio Last Supper** fresco. It's no coincidence that the cherries on the table are reminiscent of the red balls of the Medici coat of arms.*

Are you as tired as John is? WCs are immediately past the bookshop. Pass through corridors filled with a hodgepodge of architectural fragments (gathered from the ruins of the Jewish Ghetto, which stood on Piazza della Repubblica until the late 19th century) and on to the exit. On the street, turn right, then right again, and you'll see the Campanile of the Duomo.

DUOMO MUSEUM TOUR

Museo dell'Opera del Duomo

The newly remodeled Duomo Museum offers one of Italy's great artistic experiences. Five centuries ago, Italian artists decorated Florence's Duomo, Baptistery, and Campanile with amazing art. Now these treasures are gathered inside, protected from the elements, in a marvelous museum.

Brunelleschi's dome, Ghiberti's bronze doors, and Donatello's statues. These creations define the 1400s (the Quattrocento) in Florence, when the city blossomed and classical arts were reborn. Copies of the doors and statues now decorate the exteriors of the cathedral, Baptistery, and Campanile, while the original sculptured masterpieces of the complex are now restored and thoughtfully displayed here. The museum also has two powerful statues by Florence's powerhouse sculptors—Donatello's *Mary Magdalene* and Michelangelo's *Pietà,* intended as his sculptural epitaph.

Orientation

Cost: €15 combo-ticket covers all Duomo sights, valid 48 hours, covered by Firenze Card.

Hours: Daily 9:00-20:00, closed first Tue of every month, last entry one hour before closing. This is one of the few museums in Florence that's open every Monday.

Information: Tel. 055-230-2885, www.museumflorence.com.

Getting There: The museum is across from the Duomo on the east side (the far end from the Baptistery), at Via del Proconsolo 9.

Tours: A free app for the Duomo Museum is available from iTunes and Google Play.

Length of This Tour: Allow 1.5 hours. With limited time, focus on Ghiberti's doors, Michelangelo's *Pietà,* Donatello's sculptures, and the pair of finely carved choir lofts *(cantorie).*

Services: All backpacks must be checked, regardless of size; purses and messenger bags are OK. Ticket machines in the lobby allow you to make Duomo dome-climb reservations—see page 35. Several WCs are available inside. The easiest is just after the museum entrance to the right.

Starring: Brunelleschi, Ghiberti, Donatello, and Michelangelo.

The Tour Begins

GROUND FLOOR

The museum presents the 2,000-year history of Florence's Duomo, Baptistery, and Campanile.

• *Scan your ticket, and pass the hall lined with names of the many great artists and architects who helped build the Duomo over the centuries. Enter Room 4, with a large...*

❶ Model of the Duomo's Medieval Facade

The model shows the church facade circa 1500, the era of Michelangelo. Notice that only the lower third of the facade is faced with marble and statues. The rest was only bare brick. Church construction began in 1296, but after an initial burst of energy, petered out. The facade was meant to be a glorious showcase of great statues set into niches. Get close to the model and find a few: There's Mary-and-Babe over the central doorway. Above and to her left is a pope with a ridiculously tall hat. And below Mary are four seated evangelists.

• *Now let's see those actual statues, and more from the medieval facade. Continue into the large hall, Room 6, dubbed the...*

Hall of Paradise (Sala del Paradiso)

This room re-creates that lower third of the facade we saw on the model: One long wall showing the facade niches and arches, and the opposite wall exhibiting the facade and Baptistery doors. Both buildings were a showcase of the greatest art of Florence from roughly 1300 to 1600. In this room, the original statues, doors, and reliefs face each other as they once did on the buildings they were designed for.

Start with the Duomo. The Duomo began life in early medieval times as a humble church overshadowed by the more prestigious Baptistery. By the 1200s, the church wasn't big enough to

DUOMO MUSEUM

Duomo Museum—Ground Floor

STAIRS UP TO FIRST FLOOR

Room 9

Not to Scale

Rm 12

Room 8

Room 7

Room 10

DUOMO FACADE

HALL OF PARADISE

BAPTISTRY FACADE

Room 4

STAIRS & ELEV.

SHOP

STAIRS

Room 6

Room 5

TEMPORARY EXHIBITIONS

TOUR BEGINS

WC

TICKETS

COURT-YARD

ELEV.

COAT ROOM

CAFE

ENTRANCE

To Duomo Entrance

Piazza del Duomo

To Opera del Duomo Studio

❶ Model of the Duomo's Medieval Facade

❷ ARNOLFO – Madonna with the Glass Eyes

❸ DONATELLO – St. John the Evangelist

❹ ARNOLFO – Pope Boniface VIII

❺ GHIBERTI – "Gates of Paradise" Doors

❻ GHIBERTI – North Doors

❼ PISANO – South Doors

❽ DONATELLO – Mary Magdalene

❾ Relics

❿ MICHELANGELO – Pietà

contain the exuberant spirit of a city growing rich from the wool trade and banking. So in 1296, Florence set out to rebuild it, intending to make the finest church of the age.

Arnolfo di Cambio, the architect, began the construction and designed the facade. Arnolfo envisioned a three-story facade of pointed arches and white, pink, and green marble, studded with statues and gleaming with gold mosaics. In fact, it might have looked much like the Neo-Gothic version on the church today. For the next two centuries, great sculptors contributed to the facade. But, as we saw, it was never completed. Only the bottom third was faced with marble—the upper part remained bare brick.

Still, what they did complete is very impressive. It was a showcase for the city's top sculptors. In its niches were late Gothic and early Renaissance statues—some of the best of the age.

• *Let's get a closer look at some of the statues. Find the seated Madonna and Child, flanked by saints. The original is on ground level (so tourists can see it better), while a copy stands above, showing her original location on the facade.*

❷ Arnolfo di Cambio, *Madonna with the Glass Eyes (Madonna dagli Occhi di Vetro)*, c. 1300

This is the central figure over the cathedral's doorway. The building was dedicated to Mary—starry-eyed over the birth of Baby Jesus. She sits, crowned like a chess-set queen, framed with a dazzling mosaic halo. To the right is St. Zenobius, Florence's first bishop during Roman times. He raises his hand to consecrate the formerly pagan ground as Christian.

• *Flanking the Madonna in the four big niches are the Four Evangelists (left to right: Matthew, Luke, John, and Mark). Focus on...*

❸ Donatello, *St. John the Evangelist,* c. 1409

John the Evangelist and his mates would have made a solemn impression on worshippers as they filed through the church door for Mass.

John sits gazing at a distant horizon, his tall head rising high above his massive body. This visionary foresees a new age...and the coming Renaissance. With its expressive face, this work is a hundred years ahead of its time.

At 22 years old, Donatello (c. 1386-1466) sculpted this work just before becoming a celebrity for his inspiring statue of St. George (original in the Bargello, copy on the exterior of the Orsanmichele Church). Donatello ("Little Donato"), like most early Renaissance artists, was a blue-collar worker, raised as a workshop apprentice among knuckle-dragging musclemen. He proudly combined physical skill with technical know-how to create beauty (Art + Science = Renaissance Beauty). His statues are thinkers with big hands who can put theory into practice.

• *At the far left of the room is the original statue of the pope with the tall hat. The copy sits high up on the facade, just left of center.*

❹ Arnolfo di Cambio, *Pope Boniface VIII*

Despised by Dante for his meddling in politics, Pope Boniface paid 3,000 florins to get his image in a box seat high on the facade. While he looks stretched out when viewed at ground level, Arnolfo portrayed him out of proportion intentionally. His XXL shirt size looks right when he's up above and viewed from street level.

• *Facing the facade of the church, as they did in the Middle Ages, are the famous doors of the Baptistery. Here's your chance to study the original panels of those famous bronze doors. Three sets are displayed: the oldest doors on the left by Pisano (South Doors, c. 1330); the original competition doors on the right by Ghiberti (North Doors, 1403-1424); and the famous Gates of Paradise by Ghiberti in the center (East Doors, 1425-1452). Start with the most famous of the three...*

❺ Ghiberti's Gates of Paradise

The Renaissance began in 1401 with a citywide competition to build new doors for the Baptistery (see page 81 for more on this contest). Lorenzo Ghiberti (c. 1378-1455) won the job and built the doors for the north side of the building. Everyone loved them, so he was then hired to make another set of doors for the east entrance, facing the Duomo. These bronze "Gates of Paradise" revolutionized the way Renaissance people saw the world around them.

Ghiberti, the illegitimate son of a goldsmith, labored all his working life (more than 50 years) on the two sets of Baptistery

doors, including 27 years (1425-1452) working on the panels for the Gates of Paradise. The doors' execution was a major manufacturing job, requiring a large workshop of artists and artisans for each stage of the process: making the door frames that hold the panels; designing and forming models of the panels in wax (to cast them in bronze); gilding the panels (by painting them with powdered gold dissolved in mercury, then heating the panels until the mercury burned off, leaving the gold); polishing and mounting the panels; installing the doors...and signing paychecks for everyone along the way. Ghiberti was as much businessman as artist.

Each panel is bronze with a layer of gold on top. They tell several stories in one frame using perspective and realism as never before. Ghiberti poured his energy and creativity into these panels. That's him in the center of the door frame, atop the second row

Ghiberti's "Gates of Paradise"

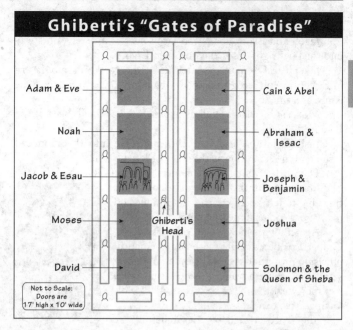

Adam & Eve — Cain & Abel

Noah — Abraham & Issac

Jacob & Esau — Joseph & Benjamin

Moses — Ghiberti's Head — Joshua

David — Solomon & the Queen of Sheba

Not to Scale: Doors are 17' high x 10' wide

of panels—the head on the left with the shiny male-pattern baldness. His son (and assistant) is to his right.

These original 10 panels were moved from the Baptistery to the museum to better preserve them. (Copies now adorn the Baptistery itself.) But even indoors, corrosive oxides gathered between the bronze panels and their gilding. Now they are under glass to protect against natural light and preserved in nitrogen to guard them from oxygen and humidity.

Moving from left to right and top to bottom, here are the Old Testament stories depicted in each panel:

Adam and Eve: God creates Adam, Eve, the snake, the apple, and original sin, then expels the humans.

Cain and Abel: Cain and Abel tend sheep, till the soil, and make a sacrifice, then Cain kills Abel and talks to God.

Noah: Noah and sons emerge from the ark (shown as a pyramid) after the flood, then Noah makes a sacrifice and gets drunk.

Abraham and Isaac: An angel prevents the sacrifice of Isaac.

Jacob and Esau: Isaac's son Jacob buys and deceives his way into the birthright of his elder brother, Esau.

Joseph and Benjamin: After his brothers sell him into slavery in Egypt, Joseph recognizes them when they visit and frames Benjamin as a thief.

Moses: Onlookers exult as Moses receives the Tablets of the Law from God.

Joshua: Joshua leads the chosen people into the Promised Land and in celebration as the walls of Jericho fall.

David: The young hero conquers the giant Goliath.

Solomon and the Queen of Sheba: After traveling to Jerusalem with a great retinue and many gifts, a queen meets a king.

Armed with new rules of perspective, Ghiberti rendered reality with a mathematical precision revolutionary for the time. To understand how these advances made visual space feel more real than ever before, study the following three panels:

The space created by the arches in the **Jacob and Esau panel** is as interesting as the scenes themselves.

At the center is the so-called vanishing point on the distant horizon, where all the arches and floor tiles converge. Those closest to us, at the bottom of the panel, are big and clearly defined. Distant figures are smaller, fuzzier, and higher up. Ghiberti has placed us as part of this casual crowd of holy people—some with their backs to us—milling around an arcade.

In the **Joseph and Benjamin panel,** notice how, with just the depth of a thumbnail, Ghiberti creates a temple in the round that's inhabited by workers. This round temple wowed the Florentines. Suddenly the world acquired a whole new dimension—depth.

The receding arches stretch into infinity in the **Solomon and the Queen of Sheba panel,** giving the airy feeling that we can see forever. All the arches and steps converge at the center of the panel, where the two monarchs meet, uniting their respective peoples. Ghiberti's subject was likely influenced by the warm ecumenical breeze blowing through Florence in 1439, as religious leaders convened here in an attempt to reunite the eastern (centered on Constantinople) and western (Rome) realms of Christendom.

Other Baptistery Doors

Displayed on either side of the Gates of Paradise you'll find the Baptistery's other doors.

❻ North Doors: Ghiberti made these doors after winning the 1401 competition, showing scenes from the life of Christ. Though they dazzled people at the time with their 3-D realism, they're most noteworthy today to illustrate how much further Ghiberti took the concept with the Gates of Paradise 25 years later.

❼ South Doors: These doors preceded Ghiberti and the Renaissance by 70 years. They tell stories from the life of St. John the Baptist, patron saint of Florence. Created by Andrea Pisano in the 1330s, they're not as renowned as Ghiberti's Renaissance doors—and with good reason: The static, expressionless Gothic figures make clear how revolutionary Ghiberti's enhancements in perspective and depth really were.

• *Before leaving Room 6, check out the* **Roman sarcophagi.** *They remind us that Florence's religious history stretches back to ancient times. The Baptistery (11th century) was likely built on the site of a pagan Roman temple. Exit the Hall of Paradise and pass through Room 7 and into Room 8 to find an evocative wooden statue of an emaciated woman.*

❽ Donatello, *Mary Magdalene (Santa Maria Maddalena),* c. 1455

Carved from white poplar and originally painted with realistic colors, this statue is a Renaissance work of intense devotion. Mary Magdalene—the prostitute rescued from the streets by Jesus—folds her hands in humble prayer. Her once-beautiful face and body have been scarred by fasting, repentance, and the fires of her own remorse. The matted hair sticks to her face; veins and tendons line the emaciated arms and neck. The rippling hair suggests emotional turmoil within. But in her hollow, tired eyes, you see a deep need for repentance, not idealized, praying to be forgiven. The rendering of her feet, arms, chest, and face make clear that Donatello understood the body and had a passion to show it realistically.

• *Duck into Room 9 to see a collection of...*

❾ Relics

Impressive, shiny vessels contain the mortal remains of saints, which helped connect the devout to the long-dead. Among the reliquaries, you'll find a slender Gothic pillar in the shape of a steeple. It holds John the Baptist's finger. This severed index finger of the beheaded prophet is the most revered relic of all the holy body parts in this museum. Also notice the large gem-studded gold cross that holds a purported fragment of the True Cross. Study the exquisite containers, which illustrate the importance of holy relics in medieval times.

• *Backtrack into Room 8, pass Mary, and continue to Room 10 and meet the maestro...*

❿ Michelangelo, *Pietà*, 1547-1555

Three mourners tend the broken body of the crucified Christ. We see Mary, his mother (the shadowy figure on our right); Mary Magdalene (on the left, polished up by a pupil); and Nicodemus, the converted Pharisee, whose face is that of Michelangelo himself. The polished body of Christ stands out from the unfinished background. Michelangelo (as Nicodemus), who spent a lifetime bringing statues to life by "freeing" them from the stone, looks down at what could be his final creation, the once-perfect body of Renaissance Man that is now twisted, disfigured, and dead.

A pietà—by definition—shows Mary mourning her dead son, taken off the cross. The theological point: Jesus died to save us. The artist's goal: to show him dead. Michelangelo made the dead weight of Jesus' body profound—you feel the downward pull. In fact, he sculpted Jesus in a Z-shape, taller than he probably was to accentuate the weight of his dead body. Notice also the intimacy of mother and son—Mary was with her son at his birth and at his death...struggling to support him.

The aging Michelangelo (1475-1564) designed his own tomb, with this as the centerpiece. He was depressed by old age, and the grim reality that by sculpting this statue, he was writing his own obituary. As it was done on his own dime, it's fair to consider this an introspective and very personal work.

• *Before leaving, look at the doorway to the left of the* Pietà *and find the tiny plaque indicating the level of the water during the terrible flooding of the Arno on November 4, 1966. The flood damaged many of these works, then in their original setting inside the Duomo. After being restored, they were moved here to be kept in a more secure environment.*

Duomo Museum—First Floor

STAIRS FROM GROUND FLOOR

Not to Scale

Room 25

Rm 24

STAIRS & ELEVATOR TO TERRAZZA & 2ND FLOOR

HALL OF PARADISE (BELOW)

VIEW HALL OF PARADISE

Room 16

Room 14

Room 15

Room 22

Room 26

Room 23

STAIRS

WC

STAIRS & ELEVATOR

TOUR ENDS

⓫ PISANO (& Others) – Campanile Panels

⓬ DONATELLO – Jeremiah & Habakkuk

⓭ Tools & Scaffolding

⓮ BRUNELLESCHI – Models of the Cupola & Lantern

⓯ Brunelleschi's Death Mask

⓰ DELLA ROBBIA – Cantoria

⓱ DONATELLO – Cantoria

⓲ Evolution of the Facade

DUOMO MUSEUM

Now, exit through the doorway on the right to the staircase. Go up the steps and, at the landing, turn right into the...

FIRST FLOOR
Gallery of Campanile Decorations
(Galleria del Campanile)

The Duomo's bell tower, designed by Giotto and augmented by Arnolfo di Cambio, also served as a colorful sculpture gallery. The museum has the original 16 statues (by several sculptors) from the bell tower's third story, where copies stand today. There are also small relief panels that once ringed the Campanile.

• *Start with the panels immediately on the left and work your way down the row. We'll focus on the statues later.*

⓫ Andrea Pisano (and Others), Campanile Panels, c. 1334-1359

These 28 hexagonal and 28 diamond-shaped, blue-glazed panels decorated the Campanile, seven per side. The original design scheme may have been Giotto's, but his successor, Andrea Pisano, and assistants executed the work.

The panels celebrate technology, showing workers, inventors, and thinkers. Allegorically, they depict humanity's long march to "civilization"—a blend of art and science, brain and brawn. But realistically, they're snapshots of the industrious generation that helped Florence bounce back ferociously from the plague, or Black Death, of 1348.

Start with the **hexagonal panels.** Reading left to right, you'll first see scenes from the Bible: God creates Adam, then Eve, who then get to work. Jabal learns to domesticate sheep while Jubal invents music on his horn. Tubalcain works as a blacksmith, and Noah invents wine. Next come scenes showing Florence's proto-scientific age: An astronomer charts the heavens and the (round, tilted-on-axis, pre-Columbian) Earth. Builders construct a brick wall. And a doctor holds a flask of urine to the light for analysis (yes, that's what it is). Skipping ahead a dozen panels—just after the last door—find the famed invention of sculpture, as an artist chisels a figure to life.

The upper **diamond-shaped panels,** made of marble on blue majolica (tin-glazed pottery tinged blue with cobalt sulfate), add religion (sacraments and virtues) to the march-of-civilization equation.

• *Now turn your attention to the other side of the room—the line of 16 **statues** that adorned the bell tower. Notice that the statues differ in quality, as they were made by different sculptors from different generations. The four statues closest to where you entered the room are some of the earliest, done by Nino and Andrea Pisano. They're less realistic, and more stylized and stiff than those farther down the wall. The sixth and seventh statues in line, in particular, stand out. These are the prophets Jeremiah and Habakkuk by the early Renaissance master Donatello.*

⑫ Donatello, *Jeremiah (Geremia,* **1427-1436) and** *Habakkuk (Abacuc,* **1434-1436)**

Donatello did several statues of the prophets, plus some others with collaborators. In the process, he developed the Renaissance style that Michelangelo would later perfect—powerful, expressive, and ultrarealistic, sculpted in an "unfinished" style by an artist known for experimentation and his prickly, brooding personality.

Start with *Jeremiah.* Watching Jerusalem burn in the distance, the prophet reflects on why the Israelites wouldn't listen when he warned them that the Babylonian kings would conquer the city. He purses his lips bitterly, and his downturned mouth is accentuated by his plunging neck muscle and sagging shoulders. The folds in the clothes are very deep, evoking the anger, sorrow, and disgust that *Jeremiah* feels but cannot share, as it is too late. Movement, realism, and human drama were Donatello's great contributions to sculpture.

Next, find the bald prophet *Habakkuk*. Donatello's signature piece shows us the wiry man beneath the heavy mantle of a prophet. From the deep furrows of his rumpled cloak emerges a bare arm with well-defined tendons and that powerful right hand. His long, muscled neck leads to a bald head (the Italians call the statue *Lo Zuccone*, meaning "pumpkin head"). This is realism.

The ugly face, with several days' growth of beard, crossed eyes, and tongue-tied mouth, looks crazed. This is no confident Charlton Heston prophet, but a man who's spent too much time alone, fasting in the wilderness, searching for his calling, and who now returns to babble his vision on a street corner.

Donatello, the eccentric prophet of a new style, identified with this statue, talking to it, swearing at it, yelling at it: "Speak!"

• *Wander the rest of these statues and imagine them looking down on the people of Florence from their bell-tower perches in 1400—at the dawn of a new age.*

Now pass into Room 15, with a large cutaway model of the dome suspended from the ceiling.

Gallery of the Dome (Galleria della Cupola)

Room 15 is dedicated to the dome that defined the Florentine Renaissance (and the man who built it). Designed by Filippo Brunelleschi (1377-1446), the dome was the final component of the cathedral complex's construction. Start by watching a fine short **video** about Brunelleschi's masterpiece (runs constantly, alternating between English and Italian).

• *Now find the following items.*

⑬ Tools and Scaffolding

The dome weighs an estimated 80 million pounds—as much as the entire population of Florence—so Brunelleschi had to design special tools and machines to lift and work all that stone. (The lantern alone—which caps the dome—is a marble building nearly as tall as the Baptistery.) You'll see sun-dried bricks, brick molds, rope, a tool belt, compasses, stone pincers, and various pulleys for lifting.

Pop. 100,000...But Still a Small Town

At the dawn of the Renaissance, Florence was bursting with creative geniuses, all of whom knew each other and worked together. For example, after Ghiberti won the bronze-door competition, Brunelleschi took teenage Donatello with him to Rome. Donatello returned to join Ghiberti's workshop. Ghiberti helped Brunelleschi with dome plans. Brunelleschi, Donatello, and Luca della Robbia collaborated on the Pazzi Chapel. And so on, and so on.

Although no scaffolding supported the dome itself, the stonemasons needed exterior scaffolding to stand on as they worked. Support timbers were stuck into postholes in the drum (some are visible on the church today).

The dome rose in rings. First, the workers stacked a few blocks of white marble to create part of the ribs, then connected the ribs with horizontal crosspieces before filling in the space with red brick, in a herringbone pattern. When the ring was complete and self-supporting, they'd move the scaffolding up and do another section.

⑭ Models of the Cupola and Lantern
(Modello Architettonico della Lanterna della Cupola)

These wooden models, done by Brunelleschi, show the dome he was constructing, including the top portion that would cap it. Brunelleschi's actual dome, a feat of engineering that was both functional and beautiful, put mathematics in stone. It rises 330 feet from the ground, with eight white, pointed-arch ribs, filled in with red brick and capped with a lantern, or cupola, to hold it all in place.

In designing the dome, Brunelleschi faced a number of challenges. The dome had to cover a gaping 140-foot hole in the roof of the church (a drag on rainy Sundays), a hole too wide to be spanned by the wooden scaffolding that traditionally supported a dome under construction. (An earlier architect suggested supporting the dome with a great mound of dirt inside the church...filled with coins, so peasants would later cart it away for free.) In addition, the eight-sided "drum" that the dome was to rest on was too weak to support its weight, and there were no side buildings on the church on which to attach Gothic-style buttresses.

The solution was a dome within a dome, leaving a hollow space between to make the structure lighter. And the dome had to be self-supporting, both while being built and when finished, so as not to require buttresses.

Brunelleschi used wooden models such as these to demonstrate his ideas to skeptical approval committees.

• *Now consider the remarkable man who built the dome, by pondering his "portrait," made on his deathbed.*

⑮ Brunelleschi's Death Mask *(Maschera Funebre)*

Brunelleschi was uniquely qualified to create the dome. Trained in sculpture, he gave it up in disgust after losing the gig for the Baptistery doors. In Rome, he visualized placing the Pantheon on top of Florence's Duomo, and dissected the Pantheon's mathematics and engineering.

In 1420 Brunelleschi was declared *capomaestro* of the dome project. He was a jack-of-all-trades and now master of all as well, overseeing every aspect of the dome, the lantern (the decorative tip-top), and the machinery to build it all.

The dome was completed in 16 short years, capping 150 years of construction on the church. Brunelleschi enjoyed the dedication ceremonies, but he died before the lantern was completed. His legacy is a dome that stands as a proud symbol of man's ingenuity, proving that art and science can unite to make beauty.

• *With the dome nearing completion, the Florentines began to decorate the church interior. Let's see some exquisite pieces. Exit Room 15 into Room 22 and turn left into Room 23 to see the...*

Room of the *Cantorie* (Sala delle *Cantorie*)

This room displays two marble choir lofts *(cantorie)* that once sat above the sacristy doors inside the Duomo. Both are from the 1430s. The one on the right is by Luca della Robbia, the one on the left by Donatello.

⑯ Luca della Robbia, *Cantoria,* 1430–c. 1438

After almost 150 years of construction, the cathedral was nearly done, and the Opera del Duomo, the workshop in charge, began preparing the interior for the celebration. Brunelleschi hired a little-known sculptor, 30-year-old Luca della Robbia, to make this *cantoria,* a balcony choir box for singers in the cathedral. It sums

up the exuberance of the Quattrocento. The panels are elegant, composed, contained within their columns: a celebration of music, song, and dance performed by toddlers, children, and teenagers (originals are below).

The *cantoria* brings Psalm 150 ("Praise ye the Lord") to life like a YouTube video. Starting in the upper left, the banner reads

"*Laudate...*"—"Praise the Lord"— while children laugh and dance to the sound of trumpets (*"sono Tubae"*) and guitars, autoharps, and tambourines (*"Psaltero... Cythera... Timpano"*). In the next level down, kids dance ring-around-the-rosy, a scene in the round on an almost flat surface, showing front, back, and in-between poses. At bottom right, the Psalm ends: "Everybody praise the Lord!" Della Robbia's choir box was a triumph, a

celebration of Florence's youthful boom time. (The Della Robbia family is best known for their colorful glazed terra-cotta, some of which you'll likely see here in the Duomo Museum and around town.)

⑰ Donatello, *Cantoria*, 1433-c. 1440

If Della Robbia's balcony looks like afternoon recess, Donatello's looks like an all-night rave. Donatello's figures are sketchier, murky

and frenetic, as the dancing kids hurl themselves around the balcony. Imagine candles lighting this as the scenes seem to come to life.

Recently returned from a trip to Rome, Donatello carved in the style of classical friezes of dancing *putti*

(chubby, playful toddlers). This choir box stood in a dark area of the Duomo, so Donatello chose colorful mosaics and marbles to catch the eye, while purposely leaving the dancers unfinished and shadowy, tangled figures flitting inside. In the dim light, worshippers swore they saw them move.

• Now let's bring the Duomo up to the church we see today. Backtrack *through Room 22, and down the corridor of Room 26. You'll pass by various diagrams, paintings, and photos that chart the multicentury...*

⑱ Evolution of the Facade

In 1587, the Duomo's medieval facade by Arnolfo di Cambio was considered hopelessly outdated and torn down like so much old linoleum. But work on a replacement never got off the ground, and the front of the church sat bare for nearly 300 years while church fathers debated proposal after proposal by many famous architects—that is, the designs in this room. Most versions championed the Renaissance style to match Brunelleschi's dome, rather than Gothic to fit the church. None of them were acted on. Near the end of Room 26, you'll see how it all played out.

Finally, in the 1800s, as Italy was unifying and filled with a can-do spirit, there was a push to finish the facade. A competition was held for the best design, and one of the contestants was Emilio De Fabris—find his portrait near the end of Room 26. He proposed to build a Neo-Gothic facade that echoed the original work of Arnolfo. Critics charged that De Fabris' design was too retro and too ornate. But they had to admit it was the style beloved by no less than Ghiberti, Donatello, Brunelleschi, and the industrious citizens of Florence's Quattrocento, who saw it as Florence's finest art gallery. De Fabris was declared the winner. Everyone got on board with it, and the new-old facade was completed in a remarkably short time, and dedicated in 1887. After almost 600 years, the Duomo was finally done.

REST OF THE MUSEUM

Browse the two floors above this one—they're accessed by a staircase near Room 15 (the Brunelleschi room). The second floor has a number of wooden models of various proposals for the facade—all rejected.

Don't miss the Terrazza Brunelleschiana on the third floor—an **outdoor terrace** with an up-close, rooftop view of the Duomo. It's an ideal place to pause at the end of your visit (and use the adjacent WC) and reflect on the engineering marvel that inspired so many other architects and marked the pinnacle of Renaissance achievement.

ART STUDIO

After leaving the Duomo Museum, make one more stop for a fascinating behind-the-scenes peek at the Duomo's restoration workshop: Head to the left around the back of the Duomo to find Via dello Studio (near the south transept), then walk a block toward the river to #23a (freestanding yellow house on the right; see map

on page 45). Here you can look through the open doorway of the **Opera del Duomo art studio** and see workers sculpting new statues, restoring old ones, or making exact copies. It's run by the Opera del Duomo, the organization that does the continual work required to keep the cathedral's art in good repair (*opera* is Italian for "work"). They're carrying on an artistic tradition that dates back to the days of Brunelleschi. The "opera" continues.

PALAZZO VECCHIO TOUR

With its distinctive castle turret and rustic stonework, this fortified "Old Palace"—Florence's past and present Town Hall—is a
Florentine landmark. The highlight of the interior is the Grand
Hall: With a Michelangelo sculpture and epic paintings of great
moments in Florentine history, it was the impressive epicenter
of Medici power. The richly decorated rooms of the royal apartments—though hardly the most sumptuous royal quarters in Europe—show off some famous art, creative decorative flourishes,
and aristocratic curiosities. It's open very late in summer, making it
a fine after-dinner activity.

While there are several sightseeing options here, this tour focuses on the "museum" part of the palace.

Orientation

Cost: Courtyard-free, museum-€10, tower climb-€10, museum
plus tower-€14, excavations-€4, combo-ticket that includes all
three-€18, free for kids 17 and under.

All three sights are covered by the Firenze Card (for the
museum and excavations, get your ticket at the ground-floor
info desk before heading upstairs; for the tower, simply present your card at the base of the stairs). This is also a convenient
place to buy the Firenze Card or to make reservations for the
Brancacci Chapel.

Hours: Museum and excavations open Fri-Wed 9:00-23:00 (Oct-
March until 19:00), Thu 9:00-14:00 year-round; tower open
Fri-Wed 9:00-21:00 (Oct-March 10:00-17:00), Thu 9:00-
14:00 (Oct-March from 10:00), last entry one hour before
closing, closed in bad weather. The ticket office closes one hour
early.

Information: Tel. 055-276-8224, www.musefirenze.it.

Tours: A videoguide is available for €5 (€8/2 people). Tours in English are offered daily, last 1.25 hours, and cost €4. The tour schedule varies, and it's wise to reserve ahead (tel. 055-276-8224).

Other Sights at the Palazzo Vecchio: Ascending Florence's landmark civic **tower** requires climbing 418 steps from ground level—though if you're touring the museum first, you'll already be about halfway there. (And if you have a museum ticket, you can ride the elevator up that far—ask.) The entrance to the tower is at the very end of the museum tour, on the second floor. If you're skipping the museum and doing only the tower, use the staircase opposite the one that leads up to the museum (on the left as you enter the courtyard).

Underneath the Palazzo Vecchio are **Roman-era excavations**—the ruins of a 2,000-year-old theater from ancient Florentia. Other than heavily restored brickwork and an interesting 10-minute video about the city's evolution over 22 centuries, there's little to see. But, it's worthwhile for antiquities enthusiasts or Firenze Card holders with 20 minutes to spare, and serves as a reminder that underneath much of the city center lie the remains of its glorious origins.

Nighttime Terrace Visits: In summer, you can join an escort for an unnarrated walk along the "patrol path"—the balcony that runs just below the crenellated top of the building (€4, no need to buy a museum or tower ticket, every 30 minutes between 21:00 and 22:30, no tours Oct-March). Note that this tour doesn't go to the top of the tower.

Activities for Kids: The palace's family program offers an ever-changing range of activities, usually requiring reservations—call the tours number above, or ask at the ticket office info desk. See page 307 for details.

Length of This Tour: One hour.

Services: Show your ticket to access the WCs, located on the ground floor, to the right of the ticket office.

Starring: The spacious grand hall known as the Salone dei Cinquecento, lavish royal apartments, and statues by Michelangelo and Donatello.

The Tour Begins

• *Stand in Florence's main square, Piazza della Signoria, and take in the palace's grand facade.*

Exterior

Around the year 1300, the citizens of Florence broke ground on a new Town Hall, designed by Arnolfo di Cambio, who also did the Duomo. Arnolfo's design expanded on an earlier palace on the site, turning its small tower into today's 308-foot spire and increasing the building's architectural footprint, which is why the tower ended up slightly off-center.

In Renaissance times, Florence was a proud, self-governing republic, and this

building is where its governing council met. The entrance sported a statue that symbolized the city's independent spirit—Michelangelo's *David*. (The statue standing here today is a copy—the original *David* was moved to the Accademia for safekeeping in 1873.) The palace's imposing, castle-like exterior announced to all of Europe's kings, popes, princes, and tyrants that Florence was determined to remain an independent city governed by its citizens.

But then came Cosimo I, who changed everything. (See a statue of him riding a horse, left of the palace.) In the 1530s, Cosimo assumed power and turned Florence's republic into a tyrannical dukedom. He and his wife Eleonora moved into the Palazzo Vecchio and transformed it from a symbol of the people to a luxury palace of the aristocracy. Let's go in and see what kind of extreme makeover they did to the place.

• Enter the courtyard (free admission), walking past the fake *David*.

Courtyard

This courtyard has long been a showcase for great Florentine art—art that made a statement to the city's populace.

Anchoring the courtyard is a copy of *Putto with Dolphin*, an innovative work of Renaissance 3-D by Verrocchio, Leonardo da Vinci's teacher (you'll see the original later, in the museum). With a twisting spiral form, this statue was one of the first intended to be equally enjoyable from any angle—an improvement on medieval statues that only worked when seen from the front.

Verrocchio's cherub took the place of Donatello's bronze *David* (now in the Bargello, and described on page 132), an even more groundbreaking statue—the first male nude sculpted in a thousand years. Donatello's *David* also made a bold populist statement, with an inscription on the base that said, "Behold, a boy defeated a tyrant, so fight on, citizens!"

Stroll around. The faded maps feature Austrian towns, designed to make the Habsburg princess feel welcome and at home for her 1565 marriage into the Medici family. The squiggly wall painting (called "grotesque") was all the rage around 1500, inspired by ancient Roman art, which was being excavated at the time.

While the Palazzo Vecchio's exterior and courtyard reflect the tastes and ideas of the Florentine Republic, most of the interior decoration dates from a later era. When Florence came under the rule of Cosimo I de' Medici, he suspended the city council and ruled as a "Grand Duke." He transformed this building from a civic center of the people into his personal palatial residence.

• *Deeper inside the palace is an interesting and free history exhibit.*

The **Tracce di Firenze exhibit,** near the ticket office, is a peaceful room with an interesting collection of paintings showing historic views of Florence, and a fascinating set of maps (well-described in English). Compare the big painting of the city "Fiorenza" (from 1490) with the version at the opposite end of the room (from 1936) to see how much—or how little—the city has changed over the centuries.

• *To see the rest of the palace, buy a ticket and head upstairs, following signs to the* Museo. *(Firenze Card holders must get a paper ticket on the ground floor before ascending.) On the first floor, enter one of the highlights of the palace, the 13,000-square-foot...*

Grand Hall (Salone dei Cinquecento)

This vast room—170' by 75'—is also called the Salone dei Cinquecento (Hall of Five Hundred). Originally built under Savonarola in 1494 to house the Florentine Republic's 500 Grand Councilors, it was expanded under Cosimo I to accommodate 500 partygoers. The ceiling and huge wall paintings, all by Giorgio Vasari and his assistants, are a celebration of the power of Florence, specifically the power of the Medici. Consider this magnificent room in

Palazzo Vecchio—First Floor

50 Meters
50 Yards

Not to Scale

■ STATUE OF LEO X

GRAND HALL
SALONE DEI CINQUECENTO

PISA

SIENA

Courtyard

■ MICHELANGELO'S VICTORY

COSIMO THE ELDER ROOM

LORENZO THE MAGNIFICENT ROOM

Piazza della Signoria

Court-yard

STAIRS UP FROM ENTRY COURTYARD

SHADED AREA SHOWS ROOMS OPEN TO VISIT

STUDIO OF FRANCESCO I

STAIRS UP TO 2ND FLOOR

LEO X ROOM

APARTMENTS OF LEO X

PALAZZO VECCHIO

its proper context: In an age when there was no mass media to use as a mouthpiece, this was how a fabulously wealthy person waged a public-relations campaign (and kept the people down).

Cosimo I is the star here, looking down from the circular medallion in the center of the ceiling. He's dressed as an emperor, with his highness-ness affirmed by the crown of the Holy Roman Emperor and blessed by the staff and cross of the pope. He's encircled by a kaleidoscope of symbols representing Florentine craft and art guilds, along with

the shields of his domain—all asserting and celebrating his power.

In the square frame, find the letters "SPQF." In place of the Roman motto of SPQR (*Senatus Populusque Romanus*—the Senate and People of Rome), Cosimo used "SPQF," implying that Florence is the new Rome. From the stage at the far end of the room, Cosimo sat on his throne, overseeing his fawning subjects.

But now sitting in the front of the room is a statue of **Pope Leo X,** looking down from his own throne. The son of Lorenzo the Magnifi-

Mannerism

While Florence is famous as the birthplace of the Renaissance, the art style that followed that period, Mannerism, is also showcased here—especially in the Palazzo Vecchio. It's hard to get a concise and clear definition of Mannerism. Michelangelo painted with bold colors and exaggerated the musculature and movement of the body in contrast to the mellow, graceful, and stable balance of the High Renaissance (think Raphael). Michelangelo died in 1564 and in the decades after that, artists tended to paint in the "manner" of the great master. No one could improve on Michelangelo, but you could enhance his bold, colorful, contorted muscular style. Call it "Mannerism."

cent, Leo X was the first of three Medici popes. When he became pope in 1513, the family suddenly had religious authority and some seriously good connections, helping them eventually become bankers to the Vatican and Grand Dukes of Tuscany.

Giorgio Vasari's wall paintings show great Florentine victories: over Pisa in 1497 (on the left) and over Siena in 1555 (on the right). In the Pisa paintings, check out the painting closest to the front: In the upper-left corner you can see the Field of Miracles, with its church and Leaning Tower. In the Siena paintings, watch the Florentines storm Siena's gate by lantern light. Vasari's style features crowded canvases, contorted bodies in every imaginable pose, bright color, and a "flat" surface design. If you're into Mannerism, this is your Sistine Chapel.

While Vasari's battle scenes are impressive, they pale in comparison to what some scholars believe was first painted on these walls. Around 1500, this hall was the scene of a painting contest between two towering geniuses—young Michelangelo and aging Leonardo da Vinci. Unfortunately, Michelangelo never got around to starting his proposed *Battle of Cascina* (and his paper sketch of it is lost to history). But Leonardo may have painted the *Battle of Anghiari* here. Art historians have long suspected that this famous-but-unseen Leonardo masterpiece lies hidden beneath Vasari's *Battle of Marciano* (on the Siena wall, third painting from the left). Vasari himself may have hinted at it to later scholars by painting an enigmatic clue: a banner (40 feet up, hard to find without binoculars) that reads *Cerca trova*—"He who seeks, finds."

Underneath Siena, in the middle of the right wall, stands Michelangelo's *Victory* (*La Vittoria*, 1533-1534), showing a young man triumphing over an older man. It was designed to ornament the never-finished tomb of Pope Julius II in St. Peter's Basilica in Rome. *Victory* was the prototype of the hall's many spiral-shaped statues by other artists. Taking their cue from Michelangelo, later

artists twisted and contorted their sculpted figures into almost ridiculous acrobatics. Six of the statues are the *Labors of Hercules.* The Medici were quick to associate themselves with Hercules—who was not a god but a demigod, as close to divine as a mortal can get.

Before leaving for the ducal apartments, see if a small, richly ornamented room is open to the immediate right of where you entered. The Studio of Francesco I is an exquisite little room covered in fine and richly symbolic art. Pick up the flier in English for a full explanation.

• *From the Grand Hall, we enter the royal apartments that housed Cosimo I and his family and guests. Be aware that some rooms on our tour may be temporarily closed to visitors—the palace is a working city hall, after all.*

Exit the Grand Hall through the door diagonally to the right of where you entered, and find the first of the royal apartments, known as the...

Apartments of Leo X

In 1540, Cosimo I and his wife Eleonora of Toledo moved into the Palazzo Vecchio, turning the Town Hall into their private residence. They set about redecorating with frescoes and coffered ceilings in the Mannerist style. They wanted each room to have a theme. These rooms were dedicated to great members of the Medici family who preceded Cosimo I.

Loop clockwise through these apartments. The first room (immediately to the left as you enter this wing) honors Cosimo the Elder, who launched the Medici dynasty in the 1400s. You'll see Cosimo portrayed on the ceiling, including one scene where he greets Brunelleschi and Ghiberti. The lower walls are decorated in the bizarre grotesque style popular in the late 16th century following the discovery of similar paintings underground in the ancient ruins of Emperor Nero's palace in Rome. You'll see similar motifs throughout Italy, including on ceilings of the Uffizi Gallery and Rome's Vatican Museums. (Find all the details on the information charts in each room.)

The next room is dedicated to the greatest of the Medici, Lorenzo the Magnificent, shown in the central ceiling painting on a throne in his purple robe. In the commotion of adoration are exotic animals. The giraffe, a gift from Tunisia, survived only a couple of months in the Medici court. Here you feel the passion of this avid patron of the arts. Lorenzo died in 1492, when Florence was at

PALAZZO VECCHIO

Cosimo I de' Medici
(1519-1574)

This palace is all about Cosimo I de' Medici. His presence is everywhere. In the famous statue on the square outside the palace, he sits like a Roman emperor astride a horse. Inside, in the Grand Hall, he looms high above in a ceiling painting. And his aesthetic vision is on full display in the Royal Apartments, which were personally decorated with care by Cosimo and his high-maintenance wife Eleonora.

Cosimo's Medici forebears had been Florentine big shots, but Cosimo was the first to have a royal title, after the pope made him a Grand Duke in 1569. Don't confuse Grand Duke Cosimo I with his equally famous ancestor, Cosimo the Elder, who established the Medici dynasty a century earlier. To see how Cosimo I fits into the Medici family tree, see the chart on page 57.

Before Cosimo I took charge, the loggia in front of the palace (Loggia dei Lanzi) had been used as a gathering place, where Florentines discussed the issues of the day. Cosimo changed it into an art gallery, swapping out public discourse for statues that personified the power and strength of his family. Perseus, holding the head of Medusa, sent a clear message about how the Medici dealt with their enemies.

It was Cosimo I who moved the family out of the Medici-Riccardi Palace and into these digs—officially called Palazzo della Signoria. Cosimo left the exterior as-is, which is why it still looks like a medieval fortress. But he completely revamped the inside, updating it to match the outlook of the Renaissance. Later, when his wife Eleonora complained about needing a fancier place with a bigger yard, they moved across the river to the Pitti Palace, where she could stroll the sprawling Boboli Gardens. The Vasari Corridor was built over Ponte Vecchio to connect the two palaces. After they'd moved out, Palazzo della Signoria began to be known as the "old" palace—Palazzo "Vecchio."

its pinnacle (and a self-governing republic), when the New World was still a mystery, and the center of European power hadn't yet moved to Spain, France, and England. Enjoy the fine examples of the erotic, mystical, and fanciful art of his time. After Lorenzo the Magnificent died, the Medici were exiled from Florence for 20 years.

Continue into the final room to see what came next. The room honors Lorenzo's son, who was exiled but eventually became Pope Leo X. A wall painting shows Leo's triumphal return to Florence,

Giorgio Vasari
(1511-1574)

Giorgio Vasari—painter, architect, and writer—has been dismissed by history as a Renaissance hack, a man who was 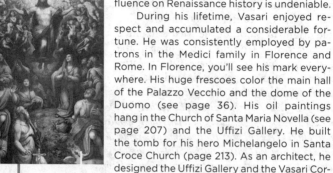 equally mediocre at many things. But his influence on Renaissance history is undeniable.

During his lifetime, Vasari enjoyed respect and accumulated a considerable fortune. He was consistently employed by patrons in the Medici family in Florence and Rome. In Florence, you'll see his mark everywhere. His huge frescoes color the main hall of the Palazzo Vecchio and the dome of the Duomo (see page 36). His oil paintings hang in the Church of Santa Maria Novella (see page 207) and the Uffizi Gallery. He built the tomb for his hero Michelangelo in Santa Croce Church (page 213). As an architect, he designed the Uffizi Gallery and the Vasari Corridor over Ponte Vecchio, which connects the Uffizi with the Pitti Palace.

Vasari is most famous, though, as the first Italian art historian. His book, *The Lives of the Artists,* was an early work that chronicled the Renaissance (with a bias that favored Florentine painters, sculptors, and architects). For that classic alone, we can say, *"Grazie tante!"*

where citizens celebrate outside the Palazzo Vecchio. Note Michelangelo's *David* guarding the entrance.

• *From here, go up the staircase to the second floor, then turn left, entering the...*

Apartments of the Elements
(Quartiere degli Elementi)

As Cosimo considered himself an enlightened Renaissance Man, he wanted his apartments decorated in the spirit of the classical world. Each of his personal living rooms has a name, usually derived from the ceiling and wall paintings.

The first room (with paintings by Vasari and assistants) depicts the four classical elements. On the far wall (as you enter) is "Water," showing the birth of a muscular (Mannerist) Venus from the foam of the waves. To the left is "Fire," with Vulcan at the forge hammering away while cupids pump the bellows and sharpen their arrows. On the third wall, "Earth" shows the abundant cornucopia of the world's produce. And on the ceiling, representing "Air," are scenes from the sky—the chariots of the sun and moon, and Cronos defeating Saturn to create the world.

Circle counterclockwise around this wing, starting with the balcony that offers a stunning view of Piazzale Michelangelo, the San Miniato Church on the hill in the distance, and Santa Croce Church, a bit closer to the left (closed in off-season). One room displays Verrocchio's original *Putto with Dolphin* (1476), from the courtyard downstairs. The statue originally stood in the Medici family's rural villa before Cosimo I brought it to the Palazzo Vecchio. It may have captured the newlywed couple's innocent joy and abandon as they moved into their new home together.

• *Return to the top of the stairs and cross over to the Apartments of Eleonora of Toledo. On the way, you'll pass along a* **balcony** *overlooking the Grand Hall. Gaze out over the opulence and imagine it filled by a lavish Medici wedding celebration with a 500-person guest list. Now enter the apartments of the duchess, starting in the Green Room.*

Private Apartments of Eleonora di Toledo

Eleonora of Toledo (1522-1562) married Cosimo I in 1539. Their marriage united the Medici clan with royal bloodlines all over Europe. The following year, the couple moved out of the Medici-Riccardi Palace (as it's now known) and settled in here. As Florence's "first lady," Eleonora used her natural grace and beauty to mollify Florentine democrats chafing under Cosimo's absolutist rule.

In the Green Room (Sala Verde), you'll find the Chapel of Eleonora, brightly painted by Agnolo Bronzino (1540-1565). After serving as their artistic wedding planner, Bronzino became Cosimo and Eleonora's court painter. The chapel's ceiling features St. Michael with a sword, battling a demon; St. John with his symbolic eagle; St. Francis receiving the stigmata; and St. Jerome with his companion the lion. In the center is the three-faced Trinity. Bronzino and Vasari were the two big stars of the Mannerist style, and this palace was their enormous blank canvas.

Before leaving the Green Room, find the other little room (likely Eleonora's private study) and a door, locked tight with a padlock, which leads onto the Vasari Corridor. From here, Eleonora and Cosimo could enter a private passageway that led through the Uffizi, across Ponte Vecchio, and into their other home across the river—the Pitti Palace.

Continue through the next half-dozen rooms, making your way to the large Hall of Lilies. Each of these rooms features virtuous women of history, thus putting Eleonora in their company. In the Room of the Sabines, the ceiling painting shows the Sa-

Palazzo Vecchio—Second Floor

bine women bravely stepping between their men and the enemy Romans to appeal for peace. In the next room, Esther kneels before the Persian king to plead for her Jewish people. Notice the fun panels with images of *putti* (chubby toddlers) playing in the letters: LEONORA on one side and, opposite, FLORENTIA. Next, Penelope spins at her wheel, faithfully awaiting the return of her lost husband Odysseus. The Penelope Room also has a *Madonna and Child* from the school of Botticelli.

• *Continue through these rooms (passing by **Dante's Death Mask**) to reach the large hall with the high, gilded ceiling.*

Hall of Lilies (Sala dei Gigli)

The coffered ceiling (from the 1460s) sports the fleur-de-lis—the three-petaled lily that's the symbol of Florence. Check out the great view of the Duomo out the window, and compare it with a painting on the wall (by Ghirlandaio) showing a glimpse of the Duomo, circa 1482. (Can't find the Duomo in the painting? Let the lion point the way.)

The room's highlight is Donatello's 11-piece bronze, *Judith and Holofernes*—

cast in 1457, when the artist was in his prime. It shows a Biblical scene easily interpreted by its Renaissance audience: the victory of the weak-but-virtuous Judith over Holofernes the tyrant. The statue was commissioned by Cosimo the Elder to use as a fountain in the garden of the Medici-Riccardi Palace (note the holes in the cushion's corners). Since then, it's served as Florentine propaganda, displayed to justify the strength of whoever was in power. The Medici saw themselves as the noble Judith slaying their (drunken, sleepy) enemies. But when the Medici were driven out by Savonarola in the 1490s, the Florentines took the statue from the Medici-Riccardi Palace and placed it at the Palazzo Vecchio's doorway (where the fake *David* now stands) as a symbol of their triumph over the corrupt family. A decade later, it was replaced by Michelangelo's *David*, the symbol of Florence victorious.

• *End your tour with a visit to two nearby rooms (starting at the far left from where you entered).*

Old Chancellery and Hall of Geographical Maps

The **Old Chancellery** (Sala della Cancelleria) was once the office of Niccolò Machiavelli (1469-1527). Ponder the bust and portrait of the man who faithfully served the Florentine Republic as a civil servant from 1498 to 1512, while the Medici were exiled as tyrants. When the Medici returned to power (under Pope Leo X), they tortured and exiled Machiavelli. He then wrote *The Prince*, a poli-sci treatise about how a ruler can ruthlessly gain and maintain power. Ironically, Machiavelli's cautionary advice soon came to be exploited by the man who would end the Florentine Republic for good—Grand Duke Cosimo I.

Finally, the **Hall of Geographical Maps** (Sala delle Carte Geografiche, the palace's former wardrobe) is full of maps made in a fit of post-1492 fascination with the wider world. Most date from about 1560 and show how serious cartography had become in the first 70 years after Columbus landed in the New World. They also say a great deal about what 16th-century Europeans did—and didn't— know about faraway lands. For  example, Cosimo's huge *mappa mundi* globe was obviously made before the discovery of Australia. On other maps, some Texans and Southern Californians can even find their hometowns (far right corner of the hall, upper level). Florentines excelled at creating and publishing maps—which is why, even though Columbus beat the Florentine Amerigo Vespucci to the New World, our continent isn't called "North Columbia."

• *To exit, return to the Hall of Lilies; the door on the left leads to a landing. From here, more than 200 stairs lead to the top of the* **tower** *(show your ticket or Firenze Card to ascend); the stairs leading down take you to the courtyard and exit.*

You're at the center of Florence—the city awaits.

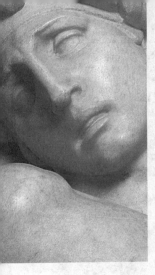

MEDICI CHAPELS TOUR

Cappelle Medicee

The Medici Chapels contain tombs of Florence's great ruling family, from Lorenzo the Magnificent to those less so. The highlight is a chapel designed by Michelangelo when he was at the height of his creative powers. This is Renaissance Man's greatest "installation," a room completely under one artist's control, featuring innovative architecture, tombs, and sculpture. His statues tell of a middle-aged man's brooding meditation on mortality, the fall of the Medici Golden Age, and the relentless passage of time—from *Dawn* to *Day* to *Dusk* to *Night*.

Orientation

Cost: €8, free and crowded on first Sun of the month, covered by Firenze Card.

Hours: Tue-Sat 8:15-17:00, Nov-March until 13:50, last entry 40 minutes before closing; also open second and fourth Mon and first, third, and fifth Sun of each month. Reservations are possible but unnecessary (€3 fee).

Information: Tel. 055-238-8602.

Crowd Alert: The bottleneck entrance (tickets and metal detector) can make for a slow entry. If you have a Firenze Card, let them know and they'll likely let you skip to the front of the security line.

Dress Code: No tank tops, short shorts, or short skirts.

Getting There: It's at the back (west end) of the Basilica of San Lorenzo—the one with the smaller dome on Florence's skyline (five-minute walk northwest of Duomo). See page 46 for more about the Basilica of San Lorenzo.

Tours: Audioguide rental is €6 (€10/2 people).

Length of This Tour: Allow 45 minutes. With limited time, make a beeline to Michelangelo's New Sacristy.

Starring: Michelangelo's statues *Day, Night, Dawn,* and *Dusk.*

OVERVIEW

The Medici Chapels consist of three burial places: the unimpressive Crypt; the large and gaudy Chapel of Princes; and—the highlight—Michelangelo's New Sacristy, a room completely designed by him to honor four Medici. Due to restoration work, scaffolding in the Chapel of Princes may obscure some (lesser) sights when you visit. For a quick overview of the Medici family tree, see page 57.

The Tour Begins

• *Enter the Chapel and buy tickets. Immediately after you show your ticket, you're in...*

The Crypt

This gloomy, low-ceilinged room with gravestones underfoot reminds us that these "chapels" are really tombs. You'll see a few Lorenzos buried in this room (after all, "Laurentius," or Lawrence, was the family's patron saint)...but none that is "Magnificent" (he's later). The collection of ornate silver and gold reliquaries is appropriately macabre and worth a quick look.

• *Head upstairs via the righthand staircase. First find your way into the large, domed, multicolored chapel, which is* not *by Michelangelo.*

Chapel of Princes
(La Cappella dei Principi), 1602-1743

The impressive **dome** overhead (seen from outside, it's the big, red-brick "mini-Duomo") tops an octagonal room that echoes the Baptistery and Duomo drum. It's lined with six tombs of Medici rulers and is decorated everywhere with the **Medici coat of arms**—a shield with six balls thought to represent the pills of doctors *(medici)*, reputedly the family's original occupation. Along with many different-colored marbles, geologists will recognize jasper, porphyry, quartz, alabaster, coral, mother-of-pearl, and lapis lazuli.

Sixteen shields ring the room at eye level, each representing one of the Tuscan cities ("Civitas") ruled by Florence's dukes. Find Florence, with its fleur-de-lis ("Florentiae"), and Pisa ("Pisarum"), both just left of the altar.

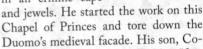

The bronze statues honor two of the "later" Medici, the cultured but oppressive dukes who

ruled Florence after the city's glorious Renaissance. In the first niche to the right (as you face the altar) stands Ferdinando I (ruled 1587-1609), dressed in an ermine cape and jewels. He started the work on this Chapel of Princes and tore down the Duomo's medieval facade. His son, Cosimo II (ruled 1609-1621, to the right), appointed Galileo "first professor" of science at Pisa U., inspiring him to label the moons of Jupiter "the Medici Stars."

The **altar** was finished in 1939 for a visit from Hitler and Mussolini. The altar itself is the only Christian symbolism in this spacious but stifling temple to power, wealth, and mediocre Medici.

(*Psst.* A room behind the altar to the right displays relics and the pastoral staff of Pope Leo X, who was Lorenzo the Magnificent's son and Michelangelo's classmate.)

• *Continue down the hall, passing statues of Roman armor with worms sprouting out, to Michelangelo's New Sacristy.*

Michelangelo's New Sacristy (Sacrestia Nuova)

The entire room—architecture, tombs, and statues—was designed by Michelangelo over a 14-year period (1520-1534) to house the bodies of four of the Medici family. Michelangelo, who spent his teen years in the Medici household and personally knew three of the four family members buried here, was emotionally attached to the project. This is the work of a middle-aged man (he started at age 45 and finished at 59)

New Sacristy

reflecting on his contemporaries dying around him, and on his own mortality.

• *There are tombs decorated with statues against three of the walls, and an altar on the fourth. Start with the tomb on the left wall (as you enter and face the altar).*

Tomb of Lorenzo II, Duke of Urbino

Lorenzo II—the grandson of Lorenzo the Magnificent—is shown as a Roman general, seated, elbow resting on a Medici-bank money box, and bowing his head in contemplation. He had been the model for Machiavelli's *The Prince*, and when he died at 27 (of tuberculosis and syphilis) without a male heir, the line of great princes stretching back to Cosimo the Elder died with him.

His sarcophagus, with a curved, scrolled lid, bears the reclining statues that Michelangelo named *Dusk* and *Dawn*. **Dusk** (the

man), worn out after a long day, slumps his chin on his chest and reflects on the day's events. **Dawn** (the woman) stirs restlessly after a long night, with an anguished face, as though waking from a bad dream. *Dusk* and *Dawn*, with their counterparts *Day* and *Night* (opposite wall), represented to Michelan-

gelo the swift passage of time, which kills everyone and causes our glorious deeds on earth to quickly fade.

During the years he worked here, Michelangelo suffered the deaths of his father, his favorite brother, and his unofficial step-brother, Pope Leo X Medici. In addition, plagues in 1522 and 1527 killed thousands in Florence. In 1527, his adopted city of Rome was looted by mercenaries. Michelangelo's letters reveal that, upon turning 50, he was feeling old, tired ("If I work one day, I need four to recuperate"), and depressed (he called it *mio pazzo*, "my madness"). He was also facing up to the sad fact that the masterpiece of his youth—the grand tomb of Pope Julius II—was never going to be completed.

Overachievers in severe midlife crises may wish to avoid the Medici Chapels.

• *On the opposite wall is the...*

Tomb of Giuliano, Duke of Nemours

Overshadowed by his famous father (Lorenzo the Magnificent) and big brother (Pope Leo X), **Giuliano** led a wine-women-and-song life, dying young without a male heir. His statue as a Roman

MEDICI CHAPELS

general, with scepter, powerful Moses-esque pose, and alert, intelligent face, looks in the direction of the Madonna statue, as though asking forgiveness for a wasted life. The likeness is not at all accurate. Michelangelo said, "In a thousand years, no one will know how they looked."

Giuliano's "active" pose complements the "contemplative" one of Lorenzo, showing the two elements (thought + action) that Plato and Michelangelo believed made up the soul of man.

Night (the woman) does a crossover sit-up in her sleep, toning the fleshy abs that look marvelously supple and waxlike, not

like hard stone. She's highly polished, shimmering, and finished with minute details. Michelangelo's females—musclemen with coconut-shell breasts—are generally more complete and (some think) less interesting than his men.

Michelangelo was homosexual. While his private sex life (or lack thereof) remains a mystery, his public expressions of affection were clearly weighted toward men. Some say he was less interested in female bodies and felt he could easily sum them up in a statue.

Day (the man) works out a crick in his back, each limb twisting a different direction, turning away from us. He looks over his shoulder with an expression (suspicious? angry? arrogant?) forever veiled behind chisel marks suggestive of Impressionist brush strokes. In fact, none of the four reclining statues' faces expresses a clear emotion, as all are turned inward, letting body language speak.

If, as some say, Michelangelo purposely left these statues "unfinished" while liberating them from their stone prison, it certainly adds mystery and a contrast in color and texture. *Night*'s moonlit clarity and *Day*'s rough-hewn grogginess may also reflect Michelangelo's own work schedule—a notorious day-sleeper and guilt-ridden layabout ("Dear to me is sleep") who, when inspired (as a friend wrote), "works much, eats little, and sleeps less."

Among *Night*'s symbols (the crescent moon on her forehead, owl under knee, and poppies underfoot) is a grotesque **mask** with, perhaps, a self-portrait. Michelangelo, a serious poet (so much so that he almost considered sculpting his "day job"), has *Night* say in one of his poems: "As long as shame and sorrow exist / I'd rather not see or hear / So speak softly and let me sleep."

Day, Night, Dawn, and *Dusk*—brought to life in this room where Michelangelo had his workshop, and where they've been ever since—meditate eternally on Death, squirming restlessly, unable to come to terms with it.

• *On the entrance wall is the...*

Tomb of Lorenzo the Magnificent and His Brother Giuliano

Because the tomb was never completed, all that really marks where The Magnificent One's body lies is a marble slab, now topped with

a statue of the Madonna flanked by saints. Perhaps Michelangelo was working up to the grand finale to honor the man who not only was the greatest Medici, but who also plucked a poor 13-year-old Michelangelo from an obscure apprenticeship to dine at the Medici table with cardinals and kings.

Lorenzo's beloved younger brother, Giuliano, died in 1478 in a "hit" by a rival family, stabbed to death before the altar of the Duomo during Easter Mass. (Lorenzo, wounded, drew his sword and backpedaled to safety. Enraged supporters grabbed the assassins—including two priests planted there by the pope—and literally tore them apart.)

The **Medici Madonna,** unlike many Michelangelo women, is thin, vertical, and elegant, her sad face veiled under chisel marks. Aware of the hard life her son has ahead of him, she tolerates the squirming, two-year-old Jesus, who seems to want to breast-feed. Mary's right foot is still buried in stone, so this unfinished statue was certainly meant to be worked on more. The saints **Cosmas** and **Damian** were done by assistants.

The Unfinished Project

The Chapel project (1520-1534) was plagued by delays: design changes, late shipments of Carrara marble, the death of patrons, Michelangelo's other obligations (including the Laurentian Medici Library next door), his own depression, and...revolution.

In 1527, Florence rose up against the Medici pope and declared itself an independent republic. Michelangelo, torn between his love of Florence and loyalty to the Medici of his youth, walked a fine line. He continued to work for the pope while simultaneously designing fortified city walls to defend Florence from the pope's troops. In 1530, the besieged city fell, republicans were rounded up and executed, and Michelangelo went into hiding (perhaps in the chapel basement, down the steps to the left of the altar). Fortunately, his status as both an artist and a staunch Florentine spared him from reprisals.

In 1534, a new pope enticed Michelangelo to come back to Rome with a challenging new project: painting the *Last Judgment* over the altar in the Sistine Chapel. Michelangelo left, never to return to the Medici Chapels. Assistants gathered up statues and fragments from the chapel floor (and the Madonna from Michelangelo's house) and did their best to assemble the pieces according to Michelangelo's designs.

• *The apse is the area behind the altar. This has the best view of the chapel as a whole, as well as a few benches.*

Sketches on the Walls of the Apse

Michelangelo's many design changes and improvisational style come to life in these (dimly lit and hard to see behind Plexiglas) black chalk and charcoal doodles, presumably by Michelangelo and assistants.

• *Starting on the left wall and working clockwise at about eye level...*

Look at all the marks: hash marks counting off days worked, a window frame for the Laurentian Medici Library, scribbles, a face, an arch, a bearded face, and (on the right wall) a horse, a nude figure crouching under an arch, a twisting female nude with her dog, and a tiny, wacky, cartoon Roman soldier with shield and spurs. You really do get a sense of Michelangelo and staff working, sweating, arguing, and just goofing off as the hammers pound and dust flies.

The Whole Ensemble—Michelangelo's Vision

The New Sacristy was the first chance for Michelangelo to use his arsenal of talents—as sculptor, architect, and Thinker of Big Ideas—on a single multimedia project. The resulting "installation" (a 20th-century term) produces a powerful overall effect that's different for everyone—"somber," "meditative," "redemptive," "ugly."

The room is a cube topped with a Pantheon-style dome, with three distinct stories—the heavy tombs at ground level, upper-level windows with simpler wall decoration, and the dome, better-lit and simpler still. The whole effect draws the eye upward, from dark and "busy" to light and airy. (It's intensified by an optical illusion—Michelangelo made the dome's coffers, the upper windows, and round lunettes all taper imperceptibly at the top so they'd look taller and higher.)

The white walls are lined in gray-brown-green stone. The half-columns, arches, and triangular pediments are traditional Renaissance forms, but with no regard for the traditional "orders" of the time (matching the right capital with the right base, the correct width-to-height ratio of columns, upper story taller than lower, etc.). Michelangelo had Baroque-en the rules, baffling his contemporaries and pointing the way to a new, more ornate style that used old forms as mere decoration.

Finally, Michelangelo, a serious Neo-Platonist, wanted this room to symbolize the big philosophical questions that death presents to the living. Summing up these capital-letter concepts (far, far more crudely than was ever intended), the room might say:

Time (the four reclining statues) kills Mortal Men (statues of Lorenzo and Giuliano) and mocks their Glory (Roman power symbols). But if we Focus (Lorenzo and Giuliano's gaze) on God's Grace (Madonna and Child), our Souls (both Active and Contemplative parts) can be Resurrected (the Chapel was consecrated to this) and rise from this drab Earth (the dark, heavy ground floor) up into the Light (the windows and lantern) of Heaven (the geometrically perfect dome), where God and Plato's Ideas are forever Immortal.

And that, folks, is a mouthful.

MEDICI-RICCARDI PALACE TOUR

Palazzo Medici-Riccardi

Cosimo the Elder, the founder of the ruling Medici family dynasty, lived here with his upwardly mobile clan, including his grandson, Lorenzo the Magnificent. Besides the immediate family, the palace also hosted many famous Florentines: teenage Michelangelo, who lived almost as an adopted son; Leonardo da Vinci, who played the lute at Medici parties; and Botticelli, who studied the classical sculpture that dotted the gardens. The historical ambience is captured in a few well-preserved rooms and in a 15th-century fresco that brings the colorful Medici world to life.

Orientation

Cost: €10, cash only, covered by Firenze Card.

Hours: Thu-Tue 8:30-19:00, closed Wed.

Information: Tel. 055-276-0340, www.palazzo-medici.it.

Crowd Alert: While the palace is rarely mobbed, you may encounter a slight bottleneck at the tiny Chapel of the Magi (Cappella di Benozzo Gozzoli). Only 10-15 people are allowed in at a time, but the line moves quickly.

Getting There: It's one block north of the Duomo at Via Cavour 3. The ticket entrance is a bit north of the gated (and often shut) courtyard.

Visitor Information: The €1 "Short Illustrated Guide" brochure, available at the shop at the entrance, is worth considering.

Tours: The €4 videoguide includes 25 minutes of commentary and interactive maps.

Length of This Tour: Allow 45 minutes. With limited time, focus on the Chapel of the Magi.

Services: WCs are in the garden (down the stairs on the right).

Starring: Cosimo the Elder and Lorenzo the Magnificent as depicted in Gozzoli's colorful Magi frescoes.

The Tour Begins

Exterior

Cosimo the Elder hired the architect Michelozzo to build the palace (1444), whose three-story facade set the tone for the rest of Florence—rough stones at bottom, rising to smooth and elegant on top. Two generations later, Michelangelo added the distinctive "kneeling windows" (with scrolls), an innovation that later cropped up on palaces the world over. In the 1700s, the palace was extended northward (keeping the same style) by its next owners, the Riccardi family.

• *Buy your ticket, pass through one small courtyard, and continue left into the...*

Courtyard

As with many Italian homes, the courtyard served as an open-air meeting point and "living room" for the extended family. The stat-

ue of Orpheus (who calmed wild animals with his harp) reminded visitors that the Medici family calmed wild Florence with smart and soothing politics. Find the family shield above the arches, with the six pills of these doctors *(medici)*-turned-cloth merchants-turned-international bankers. The Riccardi family later gilded this Renaissance lily with Baroque decor and adorned this courtyard with their collection of classical sculpture. Temporary exhibits (included in your ticket) often inhabit rooms adjoining the courtyard.

Garden

Pop into the fragrant garden with its greenhouse for lemon trees. This tiny oasis is a mere fraction of the once-spacious gardens that stretched for a city block to the north. In the past, the grounds were studded with many more fountains and statues, including the *Venus de' Medici* (Uffizi). Donatello's *David* (Bargello) likely stood in the courtyard. Teenage Michelangelo studied sculpture and liberal arts in the family school located in the gardens. In 1494, angry

Florentine mobs exiled the Medici and looted the garden's precious statues.

On the right at the end of the garden and down the stairs is the **Museo dei Marmi,** included with your ticket. At some point, you may want to visit its small collection of rare busts of ancient gods (Hercules, or Ercole), shaggy artists (the playwright Euripides), philosophers, emperors (cruel-looking Caracalla in a multicolored toga), and ordinary citizens (a *bambino* and the handsome Riccardi Athlete).

· *Head back to the courtyard, and check out any temporary exhibits (in adjoining rooms). Then find the staircase in the corner of the courtyard. This leads up to the...*

Chapel of the Magi
(Cappella di Benozzo Gozzoli)

MEDICI-RICCARDI PALACE

This sumptuous little room was the nuclear family's private chapel, where they could kneel at the altar and pray to a *Madonna and Child* by Fra Filippo Lippi (where a copy stands now). At the time, it was rare and highly prestigious for a family to have a private chapel (this is one of only three in Florence). But Cosimo the Elder was the pope's banker—he even bankrolled one of the Crusades. He could afford it.

The three walls around the altar display *The Journey of the Magi* (the three kings—one king per wall) by Benozzo Gozzoli (1459).

On the biggest wall to the right of the altar, ❶ **a curly-haired young king,** dressed in gold and riding a white horse, leads a parade of men through a rocky landscape. (Some scholars have suggested that the young Magus may be Lorenzo the Magnificent, but others dismiss the idea. Lorenzo is pictured elsewhere—read on.) The scene takes you not to Bethlehem, but to 15th-century Medici-populated Tuscany. Riding behind the king is ❷ **Piero the Gouty,** Lorenzo the Magnificent's dad (wearing a red hat, on a gray-white horse). Accompanying him is his father, ❸ **Cosimo the Elder,** who founded the family dynasty and hired Gozzoli to paint this room (in red hat, riding a modest brown donkey). In the line of young men behind them is Piero's 10-year-old son and future ruler— ❹ **Lorenzo the Magnificent** (sixth in from the left, in red cap with

scoop nose and brown bowl-cut hair; he looks to the right with an intense gaze). Little Lorenzo grew up surrounded by these beautiful frescoes that celebrate the natural world. One day, he would commission his own great art.

Above Lorenzo (and slightly to the right) is ❺ **Gozzoli** himself. The sour-faced man in the brightest red cap above Gozzoli is ❻ **Pope Pius II,** often called "the first humanist" (see "Pic-colomini Library" on page 380). Lost? Ask the attendant where they are: *"Dov'è* (doh-VEH) *Benozzo Gozzoli? Dov'è Cosimo? Dov'è Lorenzo?"*

The next wall (working clockwise) sets the king and his en-tourage in a green, spacious, and obviously Tuscan landscape. The stylish men wear colorful clothes that set trends throughout Europe. Every year on Epiphany (January 6), the Medici men would actually dress up like this and parade through the streets to celebrate the holiday of the three kings. The family invented this tradition to give them a chance to present themselves as roy-als to their citizenry.

On the last wall, notice that the white-bearded king on his white donkey (far left) got cut off when the room was later re-modeled. But the fresco was preserved: Facing the fresco, back up and you'll find the horse's ass on the other side of the doorway.

Gozzoli's crystal-clear, shadowless scenes reflect the style of his teacher, Fra Angelico. The portraits are realistic, showing the leading characters of 1459 Florence.

The room itself functioned both as a chapel and as the place where Cosimo the Elder received VIPs. By portraying his own family in this religious setting, Cosimo made a classy display of cool power and sophistication. When learned rival powers came here, they thought, "Damn, these Medici are good."

• *Exit the Gozzoli room into several...*

Palatial Rooms with Temporary Exhibitions

Though the displays change often, the rooms themselves give a small sense of the former luxury of the palace—chandeliers, tapestries, claw-foot chairs, coffered ceilings, and such. From roughly 1400 to 1700, the city of Florence set the tone for fashion and interior decor throughout Europe. This palace was ground zero of international style.

• *Eventually you'll reach a room displaying a painting in a glass case.*

Fra Filippo Lippi, *Madonna and Child*

Lippi's cheek-to-cheek *Madonna and Child* demonstrates his specialty—humanizing the son of God and the Virgin. Baby Jesus' transparent shirt, Mary's transparent scarf, and their transparent halos make this late Lippi work especially ethereal. Mary's eyes are sad, while Jesus stares into his spiritual future. She gives him a tender hug before he's off on his mission.

• *Several rooms branching off the Lippi room are government offices.*

The Palace as Civic Center

Today, the palace is a functioning county government building. As you wander around, notice the bureaucrats at work. Occasionally, the provincial council meeting room (Sala Quattro Stagioni) is open for viewing. You'll see a few dozen modern-looking seats for the council members, amid chandeliered elegance. The tapestries on the wall depict the four seasons *(quattro stagioni)*.

• *Complete your visit in the nearby...*

Luca Giordano Room

This Baroque, Versailles-like former reception hall was added by the Riccardi family. The ceiling (*The Apotheosis of the Medici Family,* frescoed in 1685 by the Naples art-

ist Luca Giordano) features Medici big shots (with starbursts over their heads) frolicking with Greek gods. Walk slowly toward the center of the room and watch as the Medici appear to rise up into heaven to be crowned by Zeus. Ringing the base of the ceiling are various Greek myths—find Poseidon with his trident (to the left) and Hades carrying off Persephone (to the right).

Claiming her place among the ancients, the blue-robed woman over the entrance is Florence, who re-birthed the classical world.
• *Your tour is done. Now head back out into the modern world and take your place among the ancients—and youth—of Florence.*

SANTA MARIA NOVELLA TOUR

Chiesa di Santa Maria Novella

The Church of Santa Maria Novella, chock-full of groundbreaking paintings and statues, is a reminder that the Renaissance was not simply a secular phenomenon. Many wealthy families paid for chapels inside this church. They were often bankers who made their money by charging interest—considered a sin by many Christians. Their need for forgiveness made their investment in a glorious chapel a very good value, and the results are the chapels that today are appreciated for their fine art.

Masaccio's fresco *The Trinity* (1427), the first painting of modern times to portray three-dimensional space, blew a "hole in the wall" of this church. From then on, a painting wasn't just a decorated panel, but a window into the spacious 3-D world of light and color. With Masaccio's *Trinity* as the centerpiece, Santa Maria Novella traces Florentine art from the medieval era to the Quattrocento (1400s) to the onset of Baroque.

Orientation

Cost: €5 covers church and museum (in the adjoining cloister), covered by Firenze Card.

Hours: Mon-Thu 9:00-19:00 (Oct-March until 17:30), Fri 11:00-19:00 (Oct-March until 17:30), Sat 9:00-17:30, Sun 13:00-17:30; last entry 45 minutes before closing.

Information: Tel. 055-219-257, www.chiesasantamarianovella.it.

Dress Code: No bare shoulders, short skirts, or short shorts for adults. Clothing must cover the knees. Free poncho-like coverings are available.

Getting There: It's on Piazza Santa Maria Novella, across the street from (and south of) the train station.

Getting In: To buy tickets, enter the courtyard to the right of the

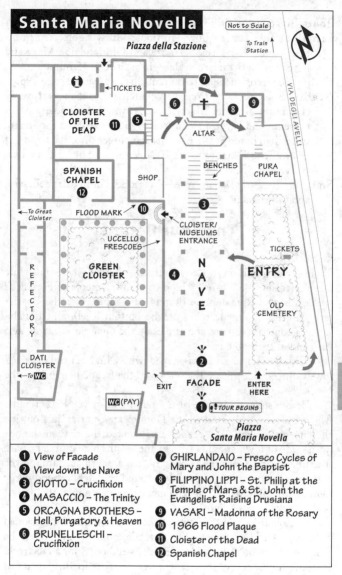

Santa Maria Novella

Not to Scale

Piazza della Stazione

To Train Station

VIA DEGLI AVELLI

TICKETS

CLOISTER OF THE DEAD

SPANISH CHAPEL

SHOP

To Great Cloister

FLOOD MARK

UCCELLO FRESCOES

GREEN CLOISTER

REFECTORY

DATI CLOISTER
To WC

ALTAR

BENCHES

PURA CHAPEL

CLOISTER/ MUSEUMS ENTRANCE

NAVE

ENTRY

TICKETS

OLD CEMETERY

EXIT   FACADE   ENTER HERE

WC (PAY)

TOUR BEGINS

Piazza Santa Maria Novella

SANTA MARIA NOVELLA

- ❶ View of Facade
- ❷ View down the Nave
- ❸ GIOTTO – Crucifixion
- ❹ MASACCIO – The Trinity
- ❺ ORCAGNA BROTHERS – Hell, Purgatory & Heaven
- ❻ BRUNELLESCHI – Crucifixion
- ❼ GHIRLANDAIO – Fresco Cycles of Mary and John the Baptist
- ❽ FILIPPINO LIPPI – St. Philip at the Temple of Mars & St. John the Evangelist Raising Drusiana
- ❾ VASARI – Madonna of the Rosary
- ❿ 1966 Flood Plaque
- ⓫ Cloister of the Dead
- ⓬ Spanish Chapel

church's main door (no Firenze Cards sold here). Firenze Card holders use the line to the left.

You can also go in through the back door—facing the train station at Piazza della Stazione 4—where you can buy either tickets or a Firenze Card. You'll enter directly into the Cloister of the Dead. (The church's back entrance is also the entry-point for the main TI.)

Tours: The tablet multimedia guide is €3.

Length of This Tour: Allow 45 minutes. Busy sightseers can hit the biggies—Masaccio's *Trinity* and Ghirlandaio's Mary and John the Baptist fresco cycles—in as little as 15 minutes.

Eating: For recommended restaurants in the area, see page 296.

Nearby: A block away from the church is a fancy **perfumery** (Farmacia di Santa Maria Novella) which feels like a small museum and is fun to visit (see page 318). Across the square from the church is the new **Museo Novecento.** It's a must if you came to Florence to see 20th-century art by Italian artists you've never heard of.

Starring: The early Renaissance—Masaccio, Giotto, Brunelleschi, and Ghirlandaio.

The Tour Begins

❶ Facade

There's a lot going on in Leon Battista Alberti's green-and-white marble facade (1456-1470), which contains elements of Florence's whole history: Romanesque (horizontal stripes, like the Baptistery), Gothic (pointed arches on the bottom level), and Renaissance (geometric squares and circles on the upper level). Note also the sundial sticking out.

The church itself is cross-shaped, with a high central nave and low-ceilinged side aisles. The scrolls on the facade help bridge the two levels.

Before stepping inside, turn around and survey Piazza Santa Maria Novella. This marked the Dominican Quarter, just outside the city walls, while the Franciscans flanked the city on the opposite side of town at Santa Croce. The monks here built a hospice (the fine arcade opposite the church), ran a pharmacy (around the corner), and for centuries provided a kind of neighborhood clinic (which still functions as an emergency room—notice the ambulances parked on the right).

The obelisks at either end of the square were commissioned by Cosimo I. His symbol was the turtle, and turtles seem to be holding up the obelisks, which served as end posts for a racetrack. Imagine high-energy, 16th-century horse races in this square as jockeys rode bareback to the delight of Florentine spectators.

• *Enter the courtyard to the right of the main door, passing through the cemetery, where you'll pay to enter. As you go inside the church, Masaccio's* Trinity *is on the opposite wall from the entrance. But we'll start our tour at the far end of the nave, looking down the long nave to the altar.*

❷ View down the Nave

From the wall facing the altar, the long, 330-foot nave looks even

longer, thanks to a 14th-century perspective illusion. The columns converge as you approach the altar, the space between them gets smaller, the arches get lower, and the floor gets higher, creating the illusion that the nave stretches farther into the distance than it actually does. Gothic architects were aware of the rules of perspective and used them in their designs.

Notice the pulpit attached to a column partway up the nave on the left. The Dominicans who occupied this church stressed teaching, so they always had prominent pulpits. And from this particular pulpit (designed by Brunelleschi), the astronomer and scientist Galileo was first accused of heresy.

• *Hanging from the ceiling in the middle of the nave is a painting by Giotto.*

❸ Giotto, *Crucifixion*

The altarpiece by Giotto (c. 1266-1337) originally stood on the main altar. Stately and understated, it avoids the gruesome excesses of many medieval crucifixes. The tragic tilt of Christ's head, the parted lips, and the stretched rib cage tell more about human suffering than an excess of spurting blood.

On either side of the crossbar, Mary and John sit in a golden, iconic heaven, but they are fully human, turned at a three-quarter angle, with knowing, sympathetic expressions. Giotto, the proto-Renaissance experimenter in perspective, creates the illusion that Christ's hands are actually turned out, palms down, and not hammered flat against the cross. Still, it would be another century before painters could fully make 3-D realism a reality.

• *Masaccio's* Trinity *is on the left wall, about midway along the nave (opposite the entrance). For the best perspective, stand about 20 feet from it, then take four steps to your left, standing on the shield with a crown. Masaccio positioned it to be seen by the faithful as they dipped fingers into a (missing) font and crossed themselves—"Father, Son, and Holy Ghost."*

❹ Masaccio, *The Trinity*, 1425-1427

In his short but influential five-year career, Masaccio (1401-1428)

was the first painter since ancient times to portray Man in Nature—real humans with real emotions, in a spacious three-dimensional world. (Unfortunately for tourists, his best portrayal of 3-D space is here, but his best portrayal of humans is in the Brancacci Chapel across the river.)

With simple pinks and blues (now faded), Masaccio creates the illusion that we're looking into a raised, cube-shaped chapel (about nine feet tall) topped with an arched ceiling and framed at the entrance with classical columns. Inside the chapel, God the Father stands on an altar, holding up the cross of Christ. (Where's the dove of the Holy Spirit? Why is God's "white collar" crooked?) John looks up at Christ while Mary looks down at us. Note the realism in the face of Mary, now a 50-year-old mother. Two donors (husband and wife, most likely) kneel on the front step outside the chapel, their cloaks spilling out of the niche. Below this fake chapel sits a fake tomb with the skeleton of Adam; compare it with the real tomb and niche to the right.

The checkerboard-coffered ceiling creates a 3-D tunnel effect, with rows of panels that appear to converge at the back, the panels getting smaller, lower, and closer together. Earlier painters had played with tricks like this, but Masaccio went further, depicting the painting's imagery on at least five planes—the donors, Mary and John, Christ, God, and the background—and each one takes you deeper into the scene. He gave such thought to the proper perspective that we, as viewers, know right where we stand in relation to this virtual chapel.

The artist knew that, in real life, the rows of coffers would, if extended, stretch to the distant horizon. Lay a mental ruler along them, and you'll find the "vanishing point"—where all the lines intersect—all the way down below the foot of the cross. Masaccio places us there, looking "up" into the chapel.

Having fixed where the distant horizon is and where the viewer is, Masaccio draws a checkerboard grid in between, then places the figures on it (actually underneath it) like chess pieces.

Together, Masaccio and Brunelleschi did the math and developed the laws of perspective. Alberti (who designed the facade) codified the laws in his famous 1435 treatise, *On Painting*. Soon, artists everywhere were drawing Alberti checkerboards on the ground, creating spacious, perfectly lit, 3-D scenes filled with chess-piece humans.

• *The Orcagna Chapel is at the far end of the left transept. As you ap-*

proach, view the chapel from a distance. This is the illusion that Masaccio tried to create—of a raised chapel set in a wall with people inside—using only paint on a flat surface. Climb the steps to see...

❺ Orcagna Brothers, Frescoes of the Last Judgment, 1340-1357

In 1347-1348, Florence was hit with the terrible Black Death (bubonic plague) that killed half the population. Here, in the Orcagna Chapel, the fading frescoes from that grim time show hundreds of figures, and not a single smile.

It's the Day of Judgment (center wall), and God (above the stained-glass window) spreads his hands to divide the good from the evil.

In *Heaven* (left wall), Hotel Paradiso is *completo*, stacked with gold-haloed

saints. *Hell* (faded right wall) is a series of layers, the descending rings of Dante's Inferno. A river of fire runs through it, dividing *Purgatory* (above) and *Hell* (below). At the bottom of the pit, where dogs and winged demons run wild, naked souls in caves beg for mercy and get none. For something a bit lighter, enjoy the hats, hairstyles, and clothing—all in vogue around 1350 in Florentine upper society.

• *In a chapel to the left of the church's main altar, you'll find...*

❻ Filippo Brunelleschi, *Crucifixion*

Filippo Brunelleschi (1377-1446)—architect, painter, sculptor—used his skills as an analyst of nature to carve (in wood) a perfectly

realistic *Crucifixion*, neither prettified nor with the grotesque exaggeration of medieval religious objects. His Christ is buck naked, not particularly muscular or handsome, with bulging veins, armpit hair, tensed leg muscles, and bent feet. The tilt of Christ's head frees a tendril of hair that directs our eye down to the wound and the dripping blood, dropping straight from his side to his thigh to his calf—a strong vertical line that sets off the curve of Christ's body. Brunelles-

SANTA MARIA NOVELLA

chi carved this to outdo a crucifix his friend Donatello had done elsewhere. He thought Donatello's Christ looked like an agonized peasant; Brunelleschi's was a dignified noble. (BTW, Donatello was impressed.)

• *In the choir area behind the main altar (the Tornabuoni Chapel) are Ghirlandaio's 21 frescoes, stacked seven to a wall. We'll concentrate on just the six panels on the bottom.*

❼ Domenico Ghirlandaio, Fresco Cycles of Mary and John the Baptist, 1485-1490

This well-preserved fresco cycle, one of the most complete in Florence, is by Domenico Ghirlandaio (1449-1494) and his workshop. This chapel was the choir, where monks gathered to worship, chanting from huge illuminated hymnals that sat on the fine lectern (from 1615).

The 15th-century stained-glass window shows the founder of the order, St. Dominic, and Dominican monks in their black robes. Above the window is the coronation of the Virgin Mary. The frescoes tell stories: the life of the Virgin (on the left), from Mary's birth to her ascendance to heaven (on top), and the life of St. John the Baptist, the patron of Florence (on the right), which shows the angel announcing John's coming, his birth, his preaching, his baptism of Jesus, the banquet where Salome requests John's head, and so on.

At the peak of Florence's power, wealth, and confidence, Ghirlandaio painted portraits of his fellow Florentines in their Sunday best, inhabiting video-game landscapes of mixed classical and contemporary buildings, rubbing shoulders with saints and angels. The religious subjects get lost in the colorful scenes of everyday life—perhaps a metaphor for how Renaissance humanism was marginalizing religion. Or perhaps it was simply more effective to communicate a message by using everyday scenes from contemporary and local life.

Here are a few panels worth a closer look:

• *Start with the left wall and work clockwise along the bottom. The first scene shows the...*

Expulsion of Joachim from the Temple

Proud, young Florentine men (the group at left) seem oblivious to the bearded, robed saints rushing from the arcade. There's Ghirlandaio himself (in the group on the right) looking out at us, with one hand proudly on

SANTA MARIA NOVELLA

his hip and the other gesturing, "I did this." The scene is perfectly lit, almost shadow-free, allowing us to look deep into the receding arches.

• *The next scene, on the right, is the...*

Birth of the Virgin

Five beautiful young women, led by the pregnant daughter of Ghirlandaio's patron, parade up to newborn Mary. Her mother, Anne, is

still in bed, overlooking the happy scene. The pregnant girl's brocade dress is a microcosm of the room's decorations. Dancing babies in the room's classical frieze celebrate Mary's birth, obviously echoing Donatello's beloved cantoria in Florence's Duomo Museum.

True, Ghirlandaio's works are "busy"— each scene crammed with portraits, designs, fantasy architecture, and great costumes—but if you mentally frame off small sections, you discover a collection of mini-masterpieces.

• *On the lowest part of the center wall, flanking the stained-glass window, are two matching panels.*

Giovanni Tornabuoni and His Wife Francesca Kneeling

Giovanni Tornabuoni, who paid for these frescoes, was a successful executive in the Medici Company (and Lorenzo the Magnificent's uncle). However, by the time these frescoes were being finished, the Medici bank was slipping seriously into the red, and soon the family had to flee Florence, creditors on their heels.

• *On the right wall...*

Mary Meets Elizabeth

In a spacious, airy landscape (with the pointed steeple—now gone—of this church, Santa Maria Novella, in the distance), Mary and Elizabeth embrace, uniting their respective entourages. The parade of ladies in contemporary dress echoes the one on the opposite wall. This panel celebrates youth, beauty, the city, trees, rocks, and life.

A generation after Brunelleschi and Alberti, all artists—including the near-genius Ghirlandaio—had mastered perspective tricks. Here, Alberti's famed checkerboard is laid on its side, making a sharply receding wall to create the illusion of great distance.

Ghirlandaio employed many assistants in his productive work-

shop: "Johnson, you do the ladies' dresses. An-
derson, you're great at birds and trees. And
Michelangelo...you do young men's butts."
The three small figures leaning over the wall
(above Mary and Elizabeth) were likely done
by 13-year-old Michelangelo, an apprentice
here before being "discovered" by Lorenzo the
Magnificent. Relaxed and natural, they cast
real shadows, as true to life as anyone in Ghirlandaio's   perfect-posture,   face-the-camera
world.

Ghirlandaio was reportedly jealous of talented Michelangelo
(who in turn was contemptuous of Ghirlandaio), but, before they
parted ways, Michelangelo learned how to lay fresco from the man
who did it as well as anyone in Florence.

• *On the far right, find the...*

Appearance of an Angel to Zechariah

In a crowded temple, old Zechariah is going about his business
when an angel strolls up. "Uh, excuse me..." The event is supposedly miraculous, but there's nothing supernatural about this scene:
no clouds of fire or rays of light. The crowd doesn't even notice the
angel. Ghirlandaio presents the holy in a completely secular way.
The cast here is the economic and social elite of late 15th-century
Florence.

• *In the chapel to the right of the altar, Filippino Lippi did the frescoes on
the left and right walls. Look first at the right wall, lower level...*

❽ Filippino Lippi
St. Philip at the Temple of Mars

In an elaborate shrine, a statue of the angry god Mars waves his
broken lance menacingly. The Christian Philip points back up at

him and says, "I'm not afraid of him—
that's a false god." To prove it, he opens
a hole in the base of the altar, letting
out a little dragon, who promptly farts
(believe it when you see it), causing the
pagan king's son to swoon and die. The
overcome spectators clutch their fore-
heads and noses.

If Ghirlandaio was "busy," Lippi
is downright hyperactive, filling every
square inch with something frilly—
rumpled hair, folds in clothes, dramatic gestures, twisting friezes,
windblown flags, and flatulent dragons.

• *On the left wall, lower level, is...*

St. John the Evangelist Raising Drusiana from the Dead

The miracle takes place in a spacious 3-D architectural setting, but Lippi has all his actors in a chorus line across the front of the stage.

Filippino Lippi (1457-1504, the son of the more famous Fra Filippo Lippi) studied with and was influenced by Botticelli and exaggerated his bright colors, shadowless lighting, and elegant curves.

The sober, dignified realism of Florence's Quattrocento was ending. Michelangelo would extend it, building on Masaccio's spacious, solemn, dimly lit scenes. But Lippi championed a style (later called Mannerism, which led to Baroque) that loved color, dramatic excitement, and the exotic.

• *In the next chapel to the right of the altar, on the central wall, find...*

❾ Giorgio Vasari, *Madonna of the Rosary*

The picture-plane is saturated with images from top to bottom. Saints and angels twist and squirm around Mary (the red patch in the center), but their body language is gibberish, just an excuse for Vasari to exhibit his technique.

Giorgio Vasari (1511-1574) was a prolific artist. As a Mannerist, he copied the "manner" of, say, a twisting Michelangelo statue, but violated the sober spirit, multiplying by 100 and cramming the canvas. I've tried to defend Vasari from the art critics who unanimously call his art superficial and garish...but doggone it, they're right. With Vasari, who immortalized the Florentine Renaissance with his writing, the Renaissance ended.

• *Exit the church out the left side, descending stairs into the* museo *part of the visit. Pause at the bottom of the steps and take in the peaceful Green Cloister.*

Museum of Santa Maria Novella

The church was part of a Dominican monastery. Imagine monks circling this shaded courtyard (cloister), as well as several adjoining ones.

At the bottom of the steps, on the right, find a ❿ **small plaque** on the wall that marks the height of the 1966 flood ("Il 4 Novembre 1966..."). The horrendous flood of the Arno inundated the church and monastery with eight feet of water. It destroyed the precious frescoes by Paolo Uccello (1397-1475) that once lined the Green Cloister (so named for Uccello's dominant color). Today, most of the walls have been completely redone by other artists, but some of Uccello's original (and very faded) frescoes can be seen on the east wall. Ironically, these depict...the Great Flood. Nearby, check out the gravestones of the ⓫ **Cloister of the Dead,** filled with the leading patrons of this monastery.

The highlight of the museum is its breathtaking ⓬ **Spanish Chapel** (a.k.a. la Sala Capitular). Once the former chapter house of the monastery, the sheer size of the vault put this place on the map when it was built in the 1320s (it became known as the Spanish Chapel after Cosimo I gave it to his bride, Eleonora of Toledo). Covering the chapel's walls is Andrea di Bonaiuto's 14th-century fresco series, *Allegory of the Active and Triumphant Church and of the Dominican Order* (c. 1365). The fresco is a visual Sunday-school class—complete with Peter's fishing boat. Follow the long and tricky road to salvation, ending high above, where the saved are finally greeted by Peter at his gate (shown upstairs in the big yellow building).

On the left wall, find the 13th-century Dominican theologian Thomas Aquinas (in a dark robe and with the Bible he translated from Greek into Latin) seated in glory amid virtues, authors of books of the Bible, and angels. The central wall tells the Passion story: Christ carries his cross (lower left), is crucified between two thieves (center), then rises triumphant (right) to trample and spook the demons of death. On the right wall, the pinkish church was inspired by designs for the Duomo, which was then under construction. Using the museum's chart, find medieval celebrities in the fresco, including Dante and Beatrice, and artists Giotto and Cimabue. Along the bottom of the fresco, dogs fight off the wolves of heresy. They're led by St. Dominic, whose fiercely loyal Dominicans (*Dominicanus* in Latin) rightly earned their medieval play-on-words nickname of "Domini canes"—God's dogs.

SANTA CROCE TOUR

Chiesa di Santa Croce

Santa Croce, one of Florence's biggest and oldest churches, gives us a glimpse into the medieval roots of the Renaissance. The church was the centerpiece of a monastery for Franciscans; it was designed by Arnolfo di Cambio (c. 1290), who also did the Duomo, and frescoed by Giotto, the proto-Renaissance pioneer.

In the cloisters is a small chapel that some consider the finest example of early Renaissance architecture. The church was host to many famous Florentines, including Michelangelo and Galileo, who are both buried here. Today, the church complex houses a leather school, a display on the disastrous 1966 flood, and a museum housed in the monks' former dining hall.

Orientation

Cost: €8 includes the church, Pazzi Chapel, museum, and cloisters; covered by Firenze Card. The leather school is always free.

Hours: Church—Mon-Sat 9:30-17:30, Sun 14:00-17:30. Leather school—daily 10:00-18:00, closed Sun Nov-March.

Information: Tel. 055-246-6105, www.santacroceopera.it. The leather school has its own website (www.scuoladelcuoio.com).

Crowd-Beating Tips: A limited number of people are allowed to enter at one time, sometimes resulting in waits of up to 40 minutes in summer. Firenze Card holders have a priority line. Otherwise, go early or late in the day, or use the...

Back Door Entrance: The leather school, tucked in the back of the church, is never crowded, and also sells entrance tickets to the church, letting you skip the line. It's less than a five-minute walk away: Head east along the left side of the church, and enter the doorway at Via San Giuseppe 5 red (labeled *Leather School of Florence*). Follow *Scuola del Cuoio* signs through the small garden and humble parking lot to the low-key back entrance of the school (#13 on the Santa Croce map). Don't be shy—they want you to visit their store. Once inside, pass through the workshops and displays to the room with the cash register, and tell the cashier you want a church ticket. From here, you can enter directly into the church (go down the hallway to pop out at #10 on the Santa Croce map; from there, make your way to the nave to start this tour).

Dress Code: A modest dress code (no short shorts or bare shoulders) is enforced. Disposable ponchos (€1) are available at the bookshop.

Getting There: It's a 10-minute walk east of the Palazzo Vecchio along the street called Borgo de' Greci.

Tours: Tablets loaded with a tour and lots of information rent for €6 (€8/2 people).

Length of This Tour: Allow one hour. With less time, focus on the tombs of VIFs (Very Important Florentines) and the Giotto frescoes.

Eating: Recommended eateries are nearby (see page 295).

Shopping: While the church's leather school is famous, it's also pricey; other leather shops abound in this area, including several cut-rate outfits and the pricier, recommended **Atelier Classe.** An excellent fragrance shop, **Aquaflor,** is also nearby. And to break out of the touristy rut, head a few blocks north and east to shop with the Florentines along **Via Pietrapiana** and **Borgo La Croce.** For more on all of these options, see the Shopping in Florence chapter.

Starring: Tombs of Michelangelo and Galileo, Giotto's frescoes, and Brunelleschi's Pazzi Chapel.

The Tour Begins

• *Begin on the square in front of the church.*

Piazza Santa Croce

Santa Croce Church, the largest Franciscan church in the world, was built from 1294 to 1442. Architect Arnolfo di Cambio's design was so impressive, the city also hired him to do the Duomo and the Palazzo Vecchio.

The church's colorful marble facade, left unfinished for centuries, was finally added in the 1850s. A statue of the medieval poet Dante adorns the church steps.

The church presides over a vast square ringed with a few old palazzos, notably the late Renaissance building at the far end. Piazza Santa Croce has always been one of Florence's gathering spots, for Carnival, May Day, and community events. If you're here in the third week of June, the square is covered with dirt and surrounded by bleachers for an annual rugby-like contest that pits neighborhood against neighborhood, while commemorating games played here as long ago as the 16th century.

If you were here on November 4, 1966, you would have found the square covered with 15 feet of water. The Arno flooded that day, submerging the church steps and rising halfway up the central doorway (more on the flood later).

• *Buy your ticket and enter. Start at the far end of the nave (farthest from the altar). Face the altar and gaze down the long nave.*

❶ The Nave

The effect here is one of great spaciousness. Franciscans liked things bright and open. The nave is 375 feet long, lined with columns that are tall, slender, and spaced far apart, supporting wide, airy arches. As in most Gothic churches, there's no attempt to hide the structural skeleton of columns and pointed arches. Instead, they're the stars of this show, demonstrating the mathematical perfection of the design and the builders' technical prowess.

Although the building is much older, it is decorated (like many Florentine churches) in the 17th-century "Counter-Reformation" style: Colorful medieval frescoes that once adorned the walls were whitewashed, the wall dividing the people from the holy area behind the altar—where the religious heavy-lifting occurred—was removed so that priests could be closer to parishioners, and side altars were added with Mannerist paintings that preached Counter-Reformation, pro-Rome values.

The Tombs

Hundreds of people are buried in the Santa Croce complex, includ-

SANTA CROCE

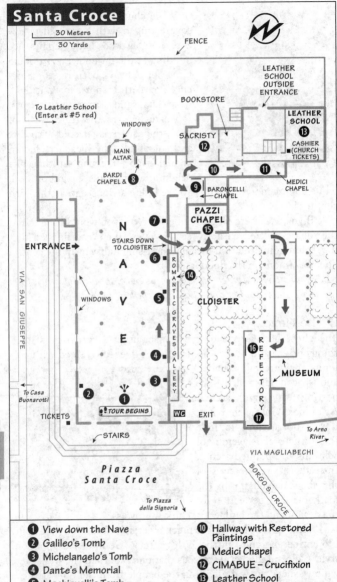

Santa Croce

30 Meters
30 Yards

FENCE

To Leather School
(Enter at #5 red)

WINDOWS

LEATHER
SCHOOL
OUTSIDE
ENTRANCE

BOOKSTORE

LEATHER
SCHOOL
13

SACRISTY
12

CASHIER
(CHURCH
TICKETS)

MAIN
ALTAR

BARDI
CHAPEL & **8**

10

11

MEDICI
CHAPEL

9

BARONCELLI
CHAPEL

7

PAZZI
CHAPEL
15

N

ENTRANCE ➤

STAIRS DOWN
TO CLOISTER

6

ROMANTIC GRAVES GALLERY

14

CLOISTER

A

5

V

WINDOWS

E

4

16

REFECTORY

MUSEUM

3

2

1

TICKETS

TOUR BEGINS

WC

EXIT

17

To Casa
Buonarotti

VIA SAN GIUSEPPE

STAIRS

To Arno
River

Piazza
Santa Croce

VIA MAGLIABECHI

BORGO S. CROCE

To Piazza
della Signoria

❶ View down the Nave	❿ Hallway with Restored Paintings
❷ Galileo's Tomb	
❸ Michelangelo's Tomb	⓫ Medici Chapel
❹ Dante's Memorial	⓬ CIMABUE – Crucifixion
❺ Machiavelli's Tomb	⓭ Leather School
❻ DONATELLO – Annunciation	⓮ Romantic Graves Gallery
❼ Rossini's Tomb	⓯ Pazzi Chapel (lower level)
❽ GIOTTO – Death of St. Francis	⓰ VASARI – The Last Supper
❾ GADDI – Frescoes in the Baroncelli Chapel	⓱ GADDI – Tree of the Cross and Last Supper

SANTA CROCE

ing 276 of them under your feet, marked by plaques in the floor. More famous folk line the walls. Just like real estate in general, it's location, location, location. The cheaper spots were by the door. People with more money landed closer to the altar.

• *Near the rear of the nave, find the tombs of two particularly well-known people.*

On the left wall (as you face the altar) is the ❷ **tomb of Galileo Galilei** (1564-1642), the Pisan who lived his last years under house arrest near Florence. His crime? Defying the Church by saying that the earth revolved around the sun. His heretical remains were only allowed in the church long after his death. (For more on Galileo, see his relics in the Galileo Science Museum.)

Directly opposite (on the right wall) is the ❸ **tomb of Michelangelo Buonarroti** (1475-1564). Santa Croce was Michelangelo's childhood church, as he grew up a block west of here at Via dei Bentaccordi 15 (where nothing but a plaque marks the spot). He took Florentine culture and spread it across Europe. In his later years, Michelangelo envisioned that his tomb would be marked with a pietà he carved himself. (Left unfinished, it's now in the Duomo Museum.) The garish tomb he actually got—with the allegorical figures of painting, architecture, and sculpture—was designed by Michelangelo's great admirer, the

artist/biographer Giorgio Vasari. (The portrait bust is considered an accurate likeness of Michelangelo.) Vasari also did the series of paintings that line the left side of the nave, using the twisting poses and bulky muscles that Michelangelo pioneered.

• *Stroll up the nave, finding more tombs and monuments along the right wall.*

At the memorial to the poet ❹ **Dante Alighieri** (1265-1321), there's no body inside, since Dante was banished by his hometown because of his politics and was buried in Ravenna. Exiled Dante looks weary, the Muse of Poetry mourns, and Lady Florence gestures to say, "Look what we missed out on."

Two tombs ahead, the ❺ **tomb of**

SANTA CROCE

Niccolò Machiavelli (1469-1527) features Lady Justice presenting a medallion with his portrait on it. Machiavelli, a champion of democratic Florence, opposed the Medici as tyrants. When they returned to power, he was arrested. He retired to his farm to write *The Prince*, a how-to manual on hardball politics—which later Medici rulers found instructive.

A few steps farther along, Donatello's carved gray-and-gold relief (1430-1435) depicting the ❻ **Annunciation** shows a kneeling angel gently breaking the news to an astonished Mary. Notable for its then-unprecedented realism, the wispy Mary (on the right) is considered one of the artistic breakthroughs that marked the beginning of the long-overdue Renaissance.

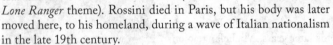

Two tombs up is ❼ **Gioacchino Rossini** (1792-1868), the Italian composer of many operas and the *William Tell Overture* (a.k.a. the *Lone Ranger* theme). Rossini died in Paris, but his body was later moved here, to his homeland, during a wave of Italian nationalism in the late 19th century.

• *Head for the main altar. In the first chapel to the right of the altar are the...*

Giotto Frescoes in the Bardi Chapel (c. 1325)

The left wall has the famous ❽ *Death of St. Francis*. With simple but eloquent gestures, Francis' brothers bid him a sad farewell.

One folds his hands and stares longingly at Francis' serene face. Another bends to kiss Francis' hand, while others raise their arms in grief. It's one of the first expressions of human emotion in modern painting. It's also one of the first to create a real three-dimensional grouping of figures. Giotto places three kneeling men (with their backs to us) in the foreground, puts some others standing behind Francis, and turns the rest to profile.

Giotto and his army of assistants were hired to plaster much of the church in colorful frescoes. But over the years, most were chiseled off, replaced by more modern works (like Vasari's). This chapel was only whitewashed over, and the groundbreaking frescoes were rediscovered in the 19th century.

• *Facing the altar, turn right, and head into the right (south) transept. At the far end, enter the chapel decorated with colorful frescoes.*

❾ Gaddi Frescoes in the Baroncelli Chapel (c. 1328-1338)

After assisting Giotto in the Bardi Chapel, Taddeo Gaddi (1300-1366)—Giotto's beloved godson—was charged with painting this chapel. His lively frescoes cover both the wall to the left (as you enter), and the wall straight ahead (with stained-glass windows by Gaddi and an altar by Giotto).

Start with the wall to the left. The story of Mary, the mother of Jesus, unfolds from top to bottom, left to right. At the very top (under the pointed arch) is a temple scene. Mary's future dad, Joachim (with a beard and a halo), is turned away from the temple because he's childless. Ashamed, he retreats to the wilderness (right side), where an angel promises him a daughter. Overjoyed, Joachim rushes to his wife, Anna, and they embrace (next level down, left panel). Anna soon gives birth to baby Mary (badly damaged panel, right side). Still a child, Mary climbs the steps of the temple (bottom level, left panel; most of her body is missing from peeling plaster) to the chief priest (cone-shaped hat), who would raise her.

When it comes time for Mary to marry, the priest assembles all the eligible bachelors (bottom-right panel). Joseph's staff sprouts

leaves and a dove (center of scene, to left of priest), signaling that he is chosen. In the foreground, a sore loser bends over and breaks his own staff.

Mary's life continues on the altar/stained-glass wall. At the top left, an angel swoops down to tell Mary that she'll give birth to Jesus. Perhaps Gaddi's most impressive scene is just below: A sleeping shepherd is awakened by an angel, who announces that Christ is born. Gaddi, an early pioneer in lighting effects, placed these windows where the natural light coming through would mix with the supernatural light from the radiant angel. Finally, Mary's story comes to its culmination (right of window): She gives birth to the Son of God in a stable.

• *From here, exit the chapel and do an immediate U-turn right, into a* ❿ *hallway, which leads to the...*

Medici Chapel and Sacristy

Lining the hallway are paintings that were victims of the devastating 1966 flooding of the Arno River. After years of restoration, they've been rehung here, at a safe height. (For more on the floods, see the sidebar on page 217.)

The ⓫ **Medici Chapel** is straight ahead, at the end of the hall.

SANTA CROCE

It was commissioned by Cosimo de' Medici the Elder in the 15th century so his family could have a private place of worship at this end of town. To design it, he hired his favorite architect, Michelozzo—who also built the Medici-Riccardi Palace.

The **Sacristy** (first door on the left from the main church) has an impressive wooden ceiling, decorated with Franciscan saints. The Franciscans who founded Santa Croce were dedicated to the principles of St. Francis, whose humanistic outlook and appreciation for the beauty of nature helped sow the seeds that would bloom into the Florentine Renaissance.

⑫ **Cimabue's** *Crucifixion* (before 1288) hangs high overhead in the Sacristy. Cimabue's Christ isn't a remote figure, but a real man experiencing human suffering. The crucifix is another survivor of the 1966 flood. Most of Christ's face and body were washed away. Rescued and restored (as best as possible), it became a symbol of the flood's destruction and the international community's efforts to recover the city's historic artworks.

• *Continue through a couple more rooms to find the entrance to Santa Croce's famous Leather School.*

⑬ Leather School (Scuola del Cuoio)

After World War II, the Franciscan monks created a "Boys Town" here to give war orphans a trade: making leather products. It was the first shop in what is now a popular leather district. The Gori family of merchants helped found the school and the grandson still runs it today. Wander through the former dorms for monks, watch the leatherworking in action, and browse the finished products for sale. Angled mirrors let you look over the shoulders of the busy leatherworkers. At the start of the long hallway, see the photos of visiting celebrities, from popes, Jimmy Stewart, and "Miss" Barbara Bush to Ozzy Osbourne. If you're in the market for leather, be aware that this shop—while top-quality—has some of the highest prices in Florence (for leather-buying tips, see page 312).

• *Head back toward the main part of the church, exit on the left between the Rossini and Machiavelli tombs, and descend the staircase into the delightful open-air cloister. At the bottom of the stairs, immediately to the right, is the doorway into the ⑭ Romantic Graves Gallery, a collection of 19th-century headstones. But let's go straight ahead to find (on your left), the entrance to the...*

⑮ Pazzi Chapel

Begun in 1430 by Brunelleschi, this small chapel captures the Renaissance in miniature. As with his Duomo dome, Brunelleschi

Floods in Florence

Summer visitors to Florence gaze at the lazy green creek called the Arno River and have a tough time imagining it being a destructive giant. But rare, powerful flooding is a part of life in this city. The Arno River washed away Ponte Vecchio in 1177 and 1333. And on November 4, 1966, a huge rainstorm turned the Arno into a wall of water, inundating the city with mud stacked as high as 20 feet. Nearly 14,000 families were left homeless, and tens of thousands of important frescoes, paintings, sculptures, and books were destroyed or damaged.

Almost as impressive as the flood was the huge outpouring of support, as the art-loving world came to the city's rescue. While money poured in from far and wide, volunteers, nicknamed "mud angels," mopped things up. After the flood, scientists made great gains in restoration techniques as they cleaned and repaired masterpieces from medieval and Renaissance times. Cimabue's *Crucifixion,* now displayed in Santa Croce's Sacristy, is a prime example.

You'll see plaques around town showing the high-water marks from 1966 (about six feet high at the Duomo). Now that a dam has tamed the Arno, rowers glide peacefully on the river, sightseers enjoy the great art with no thought of a flood, and locals...still get nervous after every heavy rain.

was inspired by Rome's ancient Pantheon. The circle-in-square design reflects the ancient Romans' (and Renaissance Florentines') belief in the unity and harmony

of perfect shapes. Notice how the color scheme of white plaster and gray sandstone accentuates the architectural lines so that only a little decoration is needed. The creamy colors help diffuse the light from the dome's windows, making the chapel evenly lit and meditative. The four medallions showing the evangelists (at the base of the dome) may be by Donatello; the medallions of apostles (on the walls) are by Luca della Robbia. While originally used as a monk's assembly room (chapter house), this later became the Pazzi family's private chapel. Imagine how modern this chapel—capped by a Brunelleschi dome—must have seemed. The chapel's portico is freshly restored thanks to a decidedly modern method of fundraising: A 2014 Kickstarter campaign quickly raised long-awaited funds, and the restoration was completed within months.

• *Exiting into the big cloister, to your left is the entrance to the...*

Museum and Refectory

Stroll through several rooms of paintings, statues, frescoes, and altarpieces by Andrea della Robbia until you come into the large room that was originally the monks' refectory, or dining hall, under heavy timber beams. The wall in front of you as you enter displays Giorgio Vasari's ⑯ *The Last Supper.* Vasari was commissioned to paint this three years before he became better known for his tell-all biography, *The Lives of the Artists.* The bright colors and dramatic poses reveal Michelangelo's influence on the next generation of artists. This painting was one of the most badly damaged victims of the 1966 flood, when it was submerged for 12 hours in polluted water. Restored in 2016, it now hangs on a pulley system so it can be quickly raised in case the waters surge again.

The refectory's entire far wall is frescoed with the impressive, 1,300-square-foot ⑰ *Tree of the Cross and Last Supper,* by Taddeo Gaddi. A crucifix sprouts branches blossoming with medieval symbolism, which dining monks ate up. Francis kneels at the base of the cross and makes sympathetic eye contact with Jesus. In one of the scenes that flank the cross (upper left), Francis has a vision in which he receives the stigmata—the same wounds in his hands, feet, and side that Christ suffered when he was crucified. Beneath the Tree of the Cross is the Last Supper, a scene that gave the monastery's residents the illusion that they were eating in the symbolic company of Jesus and the apostles.

The concept of decorating a monastery's refectory with a grand Last Supper scene started in Florence. For example, Leonardo da Vinci, a Florentine, painted this theme in the refectory of the Santa Maria delle Grazie monastery in Milan. And as we've seen from this tour, it's the genius of great Florentines—from Giotto to Brunelleschi to Michelangelo to Galileo—that helped create our modern world.

OLTRARNO WALK

*From Ponte Vecchio to
Ponte Santa Trinità*

Staying in the tourist zone leaves you with an incomplete impression of Florence. Most of its people live and work outside the touristy center. The best place to get a sense of rustic, old Florence is in the Oltrarno neighborhood, south of the Arno River. While the essence of the Oltrarno is best enjoyed by simply wandering, this walk gives you a structure you can use to cover its highlights.

We'll start at Ponte Vecchio, walk to the Pitti Palace, explore some colorful (and slightly seedy) back streets, pass by the Brancacci Chapel, peruse the artisan shops along Via di Santo Spirito, and end with a classic Ponte Vecchio view from Ponte Santa Trinità. This walk is a helpful way to link some of the Oltrarno sights worth seeing.

Orientation

Length of This Walk: Allow about an hour, not including visits to church interiors, the Brancacci Chapel, or the Pitti Palace. With less time, finish the walk at Piazza di Santo Spirito.

When to Go: What you'll see on this walk varies with the time of day, but mornings and evenings are best. Midafternoon is sleepy, and many shops and churches are closed. Most of the artisan shops are closed on weekends. In the evening, cafés, restaurants, and strolling people—both locals and tourists—leave the strongest impression, but most shops close by 19:00 or 19:30.

Getting There: Start at Ponte Vecchio, which crosses the Arno River (a 10-minute walk south of the Duomo).

Pitti Palace: €10-13 for various combo-tickets covering different parts of the palace; Palatine Gallery open Tue-Sun 8:15-18:50, closed Mon.

Santo Spirito Church: Church—free, Thu-Tue 10:00-12:30 & 16:00-18:00, except Sun opens at 11:30, closed Wed; cloister and Michelangelo crucifix—€3, Mon-Sat 10:00-18:00, Sun 14:00-17:00.

Santa Maria del Carmine: Free, daily 8:00-12:00 & 17:00-18:30.

Brancacci Chapel: €6, cash only, Wed-Mon 10:00-17:00 except Sun opens at 13:00, closed Tue; free reservations are required, but on weekdays and any day off-season, it's usually possible to walk in, especially before 15:30 (reservation tel. 055-276-8224, English spoken).

Eating and Shopping: The Oltrarno is a great destination for dining and shopping (jewelry, clothes, leather goods, woodwork, prints, home decor, and more). This walk takes you past some of my recommended restaurants and shops (for dining, see page 298; for shops, see page 323).

Starring: Views of the Arno, Florence's medieval past, present-day artisans at work, and few tourists.

The Walk Begins

• *Start in the middle of Ponte Vecchio.*

❶ Ponte Vecchio

The Arno River separates the city center from the Oltrarno—the neighborhood on the "other" *(altro)* side of the river. The two sides have historically been connected by this oldest bridge—Ponte Vecchio (current version built in 1345)—lined with its characteristic shops.

Florence was born on the north bank (founded by the Romans in the first century B.C.), and since the 1200s, the Oltrarno has been the city's poorer, working-class cousin. As the Oltrarno grew in medieval times, the wooden walls were replaced by stone, and two more bridges were added, connecting it with the city center. Looking upstream (east), you'll see the lone crenellated tower that marks the wall that once defined the medieval city. By Michelangelo's day, the Oltrarno had grown enough that Ponte Vecchio was located about mid-Florence.

Look above to see the Vasari Corridor (the yellow wall with the round windows), which was named for its architect, Giorgio Vasari. This was the personal passageway built for the Medici family to give them a private commute from the Palazzo Vecchio and Uffizi (center of

OLTRARNO

city government) to the Pitti Palace, their palatial home (which we'll see a bit later). The corridor, built in five months in 1565, drilled straight through people's homes. The only detour is where it curves around the tower at the end of the bridge. (The family who owned that tower must have had a lot of clout.) With Medici princes prancing back and forth in their corridor, the smells of the traditional shops had to go. That's when Ponte Vecchio's original merchants—butchers and fishmongers—were replaced by today's gold- and silversmiths.

Ponte Vecchio has seen a lot of turmoil. The plaque above the crowds on the uphill side honors Gerhard Wolf, the German con-

sul in Florence who is credited with saving the bridge (as well as other art treasures) from destruction during World War II. In August 1944, as Hitler's occupying troops fled the city, they were ordered to destroy all of Florence's bridges to cover their retreat. Ponte Santa Trinità, where this walk ends, was demolished (rebuilt in 1958)—and Ponte Vecchio was next in line. But thankfully, Wolf understood the bridge's historic value, and instead of destroying it, he had the buildings at either end blown up to render the bridge unusable. The flood of 1966, which later inundated the city, destroyed still more bridges and dramatically thrust entire trees like spears through buildings on Ponte Vecchio.
• *Cross the bridge, turn right on Borgo San Jacopo, and walk one block. You'll pass ugly buildings from the 1950s, built after the damage from WWII bombs. Stop at the twin towers.*

❷ Torre dei Barbadori, Torre dei Belfredelli, and Photo Op

The tower of the Barbadori family is typical of countless towers that created Florence's 12th-century skyline. Across the street is

the ivy-covered tower of the Belfredelli, another noble family. Just as the Montagues and Capulets feuded in nearby Verona, neighbors here also needed to fortify their mansions. At the corner of the Barbadori tower, next to the red and white "do not enter" sign, notice the high-water mark from the 1966 flood.

Step out to Hotel Lungarno's little riverside viewpoint for a good look at Ponte Vecchio. Envision a city turned inward, facing its main commercial artery, the river. Barges of

Oltrarno Walk

To Porta
San Frediano →

BORGO
SAN FREDIANO

#12 B

GELATERIA
LA CARRAIA

← PONTE ALLA
CARRAIA

Piazza
Nazaro
Sauro

LA CITÉ
LIBRERIA CAFÉ

BORGO STELLA

Piazza del
Carmine

VIA DEL LEONE

VIA DE' SERRAGLI

VIA MAFFIA

VIA DI SANTO SPIRITO

VIA DE' COVERELLI

8

VIA SANTA MONACA

O L T R A R N O

7

BRANCACCI
CHAPEL

SANTA MARIA
DEL CARMINE

VIA S. AGOSTINO

VIA S. AGOSTINO

SANTO
SPIRITO

VIA D. P. MARTINO

MICHELOZZI

Piazza
Santo Spirito

6

SPRUCCIOLO
DE' PITTI

VIA MAGGIO

N

200 Meters

200 Yards

VIA DELLA CHIESA

VIA DELLE CALDAIE

BORGO

VIA MAZZETTA

TEGOLAIO

PAL. DE
COSIMO
RIDOLFI

VIA MARSILI

VIA DE'

Piazza di
San Felice

1 Ponte Vecchio
2 Torre dei Barbadori, Torre
dei Belfredelli & Photo Op
3 Borgo San Jacopo
4 Via Toscanella
5 Pitti Palace
6 Piazza di Santo Spirito
7 Piazza del Carmine
8 Via di Santo Spirito
Artisan Shops
9 Ponte Santa Trinità

VIA ROMANA

Giardino
di Analena

To Porta
← Romana

TICKET
OFFICE

OLTRARNO

goods from Pisa moored here through the ages (loaded with cargo,
including marble for artists such
as Michelangelo). Today's strict
building codes leave the view essentially the same as you see in
engravings from 1700. In a more
poetic vein (see the plaque), this
is a good spot to watch the rippling Arno and sail into the beyond with your thoughts.

• *Continue down* **3** *Borgo San
Jacopo a half-block to the intersec-
tion (on the left) with the tiny street called Via Toscanella. On the corner,
look up to find a little modern statue of a woman holding her nose—a
dumpster is often left here. This is just one of countless bits of fun street art
in the Oltrarno. Turn left and enter Via Toscanella, following the lane
away from the river...and deeper into the Oltrarno.*

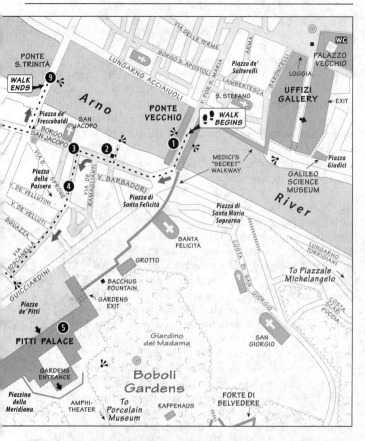

❹ Via Toscanella

You're on a quiet and characteristic lane typical of the Oltrarno. A high stone wall hides a private garden (common in this city). For a glimpse of the clothing styles of today's locals, look up at their laundry.

The little square ahead is **Piazza della Passera.** Also known as Canto ai Quattro Leoni, the piazza was officially renamed "Passera" (sparrow) in 2005. The legend goes that in 1348, the inhabitants of this neighborhood tried to help a sick little bird, which then brought the plague to the city.

Some Florentines opt for a more titillating interpretation—the area around the square was occupied by brothels, and the word *passera* is somewhat vulgar slang for the female genitalia.

The recommended **Trattoria 4 Leoni** dominates the square, and the classic little **Caffè degli Artigiani** (good for a light meal or drink) is a reminder of the earthy pride of this once rustic district, now gaining affluence as it becomes trendier. Demographically, the Oltrarno is an interesting melting pot of traditional craftspeople, immigrants, retired people, and artsy, alternative types.

Continue down Via Toscanella. You'll pass artisan shops on this and neighboring streets. Their doors are open to welcome browsers. Be comfortable stepping in and enjoying the proud work of the artisan. It's polite to say *"Buon giorno"* (in the morning and early afternoon) or *"Buona sera"* (in the late afternoon and evening). "Can I take a look?" is *"Posso guardare?"* (POH-soh gwahr-DAH-ray). Long a working-class neighborhood, the Oltrarno is where artisans still ply the traditional trades of their forebears. You'll find handmade furniture, jewelry, leather items, shoes, pottery, and picture frames in a centuries-old style. Craftsmen bind books and make marbled paper. Antique pieces are refurbished

by people who've become curators of the dying techniques of gilding, engraving, etching, enameling, mosaics, and repoussé metal work. It was in artisan workshops like these that boys like Leonardo, Michelangelo, and little Sandy Botticelli apprenticed. (We'll hit a great artisan street—Via di Santo Spirito—later.)

• *Continue to the end of Via Toscanella and turn left. You'll soon see the stony facade of a huge palace.*

❺ Pitti Palace

The massive palace, with its rusticated stonework so pleasing to noble egos, sits conveniently in front of the quarry from where all

that stone was cut. This behemoth shows the Renaissance aesthetics of symmetry and mathematical order on a giant scale.

Originally built for the Pitti family (15th century), the palace was later bought and enlarged by the Medici (16th century). In the 1860s, when Florence briefly ruled Italy as the interim capital, the palace was the "White House" for the ruling Savoy family.

OLTRARNO

While stark on the outside, it is much warmer (and Baroque) on the inside, and its bulk hides the lush Boboli Gardens. It's been a museum since the early 1900s (📖 see the Pitti Palace Tour chapter).

• *Turn 180 degrees and—with your back to the Pitti Palace—double back down the street called Sdrucciolo de' Pitti (enjoy wrapping your tongue around that "sdr"). Continue west, to busy Via Maggio—lined with galleries, antique dealers, and palazzos. Crossing Via Maggio, walk straight for another block (passing one of the last surviving custom shoemakers in town, at #17), and you come to a big church facing a square.*

❻ Piazza di Santo Spirito

Piazza di Santo Spirito, with its bald-faced church, is the community center, hosting a small but colorful produce-and-merchandise

market in the morning. You can feel the friendly scene here. Later in the day, bohemians and winos move in to drink and strum guitars on the church steps. Steer clear of any seedy characters camping out near the fountain.

Santo Spirito Church is worth a visit (see page 66) for its Brunelleschi-designed interior and crucifix by Michelangelo. As a teenager, Michelangelo was allowed to dissect bodies from the adjacent monastic mortuary in order to learn the secrets of anatomy—something he considered key to portraying bodies accurately. As thanks, he made the crucifix.

The church's blank facade prompted the neighborhood to have a contest to design a fun finish: **Caffè Ricchi** displays the hundred or so entries on its walls. Choose your favorite while enjoying a gelato or a drink.

• *To end the walk here: To return to the Arno River, face Santo Spirito Church and walk north, along the right side of the church, up Via del Presto di San Martino. At the end of the block, turn right and enter a busy five-way intersection, Piazza de' Frescobaldi. From here, you can cross back over the Arno on Ponte Santa Trinità (decorated with statues on the end). Or you could head back to Ponte Vecchio along Borgo San Jacopo (good for shopping—see page 324).*

To continue the walk: From the far end of Piazza di Santo Spirito (opposite the church), turn right on Via Sant'Agostino. Stroll westward for 5-10 minutes, enjoying more people-watching and browsing the small antique and clothing shops, until you reach a big square.

Porta San Frediano

Porta San Frediano (c. 1333) is one of the gates in Florence's medieval wall, which stretches impressively from here to the river. This gate straddled the road to Pisa. In medieval times, a three-quarter-mile-wide strip outside the wall was cleared to deny attackers any cover. The tower, originally twice as high, was built when gravity ruled warfare. During the Renaissance, gunpowder became the weapon of choice, and the tower—now just an easy target—was lopped. Florence's symbol, the lily (fleur-de-lis), decorates the top of the tower. The 40-foot doors weigh 16 tons each and are studded with fat iron nails to withstand battering rams. Take a close look at the hardware. Touch it. Clang a ring.

❼ Piazza del Carmine

Piazza del Carmine hosts the Church of Santa Maria del Carmine, with its famous Brancacci Chapel and Masaccio frescoes.

Step into Santa Maria del Carmine. Redone after a 1714 fire, the church offers a good look at textbook Baroque art. Don't miss the impressive 3-D work on the ceiling. Just as the Renaissance originated in Florence and went from here to Rome, Baroque originated in Rome and went from there to Florence. The adjacent Brancacci Chapel is covered with frescoes by Masaccio—some of the most exquisite art in Florence (📖 see the Brancacci Chapel Tour chapter).

• *With your back to the church, head straight, toward the river. At Borgo San Frediano, consider detouring a few blocks left to see the **Porta San Frediano** city gate (see sidebar) and recommended Trattoria Sabatino. Otherwise, turn right onto Borgo San Frediano, which passes the delightful **La Cité Libreria Café** (at #20 red) and becomes Via di Santo Spirito.*

❽ Via di Santo Spirito Artisan Shops

A block in from the Arno River, this nearly traffic-free stretch of Via di Santo Spirito is home to shops run by a variety of artisans. Along the way look for **Clet art**—street signs that have been creatively and whimsically painted over by the local street artist, Clet Abraham (who has a small shop in the San Niccolò neighborhood; see page 319). And you'll pass many **old palazzos** (palaces) that

OLTRARNO

today are divided into apartments, offices, and shops, as indicated by the many doorbells at their grand doorways.

The following places are worth a look. **Angela Caputi** has a jewelry workshop at #58 (on the left). **Ponziani,** at #27 (right), is a restoration workshop housed in a big warehouse of old furniture and picture frames. At #23 (right), note the tiny arches in the wall that recall the days when Tuscan wine barons had city addresses, and thirsty locals would pass in empty jugs and a few coins to have them refilled. **Castorina,** at #15 (right), is a woodcarver's shop. The palazzo at #11 (right), is still home to the aristocratic winemaking family, **Frescobaldi. L'Ippogrifo,** at #5 (right), offers an opportunity to see engraving and etching in action. (See page 323 for additional information on some of these places and a listing of more shops along this street.)

• *When you reach Via Maggio, just before the delightful little 16th-century fountain and colorful produce shop, head left past a high school and a popular* gelateria *onto...*

❾ Ponte Santa Trinità

From this bridge, enjoy a great view of the cityscape flanking the Arno River and the venerable Ponte Vecchio, where this walk began. If the medley of shops on Via di Santo Spirito stoked your consumerism, then continue across the bridge to one of the most elegant shopping streets in Florence, Via de' Tornabuoni—where you'll find not a hint of the Oltrarno.

BRANCACCI CHAPEL TOUR

Cappella Brancacci

In the Brancacci (bran-KAH-chee) Chapel, Masaccio created a world in paint that looked like the world we inhabit. For the first time in a thousand years, Man and Nature were frozen for inspection. Masaccio's painting techniques were copied by many Renaissance artists, and his people—sturdy, intelligent, and dignified, with expressions of understated astonishment—helped shape Renaissance men and women's own self-images.

Orientation

Cost: €6, cash only, covered by Firenze Card.

Hours: Mon and Wed-Sat 10:00-17:00, Sun 13:00-17:00, closed Tue, last entry 45 minutes before closing.

Information: Tel. 055-284-361, http://museicivicifiorentini. comune.fi.it.

Reservations: Reserving an entry time is required (and free), but on weekdays and any day off-season, it's often possible to walk right in, especially if you come before 15:30. Officially, reservation times begin every 30 minutes, with a maximum of 30 visitors per time slot (you have 25 minutes inside the chapel). But when it's not too busy, they generally let people come and go at will and stay as long as they like.

To find out beforehand if there's a long line, you can call the ticket desk (tel. 055-284-361).

Firenze Card holders don't need a reservation and can walk in whenever they like.

To reserve in advance, stop by the information desk in Palazzo Vecchio or call the chapel a day ahead (tel. 055-276-8224, English spoken, call center open Mon-Sat 9:30-13:00 & 14:00-17:00, Sun 9:30-12:30). If you get a busy signal, keep trying; it's best to call in the afternoon. You can also try via email—info@muse.comune.fi.it.

Dress Code: Modest dress (covered shoulders and knees—a scarf will do) is requested when visiting the church and chapel (if it's very hot, they might be lenient—but better not to chance it).

Getting There: The Brancacci Chapel is in the Church of Santa Maria del Carmine, on Piazza del Carmine, in the Oltrarno neighborhood south of the Arno River. It's about a 10-minute walk from Ponte Vecchio and a stop on my 📖 Oltrarno Walk (previous chapter).

Getting In: The chapel is accessible only through the paid entrance to the right of the church.

Film: Your ticket includes a 20-minute film (English subtitles) on the chapel, the frescoes, and Renaissance Florence (find it in the room next to the bookstore). The film's computer animation brings the paintings to 3-D life—they appear to move—while narration describes the events depicted in the panels. The film takes liberties with the art, but it's visually interesting and your best way to see the frescoes up close.

Tours: A good videoguide describes the frescoes (€3, leave ID as deposit). You're allowed to keep it for 25 minutes. I'd view most of it in the courtyard—then you can maximize your time face to face with the art inside. Skip the videoguide if you watch the film.

Length of This Tour: Allow 30 minutes (plus 30 minutes if you see the film or rent the videoguide).

Starring: Masaccio, Masolino, and Filippino Lippi.

OVERVIEW

In 1424, Masolino da Panicale (1383-1435) was hired by the Brancacci family to decorate this chapel with the story of Peter (beginning with the Original Sin that Peter's "Good News" saves man from). Masolino, a 40-year-old contractor with too many other commitments, invited 23-year-old Masaccio (1401-1428) to help him. The two set up scaffolding and worked side by side—the older, workmanlike master and the younger, intuitive genius—in a harmonious collaboration. They divvied up the panels, never (or rarely) working together on the same scene.

Half of the chapel's frescoes are by Masaccio, and half by either Masolino or Filippino Lippi (the son of Filippo Lippi), who completed the chapel more than 50 years later. The panels are displayed roughly in the order they were painted, from upper left to lower right—the upper six by Masaccio and Masolino (1424-1425), the lower ones by Masaccio (1426-1427) and Lippi (1481-1485). Although Masaccio is the star (his works are sprinkled among the

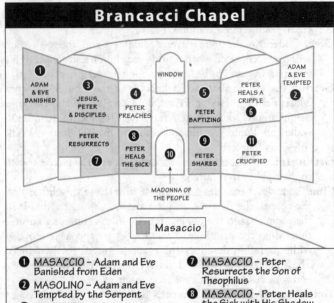

Brancacci Chapel

Masaccio (shaded panels)

1. MASACCIO – Adam and Eve Banished from Eden
2. MASOLINO – Adam and Eve Tempted by the Serpent
3. MASACCIO – Jesus, Peter & Disciples Pay the Tribute Money
4. MASOLINO – Peter Preaches to a Crowd
5. MASACCIO – Peter Baptizing Converts
6. MASOLINO – Peter Heals a Cripple and Resurrects Tabitha
7. MASACCIO – Peter Resurrects the Son of Theophilus
8. MASACCIO – Peter Heals the Sick with His Shadow
9. MASACCIO – Peter Shares the Wealth with the Poor
10. ANONYMOUS – The Madonna of the People
11. FILIPPINO LIPPI – Peter Crucified

others, mostly on the left and center walls), the panels by his colleagues are interesting and provide a good contrast in styles.

It's best to read this chapter before you enter, because if the chapel is busy, you'll have only 20 minutes inside.

The Tour Begins

• *Start with the left wall, the small panel in the upper left.*

❶ Masaccio, *Adam and Eve Banished from Eden*

Renaissance man and woman—as nude as they can be—turn their backs on the skinny, unrealistic, medieval Gate of Paradise and take their first step as mortal humans in the real world. For the first time in a thousand years of painting, these figures cast a realistic shadow, seemingly lit

by the same light we are—the natural light through the Brancacci Chapel's window.

Eve wails from deep within. (The first time I saw her, I thought Eve's gaping mouth was way over the top, until I later saw the very same expression on someone dealing with a brother's death.) Adam buries his face in shame. These simple human gestures speak louder than the heavy-handed religious symbols of medieval art.

• *Compare Masaccio's* Adam and Eve *with the one on the opposite wall, by his colleague Masolino.*

❷ Masolino, *Adam and Eve Tempted by the Serpent*

Masolino's elegant, innocent First Couple float in an ethereal Garden of Eden with no clear foreground or background (Eve hugs

a tree or she'd float away). Their bodies are lit evenly by a pristine, all-encompassing, morning-in-springtime light that casts no shadows. Satan and Eve share the same face—a motif later Renaissance artists would copy.

• *Return to the left wall, upper level. From here, we'll work clockwise around the chapel. After* Adam and Eve, *the second panel is...*

❸ Masaccio, *Jesus, Peter, and the Disciples Pay the Tribute Money*

The tax collector (in red miniskirt, with his back to us) tells Jesus that he must pay a temple tax. Jesus gestures to say, "OK, but the money's over there." Peter, his right-hand man (gray hair and beard, brown robe), says, "Yeah, over there." Peter goes over there to the lake (left side of panel), takes off his robe, stoops down at an odd angle, and miraculously pulls a coin from the mouth of a fish. He puts his robe back on (right side of panel) and pays the man.

Some consider this (which dates from the 1420s) the first modern painting, placing real humans in a real setting, seen from a single viewpoint—ours. Earlier painters had done far more detailed landscapes than Masaccio's sketchy mountains, lake, trees, clouds, and buildings, but they never fixed where the viewer was in relation to these things.

Masaccio tells us exactly where we stand—near the crowd, farther from the trees, with the sun to our right casting late-afternoon shadows. We're no longer detached spectators, but an extension of the scene. Masaccio lets us stand in the presence of the human Jesus. While a good attempt at three-dimensionality, Masaccio's work is far from perfect. Later artists would perfect mathematically what Masaccio eyeballed intuitively.

The disciples all have strong, broad-shouldered bodies, but each face is unique. Blond, curly-haired, clean-shaven John is as handsome as the head on a Roman coin (Masaccio had just returned from Rome). Thomas (far right, with a five-o'clock shadow) is intense. Their different reactions—with faces half in shadow, half in light—tell us that they're divided over paying the tax.

Masaccio's people have one thing in common—a faraway look in the eye, as though hit with a spiritual two-by-four. They're deep in thought, reflective, and awestruck, aware they've just experienced something miraculous. But they're also dazzled, glazed over, and a bit disoriented, like tourists at the Brancacci Chapel.

• *Continuing clockwise, we move to the next panel on the center wall.*

❹ Masolino, *Peter Preaches to a Crowd*

Masolino and Masaccio were different in so many ways, but they were both fans of Giotto (c. 1266-1337), who told stories with

simple gestures and minimal acting, adding the human drama by showing the reaction of bystanders. Here, the miraculous power of the sermon is not evident in Peter (who just raises his hand) but in the faces of the crowd. The lady in the front row is riveted, while others close their eyes to meditate. The big nun (far right) is skeptical, but wants to hear more. The tonsured monk's mouth slips open in awe, while the gentleman to the left finds it interesting enough to come a little closer.

Masolino never mastered 3-D space like Masaccio. Peter's extreme profile is a cardboard cutout, his left leg stands too high to plant him realistically on flat ground, the people in the back have their gazes fixed somewhere above Peter, and the "Masacciesque" mountains in the background remain just that, background.

• *Continuing clockwise to the other side of the window, come to...*

❺ Masaccio, *Peter Baptizing Converts*

A muscular man kneels in the stream to join the cult of Jesus. On the bank (far right), another young man waits his turn, shivering in

his jockstrap. Among the crowd, a just-baptized man wrestles with his robe, while the man in blue, his hair still dripping, buttons up.

The body language is eloquent: The strongman's humility, the shivering youth's uncertainty, and the bowed heads of the just-baptized communicate their reflection on the life-altering choice they've just made.

Masaccio builds these bodies with patches of color (an especially effective technique in fresco, where

colors can bleed together). He knew that a kneeling man's body, when lit from the left (the direction of the chapel window), would look like a patchwork of bright hills (his pecs) and dark crevasses (his sternum). He assembles the pieces into a sculptural, 3-D figure, "modeled" by light and shade.

Again, Masaccio was the first artist to paint real humans— with 3-D bodies and individual faces, reflecting inner emotions— in a real-world setting.

• *Continue clockwise to the right wall.*

❻ Masolino, *Peter Heals a Cripple* (left side) and *Resurrects Tabitha* (right side)

Masolino takes a crack at the 3-D style of his young partner, setting two separate stories in a single Florentine square, defined by an arcade on the left and a porch on the right. Crude elements of

the future Renaissance style abound: The receding buildings establish the viewer's point of reference; the rocks scattered through the square define 3-D space; there are secular details in the background (mother and child, laundry on a balcony, a monkey on a ledge); and the cripple (left) is shown at an odd angle (foreshortening). Masaccio may have helped on this panel.

But the stars of the work are the two sharply dressed gentlemen strolling across the square, who help to divide (and unite) the two stories of Peter. The

patterned coat is a textbook example of the International Gothic style that was the rage in Florence—elegant, refined, graceful, with curvy lines creating a complex, pleasing pattern. The man walking is at a three-quarters angle, but Masolino shows the coat from the front to catch the full display. The picture is evenly lit, with only a hint of shadow, accentuating the colorful clothes and cheerful atmosphere.

In mid-project (1426), Masolino took another job in Hungary, leaving Masaccio to finish the lower half of the chapel. Masolino never again explored the Renaissance style, building a successful career with the eternal springtime of International Gothic.

• *Move to the lower level of the opposite side. Start on the left wall with the second panel and work clockwise.*

❼ Masaccio, *Peter Resurrects the Son of Theophilus*

Peter (in that same brown robe...like Masaccio, who was careless about his appearance) raises the boy from the world of bones,

winning his freedom from stern Theophilus (seated in a niche to the left).

The courtyard setting is fully 3-D, Masaccio having recently learned a bit of the mathematics of perspective from his (older) friends Brunelleschi (with the long black hood) and Donatello. At the far right of the

painting are three of the Quattrocento (1400s) giants who invented painting perspective (from right to left): Brunelleschi, who broke down reality mathematically; Alberti, who popularized the math with his book, *On Painting;* and Masaccio himself (looking out at us), who opened everyone's eyes to the powerful psychological possibilities of perspective.

Little is known of Masaccio's short life. "Masaccio" is a nickname (often translated as "Sloppy Tom") describing his person-

ality—stumbling through life with careless abandon, not worrying about money, clothes, or fame...a lovable doofus. Imagine the absent-minded professor, completely absorbed in his art.

Next to Masaccio's self-portrait is a painting within a painting of Peter on a throne. On a flat surface with a blank background, Masaccio has created a hovering hologram, a human more 3-D than even a statue made in medieval times.

"Wow," said Brother Philip, a 20-year-old Carmelite monk stationed here when Masaccio painted this. Fra Filippo ("Brother Philip") Lippi was inspired by these frescoes and went on to become a famous painter himself. At age 50, while painting in a convent, he fell in love with a young nun, and they eloped. Nine months later, "Little Philip" was born, and he too grew to be a famous painter—Filippino Lippi, who in 1481 was chosen to complete the Brancacci Chapel.

Filippino Lippi painted substantial portions of this fresco, including the group in the far left (five heads but only eight feet).

• *Moving clockwise to the center wall, you'll see...*

❽ Masaccio, *Peter Heals the Sick with His Shadow*

Peter is a powerful Donatello statue come to life, walking toward us along a Florentine street. Next to him, in the red cap, is bearded

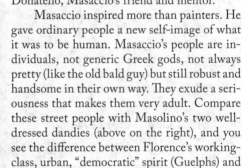

Donatello, Masaccio's friend and mentor.

Masaccio inspired more than painters. He gave ordinary people a new self-image of what it was to be human. Masaccio's people are individuals, not generic Greek gods, not always pretty (like the old bald guy) but still robust and handsome in their own way. They exude a seriousness that makes them very adult. Compare these street people with Masolino's two well-dressed dandies (above on the right), and you see the difference between Florence's working-class, urban, "democratic" spirit (Guelphs) and the courtly grace of Europe's landed gentry (Ghibellines).

• *The next panel, on the other side of the altar, is...*

❾ Masaccio, *Peter Shares the Wealth with the Poor*

Early Christians practiced a form of communal sharing. The wealthy Ananias lies about his contribution, and he drops dead at Peter's feet. Peter takes the missing share and gives it to a poor lady who can't even afford baby pants. The shy baby, the grateful woman, and the admiring man on crutches show Masaccio's blue-collar sympathies.

The scene reflects an actual event in Florence—a tax-reform measure to make things equal for everyone. Florentines were championing a new form of government where, if we all contribute our fair share through taxes, we don't need kings and nobles.

• *The altar under the window holds an 11th-century icon that is not by Masaccio, Masolino, or Lippi.*

⑩ Anonymous (possibly Coppo di Marcovaldo), *The Madonna of the People*

This medieval altarpiece replaces the now-destroyed fresco by Masaccio that was the centerpiece of the whole design—Peter's crucifixion.

With several panels still unfinished, Masaccio traveled to Rome to meet up with Masolino. Masaccio died there (possibly poisoned) in 1428, at age 27. After his death, the political and artistic climate changed, the chapel was left unfinished (the lower right wall), and some of his frescoes were scraped off whole (his *Crucifixion of Peter*) or in part (in *Peter Resurrects the Son of Theophilus,* several exiled Brancaccis were erased from history, later to be replaced).

Finally, in 1481, new funding arrived and Filippino Lippi, the son of the monk-turned-painter, was hired to complete the blank panels and retouch some destroyed frescoes.

• *The right wall, lower section, contains two panels by Filippino Lippi. The first and biggest is...*

⑪ Filippino Lippi, *Peter Crucified*

Lippi completes the story of Peter with his upside-down crucifixion. Lippi tried to match the solemn style of Masaccio, but the compositions are busier, and his figures are less statuesque, more colorful and detailed. Still, compared with Lippi's other, more hyperactive works found elsewhere, he's reined himself in admirably here to honor the great pioneer.

In fact, while Masaccio's perspective techniques were enormously influential and learned by every Tuscan artist, his sober style was not terribly popular. Another strain of Tuscan painting diverged from Masaccio. From Fra Filippo Lippi to Botticelli, Ghirlandaio, and Filippino Lippi, artists mixed in the bright colors, line patterns, and even lighting of International Gothic. But Masaccio was definitely a pioneer. His legacy remained strong, emerging in the grave, statuesque, harsh-shadow creations of two Florentine giants—Leonardo da Vinci and Michelangelo.

PITTI PALACE TOUR

Palazzo Pitti • Galleria Palatina

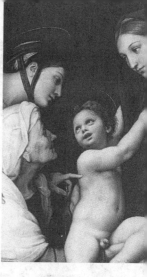

The Pitti Palace offers many reasons for a visit: the palace itself, with its imposing exterior and lavish interior; the second-best collection of paintings in town; the statue-dotted Boboli Gardens; and a host of secondary museums. However, seeing it all is impossible, and choosing where to spend your time can be confusing. While famous, the Pitti Palace exhausts tourists.

Do yourself a favor and stay focused on the highlights: Stick to the Palatine Gallery, which has the painting collection, plus the sumptuous rooms of the Royal Apartments. The paintings pick up where the Uffizi leaves off, at the High Renaissance. Lovers of Raphael's Madonnas and Titian's portraits will find some of the world's best of each at the Pitti Palace. For fashionistas, the Costume Gallery is worth a peek. And if it's a nice day, take a stroll in the Boboli Gardens, a rare and inviting patch of extensive green space within old Florence.

Orientation

Cost: Ticket #1 (the tour described in this chapter) costs €13 (€8.50 if no special exhibits) and covers the recommended Palatine Gallery, Royal Apartments, and Gallery of Modern Art (you can't buy a ticket for just the Palatine Gallery). **Ticket #2** is €10 (€7 if no special exhibits) and covers the Boboli and Bardini Gardens, Costume Gallery, Argenti/Silverworks Museum (the Medici treasures), and Porcelain Museum. All of the palace sights are covered by the Firenze Card and are free (and crowded) on the first Sun of the month.

Hours: The **ticket #1** sights (Palatine Gallery, Royal Apartments, and Gallery of Modern Art) are open the same hours year-

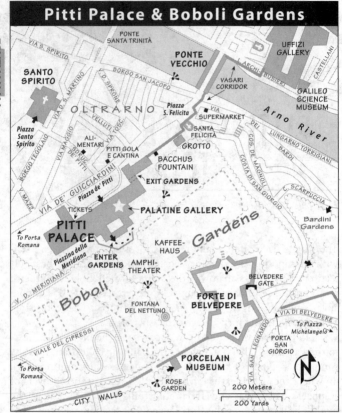

Pitti Palace & Boboli Gardens

round: Tue-Sun 8:15-18:50, closed Mon, last entry 45 minutes before closing.

Hours for the **ticket #2** sights (Boboli and Bardini Gardens, Costume Gallery, Argenti/Silverworks Museum, and Porcelain Museum) vary with the season: daily June-Aug 8:15-19:30, April-May and Sept 8:15-18:30, March and Oct 8:15-17:30, Nov-Feb 8:15-16:30; closed first and last Mon of each month, last entry one hour before closing.

Information: Tel. 055-238-8614, www.uffizi.beniculturali.it.

Avoiding Lines: Reservations are generally not necessary. But if there's a long line, you can try asking at window 3 at the ticket office (marked *Reservation Desk*) if they'll let you make a €3 reservation on the spot (not always possible). You can also skip lines if you have a Firenze Card.

Getting There: The Pitti Palace is located several blocks southwest of Ponte Vecchio, in the Oltrarno neighborhood. Bus #C3 from the Santa Croce Church and bus #D from the train station stop right in front.

Getting In: The ticket office is at the far right of the massive facade. Once you have your ticket, enter through the main doorway in the center of the facade. Firenze Card holders should go directly to the main entrance (where you may be ushered to the head of the security checkpoint); then go to the bookstore on the left side of the courtyard to have your card swiped and get your tickets.

Tours: An €8 audioguide (€13/2 people) is available from the ticket office and covers the Palatine Gallery and the Gallery of Modern Art.

Length of This Tour: Allow one hour for the Palatine Gallery and Royal Apartments.

Services: WCs are in the basement corridor underneath the café and the Palatine Gallery/Royal Apartments staircase.

Eating: The basic café in the palace courtyard is disappointing and overpriced. It's a better idea to eat nearby before or after your visit. Several recommended Oltrarno restaurants are a few blocks away (see page 298). Across the piazza is the **$$ Pitti Gola e Cantina,** a cozy wine-by-the-glass *enoteca* that also serves a range of *antipasti* plates, homemade pastas, and other dishes (food served 13:00-24:00, closed Tue, Piazza Pitti 16, tel. 055-212-704). For picnics, a tiny *alimentari* offers made-to-order sandwiches a half-block from the palace (Sdrucciolo de' Pitti 6). A drinking fountain is in front of the palace, at the base of the square, across the street from Banca Toscana.

Shopping: The area around the Pitti Palace is a busy shopping zone, with no shortage of high-profile shops. (The recommended **La Pelle** leather shop is between here and Ponte Vecchio.) I enjoy browsing two different streets near the Pitti Palace: the narrow lane called **Sdrucciolo de' Pitti,** directly across from the entrance courtyard; and, a block north, the very local-feeling **Via Romana** (which conveniently connects the palace entrance with the rear gate of Boboli Gardens). For tips on exploring these shopping zones, see page 323.

Starring: Raphael, Titian, and the most ornate palace you can tour in Florence.

The Tour Begins

The plain and brutal Pitti Palace facade is like other hide-your-wealth palace exteriors in Florence. The Pitti family (rivals of the Medici family) began building it in 1458 but ran out of money. It sat unfinished until the Medici bought it, expanded it, and moved in during the mid-1500s, choosing to keep the name. It's an imposing facade—more than two football fields long, made of heavy blocks of unpolished stone, and set on a hill. For nearly two centuries (1549-1737), this palace was arguably Europe's cultural center, setting trends in the arts, sciences, and social mores.

• *Enter the palace through the central doorway and into the courtyard. From here, all of the sights are well marked: The Palatine Gallery entrance is to your right, the Boboli Gardens entrance is straight ahead, and the Argenti/Silverworks Museum is to the left. Climb several flights of stairs to the Palatine Gallery (Galleria Palatina).*

PALATINE GALLERY

• *Enter Room 1 of the Palatine Gallery. (If there's a temporary exhibit, your visit may begin in the large white ballroom, which then leads into Room 1.)*

The collection is all on one floor. To see the highlights, walk straight down the spine through a dozen or so rooms. (Avoid the rooms that branch off to the side.) At the far end, make a U-turn left and double back. After the Palatine Gallery, the route flows naturally into the even-more-lavish rooms of the Royal Apartments.

You'll walk through one palatial room after another, with frescoed ceilings that celebrate the Medici family and give the rooms their names (the Venus Room, Apollo Room, and so on). The walls sag with floor-to-ceiling paintings in gilded frames, stacked three and four high, different artists and time periods all jumbled together. Use the information folders in each room to help find the featured paintings. Even with their help, it's still difficult to pick out the masterpieces from the minor pieces. Focus on my recommended highlights first, then let yourself browse.

Rooms 1 and 2

• *Immediately to your right as you enter is the...*

Bronze Bust of Cosimo I

Thank Cosimo I de' Medici (1519-1574, with beard and crown) for this palace. Cosimo I (not to be confused with Cosimo the Elder, the 15th-century founder of the Medici clan) was the first Grand Duke, and the man who revived the Medici family's dominance a generation after the death of Lorenzo the Magnificent. Cosimo I's wife, Eleonora, bought the palace from the Pittis and convinced him and their 11 children to move there from their home in the Palazzo Vecchio. They used their wealth to expand Pitti, building

Pitti Palace—Palatine Gallery

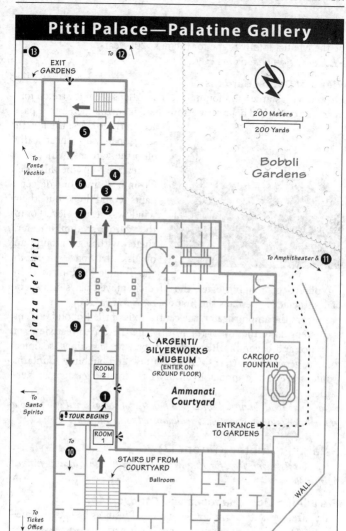

1. Bust of Cosimo I & Garden Views
2. FILIPPO LIPPI – Madonna and Child
3. RAPHAEL – Holy Family
4. Napoleon's Bathroom
5. RAPHAEL – Portrait of a Woman
6. RAPHAEL – Madonna of the Grand Duke; Tommaso Inghirami; Agnolo and Maddalena Doni; Madonna with Child and St. John the Baptist
7. RAPHAEL – Veiled Woman
8. TITIAN – Mary Magdalene; Portrait of a Man
9. TITIAN – Portrait of a Lady; Pietro Aretino; The Concert CANOVA – Venus Italica
10. To Royal Apartments
11. To Porcelain Museum & City Views
12. To Grotto of Buontalenti
13. Bacchus Fountain

the gardens and amassing the rich painting collection. This would be the Medici family home for the next 200 years.

• *Look out the windows to enjoy...*

Views of Boboli Gardens

Dotted with statues and fountains, the gardens seem to stretch forever. The courtyard below (by Ammanati) is surrounded by the pal-

ace on three sides; the fourth side opens up theatrically onto the gardens, which rise in terraces up the hillside. Cosimo I and his descendants could look out their windows at eye level onto the garden's amphitheater, ringed with seats around an obelisk that once stood in the Temple of Ramses II in

Egypt. At this amphitheater, the Medici enjoyed plays and spectacles, including perhaps the first opera, *Euridice* (1600).

From the amphitheater, the central axis of the Boboli Gardens stair-steps up to the top of the hill (where there are great views of Florence and beyond). The gardens' expansive sightlines, sculpted foliage, geometric patterns, Greek statues, and bubbling fountains would serve as the model a century later for the gardens at Versailles.

• *Continue straight ahead through a handful of rooms until you reach a green-and-gold room virtually wallpapered with paintings.*

Sala di Prometeo (Room 17)

• *Inside this room, look for the fireplace topped with a round-framed painting.*

Fra Filippo Lippi, *Madonna and Child*, c. 1452

This pure, radiant Virgin cradles a playful Jesus as he eats a pomegranate. Lippi's work combines medieval piety with new Renaissance techniques. It may be Florence's first tondo (circular artwork), an innovative format that soon became a Renaissance staple. Seed-eating Jesus adds a human touch, but the pomegranate was also a medieval symbol for new life and the Resurrection. In medieval style, the background relates episodes from different places and times, including Mary's birth to Anne (in bed, at left) and the meeting of

Mary's parents (distant background, right). But these stories are set in rooms that are textbook Renaissance 3-D, with floor tiles and ceiling coffers that create the illusion of depth. The ladies bringing gifts to celebrate Mary's birth add another element of everyday Renaissance realism.

Compare Lippi's Madonna with two by Lippi's star pupil, **Botticelli** (one on the left wall, one on the right, both hung high). Botticelli borrowed much from Lippi, including the same facial features, pale skin, precise lines, and everyday details.

• *The next room is the...*

Sala di Ulisse (Room 22)

This was the Grand Duke's bedroom. One of Cosimo I's favorite paintings hangs above the fireplace.

Raphael, *Holy Family (Sacra Famiglia, a.k.a. Madonna dell'Impannata),* 1512-1514

This work introduces us to the range of this great artist. There's the creamy, rosy beauty of the Virgin alongside the gritty wrinkles of St. Anne/Elizabeth. At first glance, it seems like a stately scene, until you notice that Jesus is getting tickled. Everyone is in motion—gazes pointed in all different directions—but they're also posed in a harmonious pyramid, with Jesus' crotch at the center. Little John the Baptist  sticks a foot in our face and points to Jesus as The One. Also typical of the always-busy Raphael: The work was probably completed by some of his 50-plus assistants.

• *The next small room you pass by is known as...*

Napoleon's Bathroom (Bagno di Napoleone)

The white-marble luxury and sarcophagus-shaped bathtub were intended for the great French conqueror, Napoleon Bonaparte, when he ruled Florence (1799-1814). Napoleon installed his little sister Elisa as Grand Duchess, and she spent her years here redecorating the palace, awaiting her brother's return. But Napoleon was not destined to meet this water loo. After he was toppled from power, the palace returned to its previous owners.

Over the centuries, the palace hosted several rulers: 200 years of Medici (c. 1549-1737); 100 years of Austrians (the Habsburg-Lorraines, 1737-1860); 15 years of Napoleon (1799-1814); and 60 years under the Savoys, Italy's first royal family (1860-1919), who made Pitti their "White House" when Florence was briefly the capital of modern Italy.

• *Pass through the final rooms and exit out the far end into the stairwell (with some handy benches). Ahhh. Admire the views of the Duomo, the Palazzo Vecchio, and the green hills of Fiesole in the distance. The Medici could commute from here to downtown Florence by way of a private, covered passageway (Vasari Corridor) that goes from the Pitti Palace and across Ponte Vecchio to the Palazzo Vecchio. If you look down into the Boboli Gardens, you can see the melted-frosting entrance to the Buontalenti Grotto.*

As you continue on through the second half of the collection, the first room you enter is the...

Sala dell' Iliade (Room 27)

This is the first of several former staterooms, used for grand public receptions. For centuries, Europe's nobles, ladies, and statesmen passed through these rooms as they visited the Medici. They wrote home with wonder about the ceiling frescoes and masterpiece-covered walls. The ceiling frescoes depict the Greek gods cavorting with Medici princes, developing the idea of rule by divine right—themes that decades later would influence the decoration of Versailles. Turn your attention to the painting by the entrance door.

Raphael, *Portrait of a Woman* (*Ritratto di Donna, a.k.a. La Gravida*), 1505-1506

This rather plain-looking woman has one hand on her stomach and a serious expression on her face. She's pregnant. Though she is no Madonna, and her eyes don't sparkle, the woman has presence. Raphael's sober realism cuts through the saccharine excesses of the surrounding paintings.

As one of Raphael's earliest portraits from his time in Florence, it shows the influence of Leonardo da Vinci. Like Mona Lisa, she's a human pyramid turned at a three-quarters angle, supporting her arm on an armrest that's almost at the level of the frame itself. It's as if she's sitting near the edge of an open window, looking out at us.

• *Enter the next room, straight ahead.*

Sala di Saturno (Room 28)

This room boasts the second-biggest Raphael collection in the world—the Vatican beats it by one. A half-dozen Raphael paintings ring the room at eye level, ranging from dreamy, soft-focus Madonnas to down-to-earth, five-o'clock-shadow portraits.

• *Next to the door you just came through, find...*

Raphael, *Madonna of the Grand Duke (Madonna del Granduca),* 1505

Raphael presents Mary in an unusually simple pose—standing, while she cradles Baby Jesus under his bum. With no background, the whole focus is on Mother, lost in thought, and Child, looking right at us. Mary's dreamy face and Jesus' golden body seem to emerge from the shadows. Try as you might, you can't quite discern the outlines of the figures, as they blend seamlessly into the dark background (Leonardo's sfumato technique).

The apparently simple pose is actually a skillful, geometric composition. Mary's head and flowing mantle form a triangle. The triangle's base is: first, the neckline of her dress, then her belt, then the horizontal line formed by her arm and Jesus' thighs. The geometric symmetry is enlivened by an off-kilter touch of reality: Mary's head tilts ever-so-slightly to the side.

This Madonna radiates tenderness and holiness, the divine embodied in human form. The iconic face, the pale colors, the simple pose, the geometric perfection—all are classic Raphael.

• *Now survey a few more paintings, moving clockwise through the room. At the right end of the same wall as the* Madonna del Granduca *is...*

Raphael, *Portrait of Tommaso Inghirami,* c. 1510

Wearing his bright red Cardinal's suit, Tommaso was the friend and librarian of the Medici pope, Leo X. Raphael captures him during an unposed moment, as he pauses to think while writing. Without glossing over anything, Raphael shows us the man just as he was, complete with cleft chin, jowls, lazy eye, and all.

• *On the next wall, look for...*

Raphael, *Companion Portraits of Agnolo and Maddalena Doni,* c. 1505-1506

These portraits are as crystal clear as the *Madonna del Granduca* is hazy. They're a straightforward look at an upwardly mobile Florentine couple. He was a successful businessman in the textile trade (who commissioned Michelangelo's *Holy Family* in the Uffizi), and she was the daughter of one of the city's richest families. Raphael places them right at the edge of the picture plane, showing off his fine clothes and her jewelry.

• *Immediately to the left of the door leading to the next room is...*

Raphael
(1483-1520)

Raphael (like most Renaissance greats, known by a single name) is considered the culmination of the High Renaissance. (Note that the museum uses his Italian name Raffaello, or Raffaello Sanzio.) He combined symmetry, grace, beauty, and emotion. With his debonair personality and lavish lifestyle, Ra-

phael also epitomized the worldly spirit of the Renaissance.

Raphael lived a charmed life. Handsome and sophisticated, he quickly became a celebrity in the Medici family's high-living circle of bankers, princes, and popes. He painted masterpieces by day and partied by night. Both in his life and art, he exuded what his contemporaries called *sprezzatura*—an effortless, unpretentious elegance. In a different decade, he might have been thrown out of the Church as a great sinner, but his love affairs and devil-may-care personality were perfectly in keeping with the optimism of the times.

Raphael employed a wide range of styles and techniques, but there are some recurring elements. His paintings are bathed in an even light, with few shadows. His brushwork is smooth and blended, and colors are restrained. Works from the Florence years (1504-1508) show Leonardo's influence: Mona Lisa poses,

Raphael, *Madonna with Child and St. John the Baptist (Madonna della Seggiola)*, c. 1514-1516

This colorful, round painting (also known as the *Madonna of the Chair*) is one of Raphael's best-known and most-copied works. Mary hugs Baby Jesus, squeezing him along with little John the Baptist. This Mary is no distant Madonna;

she wears a peasant's scarf and a colorful dress and looks directly out at us with a cheerful half-smile. The composition plays on the theme of circles and spheres. The whole canvas is patterned after round sculpture-relief *tondi*. Mary's halo is a circle, her scarf forms a half-circle, and her face is an oval. The pudgier-than-normal Bambino exaggerates the overall roundness of the scene. Mother and child fit together like inter-

sfumato brushwork (soft outlines), and lots of sweet Madonnas and Holy Families in a pyramid format. On the other hand, Raphael's portraits are never saccharine. The poses are natural, and individual quirks are never glossed over. He captures the personality without a hint of caricature.

In his later years, Raphael experimented with more complex compositions and stronger emotions. In group scenes, Raphael wants you to follow his subjects' gazes as they exchange glances or look off in different directions. This adds a sense of motion and psychological tension to otherwise well-balanced scenes. Raphael's compositions always have a strong geometric template. Figures are arranged into a pyramid or a circle. Human bodies are composed of oval faces, cylindrical arms, and arched shoulders. Subconsciously, this evokes the feeling that God's created world is geometrically perfect. But Raphael always lets a bit of messy reality spill over the lines so his scenes don't appear static. His work comes across as simple and unforced...*sprezzatura.*

When Raphael died in 1520, he was one of Europe's most celebrated painters (along with Michelangelo and Titian). His style went out of fashion with the twisted forms of Mannerism and the over-the-top drama of Baroque. The 1700s saw a revival, and today's museums are stuffed with sappy Madonnas by Raphael's many imitators. It's easy to dismiss his work and lump him in with his wannabes. Don't. This is the real deal.

locking half-circles. As in a cameo, the figures seem to bulge out from the surface, suggesting roundness. Bathed in a golden glow, Mary enfolds her child into the safe circle of motherly love.
• *Head into the next room.*

Sala di Giove (Room 29)

Here in the throne room, the Grand Duke once saw visitors beneath a ceiling fresco showing Jupiter receiving legendary guests.
• *To the left of the door leading into the next room is...*

Raphael, *Veiled Woman (La Velata),* 1514-1515

The dark-haired beauty's dark eyes stare intently at the viewer. The elaborate folds of her shiny silk dress contrast with her creamy complexion. It's a study in varying shades of white and brown, bathed in a diffuse golden glow. A geometric perfection underlies this woman's soft, flesh-and-blood beauty: Her ovoid face, almond eyes, arch-shaped eyebrows, and circular necklace are all framed by a triangular veil. She is the very picture of perfection...except for that single wisp of loose hair that gives her the added charm of human imperfection.

Who is she? She may be the same woman Raphael depicted topless for a painting in Rome and as a Virgin (in Dresden). The biographer Vasari claims (and scholars debate) that La Velata is Raphael's beloved girlfriend Margherita Luti, known to history as La Fornarina, or the baker's daughter. Raphael became so obsessed with her that he had to have her near him to work. Vasari says that Raphael's sudden and premature death at age 37 came after a night of wild sex with her. Whoever La Velata is, she's one of the beauties of Western art.

• *Pass through the Sala di Marte (Room 30) and into the Sala di Apollo (Room 31). Two paintings by Titian flank the entrance door.*

Sala di Apollo (Room 31)
Titian, *Mary Magdalene (La Maddalena),* c. 1530-1535
According to medieval lore (but not the Bible), Mary Magdalene was a prostitute who repented when she heard the message of Jesus.

Titian captures her right on the cusp between whore and saint. She's naked, though covered by her hair, which she pulls around her like a cloak as she gazes heavenward, lips parted. Her hair is a rainbow of red, gold, and brown, and her ample flesh radiates gold. The rippling locks (echoed by gathering clouds in the background) suggest the inner turmoil and spiritual awakening of this passionate soul.

Among the upper classes in Renaissance times, Mary Magdalene was a symbol of how sensual enjoyment (food, money, sex) could be a way of celebrating God's creation. The way this Mary Magdalene places her hand to her breast and gathers her hair around her is also the classic "Venus Pudica" pose of many ancient Greek statues. It's simultaneously a gesture of modesty and a way of drawing attention to her voluptuous nudity.

Titian, *Portrait of a Man (Ritratto Virile),* c. 1545
This unknown subject has so mesmerized viewers that his portrait has become known by various monikers, including *The Young Englishman, The Gray-Eyed Nobleman,* and *Doctor McDreamy's Evil*

Twin. The man is dressed in dark clothes and set against a dim background, so we only really see his face and hands, set off by a ruffled collar and sleeves. He nonchalantly places his hand on his hip while holding a glove, and stares out. The man is unforgettable, with a larger-than-life torso and those piercing blue-gray eyes that gaze right at us with extreme intensity. Scholars have speculated that the man could be a well-known lawyer...eternally cross-examining the museumgoers.

• *In the next room, you'll find several more Titians.*

Sala di Venere (Room 32)

• *Survey the room in clockwise order. First up, turn around and face the door you just came through. Immediately to the right is...*

Titian, *Portrait of a Lady (Ritratto di Donna, a.k.a. La Bella),* c. 1536

Titian presents a beautiful *(bella)* woman in a beautiful dress to create a beautiful ensemble of colors: the aqua-and-brown dress, the gold necklace, pearl earrings, creamy complexion, auburn hair, and dark jewel-like eyes. She embodies the sensual, sophisticated, high-society world that Titian ran around in. The woman is likely Titian's Venus of Urbino, standing up and with her clothes on (see page 124). Scholars speculate on who she really was; perhaps she's Eleonora, the Duchess of Urbino, or the mistress of the previous Duke, or maybe she's just a paid model that Titian found to be...beautiful.

• *At the right end of the same wall is...*

Titian, *Portrait of Pietro Aretino,* c. 1545

The most notorious and outrageous figure in Renaissance high society was the writer Pietro Aretino (1492-1556). In 1527, he fled Rome, having scandalized the city with a collection of erotic/pornographic sonnets known as the *Sixteen Ways* (or sex positions). He took refuge in luxury-loving Venice, where he befriended Titian, a fellow connoisseur of eroticism and the arts. Titian and Aretino were both commoners, but they moved easily in court circles: Titian the diplomat and Aretino the fiery satirist who tweaked the noses of arrogant princes. (In fact, Aretino was part of the Rat Pack of rowdy Medici that included the father of Cosimo I.)

This portrait captures the self-confidence that allowed Aretino to stand up to royalty. Titian portrays him with the bearded face of an ancient satyr (a lecherous, untamed creature in Greek mythology). His torso is huge, like a smoldering volcano of irreverence that could erupt at any moment. Rather than the seamless brushstrokes and elaborate detail of Titian's earlier works, the figure of Aretino is composed of many rough strokes of gold and brown paint. Around age 60, Titian radically altered his style, adopting this "unfinished" look that the Impressionists would elaborate on centuries later. Aretino joked when he saw the portrait, "It breathes and moves as I do in the flesh. But perhaps [Titian] would have spent more time on my fine clothes—the robe, the silk, the gold chain—if I'd paid him more." Aretino gave the portrait to Cosimo I as a gift.

• *On the facing wall, just over the small table, find...*

Titian, *The Concert (Concerto)*, 1510-1512

An organ-playing man leans back toward his fellow musician (a monk), who's put down his cello to tap him on the shoulder. A young dandy in fancy clothes and a feathered cap looks on. The meaning of the work is a puzzle, perhaps intentionally so. Titian may have collaborated on this early painting with his colleague Giorgione, who specialized in enigmatic works used by cultured hosts as conversation starters.

Maybe it's just a slice-of-life snapshot of Venetian musicians briefly united in their common task. Or maybe it's a philosophical metaphor, in which a middle-aged man, blithely engaged in the gay music of his youth, is interrupted by a glimpse at his future—the bass notes and receding hairline of old age.

• *In the middle of the Sala di Venere stands...*

Canova, *Venus Italica (Venere)*, 1810

This pure white marble statue of Venus looks like the *Venus de' Medici* with a sheet (see page 117). Like the Medici Venus, she's nude, modestly crossing her hands in front of her (the "Venus Pudica" pose), while turning her head to the side. But Canova's Venus clutches a garment, which only highlights her naked vulnerability.

In 1796, a young French general named Napoleon Bonaparte toured the Uffizi and fell in love with the *Venus de' Medici*. A few years later, when he conquered Italy, he carried Venus off with him to Paris. To replace it, the great Venetian sculptor Canova was asked to make a copy. He refused to make an exact replica, but he

Titian
(c. 1490-1576)

Titian the Venetian (the museum uses his Italian name Tiziano or Tiziano Vecellio) captures the lusty spirit of his hometown. Titian was one of the most prolific painters ever, cranking out a painting a month for almost 80 years. He excelled in every subject: portraits of kings, racy nudes for bedrooms, creamy-faced Madonnas for churches, and pagan scenes from Greek mythology. He was cultured and witty, a fine musician and businessman—an all-around Renaissance kind of guy. Titian was famous and adored by high society, including Cosimo I and other Medici.

Titian's style changed over his long career. In his youth, he painted alongside Giorgione, even working on the same canvases (scholars still debate who did what). When he reached middle age, he found his voice: bright colors (particularly the famed "Titian red"), large-scale canvases, exuberant motion, and complex compositions, rebelling against the strict symmetry of the early Renaissance. In his 60s, his technique became more impressionistic. He applied the paint in rough, thick brushstrokes, even using his fingers. In these late works, his figures don't pop from the background; instead, they blend in, creating a moody atmosphere.

Throughout his life, his bread and butter were portraits of Europe's movers and shakers—kings, popes, countesses, mistresses, artists, and thinkers. Without ever making the people who sat for him more handsome or heroic than they were, he captured both their outer likeness and their inner essence. Their clothes and accessories tell us about their social circle, so collectively, his portraits are a chronicle of the Renaissance in all its sensual glory.

agreed to do his own interpretation, combining motifs from many ancient Venuses of the Pudica (modest) and Callipigia (ample derriere) styles. Canova's *Venus Italica* stood in the Uffizi until Napoleon was conquered and *Venus de' Medici* returned.

• *From here, the rooms of the Palatine Gallery lead into the...*

ROYAL APARTMENTS

These 14 rooms (of which only a few are open at any one time) are where Florence's aristocrats lived in the 18th and 19th centuries. The decor reflects both Italian and French styles. In the 16th century, the two countries cross-pollinated when Catherine de' Medici (Lorenzo the Magnificent's great-granddaughter) married the king of France. Soon power shifted northward, which is why many of these rooms mimic the Versailles style, rather than vice versa. You'll see rooms of different themes and color schemes. Each room features the style of a particular time period. Ogle the velvety wallpaper, heavy curtains, white-and-gold stucco ceilings, chandeliers, and Louis XIV-style chairs, canopied beds, clocks, and candelabras. Gazing over it all are portraits of some of the people who lived in these rooms. Here, you get a real feel for the splendor of the dukes' world.

THE REST OF THE PITTI PALACE

If you've got the energy and interest, it'd be a Pitti to miss the palace's other offerings: the Boboli and Bardini Gardens, Argenti/Silverworks Museum (the Medici treasures), Costume Gallery, and Porcelain Museum.

Other Palatine Gallery Works

Art lovers can hunt down Titian's *Portrait of Filippo II of Spain* and *Portrait of Ippolito de' Medici;* Giorgione's *Three Ages of Man;* Caravaggio's *Sleeping Cupid* and *Portrait of Antonio Martelli (Cavaliere di Malta);* and many more.

Gallery of Modern Art

On the second floor, this gallery features Romantic, Neoclassical, and Impressionist works by 19th- and 20th-century Tuscan painters.

Costume Gallery

Also on the second floor, this fine collection displays centuries' worth of men's and women's fashions, with thoughtful explanations about the philosophical underpinnings of clothing styles. This is worth a linger for those interested in fashion, and interesting to anybody. Don't miss the darkened room that displays the clothes that Cosimo I and Eleonora of Toledo were buried in (later retrieved from their tombs and preserved—a rare chance to see original 16th-century garments).

Argenti/Silverworks Museum

This Medici treasure chest (on the ground and mezzanine floors) holds items such as jeweled crucifixes, exotic porcelain, rock-crystal goblets, and gilded ostrich eggs, made to entertain fans of the applied arts.

Boboli and Bardini Gardens

For those eager to escape the halls upon halls of fancy apartments, two adjoining gardens are located behind the palace. Enter the Boboli Gardens directly from the Pitti Palace's courtyard. The less-visited Bardini Gardens are higher up and farther out behind the Boboli, rising in terraces toward Piazzale Michelangelo. Both gardens are similar, providing a pleasant and shady refuge from the city heat, with statues, fountains, and scenic vistas down tree-lined avenues.

A few fun little sights are in the low-lying area to the far left as you enter the Boboli Gardens. First, near the end of the palace, is the much-photographed **Bacchus Fountain** (Fontana di Bacco, 1560), starring Cosimo I's fat dwarf jester straddling a turtle—a fitting metaphor for this heavyweight palace.

Just beyond Bacchus is the **Grotto of Buontalenti,** an artificial cave crusted with fake stalactites and copies of Michelangelo's *Prisoners,* which once stood here (and are now in the Accademia). Playful figures—a hunter with his dog, goats, a monster—seem to morph into existence from the cottage cheese-like walls. At the top of the hour (check posted schedules), the grotto gates are opened to allow five minutes of frolicking among the statues.

You can also stroll up the steep terraces directly behind the palace. From the top, you're greeted by a panoramic view of the palace and Oltrarno churches (but only peek-a-boo views of the old town center, the Palazzo Vecchio, and Duomo). On your way up, you'll pass the **amphitheater** (ringed with statues). At the top, just beyond the hillcrest, is a pleasant **rose garden** with bucolic views of the rolling Tuscan hills (punctuated by cypress trees). The small building adjoining the rose garden houses the **Porcelain Museum,** with a modest and sparsely described collection of ducal dinnerware. From here, you can follow signs around to the **Belvedere Fortress,** with even higher and better views, and the Belvedere Gate, which leads to the Bardini Gardens.

GALILEO SCIENCE MUSEUM TOUR

Museo Galilei e Istituto di Storia della Scienza

Enough art, already! Forget the Madonnas and Venuses for a while to ponder weird contraptions from the birth of modern science. The same spirit of discovery that fueled the artistic Renaissance helped free the sciences from medieval mumbo jumbo. This museum offers a historical overview of technical innovations from roughly A.D. 1000 to 1900, featuring early telescopes, clocks, experiments, and Galileo's fingers in a jar.

English majors will enjoy expanding their knowledge. Art lovers can admire the sheer beauty of functional devices. Engineers will be in hog heaven among endless arrays of gadgets. Families with little kids looking for a hands-on experience may be disappointed, but students of all ages will be amused by my feeble attempts to explain technical concepts. And admission to the museum gives you access to one of the marvels of modern science: air-conditioning.

Orientation

Cost: €9, €22 family ticket covers two adults and two kids ages 18 and under, tickets good all day, covered by Firenze Card.

Hours: Wed-Mon 9:30-18:00, Tue 9:30-13:00.

Information: Tel. 055-265-311, www.museogalileo.it.

Getting There: The museum is located one block east of the Uffizi on the north bank of the Arno River at Piazza dei Giudici 1.

Tours: The 1.5-hour English-language guided tour covers the collection plus behind-the-scenes areas, and includes demonstrations of some of the devices (€65 flat fee for 2-14 people, cash only, doesn't include museum entry, book at least a week in advance, great for kids, tel. 055-234-3723, gruppi@museogalileo.it).

Length of This Tour: Allow one hour or more (especially for those interested in science).

Starring: Galileo's telescopes, experiment models, and fingers.

The Tour Begins

The collection is on the first and second floors. Excellent descriptions are posted throughout, and engaging video screens in many rooms illustrate the inventions and scientific principles.

Take advantage of the helpful English-speaking docents. They're available to answer questions about how these scientific gadgets work. In fact, the staff is happy that you're there to see this museum and not just lost on your way to the Uffizi.

• *Buy your ticket and head up the stairs to the first floor, Room I.*

Room I: The Medici Collections

In this room, you immediately get a sense of the variety of devices in the collection: everything from a big wooden quadrant and

maps to optical illusions and old science books. These belonged to that trendsetting family, the Medici, who always seemed at the forefront of Europe's arts and sciences. Many of the objects we'll see measured the world around us—the height of distant mountains, the length of a man's arm, the movement of the sun and stars across the sky. In fact, one of the bold first steps in science was to observe nature and measure it. What scientists found was that nature—seemingly ever-changing and chaotic—actually behaves in an orderly way, following rather simple mathematical formulas.

Room II: Astronomy and Time

This room has (triangle-shaped) quadrants and (round) astrolabes. In medieval times, sailors used these to help find their way at sea. They mapped the constellations as a starting point. Next they had to figure out where they stood in relation to those stars.

Quadrants: A *quad*-rant is one-*fourth* of a 360-degree circle, or 90 degrees. You'd grab this wedge-shaped object by its curved edge, point it away from you, and sight along the top edge toward, say, a distant tower or star. Then you'd read the scale etched along the curved edge to find how many degrees above the horizon the object was.

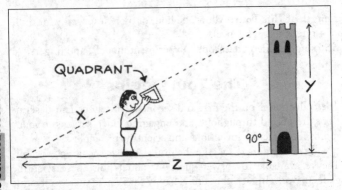

The quadrant *(quadrante)* measured the triangle formed by you, the horizon, and a distant object. Once you knew at least three of the triangle's six variables (three angles and three sides), you could calculate the others. (That's trigonometry.) Armed with this knowledge, you could use the quadrant to measure all kinds of things. On land, you could calculate how high or how far away a building was. At sea, you could figure your position relative to the sun and stars.

Astrolabes: Astrolabes—invented by the ancient Greeks and pioneered by medieval Arab sailors—combined a quadrant with a map of the sky (a star chart), allowing you to calculate your position against the stars without doing all the math. You'd hang the metal disk from your thumb and sight along the central crossbeam, locate a star, then read its altitude above the horizon on the measuring scale etched around the rim.

Next, you'd enter this information by turning a little handle on the astrolabe's face. This set the wheels-within-wheels into motion, and the constellations would spin across a backdrop of coordinates. You'd keep turning until the astrolabe mirrored the current heavens. With your known coordinates dialed in, the astrolabe calculated the unknowns, and you could read out your position along the rim.

In the center display case, find the celestial globe, the oldest object in the collection (1085 A.D.). Knowing the position of the stars and sun (using the astrolabe and celestial globe) also revealed the current time of day, which was especially useful for Arab traders (i.e., Muslims) in their daily prayers.

• *Continue to Room III, dominated by a big globe.*

Room III: The Representation of the World

The big globe is an **armillary sphere,** a model of the universe as conceived by ancient Greeks and medieval Europeans. You'd turn

a crank and watch the stars and planets orbit around the Earth in the center. This Earth-centered view of the universe—which matches our common-sense observations of the night sky—was codified by Ptolemy, a Greek-speaking Egyptian of the second century A.D.

Ptolemy (silent P) summed up Aristotle's knowledge of the heavens and worked out the mathematics explaining their movements. His math was complex, especially when trying to explain the planets, which occasionally lag behind the stars in their paths across the night sky. (We now know it's because fast-orbiting Earth passes the outer planets in their longer, more time-consuming orbits around the sun.)

Ptolemy's system dominated Europe for 1,500 years. It worked most of the time and fit well with medieval Christianity's human-centered theology. But, finally, Nicolaus Copernicus (and Galileo) made the mental leap to a sun-centered system. This simplified the math, explained the movement of planets, and—most importantly—changed Earthlings' conception of themselves forever.

Thanks to Columbus' voyages, the Europeans' world suddenly got bigger and rounder. Increasingly, maps began to portray the spherical world on a flat surface.

• *Pass through **Room IV**, with more globes and a map from 1459. Notice that, by this time, Europe is pretty well mapped. But south is up, the Holy Land marks the center, and the Western Hemisphere is nowhere to be found. Now enter...*

Room V: The Science of Navigation

This room has more quadrants and maps, plus a new navigational feature: clocks. By measuring time accurately, sailors could not only establish their latitude (north-south on the globe), but also their longitude (east-west).

In the 1700s, with overseas trade booming, there was a crying need for an accurate and durable clock to help in navigation. Sighting by the stars told you your latitude but was less certain on whether you were near Florence, Italy (latitude 44), or Portland, Maine (also latitude 44). You needed a way to time Earth's 24-hour rotation, to know exactly where you were on that daily journey—that is, your longitude. Reward money was offered for a good clock that could be taken to sea, and scientists sprang into action.

The longitude problem was finally solved—and a £20,000 prize won—by John Harrison of England (1693-1776), who developed the "chronometer" (not in this museum), a spring-driven clock that was set in a suspension device to keep it horizontal. It was accurate within three seconds a day, far better than any clock displayed here.

• *Room VI (The Science of Warfare) displays not weapons but surveyors' tools, crucial for plotting the trajectory of, say, a cannonball. Next up is one of the museum's highlights.*

Room VII: Galileo's New World

Galileo Galilei (1564-1642) is known as the father of modern science. His discoveries pioneered many scientific fields, and he was among the first to blend mathematics with hands-on observation of nature to find practical applications. Raised in Pisa, he achieved fame teaching at the University of Padua before working for the Grand Duke of Florence. The museum displays several of his possessions (lens, two telescopes, compass, and thermometer), models illustrating his early experiments, and his fingers, preserved in a jar.

• *Immediately to the right, look for the case containing...*

Galileo's Telescopes: Galileo was the first Earthling to see the moons of Jupiter. With a homemade telescope, he looked through

the lens and saw three moons lined up next to Jupiter. This discovery also irked the Church, which insisted that all heavenly bodies orbited the Earth. You could see Jupiter's moons with your own eyes if you simply looked through the telescope, but few church scholars bothered to do so, content to believe what they'd read in ancient books.

Galileo built these telescopes based on reports he'd read from Holland. He was the first person to seriously study the heavens with telescopes. Though these only magnified the image about 30 times ("30 power," which is less than today's binoculars), he saw Jupiter's four largest moons, Saturn's rings, the craters of the moon (which he named "seas"), and blemishes (sunspots) on the supposedly perfect sun.

• *In the same case is a...*

Pendulum Clock Model: Galileo's restless mind roamed to other subjects. It's said that during a church service in Pisa, Galileo looked up to see the cathedral's chandelier swaying slowly back and forth, like a pendulum. He noticed that a wide-but-fast arc took the same amount of time as a narrow-but-slow arc. "Hmmm. Maybe that regular pendulum motion could be used to time things..."

• *The last case on this wall contains a...*

Thermoscope: Galileo also invented the thermometer (or thermoscope—similar to the museum's 19th-century replica), though his glass tube filled with air would later be replaced by thermometers filled with mercury.

• *Across the room is a giant model of an...*

Inclined Plane: The large wooden ramp figures in one of the most enduring of scientific legends. Legend has it that Galileo dropped cannonballs from the Leaning Tower of Pisa to see whether heavier objects fall faster than lighter ones, as the ancient philosopher Aristotle (and most people) believed. In fact, Galileo probably didn't drop objects from the Leaning Tower, but likely rolled them down a wooden ramp like this reconstructed one. It slowed them down, making it easier to measure.

Rolling balls of different weights down the ramp, he timed them as they rang the bells posted along the way. (The bells are spaced increasingly far apart, but a ball—accelerating as it drops—will ring them at regular intervals.) What Galileo found is that—if you discount air resistance—all objects fall at the same rate, regardless of their weight. (It's the air resistance, not the weight, that makes a feather fall more slowly than a cannonball.)

He also found that falling objects accelerate at a regular rate (9.8 meters per second faster every second), summed up in a mathematical formula (distance is proportional to the time squared).

Galileo pioneered the art of experimentation. He built devices that could simulate nature on a small scale in a controlled laboratory setting, where natural forces could be duplicated and measured. In the following rooms, we'll see many of the experimental tools and techniques he inspired.

• *And last but not least, in the glass case perched on the column at the end of the benches, look for...*

Galileo's Fingers: Galileo is perhaps best known as a mar-

tyr for science. He popularized the belief (conceived by the Polish astronomer Nicolaus Copernicus in the early 1500s) that the Earth orbits around the sun. At the time, the Catholic Church (and most of Europe) preached an Earth-centered universe. At the age of 70, Galileo was hauled before the Inquisition in Rome and forced to kneel and publicly proclaim that the Earth did not move around the sun. As he walked away, legend has it, he whispered to his followers, "But it does move!"

A century after his death, Galileo's followers preserved his finger bone *(Dito Medio della Mano Destra di Galileo)*, displayed on an alabaster pedestal, as a kind of sacred relic in this shrine to science. (This case also holds two other fingers and a tooth that were rediscovered a few years ago.) Galileo's beliefs eventually triumphed over the Inquisition, and, appropriately, we have his right middle finger raised upward for all those blind to science.

• *Room VIII has early glassware and thermometers (which you'll explore in greater depth in Room XV). Continue on to...*

Room IX: Exploring the Physical and Biological World

This room has both telescopes (for observing objects far away) and microscopes (to see the world up close).

A **telescope** is essentially an empty tube with a lens at the far end to gather light, and another lens at the near end to magnify the image. The farther apart the lenses, the greater the magnification, which is why telescopes have increased in size over time. The longest ever built was 160 feet, but the slightest movement would jiggle the image.

Galileo used a "refracting telescope," made with lenses that bend (refract) light. Later on, scientists started using "reflecting telescopes," which were often thick-barreled, with the eyepiece sticking out the side. These telescopes use mirrors (not lenses) to bounce light rays back and forth through several lenses, thereby increasing magnification without the long tubes and distortion of refractors.

• *Ascend to the second floor and enter...*

Room X: The Lorraine Collections (Medical Science)

Look at the big table with all the drawers and jars in the glass case in the center of the room. Back when the same guy who cut your

hair removed your appendix, medicine was crude. In the 1700s, there were no anesthetics beyond a bottle of wine, nor was there any knowledge of antiseptics. The best they could do was resort to the healing powers of herbs and plants. Consider what was thought to be therapeutic in the 1700s: cocaine, anise, poisonous plants like belladonna, tea, and ipecac.

The room also displays models detailing the varieties of complications that could arise during childbirth. Not a pretty sight, but crucial to finding ways to save lives.

Room XI: The Spectacle of Science

This room is filled with odd-looking devices used by scientists to instruct and amaze. Chief among them, in the middle of the room, are the turn-the-crank machines dealing with electricity.

Electromagnetism: Lightning, magnets, and static cling mystified humans for millennia. Little did they know that these quite different phenomena are all generated by the same invisible force—electromagnetism.

In the 1700s, scientists began to study, harness, and play with electricity. As a popular party amusement, they devised big static electricity-generating machines. You turned a crank to spin a glass disk, which rubbed against silk cloth and generated static electricity. The electricity could then be stored in a glass Leyden jar (a jar coated with metal and filled with water). A metal rod sticking out of the top of the jar gave off a small charge when touched, enough to create a spark, shock a party guest, or tenderize a turkey (as Ben Franklin attempted one Thanksgiving). But such static generators could never produce enough electricity for practical use.

• *In the corner near where you entered, look for a...*

Model for Demonstrating Newton's Mechanics: Isaac Newton (1642-1727) explained all of the universe's motion ("mechanics")—from spinning planets to rolling rocks—in a few simple mathematical formulas.

The museum's collision balls (the big wooden frame with hanging balls—labeled *Elastic and Inelastic Collisions Apparatus*), a popular desktop toy in the 1970s, demonstrate Newton's three famous laws.

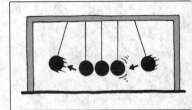

1. Inertia: The balls just sit there unless something moves them, and once they're set in motion, they'll keep moving the same way until something stops them.

2. Force = Mass × Acceleration: The harder you strike the balls, the more they accelerate (change speeds). Strike with two balls to pack twice the punch.

3. For every action, there's an equal and opposite reaction: When one ball swings in and strikes the rest, the ball at the other end swings out, then returns and strikes back.

• *Room XII has devices formerly used to teach the "new" physics of Newton. In Room XIII is another instructive model.*

Room XIII: The Archimedes Screw Model

Back in third-century B.C. Greece, Archimedes—the man who gave us the phrase "Eureka!" ("I've found it!")—invented a way

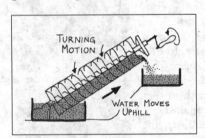

to pump water that's still occasionally used today. It's a screw in a cylinder. Simply turn the handle and the screw spins, channeling the water up in a spiral path (as seen in the video in Room XII). Dutch windmills powered big Archimedes screws to push water over dikes, reclaiming land from the sea.

Room XIV: Precision Instruments

This room shows the development of big reflecting **telescopes** and finer **microscopes.**

One day, a Dutchman picked something from his teeth, looked at it under his crude microscope, and discovered a mini-universe, crawling with thousands of "very little animalcules, very prettily a-moving" (i.e., bacteria and protozoa). Antonie van Leeuwenhoek (1632-1723) popularized the microscope, finding that fleas have fleas, semen contains sperm, and one-celled creatures are our fellow animals.

Microscopes can be either simple or compound. A simple one is just a single convex lens—what we'd call a magnifying glass. A compound microscope contains two (or more) lenses in a tube, working like a telescope: One lens magnifies the object, and the eyepiece lens magnifies the magnified image. Van Leeuwenhoek opted for a simple microscope (not in this museum), since early compound ones often blurred and colored objects around the edges. His glass bead-size lens could make a flea look 275 times bigger.

Room XV: Atmosphere and Light

Even nature's most changeable force—the weather—was analyzed by human reason, using thermometers and barometers.

Thermometers: You'll see many interesting thermometers—spiral ones, tall ones, and skinny ones on distinctive bases. All operate on the basic principle that heat expands things. So, liquid in a closed glass tube will expand and climb upward as the temperature rises.

Galileo's early thermoscope was not hermetically sealed, so it was too easily affected by changing air pressure. So scientists experimented with various liquids in a vacuum tube—first water, then alcohol. Finally, Gabriel Fahrenheit (1686-1736) tried mercury, the densest liquid, which expands evenly. He set his scale to the freezing point of a water/salt/ice mixture (zero degrees) and his own body temperature (96 degrees). With these parameters, water froze at 32 degrees and boiled at 212 degrees. Anders Celsius (1701-1744) used water as the standard, and called the freezing point 0 and the boiling point 100.

Barometers: To make a barometer, take a long, skinny glass tube (like the ones in the wood frames), fill it with liquid mercury, then turn it upside-down and put the open end into a bowlful of more mercury. The column of mercury does not drain out because the air in the room "pushes back," pressing down on the surface of the mercury in the bowl.

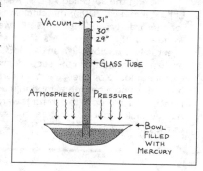

Changing air pressure signals a shift in the weather. Hot air expands, pressing down harder on the mercury's surface, thereby causing the mercury column to rise above 30 inches; this indicates the "pushing away" of clouds and points to good, dry weather. Low pressure

Tick, Tock, Clocks

Pop into the museum's ground-floor **bookshop,** where some impressive clocks are on display.

In an ever-changing universe, what is constant enough to measure the passage of time? The sun and stars passing over every 24 hours works for calendar time, but not for hours, minutes, or seconds. Since the time of the Greeks, man used sundials, or the steady flow of water or sand through an opening, but these were only approximate.

In medieval times, humans invented mechanical clocks that work similarly to the classic grandfather clock. The clock is powered by suspended weights that slowly "fall," producing enough energy to turn a series of cogwheels that methodically move the clock hands around the dial. The whole thing is regulated by a pendulum rocking back and forth, once a second. A clock has three essential components:

1. Power (falling weights).
2. An "escapement" (the cogs that transform the "falling" power into turning power).
3. A regulator (swinging pendulum) that keeps the gears turning evenly.

Later clocks were powered by a metal spring that slowly uncoiled (also used in most watches). The power was regulated by a pendulum—Galileo's contribution. Unfortunately, a rocking pendulum on a rocking ship wasn't going to work.

During the so-called Age of Reason (1600s) and Age of Enlightenment (1700s), the clock was the perfect metaphor for the orderly workings of God's well-crafted universe. So, wondered the philosophers/scientists, would the universe eventually wind down like an old clock? In fact, in every energy exchange (as stated in the second law of thermodynamics), a certain amount of energy is transformed into nonrecyclable heat, meaning a perpetual motion machine is impossible. This principle of entropy (the trend toward dissipation of energy) has led philosophers to ponder the eventual cold, lifeless fate of the universe itself.

lets the mercury drop, warning of rain. If you have a barometer at home, it probably has a round dial with a needle (or a digital read-out), but it operates on a similar principle.

• *In the next room, you'll find (among magnets, generators, and small machines) a couple of early batteries.*

Room XVI: Electricity

Alessandro Volta (1745-1827) built the first battery in Europe. (Although the museum does not have one of Volta's batteries, it does have a couple of similar devices made by Florence's own Leopoldo Nobili.) A battery generates electricity from a chemical reaction. Volta (and others) stacked metal disks of zinc and copper between disks of cardboard soaked with salt water. The zinc slowly dissolves, releasing electrons into the liquid. Hook a wire to each end of the battery, and the current flows. When the zinc is gone, your battery is dead.

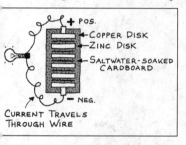

+ POS.
COPPER DISK
ZINC DISK
SALTWATER-SOAKED CARDBOARD
— NEG.
CURRENT TRAVELS THROUGH WIRE

England's Michael Faraday (c. 1831) created the first true electric motor, which could generate electricity by moving a magnet through a coil of copper wire. Faraday shocked the world (and occasionally himself), and his invention soon led to the production of electricity on a large scale.

Room XVII: Making Science Useful

Chemistry: Antoine Lavoisier (1743-1794) was the Galileo of chemistry, introducing sound methodology and transforming the mumbo jumbo of medieval alchemy into hard science. He created the precursor to our modern periodic table of the elements and used the standardized terminology of suffixes that describe the different forms a single element can take (sulfur, sulf-ide, sulf-ate, sulf-uric, etc.).

The large object with lenses nearby was used, I believe, by 18th-century dukes to burn bugs.

• *In the case to the left of this primitive bug zapper, look for the metal rod in a wooden box.*

Standard Meter: Much of the purpose of science is to use constants to measure an ever-changing universe. For centuries, one of these constants was the meter-long metal rod, established in 1790 as the fundamental unit by which all distances are measured.

The rod is exactly one meter. Or 39.37 inches. Or 1/1,000th of the distance from the Galileo Science Museum to *David*. Or 1/10,000,000th of the distance from the equator to the North Pole. Or, according to the updated definition from 1960, a meter is the length of 1,650,763.73 wavelengths in a vacuum of the orange-red radiation of krypton 86.

Ain't science wonderful?

• *On the way out,* **Room XVIII** *is filled with novelty pieces—a barometer hidden in a walking stick, a portable pharmacy kit, and an early air-conditioner (ventilator/fan). Downstairs, you'll pass through a small kids' zone with interactive exhibits.*

SLEEPING IN FLORENCE

Most of my recommended hotels are grouped in central Florence, to either side of the River Arno. Around the big sights you'll find tourist-friendly options, just steps away from everything you came to Florence to see. And across the Arno in the Oltrarno area—between the Pitti Palace and Ponte Vecchio—good budget alternatives dot an area with a neighborly vibe. If arriving by train, you can either walk (usually around 10-20 minutes) or take a taxi (roughly €6-8) to reach most of my recommended accommodations.

Outside the city, I list several rustic and serene *agriturismi*—rural farms offering accommodations in the Tuscan countryside south of Florence.

The accommodations listed here cluster around the €100-150 range, but include everything from €25 bunks to deluxe €350 doubles. Competition among hotels is stiff—when things slow down, fancy hotels drop their prices and become a much better value for travelers than the cheap, low-end places. For some travelers, short-term, Airbnb-type rentals can be a good alternative; search for places in my recommended hotel neighborhoods.

Book any accommodations well in advance, especially if you'll be traveling during peak season or if your trip coincides with a major holiday or festival (see page 673). Note, though, that Florence can be busy any time of year.

I rank accommodations from **$** budget to **$$$$** splurge. To get the best deal, contact my family-run hotels directly by phone or email. By going direct, the owner avoids a roughly 20 percent commission and may be able to offer you a discount. For more information and tips on hotel rates and deals, making reservations, and finding a short-term rental, see page 622.

Museumgoers Take Note: Your hotelier may be able to reserve entry times for you at the Uffizi Gallery and the Accademia (Michelangelo's *David*). This can be handy if you don't plan to get a Firenze Card and don't want to bother with making reservations yourself (see page 30). Ask about it when you book your room. Most likely the hotelier will book your museum visits by phone, then give you a confirmation number that you'll exchange for a ticket at the museum. Your hotel may charge a fee for this service.

Beware of Bugs: Florence is notorious for its mosquitoes. If your hotel lacks air-conditioning, request a fan and don't open your windows, especially at night. Many hotels furnish a small plug-in bulb *(zanzariere)*—usually set in the ashtray—that helps keep the bloodsuckers at bay. If not, you can purchase one cheaply at any pharmacy *(farmacia)*.

AROUND THE DUOMO

The following places are within a block of Florence's biggest church and main landmark. While touristy—and expensive—this location puts just about everything in town at your doorstep.

$$$$ Palazzo Niccolini al Duomo, one of five elite Historic Residence Hotels in Florence, is run by the Niccolini di Camugliano family. The lounge (where free chamomile tea is served in the evenings) is palatial, but the six rooms and seven suites, while splendid, vary wildly in size and quality. If you have the money and want a Florentine palace to call home, this can be a good bet (RS%, elevator, air-con, pay parking—reserve ahead, Via dei Servi 2, tel. 055-282-412, www.niccolinidomepalace.com, info@niccolinidomepalace.com).

$$$$ Hotel Duomo's 24 rooms are modern and comfortable enough, but you're paying for the location and the views—the Duomo looms like a monster outside the hotel's windows. If staying here, you might as well spring the extra €20 for a "superior" room with a view (RS%, air-con, historic elevator, Piazza del Duomo 1, fourth floor, tel. 055-219-922, www.hotelduomofirenze.it, info@hotelduomofirenze.it; Paolo, Gilvaneide, and Federico).

$$$ Soggiorno Battistero rents seven simple yet pristine rooms, most with great views, overlooking the Baptistery and the Duomo square. Request a view or a quieter room in the back when you book, but keep in mind there's always some noise in the city center. It's a minimalist place with no public spaces or full-time reception, but the location is great (RS%, air-con, elevator, Piazza San Giovanni 1, third floor, tel. 055-295-143, www.soggiornobattistero.it, info@soggiornobattistero.it, Francesco).

$$$ Residenza Giotto B&B offers a well-priced chance to stay on Florence's upscale shopping drag, Via Roma. Occupying the top floor of a 19th-century building, this place has six bright rooms (three with Duomo views) and a terrace with knockout views of the Duomo's tower. Reception is generally open Mon-Sat 9:00-17:00 and Sun 9:00-13:00; let them know your arrival time in advance (RS%, air-con, elevator, Via Roma 6, tel. 055-214-593, www.residenzagiotto.it, info@residenzagiotto.it, Giorgio).

$$ La Residenza del Proconsolo B&B has six older-feeling rooms a minute from the Duomo (three rooms have Duomo views). The place lacks public spaces, but the rooms are quite large and nice—perfect for eating breakfast, which is served in your room (extra cost for slightly larger "deluxe" with view, air-con, no elevator, Via del Proconsolo 18 black, tel. 055-264-5657, www.proconsolo.com, info@proconsolo.com, Susie).

NORTH OF THE DUOMO
Near the Accademia

$$$ Hotel dei Macchiaioli offers 15 fresh and spacious rooms on one high-ceilinged, noble floor in a restored palazzo owned for generations by a well-to-do Florentine family. You'll eat breakfast under original frescoed ceilings while enjoying modern comforts (RS%, air-con, Via Cavour 21, tel. 055-213-154, www.hoteldeimacchiaioli.com, info@hoteldeimacchiaioli.com, helpful Francesca and Paolo).

$$$ Hotel Loggiato dei Serviti, at a prestigious address on the most Renaissance-y square in town, gives you Old World ro-

mance with hair dryers. Stone stairways lead you under open-beam ceilings through this 16th-century monastery's monumental public rooms. The 32 well-worn rooms are both rickety and characteristic. The hotel staff is professional yet warm (RS%, family rooms, elevator, pay valet parking, Piazza S.S. Annunziata 3, tel. 055-289-592, www.loggiatodeiservitihotel.it, info@loggiatodeiservitihotel.it; Chiara B., Chiara V., and Alex). Attentive Daniel takes care

SLEEPING

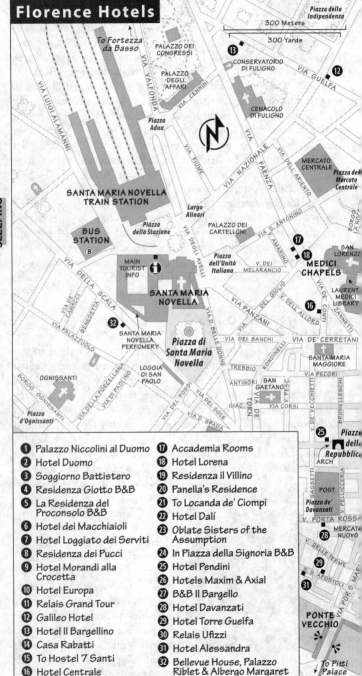

Florence Hotels

300 Meters
300 Yards

1 Palazzo Niccolini al Duomo
2 Hotel Duomo
3 Soggiorno Battistero
4 Residenza Giotto B&B
5 La Residenza del Proconsolo B&B
6 Hotel dei Macchiaioli
7 Hotel Loggiato dei Serviti
8 Residenza dei Pucci
9 Hotel Morandi alla Crocetta
10 Hotel Europa
11 Relais Grand Tour
12 Galileo Hotel
13 Hotel Il Bargellino
14 Casa Rabatti
15 To Hostel 7 Santi
16 Hotel Centrale
17 Accademia Rooms
18 Hotel Lorena
19 Residenza il Villino
20 Panella's Residence
21 To Locanda de' Ciompi
22 Hotel Dalí
23 Oblate Sisters of the Assumption
24 In Piazza della Signoria B&B
25 Hotel Pendini
26 Hotels Maxim & Axial
27 B&B Il Bargello
28 Hotel Davanzati
29 Hotel Torre Guelfa
30 Relais Ufizzi
31 Hotel Alessandra
32 Bellevue House, Palazzo Riblet & Albergo Margaret

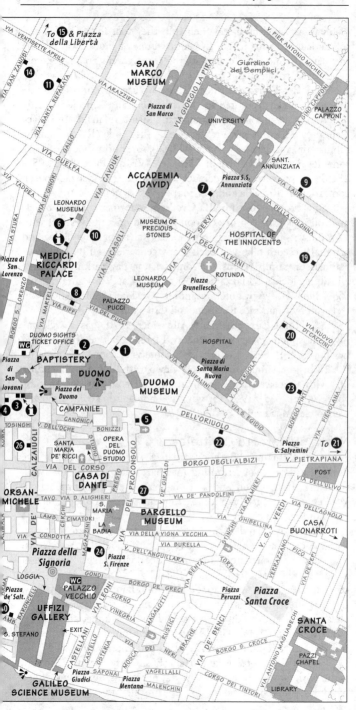

SLEEPING

of breakfast and the bar. When full, they rent five spacious and sophisticated rooms in a 17th-century annex a block away. While they lack the monastic mystique, the annex rooms are bigger, gorgeously refurnished, and cost the same.

$$$ Residenza dei Pucci rents 13 pleasant rooms (each one different) spread over three floors (with no elevator). The decor, a mix of soothing earth tones and aristocratic furniture, makes this place feel upscale for this price range (RS%—use code "RICK," family rooms, air-con, reception open 9:00-20:00, shorter hours off-season—let them know if you'll arrive late, Via dei Pucci 9, tel. 055-281-886, www.residenzadeipucci.com, info@residenzadeipucci.com, friendly Rossella and Marina).

$$$ Hotel Morandi alla Crocetta, a former convent, envelops you in a 16th-century cocoon. Located on a quiet street with 12 rooms, its period furnishings, squeaky clean parquet floors, and original frescoes take you back a few centuries and up a few social classes (family rooms, air-con, elevator, pay parking—reserve ahead, a block off Piazza S.S. Annunziata at Via Laura 50, tel. 055-234-4747, www.hotelmorandi.it, welcome@hotelmorandi.it, well-run by Maurizio, Rolando, and Cristiano).

$$ Hotel Europa, family run since 1970, has a welcoming atmosphere fostered by cheery Florence native Miriam and her husband Robert. The breakfast room is spacious, and most of the 12 bright, simple rooms have views of the Duomo, including one with a terrace (RS%, family rooms, air-con, elevator, Via Cavour 14, tel. 055-239-6715, www.webhoteleuropa.com, firenze@webhoteleuropa.com).

North of Mercato Centrale

After dark, this neighborhood can feel a little deserted, but I've never heard of anyone running into harm here. It's a short walk from the train station and a stroll to all the sightseeing action. While workaday, it's practical, with plenty of good budget restaurants and markets nearby.

$$ Relais Grand Tour has four charmingly eclectic rooms on a nondescript street between the train station and the Accademia. This cozy and thoughtfully appointed B&B will make you feel right at home and is great for families. The delightful and spacious suites come with a garden ambience on the ground floor (RS%, cash only, family suites, includes breakfast voucher for the corner bar, for cheaper rates ask to skip breakfast and daily cleaning, air-con, Via Santa Reparata 21, tel. 055-283-955, www.florencegrandtour.com, info@florencegrandtour.com, Cristina and Giuseppe).

$$ Galileo Hotel, a comfortable business hotel with 31 rooms, is run with familial warmth (RS%, family rooms, quadruple-paned windows shut out street noise, air-con, elevator, Via Nazionale

22a, tel. 055-496-645, www.galileohotel.it, info@galileohotel.it, Vincenzo).

$ Hotel Il Bargellino, run by Bostonian Carmel and her Italian husband Pino, is a good-value place with an old-time convivial atmosphere. In a residential neighborhood within walking distance of the center, the 10 summery rooms are decorated with funky antiques and Pino's modern paintings. Guests enjoy relaxing and chatting on the big, breezy, momentum-slowing terrace adorned with plants and lemon shrubs (RS%, cheaper rooms with shared bath, no breakfast, air-con extra, north of the train station at Via Guelfa 87, tel. 055-238-2658, www.ilbargellino.com, carmel@ilbargellino.com).

$ Casa Rabatti is the ultimate if you always wanted to have a Florentine mama. Its three simple, clean rooms are run with warmth by Marcella. This is a great place to practice your Italian: Marcella speaks minimal English but loves to invite guests into her kitchen to chat. Seeing decades of my family Christmas cards on their walls, I'm reminded of how long she has been keeping budget travelers happy (RS%, cheaper rooms with shared bath, family rooms, cash only but secure reservation with credit card, no breakfast, fans available, 5 blocks from station at Via San Zanobi 48 black, tel. 055-212-393, www.casarabatti.it, casarabatti@inwind.it). In the same building on the ground floor, she also rents three modern and spacious **$$ apartments** with kitchenettes and access to a tranquil garden—ideal for longer stays.

Hostel: Calling itself a "travelers' haven," **¢ Hostel 7 Santi** fills a former convent, but you'll feel like you're in an old school. It offers some of the best cheap beds in town, is friendly to older travelers, and comes with the services you'd expect in a big, modern hostel, including self-serve laundry. It's in a more residential neighborhood near the Campo di Marte stadium, about a 10-minute bus ride from the center (private rooms available, breakfast and dinner extra, no curfew; Viale dei Mille 11—from train station, take bus #10, #17, or #20, direction: Campo di Marte, to bus stop Chiesa dei Sette Santi; tel. 055-504-8452, www.7santi.com, info@7santi.com).

Near the Medici Chapels

This touristy zone has lots of budget and midrange hotels catering to an international clientele, stacks of basic trattorias, and easy access to major sights (just steps from the Medici Chapels, Basilica of San Lorenzo, and Mercato Centrale, and only a bit farther to the biggies). The mostly pedestrianized Via Faenza is the spine of this neighborhood, with lots of tourist services.

$$$$ Hotel Centrale is indeed central, just a short walk from the Duomo. The 35 spacious but overpriced rooms—with a tasteful mix of old and new decor—are over a businesslike conference center (RS%, air-con, elevator, Via dei Conti 3, check in at big front desk on ground floor, tel. 055-215-761, www.hotelcentralefirenze. it, info@hotelcentralefirenze.it, Margherita and Roberto).

$$$ **Accademia Rooms** has five quiet rooms clustered around a sunny courtyard. While overpriced and getting a bit long in the tooth, it has a convenient location (RS%, air-con, no elevator, Piazza Madonna degli Aldobrandini 1, tel. 055-293-451, www. accademiarooms.com, info@accademiarooms.com, Tea).

$ **Hotel Lorena,** just across from the Medici Chapels, has 19 simple, well-worn rooms (six with shared bathrooms) and a tiny lobby. Though it feels a little like a youth hostel, it's well located, inexpensive, and run with care by the Galli family (air-con, elevator from first floor, Via Faenza 1, tel. 055-282-785, www.hotellorena. com, info@hotellorena.com).

EAST OF THE DUOMO

While convenient to the sights and offering a good value, these places are mostly along nondescript urban streets, lacking the grit, charm, or glitz of some of my other recommended neighborhoods.

$$$ **Residenza il Villino** has 10 charming rooms and a picturesque, peaceful little courtyard. The owner, Neri, has turned part of the breakfast room into a museum-like tribute to his grandfather, a pioneer of early Italian fashion. As it's in a "little villa" (as the name implies) set back from the street, this is a quiet refuge from the bustle of Florence (RS%, family rooms, air-con, parking available, just north of Via degli Alfani at Via della Pergola 53, tel. 055-200-1116, www.ilvillino.it, info@ilvillino.it, Giovanni).

$$$ **Panella's Residence,** once a convent and today part of owner Graziella's extensive home, is a classy B&B, with five chic, romantic, and ample rooms, antique furnishings, and historic architectural touches (RS%, air-con, Via della Pergola 42, tel. 055-234-7202, mobile 345-972-1541, www.panellaresidence.com, panella_residence@yahoo.it).

$$ **Locanda de' Ciompi,** overlooking the inviting Piazza dei Ciompi in a young and lively neighborhood, is just right for travelers who want to feel like a part of the town. Alessio and daughter Lisa have five attractive rooms that are tidy, lovingly maintained, and a good value (RS%, cheaper single with private bath down the hall, includes breakfast at nearby bar, air-con, 8 blocks behind the Duomo at Via Pietrapiana 28—see map on page 18, tel. 055-263-8034, www.bbflorencefirenze.com, info@bbflorencefirenze.com).

$ **Hotel Dalí** has 10 cheery, worn rooms in a nice location for a great price. Samanta and Marco, who run this guesthouse with a charming passion and idealism, are a delight to know (request one of the quiet and spacious rooms facing the courtyard when you book, cheaper rooms with shared bath available, nearby apartments sleep 2-6 people, no breakfast, fans but no air-con, elevator, free parking, 2 blocks behind the Duomo at Via dell'Oriuolo 17 on the second floor, tel. 055-234-0706, www.hoteldali.com, hoteldali@ tin.it).

$ Oblate Sisters of the Assumption run an institutional 35-room hotel in a Renaissance building with a dreamy garden, great public spaces, appropriately simple rooms, and a quiet, prayerful ambience (family rooms, single beds only, air-con, elevator, Wi-Fi with suggested donation, 23:30 curfew, limited pay parking—request when you book, Borgo Pinti 15, tel. 055-248-0582, www.bb-oblate.com, sroblateborgopinti@virgilio.it). As there's no night porter, it's best to time your arrival and departure to occur during typical business hours.

SOUTH OF THE DUOMO
Between the Duomo and Piazza della Signoria

Buried in the narrow, characteristic lanes in the very heart of town, these are the most central of my accommodations recommendations (and therefore a little overpriced). While this location is worth the extra cost for many, nearly every hotel I recommend can be considered central given Florence's walkable, essentially traffic-free core.

$$$$ In Piazza della Signoria B&B, in a stellar location overlooking Piazza della Signoria, is peaceful, refined, and homey. The service is friendly, but the rates are high. "Partial view" rooms, while slightly larger, require craning your neck to see anything and aren't worth the extra euros. Guests enjoy socializing at the big, shared breakfast table (RS%, family apartments, air-con, tiny elevator, Via dei Magazzini 2, tel. 055-239-9546, mobile 348-321-0565, www.inpiazzadellasignoria.com, info@inpiazzadellasignoria.com, Sonia and Alessandro).

$$$$ Hotel Pendini, with three stars and 44 plush, flowery rooms, fills the top floor of a grand building overlooking Piazza della Repubblica that was built to celebrate Italian unification in the late 19th century. This place just feels classy; as you walk into the lobby, it's as if you're walking back in time. While pricey, this level of elegance makes it a good value for those looking to indulge (RS%, "deluxe" rooms come with square view and noise, family rooms, air-con, elevator, Via degli Strozzi 2, tel. 055-211-170, www.hotelpendini.it, info@hotelpendini.it).

$$$ Hotel Maxim, run by the Maoli family since 1981, has 26 straightforward rooms in a good location on the main pedestrian drag. Its narrow, painting-lined halls and cozy lounge have old Florentine charm (RS%—use code "RICK," family rooms, air-con, elevator, Via de' Calzaiuoli 11, tel. 055-217-474, www. hotelmaximfirenze.it, reservation@hotelmaximfirenze.it, Chiara).

$$$ Hotel Axial, two floors below its sister Hotel Maxim, has 14 rooms and a more forgettable, businesslike, modern feel at comparable rates (RS%—use code "RICK," air-con, elevator, Via de' Calzaiuoli 11, tel. 055-218-984, www.hotelaxial.it, info@ hotelaxial.it, Nicola).

$$ B&B Il Bargello is a home away from home, run by friendly and helpful Canadian expat Gabriella. Hike up three long flights (no elevator) to reach six smart, relaxing rooms. Gabriella offers a cozy living room, a communal kitchenette, and an inviting rooftop terrace with close-up views of Florence's towers (RS%, fully equipped apartment across the hall sleeps up to six with one shared bathroom; air-con, 20 yards off Via Proconsolo at Via de' Pandolfini 33 black, tel. 055-215-330, mobile 339-175-3110, www. firenze-bedandbreakfast.it, info@firenze-bedandbreakfast.it).

Near Ponte Vecchio

This sleepy zone is handy to several sights and some fine shopping streets (from top-end boutiques to more characteristic hole-in-the-wall shops), though it's accordingly pricey and lacks a neighborhood feel of its own.

$$$$ Hotel Davanzati, bright and shiny with artistic touches, has 25 cheerful rooms with all the comforts. The place is a family affair, thoughtfully run by friendly Tommaso and father Fabrizio, who offer drinks and snacks each evening at their candlelit happy hour, plus lots of other extras (RS%, family rooms, free tablets in every room, free on-demand videos—including my travel shows about Italy—on your room TV, air-con, 20 steep steps to the elevator, handy room fridges, next to Piazza Davanzati at Via Porta Rossa 5—easy to miss so watch for low-profile sign above the door, tel. 055-286-666, www.hoteldavanzati.it, info@hoteldavanzati.it).

$$$$ Hotel Torre Guelfa has grand public spaces and is topped by a fun medieval tower with a panoramic rooftop terrace (72 stairs take you up—and back 720 years).  Its 31 pricey rooms vary wildly in size and furnishings, but most come with the noise of the city center. Room 315, with a private terrace, is worth reserving several months in advance (RS%, family rooms, air-con, elevator, a couple of blocks northwest of Ponte Vecchio, Borgo S.S. Apostoli 8, tel. 055-239-6338, www. hoteltorreguelfa.com, info@hoteltorreguelfa. com, Niccolo and Barbara).

$$$$ Relais Uffizi is a peaceful little gem, offering a friendly welcome and tight maze of 15 classy rooms tucked away down a tiny alley off Piazza della Signoria. The lounge has a huge window overlooking the action in the piazza—a unique view (family rooms, air-con, elevator; official address is Chiasso del Buco 16—from the square, go down tiny Chiasso de Baroncelli lane—right of the loggia—and after 50 yards turn right through the arch and look for entrance on your right; tel. 055-267-6239, www.relaisuffizi.it, info@relaisuffizi.it, charming Alessandro and Elizabetta).

$$$ **Hotel Alessandra** is a tranquil and sprawling place, occupying part of a 16th-century building with 27 big, old-school rooms with frescoes and a tiny Arno-view terrace (family rooms, air-con, 30 steps to the elevator, Borgo S.S. Apostoli 17, tel. 055-283-438, www.hotelalessandra.com, info@hotelalessandra.com; Anna, son Andrea, and spunky Monti).

NEAR SANTA MARIA NOVELLA

These fine, charming little budget options are around the corner from Santa Maria Novella, near the train station. The sweet-smelling Farmacia di Santa Maria Novella perfumery is just across the street.

$$ **Bellevue House** is a third-floor (no elevator) oasis of tranquility, with six spacious, old-fashioned rooms flanking a long, mellow-yellow lobby. It's a peaceful home away from home, thoughtfully run by the Michel family (RS%, family rooms, no breakfast, air-con, Via della Scala 21, tel. 055-260-8932, www.bellevuehouse.it, info@bellevuehouse.it; Luciano, Susan, and Alessandro). Press the bell at street level, and they'll carry up your bags. On a lower floor, their other property, $$ **Palazzo Riblet,** offers three upscale rooms with frescoes and elegant furnishings (tel. 055-260-8932, www.palazzoriblet.it, info@palazzoriblet.it).

$$ **Albergo Margaret,** homey yet minimalist, offers seven tidy, simple rooms but no public lounge or breakfast (RS%, some cheaper rooms with shower but toilet down the hall, apartment, air-con in most rooms, Via della Scala 25, tel. 055-210-138, www.hotel-margaret.it, info@hotel-margaret.it; Francesco and Graziano).

THE OLTRARNO

Across the river in the Oltrarno area, between the Pitti Palace and Ponte Vecchio, you'll find small, traditional crafts shops, neighborly piazzas, and family eateries. The following places are walkable from Ponte Vecchio. Only the first two are real hotels—the rest are a ragtag gang of budget alternatives.

$$$$ **Palazzo Guadagni,** perched high above Piazza Santo Spirito, is a romantic, Grand Tour retreat from modern Florence. The 15 refined rooms are spacious, with antique furnishings and

Oltrarno Hotels & Restaurants

1 Palazzo Guadagni
2 Hotel la Scaletta
3 To Hotel Silla, Via di San Niccolò Eateries, Zeb Wine Bar; Negroni & Zoe Nightclubs
4 Soggiorno Alessandra
5 Casa Santo Nome di Gesù
6 Istituto Gould

7 Ostello Santa Monaca
8 Signorvino
9 Golden View Open Bar
10 Osteria Ponte Vecchio
11 Tamerò
12 Gusta Osteria
13 Trattoria Casalinga

frescoes. While the ample, chandeliered public spaces are pleasant, the highlight is their panoramic wrap-around loggia, a terrace with comfy, stay-awhile seating and lovely views (RS%, air-con, elevator, Piazza Santo Spirito 9, tel. 055-265-8376, www.palazzoguadagni. com, info@palazzoguadagni.com).

$$$$ Hotel la Scaletta has 36 pricey, sleek rooms hiding in a tortured floor plan. Their fabulous rooftop terrace overlooks the Boboli Gardens (RS%, family suites, breakfast extra, air-con, elevator, Via de' Guicciardini 13, tel. 055-283-028, www. hotellascaletta.it, info@hotellascaletta.it, Sara).

$$$ Hotel Silla is a classic three-star hotel with 36 cheery, spacious rooms. Across the river from Santa Croce Church, it has a breezy terrace and faces the river, overlooking a small park, with

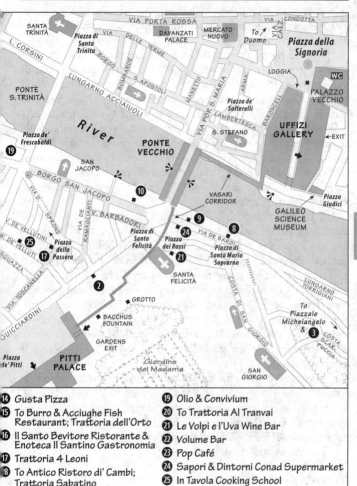

free coffee and tea for guests in the late afternoon. The surrounding neighborhood can be a bit noisy (RS%—use promo code "RICK," air-con, elevator, pricey self-service washing machine, pay parking, Via dei Renai 5, for location see map on page 278, tel. 055-234-2888, www.hotelsilla.it, hotelsilla@hotelsilla.it; Laura, Chiara, Massimo, and Stefano).

$ Soggiorno Alessandra has five bright, comfy, and smallish rooms. Because of its double-paned windows, you'll hardly notice the traffic noise (cheaper rooms with shared bath, family rooms, includes basic breakfast in room, air-con, no elevator; there's no formal reception, so let them know what time you'll be arriving; just past the Carraia Bridge at Via Borgo San Frediano 6, tel. 055-

290-424, www.soggiornoalessandra.it, info@soggiornoalessandra.it, Alessandra).

$ Casa Santo Nome di Gesù is a grand, 25-room convent whose sisters—Franciscan Missionaries of Mary—are thankful to rent rooms to tourists. Staying in this 15th-century palace, you'll be immersed in the tranquil atmosphere created by a huge, peaceful garden, generous and prayerful public spaces, and smiling nuns. As with the Istituto Gould, next, it's a good value and understandably popular—it's best to reserve a couple of months in advance (family rooms, no air-con but rooms have fans, elevator, memorable convent-like breakfast room, 1:00 in the morning curfew, pay parking, Piazza del Carmine 21, tel. 055-213-856, www.fmmfirenze.it, info@fmmfirenze.it).

$ Istituto Gould is a Protestant Church-run place with 40 clean and spartan rooms that have twin beds and modern facilities. It's located in a 17th-century palace overlooking a beautiful garden courtyard. The complex also houses kids from troubled homes, and proceeds raised from renting rooms help fund that important work (extra for garden rooms that are quieter and have air-con, family rooms, breakfast extra, non-air-con rooms have fans, Wi-Fi in lobby only, Via dei Serragli 49, tel. 055-212-576, www.firenzeforesteria.it, info@firenzeforesteria.it). If you can't arrive when the office is open (daily 9:00-13:00 & 15:00-19:30), they'll email you a code.

Hostel: ¢ Ostello Santa Monaca is a well-run, institutional-feeling hostel a long block east of the Brancacci Chapel. As clean as its guests, it attracts a young backpacking crowd (10:00-14:00 lock-out, 2:00 in the morning curfew, bike rental, Via Santa Monaca 6, tel. 055-268-338, www.ostellosantamonaca.com, info@ostellosantamonaca.com).

RURAL *AGRITURISMI*

The Tuscan countryside south of Florence is loaded with enticing rural farms offering accommodations, called *agriturismi* (for details, see page 626).

The following places are south of Florence and within 30 minutes of the city. The rustic and cozy **$$$$ Villa Salvadonica** has a gorgeous setting overlooking rolling Tuscan hills (Via Grevigiana 82, Mercatale Val di Pesa, tel. 055-821-8039, www.salvadonica.com, info@salvadonica.it). **$$$ Villa Il Poggiale** is a serene manor house with classy and spacious rooms and expansive countryside views (Via Empolese 69, San Casciano Val di Pesa, tel. 055-828-311, www.villailpoggiale.it, villailpoggiale@villailpoggiale.it). The spa hotel **$$$$ Villa I Barronci** offers a relaxing respite from sightseeing (Via Sorripa 10, San Casciano Val di Pesa, tel. 055-820-598, www.ibarronci.com, info@ibarronci.com).

Another option about 45 minutes south of Florence is in the Chianti region: **$$$ I Greppi di Silli** is a lovely, family-run *agriturismo* set among rolling hills. Owners Anna and Giuliano Alfani cultivate grapes and olive trees, and offer six carefully remodeled apartments with beds for 2-6 people, some with panoramic views and/or terraces; a seventh apartment (sleeps 8) is a mile away in an old country house (one-week minimum—Sat-to-Sat—in July-Aug, generally 4-night minimum at other times; breakfast extra, pool, kids play area, table tennis, bocce-ball court, loaner bikes, weekly farm dinners, Via Vallacchio 19, near San Casciano and just outside the village of Mercatale Val di Pesa, 45-minute drive to San Gimignano and 1 hour to Siena, tel. 055-821-7956, www. igreppidisilli.it, igreppidisilli@gmail.com).

Also a 45-minute drive south of Florence is **$$ Villa il Crocicchio,** a larger *agriturismo* set amid 20 acres of vineyards, olive trees, and greenery. The friendly Gonnelli family has restored a medieval tower-turned-farmhouse into 14 characteristic rooms and apartments, while adding another nine rooms in more modern, separate buildings. All surround a swimming pool that, combined with a small play area, makes this place especially appealing to families. Tasty Tuscan dinners are served nightly and are best enjoyed with a glass of their Sangiovese wine produced on-site (RS%, family rooms, no minimum stay, air-con, closed Nov-March; from the Incisa/Reggello exit follow the signs to Via di San Siro 35, Reggello; tel. 055-866-7262, www.crocicchio.com, info@crocicchio. com, Sonia and Simona).

If you want to go farther afield, I've listed several good choices near Siena (see page 397) and throughout the Tuscan hill towns chapters.

EATING IN FLORENCE

As a big city jammed with tourists, Florence has plenty of good restaurants—but even more bad ones. In this chapter, I've recommended a cross-section of reliably good eateries, from cafeterias and sandwich shops to classic Italian trattorias and foodie splurges. My readers fill many of the mom-and-pop eateries listed here—to escape the crowds, head away from the town center. The Oltrarno, just across the river, is a good compromise: far enough away to not be completely overrun by tourists, but close enough for an easy commute by foot.

EATING TIPS

I rank eateries from **$** budget to **$$$$** splurge. For advice on eating in Italy, including details on pricing, ordering, dining, and tipping in restaurants, where to find budget meals, picnicking help, and Italian cuisine and beverages—including wine, see page 627.

Restaurants: You may have the best luck finding local ambience at lunch, since that's when many restaurants in the center cater to office workers. Most restaurants close their kitchens between lunch and dinner, typically reopening around 19:00 or later. Before 21:00 or so, restaurants are usually filled with tourists; after that, the tourists are replaced by locals. Even if a restaurant is fully booked at night, it may accommodate walk-in diners who are willing to eat early and quickly.

Restaurants like to serve what's fresh. Seasonal ingredients are most likely featured in the *piatti del giorno* (specials of the day) section on menus. For dessert, it's all about gelato (see sidebar on page 297). Rather than eat it at the restaurant, I'd enjoy a gelato-fueled evening stroll.

Foodies appreciate Elizabeth Minchilli's app, Eat Florence, which has thorough descriptions of all things food-related in the city (www.elizabethminchilliinrome.com).

Budget Eating: To save money and time, keep lunches fast and simple by eating at one of Florence's countless sandwich shops and stands, pizzerias, or self-service cafeterias. You'll find a unique range of sandwich options. In addition to the basic *panino* (usually on a baguette), *crostini* (open-faced, toasted baguette), and *semel* (big, puffy roll), you'll see places advertising *schiaccata* (sandwich made with a "squashed," focaccia-like bread). Florence is also home to many carts selling tripe sandwiches—a prized local specialty; for details, see the sidebar on page 284.

Picnicking is easy. You can picnic your way through Mercato Centrale, near the Basilica of San Lorenzo. You'll also find good *supermercati* throughout the city—I've included some handy ones in the neighborhood listings in this chapter. I like the classy Sapori & Dintorni markets (run by Conad), which have branches near the Duomo (Borgo San Lorenzo 15 red) and just over Ponte Vecchio in the Oltrarno (Via de Bardi 45). Despar is another handy grocery chain (there's one around the corner from the Duomo Museum at Via dell'Oriuolo 66).

Cooking Classes: If you'd like to spend the morning cooking your lunch and then actually eat it, see the sidebar on page 302.

MERCATO CENTRALE AND NEARBY
In Mercato Centrale

Florence's Industrial Age, steel-and-glass Mercato Centrale (Central Market) is all about feeding people. The ground floor has always been a fun-to-explore food wonderland of vendors selling meat, fish, produce, and other staples to a mostly local clientele, plus some lunch-only food counters. And now, the upstairs is a bustling food court open late into the evening.

$ Ground Floor: The market zone, with lots of raw ingredients and a few humble food counters, is open only through lunchtime (Mon-Fri 7:00-14:00, Sat 7:00-17:00, closed Sun). Buy a picnic of fresh mozzarella cheese, olives, fruit, and crunchy bread to

Florentine Food Carts
for Those with Guts

While on a lunch break from chipping trapped statues out of blocks of marble, Michelangelo would swing by the market and dig into a bun stuffed with stewed organs. Offal sandwiches originated as an affordable source of protein for working-class Florentines. While this longstanding tradition nearly faded away a few years back, the recent worldwide foodie trend for "nose-to-tail" eating has kicked off a renaissance of food carts selling this prized local delicacy.

Tourists may find it hard to stomach, but Florentines' favorite quick lunch is a *panino* (sandwich) of *trippa* or *lampredotto*—the second and fourth stomach of a cow, respectively—slow-boiled to tender perfection. Less common variations include *poppo* (udder) and *nervetti* (tendons). While these are worth trying (be brave), most carts also offer *bollito* (stewed beef) and the always delicious—and easier to stomach—*porchetta* (roast pork with herbs). When you order, the food-cart proprietor pulls the lid off of a gently simmering pot, forks out some tender meat, and—if you're lucky—dips the bun in the broth. The sandwich is topped with *salsa piccante* (spicy red sauce) and/or *salsa verde* (tangy parsley sauce).

As it's been for centuries, these food stands are most commonly found at or near markets. Good places (described in this chapter) include **Nerbone in the Market** at Mercato Centrale; **L'Antico Trippaio,** tucked in the tight streets between the Duomo and the Palazzo Vecchio; the locally beloved *lampredotto* **cart** at Mercato Nuovo; or anywhere else that locals are excited about. Come on, have some guts...give it a try. It's offal.

munch on the steps of the nearby Basilica of San Lorenzo. The fancy deli, **Perini,** is famous for its quality (pricey) products and enticing display. For a simple sit-down meal, head for the venerable **Nerbone in the Market.** Join the shoppers and workers who crowd up to the bar to grab their inexpensive plates, and then find a stool at the cramped shared tables nearby. Of the several cheap market diners, this feels the most authentic (lunch menu served Mon-Sat 12:00-14:00, sandwiches available from 8:00 until the bread runs out, cash only, on the side closest to the Basilica of San Lorenzo). Its less-famous sisters, nearby, have better seating and fewer crowds.

$$ Upstairs: Under the old glass roof, the upper floor features a dozen upscale food counters open for lunch and dinner (daily 10:00-24:00). Before choosing, do a full circuit to get to know your options. Then grab what you want—pizza, pasta, fish, meat, *salumi*, *lampredotto*, wine, and so on—and pull up a stool at one of the food-court tables.

Near Mercato Centrale

A huge array of eateries is within a couple of blocks of the market. Each has its own distinct vibe, so scout around to find your favorite.

$$ Trattoria Mario's has served hearty lunches to market-goers since 1953 (Fabio and Romeo are the latest generation). Their simple formula: no-frills, bustling service, old-fashioned good value, and shared tables. It's *cucina casalinga*—home cooking *con brio*. This place is high-energy and jam-packed, with very tight seating. Their best dishes (*ribollita*, bean soup, *amatriciana*) often sell out first, so go early. If there's a line, put your name on the list (cash only, Mon-Sat 12:00-15:30, closed Sun and Aug, no reservations, Via Rosina 2, tel. 055-218-550).

$ Casa del Vino, Florence's oldest operating wine shop, offers glasses of wine from 25 open bottles. Owner Gianni, whose family has owned the Casa for more than 70 years, is a class act. The sandwiches, crostini, and mixed plates of meat and cheese with fine wine by the glass are perfect. During busy times, it's a mob scene. You'll eat standing outside alongside workers on a quick lunch break. But come early or late, and you can actually connect with Gianni. Ask him for *"uno etto misto €5,"* add two glasses of fine wine, and you've got a memorable and very cheap lunch (Mon-Thu 9:30-15:30, Fri-Sat 9:30-20:30; closed Sun year-round, Sat in summer, and Aug; Via dell'Ariento 16 red, tel. 055-215-609).

$$ Pepò, a colorful and charmingly unpretentious space, is tucked just around the corner from the touristy Trattoria Zà-Zà glitz on Piazza del Mercato Centrale. Pepò handles its neighbor's overflow admirably, with a short menu of simple but well-prepared Florentine classics such as *ribollita* and *pollo alla cacciatora*—chicken cacciatore (daily 12:00-14:30 & 19:00-22:30, Via Rosina 4 red, tel. 055-283-259).

$$ Trattoria Sergio Gozzi is your classic neighborhood lunch-only place, serving hearty, traditional Florentine fare to market-goers since 1915—long before the tourist crush of today. The handwritten menu is limited and changes daily, and the service can be hectic, but it remains a local favorite (Mon-Sat 12:00-15:00, closed Sun, reservations smart, Piazza di San Lorenzo 8, tel. 055-281-941).

$$ Trattoria la Burrasca offers a traditional menu featuring fine beef and good-value seasonal specials of Tuscan home cooking, served with lightning-fast service by Elio and his staff. It's small, with just 14 tables—often filled with tourists (Tue-Sun 12:00-15:00 & 19:00-22:30, closed Mon, reservations smart, Via Panicale 6, north corner of Mercato Centrale, tel. 055-215-827).

EATING

Florence Restaurants

300 Meters
300 Yards

Piazza della Indipendenza

To Fortezza da Basso

PALAZZO DEI CONGRESSI

CONSERVATORIO DI FULIGNO

30

PALAZZO DEGLI AFFARI

VIA GUELFA

VIA SAN ZANOBI

CENACOLO DI FULIGNO

Piazza Adua

VIA VALFONDA

VIA CENNINI

VIA FIUME

VIA DELL'ARIENTO

VIA NAZIONALE

VIA FAENZA

VIA PANICALE

VIA TADDEA

6

MERCATO CENTRALE

1

Piazza del Mercato Centrale

2

4

BORGO LA NOCE

VIA STUFA

3

SANTA MARIA NOVELLA TRAIN STATION

Largo Alinari

PALAZZO DEI CARTELLONI

VIA S. ANTONINO

VIA S. AMARINO

5

Piazza di San Lorenzo

MEDICI CHAPELS

SAN LORENZO

BUS STATION

B

Piazza della Stazione

Piazza dell'Unità Italiana

V. DEI MELARANCIO

VIA DEL GIGLIO

V. DELL'ALLORO

VIA DE' CONTI

LAURENTIAN MEDICI LIBRARY

VIA DE' ZANNETTI

VIA SAN LORENZO

43

WC

MAIN TOURIST INFO

SANTA MARIA NOVELLA

VIA DEGLI AVELLI

VIA PANZANI

VIA DE' CERRETANI

40

VIA DELLA SCALA

VIA DEL CANACCI

VIA BENEDETTA

VIA PALAZZUOLO

SANTA MARIA NOVELLA PERFUMERY

Piazza di Santa Maria Novella

39

VIA D. BELLE DONNE

VIA DEI BANCHI

TREBBIO

RONDINELLI

SANTA MARIA MAGGIORE

VIA PECORI

Piazza di San Giovanni

SAN GAETANO

LOGGIA DI BIGALLO & i

OGNISSANTI

37

VIA DEL PORCELLANA

VIA DI PAOLINO

LOGGIA DI SAN PAOLO

VIA DEL SOLE

ANTINORI

10

VIA CORSI

GIAC.

VIA DE' VECCHIETTI

ARCH

11

BRUNELLESCHI

TOSINGHI

ROMA

MEDICI

42

BORGO OGNISSANTI

LUNGARNO VESPUCCI

VIA DEL MORO

VIA DE' FEDERIGHI

VIA DELLA SPADA

RUCELLAI PALACE

38

13

PESCIONI

VIA D. STROZZI

STROZZI PALACE

V. D. ANSELMI

VIA DEL TORNABUONI

Piazza della Repubblica

41

ORSAN-MICHELE

45

CALIMALA

N

Piazza Carlo Goldoni

VIA DELLA VIGNA NUOVA

PALAZZO CORSINI

VIA DEL PARIONE

PARIONCINO

PURGATORIO

INFERNO

MONALDA

44

SASSETTI

POST

FELLICERIA

PONTE ALLA CARRAIA

LUNGARNO CORSINI

SANTA TRINITÀ

Piazza di Santa Trinita

Piazza de' Davanzati

VIA PORTA ROSSA

DAVANZATI PALACE

MERCATO NUOVO

15

VIA DELLE TERME

Arno River

LUNGARNO GUICCIARDINI

Piazza Nazaro Sauro

BORGO S. S. APOSTOLI

BOMBARDE

LUNGARNO ACCIAIUOLI

PONTE S. TRINITÀ

VIA POR S. MARIA

MANETTO

Piazza de' Salt

49

LAMB

S. Stefano

20

Piazza de' Frescobaldi

SANTO SPIRITO

SAN JACOPO

PONTE VECCHIO

BORGO SAN JACOPO

OLTRARNO

VIA MAGGIO

V. D. RANCI ARTI

Piazza della Passera

To Pitti Palace

Gelaterie

46 Gelateria Carabè
47 Edoardo
48 Perchè No!
49 Carapina
50 Gelateria de' Neri

EATING

1. Mercato Centrale Eateries
2. Trattoria Mario's
3. Casa del Vino
4. Pepò
5. Trattoria Sergio Gozzi
6. Trattoria la Burrasca
7. Simbiosi Organic Pizza & Lovely Food
8. La Ménagère Bistro & Rest.
9. Enoteca Coquinarius
10. Self-Service Rist. Leonardo
11. Paszkowski Café
12. EATaly
13. Procacci
14. To Lovelife Café
15. Rivoire Café
16. Osteria Vini e Vecchi Sapori
17. Frescobaldi Ristorante & Wine Bar
18. Cantinetta dei Verrazzano
19. I Fratellini
20. 'Ino Wine Bar & Sandwiches
21. L'Antico Trippaio, Pizzeria Totò & Supermarket
22. Da' Vinattieri
23. Il Cernacchino
24. Ará è Sicilia
25. Due Sorsi e un Boccone
26. La Mescita Fiaschetteria
27. Pasticceria Robiglio
28. To Antica Trattoria da Tito
29. Ristorante Cafaggi
30. Trattoria La Gratella
31. Ristorante del Fagioli
32. Trattoria Anita
33. Trattoria l'cche C'è C'è
34. All'Antico Vinaio
35. Club del Gusto
36. Istanbul Döner Kebap
37. Trattoria Sostanza-Troia
38. Trattoria Marione
39. Trattoria al Trebbio
40. Trattoria "da Giorgio"
41. Caffè La Terrazza
42. Sesto Bar
43. Groceries (3)
44. Artviva Tours & Cooking School
45. Florencetown Tours & Cooking School

EATING

$ Simbiosi Organic Pizza and Lovely Food is a happy little pizzeria under a medieval vault with a young hip crew, open fire, and healthy energy (daily 12:00-23:00, organic and gluten-free, craft beer, Via de' Ginori 56 red, tel. 055-064-0115).

$$$ La Ménagère Bistro and Restaurant is a youthful place serving nicely presented, modern Italian dishes to a smart crowd in a spacious and dressy atmosphere. The more casual bistro in front (which serves salads, sandwiches, and simple plates until 18:00) hides a fancier restaurant in back where you can choose between small tables or bigger shared ones (daily 12:00-23:00, dinner from 19:30—reservations smart, Via de' Ginori 8 red, tel. 055-075-0600, www.lamenagere.it).

AROUND THE DUOMO

At lunchtime, my first listing is more of a sit-down place; the others are better for a fast meal.

$$ Enoteca Coquinarius feels as welcoming as someone's cool and spacious living room or library. It's an unstressful, hip place with a slow-food ethic and lots of great salads and pastas (daily 12:30-15:30 & 18:30-22:30, a few steps from the Duomo workshop at Via delle Oche 11 red, tel. 055-230-2153).

$ Self-Service Ristorante Leonardo is an inexpensive, air-conditioned, quick, and handy cafeteria. While it's no-frills and old-school, the food is better than many table-service eateries in this part of town. Stefano and Luciano run the place with enthusiasm and free pitchers of tap water. It's a block from the Duomo, southwest of the Baptistery (lots of veggies, daily 11:45-14:45 & 18:45-21:45, upstairs at Via Pecori 11, tel. 055-284-446).

$$ Paszkowski Café is a venerable place on Piazza della Repubblica. While famously expensive as a restaurant, it serves up inexpensive, quick lunches. At the display case, order a salad or plate of pasta or cooked veggies (or half-and-half), pay the cashier, and find a seat upstairs or at one of the tables reserved for self-serve diners on the square (lunch served 12:00-15:00, Piazza della Repubblica 35 red—northwest corner, tel. 055-210-236).

$$ EATaly, a slick, modern space a half-block from the Duomo, is an outpost of a chain of foodie mini-malls located in big Italian cities (as well as in Chicago and New York City). Along with a world of gifty edibles, it offers several food options under one roof, including an espresso counter, a soft-serve gelato counter and tempting pastry shop, a grocery store for top-end Italian ingredients and kitchen gadgets, and a bright, modern dining area serving pastas, pizzas, salads, and *secondi*, including daily specials (food shop open daily 10:00-22:30, restaurants open 12:00-15:00 and from 19:00, Via de' Martelli 22 red, tel. 055-015-3601).

$$ Procacci, right on Florence's most genteel boutique-browsing street, is upscale yet still affordable. This wine bar, with a swanky, circa-1885 atmosphere, specializes in pungent truffle-scented ingredients: cheap mini-*panini* and €9-18 sampler plates of *salumi* and cheeses. While the platters are pricey, the sandwiches may be Florence's cheapest way to dine on truffles. Paired with a €5 glass of wine, it makes an elegant light meal (daily 10:00-21:00, Via Tornabuoni 64 red, tel. 055-211-656).

NEAR PIAZZA DELLA SIGNORIA

Piazza della Signoria, the scenic square facing the Palazzo Vecchio, is ringed by beautifully situated yet touristy eateries serving overpriced, forgettable food with an unforgettable view. If you're determined to eat on the square, have pizza at the touristy Ristorante il Cavallino, bar food at the adjacent Irish pub, or dine more elegantly at the Gucci Caffè and Restaurant. Piazza della Signoria's saving grace is **$$$ Rivoire** café, famous for its fancy desserts and thick hot chocolate (€7). While obscenely expensive, it has the best view tables on the square. Their delightful bar is perfectly affordable, and drinks often come with fine *aperitivo* munchies (Tue-Sun 8:00-24:00, closed Mon, tel. 055-214-412).

Dining near Piazza della Signoria

Two recommended places, one casual, the other fancy, are just off Piazza della Signoria, a half-block north of the Palazzo Vecchio. Facing the bronze equestrian statue in the piazza, go behind the horse's tail and into the corner to the left.

$$ Osteria Vini e Vecchi Sapori is a colorful eatery—tight and tiny, and with attitude. They serve Tuscan food—like *pappardelle* with duck—from a fun, accessible menu of delicious pastas and *secondi* (Mon-Sat 12:30-14:30 & 19:30-22:30, closed Sun, reservations smart, Via dei Magazzini 3 red, tel. 055-293-045, run by Mario while wife Rosanna cooks and son Tommaso serves).

$$$$ Frescobaldi Ristorante and Wine Bar, the showcase of Italy's aristocratic wine family, serves sophisticated dishes by candlelight under high-vaulted ceilings. They offer the same seasonal menu in their cozy interior, tight wine bar, and at a few outside tables. If coming for dinner, make a reservation and dress up (lighter wine-bar and good-value set menus at lunch, daily 12:00-14:30 & 19:00-22:30, air-con, Via dei Magazzini 2 red, tel. 055-284-724, www.deifrescobaldi.it).

Cheap, Simple Eats near Piazza della Signoria

$$ Cantinetta dei Verrazzano, a long-established bakery/café/wine bar, serves delightful sandwich plates in an old-time setting. Their *selezione Verrazzano* is a plate of four little crostini featuring different breads, cheeses, and meats from the Chianti region. The

Florentine and Tuscan Cuisine

In general, Tuscan cuisine is hearty, simple food: grilled meats, high-quality seasonal vegetables, fresh herbs, prized olive oil, and rustic bread. If a dish ends with *"alla toscana"* or *"alla fiorentina,"* it's cooked in the Tuscan or Florentine style—usually a preparation highlighting local products. In addition to specialty dishes, most restaurants also serve pasta and pizza, veal cutlets, and salad (for more on Italian cuisine, see page 636).

There's nothing wrong with your Tuscan bread—it's supposed to taste like that. *Pane alla toscana* is unsalted and nearly flavorless (from the days when salt's preservative powers made it more valuable than gold). Italians drench it in olive oil and sprinkle it with salt, or use it to scoop up sauce.

Antipasti (Appetizers)

Bruschetta: Toasted bread brushed with olive oil and rubbed with garlic, topped with chopped tomato, mushrooms, or whatever else sounds good.

Crostini: Toasted bread rounds topped with meat or vegetable pastes. *Alla toscana* generally means with chicken liver pâté.

Panzanella: A simple summer salad, made of day-old bread, chopped tomatoes, onion, and basil, tossed in a light vinaigrette.

Pecorino cheese: Fresh *(fresco)* or aged *(stagionato)*, from ewe's milk.

Porcini mushrooms: Harvested in fall; used in pasta and soups, as a topping on meats and bruschetta, and sometimes deep-fried.

Salumi: Cold cuts, usually air- or salt-dried pork. Popular kinds include prosciutto (air-cured ham hock), pancetta (cured pork belly), *lardo* (cured pork lard), and *finocchiona* (fennel salami). For a list of other *salumi,* see page 638.

Tagliere: A wooden platter with cold cuts and/or cheeses.

Primo Piatto (First Course)

Carabaccia: Onion soup.

Pappa al pomodoro: Thick stew of tomatoes, olive oil, and bread.

Pappardelle al sugo di lepre: A rich sauce with wild hare over long, broad noodles.

Pici al ragù: A fat, spaghetti-like, hand-rolled pasta served with a meat-tomato sauce.

Ribollita: "Reboiled" soup, traditionally made with leftovers including white beans *(fagioli)*, seasonal vegetables, and olive oil, with layers of day-old Tuscan bread.

Zuppa alla volterrana: Volterra-style soup, similar to *ribollita* but with fresh bread.

Secondo Piatto (Second Course)

Arrosto misto: An assortment of roasted meats, sometimes

served on a skewer *(spiedino)*.

Bistecca alla fiorentina: A thick T-bone steak, generally grilled very rare and lightly seasoned (often sold by weight—per *etto*, or 100 grams). The best—and most expensive—is from the white Chianina breed of cattle you'll see grazing throughout Tuscany.

Cinghiale: Wild boar, served grilled or in soups, stews, and pasta. It is also made into many varieties of sausage and salami.

Fegatelli: Liver meatballs.

Game birds: Squab *(piccione)*, pheasant *(fagiano)*, and guinea hen *(faraona)* are popular.

Trippa alla fiorentina: Tripe (intestines) and vegetables sautéed in tomato sauce, sometimes baked with parmesan. *Trippa* (and the similar *lampredotto*) are popular in sandwiches; see page 284.

Dolci (Desserts)

Cantucci: Florentines love to end a meal by dipping this crunchy almond cookie in vin santo wine (described below).

Gelato: The Florentines claim they invented Italian-style ice cream. Rather than order dessert in a restaurant, I like to stroll with a gelato. For more on gelato, see page 639; for tips on enjoying it here, see page 297.

Panforte: Dense, clove-and-cinnamon-spiced cake from Siena.

Local Wines

Many Tuscan wines are made with sangiovese ("blood of Jupiter") grapes. But the characteristics of the soil, temperature, and exposure make each wine unique to its area.

Brunello di Montalcino: One of Italy's best reds, this full-bodied wine comes from the slopes of Montalcino, south of Siena. Smooth and dry, it pairs well with hearty, meaty food.

Chianti: This red hails from the Chianti region (20 miles south of Florence). Varieties range from cheap, acidic basket-bottles of table wine (called *fiaschi*) to the hearty Chianti Classico.

Rosso di Montalcino: This cheaper, younger "baby Brunello," also made in Montalcino, lacks Brunello's depth of flavor and complexity—but it's still a great wine at a bargain price.

Super Tuscans: This newer wine blends traditional grapes with locally grown non-Italian grapes (such as cabernet or merlot).

Vernaccia di San Gimignano: This medium-dry white goes well with pasta and salad. Trebbiano and vermentino are two other local white grapes.

Vin Santo: Sweet and syrupy, this "holy" dessert wine is often served with a cookie for dipping.

Vino Nobile di Montepulciano: This high-quality, ruby red, dry wine pairs well with meat, especially chicken.

EATING

Cheap, Fast, and Not a Hint of Pasta

If you're on the move and crave a cheap, filling, healthy alternative to the typical plate of noodles or ham-and-cheese *panino*, you have some good options.

My favorite is the *döner kebab:* slow-roasted, ultra-thin-sliced chicken or veal stuffed into pita bread *(panino)* or a wrap *(piadina)*, along with tomatoes, onions, lettuce, tangy yogurt sauce, and (optional) hot chili sauce. A vegetarian alternative is falafel (a fried garbanzo-bean patty) served with the same works. Kebab shops are generally open from 11:00 until midnight. Dishes are about €3-5, and most places also sell refreshing *ayran* (a Turkish yogurt drink). Shops with more traffic tend to be better bets—with fresher meat and toppings. A handy spot is **Istanbul Döner Kebap** (Via dei Benci 18 red, just south of Santa Croce).

You can cover all the health-food bases at **$ Lovelife Café,** a simple, informal place with green salads, couscous and rice dishes, quiches, fruits, smoothies, and juices. Order at the counter, then eat at one of their few tables downstairs or take your meal to go (Mon-Fri 8:30-19:30, Sat 12:00-19:00, closed Sun, east of the Duomo at Via dell'Oriuolo 26 red, see map on page 18, tel. 055-263-8027).

Stands selling fresh fruit, juice, and smoothies are found throughout the center. Try **Il Chiosco** (The Kiosk). They have two stands: one facing the southeast corner of the Duomo (usually daily 9:00-19:00, Piazza delle Pallottole) and another south of Piazza della Repubblica (corner of Via Porta Rossa and Via Pellicceria).

tagliere di focacce, a sampler plate of mini-focaccia sandwiches, is also fun. Add a glass of Chianti to either of these dishes to make a fine, light meal. Office workers pop in for a quick lunch, and it's traditional to share tables. They also have benches and tiny tables for eating at takeout prices. Simply step to the back and point to a hot *focacce* sandwich, order a drink at the bar, and take away your food or sit with Florentines and watch the action while you munch. For dessert, consider their tempting display case of delicious cakes (Mon-Sat 8:00-21:00, Sun 10:00-16:30, no reservations taken, just off Via de' Calzaiuoli, at Via dei Tavolini 18 red, tel. 055-268-590).

$ I Fratellini is a hole-in-the-wall where the "little brothers" have served peasants more than 30 kinds of sandwiches and a fine selection of wine at great prices (see list on wall) since 1875. Join the local crowd to order, then sit on a nearby curb to eat, placing your glass on the wall rack before you leave. Be adventurous with the menu (easy-order by number). Consider *finocchiona e caprino* (#15, a Tuscan salami and soft goat cheese), *lardo di Colonnata* (#22, cured lard aged in Carrara marble), and *cinghiale* (#19, spicy boar salami) sandwiches. It's worth ordering the most expensive wine they're selling by the glass (daily 9:00-19:30 or until the bread runs out, 20 yards in front of Orsanmichele Church on Via dei Cimatori, tel. 055-239-6096).

$ Sandwich Shop/Wine Bar near Ponte Vecchio: 'Ino is a mod little shop filled with gifty edibles. Alessandro and his staff serve creative sandwiches and glasses of wine—you'll munch your meal while perched on a tiny, uncomfortable stool. They can also make a fine €9-12 *piatto misto* of cheeses and meats with bread (daily 11:30-15:30, immediately behind Uffizi Gallery courtyard on Ponte Vecchio side, near the potted olive tree at Via dei Georgofili 7 red, tel. 055-219-208).

Cheap Takeout on Via Dante Alighieri: Three handy places line up on this street, located between Piazza della Signoria and the Duomo. **$ L'Antico Trippaio,** a food cart, is a fixture in the town center. Cheap and authentic as can be, this is where locals come daily for sandwiches *(panini),* featuring specialties like *trippa* (tripe), *lampredotto,* and a list of more appetizing options, including *bollito* (for more on these, see sidebar on page 284). Lisa, Maurizio, and Roberto offer a free plastic glass of rotgut Chianti with each sandwich for travelers with this book (daily 9:00-21:00, on Via Dante Alighieri, mobile 339-742-5692). **$ Pizzeria Totò,** just next to the tripe stand, has good-and-cheap slices (daily 10:30-22:00, Via Dante Alighieri 28 red, tel. 055-290-406). And a few steps away is a **Carrefour Express supermarket,** with cheap drinks and snacks and a fine *antipasti* case (daily 8:30-21:30, Via Dante Alighieri 24). If you pick up lunch at any of these, the best people-watching place to enjoy your sandwich is on Piazza della Signoria (three blocks south).

More Sandwich Shops: Two well-regarded places to grab a cheap sandwich are **$ Da' Vinattieri,** a literal hole-in-the-wall (*schiaccata* sandwiches plus *trippa* and *lampredotto,* daily 10:00-19:30, next to Casa di Dante at Via Santa Margherita 4 red); and **$ Il Cernacchino** (*panino* sandwiches, Mon-Sat 9:30-19:30, closed Sun, just north of the Palazzo Vecchio at Via della Condotta 38 red, tel. 055-294-119).

NEAR THE ACCADEMIA

There aren't many appealing sit-down restaurants in the boring streets near the Accademia. But hungry tourists looking for a quick lunch between sightseeing stops find plenty of options. Picnickers can grab a takeout bite at one of these places, then hike around the block and join the bums on the traffic-free **Piazza S.S. Annunziata,** the first Renaissance square in Florence. There's a fountain for washing fruit on the square. Grab a stony seat anywhere you like.

$ Ará è Sicilia, just around the corner from *David,* is tiny, bright, and packed with Italians ordering up chef Carmelo's take on Sicilian street food: *arancini* (filled risotto balls) and *pizzole* (stuffed pizza) in fresh, inventive flavors, chased by homemade sorbet, cannoli, or pistachio biscotti. Order to takeaway or perch on one of the few stools (daily 10:00-22:00, Via degli Alfani 127 red, mobile 333-198-3927).

$ Due Sorsi e un Boccone ("Two Sips and a Bite"), a few steps down the same street, serves just that: cheap glasses of house wine, savory or sweet crêpes, and made-to-order *schiacciate* (sandwiches on flattened, foccacia-like bread). Order your food to go, or squeeze into a spot at the counter. It's run with a fresh, youthful attitude and jammed with local students at lunchtime (Mon-Fri 10:30-17:00, closed Sat-Sun, Via degli Alfani 105 red, mobile 334-264-0931).

$ La Mescita Fiaschetteria is a characteristic hole-in-the-wall, where locals enjoy a simple menu of pastas and *secondi* with tasty, cheap house wine. The place can either be mobbed by students or a peaceful time warp, depending on when you stop by. Mirco and Alessio are gregarious to the point of being a bit pushy... order carefully and check your bill (daily 11:30-15:30, Via degli Alfani 70 red, mobile 338-992-2640).

Supermarket: Carrefour Express, a half-block north of the Accademia, has a sandwich counter and picnic provisions (daily 8:00-20:00, Via Ricasoli 109 red).

Sit-Down Lunch in a Classy Café: A smart little café with friendly service, **$$ Pasticceria Robiglio,** has a stately dining area and a few tables on the sidewalk. They have a small menu of salads and daily pasta and *secondi* specials. It's good any time for a coffee and one of their pretty pastries—famous among Florentines (café open daily 7:30-20:00, lunch served 12:00-16:00, a block toward the Duomo off Piazza S.S. Annunziata at Via dei Servi 112 red, tel. 055-212-784).

Memorable Restaurants a Bit Farther from the Accademia

These two places—within a 5- to 10-minute walk of the Accademia—are worth going out of your way for.

$$$ Antica Trattoria da Tito, a 10-minute hike from the Accademia along Via San Gallo, can be fun if you want a memorable meal with a local crowd and smart-aleck service. The boss, Bobo, serves quality traditional food and lots of wine. While the food is good, there's no pretense—it's just a playground of Tuscan cuisine. The music is vintage 1980s and can be loud. To gorge on a feast of *antipasti* (cold cuts, cheeses, a few veggies, and bruschetta), consider ordering *fermami* (literally "stop me")—for €18, Bobo brings you food until you say, *"Fermami!"* A couple can get *fermami* for two, desserts, and a nice bottle of wine for around €60 total. Dinner is served in two seatings: 19:30 (more sanity) and 21:30 (less sanity), and reservations are generally necessary (€17 *gran tagliere*—big plate of cheese and meat, travelers with this book get a free after-dinner drink, Mon-Sat 12:30-15:00 & 19:00-23:00, closed Sun, Via San Gallo 112 red, tel. 055-472-475, www.trattoriadatito.it).

$$$ Ristorante Cafaggi fills a bright yet low-energy space on a drab street between the Accademia and Mercato Centrale. With a vaguely 1950s vibe, it feels like it's been retro since before it was "retro." The service can be a bit shy; the emphasis here is their generations-old passion for Florentine food. It's been family-run since 1922, with Grandma and Grandpa still puttering around (Mon-Sat 12:30-15:00 & 19:00-22:00, closed Sun and several weeks in Aug, Via Guelfa 35 red, tel. 055-294-989, www.ristorantecafaggi.com).

$$ Trattoria La Gratella, near recommended hotels north of the center, serves solid Tuscan cuisine to a mostly local crowd. The tiny entrance hides a sprawling interior and an outdoor courtyard, full of diners grilling their own *bistecca alla fiorentina* on mini barbeques at the table (daily 12:00-15:00 & 19:00-23:00, Via Guelfa 81r, tel. 055-211-292, www.lagratella.it).

BETWEEN THE PALAZZO VECCHIO AND SANTA CROCE CHURCH

$$ Ristorante del Fagioli, an enthusiastically run eatery where you can sense the heritage, just feels real, from the wood-paneled dining room to the daily specials chalked on a board. Maurizio commands the kitchen while family members Antonio and Simone keep the throngs of loyal customers returning. The cuisine: home-style bread-soups, hearty steaks, and other Florentine classics. Don't worry—while *fagioli* means "beans," that's the family name, not the extent of the menu (Mon-Fri 12:30-14:30 & 19:30-22:30, closed Sat-Sun, cash only, reserve for dinner, a block north of the Alle Grazie bridge at Corso dei Tintori 47, tel. 055-244-285).

$$ Trattoria Anita, midway between the Uffizi and Santa Croce, feels old-school, with wood paneling and rows of wine bottles. Brothers Nicola, Gianni, and Maurizio offer good value—both for their weekday lunch special featuring three hearty Tuscan courses for €11 and their à la carte dinner (Mon-Sat 12:00-14:30 & 19:00-22:15, closed Sun, on the corner of Via Vinegia and Via del Parlagio at 2 red, tel. 055-218-698).

$$ Trattoria I'cche C'è C'è is a small, family-run restaurant where Gino, Mara, and their son Jacopo serve basic Florentine dishes. A bit tired and old-fashioned, it's still cozy and welcoming (Tue-Sun 12:30-14:30 & 19:30-22:30, closed Mon, Via Magalotti 11 red, tel. 055-216-589).

Quick Lunch Places on Via dei Neri: This is *panino* lane, with five high-energy, rustic, and youthful sandwich bars. This street, which runs behind the Palazzo Vecchio and the Uffizi toward Santa Croce, seems to specialize in sightseers seeking lunch between landmarks: **$ All'Antico Vinaio,** a photogenic Florentine favorite, offers two options: stand in the street with a crusty sandwich and pour your own wine, or head across the street to their more comfortable and expensive *osteria* (sandwiches available at both shops, Mon-Sat 10:30-22:30, Sun 12:00-16:00, Via dei Neri 65 red, tel. 055-238-2723). **$ Club del Gusto,** with friendly owner/chef Paolo, is much quieter. Grab a sandwich to carry away, or enjoy a plate of mixed meats and cheeses, or a made-to-order pasta plate, with their nice house wine at a shared table in back. Enthusiastic about traditional dishes, they provide a good venue for trying *lampredotto*—that's cow stomach (daily 9:00-24:00, Via dei Neri 50 red, tel. 348-090-3142).

$ Döner Kebab: Just south of Santa Croce is **Istanbul Döner Kebap,** a good place for a quick, un-Italian meal (Via dei Benci 18 red; see sidebar on page 292).

NEAR THE CHURCH OF SANTA MARIA NOVELLA

$$$ Trattoria Sostanza-Troia, characteristic and well-established, is famous for its steaks and its *pollo al burro* (chicken in butter). Whirling ceiling fans and walls strewn with old photos evoke earlier times, while the artichoke pie *(tortino di carciofi)* reminds locals of Grandma's cooking. Crowded, with just eight shared tables, a small menu, and grumpy service, the place feels like a simple bistro. Reservations are essential for their two dinner seatings: 19:30 and 21:00 (cash only, open Mon-Sat, closed Sun year-round and Sat off-season, lunch served 12:30-14:00, Via del Porcellana 25 red, tel. 055-212-691).

$$ Trattoria Marione serves home-cooked-style meals to a mixed group of tourists and Florentines crowding very tight tables beneath hanging ham hocks. The ambience is happy, food-loving, and a bit frantic—no reservations, so arrive early (daily 12:00-17:00 & 19:00-23:00, Via della Spada 27 red, tel. 055-214-756, Fabio).

$$ Trattoria al Trebbio features all the traditional Tuscan classics at average prices in an eclectic, modern setting. Dine inside, surrounded by old movie posters and framed prosciutto legs, or grab one of the few tables outside (daily 12:00-15:00 & 19:00-23:00, half a block off Piazza Santa Maria Novella at Via delle Belle Donne 47 red, tel. 055-287-089, Giulia).

$$ Trattoria "da Giorgio" is a rustic family-style diner on a sketchy street serving up simple home cooking to happy locals and tourists alike. Their €14 three-course, fixed-price meal, including a drink, is a great value. This place is completely without pretense—head here for a taste of working-class Florence (Mon-Sat

Gelato

Italy's best ice cream is in Florence—many think they serve some of the world's best. But beware of scams at touristy joints on busy streets that turn a simple request for a cone into a €10 "tourist special" rip-off. To avoid this, survey the size options and specify what you want—for example, *un cono da tre euro* (a €3 cone). A rule of thumb: Stay away from places with heaping mounds of brightly (artificially) colored gelato. For

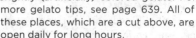

more gelato tips, see page 639. All of these places, which are a cut above, are open daily for long hours.

Near the Accademia: A Sicilian choice on a tourist thoroughfare, **Gelateria Carabè** is particularly famous for its pistachio and its luscious *granite*—Italian ices made with fresh fruit. A *cremolata* is a *granita* with a dollop of gelato (almond and pistachio work well together). If you'd like a real Sicilian cannoli, get it here (from the Accademia, it's a block toward the Duomo at Via Ricasoli 60 red—Simone clearly loves his work).

Near the Duomo: A favorite, **Edoardo** features organic ingredients and tasty handmade cones (facing the southwest corner of the Duomo at Piazza del Duomo 45 red).

Near Orsanmichele Church: This shop's name, **Perchè No!,** translates to "Why not!"—good advice when it comes to gelato. It feels touristy but serves one of the widest range of flavors around, and the quality's top notch (just off the busy main pedestrian drag, Via de' Calzaiuoli, at Via dei Tavolini 19).

Near Ponte Vecchio: Modern *gelateria* **Carapina** offers some pleasantly atypical flavors, seasonal ingredients, and a loyal following (Via Lambertesca 18 red).

Near the Church of Santa Croce: Florentines flock to **Gelateria de' Neri,** with an enticingly wide array of flavors (Via dei Neri 9 red).

12:00-14:30 & 18:30-22:00, closed Sun, Via Palazzuolo 100 red, tel. 055-284-302, Silvano).

HIDDEN ROOFTOP CAFÉ TERRACES

If you're willing to pay extra to enjoy a drink surrounded by splendid Florentine views, head to one of these rooftop terraces:

$$ Caffè La Terrazza is on the rooftop of La Rinascente department store overlooking Piazza della Repubblica. While fairly plain, it comes with commanding views of the Duomo, which looms gloriously on the horizon (€6 coffee drinks, daily 9:00-20:30).

$$$$ Sesto is a dressy bar on a partially covered terrace perched on the top floor of the luxurious Westin Hotel. While cocktails here are pricey (€15 and up; €6 coffee drinks), they come with amazing city views. To turn your spendy drink into a light dinner, come by during their *aperitivo* happy hour (19:00-21:00) when, for €18, your drink includes access to a little buffet, giving you something to nibble as you enjoy the sunset (daily 12:00-24:00, Piazza Ognissanti 3, tel. 055-27151, www.sestoonarno.com).

THE OLTRARNO

In general, dining in the Oltrarno, south of the Arno River, offers a more authentic experience. While it's just a few minutes' walk from Ponte Vecchio, this area sees far fewer tourists than the other side of the river. You may even find that Florentines outnumber my readers. For most locations, see the map on page 278.

Dining or Drinking with a Ponte Vecchio View

$$ Signorvino is an *enoteca* (wine shop) with a simple restaurant that has a rare terrace literally over the Arno River, with Ponte Vecchio views. It's a fun-loving place with no pretense yet a passion for quality Italian ingredients. They serve regional dishes and plates of fine meats and cheeses to go with a wonderful array of wines by the glass, allowing you to drink and eat your way merrily across Italy. If you're up for a full bottle, their huge selection is available for the same fair prices at a table as in their wine store (shop open daily 9:30-24:00, food served 11:30-23:00, Via dei Bardi 46 red, tel. 055-286-258, www.signorvino.com, call to reserve, especially for terrace seating).

$$$ Golden View Open Bar is a modern, noisy, and touristy bistro, good for a salad, pizza, or pasta with fine wine and a fine view of Ponte Vecchio and the Arno River. Its white, minimalist interior is a stark contrast to atmospheric old Florence. Reservations for window tables are essential. They have three seating areas (same menu and prices at each): a riverside pizza place, a classier restaurant, and a jazzy lounge. In the afternoon (12:00-18:00), they offer wine tastings (€9-15) that include three pours. Later (18:30 to 21:30), the wine bar serves a buffet of appetizers free with your €10 drink. Mixing their fine wine, river views, and live jazz makes for a wonderful evening (daily 12:00-24:00, café opens at 7:30; jazz usually Mon, Fri, and Sat nights at 21:00; 50 yards east of Ponte Vecchio at Via dei Bardi 58, tel. 055-214-502, www.goldenviewopenbar.com, run by Antonio, Paolo, and Tommaso).

$ Osteria Ponte Vecchio is a tiny place—little more than a bar—serving basic drinks, *panini*, and microwaved snacks with a couple of amazing tables on the river (daily 10:00-23:00, off-season until 20:00, a block downstream from Ponte Vecchio at Via Borgo San Jacopo 16 red, Giacomo).

On or near Piazza di Santo Spirito

Piazza di Santo Spirito is a thriving neighborhood square in the heart of the Oltrarno, with a collection of fun eateries and bars. Several bars offer *aperitivo* buffets with their drinks during happy hour. Late in the evening the area becomes a club scene (see the Nightlife in Florence chapter), filled with foreign students and young locals. And every day, when the weather's nice, the tables of Trattoria Borgo Antico and several other characteristic places spill onto the square. After noting the plain facade of the Brunelleschi church facing the square, step inside Caffè Ricchi to see pictures of the many possible ways the church might be finished.

$$ Tamerò is an arty pasta bar in an old auto mechanic's shop serving high-quality Sardinian-Tuscan dishes at reasonable prices. The pasta is freshly made and on display in the open kitchen. Sit in the funky interior with local hipsters or enjoy a lazy meal on the colorful piazza (daily 12:00-late, DJ music some nights, Piazza Santo Spirito 11 red, tel. 055-282-596, www.tamero.it).

$$ Gusta Osteria, just around the corner from the piazza, serves big salads and predictable Tuscan fare at fun, cozy indoor seating or at outdoor tables (Tue-Sun 12:00-23:00, closed Mon, Via de' Michelozzi 13 red, tel. 055-285-033). For cheaper bites, try its sister restaurant **$ Gusta Panino,** a sandwich bar directly on the square.

$$ Trattoria Casalinga, an inexpensive standby, comes with aproned women bustling around the kitchen. Florentines (who enjoy the tripe and tongue) and tourists (who opt for easier to swallow Tuscan favorites) alike pack the place and leave full and happy, with euros to spare for gelato (Mon-Sat 12:00-14:30 & 19:00-22:00, after 20:00 reserve or wait, closed Sun and Aug, just off Piazza di Santo Spirito, near the church at Via de' Michelozzi 9 red, tel. 055-218-624, www.trattorialacasalinga.it, Andrea and Paolo).

$ Gusta Pizza is your typical jam-packed, cheap, sloppy, and fun neighborhood pizzeria (Tue-Sun 11:30-15:30 & 19:00-23:30, closed Mon, two blocks off Piazza di Santo Spirito at Via Maggio 46 red, tel. 055-285-068).

Beyond Piazza del Carmine, away from Tourists

While Piazza di Santo Spirito is well known by tourists, a short walk beyond it gets you completely away from the tourist scene. These two restaurants (side by side on Via dell'Orto) are worth the five-minute walk beyond Piazza del Carmine:

$$ Burro & Acciughe Fish Restaurant ("butter and anchovies") is a new, minimalist place packed with locals enjoying enthusiastically presented fresh seafood. With just 35 seats in a long, rustic setting, it's very simple but oozes quality (closed Mon, Via dell'Orto 35 red, tel. 055-045-7286).

$$ Trattoria dell'Orto is a classic Florentine trattoria filled with classic Florentines enjoying steaks, grilled dishes, and quintessential local fare—with no tourists. It has a fun vibe and a nice covered outdoor terrace in back (closed Tue, Via dell'Orto 35a, tel. 055-224-148).

Dining Well in the Oltrarno

Of the many good and colorful restaurants in the Oltrarno, these are my favorites. You can survey most of them while following the route in the 📖 Oltrarno Walk chapter before making a choice. Reservations are a good idea in the evening.

$$$ Il Santo Bevitore Ristorante, lit like a Rembrandt painting and unusually spacious, serves creative modern Tuscan cuisine at dressy tables. They're enthusiastic about matching quality produce from the area with the right wine. This is a good break from the big, sloppy plates of pasta you'll get at many Florence eateries (good wine list by the glass or bottle, daily 12:30-14:30 & 19:30-23:00, closed Mon for lunch, reservations smart, three tables on the sidewalk, acoustics can make it noisy inside, Via di Santo Spirito 64 red, tel. 055-211-264, www.ilsantobevitore.com).

$$ Enoteca Il Santino Gastronomia, Il Santo Bevitore's smaller wine bar next door, feels like the perfect after-work hangout for foodies who'd like a glass of wine and a light bite. Tight, cozy, and atmospheric, the place has a prominent bar, where you can assemble an €8-12 *tagliere* of local cheeses and *salumi*. They also have a few affordable hot dishes. Both the food and the wine are locally sourced from small producers (daily 12:30-23:00, Via di Santo Spirito 60 red, no reservations, tel. 055-230-2820).

$$$ Trattoria 4 Leoni creates the quintessential Oltrarno dinner scene, and is understandably popular with tourists. The Tuscan-style food is made with an innovative twist and an appreciation for vegetables. You'll enjoy the fun energy and characteristic seating, both outside on the colorful square and inside, where you'll dine in exposed-stone sophistication. While the wines by the glass are pricey, the house wine is good (daily 12:00-24:00, dinner reservations smart; midway between Ponte Vecchio and Piazza di Santo Spirito, on Piazza della Passera at Via dei Vellutini 1; tel. 055-218-562, www.4leoni.com).

$$$ Antico Ristoro di' Cambi is thick with Tuscan traditions, rustic touches, and T-bone steaks. The bustling scene has a memorable, beer-hall energy. As you walk in, you'll pass a glass case filled with red chunks of Chianina beef that's priced by weight (for the famous *bistecca alla fiorentina* it's €45/kilo—figure a half-kilo per person). Before you OK your investment, they'll show you the cut and tell you the weight. While the steak comes nearly uncooked, it's air-dried for 21 days so it's not really raw, just very tasty and tender—it'll make you happy you're at the top of the food chain. Sit inside the convivial woody interior or outside on a square (Mon-Sat 12:00-14:30 & 18:30-22:30, closed Sun, reserve on weekends and to sit outside, Via Sant'Onofrio 1 red, one block south of Ponte Amerigo Vespucci, see map on page 65, tel. 055-217-134, www.anticoristorodicambi.it, run by Stefano and Fabio, the Cambi cousins).

$$$$ Olio & Convivium is primarily a catering company for top-end events, and this is where they showcase their artful, slow-food cooking (you can buy many of the ingredients on their menu). Their three intimate rooms are surrounded by fine *prosciutti*, cheeses, and wine shelves. It can seem a little formal, but well-dressed foodies will appreciate this place for its clubby atmosphere. Their list of €14-25 *gastronomia* plates offers an array of taste treats and fine wines by the glass. Take full advantage of their passion for olive oil. They also have €35-49 tasting menus and stylish €18 lunches with wine (Tue-Sun 12:00-14:30 & 19:00-22:30, closed Mon, Via di Santo Spirito 4, tel. 055-265-8198, www.oliorestaurant.it, Tommaso is the chef and owner).

Casual Oltrarno Neighborhood Eateries

$$ Trattoria Al Tranvai, with tight seating and small dark-wood tables, looks like an old-time tram filled with the neighborhood gang. A 10-minute walk from the river at the edge of the Oltrarno, it feels like a small town's favorite eatery, serving creative dishes for good prices (Mon 19:00-24:00, Tue-Sat 12:30-14:30 & 19:30-22:30, closed Sun; from the Brancacci Chapel, go south on Via del Leone 5 minutes to Piazza Torquato Tasso 14 red; tel. 055-225-197, www.altranvai.it).

$$ Le Volpi e l'Uva, a wine bar just steps from Ponte Vecchio, has a limited menu of *affettati* (cold cuts), cheese, and *crostone* (hearty bruschetta)—a nice spot for a light lunch (for details, see the listing on page 330).

$ Trattoria Sabatino, farthest away of my Oltrarno listings (and not touristy), is a spacious, brightly lit mess hall. You get the feeling it hasn't changed much since it opened—in 1956. It's disturbingly cheap, with family character and a simple menu—a super place to watch locals munch, especially since you'll likely be sharing a table. It's a 15-minute walk from Ponte Vecchio (Mon-Fri 12:00-14:30 & 19:15-22:00, closed Sat-Sun, just outside Porta San Frediano, Via Pisana 2 red, see map on page 65, tel. 055-225-955, little English spoken). Let eating here be your reward after following the stroll in my ▢ Oltrarno Walk chapter.

Via di San Niccolò and Nearby

This charming little street—just over Ponte alle Grazie, behind

EATING

EATING

Cooking Classes

Tuscany has some of Italy's best food, and Florence is a natural place to learn a thing or two from this region's prodigious culinary tradition. Cooking classes range from multiday or multiweek courses for professional and semiprofessional chefs, to two- or three-hour crash courses for tourists. If you're an efficiency fiend like I am, these are a great use of time: You're combining a unique Italian experience (learning to cook, say, pasta from scratch) with a satisfying meal, all in just a few hours.

In my experience, the best casual cooking classes are taught by trained chefs with actual restaurant experience (rather than hobbyists or unemployed Florentines embarking on a second career). They take place in a real kitchen environment (rather than a stuffy classroom or "show" kitchen) and have a spirit of fun and interaction. The classes should be conducted in smaller groups (allowing more personal interaction with the instructor) and—perhaps most important—are hands-on rather than demonstration-based.

You'll typically spend a couple of hours cooking, then sit down to a hard-earned (if not always flawlessly executed) meal. They'll send you on your way with the recipes you prepared that day. Some classes also include a shopping trip to the market. While this adds an engaging dimension to your cooking experience, it also adds time and expense, and (some think) draws the focus away from the actual cooking.

The options listed below represent only a few of your many choices. As this is a fast-changing scene, it's worth doing some homework online and booking well ahead. For additional tour companies and private guides, see page 24.

In Tavola: A dedicated cooking school in the heart of the Oltrarno, In Tavola features trained Italian chefs (they speak English) who quickly demonstrate each step before setting you loose. You'll work in a functional kitchen, then sit down to eat in the cozy wine cellar (classes ranging from €53-73/person, ideally book well ahead but you can try calling last-minute, between the Pitti Palace and Brancacci Chapel at Via dei Velluti 18 red, tel. 055-217-672, www.intavola.org, info@intavola.org, Fabrizio).

Artviva: The Artviva walking-tour company offers a range of hands-on cooking, pasta, and pastry classes (€53-68/person, 10 percent discount with this book—log in at www.artviva.com/ricksteves with username "ricksteves" and password "reader," see their listing on page 26).

Florencetown: This walking-tour company offers a five-hour experience that starts with a trip to Mercato Centrale, then settles into their kitchen for a cooking lesson (€89/person, also 3-hour pizza- and gelato-making class for €49/person, 10 percent discount with the code "RICKSTEVES," see listing on page 26).

Hotel Silla—is the Oltrarno's "hipster corner" and can be a fun place for young foodies to explore (see the map on page 65). There's a convivial neighborhood pizzeria, an *enoteca,* a good *gelateria* (**Il Gelato di Filo,** at Via San Miniato 5 red), and a rollicking bar (**Il Baretto del Rifrullo,** at Via San Niccolò 55 red), which serves a generous buffet during happy hour. Street-art lovers enjoy popping into the **Clet gallery,** run by Clet Abraham, the artist who creatively disfigures signs around town (see page 319). For those looking to dine, two good eateries anchor the square:

$$ Antica Mescita San Niccolò, with traditional decor but a modern approach, feels like the grandkids took over Nonno's trattoria. Technically a wine bar, they also serve up Tuscan standbys (like soups and stews). There's delightful seating outside in good weather; their cellar is less cozy (daily 12:00-24:00, Via San Niccolò 60 red, tel. 055-234-2836).

$$$ Zeb is a tight, mod, minimalist wine-bar/deli with one long counter (just two dozen seats). Although the name stands for *zuppe e bolliti* ("soup and boiled meats"), they dish up all types of well-executed and elegantly presented Florentine food. Portions are large and fun to share, served up by charming Mama Guiseppina and her son Alberto. Dinner reservations are smart (closed Wed, Via San Miniato 2 red, tel. 055-234-2864, www.zebgastronomia. com).

EATING

FLORENCE WITH CHILDREN

With relatively few kid-friendly activities, Florence may not be the ideal destination for a family vacation. But it does offer enough entertainment to keep kids occupied for a few days. Spend the morning hiking up to Piazzale Michelangelo or the top of the Duomo's dome. In the afternoons, wander the city's streets and squares looking for quirky sculptures or visit various interactive museums. Here are a few ideas for family fun in the art capital of Europe.

Trip Tips

EATING
Florence offers plenty of food options for children.

What to Eat (and Drink)
- Kid-friendly foods found everywhere include fresh bread *(pane)* and pasta (plain is *"pasta bianca"* and pasta with butter is *"pasta al burro";* grated cheese will be served on the side). Pizza is another popular favorite—kids like margherita (tomato, basil, and cheese) and the slightly spicy Italian version of pepperoni *(diavola, salsiccia piccante,* or *salame piccante).*
- Popular drinks are *granitas* (slushies), *frullati* (smoothies), *frappés* (shakes), Orangina (orange soda), *limonata* (lemonade), *spremuta d'arancia* (fresh-squeezed orange juice), and *cioccolata calda* (hot chocolate).
- While the official drinking age in Italy is 18, teens 16 and over are sometimes offered wine or beer in restaurants, especially when accompanied by a parent. It's best to decide on a family policy beforehand.

When to Eat

- Eat dinner early (at about 19:00) to dodge the romantic crowd. Restaurants are less kid-friendly after 21:00. Skip the famous places. Look instead for self-service cafeterias, bars (children are welcome), or fast-food restaurants where younger kids can move around without bothering others.

Where to Eat

- For a refreshing respite from the midday heat, take a gelato break or go to a casual, air-conditioned place for lunch.
- Eating *al fresco* is fun; try places on squares where kids can run free while you dine. For ready-made picnics that can please everyone, try the *rosticcerie* (delis). *Pizza al taglio* shops sell cheap takeout pizza by the slice.
- For fast and kid-approved meals in the old center, there are plenty of hamburger and pizza joints. For a good cafeteria, try Self-Service Ristorante Leonardo (a block from the Duomo). *Gelaterie* such as Perchè No! (Via dei Tavolini 19) are brash and neon, providing some of the best high-calorie memories in town. These are described in the Eating in Florence chapter.

SIGHTSEEING

The key to a successful Florence family vacation is to slow down. Tackle one or two key sights each day, mix in a healthy dose of pure fun at a park or square, and take extended breaks when needed.

One of my favorite suggestions is to buy your child a trip journal, where he or she can record observations, thoughts, and favorite sights and memories. This journal could end up being your child's favorite souvenir.

Planning Your Time

- Incorporate your child's interests into each day's plans. Let your kids make some decisions, such as choosing lunch spots or deciding which stores or museums to visit. Deputize your child to lead you on my self-guided walks and museum tours.
- Older kids and teens can help plan the details of a museum visit, such as what to see, how to get there, and ticketing details.
- Italy's national museums and Florence's municipal museums generally offer free admission to children under 18—always ask before buying tickets for your kids.
- Use the tips in the Sights in Florence chapter to avoid lines whenever possible, especially at the Uffizi and Accademia.
- Public WCs are hard to find: Try museums, bars, gelato shops, and fast-food restaurants.

Books and Films for Kids

Get your kids into the spirit of Florence with these books and movies:

Florence: Just Add Water (Monica Fintoni, Simone Frasca, and Andrea Paoletti, 2007). This guidebook, excellent for travelers ages 10 and up, makes history more accessible for kids. It's easy to find in the US or in Florence (see bookstores listed on page 21).

If You Were Me and Lived In...Renaissance Italy (Carole P. Roman and Silvia Brunetti, 2016). This award-winning book helps kids imagine life in 15th-century Florence.

Kids Go Europe: Treasure Hunt Florence (Ellen Mouchawar and Marvin Mouchawar, 2006). Pocket-size and spiral-bound, this handy little book encourages youngsters to journal and sketch.

Michelangelo (Diane Stanley, 2003). The great Renaissance artist comes to life through Stanley's vibrant narration and illustrations.

Pinocchio (1940). This classic Disney animation, based on the Carlo Collodi novel written in Florence in the late 1800s, features the misadventures of a wooden marionette in his quest to become a real boy.

Stravaganza series (Mary Hoffman, 2002-2012). This popular, imaginative adventure series follows individuals who time-travel to 16th-century Italy. The series' second book, *City of Stars,* is set in "Remora," an alternate-universe Siena, and the third book, *City of Flowers,* takes place in "Giglia," a.k.a. Florence.

The Wizards Return: Alex vs. Alex (2013). Alex Russo, from the Disney TV show *Wizards of Waverly Place,* accidentally creates an evil version of herself during a trip to Tuscany, leading to an epic battle atop the Leaning Tower of Pisa.

CHILDREN

Successful Sightseeing

- If you're visiting art museums with younger children, you could hit the gift shop first to buy postcards; then hold a scavenger hunt to find the pictured artwork.
- Museum audioguides help older children and teens get the most out of a sight.
- Bring a sketchbook to a museum and encourage kids to select a painting or statue to draw. It's a great way for them to slow down and observe.
- Context Florence offers a children's tour program run by scholarly guides who make the city's great art and culture accessible to a younger audience (see page 27). Local guide Alessandra Marchetti also does kid-tailored tours (see page 27).
- If homesickness sets in, take your kid to see a movie—Ameri-

can movies are commonplace (often shown in English with Italian subtitles).

MONEY, SAFETY, AND STAYING CONNECTED

Before setting them loose, talk to your kids about safety and money.

- Give your child a money belt and an expanded allowance; you are on vacation, after all. Let your kids budget their funds by comparing and contrasting the dollar and euro.
- If you allow older kids to explore a museum or neighborhood on their own, be sure to establish a clear meeting time and place.
- For kids of all ages, have a "what if" procedure in place in case something goes wrong. Give your kids your hotel's business card, your phone number (if you brought a mobile phone), and emergency taxi fare. Let them know to ask to use the phone at a hotel if they are lost. And if they have mobile phones, show them how to make calls in Italy.
- Teens traveling with a mobile device can keep in touch with friends at home—and Europeans they meet—via apps such as WhatsApp (common in Europe), Snapchat, Google Talk, FaceTime, or Skype. Readily available Wi-Fi helps keep on-line time affordable, or consider buying an international data plan (see page 644).

TRANSPORTATION

Kids often travel cheaper or for free.

- Children under three feet tall ride free on public buses when accompanied by an adult.
- Families with kids can sometimes get price breaks on train tickets; see page 650 for details.

Top Kids' Sights and Activities

Seek out kid-friendly sights, such as the Leonardo Museums, the Galileo Science Museum, or the Palazzo Vecchio.

MUSEUMS AND CHURCHES
Leonardo Museums

After touring a bunch of hands-off museums, squirming kids will enjoy the hands-on activities at either Le Macchine di Leonardo da Vinci or Museo Leonardo da Vinci. They can burn off some of that human energy while powering modern re-creations of the brilliant scientist's machines (see page 50).

Palazzo Vecchio

With a number of interactive activities for kids, this palace can be a good place for the whole family to explore together. For kids ages six and up, the palazzo rents €5 family kits—turtle-shaped backpacks filled with materials for helping kids learn about the Medici and uncover interesting details about the place. The palace's family program offers a variety of daily activities (in the morning and afternoon) for kids as young as four all the way up to teenagers (€4/person, reservations recommended). Enjoy brief performances portraying Medici history, or help your kids paint their own frescoes. As the offerings are always changing, call or drop by the info desk at the ticket office to find out what your options are and make reservations.

📖 See the Palazzo Vecchio Tour chapter.

Galileo Science Museum

See several of Galileo's fingers on display, plus cool old telescopes and early chemical and science lab stuff. Engaging video screens illustrate scientific principles. Private tours and special child-friendly programs are available. Be warned that some parents find the museum's displays on childbirth too graphic for kids.

📖 See the Galileo Science Museum tour chapter.

Duomo Dome Climb

Climbing the dome of the cathedral is almost like climbing an urban mountain—you'll spiral up in a strange dome-within-a-dome space, see some musty old tools used in the construction, get a bird's-eye peek into the nave from way up, and then pop out to see the best city view in town (see page 39).

Bargello Museum

While kids are likely to be more familiar with Michelangelo's *David*, they may prefer the works at the Bargello. This underappreciated sculpture museum in a former police-station-turned-prison hosts Florence's most interesting collection of statues—with many bizarre poses.

📖 See the Bargello Tour chapter.

Uffizi Courtyard

This courtyard, filled with artists and souvenir stalls, is ringed by statues of all the famous Florentines (Amerigo Vespucci, Machiavelli, Leonardo, and so on)—great for putting faces to names on a sweep through history (see page 90 of the Renaissance Walk chapter).

Museum of Precious Stones

Find 500 kinds of stones on display, demonstrating the fascinating techniques of inlay and mosaic work (see page 43).

PARKS AND SQUARES
Boboli and Bardini Gardens
These adjacent gardens outside the Pitti Palace are landscaped wonderlands. While designed to give adults a break from the city, they're kid-friendly, too.

   📖 See the Pitti Palace Tour chapter.

Parco delle Cascine
Originally constructed as a hunting ground and farm for the Medici family, Florence's sprawling public park has lots of grass, historic monuments, and a playground. For a fee, families can cool off in the park's outdoor swimming pool, the Pavoniere.

   Cost and Hours: Park—free and open year-round; swimming pool—€7 for kids 4-12, €9 for adults, open daily May-Aug 10:00-19:00, until 18:30 on Sat-Sun, Via della Catena 2, tel. 055-362-233.

   Getting There: Head west of the old center along the north side of the river (25-minute walk from Ponte Vecchio) or take tram T1 from the southwest corner of the train station to the stop Cascine.

Piazza d'Azeglio
This peaceful and breezy park, complete with playground, can be a welcome refuge from touring madness (open daily, dawn to dusk).

   Getting There: It's a 15-minute walk east from the Duomo. Or take bus #12 or #13 from the train station or the Piazza San Marco bus stop just north of the Duomo.

CHILDREN

Piazzale Michelangelo
Older children may enjoy hiking up to this panoramic piazza for the superb view of Florence and the Duomo. Or take a taxi or ride the bus up and then enjoy the easy downhill walk back into town. Bring a picnic and eat lunch on the somewhat hidden terrace, just off the west side of the piazza (see page 66).

Piazza della Repubblica
For kids running on their gelato buzz well into the evening hours, this vibrant piazza has a sparkling carousel and lively street musicians.

MORE EXPERIENCES

Open-Air Markets

Florence's various markets are fun for kids (see the Shopping in Florence chapter). Remember to haggle.

Artviva Art Classes

Local tour company Artviva offers cooking, painting, and sculpture classes that work well for older kids and teens (see page 26).

Florencetown's "I Bike Florence" Tour

This tour, led by a quick-talking guide, is a 2.5-hour, 15-stop blitz of the town's top sights. Families with younger children are provided with tandem bikes (see page 26).

Leaning Tower of Pisa

Of your day-trip options from Florence, this one is probably the most interesting for kids. Note that kids under age eight aren't allowed to climb the tower (see page 431 of the Pisa chapter).

CHILDREN

SHOPPING IN FLORENCE

Florence may be one of Europe's best shopping towns—it's been known for its sense of style since the Medici days. While most businesses are as staid and stately as the city itself, a sampling of creative, funky shops will help you appreciate the younger side of Florence.

Hours: Smaller stores are generally open about 9:00-13:00 and 15:30-19:30, usually closed on Sunday, often closed on Monday (or at least Monday morning), and sometimes closed for a couple of weeks around August 15. Bigger stores have similar hours, without the afternoon break. Many brick-and-mortar stores also run small stalls in market squares.

Information: For shopping ideas, ads, and a list of markets, see *The Florentine* newspaper or *Florence Concierge Information* magazine (free from TIs and some hotels). For authentic, locally produced wares, look for shops displaying the *Esercizi Storici Fiorentini* seal, with a picture of the Palazzo Vecchio's tower. At these city-endorsed "Historical Florentine Ventures," you may pay a premium, but quality is assured (for a list of shops, see www.esercizistorici.it).

Tax Refunds: For details on VAT refunds and customs regulations, see page 613.

Department Stores: Department store chains include **Coin,** the Italian equivalent of Macy's (Mon-Sat 10:00-20:00, Sun from 10:30, on Via de' Calzaiuoli, near Orsanmichele Church); the upscale **La Rinascente** (Mon-Sat 9:00-21:00, Sun 10:30-20:00, on Piazza della Repubblica); and **Oviesse,** a discount clothing chain, the local JCPenney (Mon-Sat 9:00-19:30, Sun from 10:00, near train station at intersection of Via Panzani and Via del Giglio).

Bargaining: At Florence's many street markets (such as San Lorenzo Market), and even at many midrange leather shops, the first price you're quoted is an opening volley; sometimes if you simply show small signs of reluctance, you'll be offered a better price. Feel free to push back with a much lower offer. Vendors may also sweeten the deal if you offer to pay cash or buy two or more of something. Some vendors are willing to help you with the VAT red tape, while others give you a discount equivalent to the tax to avoid the hassle.

What to Buy

LEATHER

With its inimitable sense of style, richly perfumed leather shops, and persuasive sales clerks, Florence has a way of turning leather browsers into leather buyers. Florence's long leatherworking tradition was born at Santa Croce Church, where Franciscan monks perfected the art of binding gorgeously illustrated manuscripts. Over the centuries, the skill evolved into a more fashion-forward form of leatherworking—designer shoes, jackets, and handbags. You'll see leather for sale all over Florence.

Leather-Buying Tips

While the following advice is focused primarily on leather jackets, much of it also applies to handbags, shoes, and other items. If you're serious about buying a big-ticket leather item, do some homework before your trip. Visit importers and boutiques in your home city so that you can smartly comparison-shop when you get to Florence.

A good-quality, authentic leather, "made in Italy" jacket starts at about €250-350. Top-quality and designer jackets can cost much more—and there's a big difference in quality between a €100 jacket, a €250 jacket, and a €500 jacket. If shopping in the €100-200 range, you'll find plenty of merchants willing to help you part with your money (particularly at San Lorenzo Market). But if you pay a lower price, you're likely sacrificing quality, craftsmanship, and durability.

Remember, bargaining is common, and the prices are as soft as that famously supple Italian leather. Don't be shy. Except at the top-of-the-line designers, assume that the first quoted price is just a starting point.

Because any item that is even partially assembled in Italy can be legally labeled "Made in Italy," many leather producers—including some famous brands—make their items abroad, then bring them home for a few final stitches. And even leather that is truly worked, from start to finish, in Italy, may originate in South America or elsewhere.

When evaluating leather, here are a few things to look for: Leather should smell like, well, leather—not chemicals. (Some vendors tout their "vegetable-tanned" wares, meaning they use only organic treatments.) But that "genuine leather" smell can be faked as well. Don't be fooled by other tricks, either, such as holding a lighter or match against the leather to show that it doesn't burn. Some leather imitators also pass this test.

The "touch test" is important: The leather should feel soft and pliable. If it's rough and thick, it's probably lower quality (or imitation). Crumple the leather to see how well it rebounds. If it remains wadded or wrinkled, it's not top-notch.

Examine the seams and stitching for flaws, consider the quality of the liner, and test the zippers. (American men find themselves fumbling with "backwards" Italian zippers, which run along the left rather than the right.)

Consider the fit. Italians prefer their jackets more fitted than Americans, and their idea of the "right size" may feel snug to you. Don't let a salesperson talk you into a jacket that doesn't fit. ("Italians like to roll their sleeves up" is one of many lines vendors may employ to try to get you to splurge on a jacket that doesn't fit properly.) Better leather shops can alter your jacket (sometimes on the spot). They may even offer to custom-make a jacket for you and ship it—though, both for matters of fit and finances, this should only be considered at a shop that has a stellar reputation.

Leather Jackets

When Italians want to shop for affordable leather, they go to suburban outlet malls (such as The Mall, with outlet stores for many top-name Italian designers, about 15 miles southeast of the Duomo, www.themall.it). Or they head for a leather factory (Piero Tucci is one of many with a good reputation, www.pierotucci.com). But this isn't practical for a carless tourist on a short visit. Most leather shops within walking distance of the historic core cater to tourists and well-heeled locals, so bargains are rare. In these neighborhoods, you have four general options, from cheap to very pricey.

1) Buy an inexpensive, likely imitation, almost certainly made-in-China jacket from a street vendor. Many of these street stalls are actually outposts of cheap leather shops.

2) Visit a hole-in-the-wall

shop with slightly better quality, though still somewhat ambiguous origin. For travelers on a budget, this is a decent option.

3) Find a midrange leather "factory" or gallery with a good reputation, authentic made-in-Italy merchandise, and higher prices. Note that some of these vendors actually make the jackets sold under designer labels. If you can afford it, I'd lean toward this option to get something of higher quality.

4) Go designer at Gucci, Prada, or another big-name boutique.

Here are a few shops with good reputations:

La Pelle, straight ahead from the Oltrarno end of Ponte Vecchio, stocks a fine variety of good-quality leather coats (€300-400); the welcome is warm but not too aggressive (Via Guicciardini 11 red, tel. 055-292-031, www.lapellesrl.it).

Atelier Classe sits down a mostly neglected alley near Piazza Santa Croce. This boutique feels classier than its cut-rate neighbors—and its prices are higher too (€400-600 for a basic jacket, on-site alterations possible, closed Sun and Mon until 14:00, Via Torta 16 red, tel. 055-268-145, www.atelierclasse.com). They also have a shoe store two doors down.

Davide Cesari sits along the embankment on the north side of the Arno, just steps from Ponte Vecchio. They make jackets for some well-known American brands. It feels tasteful but a bit pushy (€250-400 jackets, Lungarno Acciaiuoli 32 red, tel. 055-282-019).

Noi, facing Piazza Davanzati, has jackets of reputable quality as well as a good selection of well-priced bags (Via Porta Rossa 65 red, tel. 055-210-319).

Michelangelo, burrowed down a side street from the San Lorenzo Market chaos, is a bit cheaper than the others, but the quality feels less assured (€250-350 jackets, daily 10:00-19:00, Via Giovan Battista Zannoni 9/11 red, tel. 055-285-497, www.michelangeloflorentineleather.com).

On Borgo La Noce: To step down a notch, browse the aggressive shops that line Borgo La Noce between the Basilica of San Lorenzo and Mercato Centrale. While these shops—including **Massimo Leather, Raffaello,** and **Pelletteria La Noce**—have their fans (likely because of their somewhat lower prices and gregarious/"helpful" sales clerks), they feel a bit less upmarket than the ones listed above.

Handbags and Other Leather Accessories

Consider these places when shopping for leather handbags, wallets, and other items; some of the jacket shops listed earlier also sell accessories.

The venerable **Leather School** (Scuola del Cuoio) at **Santa Croce Church**—described on page 216—is the most famous place to buy leather in Florence. The quality is unsurpassed, and a splurge here will get you a top-end item that should last a lifetime (figure €70 for a simple wallet or €150 for a small purse; monogramming costs just a bit extra). But even for browsers, the school is worth a visit as the most accessible place to watch leather workers in action. Although the leather school produces mostly handbags, briefcases, travel cases, wallets, and belts, they do have a small selection of jackets (daily 10:00-18:00, artisans at work Mon-Fri 10:00-17:30, closed Sun off-season, enter around behind Santa Croce Church at Via San Giuseppe 5 red, or from inside the church; 055-244-533, www.scuoladelcuoio.com).

Of Florence's many midrange shops specializing in bags, **Via de Ginori 23r** is well worth a look. Conveniently located just a couple of blocks from the San Lorenzo Market, this family-run shop carries a tasteful collection of stylish yet practical bags—some of their own production, some from other local suppliers—and a line of eco-friendly bags made from recycled tires (Mon 15:30-19:30, Tue-Sat 10:00-14:00 & 15:00-19:30, closed Sun, may be closed Sat afternoon in summer, Via de Ginori 23 red, tel. 055-239-8031).

Not far away, **Furò e Punteruolo** ("Flatknife and Awl") sells a small selection of wallets, purses, and handbags in a more rustic style. Paulo makes everything by hand on the premises (closed Mon morning, Via del Giglio 29 red, mobile 348-437-0867).

Across the river in the Oltrarno, a couple of blocks from Ponte Vecchio, **Roberta** is another popular choice for fashionable but moderately priced handbags (Mon-Sat 10:00-19:30, closed Sun, also closed Mon Nov-Feb, Borgo San Jacopo 74 red, tel. 055-284-017, www.robertafirenze.com).

Leather Shoes

I dare not wade into this highly subjective topic. But for a reliable local standby, consider **Gilardini,** just steps from the Duomo and Baptistery. This classic and classy shop sells a variety of Italian leather shoes, for women and men (Sun-Mon 15:30-19:30, Tue-Sat 9:30-19:30, Via Cerretani 8 red, tel. 055-212-412, www.gilardinishoes.it).

PERFUME AND COSMETICS

Long ago, as part of their service to the community, Dominican friars typically served as pharmacists (a.k.a. chemists or alchemists). And—back in an age when "medicine" meant potions and herbal remedies—the pharmacy at the Dominican church of Santa Maria Novella was a local trendsetter in the art of fragrance. In the centuries since, perfumes and colognes have taken off in a big way in other parts of this fashion-forward city. Below are two fragrance experiences—both elegant, but quite different: a big, staid, historic perfumery, and a smaller, more intimate alternative.

SHOPPING

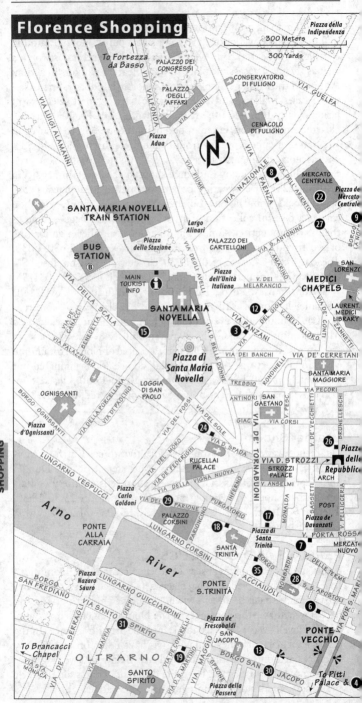

Florence Shopping

Department Stores
1. Coin
2. La Rinascente
3. Oviesse

Leather
4. To La Pelle
5. Atelier Classe
6. Davide Cesari
7. Noi
8. Michelangelo
9. Borgo La Noce Shops
10. S. Croce Leather School
11. Via de Ginori 23r (Bags)
12. Furò e Punteruolo (Bags)
13. Roberta (Bags)
14. Gilardini (Shoes)

Perfume & Cosmetics
15. Farmacia di S. Maria Novella
16. Aquaflor

Paper, Stationery & Prints
17. Il Papiro (2)
18. Alberto Cozzi

19. L'Ippogrifo
20. Fabriano Boutique
21. Johnsons & Relatives

Food
22. Mercato Centrale
23. EATaly

Gifts & Books
24. MIO Concept Store
25. Paperback Exchange
26. RED Bookstore

Shopping Areas
27. San Lorenzo Market
28. Borgo Santi Apostoli
29. Via del Parione
30. Borgo San Jacopo
31. Via di Santo Spirito
32. Piazza Santa Croce
33. To Via Pietrapiana & Borgo La Croce

Fashion Museums
34. Gucci Museum
35. Ferragamo Museum

The **Farmacia di Santa Maria Novella** was founded by the Dominicans of Santa Maria Novella back in 1612. Thick with the lingering aroma of centuries of spritzes, this palatial perfumery and cosmetics shop started as the herb garden of the Santa Maria Novella monks. Well-known even today for its top-quality products, it is extremely Florentine. It's as formal as it is historic, with dressy, no-nonsense clerks. Pick up the history sheet from the rack, and wander deep into the shop. The main sales room, where you can sample more than 60 perfumes—as well as face creams, body lotions, and talcum powders—was originally a chapel; the middle (green) room offers potpourris and incenses for the home; and the historic third room, which sells herbal products, is where the pharmacy was originally established. From here, you can peek at one of Santa Maria Novella's cloisters with its dreamy frescoes and imagine a time before Vespas and tourists. If you get serious about buying, pick up an electronic card, which the clerks load up with your selections. When you're ready to check out, bring it back to the bunker-like perfume room to pick up your purchases (daily 9:00-20:00, a block from Piazza Santa Maria Novella, 100 yards down Via della Scala at #16, tel. 055-216-276, www.smnovella.com).

Aquaflor is a rare shop where the master perfumer sells his wares in the same space where he makes them. Hidden away on a side street between Piazza della Signoria and Piazza Santa Croce, Aquaflor uses only natural extracts to pull out subtle but warmly pungent aromas, free of the acrid artificial edge of many mass-market fragrances. They're generous with samples, and the space is enjoyable to simply be in. In one of the three cavernous rooms, you'll see Sileno's "organ"—the giant cabinet stocked with little jars and bottles—where, like a musician, he finds just the right combination of notes. They can also create a custom fragrance just for you (daily 10:00-19:00, Borgo Santa Croce 6, tel. 055-234-3471, www.florenceparfum.com). After your visit, be sure to dip into the courtyard of the sprawling palazzo-turned-condominium complex that houses the shop.

PAPER, STATIONERY, AND PRINTS

Long known as a literary center, Florence offers traditional marbled stationery (with its edge dipped carefully into a bath of swirling pigments) and leatherbound journals, plus reproductions of old documents, prints, maps, and manuscripts.

Just North of the River: This area seems to specialize in high-quality stationery shops. **Il Papiro** has been selling a classy selection of marbled paper, stationery, and paper boxes for decades (closed Sun, Via Porta Rossa 76 red, tel. 055-216-593, www.ilpapirofirenze.eu). A few blocks west, **Alberto Cozzi** is a big shop with a colorfully cluttered window display of marbled paper products (Via del Parione 35 red, tel. 055-294-968).

In the Oltrarno: L'Ippogrifo makes stylish, high-quality prints of mostly Florentine scenes—a notch above the mass-produced posters you'll see around town (closed Sun, at Via di Santo Spirito 5 red, tel. 055-213-255, www.ippogrifostampedarte.com). **Legatoria La Carta** is a workshop producing all manner of marbled paper products, from blank books to desk sets. It's a few short blocks down Via Romana from the Pitti Palace's entrance, and just a block from the Boboli Gardens' rear entrance (Mon-Sat 9:30-17:30, closed Sun, Via Romana 58 red, see map on page 65, tel. 055-094-8043, www.legatoria-lacarta.com).

In the Historical Center: Fabriano Boutique, tucked in the twisty streets between the Duomo and the river, is part of a top-end chain selling leatherbound office tools and modern stationery (daily 10:00-20:00, Via del Corso 59 red, www.fabrianoboutique.com). **Il Papiro,** described above, has another branch right behind the Duomo (Piazza Duomo 24 red, tel. 055-281-628). Nearby, **Johnsons & Relatives** also sells high-end stationery and paper products, as well as fine table linens (Via del Proconsolo 26 red, tel. 055-265-8103).

EDIBLE GOODIES

Mercato Centrale is a prime spot for stocking up on culinary souvenirs (Mon-Fri 7:00-14:00, Sat 7:00-17:00, closed Sun, a block north of the Basilica of San Lorenzo). Classic purchases include olive oil and balsamic vinegar, unusually shaped and colored pasta, dried porcini mushrooms, spices, and jars of pestos and sauces (such as pesto *genovese* or *tartufo*—truffle).

EATaly, an outpost of the gourmet minimall chain, is a convenient place to pick up pricey, premium consumable souvenirs (see listing on page 288).

Wine: While many bring home a special bottle of Chianti Classico or Brunello di Montalcino, I take home only the names of my favorite wines—and buy them later at my hometown wine shop. Remember that all liquids—wine, olive oil, or otherwise—need to be placed in checked luggage.

FUNKY, ARTSY SOUVENIRS

Clet Abraham, a French-born street artist now living in Florence, has gained an international reputation for his clever alterations to traffic signs. Most commonly, he adds his flourishes to the dull "no entry" signs, a horizontal white bar in a red circle. In his most iconic piece—which you'll see around the city—he's added a figure that looks like it's sneaking off with the white bar. His message: Think before you blindly follow regulations. While you can debate whether these works blur the line between vandalism and art, Clet's Banksy-like creativity is hard to deny. The Clet gallery, where you can buy stickers and other fun souvenirs, or fork out several thousand euros for an original, is in the Oltrarno's lively, youthful San Niccolò neighborhood (Mon-Sat 9:30-18:00, closed Sun, Via dell'Olmo 8 red, see map on page 65).

MIO Concept Store feels like a hipster home sale. It has an eclectic collection of gifts, home decor, gadgets, jewelry, and accessories, much of it by local artists and designers (Mon-Sat 10:00-13:30 & 14:30-19:00, closed Sun, in a nondescript urban zone between the train station and Piazza della Signoria at Via delle Spada 34 red, tel. 055-264-5543, www.mio-concept.com).

MORE SOUVENIR IDEAS

You'll find many **art reproductions** of your favorite Florentine pieces on posters, calendars, books, prints, and so on. Major museums—such as the Uffizi and Accademia—have excellent bookstores. The bookstore at the Duomo Museum is well stocked and a bit less crowded than the shops at some of the bigger sights. For a list of other bookstores in Florence, see page 21.

Other souvenir ideas include silk ties, scarves, Tuscan ceramics, and wood-carved bowls and spoons. Goofy knickknacks featuring Renaissance masterpieces are popular: Botticelli mouse pads, Raphael lipstick holders, and plaster *David*s.

Best Shopping Areas

To explore Florence's shopping scene, make a point to break out of the heavily traveled tourist zones in the heart of town, such as the **Santa Croce** area, **Ponte Vecchio**'s gold and silver shops, the old, covered **Mercato Nuovo** (three blocks north of Ponte Vecchio; see page 58), and, to a lesser extent, the streets near the **Accademia.** Just a short walk away, you'll find several pleasant streets and neighborhoods with a (somewhat) more authentic and innovative array of shops. Some close for a mid-afternoon break, and many close for part or all day on Sunday and/or Monday.

SAN LORENZO MARKET

The market stalls between the Basilica of San Lorenzo and Mercato Centrale are no secret—this is ground zero for tourists seek-

ing cheap, cut-rate sou-
venirs, lower-end leather,
clothing, T-shirts, and
handbags. It's a fun area to
browse and bargain. You'll
find many of the stalls in
the narrow streets around
Mercato Centrale (daily
9:00-19:00, closed Mon in
winter).

If you end up going overboard on Florentine finds, you can
buy a cheap suitcase here and at the various open-air market stalls
around town. A big suitcase with wheels costs about €25 and
should last just long enough to haul your purchases home.

HISTORIC CENTER, JUST NORTH OF THE RIVER

The following streets run parallel to the river one block inland,
from near the Uffizi westward. I've listed (from east to west)
some of the more interesting shops on each. Near the start of this
stretch, you'll find jewelry shops, clothing boutiques, and touristy
but good-quality shops selling stationery and other local products;
farther along, more home-decor stores are mixed in.

Borgo Santi Apostoli

This narrow and fairly touristy street begins just one short block
up from Ponte Vecchio. Among the boutiques, designer handbag
shops, and jewelers is **Gatto Bianco** ("White Cat," on the right,
at #12 red), which sells big, chunky, modern-style jewelry. At #20
red, **T. Pestelli** is a fascinating silverwork shop where Tommaso
creates finely detailed jewelry and small sculptures. Continuing
along, you'll pass several antiques and art shops. After about two
blocks, on the right (#42 red), is an outpost of **Angela Caputi,** another local jeweler whose oversized, colorful resin accessories has
earned her a loyal following. Just after that, set back on the little
square on the left, is **La Bottega dell'Olio,** selling olive oil and
beautiful hand-carved wooden bowls, spoons, and other kitchen
utensils (Piazza del Limbo 4 red). Also on the left (#37 red) is **Solo
a Firenze** ("Only in Florence"), with a tasteful collection of cards,
prints, and paintings, as well as silverwork and jewelry made by the
family. Near the end of the street (#45 red), the stylish and upscale
Viajiyu sells a selection of their own pricey, fashionable shoes and
will custom-make some for you. Filling the stately 800-year-old
building next door is the flagship store for the famous shoemaker
Ferragamo, with its endearing shoe museum in the basement (Via
de' Tornabuoni 2; see description on page 60).

Ferragamo marks the end of Borgo Santi Apostoli, where it

SHOPPING

Florence's Upscale Boutique Streets

Florence is a bastion of high fashion, where budget travelers can enjoy high-end window shopping. The entire area between the river and the cathedral is busy with inviting boutiques that show off ritzy Italian fashions. The highest concentration of shops is along Via dei Calzaiuoli, Via de' Tornabuoni, and the streets in between (particularly around Piazza della Repubblica). In recent years, city officials have been pedestrianizing and sprucing up more and more streets in this area in an attempt to cement Florence's status as a high-fashion destination. (Many locals grouse that in so doing, they've forced out more characteristic, low-rent mom-and-pop shops that have thrived here for generations.)

Via dei Calzaiuoli mixes tourist-rip-off pizza and gelato joints with upscale chain boutiques.

Via de' Tornabuoni is a delightfully pedestrianized, flower-lined street where Prada and Gucci face each other, like bitter rivals, kicking off a string of Italian designers and international chains. The bottom half of the street features the big Italian "-i" designers (Gucci, Armani, Fendi, Tiffan-i); a pillar marks the intersection with the lower-rent, and more characteristic, Borgo Santi Apostoli.

Piazza della Repubblica has several fine shops, including the upscale La Rinascente department store, with its Duomo-view café terrace (see page 53).

If you head under that piazza's arch and down **Via degli Strozzi,** you'll pass big names—Dolce & Gabbana, Louis Vuitton, Cartier, and Bulgari—on the way to the fine Palazzo Strozzi (a good place for a coffee break; described on page 54) and the intersection with Via de' Tornabuoni.

Fashionistas will enjoy the **Ferragamo Museum** and flagship store near Ponte Santa Trinità and the **Gucci Museum,** with a prime address on Piazza della Signoria (both described on page 60).

SHOPPING

opens up into the triangular Piazza Santa Trinità. Leaving this square to the right (away from the river) is **Via de' Tornabuoni,** arguably Florence's most inviting top-of-the-line boutique browsing street. This pedestrianized street is lined with oversized flower pots, well-heeled shoppers, and international designers. But to keep within our budget, we'll continue straight ahead through Piazza Santa Trinità, jogging a bit right to angle up...

Via del Parione

Though we're gradually leaving the high-fashion district, this street still boasts plenty of trendy boutiques, handbag shops, and salons. A good paper shop (described earlier, under "Paper, Stationery, and Prints") kicks off this street: **Alberto Cozzi** (on the left, #35 red).

Letizia Fiorini (on the right, #60 red) lovingly crafts handmade puppets, most of them based on traditional commedia dell'arte figures. Across the street (#37 red), **Bazzanti** is a sprawling space with bulky statues for the home and garden.

At the end of the street, you'll pop out at a lively three-way intersection. Across the street are a trio of interesting shops: **Marioluca Giusti** sells high-quality plastic plates, glasses, and other tableware that look stylish but are durable enough for a backyard picnic (Via Lunga 133); **A. Bianda Coltelleria** is a classy gentlemen's shop, selling pocketknives and shaving gear (Via della Vigna Nuova 86 red); and **La Piccola T-Shirteria** sells unique Florentine-hipster loungewear (Via della Vigna Nuova 84 red).

From here, if you take a sharp right and head up **Via della Vigna Nuova,** you'll head back to the main upscale shopping zone (Via de' Tornabuoni), passing several smaller boutiques. Along here, step into **Controluce** (#89 red), with colorful, creative, even goofy household stuff. But mostly this street is all about clothes— it's a great place to shop for affordable, everyday apparel, with a few splurge boutiques mixed in (Petit Bateau, at #16 red, is the perfect place to outfit the li'l sailor in your life).

THE OLTRARNO

Across the river, a short walk past the tourist crowds takes you to some less-discovered zones. I've focused on two areas: near the Pitti Palace, and the main street parallel to the river (Borgo San Jacopo to Via di Santo Spirito).

The Oltrarno is known for its artisanal workshops, where craftspeople make and sell fine handmade items on their premises. I've listed the shops that are easily accessible to browsers. For a more in-depth look at Oltrarno workshops, pick up the brochure called "A Tour of Artisan Workshops," which you may find at the TI or at participating shops. Various tour operators also do tours of Oltrarno workshops (see page 24).

Near the Pitti Palace

Both of these streets are within a very short walk of the Pitti Palace.

Sdrucciolo de' Pitti: Directly across from the big courtyard in front of the Pitti Palace, poke down the narrow alley called Sdrucciolo de' Pitti. While somewhat touristy (just steps from a big sight), and therefore pricey, it's a convenient place to drop into a cluster of fine little shops. One short block down the lane, on the left, is **La Casa della Stampa** (#11 red), a cramped prints shop cluttered with old printing presses and a "bargain bin" of tattered antique documents. Just past that is **Giulia Materia** (#13 red), a hipster design boutique with colorful and creative clothes, cloth bags, and blank books. Next is **Le Telerie Toscane** (#15 red), with textiles—placemats, towels, table runners, and tablecloths—with Tuscan designs that feel less mass-produced than the ones sold at cheap souvenir stands. And across the street, **Argenteria Donato Zaccaro** (#12 red) sells silver jewelry and other goods.

Via Romana: Running southwest from the Pitti Palace into a sleepy residential quarter, this workaday street features an eclectic mix of art galleries, antique shops, and creative boutiques that offer a change of pace from the generally traditional offerings in the Oltrarno. (You can also visit this street on your way home from the Boboli Gardens—the back exit of Boboli puts you at the far end of Via Romana, so you can follow this walk backward to the Pitti Palace entry.)

Facing the palace, turn right and walk past the **Oro Nero** shop (Piazza de Pitti 1 red), which sells a wide array of "Black Gold" (as its name means): artisanal chocolates and teas (you'll encounter another tea shop later). Continuing straight past the shop and through the small, busy Piazza San Felice, you'll start down Via Romana. On the left, **Anita Russo** (#13 red), a ceramics studio, sells pottery pieces made by Anita herself. Across the street, **Erboristeria Boboli** (#12 red)—a fragrant shop with herbal/organic lotions, fragrances, candles, and so on—is worth a whiff. Passing some clothing boutiques, you'll reach **Tealicious** (on the right, #26 red), where Laura curates a fragrant selection of exotic teas, including some unusual flavor combinations. A block farther on the left, **Tabescè** (#39 red) produces quirky, modern, Murano-style glass jewelry and funky art objects that appeal to hipsters. Across the street is the characteristic **Legatoria La Carta** marbled-paper shop and book bindery (#58 red; see listing on page 319). Soon after, you reach the rear entrance to Boboli Gardens; Via Romana continues past this point, but there are fewer interesting shops.

Along the River

Borgo San Jacopo and Via di Santo Spirito, running parallel to the river through the heart of the Oltrarno, are lined with fine shops. The first stretch (Borgo San Jacopo)—with its proximity to Ponte Vecchio—feels quite touristy, with jewelry and clothing stores and souvenir shops, while Via di Santo Spirito feels increasingly more local, with several home-decor places. Crossing Ponte Vecchio from the historical center, turn right and head down...

Borgo San Jacopo: The shops along here are heavy on leather, clothing boutiques, jewelry, textiles, and prints. The **Ortiga Sicilia** fragrance shop (#12 red) is the venture of one of the founders of Crabtree & Evelyn, who lives just around the corner. **Le Sorelle** (#30 red) is a fun home and garden shop. **Domi Textile & Design** (#38 red) carries top-quality but pricey Busatti linens for the home. **Fantasie Florentine** (#50 red)—a cluttered stationery and souvenir shop—marks the lane leading to a fine river perch for viewing Ponte Vecchio. Soon after and across the street, **Argentiere Pagliai** (#41 red) is a fine, old-school Oltrarno silversmith with a real workshop in the back; while there's not much to browse inside, the window displays are worth a look. Passing a few more hole-in-the-wall jewelry shops, you'll reach **Roberta,** with leather handbags (for details, see listing on page 315); their second shop, a few doors down, has more bags, plus scarves and ties. You'll come to the busy cross-street Via Maggio, passing a characteristic fountain on your left. Crossing Via Maggio straight ahead, you'll start down...

Via di Santo Spirito: From here, the shops get a bit less touristy, with more real artisans mixed in. Passing the recommended Olio and Convivium wine and olive oil bar on the right, look across the street for **L'Ippogrifo,** a print shop (#5 red; see listing on page 319). Next is a stretch of furniture, antique, and home-decor shops—less practical for souvenir-hunting, but satisfying for window-shopping...and getting ideas for back home. There's also a smattering of clothing boutiques along here. On the right (at #16 red), watch for the cluttered, hole-in-the-wall **La Bottega di Mastro Geppetto,** with Pinocchio-themed window displays up front, but a handmade wooden frame store in back. (Written and published in Florence in 1881-1883, the original Pinocchio stories are often appropriated by local merchants for their touristic currency. You'll notice a chain of tacky, Pinocchio-themed, made-in-China wooden toy stores around Florence that act as magnets for tourists. At least this shop actually carves wood on the premises.)

Fiorile (#26 red) is a florist and housewares shop that feels like a hidden gem with modern style; it may just inspire you to pick up a bouquet for your hotel room. Next door, **Studio Puck** (#28 red) sells prints and frames with a unique, fresh take that offers a change of pace from the traditional Florentine designs. On the left, **Castorina** (#15 red) produces delicate, hand-carved wooden sculptures, frames, furniture, table legs, and so on—some gilded, others unfinished. Step inside to smell the sawdust and watch the masters hard at work in the back. Near the end of the street on the right, **Angela Caputi** (#58 red) produces big, bold, colorful, lightweight resin jewelry; she also has a shop across the river, on Borgo Santi Apostoli. Just beyond, peek in the window at **Francesco** (#62 red), an old-school cobbler's shop that makes shoes on site. The busy cross-street marks the end of Via di Santo Spirito.

For a look at one more artisan shop, turn left (away from the river) up Via dei Serragli, a busier street with more antiques and housewares. About a block up on your right is **Bianchi Lamberto e Duccio** (#10 red). Here a father-and-son team produces bronze and brass frames, door knockers, and other design features. Duccio, the son, speaks good English and enjoys explaining the family business.

NEAR PIAZZA SANTA CROCE

The area around Santa Croce Church is another popular, if touristy, shopping zone. You're just a few steps away from a more local, residential zone to the north and east. The farther you get from the church, the more real Florentines you'll see.

Touristy Shops at Piazza Santa Croce and Nearby: The piazza in front of Santa Croce Church is bordered by a high concentration of shops. Leather vendors, in particular, cling to the church, trying to entice customers who've suffered sticker shock at the church's **leather school** (for more on the Santa Croce Leather School, see page 216). These shops target tired sightseers, making this a handy, if not particularly affordable or authentic, area for buying leather. The most leather shops are along **Borgo de Greci,** the heavily touristed corridor linking Piazza della Signoria and Piazza Santa Croce. For better quality, head a couple of short blocks north to **Atelier Classe** (see listing on page 314). An excellent perfume shop, **Aquaflor,** is also nearby, just down Via Borgo Santa Croce (see page 318).

Shop with the Florentines (Via Pietrapiana and Borgo La Croce): To get off the beaten path, walk about 10 minutes northeast of Santa Croce, to the axis formed by Via Pietrapiana, Borgo La Croce, and Via Gioberti. This authentic-feeling area isn't about artsy souvenirs, but about getting a glimpse at what Florentines buy for day-to-day life.

Short but bustling **Via Pietrapiana** is lined with shops and dominated by a big, Renaissance loggia that marks the entrance to a park. Inside the park is the quirky, grubby **Piazza dei Ciompi flea market,** which blurs the boundary between antiques and junk (daily 9:00-19:30, bigger the last Sun of each month). Also along this street is **Sotto Sotto** (#67 red), where local bargain hunters browse last year's deeply discounted designer fashions (closed Sun, www.sottosotto.it).

Heading east on Via Pietrapiana, you'll reach Piazza Sant'Ambrogio, with its namesake church. To the right of the church, **Borgo La Croce** teems with local shoppers. Stroll this mostly pedestrianized street two blocks to the big piazza, passing stores selling housewares, kitchen gadgets, linens, haircuts, clocks, everyday fashions, shoes, home decor, organic body prod-

SHOPPING

ucts, ceramics, pets, candy, antiques, and bridal wear. This is the most interesting strip in the area, but at its far end, you could continue straight ahead through the big square and across the busy street, and proceed down **Via Gioberti**—which is wider, less pedestrian-friendly, and lined with more everyday shops, including inexpensive clothing chain stores.

NIGHTLIFE IN FLORENCE

With so many American and international college students in town, Florence by night can have a frat-party atmosphere. For me, nighttime is for eating a late meal, catching a concert, strolling through the old-town pedestrian zone and piazzas with a gelato, or hitting one of the many pubs.

The latest on nightlife and concerts is listed in several publications available free at the TI, such as *The Florentine* monthly (the online version is updated biweekly at www.theflorentine.net). The TI can give you a rundown of the day's musical events; also check www.firenzeturismo.it. The monthly *Firenze Spettacolo*, which has an English section, is sold cheap at newsstands (www.firenzespettacolo.it).

STROLLING AFTER DARK

The **historic center** has a floodlit ambience that's ideal for strolling. The entire pedestrian zone around the Duomo and along Via de' Calzaiuoli, between the Uffizi and the Duomo, is lively with people.

Piazza della Repubblica, lined with venerable 19th-century cafés, offers good people-watching. In the evening, it's a hub of activity, with opera singers, violinists, harpists, bizarre street performers, and a cover band that plays cheesy tunes for the seating area of one of the piazza's bars. A ride on the carousel is always fun, but more so at night.

Ponte Vecchio is a popular place to enjoy river views (and kiss), and often has a street musician after dark who encourages passersby to dance.

A few areas feel creepy after dark. Use good judgment. I'd skip the seedy area between Mercato Centrale and the train station.

SUNSETS

For the perfect end to the day, watch the sun descend over the Arno River from any of the bridges, especially Ponte Vecchio. Piazzale

Michelangelo, perched on a hilltop across the river, is also great for sunset-watching; it's packed with Romeos and Juliets on weekend evenings (for directions on how to get there, see page 66).

The nearby San Miniato Church (200 yards uphill) is quieter and comes with the same commanding view. If you're going after dark, it's more efficient to zip up there by taxi (rather than take a one-hour round-trip hike; see page 67). While side-tripping out to Fiesole for the sunset is popular (see page 70), I'd stick with Piazzale Michelangelo.

LIVE MUSIC

Frequent **live concerts** enhance Florence's beautiful setting. In the summertime, piazzas host a wide range of performers, including pop bands on temporary stages. The lovely sounds of classical music fill churches year-round for special performances. At the TI, ask about current musical events, and keep an eye open for posters as you wander around town.

Orsanmichele Church regularly holds concerts under its Gothic arches. Tickets are sold on the day of the concert from the door facing Via de' Calzaiuoli.

Orchestra della Toscana presents classical concerts from November to May in Teatro Verdi (€13-20, box office open Mon-Sat 10:00-13:00 & 16:00-19:00, closed Sun, near Bargello at Via Ghibellina 97, tel. 055-210-804, www.orchestradellatoscana.it).

St. Mark's English Church offers opera music several nights each week from February through October (less frequent in winter). Check the website or call to see what's playing (full opera performance-€35, opera concerts-€25, Via Maggio 18, mobile 340-811-9192, www.concertoclassico.info).

Dinner Theater at Teatro del Sale is a quirky place for dinner and theater. Every night (except Sun-Mon) at 19:30 they kick off a buffet with a fun array of tasty dishes for an hour and a half. Then they take away the tables for an hour-long show. Sometimes the show is great for non-Italian speakers—and sometimes it's not (call or check their website). The old theater is not technically a restaurant, so you'll pay a €7 membership fee to "join" the association, plus €30 for the evening, including drinks (10 blocks behind

NIGHTLIFE

Sights Open Late

You can extend your sightseeing day into the night at a number of sights around Florence. The Uffizi, Accademia, and the Pitti Palace (Palatine Gallery, Royal Apartments, and Gallery of Modern Art) stay open into the early evening every day but Monday.

Other sights with evening hours include the Duomo Museum, Duomo's dome (Mon-Fri), the Baptistery (Mon-Sat), the Campanile (daily), and in summer, Pitti Palace's Boboli and Bardini Gardens. The stalls at the Mercato Nuovo and San Lorenzo Market (closed Mon in winter) stay open late for shoppers every night.

In summer (April-Sept), the best late-hours sightseeing is at Palazzo Vecchio, which stays open until 23:00 (except Thu).

the Duomo, northeast of Santa Croce at Via dei Macci 111 red, tel. 055-200-1492, www.teatrodelsale.com).

The recommended **Golden View Open Bar** complements its Arno River views with live jazz (usually Mon, Fri, and Sat at 21:00; near Ponte Vecchio—see listing on page 298).

The **Box Office** sells tickets for rock concerts and theater productions in Italian (Mon-Fri 10:00-19:00, Sat 9:00-14:00, closed Sun, east of Santa Croce Church at Via delle Vecchie Carceri 1, tel. 055-210-804, www.boxofficetoscana.it).

Ponte Vecchio often hosts a fine street musician late each evening in summer. He plugs in his amp while young people get comfortable on the curb. There's also generally a street musician nightly in the **Uffizi courtyard.**

DRINKS

Grab a drink and enjoy the scene at one of the following places.

Wine Bars: An *enoteca* is fun for sampling regional wines and enjoying munchies, especially before dinnertime. Throughout the old town, *enoteche* serve fine Italian wines by the glass with memorable atmospheres. **Le Volpi e l'Uva,** specializing in small, often organic wine producers, has a cozy interior and romantic seating on a quiet little piazza. They have 40 open bottles to choose from and a short menu of appropriate dishes. For maximum tasting, they are happy to arrange a flight of half-glasses and make a little plate of mixed *affettati* (cold cuts) and cheeses (Mon-Sat 11:00-21:00, closed Sun, 65 yards south of Ponte Vecchio—walk through Piazza Santa Felicità to Piazza dei Rossi 1; see map on page 279 for location, tel. 055-239-8132, run by wine experts Riccardo, Ciro, and Emilio).

Pubs: Irish and English pubs abound in Florence, attracting a mixed crowd of locals and tourists. Most are open late daily. Popular ones include **The Old Stove** (Via Pellicceria 2 red, south of Piazza della Repubblica), **Angie's Pub** (Via dei Neri 35 red, east of the Uffizi), **The Michael Collins Pub** (Piazza della Signoria 30 red, north side of the square), **The Fiddlers Elbow** (Piazza Santa Maria Novella 7 red), and the **Dublin Pub** (Via Faenza 27, near Mercato Centrale).

Microbreweries: Italy is experiencing a craft beer fad, and Florence has several places where you can join in. Handy to many recommended hotels (and near Mercato Centrale) is **Mostodolce.** A *birrificio artigianale* (craft brewery), they serve nine original beers and basic pub grub to raucous, youthful patrons who pin their drawings to the walls and spill out onto the street (daily 11:00-24:00, Via Nazionale 114 red, tel. 055-230-2928). Or head across the river to **Archea Brewery,** a small pub that brews several of their own varieties, with a few other Italian-produced beers on tap (daily 17:00-24:00, opens at 18:00 in winter, Via de'Serragli 44 red, a 5-minute walk west of Piazza di Santo Spirito, tel. 055-219-671, Carmine).

LATE-NIGHT LOCAL SCENES

American university students in Florence seem to do more drinking than studying during their semesters abroad. Despite the college party vibe, there is something for everyone in Florence after hours.

As elsewhere in Italy, many bars have a nightly *aperitivo*, a spread of snacks intended to tide you over until dinner. For the price of a drink, anyone can sample a dish, and the frugal can stretch it to a light meal.

Piazza Santa Croce: It's a hangout at night, often with concerts in front of the church. The epicenter of American student partying is around this square, where you'll find lots of bars and more foreigners than Italians. The neighboring Via de' Benci is busy with trendy night spots. **Moyo,** a slick, gold-lit lounge, is popular with a hip, young, local crowd (no cover, €5-8 drinks, daily until late, *aperitivo* 19:00-22:30, just off Piazza Santa Croce at Via de' Benci 23 red, tel. 055-247-9738). There are tables outside, if you want to hear yourself talk, and another inviting lounge next door.

Near the Duomo: La Congrega Lounge Bar, a tiny wine/champagne/coffee bar, is a handy little retreat day or night tucked into a tiny lane, 20 yards off Via de' Calzaiuoli. It offers a chic mix of old and new (daily 9:00-24:00, *aperitivo* 18:00-21:00, between the Duomo and Piazza della Repubblica at Via Tosinghi 3 red, tel. 055-287-267, Maya).

Near Piazza della Repubblica: Slowly feels anything but slow, with loud DJ music and a trendy vibe (€10 drinks, *aperitivo*

NIGHTLIFE

with mellow music 18:30-22:00, DJ after about 22:30, south of Piazza della Repubblica at Via Porta Rossa 63 red, tel. 055-035-1335). Just a few steps up the square, **YAB** ("You Are Beautiful") is the dance club of choice for the younger set, with the action often not starting until midnight (€13-16 cover, Via Sassetti 5 red).

Piazza Demidoff: To rub elbows with the locals, head across the river toward tiny Piazza Demidoff (cross the bridge east of Ponte Vecchio and turn left, about a 10-minute walk). These two places have outdoor seating, chichi interiors, late hours, and Florentines flaunting their latest shoe purchases: **Negroni** (opens Mon-Fri at 8:30, Sat-Sun at 19:00, Via dei Renai 17 red, tel. 055-243-647) and **Zoe** (opens Mon-Sat at 9:00, Sun at 18:00, Via dei Renai 13 red, tel. 055-243-111). See map on page 64.

San Niccolò: Just a few steps around the corner from Piazza Demidoff, Via di San Niccolò has a compact and enjoyable cluster of nighttime hangouts. The bar called **Il Baretto del Rifrullo** is the center of attention, with a lively and sophisticated yet youthful setting (open daily until late, Via San Niccolò 55 red—see map on page 64, tel. 055-234-262).

Piazza di Santo Spirito: This square—long known for its riff-raff and druggies—has become a more mainstream place to enjoy the evening. It's lined with popular bars and restaurants; for locations see the map on page 278. **Volume** caters to a younger crowd with a living-room atmosphere in an old woodshop. You'll see tools still on the walls amid modern art (daily 9:00-24:00, *aperitivo* 18:00-22:00, Piazza di Santo Spirito 5 red, tel. 055-238-1460). On the opposite side of the square, **Pop Café** feels trendy, though it's plastic-plate simple, with students getting comfortable on the curbs and cobbles (€5-7 drinks, daily 9:00-late, *aperitivo* 19:00-22:00, Piazza di Santo Spirito 18, tel. 055-217-475).

MOVIES

Find first-run films in their original languages—including English—at Odeon Cinema, a beautiful historic movie house right downtown, a half-block west of Piazza della Repubblica (Piazza Strozzi, tel. 055-214-068, www.odeonfirenze.com; for schedule of original-language films, look under *"Original Sound"*).

FLORENCE CONNECTIONS

Florence is Tuscany's transportation hub, with fine train, bus, and plane connections to virtually anywhere in Italy. The city has several train stations, a bus station (next to the main train station), and an airport (and Pisa's airport is nearby). Livorno, on the coast west of Florence, is a major cruise-ship port.

By Train

Florence's main train station is called **Santa Maria Novella** (*Firenze S.M.N.* on schedules and signs). Florence also has two suburban train stations: **Firenze Rifredi** and **Firenze Campo di Marte.** Note that some trains don't stop at the main station—before boarding, confirm that you're heading for S.M.N., or you may overshoot the city. (If this happens, don't panic; the other stations are a short taxi ride from the center.)

For general information on train travel in Italy—including ticket-buying options—see page 650.

SANTA MARIA NOVELLA STATION

Built in Mussolini's "Rationalism" style back between the wars, in some ways the station seems to have changed little—notice the 1930s-era lettering and architecture. The signage still refers to long-gone services while the photographs and artwork also evoke an earlier era. As at any busy train station, be on guard: Don't trust "porters" who want to help you find your train or carry your bags (they're not official), and politely decline offers of help using the ticket machines by anyone other than uniformed staff.

To orient yourself to the station, stand with your back to the tracks. Look left to see the green cross of a 24-hour pharmacy *(farmacia)* and the exit to the taxi queue. Baggage storage *(deposito bagagli)* is also to the left, halfway down track 16 (long hours daily, passport required). Fast-food outlets and a bank are also along track 16. Directly ahead of you is the main hall *(salone biglietti)*, where you can buy train and bus tickets. Pay WCs are to the right, near the head of track 5.

To reach the **TI,** walk away from the tracks and exit the station; it's straight across the square, 100 yards away, by the stone church.

Buying Tickets: Be aware that there are two train companies: Trenitalia, with most connections (toll tel. 892-021, www. trenitalia.it), and Italo, with high-speed routes between larger cities (no rail passes accepted, tel. 06-0708, www.italotreno.it).

For travel within Italy, there's no reason to stand in line at a ticket window. It's quick and easy to buy tickets online; with a smartphone, you can even purchase them minutes before the train departs.

If you decide to buy tickets at the station, take advantage of the ticket *(biglietti)* machines that display schedules, issue tickets, and even make reservations for rail-pass holders. Some take only credit cards; others take cards and cash. Using them is easy—just select "English." Both companies have bright-red machines, so be sure you use the right one.

For most international tickets, you'll need to either go to a Trenitalia ticket window (in the main hall) or a travel agency (ask at your hotel for the nearest one).

For Trenitalia information, use window #18 or #19 (take a number). For Italo tickets and information, use window #10 or #11, or visit their main office, opposite track 5, near the exit. Also near track 5, you'll find the Trenitalia Frecciaclub (first-class lounge).

To buy ATAF city bus tickets, stop at windows #8-9 in the main hall—and ask for a transit map while you're there (TIs do not have them).

Eating: $ **VyTA,** across from track 13, has good sandwiches, snacks, and pastries. Modern and refined $$ **Reale** serves drinks, salads, and other goodies and offers perhaps the best seats in the station (daily 8:00-24:00, 100 yards down track 16, just beyond baggage storage, tel. 055-264-5114). A food court is near track 16. The handiest supermarket is the classy **Sapori & Dintorni Conad,** across the busy street toward the Duomo (daily until 21:00, Largo Alinari 6).

Services: **Feltrinelli** has English language books and magazines and a café (across from track 14) while a modern **shopping gallery** with clothing stores and another café is down the escalator, across from tracks 11-12.

Getting to the Duomo and City Center

The Duomo and town center are to your left (with your back to the tracks). Out the doorway to the left, you'll find city buses and the taxi stand. **Taxis** cost about €6-8 to the Duomo, and the line moves fast, except on holidays. **Buses** generally don't cover the center well and probably aren't the best way to reach your hotel (walking could be faster), but if you need to take one, buy a ticket at the ATAF ticket window inside the main station hall. Minibus #C2 (which runs through the middle of town) departs from across the square, at the corner beyond the TI and Santa Maria Novella underpass; however, by the time you walk to the stop, you're already halfway to downtown.

To **walk** into town (10-15 minutes), exit the station straight ahead (with your back to the tracks), through the main hall and head straight across the square outside (toward the Church of Santa Maria Novella). On the far side of the square, keep left and head down the main Via dei Panzani, which leads directly to the Duomo.

Train Connections

Note that unless otherwise specified, the following connections are for Trenitalia.

From Florence by Train to: Pisa (2-3/hour, 45-75 minutes), **Lucca** (2/hour, 1.5 hours), **Siena** (direct trains hourly, 1.5-2 hours; bus is better because Siena's train station is far from the center), **Camucia-Cortona** (hourly, 1.5 hours), **Livorno** (hourly, 1.5 hours, some change in Pisa), **La Spezia** (for the Cinque Terre, 5/day direct, 2.5 hours, otherwise nearly hourly with change in Pisa), **Milan** (Trenitalia: hourly, 2 hours; Italo: 2/hour, 2 hours), **Venice** (Trenitalia: hourly, 2-3 hours, may transfer in Bologna, often crowded—reserve ahead; Italo: 4/day, 2 hours), **Assisi** (8/day direct, 2-3 hours), **Orvieto** (hourly, 2 hours, some with change in Campo di Marte or Rifredi Station), **Rome** (Trenitalia: 2-3/hour, 1.5 hours, most require seat reservations; Italo: 2/hour, 1.5 hours), **Naples** (Trenitalia: hourly, 3 hours; Italo: hourly, 3 hours), **Brindisi** (8/day, 8 hours with change in Bologna or Rome), **Interlaken** (2/day, 5.5 hours, 2 changes), **Frankfurt** (6/day, 10-11.5 hours, 2 changes), **Paris** (5/day, 9-10.5 hours, 1-2 changes; 1 night train with change in Milan, 13 hours, important to reserve ahead at www.thello.com), **Vienna** (5/day, 10-11 hours, 1-2 changes).

By Bus

BUSITALIA BUS STATION

BusItalia Station (100 yards west of the train station on Via Santa Caterina da Siena) is a big, old-school lot with numbered stalls and all the services you'd expect. Schedules for regional trips are posted, and video monitors show imminent departures. Bus service drops dramatically on Sunday. Generally it's best to buy tickets in the station, as you'll pay 30 percent to buy tickets onboard. Bus info: Tel. 800-373-760 (Mon-Fri 9:00-15:00, closed Sat-Sun), www.fsbusitalia.it.

Getting to the Train Station and City Center: Exit the station through the main door, and turn left along the busy street toward the brick dome. The train station is on your left, while downtown Florence is straight ahead and a bit to the right.

From Florence by Bus to: San Gimignano (hourly, fewer on Sun, 1.5-2 hours, change in Poggibonsi), **Siena** (roughly 2/hour, 1.5-hour *rapida/via superstrada* buses are faster than the train, avoid the slower *ordinaria* buses, www.sienamobilita.it), **Volterra** (4/day Mon-Sat, 1/day Sun, 2 hours, change in Colle di Val d'Elsa to CTT bus #770, www.pisa.cttnord.it; or faster train to Pontedera-Casciana Terme and then CTT bus #500 to Volterra, 7/day, fewer on Sun, 1.5 hours, www.pisa.cttnord.it), **Montepulciano** (1-2/day, 2 hours, change in Bettolle, LFI bus, www.lfi.it; or train to Chiusi, then Siena Mobilità bus to Montepulciano, www.sienamobilita.it), **Florence airport** (2/hour, 30 minutes, pay driver and immediately validate ticket, usually departs from platform 1, first bus departs at 5:30).

As some Tuscan towns (including Volterra and Montepulciano) have few connections, day-trippers could instead consider a guided tour such as those offered by Artviva (see page 26).

By Taxi

For small groups with more money than time, zipping to nearby towns by taxi can be a good value (e.g., €120 from your Florence hotel to your Siena hotel).

A more comfortable alternative is to hire a private car service. Florence-based **Transfer Chauffeur Service** has a fleet of modern vehicles with drivers who can whisk you between cities, to and from the cruise ship port at Livorno, and through the Tuscan countryside for around the same price as a cab (tel. 338-862-3129, www.transfercs.com, marco.masala@transfercs.com, Marco). **Prestige Rent** also has friendly, English-speaking drivers and offers similar services (office near Piazza della Signoria at Via Porta Rossa 6 red, tel. 055-398-6598, mobile 333-842-4047, www.prestigerent.com, usa@prestigerent.com, Saverio).

By Car

For general information on car rental and driving in Italy, see page 665. For tips on driving in Tuscany, see page 666. Renting a car at the Florence airport, with easy access to the Autostrada, is the best option.

DRIVING IN FLORENCE

Don't even attempt driving into the city center. The autostrada has several exits for Florence. Get off at the Nord, Scandicci, Impruneta (formerly Certosa), or Sud exits and follow signs toward—but not into—the *Centro*. Park on the outskirts—see the next section—and take a bus, tram, or taxi in.

Florence has a traffic-reduction system that's complicated and confusing even to locals. Every car passing into the "limited traffic zone" (*Zona Traffico Limitato*, or *ZTL*) is photographed; those who haven't jumped through bureaucratic hoops to get a permit can expect a €100 ticket in the mail (and an "administrative" fee from the rental company). If you get lost and cross the line several times...you get several fines. Since this is Italy, it can take as long as a year for your ticket to

show up. If you have a reservation at a hotel within the ZTL area—and it has parking—ask in advance if they can get you permission to enter town.

The no-go zone (defined basically by the old medieval wall, now a boulevard circling the historic center of town—watch for *Zona Traffico Limitato* signs) is roughly the area between the river, main train station, Piazza della Libertà, Piazza Donatello, and Piazza Beccaria; across the river, in the Oltrarno, the area around the Pitti Palace and Santo Spirito is also a ZTL. Some streets are classified ZTL only at certain times of day; at the beginning of each block, watch for a stoplight with instructions (in Italian and English)—the green light means it's currently OK to drive there, while the red light means, well...

Another potentially expensive mistake drivers make in Florence is using the lanes designated for buses only (usually marked with yellow stripes). Driving in these lanes can also result in a ticket in the mail. Pay careful attention to signs.

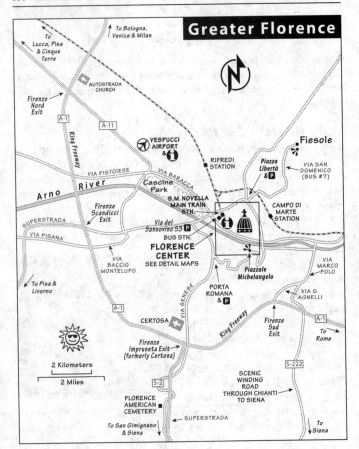

Greater Florence

To Bologna, Venice & Milan

To Lucca, Pisa & Cinque Terre

AUTOSTRADA CHURCH

Firenze Nord Exit

A-1

A-11

VESPUCCI AIRPORT & ℹ

Fiesole

RIFREDI STATION

Piazza Libertà & 🅿

VIA SAN DOMENICO (BUS #7)

VIA PISTOIESE

VIA BARACCA

Arno River

Cascine Park

S.M. NOVELLA MAIN TRAIN STN.

CAMPO DI MARTE STATION

Firenze Scandicci Exit

Via del Sansovino 53 🅿

BUS STN.

SUPERSTRADA

VIA PISANA

FLORENCE CENTER
SEE DETAIL MAPS

VIA BACCIO MONTELUPO

Piazzale Michelangelo

VIA MARCO POLO

To Pisa & Livorno

VIA SENESE

PORTA ROMANA & 🅿

VIA G. AGNELLI

A-1

CERTOSA

Ring Freeway

Firenze Sud Exit

A-1

To Rome

2 Kilometers

2 Miles

Firenze Impruneta Exit (formerly Certosa)

S-222

S-2

SCENIC WINDING ROAD THROUGH CHIANTI TO SIENA

FLORENCE AMERICAN CEMETERY

To San Gimignano & Siena

SUPERSTRADA

To Siena

PARKING IN FLORENCE

The city center is ringed with big, efficient parking lots (signposted with a big *P*). From these, you can ride into the center (via taxi, bus, or possibly tram). Check www.firenzeparcheggi.it for details on parking lots, availability, and prices. From the freeway, follow the signs to *Centro,* then *Stadio,* then *P.*

I usually head for Parcheggio del Parterre, just beyond Piazza della Libertà (€2/hour, €10/day, €70/week, open 24 hours daily, tel. 055-500-1994, 650 spots, automated, pay with cash or credit card, never fills up completely). To get into town, find the taxi stand at the elevator exit, or ride one of the minibuses that connect all the major parking lots with the city center (see www.ataf.net for routes).

Parcheggio Sansovino, a convenient lot for drivers coming from the south, is on the Oltrarno side of the river, right at a tram stop. Park, then ride four quick stops to Santa Maria Novella Sta-

CONNECTIONS

tion (€1/hour, €12/day, open 24 hours daily, Via Sansovino 53—from A-1 take the Firenze Scandicci exit, tel. 055-363-362, www.scaf.fi.it).

You can park for free along any suburban curb that feels safe; pick a place near a bus stop and bus into the city center. Check for signs that indicate parking restrictions—for example, a circle with a slash through it and *"giovedì dispari,* 0,00-06,00" means "don't park on Thursdays between midnight and six in the morning."

By Plane

For information on Pisa's **Galileo Galilei Airport,** see page 453.

AMERIGO VESPUCCI AIRPORT
Also called Peretola Airport, Florence's compact, manageable airport is about five miles northwest of the city (open 4:00-24:30, no overnighting allowed, TI, airport code: FLR, tel. 055-306-1830, www.aeroporto.firenze.it).

If you need a customs stamp for your VAT refund, you'll find the customs desk upstairs, facing the check-in area (follow *customs* signs); to mail your paperwork after getting it stamped, look for the red mailbox at the small building straight ahead as you exit the airport.

Getting Between the Airport and City Center: Shuttle buses (to the far right as you exit the arrivals hall) connect the airport with Florence's train and bus stations (2/hour until 22:00, 1/hour until 00:30, 30 minutes, runs 5:00-00:30, €6 one-way—buy ticket on board, €10 round-trip—buy ticket inside airport). If you're changing to a different intercity bus in Florence (for instance, one bound for Siena), stay on the bus through the first stop (at the train station); it will continue on to the bus station nearby.

Official **taxi** companies have fixed rates for the 20- to 30-minute ride between the airport and downtown: €22 during the day (6:00-22:00), €25.30 at night, and €24 on Sunday. They may tack on €1 per bag, and €2 if you call for a cab rather than hailing one. Be sure to use an official taxi (white, marked with *Taxi/Comune di Firenze* and a red fleur-de-lis).

Car Rental: The airport's rental-car offices share one big parking lot that's a three-minute drive away. However, the streets around the airport (which is tucked behind a big elevated highway) are a dizzying maze, making it tricky to find the place to drop off your car. One option is to drive to the airport, wait for the rental-car shuttle bus to show up, then follow that bus to the lot.

By Cruise Ship

FLORENCE'S CRUISE PORT: LIVORNO

Cruise ships dock in the coastal town of Livorno (sometimes called "Leghorn" in English), about 60 miles west of Florence. For more details, see my *Rick Steves Mediterranean Cruise Ports* guidebook.

Getting to Florence: To reach Florence by train, ride the cruise line's shuttle bus from the port to downtown Livorno, then walk to Piazza Grande; just beyond the square is the stop for buses for Livorno Centrale Station. From there, trains zip to Florence about hourly (1.5 hours). Other options include sharing a minibus taxi with other travelers (about one hour each way), or joining your cruise line's excursion.

Getting to Pisa and Lucca: To get to Pisa by train, follow the directions above to reach Livorno Centrale Station, then hop on a train to Pisa (2-3/hour, 20 minutes). Alternatives include cheap shuttle buses arranged by the Livorno TI, or the public bus that departs downtown Livorno and drops off near the Pisa train station (1-2/hour, fewer Sat-Sun, 1.25 hours; see page 422 for details on how to reach the Leaning Tower from the Pisa train station).

To also visit the neighboring town of Lucca, take the train there first to avoid the morning cruise-ship crowds in Pisa (trains depart Livorno about hourly, 1-1.5 hours, transfer at Pisa Centrale). A handy bus connects Lucca's Piazzale Giuseppe Verdi to Pisa's Field of Miracles, or take a train from Lucca to Pisa San Rossore Station, near the Field of Miracles (see page 481).

If you value convenience over cost, consider sharing a taxi or taking a cruise-line excursion for your Pisa/Lucca sightseeing.

Local Guide: Karin Kibby, an Oregonian living in Livorno who leads Rick Steves tours, offers a morning "slice of Italian life" walk through Livorno, focusing on local culture (includes its fantastic food market), as well as day trips throughout Tuscany (2-10 people, mobile 333-108-6348, karinkintuscany@yahoo.it).

TUSCANY
Toscana

TUSCANY

Toscana

When travel dreams take people to Italy, Tuscany is often their first stop. Wedged between Florence and Rome, this region offers the quintessential Italian experience: well-preserved medieval cities, sun-soaked hill towns, green and rolling fields, romantic farms, and cypress trees marching single file up lonely ridges.

Connoisseurs of Italy find a blissful mix of scenic beauty and rich history in Tuscany's emblematic hill towns. Built for defensive purposes in ancient and medieval times, today their lofty perches protect them from the modern world.

Proud locals will remind you that their ancestors—the Etruscans (the word Tuscany comes from "Etruscan")—thrived here long before anyone had heard of Julius Caesar. Many Tuscan hill towns date back to the Etruscan era—well before ancient Rome. Others date to the last days of Rome: when Rome fell, chaos followed, and people naturally grabbed the high ground to escape marauding Dark Ages barbarians. Over time, these hilltop towns were fortified and eventually functioned as independent city-states.

The Middle Ages were formative, when warring factions divided towns between those loyal to the pope and those supporting the Holy Roman Emperor. Cities developed monumental defensive walls and built great towers. Then, in 1348, the Black Death—an epidemic of bubonic plague—swept through Tuscany, devastating the region. The plague, plus the increasing dominance of Florence, turned many bustling cities into docile hamlets. Ironically, what was bad news in the 14th century is good news today: Tuscany and its hill towns enjoy a tourist-fueled affluence and retain a unique, medieval charm.

Slow down and savor the delights that this region offers. Spend the night in a hill town to experience the quiet after the day-trippers go home. In Florence you experience the finesse of Italy,

but it's in Tuscany that you'll find the rustic-yet-elegant essence of "Italia."

Visiting Tuscany

It's a joy to downshift to the more peaceful pace of Italy's small cities...and even smaller hill towns. I've covered my favorites in the following chapters.

Siena, Pisa, and Lucca are in a category of their own, with more artistic and historic sights. **Siena** is the ultimate (and biggest) hill town, with an unrivalled spirit any visitor can enjoy. Like a medieval stage set, its pedestrian-friendly old town is surrounded by its fortified wall. Siena's stunning main square—the gently tilted red-brick Campo—is the city's proud centerpiece. As Tuscany's hub, Siena is well-connected by bus to Florence and the surrounding hill towns. For drivers it's a convenient jumping-off point for my loop drive through the clay hills of the Crete Senesi.

Pisa's iconic Leaning Tower draws flocks of tourists, but this mid-size city also offers plenty of history and beautiful architecture, along with a thriving student scene. Lesser-known and smaller, charming **Lucca** is a "flat hill town" with winding streets ringed by a well-preserved Renaissance wall, perfect for circling on a bike. Both lie an hour or so west of Florence and are easily reached by train or bus.

But how in Dante's name does one choose from among Tuscany's hundreds of small hill towns? The one(s) you visit will depend on your interests, time, and mode of transportation.

Volterra—with its rustic vitality—is a beautifully preserved jewel. Its out-of-the-way location keeps this town from being trampled by tourist crowds, and its Etruscan history makes for compelling sightseeing. With 14 surviving medieval towers, walled **San Gimignano** is a classic. But because it's easy to visit from Florence—about 1.5 hours by bus—midday crowds can overwhelm its charms (it's an evocative delight early and late in the day). Both Volterra and San Gimignano work best for drivers, but can be reached by public transportation.

South of Siena, in the region I call the "Heart of Tuscany," drivers have their pick of hill towns. Ridge-hugging **Montepulciano**'s medieval cityscape resembles a miniature Florence. With several historic wine cellars and easy access to wine country, it attracts wine aficionados, as does **Montalcino,** itself a happy gauntlet of wine shops and art galleries. Fans of architecture and urban design appreciate little **Pienza**'s well-planned streets and squares. All three towns are covered in the Heart of Tuscany chapter, which also includes driving routes tying together the sights, villages, *agriturismi,* and wineries in the countryside.

Finally, those enamored with Frances Mayes' memoir, *Under the Tuscan Sun,* can make the pilgrimage to thriving **Cortona.** It soars high above a scenic landscape near the border of neighboring Umbria and is dotted with grand churches, Renaissance art, and Etruscan ruins. It's possible to reach by train but best by car.

Getting Around Tuscany

By Bus or Train: Buses are often the only public-transportation choice to get between small hill towns. Train stations are likely to be in the valley below the town center, connected by a local bus.

By Car: Exploring Tuscany and its hill towns by car can be a great experience. Wait to pick up your car until the last sizable town you visit (or at the nearest airport to avoid big-city traffic), and carry a good, detailed road map in addition to any digital navigation systems. Freeways (such as the toll autostrada and the non-toll *superstrada*) are the fastest way to connect two points, but smaller roads, including the super-scenic S-222, connecting Florence and Siena, are more rewarding.

Some towns don't allow visitors to drive or park in the city center. Be alert for "ZTL" *(Zona Traffico Limitato)* signs, indicating no cars allowed. Leave your car outside the walls and walk into town. Lots are usually free and plentiful outside city walls (and sometimes linked to the town center by elevators or escalators). For more driving and parking tips, see page 666.

Eating in Tuscany

One of the greatest Tuscan treats—the food—varies wildly depending on where you are. The areas around Florence and Siena are famed for serving hearty "farmer food," but as you move west, dishes become lighter, based more on seafood and grains. Each town proudly boasts local specialties—ask for the *specialità della città*. For an overview of Tuscan cuisine, see the sidebar on page 290. Wine is good throughout Tuscany, with pleasing selections for both amateurs and connoisseurs (see page 560).

Sleeping in Rural Tuscany

For a relaxing break from big-city Italy, settle down in an *agriturismo*—a farmhouse that rents out rooms to travelers (usually for a minimum of a week in high season). These rural B&Bs—almost by definition in the middle of nowhere—provide a good home base from which to find the magic of Italy's hill towns. Many provide memorable meals from locally sourced ingredients. I've listed several good options throughout these chapters. For more information, see *"Agriturismi"* on page 625.

SIENA

Siena was medieval Florence's archrival. And while Florence ultimately won the battle for political and economic superiority, Siena still competes for the tourists. Sure, Florence has the heavyweight sights. But Siena seems to be every Italy connoisseur's favorite town. In my office, whenever Siena is mentioned, someone exclaims, "Siena? I looove Siena!"

Situated atop three hills, Siena qualifies as Italy's ultimate "hill town." Its thriving historic center, with red-brick lanes cascading every which way, offers Italy's best medieval city experience. Most people visit Siena, just 35 miles south of Florence, as a day trip, but it's best experienced at twilight. While Florence has the blockbuster museums, Siena has an easy-to-enjoy soul: Courtyards sport flower-decked wells, alleys dead-end at rooftop views, and the sky is a rich blue dome.

For those who dream of a Fiat-free Italy, Siena is a haven. Pedestrians rule in the old center of town, as the only drivers allowed are residents and cabbies. Sit at a café on the main square. Wander narrow streets lined with colorful flags and studded with iron rings to tether horses. Take time to savor the first European city to eliminate automobile traffic from its main square (1966) and then, just to be silly, wonder what would happen if they did it in your hometown.

PLANNING YOUR TIME

On a quick trip, consider spending two nights in Siena (or three nights with a whole-day side-trip into Florence). Whatever you do, be sure to enjoy a sleepy medieval evening in Siena. The next morning, you can see the city's major sights in half a day. Or consider using Siena as your jet-lag pillow. With its lazy small-town ambience, impressive but user-friendly sights, and easy connection by bus to Florence's airport (simply change at downtown Florence's bus station), this is a fine way to settle into Italian life.

Drivers home-basing in Siena can consider my scenic Crete Senesi Drive, a countryside loop tour described at the end of this chapter.

Orientation to Siena

Siena lounges atop a hill, stretching its three legs out from Il Campo. This pedestrianized main square is the historic meeting point of Siena's neighborhoods.

Just about everything mentioned in this chapter is within a 15-minute walk of the square. Navigate by three major landmarks (Il Campo, Duomo, and Church of San Domenico), following the excellent system of street-corner signs. The typical visitor sticks to the Il Campo-San Domenico axis. Make it a point to stray from this main artery. Sienese streets go in anything but a straight line, so it's easy to get lost—but equally easy to get found. Don't be afraid to explore.

Siena itself is one big sight. Its individual attractions come in two little clusters: the square (Civic Museum and City Tower) and the cathedral (Baptistery and Duomo Museum, with its surprise viewpoint), plus the Pinacoteca for art lovers. Check off these sights, and then you're free to wander.

TOURIST INFORMATION

The TI is just across from the cathedral (daily 9:00-18:00, until 17:30 off-season; Piazza del Duomo 1, tel. 0577-280-551, www.enjoysiena.it). They hand out a few pretty booklets (including the regional *Terre di Siena* guide) and a free map. The bookshop next to the information desk sells more detailed Siena maps.

ARRIVAL IN SIENA
By Train

The small train station is at the base of the hill, on the edge of town. It has a bar/tobacco shop, a bus office (Mon-Fri 7:15-19:30, Sat until 17:45, Sun 7:15-12:00 & 15:15-18:30, opens later in winter), and a newsstand (which sells local bus tickets—buy one now if you're taking the city bus into town), but no baggage check or lockers (stow bags at Piazza Gramsci—see "By Intercity Bus," later). A shopping mall with a Pam supermarket is across the plaza right in front of the station. WCs are at the far north on track 1, past the pharmacy to the left.

Getting from the Train Station to the City Center: To reach central Siena, you can hop aboard the city bus, ride a long series of escalators, or take a taxi.

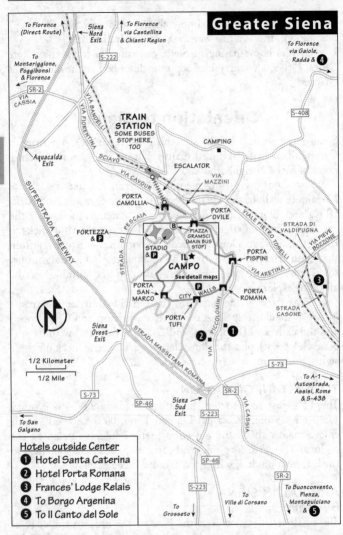

Greater Siena

To Florence
(Direct Route)

Siena
Nord
Exit

To Florence
via Castellina
& Chianti Region

To Florence
via Gaiole,
Radda & **4**

To Monteriggioni,
Poggibonsi
& Florence

SR-2
VIA CASSIA

S-222

VIA BANDELLI

VIA FIORENTINA

S-408

Aquacalda
Exit

TRAIN STATION
SOME BUSES
STOP HERE,
TOO

CAMPING

SCIAVO

VIA CAVOUR

ESCALATOR

VIA MAZZINI

SUPERSTRADA FREEWAY

PORTA CAMOLLIA

PORTA OVILE

VIALE PIETRO TOSELLI

STRADA DI VALDIPUGNA

VIA PIEVE BOZZONE

STRADA DI PESCAIA

FORTEZZA & **P**

B

PIAZZA GRAMSCI
(MAIN BUS STOP)

STADIO & **P**

P

IL CAMPO

See detail maps

PORTA PISPINI

VIA ARETINA

3

PORTA SAN MARCO

P

CITY WALLS

PORTA ROMANA

STRADA CASONE

PORTA TUFI

N

Siena
Ovest
Exit

2

1

VIA PICCOLOMINI

1/2 Kilometer

1/2 Mile

STRADA MASSETANA ROMANA

S-73

S-73

SP-46

Siena
Sud
Exit

SR-2

S-223

VIA CASSIA

To A-1
Autostrada,
Assisi, Rome
& S-438

To San
Galgano

SP-46

SR-2

To Buonconvento,
Pienza,
Montepulciano
& **5**

To
Grosseto

To
Ville di Corsano

Hotels outside Center
1 Hotel Santa Caterina
2 Hotel Porta Romana
3 Frances' Lodge Relais
4 To Borgo Argenina
5 To Il Canto del Sole

By Bus or Escalator: To reach either the bus or the escalators, head for the shopping mall across the square. From the tracks, go down the stairs into the tunnel that connects the platforms; this leads (with escalators) right up into the mall. Alternatively, you can exit the station out the front door, bear left across the square, and use the corner entrance marked *Galleria Porta Siena* (near the Pam supermarket).

To ride the **city bus,** go through the shopping mall's right-hand door at the corner entrance and take the elevator down to the subterranean bus stop. If you didn't buy bus tickets in the train station, you can get them from the blue machine (press "F" to toggle to English, then select "A" for type of ticket) or buy them onboard. Buses leave frequently (6/hour, fewer on Sun and after 22:00, €1.20, exact change required onboard, about a 10-minute ride into town). Smaller shuttle buses go up to Piazza del Sale, while bigger city buses head to nearby Piazza Gramsci (both at the north end of town, and walkable to most of my recommended hotels). Before boarding, double-check the destination with the driver by asking "*Centro?*" Validate your ticket in the machine onboard.

Riding the **escalator** into town takes a few minutes longer (about 15 minutes to Piazza Gramsci) and requires more walking than the bus. From the station, enter the mall at the far-left end as described above. Once inside, go straight ahead and ride the escalators up two floors to the food court. Continue directly through the glass doors to another escalator (marked *Porta Camollia/Centro*) that takes you gradually, up, up, up into town. Exiting the escalator, turn left down the big street, bear left at the fork, then continue straight through the town gate. From here, landmarks are well-signed (go up Via Camollia).

By Taxi: The taxi stand is to your left as you exit the train station, but as the city is chronically short on cabs, getting one here can take a while (about €10 to Il Campo, taxi tel. 0577-49222).

Returning to the Train Station from the City Center: You can ride a smaller shuttle bus directly to the station from Piazza del Sale, or catch an orange or red-and-silver city bus from Piazza Gramsci (which may take a more roundabout route). Multiple bus routes make this trip—look for *Ferrovia* or *Stazione* on schedules and marked on the bus, and confirm with the driver that the bus is going to the *stazione* (staht-see-OH-nay).

By Intercity Bus

Most buses arrive in Siena at Piazza Gramsci, a few blocks north of the city center. (Some buses only go to the train station; others go first to the train station, then continue to Piazza Gramsci—to confirm, ask your driver, "pee-aht-sah GRAHM-shee?") The main bus companies are Sena/Baltour and Tiemme/Siena Mobilità. Day-trippers can store baggage in the Sottopassaggio la Lizza passageway underneath Piazza Gramsci at the Tiemme/Siena Mobilità office (daily 7:00-19:00, carry-on-sized luggage no more than 33 pounds, no overnight storage; bus tickets and WC available). From Piazza Gramsci, it's an easy walk into the town center—just head in the opposite direction of the tree-filled park. For more on buses, see page 404.

SIENA

By Car

Siena is not a good place to drive. Plan on parking in a big lot or garage and walking into town.

Drivers coming from the autostrada take the *Siena Ovest* exit and follow signs for *Centro*, then *Stadio* (stadium). The soccer-ball signs take you to the stadium lot (Parcheggio Stadio, €2/hour, pay when you leave) near Piazza Gramsci and the huge, bare-brick Church of San Domenico. The nearby Fortezza lot charges the same amount.

Another good option is the underground Santa Caterina garage (you'll see signs on the way to the stadium lot, same price). From the garage, hike 150 yards uphill through a gate to an escalator on the right, which carries you up into the city. Take a left at the top onto Siena's main street.

If you're staying in the south end of town, try the Il Campo lot, near Porta Tufi.

On parking spots, blue stripes mean pay and display; white stripes mean free parking. You can park for free in the lot west of the Fortezza; in white-striped spots south of the Fortezza; and overnight in most city lots (20:00-8:00). Signs showing a street cleaner and a day of the week indicate when the street is closed to cars for cleaning.

Driving within Siena's city center is restricted to local cars and is policed by automatic cameras. If you drive or park anywhere marked *Zona Traffico Limitato (ZTL)*, you'll likely have a hefty ticket waiting for you in the mail back home. Check with your hotel in advance if you plan to drop off your bags before parking.

HELPFUL HINTS

Combo-Tickets: Siena often experiments with different combo-tickets, but in general, only three are worth considering: the €13 Opa Si Pass that includes the Duomo, Duomo Museum, Crypt, and Baptistery (valid 3 days; sold only at ticket office next to Santa Maria Della Scala); the €13 combo-ticket covering the Civic Museum and Santa Maria della Scala; and the €20 combo-ticket covering the Civic Museum, Santa Maria della Scala, and City Tower (valid 2 days). All combo-tickets allow only one entry per sight.

Markets: Every Wednesday morning a market of clothes, knick-knacks, and food sprawls between the Fortezza and Piazza Gramsci along Viale Cesare Maccari and the adjacent Viale XXV Aprile. Friday mornings see an organic food market in the same location.

Post Office: It's on Piazza Matteotti (Mon-Fri 8:15-19:00, Sat until 12:30, closed Sun).

Bookstores: For books and magazines in English, try **Libreria**

Siena's Big Plans and Slow Fade

Once upon a time (about 1260-1348), Siena was a major banking and trade center, and a military power in a class with Florence, Venice, and Genoa. With a population of about 50,000, it was even bigger than Paris. Situated on the north-south road to Rome (Via Francigena), Siena traded with all of Europe.

After rival republic Florence began its grand cathedral (1296), proud Siena planned to build one even bigger—the biggest church in all Christendom. Construction began in the 1330s on an extension off the right side of the existing Duomo (today's cathedral would have been used as a transept). The vision was grand, but it underestimated the complexity of constructing such a building without enough land for it to sit upon.

When the Black Death raged across Europe in 1348, Siena's population was cut by more than a third. Many Sienese saw the plague as a sign from God, punishing them for their pride. Plans for the cathedral expansion were cancelled and the city began a slow fade into the background of Tuscan history.

In the 1550s, Florence, with the help of Philip II's Spanish army, conquered the flailing city-state, forever rendering Siena a nonthreatening backwater. Siena's loss became our sightseeing gain, as its political and economic irrelevance pickled the city in a purely medieval brine. Today, Siena's population is again at its medieval level of 50,000, although only 18,000 of those live within the walls.

Senese (daily 9:00-20:00, Via di Città 62, tel. 0577-280-845) and the **Feltrinelli** bookstore at Banchi di Sopra 52 (Mon-Sat 9:00-19:45, closed Sun, tel. 0577-271-104).

Laundry: Lavanderia Barbara is one of the few laundromats in the historic center (Mon-Fri 8:30-12:30 & 16:00-19:30, morning hours only Sat, closed Sun, near Porta Romana at Via Pantaneto 129, tel. 0577-289-501).

Travel Agency: Carroccio Viaggi sells train, plane, and some bus tickets for a small fee (Mon-Fri 9:00-12:30 & 15:30-19:00, Sat 9:30-12:00, closed Sun, Via Montanini 20, tel. 0577-226-964, www.carroccioviaggi.com, info@carroccioviaggi.com).

Wine Classes: The **Tuscan Wine School** gives two-hour classes on Italian wine and food. The midday class (12:00) focuses on local food culture with tastings at vendors around town. Afternoon classes (16:00) teach Tuscan wines and stay in the classroom (€45/person, 20 percent discount for afternoon class with this book; classes Mon-Sat, closed Sun; Via di Stalloreggi 26, 30 yards from recommended Hotel Duomo, tel. 0577-221-704, mobile 333-722-9716, www.tuscanwineschool.com,

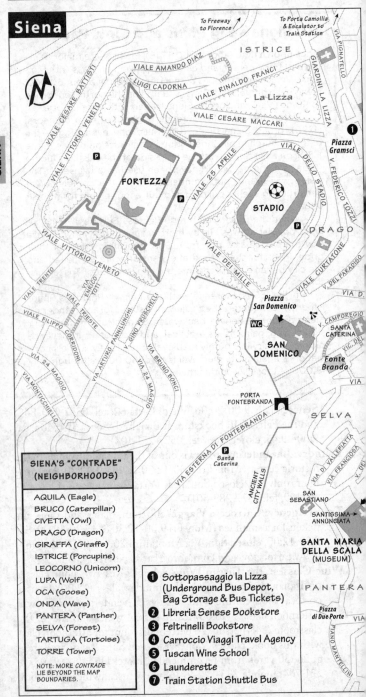

Siena

To Freeway to Florence

To Porta Camollia & Escalator to Train Station

ISTRICE

VIALE AMANDO DIAZ

V. LUIGI CADORNA

VIALE RINALDO FRANCI

La Lizza

GIARDINI LA LIZZA

VIA PIGNATELLO

VIALE CESARE BATTISTI

VIALE CESARE MACCARI

VIALE VITTORIO VENETO

❶ Piazza Gramsci

V. FEDERICO TOZZI

P

FORTEZZA

VIALE 25 APRILE

VIALE DELLO STADIO

STADIO

P

P

DRAGO

VIALE DEI MILLE

VIALE CURTATONE

V. PEL PARADISO

VIALE VITTORIO VENETO

VIA ENRICO TOTI

VIALE TRENTO

VIALE TRIESTE

Piazza San Domenico

VIA D.

VIA CAMPOREGIO

VIALE FILIPPO CORRIDONI

VIA GINO FRUSCHELLI

WC

SAN DOMENICO

SANTA CATERINA

VIA ARTURO PANNILUNGHI

VIA BRUNO BONCI

VIG. DEL

Fonte Branda

VIA 24 MAGGIO

VIA 24 MAGGIO

VIA

VIA MONTUCCHIELLO

PORTA FONTEBRANDA

SELVA

VIA ESTERNA DI FONTEBRANDA

P

Santa Caterina

VIA DI VALLEPIATTA

VIA ERANGIOSA

V. DEL

ANCIENT CITY WALLS

SAN SEBASTIANO

SANTISSIMA ANNUNCIATA

SANTA MARIA DELLA SCALA (MUSEUM)

PANTERA

Piazza di Due Porte

PIANO MANTELLIN

SIENA'S "CONTRADE" (NEIGHBORHOODS)

AQUILA (Eagle)
BRUCO (Caterpillar)
CIVETTA (Owl)
DRAGO (Dragon)
GIRAFFA (Giraffe)
ISTRICE (Porcupine)
LEOCORNO (Unicorn)
LUPA (Wolf)
OCA (Goose)
ONDA (Wave)
PANTERA (Panther)
SELVA (Forest)
TARTUGA (Tortoise)
TORRE (Tower)

NOTE: MORE *CONTRADE* LIE BEYOND THE MAP BOUNDARIES.

❶ Sottopassaggio la Lizza (Underground Bus Depot, Bag Storage & Bus Tickets)
❷ Libreria Senese Bookstore
❸ Feltrinelli Bookstore
❹ Carroccio Viaggi Travel Agency
❺ Tuscan Wine School
❻ Launderette
❼ Train Station Shuttle Bus

SIENA

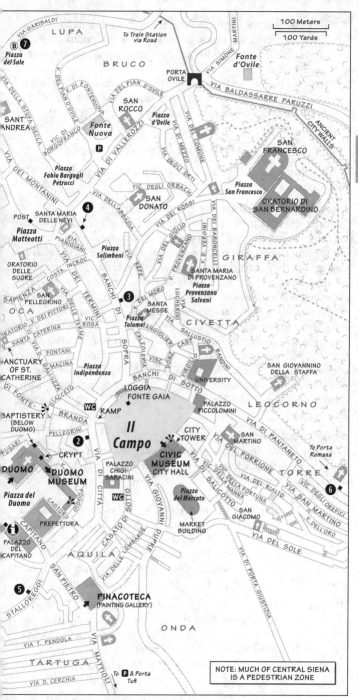

tuscanwineschool@gmail.com, Rebecca and Riikka Sofia). They also offer countryside food- and wine-oriented tours, convenient for those without their own wheels (www.siena-wine-tour.com).

Souvenirs: For easy-to-pack souvenirs, consider one of the large, colorful scarves/flags that depict the symbols of Siena's 17 neighborhoods (such as the wolf, the turtle, or the snail).

Tours in Siena

∩ To sightsee on your own, download my free Siena City Walk audio tour.

Tours by Roberto: Tuscany Minibus Tours

Tours by Roberto, led by Roberto Bechi or one of his guides, offers off-the-beaten-path minibus tours of the surrounding countryside (up to eight passengers, pickup at hotel). Regardless of the size of your group, they charge per person, so these minibus tours are economical. The first participants to book choose one of seven itineraries—then others join until the van fills. Roberto and his team share the same passion for Sienese culture, Tuscan history, and local cuisine (tour options explained on website, special Rick Steves discount prices: full-day minibus tours-€90/person, 4-hour off-season tours-€60/person, entry fees extra; also offers Siena walks and multiday tours, booking mobile 320-147-6590, Roberto's mobile 328-425-5648, www.toursbyroberto.com, toursbyroberto@gmail.com). Roberto also provides private van connections to Volterra—see page 507.

Other Local Guides

Federica Olla, who leads walking tours of Siena, is a smart, friendly guide with a knack for creative teaching (€55/hour, minimum 2 hours, mobile 338-133-9525, www.ollaeventi.com, info@ollaeventi.com).

GSO Guides Co-op is a group of 10 young professional guides who offer good tours covering Siena and all of Tuscany and Umbria (€140/half-day, €260/full day, they don't drive but can join you in your car, 10 percent discount for Rick Steves readers, www.guidesienaeoltre.com). Among them, **Stefania Fabrizi** stands out (mobile 338-640-7796, stefaniafabriziguide@gmail.com).

Walking Tours

The **TI** offers walking tours of the old town. Guides usually conduct their walks in both English and Italian (€20—pay guide directly, daily April-Oct at 11:00, 2 hours, no interiors except for the Duomo, depart from TI, Piazza del Duomo 1, tel. 0577-280-551).

Siena at a Glance

▲▲▲**Il Campo** Best square in Italy. See page 356.

▲▲▲**Duomo** Art-packed cathedral with mosaic floors and statues by Michelangelo and Bernini. **Hours:** Mon-Sat 10:30-19:00, Sun 13:30-18:00, Nov-Feb closes daily at 17:30. See page 374.

▲▲**Civic Museum** City museum in City Hall with Sienese frescoes, the *Effects of Good and Bad Government.* **Hours:** Daily 10:00-19:00, Nov-mid-March until 18:00. See page 366.

▲▲**Duomo Museum** Siena's best museum, with cathedral art (Duccio's *Maestà*) and sweeping Tuscan views. **Hours:** Daily 10:30-19:00, Nov-Feb until 17:30. See page 383.

▲**City Tower** Siena's 330-foot tower climb. **Hours:** Daily 10:00-19:00, mid-Oct-Feb until 16:00. See page 371.

▲**Pinacoteca** Fine Sienese paintings. **Hours:** Tue-Sat 8:15-19:15, Sun-Mon 9:00-13:00. See page 371.

▲**Baptistery** Cave-like building with baptismal font decorated by Ghiberti and Donatello. **Hours:** Daily 10:30-19:00, Nov-Feb until 17:30. See page 387.

▲**Santa Maria della Scala** Museum with much of the original Fountain of Joy, Byzantine reliquaries, and vibrant frescoes depicting day-to-day life in a medieval hospital. **Hours:** Daily 10:00-19:00, Fri until 22:00; closes earlier mid-Oct-mid-March. See page 388.

Sanctuary of St. Catherine Home of St. Catherine. **Hours:** Daily 9:00-18:00, Chapel of the Crucifixion closed 12:30-15:00. See page 390.

Near Siena

▲▲▲**Abbey of Monte Oliveto Maggiore** Rural abbey buried in a cypress forest, with vivid Renaissance art in an untrampled setting (if old frescoes bore you, don't bother). **Hours:** Daily 9:15-12:00 & 15:15-18:00, Nov-March until 17:00. See page 410.

▲▲**Crete Senesi** Rugged region tucked between Siena and the "Heart of Tuscany," with breathtaking scenery, workaday towns of Asciano and Buonconvento, and Abbey of Monte Oliveto Maggiore. See page 405.

Bus Tours

Aggressively utilizing commissions, a company called **My Tour** has a lock on all hotel tour-promotion space. Every hotel has a rack of their brochures, which advertise a variety of five-hour bus tours into the countryside (www.mytours.it, depart from Piazza Gramsci).

Siena City Walk

It's easy to get to know Siena on foot, and this short self-guided walk laces together its most important sights. You can do this walk as a quick orientation, or use it to lace together visits to the major sights (breaking the narration to tour City Hall, the Duomo, the Duomo Museum, and Santa Maria della Scala—all described in more detail under "Sights in Siena"). If you do the walk without entering the sights, it works great at night when the city is peaceful.

∩ This walk is also available as a free Rick Steves audio tour.
• *Start in the center of the main square, Il Campo, standing just below the fountain.*

❶ Il Campo

This square is the heart of Siena, both geographically and metaphorically—and it's worth ▲▲▲. First laid out in the 12th century, today Il Campo (officially the Piazza del Campo) is the only town square I've seen where people stretch out as if at the beach. At the flat end of its clamshell shape is City Hall, where you can tour the Civic Museum and climb the City Tower. From there it fans out as if to create an amphitheater. Twice each summer, all eyes are on Il Campo when it hosts the famous Palio horse races (see sidebar on page 360).

Originally, this area was just a field *(campo)* located outside the city walls (which encircled the cathedral). Bits of those original walls, which curved against today's square, can be seen above the pharmacy (the black-and-white stones, third story up, to the right as you face City Hall). In the 1200s, with the advent of the Sienese republic, the city expanded. The small medieval town wrapped around its cathedral became a larger, human-istic city gathered around its towering City Hall. In this newer and relatively secular age, the focus of power shifted from the bishop to the city council.

As the city expanded, Il Campo became its marketplace and the historic junction of Siena's various competing *contrade* (neighborhood districts). The square and its buildings are the color of the soil upon which they stand—a color known to artists and Crayola users as "Burnt Sienna."

City Hall (Palazzo Pubblico), with its looming tower, dominates the square. In medieval Siena, this was the center of the city, and the whole focus of Il Campo still flows down to it.

The building's facade features the various symbols of the city. The **stylized sun** hearkens back to St. Bernardino of Siena, who preached devotion to the Holy Name of Jesus. (The "IHS" inside is a shortening of Jesus' name in Greek.) Born on the day that St. Catherine of Siena died, Bernardino grew up here and went on to travel throughout Italy, giving spirited sermons that preached peace between warring political factions. His sermons often ended with reconciling parties exchanging a *bacio di pace* (kiss of peace). Bernardino, who personally designed the sun logo, later became the patron saint of advertising.

Flanking the sun logo, **she-wolf gargoyles** lean out and snarl, "Don't mess with Siena, Mister Pope!" This Ghibelline city prided itself on its political independence from the papacy; it embraced as a city symbol the pagan she-wolf who suckled Romulus and Remus (Remus' son was Siena's legendary founder). The black-and-white **shields** over the windows are another city symbol. Near ground level, the iron rings are for tying your horse, while the fixtures above once held flags.

The **City Tower** was built around 1340. At 330 feet, it's one of Italy's tallest secular towers. Medieval Siena was a proud repub-

lic, and this tower stands like an exclamation point—an architectural declaration of independence from papacy and empire. The tower's Italian nickname, Torre del Mangia, comes from a hedonistic bell-ringer who consumed his earnings like a glutton consumes food. (His chewed-up statue is just inside City Hall's courtyard, to the left as you enter.)

The open **chapel** located at the base of the tower was built in 1348 as thanks to God for ending the Black Death (after it killed more than a third of the population). It should also be used to thank God that the top-heavy tower—plunked onto the building with no extra foundation and no iron reinforcement—still stands. These days, the chapel is used to bless Palio contestants (and to provide an open space for EMTs who stand by during the race).

You can visit the Civic Museum inside City Hall and climb

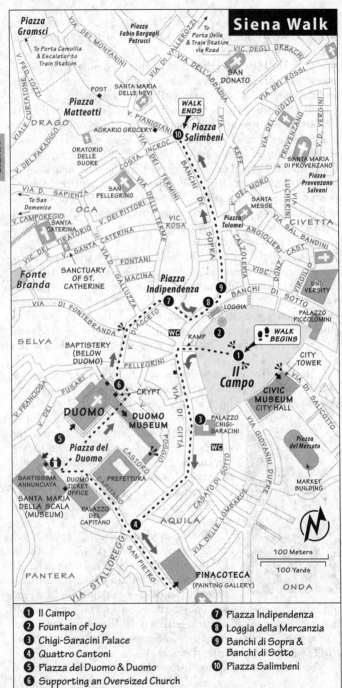

Siena Walk

① Il Campo
② Fountain of Joy
③ Chigi-Saracini Palace
④ Quattro Cantoni
⑤ Piazza del Duomo & Duomo
⑥ Supporting an Oversized Church

⑦ Piazza Indipendenza
⑧ Loggia della Mercanzia
⑨ Banchi di Sopra & Banchi di Sotto
⑩ Piazza Salimbeni

the tower (see page 367 for a self-guided tour of the Civic Museum).

• *Now turn around and take a closer look at the fountain in the top center of the square.*

❷ Fountain of Joy (Fonte Gaia)

This fountain—a copy of an early 15th-century work by Jacopo della Quercia—marks the square's high point. The joy is all about

how the Sienese republic blessed its people with water. Find Lady Justice with her scales and sword (right of center), overseeing the free distribution of water to all. Imagine residents gathering here in the 1400s to fill their jugs. The Fountain of Joy still reminds locals that life in Siena is good. Notice the pigeons politely waiting their turn to tightrope gingerly down slippery spouts to slurp a drink from wolves' snouts. The relief panel on the left

shows God creating Adam by helping him to his feet. It's said that this reclining Adam (carved a century before Michelangelo's day) influenced Michelangelo when he painted his Sistine Chapel ceiling. The original fountain is exhibited indoors at Santa Maria della Scala (see page 388).

Siena and Florence have always been very competitive. In medieval times, a statue of Venus stood on Il Campo. After the plague hit Siena, the monks blamed the pagan statue. According to legend, the people of Siena cut the statue to pieces and buried it along the walls of Florence.

• *Leave Il Campo uphill on the widest ramp. With your back to the tower, it's at 10:00. After a few steps you reach Via di Città. Turn left and walk 100 yards uphill toward the imposing white palace with brick crenellations on top.*

Halfway there, at the first corner, notice small plaques on the first level of the building facades—these mark the neighborhood, or **contrada.** *If the flags are flying, they reinforce the point. You are stepping from the* contrada *of the Forest* (Selva) *into the* contrada *of the Eagle* (Aquila). *Notice also the once mighty and foreboding medieval* **tower house.** *Towers once soared all around town, but they're now truncated and no longer add to the skyline—look for their bases as you walk the city. As you stroll, consider the density of this city over the years. Siena had about 50,000 people living within its walls before the plague hit in 1348. Today, only 18,000 live within the walls.*

On the left, you reach the big...

❸ Chigi-Saracini Palace (Palazzo Chigi-Saracini)

This old fortified noble palace is today home to a prestigious music

SIENA

Siena's *Contrade* and the Palio

Siena's 17 historic neighborhoods, or *contrade*—each with a parish church, well or fountain, and square—still play an active role in the life of the city. Each is represented by a mascot (porcupine, unicorn, wolf, etc.) and unique colors worn proudly by residents.

Contrada pride is evident year-round in Siena's parades and colorful banners, lamps, and wall plaques. If you hear the thunder of distant drumming, run to it for some medieval action—there's a good chance it'll feature flag throwers. Buy a scarf in *contrada* colors, and join in the merriment of these lively neighborhood festivals.

Contrade rivalries are most visible twice a year—on July 2 and August 16—during the city's world-famous horse race, the **Palio di Siena.** Ten of the 17 neighborhoods compete (chosen by rotation and lot), hurling themselves with medieval abandon into several days of trial races and traditional revelry. Jockeys—usually from out of town—are considered hired guns, no better than paid mercenaries. Bets are placed on which *contrada* will win...and lose. Despite the shady behind-the-scenes dealing, on the big day the horses are taken into their *contrada*'s church to be blessed. ("Go and return victorious," says the priest.) It's considered a sign of luck if a horse leaves droppings in the church.

On the evening of the race, Il Campo is stuffed to the brim with locals and tourists. Dirt is brought in and packed down to create the track's surface, while mattresses pad the walls of surrounding buildings. The most treacherous spots are the sharp corners, where many a rider has bitten the dust.

Picture the scene: Ten snorting horses and their nervous riders line up near the pharmacy (on the west side of the square) to

academy, the Accademia Musicale Chigiana. If open, step into the courtyard with its photogenic well (powerful medieval families enjoyed direct connections to the city aqueduct). The walls of the loggia are decorated with the busts of Chigi-Saracini patriarchs, and the vaults are painted in the "grotesque" style popular during the Renaissance. What look like pigeonholes in the other walls are actually for scaffolding, for both construction and ongoing maintenance. (Notice the wire mesh to keep pigeons from nest-

await the starting signal. Then they race like crazy while spectators wave the scarves of their neighborhoods.

Every possible vantage point and perch is packed with people straining to see the action.  One lap around the course is about a third of a mile (350 meters); three laps make a full circuit. In this no-holds-barred race—which lasts just over a minute—a horse can win even without its rider (jockeys ride precariously without saddles and often fall off the horses' sweaty backs).

SIENA

When the winner crosses the line, 1/17th of Siena—the prevailing neighborhood—goes berserk. Winners receive a *palio* (banner), typically painted by a local artist and always featuring the Virgin Mary (the race is dedicated to her). But the true prizes are proving that your *contrada* is *numero uno,* and mocking your losing rivals.

All over town, sketches and posters depict the Palio. This is not some folkloric event—it's a real medieval moment. If you're packed onto the square with 60,000 people, all hungry for victory, you may not see much, but you'll feel it. Bleacher and balcony seats are expensive, but it's free to join the masses in the square. Go with an empty bladder as there are no WCs, and be prepared to surrender any sense of personal space.

While the actual Palio packs the city, you can more easily see the horse-race trials—called *prove*—on any of the three days before the main event (usually at 9:00 and after 19:00, free seats in bleachers). Good sources for more information include www.ilpalio.org, www.comitatoamicidelpalio.it, and the free "Contrada è...Palio è..." app.

ing.) The palace, which dates back to the 13th century, was owned by the Saracini family, then the Chigi family. Its last owner, Guido Chigi-Saracini, loved music and had no heirs. So he left his estate to house and fund this music academy. It hosts a festival each July and August with popular concerts almost nightly, international talent, and affordable tickets (box office just off courtyard; €7 one-hour tours of the palace's library, art, and musical instruments run Mon-Sat at 11:30 plus Thu-Fri at 16:00, closed Sun, call to confirm English tour is being offered; Via di Città 89, tel. 0577-22091, www.chigiana.it).

• *Continue up the hill on Via di Città to the next big intersection. As you walk, notice how strict rules protect the look of exteriors. Many families live in each building, but all shutters are the same color. Inside, apartments can be modern, and expensive—some of the priciest in Italy. I think it's classy that the local government prohibits unlicensed vendors from selling their wares on the streets (a practice that is becoming a big problem elsewhere).*

❹ Quattro Cantoni

The intersection known as Quattro Cantoni (the Four Corners) offers a delightful perch from which to study the city. The modern column (from 1996) with a Carrara marble she-wolf on top functions as a flag holder for the *contrada*. You are still in the Eagle district (see the fountain and the corner plaque)—but beware. Just one block up the street, a ready-to-pounce panther—from the rival neighboring district—awaits.

Only the very rich could afford stone residences. The fancy buildings here hide their economical brick construction behind a stucco veneer. The stone tower on this corner had only one door—30 feet above street level and reached by ladder, which could be pulled up as necessary. Within a few doors, you'll find a classy bar, an elegant grocery store, and a *gelateria*.

Take a little side-trip, venturing up Via di San Pietro. Interesting stops include the window with Palio video clips playing (at #1), Simon and Paula's art shop with delightful Palio and *contrade* knickknacks (#5), a weaver's shop (#7), the recommended La Vecchia Latteria *gelateria* (#10), an art gallery (#11), and four enticing little osterias. After a block you'll reach the best art museum in town, the **Pinacoteca** (for a self-guided tour of its interior, see page 372). From there to the former town gate (Porta all'Arco), a couple of short blocks ahead, the street becomes more workaday, with local shops and no tourists.

• *Back at the Four Corners, head up Via del Capitano, passing another massive Chigi family palace (bankers sure know how to get their hands on people's money) to the cathedral and Piazza del Duomo. Find a shady seat on the stone bench against the wall of the old hospital opposite the church.*

❺ Piazza del Duomo and the Duomo

The pair of she-wolves atop columns flanking the cathedral's facade says it all: The church was built and paid for not by the pope but by the people and the republic of Siena.

This 13th-century Gothic cathedral, with its striped bell tower—Siena's ultimate tribute to the Virgin Mary—is heaped with statues, plastered with frescoes, and paved with art. Take in this architectural festival of green, white, pink, and gold. Imagine pilgrims arriving at this church, its facade trumpeting the coming of Christ and the true path to salvation.

The current structure dates back to 1215, with the major decoration done during Siena's heyday (1250-1350). The lower story, by Giovanni Pisano (who worked from 1284 to 1297), features remnants of the fading Romanesque style (round arches over the doors), topped with the pointed arches of the new Gothic style that was seeping in from France. The upper half, in full-blown frilly Gothic, was designed and built a century later.

The six-story bell tower (c. 1315) looks even taller, thanks to an optical illusion: The white marble stripes get narrower toward the top, making the upper part seem farther away.

The she-wolf columns flanking the entrance honor Romulus and Remus, the mythical founders of Rome. Legend has it that Remus' son Senio ("Siena") rode north on a black horse to found the city of Siena.

The interior is a Renaissance riot of striped columns, remarkably intricate inlaid-marble floors, a Michelangelo statue, evocative Bernini sculptures, and the amazing Piccolomini Library. (If you want to enter now, you'll need a ticket from the booth around to the right; for a self-guided tour of the interior, see page 376.)

At your back, facing the cathedral, is Santa Maria della Scala, a huge building that housed pilgrims and, until the 1990s, was used as a hospital. Its labyrinthine 12th-century cellars—carved out of volcanic tuff and finished with brick—go down several floors, and during medieval times were used to store supplies for the hospital upstairs. Today, the exhibit-filled hospital and cellars can be a welcome refuge from the hot streets (for a self-guided tour, see page 388).

Grand as Siena's cathedral is, it's actually the rump of a failed vision. After rival republic Florence began its grand cathedral (1296), proud Siena planned to build an even bigger one, the biggest in all Christendom. But Siena is so hilly that there wasn't enough flat ground upon which to build a church of that size. What to do? Build a big church anyway, and prop up the overhanging edge with the Baptistery (which we'll pass shortly).

Walk to the right of the church and find the unfinished wall with see-through windows (circa 1330). From here you can envision the audacity of this vision—today's cathedral would have been just a transept. But the vision underestimated the complexity of constructing such a building without enough land. That, coupled with the devastating effects of the 1348 plague, killed the city's ability and will to finish the project. Many Sienese saw the Black Death as a sign from God, punishing them for their pride. They canceled their plans and humbly faded into the background of Tuscan history.

• *Walk to the rear of the church (past the Duomo Museum) and pause at the top of the marble stairs leading down. The Duomo Museum (to your right) houses the church's art (for a self-guided tour, see page 383).*

❻ Supporting an Oversized Church

From here, look down the stairs leading behind the church and see the architect's quandary. The church sticks out high above the lower street level. Partway down the stairs is the Crypt, and below that is the Baptistery. Each is an integral part of the foundation for the oversized structure. (Both the Baptistery and the Crypt are worth entering; see page 387.)

• *Descend the stairs, nicknamed "The Steps of St. Catherine," as she would have climbed them each day on her walk from home to the hospital. Below the Baptistery, jog right, then left, and through a tunnel down Via di Diacceto. Pause for a beautiful view of the towering brick Dominican church in the distance on the left. Then continue straight up the lane until you reach the next big square.*

❼ Piazza Indipendenza

This square celebrates the creation of a unified Italy (1860) with a 19th-century loggia sporting busts of the first two Italian kings. Stacking history on history, the neo-Renaissance loggia is backed by a Gothic palace and an older medieval tower.

• *Head right downhill one block (on Via delle Terme), back to the grand Via di Città, and take a few steps to the left to see another, fancier loggia.*

❽ Loggia della Mercanzia

This Gothic-Renaissance loggia was built about 1420 as a kind of headquarters for the union of merchants (it's just above Il Campo). Siena's nobility purchased it, and eventually it became the clubhouse of the local elites. To this day, it's a private, ritzy, and notoriously out-of-step-with-the-times men's club. The "Gli Uniti" above the door is a "let's stick together" declaration.

• *From here, steep steps lead down to Il Campo, but we'll go left and uphill on Banchi di Sopra. Pause at the intersection of...*

❾ Banchi di Sopra and Banchi di Sotto

These main drags are named "upper row of banks" and "lower row of banks." They were once lined with market tables *(banchi)*, and vendors paid rent to the city for a table's position along the street. If the owner of a *banco* neglected to pay up, thugs came along and literally broke *(rotto)* his table. It is from this practice—*banco rotto*, broken table—that we get the English word "bankrupt."

In medieval times, these streets were part of the Via Francigena, the main thoroughfare linking Rome with northern Europe. The medieval Sienese traded wool with passing travelers, which required moneychangers, which led to banks. As Siena was a secular town, local Christians were allowed to loan money and work as bankers. Today, strollers—out each evening for their *passeggiata*—fill Banchi di Sopra. Join the crowd, strolling past Siena's finest shops. You could nip into Nannini, a venerable café and *pasticceria* famous for its local sweets. The traditional Sienese taste treats *(cantucci, ricciarelli,* and various kinds of fruity and nutty *panforte)* are around the far end of the counter in the back (sold by weight, small amounts are fine, a little slice of panforte costs about €3).

A block or so farther up the street, Piazza Tolomei faces the imposing Tolomei family palace (now an imposing bank). This is a center for the Owl *contrada*. The column in the square, topped by the she-wolf, is for *contrada* announcements of births, deaths, parties, festivals, and so on.

• *Continue on Banchi di Sopra to Piazza Salimbeni; this gets my vote for Siena's finest stretch of palaces.*

❿ Piazza Salimbeni

The next square, Piazza Salimbeni, is dominated by Monte dei Paschi, the head office of a bank founded in 1472. It's amazing to think this bank has been in business on this square for over 500 years. Originally a kind of community bank for common people, in this generation, Monte dei Paschi's image has sunk to become the poster child for Italian bank scandals. Notice the Fort Knox-style base

of the building. The statue in the center honors Sallustio Antonio Bandini. His claim to fame: He invented the concept of collateral.

Directly across from Piazza Salimbeni, the steep little lane called Costa dell'Incrociata leads straight (down and then up) to the Church of San Domenico (it's worth the hike; see page 389). Also nearby (behind the cute green newsstand) is the most elegant grocery store in town, Consorzio Agrario di Siena. This farming consortium has been around since 1901, and today lets a group of local producers showcase their finest olive oils, pastas, wines, sweets, and various sauces and pastes. It's like a museum of local edibles (for more on this store, see page 403).

• *With this walk under your belt, you've got the lay of the land. The city is ready for further exploration—the sights associated with City Hall and the Duomo are all just a few minutes away. Enjoy delving deeper into Siena.*

Sights in Siena

IL CAMPO AND NEARBY

The gorgeous red-brick square known as Il Campo—worth ▲▲▲—is the best in Italy (for more on the square itself, see page 356). It's also home to City Hall (with the Civic Museum and City Tower) and other sights.

▲▲Civic Museum (Museo Civico)

Siena's City Hall (Palazzo Pubblico), still the seat of city government, symbolizes a republic independent from the pope and the

Holy Roman Emperor. It also represents a rising secular society, one that appeared first in Tuscany and then spread throughout Europe in the Renaissance. City Hall also has a fine and manageable museum that displays a good sampling of Sienese art, including Siena's first fresco (with a groundbreaking, down-to-earth depiction of the Madonna). It's worth strolling through the dramatic halls to see fascinating frescoes and portraits extolling Siena's greats, saints, and the city-as-utopia, when this proud town understandably considered itself the vanguard of Western civilization.

Siena's Civic Museum

Piazza del Mercato

SALA DELLA PACE (SALA DEI NOVE)

GIFT SHOP

COURT-YARD

SALA DEL MAPPAMONDO

CHAPEL

SALA DI BALIA

TOUR BEGINS

SALA DEL RISORGI-MENTO

VIA SALICOTTO

VIA GIOVANNI DUPRÈ

WC

TORRE DEL MANGIA (TOWER)

Il Campo

20 Meters
20 Yards

SIENA

❶ Victor Emmanuel II at Battle of San Martino
❷ Victor Emmanuel II Receives Politicians
❸ Chapel
❹ MARTINI – Maestà
❺ MARTINI (?) – Guidoriccio da Fogliano
❻ DUCCIO – The Surrender of the Castle of Giuncarico
❼ St. Bernardino & St. Catherine Frescoes
❽ LORENZETTI – Good Government
❾ LORENZETTI – Bad Government

Cost and Hours: Museum-€9, €13 combo-ticket with Santa Maria della Scala, €20 combo-ticket includes City Tower and Santa Maria della Scala (valid 2 days), ticket office is straight ahead as you enter City Hall courtyard; open daily 10:00-19:00, Nov-mid March until 18:00, last entry 45 minutes before closing; videoguide-€5 in bookshop, tel. 0577-292-232, www.comune.siena.it.

❍ Self-Guided Tour

• *Climb two flights of stairs (elevator on request—ask at ticket desk), pass through the gift shop, and on the left enter the...*

Sala del Risorgimento (Hall of Italian Unification)

This hall has dramatic scenes of the 19th-century unification of Italy (surrounded by statues that don't seem to care). In the paintings, see Victor Emmanuel II (left wall as you enter, on the white horse, with beard and pointy moustache), king of a small northern Italian province. His status as the only Italian-blooded provincial king made him a natural to become the first king of a united Italy. Here we see him at the ❶ **Battle of San Martino** (1859) while leading a united Italian nation against its Austrian oppressors. Beneath that, you'll see the coat he's wearing in the painting. Next (clockwise above the windows), the king's red-shirted troops cheer as he shakes hands with the dashing general Giuseppe Garibaldi. There was a concern that Garibaldi, the charismatic revolutionary who had won the south, might not submit to the king. In this scene, even as the king's white horse seems to honor Garibaldi, the revolutionary famously says, "I obey." Victorious, ❷ **the king receives politicians** (next painting), who bow and present the election results that made Italy united and democratic, with Victor Emmanuel II as a symbolic head. When he died in 1878 (see his funeral procession passing through Rome's Pantheon portico, filled with real portraits, on the far wall), Italy was well on the way to modern nationhood. The mythological grandeur on the ceiling seems designed to legitimize the Italian Republic, a latecomer to the European family of nations.

• *Pass through the hallway to the left, and walk through the Sala di Balia (which celebrates an early Sienese pope and was painted in the 1400s). In the next room, turn left and pass to the...*

❸ Chapel

This is where the city's governors and bureaucrats prayed. Back in the 14th century, Siena was overseen by a "revolving" government (like Switzerland today), with a group of nine representatives serving for two-month stints. The system was designed to combat corruption in government by keeping any one politician from becoming famous or powerful. "The Nine" were cloistered within this building, and therefore they needed their own chapel. The fine frescoes from the early 1400s show scenes from the life of the Virgin by Taddeo di Bartolo. Note also the inlaid choir chairs and how the artist struggled valiantly with perspective.

• *Continue into the large...*

Sala del Mappamondo (Hall of the World Map)

This room, where the Grand Council met, pumped up governors and citizens alike with its images of military victories and the blessings of Mary. On opposite ends of the room, you'll find two large frescoes. The beautiful ❹ *Maestà* (*Enthroned Virgin*, 1315), by Siena's great Simone Martini (c. 1280-1344), was the secular counterpart to Duccio's *Maestà* (then in the Duomo, now in the Duomo Museum). Mary sits on a throne under a red silk canopy, a model to Siena's city council of what a just ruler should be. Siena's black-and-white coat of arms is woven into both the canopy and the picture frame. Mary is surrounded by saints and angels, clearly echoing the *Maestà* of Simone's teacher, Duccio.

But this is a groundbreaking work. It's Siena's first fresco showing a Madonna not in a faraway, gold-leaf heaven, but under the blue sky of a real space that we inhabit. As Mary delicately holds Baby Jesus, her expressive face anticipates the sacrifice of her son. A scraggly John the Baptist (on the right) looks out, connecting viewers with the scene.

The canopy creates a 3-D stage, with saints in front of, behind, and underneath it. Some saints' faces are actually blocked by the support poles. These saints are not a generic conga-line of Byzantine icons, but a milling crowd of 30 individuals with expressive faces. Some look straight out, some are in profile, and some turn at that difficult-to-draw three-quarter angle, grabbing onto the canopy poles.

With unbeatable Florence to its north, Siena expanded south. Facing the *Maestà* is the famous ❺ *Equestrian Portrait of Guidoriccio da Fogliano* (1330; long attributed to Simone Martini, but more recently art historians have debated its authorship). The year is MCCCXXVIII (1328), and Siena's renowned mercenary commander Guidoriccio da Fogliano rides across a barren landscape and surveys the imposing castle that his armies have just conquered. He has successfully finished a six-month-long siege—see his camp on the right. This is one of Europe's first secular portraits. (Guido and his horse have the same tailor.)

On the same wall, just below the horse and rider, ❻ *The Surrender of the Castle of Giuncarico* (1314), attributed to Duccio, shows a man in green about to hand over his sword to a representative of the Sienese republic (not pictured—the scene was obliterated when it was covered by a later fresco). In the background is the man's castle and village on a rocky outcrop. Duccio's *Surrender* apparently inspired the 3-D landscape of *Guidoriccio da Fogliano*.

Also in the room (among those painted on pillars between the arches) are frescoes of two saints with local connections, ❼ **St. Bernardino** and **St. Catherine** (see page 390). Bernardino's charismatic sermons in Siena would famously hold a Campo crowd for several days. At sunset, he'd announce that he would begin speaking again at sunrise...and people would come back. His words brought together sworn enemies to share a *bacio di pace*—kiss of peace.

• *Continue into the next room.*

Sala della Pace, a.k.a. Sala dei Nove (Hall of Peace/Hall of the Nine)

The Council of Nine, who ruled Siena from 1287 to 1355, met in this room. Looking down on the oligarchy during their meetings was a fascinating fresco series showing the *Effects of Good and Bad Government,* by Ambrogio Lorenzetti (1337-1340).

The short wall opposite the window features the ❽ *Allegory of Good Government,* which celebrates the Sienese social system: "Siena," the stately, bearded man on the throne, is flanked by the six virtues. The central virtue, Peace (Pax), lounges on a pile of discarded armor. Justice (in red on the left) is punishing and forgiving under the figure of wisdom. Justice holds a scale, with angels on either side, to execute her judgments. Wrongdoers (lower right) are rounded up by the authorities. At the foot of the stage, prominent Sienese citizens file by. Concordia (below the figure of Justice) makes society just and equal—leveling the playing field with the wooden plane on her lap. And the symbolic foundation of it all is the she-wolf with Romulus and Remus (under the bearded "Siena"), recalling a myth meant to connect Siena's origins to the glory of ancient Rome.

The allegory continues on the long wall to the right with a well-preserved fresco depicting the effects of good government in town and country. Notice the whistle-while-you-work happiness of the utopian community ruled by the utopian government. The city and the countryside are exactly the same width (20 feet), an indication that they work together and need each other. Amid Siena's skyline (find the Duomo in the upper left corner), young people dance to the beat of a tambourine, workers repair roofs, a professor teaches, and the conversation flows. The blessings of a good government extend even to the countryside, which feels safe and prosperous. Bringing stability and safety to the land outside the city walls was a big accomplishment in the 14th century. The fields are tilled, the Via Francigena is busy with pilgrim traffic, and angels fly overhead.

Study this intimate and rare look at medieval commerce, and take in the details of the 14th-century cityscape. Notice, for instance, how today's exposed brick work, so "typical" of Siena, had then been stuccoed over and brightly painted. Notice also the pointy skyline, showing the city's proud towers before they were lopped off by the Florentines. The toppled towers ended up providing building material for the huge Fortezza—a repurposing that wasn't just practical but also psychological, serving as a reminder of the Florentine Medicis' success in keeping the Sienese down.

On the opposite long wall, in the
❾ *Allegory of Bad Government* (badly
damaged), a horned, fanged, wine-
drinking devil sets the vices loose ("Ava-
rice," "Vainglory"). Rather than dancing
in the streets, people are being arrested.
Arsonists torch homes and fields, soldiers rape and pillage, crime is rampant,
fields are barren, and frescoes get damaged. The only person still working is
making weapons. Justice slumps at the
devil's feet, bound, too depressed to look
up. The countryside is dark and devas-

tated, and no one leaves the city unarmed. The message: Without
justice, there can be no prosperity.

• *An enlightened city government also provides convenient toilets for the
public—which you'll find just off this room. Backtracking to the exit, just
before the Sala del Risorgimento, the lo-o-o-o-ong stairs lead to...*

A Grand View

You can cap your visit by climbing up to the loggia for a sweeping
view of the city and its surroundings. (For a less impressive version
of this view, you could skip the stairs and simply peek behind the
curtains in the Sala della Pace.)

Other Sights on or near Il Campo
▲City Tower (Torre del Mangia)

The tower's nearly 400 steps get pretty skinny at the top, but the
reward is one of Italy's best views. For more on the tower, see page
357.

Cost and Hours:
€10, €20 combo-ticket
with Civic Museum and
Santa Maria della Scala,
daily 10:00-19:00, mid-
Oct-Feb until 16:00, last
entry 45 minutes before
closing, closed in rain, free
and mandatory bag check.

Crowd Alert: Admission is limited to 50 people at a time.
Wait at the bottom of the stairs for the green *Avanti* light. Try to
avoid midday crowds (up to an hour wait at peak times).

▲Pinacoteca

If you're into medieval art, you'll likely find this quiet, uncrowded, colorful museum delightful. The museum walks you through

Siena's art chronologically, from the 12th through the 16th century, when a revolution in realism was percolating in Tuscany.

Cost and Hours: €4, Tue-Sat 8:15-19:15, Sun-Mon 9:00-13:00, free and mandatory bag check. From Il Campo, walk out Via di Città and go left on Via San Pietro to #29; tel. 0577-281-161, www.pinacotecanazionale.siena.it.

❯ Self-Guided Tour: In general, the collection lets you follow the evolution of painting styles from Byzantine to Gothic, then to International Gothic, and finally to Renaissance. The Medieval and early Renaissance core of the collection is on the second floor (rooms 1-19). The also impressive later art of the Cinquecento is downstairs, on the first floor.

· *Start your visit by climbing to the second floor and room 1.*

Long after Florentine art went realistic, the Sienese embraced a timeless, otherworldly style glittering with lots of gold. But Sienese art features more than just paintings. In this city of proud craftsmen, the gilding and carpentry of the frames almost compete with the actual paintings. The exquisite attention to detail gives a glimpse into the wealth of the 13th and 14th centuries, Siena's Golden Age. As you walk through the museum, take time to trace the delicate features with your eyes. The woven silk and gold clothing you'll see was worn by the very people who once walked these halls, when this was a private mansion (appreciate the colonnaded courtyard).

Room 1 mostly features early Sienese works of the 13th century, with the intense color, stylized compositions, and gold backgrounds of the Byzantine style. The altarpieces here emphasize the heavenly and otherworldly.

Rooms 2-4 contain a number of works by Duccio di Buoninsegna, who revolutionized a more human realism in the Sienese approach to painting. His groundbreaking innovations are subtle: less gold-leaf background, fewer gold creases in robes, translucent garments, inlaid-marble thrones, and a more human Mary and Jesus. Notice that the Madonna-and-Bambino pose is eerily identical in each version. While artists had yet to master depth and perspective, they appreciated it—see how in the crucifixes, Jesus' head actually tilts out. (Duccio also created the *Maestà* in the Duomo Museum, the Duomo's big stained-glass window, and a fresco in the Civic Museum.)

In **Room 5** are works by Duccio's one-time assistant, Simone Martini, including his *St. Augustine of Siena*. Scenes from the saint's life appear in an attempt at realistic Sienese streets, buildings, and landscapes. In each panel, the saint pops out at the oddest (difficult to draw) angles to save the day by performing one of his many miracles, to the obvious relief of those involved—notice the dramatic emotion on their faces. (Simone Martini also did the *Maestà* and possibly the Guidoriccio frescoes in the Civic Museum.)

Room 7 includes religious works by the hometown Lorenzetti brothers (Ambrogio is best known for the secular masterpiece, the *Effects of Good and Bad Government,* in the Civic Museum). The rest of the rooms on this floor are a menagerie of gold-backed saints and Madonnas.

In **Room 11** find the powerful *Crucifixion* (c. 1400) by Taddeo di Bartolo. In the dreamy, delicate *Annunciation* (also by Bartolo), follow the exciting action between the cast: God, Holy Spirit, Mary, and the angel Gabriel with patron saints looking out, connecting us with the scene. The adjacent chapel is a reminder that this was formerly the home of a noble family.

In **Room 12** are two famous small wooden panels: *Città sul Mare (City by the Sea)* and *Castello in Riva al Lago (Castle on the Lakeshore).* These beautifully drawn pieces, done by an early 15th-century Sienese painter, feature a strange, medieval-landscape Cubism. Notice the weird, melancholy light that captures the sense of the Dark Ages.

• *Loop through Rooms 13 to 17 and notice how, even in the 15th century, Siena stays retro, clinging to its Gothic glory. Then descend one floor to view an entertaining collection of later Renaissance art.*

In **Room 20,** suddenly the gold is gone—Madonna is set on Earth. See works by the painter/biographer Giorgio Vasari **(Room 22),** a stunning view out the window **(Room 26),** and several colorful rooms **(27-30)** dedicated to Domenico Beccafumi (1486-1551). Beccafumi designed many of the Duomo's inlaid pavement panels (including *Slaughter of the Innocents*), and his original cartoons are displayed in **Room 30.** With strong bodies, twisting poses, and dramatic gestures, Beccafumi's works epitomize the Manner-

ist style. In the center of the room stand two finely painted end panels (1540) for a stretcher used to carry the sick and dead.

Room 31 has the sympathetic *Christ on the Column* by Sodoma (Giovanni Bazzi), and the long **Room 32** displays large-scale works by Sodoma, Beccafumi, and others. In **Room 33,** Bernardino Mei gives a Sienese take on the wrinkled saints and dark shadows of Caravaggio.

SIENA

SIENA

CATHEDRAL AREA
▲▲▲Duomo

Siena's 13th-century cathedral and striped bell tower are one of the most illustrious examples of Romanesque-Gothic style in Italy.

This ornate but surprisingly secular shrine to the Virgin Mary is slathered with colorful art inside and out, from inlaid-marble floors to stained-glass windows. The cathedral's interior showcases the work of the greatest sculptors of every era—Pisano, Donatello, Michelangelo, and Bernini—and the Piccolomini Library features a series of 15th-century frescoes chronicling the adventures of Siena's philanderer-turned-pope, Aeneas Piccolomini.

Cost: €4, €5 mid-Aug-Oct when marble floors are on display, includes cathedral and Piccolomini Library, buy ticket at Duomo ticket office (facing the cathedral entry, the ticket office is behind you to the right).

Combo-Tickets: To see the Duomo, Duomo Museum, Crypt, and Baptistery, consider the €13 Opa Si Pass. To add an escorted visit into the dome and rooftop (described next), pay €15 for the Opa Si Pass + Porta del Cielo. The €18 Acropoli Pass adds Santa Maria della Scala to the Opa Si Pass, and the €20 Acropoli Pass Plus includes both Santa Maria della Scala and the dome/rooftop tour.

Hours: Mon-Sat 10:30-19:00, Sun 13:30-18:00, Nov-Feb closes daily at 17:30. Tel. 0577-286-300, www.operaduomo.siena.it.

Avoiding Lines: Check the line to get into the Duomo before buying tickets—if there's a long wait, you can pay an extra €1 for a "reservation" that lets you skip the line (available at the "reserved/fast entrance" queue).

Tours: The €8 videoguide covers the all of the sights included in the combo-ticket and is informative but dry; I'd stick with the commentary in this chapter.

Going to Church: It's free to enter the cathedral if you are attending Mass; use the entrance to the right of the main one (Mon-Sat at 9:00 and 10:00, Sun at 8:00, 11:00, 12:15, and 18:30, no mass mid-Aug-Oct).

Dress Code: Modest dress is required, but stylish paper ponchos are provided for the inappropriately clothed.

Cathedral Roof Visit: The Opa Si Pass + Porta del Cielo in-

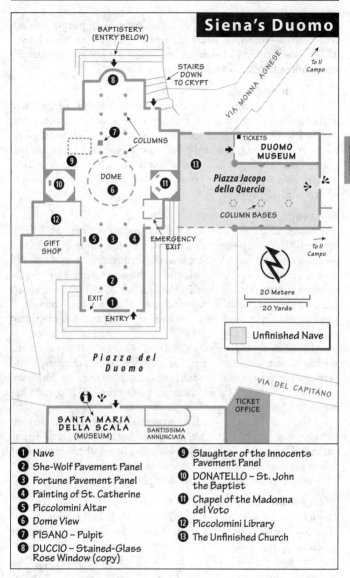

Siena's Duomo

BAPTISTERY (ENTRY BELOW)

STAIRS DOWN TO CRYPT

VIA MONNA AGNESE

To Il Campo

TICKETS

DUOMO MUSEUM

COLUMNS

Piazza Jacopo della Quercia

DOME

COLUMN BASES

EMERGENCY EXIT

To Il Campo

GIFT SHOP

20 Meters
20 Yards

Unfinished Nave

EXIT

ENTRY

Piazza del Duomo

VIA DEL CAPITANO

TICKET OFFICE

SANTA MARIA DELLA SCALA (MUSEUM)

SANTISSIMA ANNUNCIATA

1 Nave
2 She-Wolf Pavement Panel
3 Fortune Pavement Panel
4 Painting of St. Catherine
5 Piccolomini Altar
6 Dome View
7 PISANO – Pulpit
8 DUCCIO – Stained-Glass Rose Window (copy)

9 Slaughter of the Innocents Pavement Panel
10 DONATELLO – St. John the Baptist
11 Chapel of the Madonna del Voto
12 Piccolomini Library
13 The Unfinished Church

SIENA

cludes all of the cathedral sights plus a 30-minute accompanied Porta del Cielo ("Heaven's Gate") visit to the dome's cupola and roof. For spectacular interior and exterior views, you'll climb 79 steps to see restored rooms with impressive inlaid floors and get a close-up look at the cupola, with its blue, star-decorated panels and 12 windows (representing the 12 apostles) by Ulisse De Matteis. You'll also walk briefly outside on the rooftop for a breathtaking view (timed-entry ticket, escorted visits of 18 people go each half-hour, March-Oct Mon-Sat from 10:30-18:00, Sun 13:30-17:00, less frequent off-season, tel. 0577-286-300 or opasiena@operalaboratori.com for advance reservations).

◐ Self-Guided Tour

The Duomo sits atop Siena's highest point, with one of the most extravagant facades in all of Europe. Like a medieval altarpiece, the facade is divided into sections, each frame filled with patriarchs and prophets, studded with roaring gargoyles, and topped with prickly pinnacles (for more about the facade, see page 362).

• *Step inside, putting yourself in the mindset of a pilgrim as you take in this trove of religious art.*

❶ Nave

The heads of 172 popes—who reigned from the time of St. Peter to the 12th century—peer down from above, looking over the fine inlaid art on the floor. With a forest of striped columns, a coffered dome, a large stained-glass window at the far end (it's a copy—the original is viewable up close in the Duomo Museum), and an art gallery's worth of early Renaissance art, this is one busy interior. If you look closely at the popes, you'll see the same four faces repeated over and over.

For almost two centuries (1373-1547), 40 artists paved the marble floor with scenes from the Old Testament, allegories, and intricate patterns. The series starts near the entrance with historical allegories; the larger, more elaborate scenes surrounding the altar are mostly stories from the Old Testament.

Many of the floor panels are roped off and covered to prevent further wear and tear. But from mid-August through October, the cathedral uncovers them and holds mass in another church. The following two panels are always visible.

• *On the floor, find the second pavement panel from the entrance.*

❷ She-Wolf Pavement Panel

Depicted as a she-wolf, the proud city of Siena is the center of the Italian universe, orbited by such lesser lights as Roma, Florentia (Florence), and Pisa. This is pretty secular stuff for such prime church real estate. Five yards to the left and right are panels with pre-Christian imagery of the ancient Greek prophetesses known as the sibyls. The sibyls parade up both aisles to the front as the faithful process to redemption at the main altar. This church's mix

of pre-Christian wisdom, secular humanism, and Christian piety gives an insight into the Sienese approach to religion.

• *The fourth pavement panel from the entrance is the...*

❸ Fortune Pavement Panel

Lady Luck (lower right) parachutes down to earth, where she teeters back and forth on a ball and a tipsy boat. The lesson? Fortune is an unstable foundation for life. Truth seekers wind their way up the precarious path to the top, where Socrates accompanies Lady Wisdom. Having attained wisdom, the world's richest man ("Crates," upper right) realizes that money doesn't buy happiness, and he dumps his jewels out. They fall to earth, and the cycle of Fortune begins again.

On the right wall hangs a dim ❹ **painting of St. Catherine** (fourth from entrance). Siena's homegrown saint (see page 390) had a vision in which she mystically married Christ. Here's the wedding ceremony in heaven. Jesus places the ring on Catherine's finger as her future mother-in-law, Mary, looks on.

• *On the opposite wall is a marble altarpiece decorated with statues (next to a doorway leading to a shop, snacks, and WC).*

❺ Piccolomini Altar

The Piccolomini Altar was commissioned by the Sienese-born Pope Pius III (born Francesco Piccolomini) as a memorial honor-

ing his uncle Pius II. As the cardinal of Siena at the time, Piccolomini also expected this fancy tomb to be his own final resting place, but because he later became pope he was buried in the Vatican instead. (If you look high above to the right, you'll see the colorful fresco of the coronation of Pope Pius, wearing a golden robe.)

The Piccolomini Altar is most interesting for its statues: one by Michelangelo and three by his students. Michelangelo was originally contracted to do 15 statues, but another sculptor had started the marble blocks, and Michelangelo's heart was never in the project. He personally finished only the figure of St. Paul (lower right, clearly more interesting than the bland, bored popes above him).

Paul has the look of Michelangelo's *Moses*, the broken-nosed self-portrait of the sculptor himself, and the relaxed hand of his *David*. It was the chance to sculpt *David* in Florence that convinced Michelangelo to abandon the Siena project.

• *Now grab a seat under the dome to study the...*

❻ Dome and Surrounding Area

The dome sits on a 12-sided base, but its "coffered" ceiling is actually a painted illusion.

Get oriented to the array of sights we'll see by thinking of the church floor as a big 12-hour clock. You're the middle, and the altar is high noon: You'll find the *Slaughter of the Innocents* roped off on the floor at 10 o'clock, Pisano's pulpit between two pillars at 11 o'clock, a copy of Duccio's round stained-glass window at 12 o'clock, Bernini's chapel at 3 o'clock, the Piccolomini Altar at 7 o'clock, the Piccolomini Library at 8 o'clock, and a Donatello statue at 9 o'clock.

Attached to columns (easy to miss, at 7 o'clock and 5 o'clock) are two 60-foot-tall wooden poles that are dear to any Sienese heart. These **flagpoles**—bearing the Florentine flag—were captured during the pivotal Battle of Montaperti (1260, fought near Siena), when 20,000 Sienese squared off against 35,000 soldiers from their archrival city, Florence. The two armies battled back and forth all day, until one of the Florentine soldiers—actually, a Sienese spy under cover—attacked the Florentine standard-bearer from behind. Florence's flag fell to the ground, the army lost its bearings and confidence, and Siena seized the moment to counterattack and win. It was the city's finest hour, ushering in its 88-year Golden Age (it lasted from 1260 until the plague hit in 1348).

The church was intended to be much larger. Look into the right transept and mentally blow a hole in the wall. You'd be looking down the nave of the massive extension of the church—that is, if the original grandiose plan had been completed (see sidebar, page 351).

❼ Pisano's Pulpit

The octagonal Carrara marble pulpit (1268) rests on the backs of lions, symbols of Christianity triumphant. Like the lions, the Church eats its catch (devouring paganism) and nurses its cubs. The seven relief panels tell the life of Christ in rich detail. The pulpit is the work of Nicola Pisano (c. 1220-1278), the "Giotto of sculpture," whose revival of classical forms (columns, sarcophagus-like relief panels) signaled the coming Renaissance. His son Giovanni (c. 1240-1319) carved many of the panels, mixing his dad's classicism and realism with the decorative detail and curvy lines of French Gothic—a style that would influence Donatello and other Florentines.

The Crucifixion panel (facing the nave under the eagle) is proto-Renaissance. Christ's anatomy is realistic. Mary (bottom left) swoons into the arms of the other women, a very human outburst of emotion. And a Roman soldier (to the right, by Giovanni) turns to look back with an easy motion that breaks the stiff, frontal Gothic mold.

Look at the two panels facing the altar. It's Judgment Day, and Christ is flanked by the saved (on his right, almost hypnotized by the presence of their savior) and, on his left, the desperate damned.

If you visit Pisa, you'll see two similar Pisano pulpits there. (See pages 439 and 444 for more on the Pisanos and their pulpits.)

❽ Duccio's Stained-Glass Rose Window

This is a copy of the original window (now in the Duomo Museum). The famous rose window was created in 1288 and dedicated to the Virgin Mary (description on page 384).

• *As you face the window, in the floor to the left (in the transept) is the...*

❾ Slaughter of the Innocents Pavement Panel

Herod (left), sitting enthroned amid Renaissance arches, orders the massacre of all babies to prevent the coming of the promised Messiah. It's a chaotic scene of angry soldiers, grieving mothers, and dead babies, reminding locals that a republic ruled by a tyrant will always experience misery. The work was designed by the Sienese Matteo di Giovanni (late 1400s) and inlaid with a colorful array of marble, including yellow marble, a Sienese specialty quarried nearby.

• *Step into the chapel just behind you (next to the Piccolomini Library) to see...*

❿ Donatello's St. John the Baptist

The rugged saint in his famous rags stands in a quiet chapel. Donatello, the aging Florentine sculptor, whose style was now considered passé in Florence, came here to build bronze doors for the church (similar to Ghiberti's in Florence). Donatello didn't complete the door project, but he did finish  this bronze statue (1457). Appreciate John's expressive face and the realistic stance of his body—done before Michelangelo was even born. Notice the cherubs high above in the dome, playfully dangling their feet.

• *Cross the church. Directly opposite find the Chigi Chapel, also known as the...*

⓫ Chapel of the *Madonna del Voto*

To understand why Bernini is considered the greatest Baroque sculptor, step into this sumptuous chapel (designed in the early 1660s for Fabio Chigi, a.k.a. Pope

Alexander VII). Move up to the altar and look back at the **two Bernini statues:** Mary Magdalene in a state of spiritual ecstasy and St. Jerome playing the crucifix like a violinist lost in beautiful music.

The chapel is classic Baroque, combining colored marble, statues, stained glass, a dome, and golden angels holding an icon-like framed painting, creating a multimedia extravaganza that offers a glimpse of heaven. It's enough to make even a Lutheran light a candle.

The painting over the altar is the *Madonna del Voto,* a Madonna and Child adorned with a real crown of gold and jewels (painted by a Sienese master in the mid-13th century). In typical medieval fashion, the scene is set in the golden light of heaven. Mary has the almond eyes, long fingers, and golden folds in her robe that are found in orthodox icons of the time. Still, this Mary tilts her head and looks out sympathetically, ready to listen to the prayers of the faithful. This is the Mary to whom the Palio is dedicated, dear to the hearts of the Sienese.

For untold generations, the Sienese have prayed to the *Madonna del Voto* for help. In thanks, they give **offerings** of silver hearts and medallions, many of which now hang on the wall just to the left as you exit the chapel. On the other side of the chapel door, the glass display case on the wall looks like a jewelry store's front window—with rings, necklaces, and other precious items given by thankful worshippers. To leave an offering yourself, light a candle for a small donation.

• *Cross back to the other side of the church and head toward the main door. On the right, just before the big Piccolomini Altar we saw earlier, look for the door to the...*

⑫ Piccolomini Library

If crowds slow your way into this library, spend your waiting time reading ahead. Brilliantly frescoed, the library captures the exuberant, optimistic spirit of the 1400s, when humanism and the Renaissance were born. The never-restored frescoes look nearly as vivid now as the day they were finished 550 years ago. (With the bright window light, candles were unnecessary in this room—and didn't sully the art with soot.) The painter Pinturicchio (c. 1454-1513) was hired to celebrate the life of one of Siena's hometown boys—a man many call "the first humanist," Aeneas Piccolomini (1405-1464), who became Pope Pius II. Each of the 10 scenes is framed with an arch, as if Pinturicchio were opening a window onto the spacious 3-D world we inhabit. View the paintings from across the room and begin with the episode to the right of the window. Let your eyes follow the frescoes clockwise:

1. Leaving for Basel: Twenty-seven-year-old Aeneas, riding

a white horse and decked out in an outrageous hat, pauses to take one last look back as he leaves Siena to charge off on the first of many adventures in his sometimes sunny, sometimes stormy life. Born poor but noble, he got all A's in his classics classes in Siena. Now, having soaked up all the secular knowledge available, he leaves home to crash a church council in Switzerland, where he would take sides against the pope.

2. Meeting James II of Scotland: Aeneas (with long brown hair) charmed King James and the well-dressed, educated, worldly crowd of Europe's courts. Among his many travels, he visited London (writing home about Westminster Abbey and St. Paul's), barely survived a storm at sea, negotiated peace between England and France, and fathered (at least) two illegitimate children.

3. Crowned Poet by Frederick III: Next we find Aeneas in Vienna, working as secretary to the German king. Aeneas kneels to ceremonially receive the laurel crown of a poet. Aeneas wrote love poetry, bawdy stories, and a play, and is best known for his candid autobiography. Everyone was talking about Aeneas—a writer, speaker, diplomat, and lover of the arts and pretty women, who was the very essence of the *uomo universale*, a.k.a. Renaissance Man.

4. Submitting to Pope Eugene IV: At age 40, after a serious illness, Aeneas changes his life. He journeys to Rome and kisses the pope's foot, apologizing for his heretical opposition. He repents for his wild youth and becomes a priest. (In his autobiography, he says it was time to change anyway, as women no longer aroused him...and he no longer attracted them.)

5. Introducing Frederick III and Eleanora: Quickly named Bishop of Siena, Aeneas (in white pointed bishop's hat) makes his hometown a romantic getaway for his friend Frederick and his fiancée. Notice the Duomo's bell tower in the distance and the city walls (upper left). Aeneas always seemed to be present at Europe's most important political, religious, and social events.

6. Made Cardinal: Kneeling before the pope, with shaved head and praying hands, Aeneas receives the flat red hat of a cardinal. In many of these panels, the artist Pinturicchio uses all the latest 3-D effects—floor tiles and carpets, distant landscapes, receding lines—to suck you into the scene. He tears down palace walls and lets us peek inside, into the day's centers of power.

7. Made Pope: In 1458, at age 53, Aeneas is elected to be Pope Pius II. Carried in triumph, he blesses the crowd. One of his first acts as pope is to declare as heresy the antipope doctrines he championed in his youth. (Pius II fans can visit his birthplace in Pienza, described in the Tuscan Hill Towns chapter.)

8. Proclaims a Crusade: He calls on all of Europe to liberate the Christian city of Constantinople, which had recently fallen (in 1453) to the Ottoman Turks. Europe is reluctant to follow his call, but Aeneas pushes the measure through.

9. Canonizes St. Catherine: From his papal throne, Aeneas looks down on the mortal remains of Catherine (clutching her symbol, the lily) and proclaims his fellow Sienese a saint. The well-dressed candle-holders in the foreground pose proudly.

10. Arrival in Ancona: Old and sick, the pope has to be carried everywhere on a litter because of rheumatic feet. He travels to Ancona, ready to board a ship to go fight the Turks. But only a handful of Venetian galleys arrive at the appointed time, the crusade peters out, and Aeneas, disheartened, dies. He wrote: "I do not deny my past. I have been a great wanderer, wandering away from the right path. But at least I know it, and hope the knowledge has not come too late."

Circle around a second time to appreciate the library's intricately decorated, illuminated music scores and a statue (a Roman copy of a Greek original) of the Three Graces, who almost seem to dance to the beat. The oddly huge sheepskin sheets of music are from the days before individual hymnals—they had to be big so that many singers could read the music from a distance. If the musical notation looks off, that's because 15th-century Italians used a sliding C clef, not the fixed C, F, and G clefs musicians know today. This

clef marked middle C, and the melodies could be chanted in relation to it. Appreciate the fine painted decorations on the music—the gold-leaf highlights, the blue tones from expensive ultramarine (made from precious lapis lazuli), and the miniature figures. All of this exquisite detail was lovingly crafted by Benedictine monks for the glory of God. Find your favorite—I like the blue, totally wild god of wind with the big hair (in the fourth case from the right of the window).

• *Exit the Duomo and make a U-turn to the left, walking alongside the church to Piazza Jacopo della Quercia.*

⑬ The Unfinished Church

Had the massive church Siena envisioned been built, the nave would be where the piazza is today. Worshippers would have en-

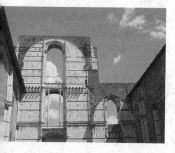

tered the church from the far end of the piazza through the unfinished wall. (Look way up at the highest part of the wall. That viewpoint is accessible from inside the Duomo Museum.) Some of the nave's green-and-white-striped columns were built, but are now filled in with a brick wall. White stones in the pavement mark where a row of pillars would have been.

Look through the unfinished entrance facade, note blue sky where the stained-glass windows would have been, and ponder the struggles, triumphs, and failures of the human spirit.

▲▲Duomo Museum

Located in a corner of the Duomo's grand but unfinished extension (to the right as you face the main facade), Siena's most enjoyable museum (Museo dell'Opera e Panorama) was built to house the cathedral's art. Stand eye-to-eye with the saints and angels who once languished, unknown, in the church's upper reaches (where copies are found today). The ground floor features the original Duccio stained-glass window that once hung over the high altar, along with an army of statues from the facade. Upstairs is Duccio's *Maestà* (*Enthroned Virgin*, 1311), a masterpiece of medieval art. The flip side of the *Maestà* (displayed on the opposite wall) has 26 panels—the medieval equivalent of pages—showing scenes from the Passion of Christ. And the museum's high point is one of the loftiest viewpoints in town, offering expansive views of the church and the city.

Cost and Hours: €8, daily 10:30-19:00, Nov-Feb until 17:30, videoguide-€4 (€6/2 people) but you'll do fine with just the commentary in this listing, tel. 0577-286-300, www.operaduomo. siena.it.

↻ Self-Guided Tour

• *Start on the ground floor, which houses the church's original statues, mainly from the facade and exterior. After descending a few steps (if you spot an exit sign, ignore it for now), turn your back on the hall of statues and wrought-iron gate. You're now face-to-face with...*

Donatello's Madonna and Child

In this round, carved relief, a slender and tender Mary gazes down at her chubby-cheeked baby. The thick folds of her head-

dress stream down around her smooth face. Her sad eyes say that she knows the eventual fate of her son. Donatello creates the illusion of Mary's three-dimensional "lap" using only a few inches of depth cut into the creamy-rose stone. Move to the far right and look at Mary's face from an angle (try not to notice impish Jesus); think of the challenge involved in carving the illusion of such depth.

• *On the opposite side of the room is...*

Duccio's Stained-Glass Window

Until recently, this splendid original window was located above and behind the Duomo's altar. Now the church has a copy, and art lovers can enjoy a close-up look at this masterpiece. The rose window—20 feet across, made in 1288—is dedicated (like the church and the city itself) to the Virgin Mary. In the window's bottom panel, Mary (in blue) lies stretched across a red coffin while a crowd of mourners looks on. Miraculously, Mary was spared the pain of death (the Assumption, central panel); winged angels carry her up in a holy bubble to heaven (top panel), where Christ sets her on a throne beside him and crowns her.

The work is by Siena's most famous artist, Duccio di Buoninsegna (c. 1255-1319). Duccio combined elements from rigid Byzantine icons (Mary's almond-shaped bubble, called a *mandorla*, and the full-frontal saints that flank her) with a budding sense of 3-D realism (the throne turned at a three-quarter angle to simulate depth, with angels behind). Also notice how the angels in the central panel spread their wings out beyond the border of the window frame.

The Sienese army defeated Florence in the bloody battle of Montaperti, thanks, many believed, to the divine intervention of the Virgin. For the next 80 years of prosperity, Sienese artists cranked out countless Madonnas as a way of saying *grazie*. Bear in mind that the Duomo's main altar was originally dominated by Duccio's *Maestà*, a huge golden altarpiece of the Virgin in Majesty (which you'll see upstairs) that was bathed in the golden-blue light from this window.

• *Lining this main room are...*

Pisano's Statues

Giovanni Pisano spent a decade (c. 1285-1296) carving and orchestrating the decoration of the cathedral—saints, prophets, sibyls, animals, and the original she-wolf with Romulus and Remus. These life-size, robed saints stand in a relaxed *contrapposto*, with open mouths and expressive gestures. Their heads jut out—Pisano's way of making them more visible from below. Some turn and seem to converse with their neighbors, especially evident with Moses *(Mosè)* and the sister who raised him like a mother, Miriam *(Maria di Mosè*, on the left side of the room). The copies of these two stand on the right side of the church, where they appear to interact.

Down a few steps in Room 11 are the two lions that once looked down from the church's main entrance, and Pisano's 12 apostles, who originally lined the nave. (See old photos on the wall.) Tastes changed over the centuries, and the apostles were later moved up to the roof, where they eroded. Pisano's relaxed realism and expressive gestures were a major influence on later Florentine sculptors like Donatello.

• *Retrace your steps and go up to the first floor. Head to the left, through a glass door into the darkened Room 6, for a private audience with Duccio's Madonna.*

Duccio, *Maestà* and Passion Panels, 1311

The panels in this room were once part of the Duomo's main altarpiece. Grab a seat and study one of the great pieces of medieval art. Although the former altarpiece was disassembled (and the frame was lost), most of the pieces are displayed here, with the front side (*Maestà*, with Mary and saints; pronounced my-STAH) at one end of the room and the back side (26 Passion panels) at the other.

Imagine these separate panels pieced together, set into their original gold, prickly, 15-by-15-foot wood frame and placed on the main altar in the Duomo.

Maestà (Enthroned Virgin): At the center of the front side sit the Virgin and Child, surrounded by angels and saints. Mary is a melancholy queen on an inlaid-marble throne. Young angels lean their elbows on the back of the throne and sigh. We see the throne head-on, unnaturally splayed open (a Byzantine style popular at the time in Siena). Mary is massive, twice the size of the saints around her, and she clearly stands out from the golden background. Unlike traditional full-frontal Byzantine icons, she turns slightly sideways to touch her baby, who does not bless us.

The city of Siena is dedicated to this Lady, who backed the Sienese against Florence in the bloody battle of Montaperti in 1260. Here, she's triumphant, visited by Siena's four patron saints (kneeling in front), John the Baptist and other saints (the first choir row), more angels in a row (soprano section), and, chiming in from up in the balcony, James the Great and the 12 apostles.

The painting was revolutionary for the time in its sheer size and opulence, and in Duccio's budding realism, which broke standard conventions. Duccio, at the height of his powers, used every innovative arrow in his quiver. He replaced the standard gold-leaf background (symbolizing heaven) with a gold, intricately patterned curtain draped over the throne. Mary's blue robe opens to reveal her body, and the curve of her knee suggests real anatomy beneath the robe. Baby Jesus wears a delicately transparent garment. Their faces are modeled with light—a patchwork of bright flesh and shadowy valleys, as if lit from the left (a technique he likely learned from his contemporary Giotto during a visit to Florence).

Along the base of Mary's throne is an inscription (*"Mater sancta dei..."* or "Holy Mother of God...") asking Mary to bring peace to Siena *(Senis)* and long life to Duccio *(Ducio)*—quite a tribute in a time when painters were usually treated as anonymous craftsmen.

The Passion of Christ: The flip side of the altarpiece featured 26 smaller panels showing colorful scenes from the Passion of Christ.

The panels showcase the budding Tuscan style that united realism and storytelling. It doesn't take a Bible scholar to "read" these panels, left to right. Christ on a donkey (lower left) makes his triumphal entry into the city gate of Jerusalem (or is it Siena?). Next, he washes his disciples' feet in a realistic, three-dimensional room. But Duccio hasn't fully mastered perspective—in the Last Supper, we see Christ eye-to-eye, but view the table from above. Christ is arrested in Gethsemane, and so on, until the climactic Crucifixion. The Crucifixion is given the standard gold background, but the cross is set in a real-world location: on a terraced hillside, amid the crowd. Jesus' followers express human emotion rarely seen in earlier art.

The crowd scenes in the Passion panels aren't arranged in neat choir rows, but in more natural-looking groups. Duccio sets figures in motion, with individual faces expressing sorrow, anger, and agitation. Duccio's human realism would be taken to the next level by his Florentine counterpart Giotto, often called the proto-Renaissance painter.

Duccio and assistants (possibly including Simone Martini) spent three years on this massive altarpiece. It was a triumph, and at its dedication the satisfied Sienese marched it around the Campo and into the church in a public procession.

But by 1506, at the height of the Renaissance, Duccio's medieval altarpiece looked musty and old-fashioned, and was moved to a side altar. In 1771 it was disassembled and stored in the church offices (now the Duomo Museum). Today, scholars debate how to reassemble it accurately, and hail it as a quantum leap in the evolution of art.

Room 9, to the left and behind the *Maestà*, contains wooden models of the Duomo's inlaid-marble floor and close-ups of the individual floor panels for easier inspection.

• *Return to the stairs and continue up. Take a right at the first landing. At the landing just before the top floor, turn right and walk past the rooms, going through the small doorway to the stairwell. If the line is all the way to the middle of the room, you're facing a 40-minute wait. Eventually you'll climb down the steps and then up about 40 tight and claustrophobic spiral stairs to the first viewpoint. You can continue up another 100 steps of a similar spiral staircase to reach the very top.*

SIENA

Panorama dal Facciatone

Standing on the wall from this high point in the city, you're rewarded with a stunning view of Siena...and an interesting perspective.

Look toward the Duomo and remember this: To outdo Florence, Siena had planned to enlarge this cathedral by turning it into a transept and constructing an enormous nave. You're standing on top of what would have been the new entrance facade. Columns would have stood where you see the rows of white stones in the pavement below. Had the church been completed, you'd be looking straight down the nave toward the altar.

Other Cathedral-Area Sights
▲Baptistery (Battistero)

This richly adorned and quietly tucked-away cave of art is worth a look for its cool tranquility and exquisite art, including an ornately painted vaulted ceiling. The highlight is the baptismal font designed by Jacopo della Quercia and adorned with bronze panels and angels by Quercia, Ghiberti, and Donatello. It dates from the 1420s, the start of the Renaissance.

Cost and Hours: €4, daily 10:30-19:00, Nov-Feb until 17:30.

Crypt (Cripta)

The cathedral "crypt" is archaeologically important. The site of a small 12th-century Romanesque church, it was filled in with dirt a century after its creation to provide a foundation for the huge church that sits atop it today. Recently excavated (with modern metal supports from the 1990s), the several rediscovered rooms show off what are likely the oldest frescoes in town (well-described in English).

Cost and Hours: €8, daily 10:30-19:00, Nov-Feb until 17:30, entrance near the top of the stairs between the Baptistery and Duomo Museum.

▲Santa Maria della Scala

This museum, opposite the Duomo, operated for centuries as a hospital, foundling home, and pilgrim lodging. Many of those activities are visible in the 15th-century frescoes of its main hall, the Pellegrinaio. Today, the hospital and its cellars are filled with fascinating exhibits (well-described in English). You'll exit through a cool and quiet air-conditioned lobby, where you'll find a fine bookshop and the TI, all under great 15th-century timbers.

Cost and Hours: €9, €13 combo-ticket with Civic Museum, €20 combo-ticket includes the Civic Museum and Tower (valid 2 days); daily 10:00-19:00, Fri until 22:00; closes earlier mid-Oct-mid-March; tel. 0577-534-571, www.santamariadellascala.com.

◐ Self-Guided Tour: It's easy to get lost in this gigantic complex, so stay focused on the main attractions—the fancily frescoed Pellegrinaio Hall (ground floor), most of the original Fountain of Joy and some of the most ancient Byzantine reliquaries in existence (first basement), and the Etruscan collection in the Archaeological Museum (second basement), where the Sienese took refuge during WWII bombing.

• *From the entrance, go left into the second room to reach the Pellegrinaio—the long room with the colorful frescoes.*

The sumptuously frescoed walls of **Pellegrinaio Hall**—originally a reception hall for visiting pilgrims, then a hospital—show medieval Siena's innovative health care and social welfare system in action (by Sienese painters, c. 1442, wonderfully described in English). Starting in the 11th century, the hospital nursed the sick and cared for abandoned children, as is vividly portrayed in these frescoes. The good works paid off, as bequests and donations poured in, creating the wealth that's evident throughout this building. The video, projected on the left side of the wall, gives interesting insight into medieval life depicted in the scenes.

• *Head down the stairs, then continue straight into the darkened rooms with pieces of Siena's landmark fountain—follow signs to La Fonte Gaia.*

An engaging exhibit explains Jacopo della Quercia's early 15th-century **Fountain of Joy** (Fonte Gaia)—and displays the disassembled pieces of the original fountain itself. In the 19th century, after serious deterioration, the ornate fountain was dismantled and plaster casts were made. (These casts formed the replica that graces Il Campo today.) Here you'll see the eroded original panels paired with their restored casts, along with the actual statues that once stood on the edges of the fountain.

• *To visit the reliquaries, retrace your steps and follow the signs for* Il Tesoro.

You'll enter a winding labyrinth with glass cases of some **powerful relics,** including a nail from Jesus' cross *(sacro chiodo),* a piece of the Virgin's robe *(beata Vergine),* some of Jesus' blood in a veil *(sangue di Christo),* and lots of bones. They're all contained in cases or reliquaries that befit the preciousness of these sacred bits and saintly pieces.

Many of these **Byzantine reliquaries** are made of gold, silver, and precious stones. Legend has it that some were owned by Helen, Constantine's mother. They were "donated" (around 1350) to the hospital shortly after the plague that decimated the city (and the rest of Europe), since the sale of reliquaries was forbidden. The hospital then used them very effectively for fundraising from the many visiting pilgrims.

• *Now, descend into the cavernous second basement. After a peek at the Siena City Museum (Racconto della Città), cross a carriageway, and head into the Archaeological Museum.*

Under the groin vaults of the **Archaeological Museum,** you're alone with piles of ancient Etruscan stuff excavated from tombs dating centuries before Christ (displayed in another labyrinthine exhibit). Remember, the Etruscans dominated this part of Italy before the Roman Empire swept through. About all we have from the Etruscans came from the tombs of their aristocracy. These wealthy people had exquisite treasures they really wanted to take with them into the next life. You'll see terra-cotta funeral urns for ashes (the design was often a standard body with the heads personalized) and piles of domestic artifacts from the 8th to the 5th century B.C.—none of which stayed with the dead aristocrats.

SAN DOMENICO AREA
Church of San Domenico
This huge brick church is worth a quick look. Spacious and plain (except for the colorful flags of the city's 17 *contrade*), the Gothic interior fits the austere philosophy of the Dominicans and invites meditation on the thoughts and deeds of St. Catherine. Walk up the steps in the rear to see paintings from her life. Halfway up the church on the right, find a copper bust of St. Catherine (for four centuries it contained her skull), a small case housing her thumb (on the right), and a page from her personal devotional book (12th century, on the left). In the chapel (10 feet to the left) surrounded with candles, you'll see Catherine's head (a clay mask around her skull with her actual teeth showing through) atop the altar. Through the door just beyond are the sacristy and the bookstore.

Cost and Hours: Free, daily 7:00-18:30, shorter hours off-season, www.basilicacateriniana.com.

St. Catherine of Siena (1347-1380)

The youngest of 25 children born to a Sienese cloth dyer, Catherine began experiencing heavenly visions as a child. At 16 she became a member of the Dominican order, locking herself away for three years in a room in her family's house. She lived the life of an ascetic, which culminated in a vision wherein she married Christ. Catherine emerged from solitude to join her Dominican sisters, sharing her experiences, caring for the sick, and gathering both disciples and enemies. At age 23, she lapsed into a spiritual coma, waking with the heavenly command to spread her message to the world. She wrote essays and letters to kings, dukes, bishops, and popes, imploring them to find peace for a war-ravaged Italy. While visiting Pisa during Lent in 1375, she had a vision in which she received the stigmata, the wounds of Christ.

Still in her 20s, Catherine was invited to Avignon, France, where the pope had taken up residence. With her charm, sincerity, and reputation for holiness, she helped convince Pope Gregory XI to return the papacy to the city of Rome. Catherine also went to Rome, where she died young. She was canonized in the next generation (by a Sienese pope), and her relics were distributed to churches around Italy.

Because of her intervention in the papal schism, today Catherine is revered (along with St. Benedict) as the patron saint of Europe and remembered as a rare outspoken medieval woman still appreciated for her universal message: that this world is not a gift from our fathers, but a loan from our children.

Sanctuary of St. Catherine (Santuario di Santa Caterina)

Step into the cool and peaceful site of Catherine's home. Siena remembers its favorite hometown gal, a simple, unschooled, but mystically devout soul who helped convince the pope to return from France to Rome (see sidebar). Pilgrims have visited this place since 1464, and architects and artists have greatly embellished what was probably once a humble home (her family worked as wool dyers). You'll see paintings throughout showing scenes from her life.

Enter through the courtyard, and walk down the stairs at the far end. The church on your right contains the wooden crucifix upon which Catherine was meditating when she received the stigmata. Take a pew, and try to imagine the scene. Back outside, the oratory across the courtyard stands where the kitchen once was. Go down the stairs (left of the gift shop) to reach the saint's room. Catherine's bare cell is behind wrought-iron doors.

Cost and Hours: Free, daily 9:00-18:00, Chapel of the Crucifixion closed from 12:30-15:00 but church stays open, a few down-hill blocks toward the center from San Domenico—follow signs to *Santuario di Santa Caterina*—at Costa di Sant'Antonio 6.

NEAR SIENA

You'll need a car to reach the Abbey of Monte Oliveto Maggiore, but for Renaissance art pilgrims it's well worth the 40-minute drive from town. You can combine a visit to the abbey with a loop drive through the scenic countryside. For details on the abbey and driving directions, see my "Crete Senesi Drive" on page 405.

Sleeping in Siena

Finding a room in Siena is tough during Easter (April 1 in 2018) or the Palio (July 2 and Aug 16). Many hotels won't take reservations until the end of May for the Palio, and even then they might require a four-night stay. While day-tripping tour groups turn the town into a Gothic amusement park in midsummer, Siena is basically yours in the evenings and off-season.

Part of Siena's charm is its lively, festive character—this means that all hotels can be plagued with noise, even (and sometimes especially) the hotels in the pedestrian-only zone. If tranquility is important for your sanity, ask for a room that's off the street, or consider staying at one of the recommended places outside the center. If your hotel doesn't provide breakfast, eat at a bar on Il Campo or near your hotel.

BIGGER HOTELS NEAR IL CAMPO

These places are a 10-minute walk from Il Campo. If driving, get parking instructions from your hotel in advance and make sure that you don't violate the *Zona Traffico Limitato (ZTL)* restrictions. You'll go through Porta San Marco, turn right, and follow signs to your hotel—drop your bags, then park as they instruct.

$$$$ Pensione Palazzo Ravizza is elegant, friendly, and well-run, with 40 rooms and an aristocratic feel—fitting, as it was once the luxurious residence of a noble. Guests enjoy a peaceful garden set on a dramatic bluff, along with a Steinway in the upper lounge (RS%, family rooms, rooms in back overlook countryside, air-con, elevator, Via Piano dei Mantellini 34, tel. 0577-280-462, www.palazzoravizza.it, bureau@palazzoravizza.it). As parking here is free and the hotel is easily walkable from the center, this is a particularly good value for drivers.

$$$ Hotel Duomo is dreary but well located, with 20 spacious but overpriced rooms (some with Duomo views—request when booking), a picnic-friendly roof terrace, and a bizarre floor plan (family rooms, elevator with some stairs, air-con, expensive pay parking; Via di Stalloreggi 38, tel. 0577-289-088, www. hotelduomo.it, booking@hotelduomo.it, Alessandro and Tony).

SIMPLE PLACES NEAR IL CAMPO

Most of these listings are forgettable but well-priced, and just a horse-wreck away from one of Italy's most wonderful civic spaces.

$$ Piccolo Hotel Etruria, with 20 simple, recently redecorated rooms, is well located, restful, and a fine value (RS%—use code "RSITA," family rooms, breakfast extra, air-con May-Oct only, elevator, at Via delle Donzelle 3, tel. 0577-288-088, www. hoteletruria.com, info@hoteletruria.com, friendly Leopoldo and Lucrezia). They also rent apartments nearby.

$ Albergo Tre Donzelle, run by the same family, is a fine budget value with welcoming hosts and 20 homey rooms—these may be the best-value rooms in the center. Il Campo, a block away, is your terrace (RS%—use code "RSITA," cheaper rooms with shared bath, family rooms, breakfast extra, fans, no elevator; with your back to the tower, head away from Il Campo toward 2 o'clock to Via delle Donzelle 5; tel. 0577-270-390, www.tredonzelle.com, info@tredonzelle.com, Leopoldo and Lucrezia).

$ Hotel Cannon d'Oro, a few blocks up Banchi di Sopra, is a labyrinthine slumbermill renting 30 institutional, overpriced rooms (RS%, family rooms, fans, Via dei Montanini 28, tel. 0577-44321, www.cannondoro.com, info@cannondoro.com; Maurizio, Tommaso, and Rodrigo).

$ Casa Laura has eight clean, charming, well-maintained budget rooms, some with brick-and-beam ceilings (RS%, more expensive rooms with air-con, no elevator, Via Roma 3, about a 10-minute walk from Il Campo toward Porta Romana, tel. 392-811-0364, www.casalaurasiena.com, info@casalaurasiena.com).

B&BS IN THE OLD CENTER

$$ Antica Residenza Cicogna is a seven-room guesthouse with a homey elegance and an ideal location. It's warmly run by the young and charming Elisa and her friend Ilaria, who set out biscotti, vin santo, and tea for their guests in the afternoon. With artfully frescoed walls and ceilings, this is remarkably genteel for the price (air-con, no elevator, Via delle Terme 76, tel. 0577-285-613, mobile 347-007-2888, www.anticaresidenzacicogna.it, info@ anticaresidenzacicogna.it).

$$ Palazzo Masi B&B, run by friendly Alizzardo and Daniela, is just below Il Campo. They rent six pleasant, spacious, antique-furnished rooms with shared common areas on the second and third floors of a restored 13th-century building (RS%—use code "RICK," cheaper rooms with shared bath, no elevator; from City Hall, walk 50 yards down Casato di Sotto to #29; mobile 349-

600-9155, www.palazzomasi.com, info@palazzomasi.it). The place is sometimes unstaffed, so confirm your arrival time in advance.

$$ B&B Alle Due Porte is a charming little establishment renting three big rooms with sweet furniture under medieval beams. The shared breakfast room is delightful. Manager Egisto is a phone call and 10-minute scooter ride away (3 rooms have air-con, Via di Stalloreggi 51, mobile 368-352-3530, www.sienatur.it, soldatini@interfree.it).

$ Le Camerine di Silvia, a romantic hideaway perched near a sweeping, grassy olive grove, rents five simple rooms in a converted 16th-century building. A small breakfast terrace with fruit trees and a private hedged garden lends itself to contemplation (cash only, view room on request, no breakfast, fans, free parking nearby, Via Ettore Bastianini 1, just below recommended Pensione Palazzo Ravizza, mobile 338-761-5052 or 339-123-7687, www.lecamerinedisilvia.com, info@lecamerinedisilvia.com, Conti family).

$ B&B Siena in Centro is a clearinghouse managing 15 rooms and five apartments. Their handy office functions as a reception area; stop by to pick up your key and be escorted, or meet the owners at your room. The rooms are generally spacious, quiet, and comfortable. Their website lets you visualize your options (RS%, some with air-con and others with fans, family rooms, reception open 9:00-13:30 & 15:00-22:00, Via di Stalloreggi 16, tel. 0577-48111, mobile 331-281-0136 or 347-465-9753, www.bbsienaincentro.com, info@bbsienaincentro.com, Gioia or Michela).

NEAR SAN DOMENICO CHURCH

These hotels are within a 10- to 15-minute walk northwest of Il Campo. Both Albergo Bernini and Alma Domus are in the old town with fine views and reasonable prices. The other two are farther out, in the modern world.

$$$ Hotel Chiusarelli, with 48 classy rooms in a beautiful, frescoed Neoclassical villa, is just outside the medieval town center on a busy street. Expect traffic noise at night—ask for a quieter room in the back, which can be guaranteed with reservation (RS%, family rooms, air-con, several free parking spots, nearby pay parking, across from San Domenico at Viale Curtatone 15, tel. 0577-280-562, www.chiusarelli.com, info@chiusarelli.com).

$$$ Hotel Villa Elda rents 11 bright and light rooms in a recently renovated villa. It's classy, stately, pricey, and run with a feminine charm (view rooms extra, air-con, no elevator, garden and view terrace, closed Nov-March, Viale Ventiquattro Maggio 10, tel. 0577-247-927, www.villaeldasiena.it, info@villaeldasiena.it).

$$ Albergo Bernini makes you part of a Sienese family in a modest, clean home with 10 traditional rooms. Giovanni, charm-

Siena Hotels & Restaurants

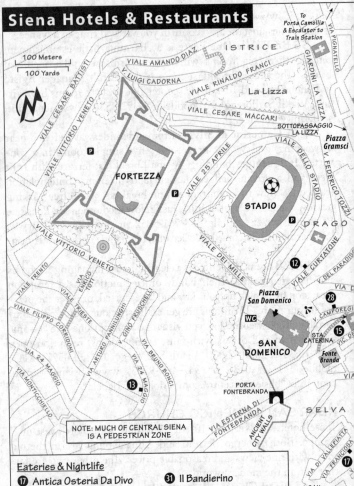

To
Porta Camollia
& Escalator to
Train Station

100 Meters
100 Yards

ISTRICE

VIALE AMANDO DIAZ

V. LUIGI CADORNA

VIALE RINALDO FRANCI

La Lizza

VIALE CESARE MACCARI

SOTTOPASSAGGIO
LA LIZZA

Piazza
Gramsci

VIALE CESARE BATTISTI

VIALE VITTORIO VENETO

FORTEZZA

VIALE 25 APRILE

VIALE DELLO STADIO

V. FEDERICO TOZZI

STADIO

DRAGO

VIALE VITTORIO VENETO

VIALE DEI MILLE

VIALE CURTATONE

VIALE DEL PARADIS

VIA D

VIALE TRENTO

VIA ENRICO TOTI

VIALE TRIESTE

VIA GINO FRUSCHELLI

Piazza
San Domenico

WC

SAN
DOMENICO

VIA CAMPOREGI

STA.
CATERINA

Fonte
Branda

VIA DE

VIALE FILIPPO CORRIDONI

VIA ARTURO PANNILUNGHI

VIA BRUNO BONCI

VIA 24 MAGGIO

VIA 24 MAGGIO

VIA MONTICCHELLO

PORTA
FONTEBRANDA

SELVA

NOTE: MUCH OF CENTRAL SIENA
IS A PEDESTRIAN ZONE

VIA ESTERNA DI
FONTEBRANDA

ANCIENT
CITY WALLS

VIA DI VALLERIATA

VIA FRANCIOSA

SAN
SEBASTIANO

SANTISSIMA
ANNUNCIATA

SANTA MARIA
DELLA SCALA
(MUSEUM)

PANTERA

Piazza
di Due Porte

PIANO MANTELLINI

To
10

Eateries & Nightlife

17 Antica Osteria Da Divo
18 Osteria le Logge
19 Enoteca I Terzi
20 Ristorante Guidoriccio
21 Ristorante Tar-Tufo
22 Compagnia dei Vinattieri
23 Osteria Il Carroccio
24 Trattoria Papei
25 La Taverna Di Cecco
26 Trattoria La Torre; Sapori
  & Dintorni Conad Grocery
27 Osteria del Gatto
28 Il Pomodorino
29 Osteria il Grattacielo
30 Ristorante Alla Speranza
  & Bar Paninoteca San Paolo

31 Il Bandierino
32 Bar Il Palio
33 Osteria Liberamente
34 Gelateria Costarella
35 Key Largo Bar
36 Antica Pizzicheria al
  Palazzo della Chigiana
37 Pizzeria San Martino
38 Pizzeria Poppi
39 Consorzio Agrario di
  Siena Grocery
40 Morbidi
41 Nannini Pastry Shop
42 Venchi Gelato
43 La Vecchia Latteria
  Gelato

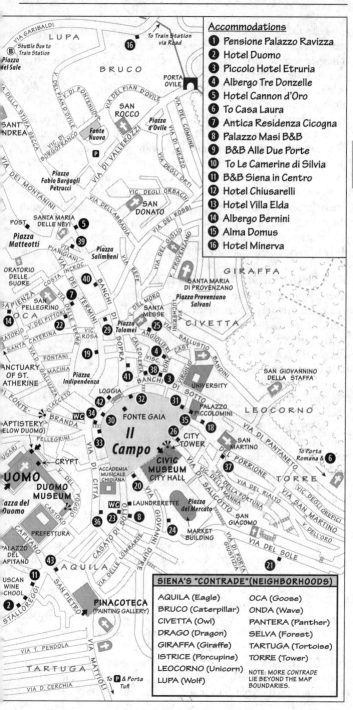

Accommodations

1. Pensione Palazzo Ravizza
2. Hotel Duomo
3. Piccolo Hotel Etruria
4. Albergo Tre Donzelle
5. Hotel Cannon d'Oro
6. To Casa Laura
7. Antica Residenza Cicogna
8. Palazzo Masi B&B
9. B&B Alle Due Porte
10. To Le Camerine di Silvia
11. B&B Siena in Centro
12. Hotel Chiusarelli
13. Hotel Villa Elda
14. Albergo Bernini
15. Alma Domus
16. Hotel Minerva

SIENA'S "CONTRADE" (NEIGHBORHOODS)

AQUILA (Eagle)	OCA (Goose)
BRUCO (Caterpillar)	ONDA (Wave)
CIVETTA (Owl)	PANTERA (Panther)
DRAGO (Dragon)	SELVA (Forest)
GIRAFFA (Giraffe)	TARTUGA (Tortoise)
ISTRICE (Porcupine)	TORRE (Tower)
LEOCORNO (Unicorn)	
LUPA (Wolf)	

NOTE: MORE CONTRADE LIE BEYOND THE MAP BOUNDARIES.

ing wife Daniela, and their daughters welcome you to their spectacular view terrace—a great spot for a glass of wine or a picnic (cheaper rooms with shared bath, family rooms, breakfast extra, fans, on the main Il Campo-San Domenico drag at Via della Sapienza 15, tel. 0577-289-047, www.albergobernini.com, info@albergobernini.com).

$ Alma Domus is a church-run hotel featuring 28 tidy rooms with quaint balconies, some fantastic views (ask for a room *con vista*), stately public rooms, and a pleasant atmosphere. However, the thin doors, echoey halls, and nearby church bells can be drawbacks, particularly on upper floors. Consider upgrading to a snazzy superior room for slightly more (RS%, family rooms, air-con, elevator; from San Domenico, walk downhill toward the view with the church on your right, turn left down Via Camporegio, make a U-turn down the brick steps to Via Camporegio 37; tel. 0577-44177, www.hotelalmadomus.it, info@hotelalmadomus.it, Louis).

FARTHER FROM THE CENTER

These options, a 10- to 20-minute walk from the center, are convenient for drivers. These first two are about 200 yards outside the Porta Romana (for locations, see the map on page 348). To get to the historic center from here, catch minibus line A uphill to Piazza al Mercato, just behind Il Campo (€1.20). To reach the bus and train stations, take bus #2 (which becomes #17 at Piazza del Sale; when arriving, catch #17 from the station). If driving, take the Siena Sud exit from the freeway, continue in direction *Romana*, then follow *Pta Romana/Centro* signs until you see the big city gate.

$$$ Hotel Santa Caterina is a three-star, 18th-century place renting 22 comfy rooms. It's professionally run with real attention to quality. While it's on a busy street, it has a delightful garden terrace with views over the countryside (RS%, family rooms, garden side is quieter, air-con, elevator, pay parking—request when you reserve, Via E.S. Piccolomini 7, tel. 0577-221-105, www.hotelsantacaterinasiena.com, info@hotelsantacaterinasiena.com, Lorenza).

$$ Hotel Porta Romana, on the same busy road, has simple rooms with cheap finishes. Request one of the 14 rooms that face the open countryside and the hotel's terraced footpaths into the valley. Breakfast is served in the scenic garden (RS%, air-con in most rooms, free parking, inviting sun terrace, outdoor hot tub open April-Oct free to guests with this book, Via E.S. Piccolomini 35, tel. 0577-42299, www.hotelportaromana.com, info@hotelportaromana.com, Marco and Evelia).

$$ Hotel Minerva is your big, professional, plain, efficient option. It's impersonal, with zero personality and mediocre views, but offers predictable business-class comfort in its 56 rooms. It works best for those with cars—its pay parking is reasonable, and it's only a 10-minute walk from the action (RS%, view rooms extra, air-con, elevator, just inside Porta Ovile at the north end of town at Via Garibaldi 72, tel. 0577-284-474, www.albergominerva.it, info@albergominerva.it).

OUTSIDE SIENA

The following accommodations are set in the lush, peaceful countryside surrounding Siena, and are best for those traveling by car. The first is just a mile east of town; the others are farther out (see map on page 348). For options in the Crete Senesi, including one just six miles from the Porta Romana gate, see page 528.

$$$$ Frances' Lodge Relais is a tranquil and delightfully managed farmhouse B&B. Each of its six rooms is bursting with character (well-described on their website). Franca and Franco run this rustic-yet-elegant old place, which features a 19th-century orangery that's been made into a "better homes and palaces" living room, as well as a peaceful garden, eight acres of olive trees and vineyards, and great views of Siena and its countryside—even from the swimming pool (RS%, no kids, air-con, free parking, Strada di Valdipugna 2, tel. 0577-42379, mobile 337-671-608, www.franceslodge.eu). To the center, it's a five-minute walk plus a five-minute bus ride (€1.60), or €10 by taxi. Consider having an al fresco dinner in the gazebo, complete with view (make your own picnic, or have your hosts assemble a very fancy one).

$$$ Borgo Argenina has seven rooms in a well-maintained splurge of a B&B, 20 minutes north of Siena by car in the Chianti region. Helpful hostess Elena offers cooking classes, can arrange wine tastings, and provides lots of thoughtful touches (air-con, beautiful gardens, mobile 345-353-7673, www.borgoargenina.it, info@borgoargenina.it).

$$ Il Canto del Sole is a restored 18th-century farmhouse turned family-friendly B&B located just six miles outside the Porta Romana city gate. The Lorenzetti family (Laura, Luciano, and son Marco) enjoy engaging with their guests. They have 10 bright and airy rooms, a plush lawn surrounding a saltwater swimming pool, a game room, a piano, and bike rentals. Their two apartments with original antique furnishings fit six to eight people (RS%, air-con, free parking, free town shuttle service and pickup/drop-off from train/bus station, dinner available some nights, Val di Villa Canina 1292, 53014 Loc. Cuna, tel. 0577-375-127, www.ilcantodelsole.com, info@ilcantodelsole.com).

Eating in Siena

Sienese restaurants are reasonably priced by Florentine and Venetian standards. You can enjoy ordering high on the menu here without going broke. For pasta, a good option is *pici* (PEE-chee), a thick Sienese spaghetti that seems to be at the top of every menu.

IN THE OLD TOWN
Fine Dining

These places deliver an upscale ambience, interesting menus, and generally finer food than my less dressy recommendations. Reservations are a good idea at all of them; otherwise arrive early. The first two have no outside seating.

$$$$ Antica Osteria Da Divo is a great splurge. The kitchen is inventive, the ambience is flowery and candlelit, some of the seating fills old Etruscan tombs, and the food is delicate and top-notch. Fanatical for fresh ingredients and giving traditional dishes a creative spin, Claudia will make you feel at home (reserve in advance, wine by the glass on request, Wed-Mon 12:00-14:30 & 19:00-22:30, closed Tue; facing Baptistery door, take the far right street to Via Franciosa 29; tel. 0577-284-381, www.osteriadadivo. it). Show this book to finish with a complimentary biscotti and vin santo or coffee.

$$$$ Osteria le Logge caters to a fancy crowd and offers Tuscan favorites with a gourmet twist, made with seasonal local ingredients. Inside you'll enjoy a gorgeous living-room setting (books, wood, and wine bottles), and outside there's fine seating on a pedestrian street. This is an excellent choice for dining al fresco (Mon-Sat 12:00-15:00 & 19:00-23:00, closed Sun, two blocks off Il Campo at Via del Porrione 33, tel. 0577-48013, www. osterialelogge.it).

$$$ Enoteca I Terzi is dressy and modern under medieval vaults, with a simple yet enticing menu of creative dishes—and one of the most extensive wine selections in town. They have a few tables on a quiet square out front and an elegant main dining area, but I'd avoid the back room (daily 12:30-15:00 & 19:30-23:00, Via dei Termini 7, tel. 0577-44329, www.enotecaiterzi.it).

More Dining Options

$$ Ristorante Guidoriccio, just a few steps below Il Campo, feels warm and welcoming. You'll get smiling service from Ercole and Flora—the place has charm—especially if you let gentle Ercole explore the menu with you and follow his suggestions (Mon-Sat 12:30-14:30 & 19:00-22:30, closed Sun, air-con, Via Giovanni Dupre 2, tel. 0577-44350).

$$$$ Ristorante Tar-Tufo, on the back side of Il Campo, is the only place in the old center offering a gourmet meal on a countryside view terrace. Tucked in the basement of a former school, the restaurant specializes in modern Tuscan cuisine garnished with truffles (daily 12:00-14:30 & 16:30-22:00, Via del Sole 6, tel. 0577-284-031).

$$$ Compagnia dei Vinattieri is a good bet for wine lovers and serves Tuscan dishes with a creative touch. In this elegant space, you can enjoy a romantic meal under graceful brick arches. The menu is small and accessible. Owners Marco and Gianfranco are happy to take you down to the marvelous wine cellar (beef is big here, leave this book on the table for a complimentary *aperitivo* or *digestivo,* daily 12:30-15:00 & 19:30-23:00, enter at Via dei Pittori 1 or Via delle Terme 79, tel. 0577-236-568).

$$ Osteria Il Carroccio, artsy and convivial, seats guests in a characteristic but tight dining room. They serve traditional "slow food" recipes with innovative flair at affordable prices (€30 tasting *menu*—minimum two people, reservations wise, Thu-Tue 12:30-15:00 & 19:30-22:00, closed Wed, Casato di Sotto 32, tel. 0577-41165).

Traditional and Rustic Places

$$ Trattoria Papei has a casual, rollicking family atmosphere and friendly servers dishing out generous portions of rib-stickin' Tuscan specialties and grilled meats. This big, sprawling place has festive outdoor seating under brown awnings and is often jammed—so call to reserve (daily 12:00-15:00 & 19:00-22:30, on the market square behind City Hall at Piazza del Mercato 6, tel. 0577-280-894; Amedeo and Eduardo speak English).

$$ La Taverna Di Cecco is a simple, comfortable little eatery on an uncrowded back lane where grandma Olga cooks and earnest Luca and Gianni serve. They offer a simple menu of traditional Sienese favorites made with fresh ingredients, along with hearty salads (daily 12:00-16:00 & 19:00-23:00, Via Cecco Angiolieri 19, tel. 0577-288-518).

$$ Trattoria La Torre is an unfussy family-run *casalinga* (home-cooking) place, popular for its homemade pasta, a table of which entices customers as they enter. Its open kitchen and 10 tables are packed under one medieval brick arch. Service is brisk and casual—because the only menu is posted outside, they'll explain your options individually. Still, come here more for the fun atmosphere than the cuisine. Even with its priceless position below the namesake tower, it feels more like a local hangout than a tourist trap (Fri-Wed 12:00-15:00 & 19:00-22:00, closed Thu, just steps below Il Campo at Via di Salicotto 7, tel. 0577-287-548).

$ Osteria del Gatto is another classic little hole-in-the-wall, thriving with townspeople and powered by a passion for good

Sienese cuisine. Friendly Marco Coradeschi and his staff cook and serve daily specials with attitude. As it's so small and popular, it can get loud (Mon-Sat 12:30-15:00 & 19:30-22:00, closed Sun, reservations recommended, 10-minute walk from Il Campo at Via San Marco 8, look for *La Vecchia Osteria* sign, tel. 0577-287-133).

$ Il Pomodorino is a lively good-value restaurant serving meal-size salads, some of the best pizza in town, and a wide selection of beer—unusual in wine-crazy Tuscany. The intimate modern interior is covered by brick vaulting, but the real appeal is the outdoor terrace with a great view of the Duomo (daily 12:00-late, a few steps above the recommended Alma Domus hotel at Via Camporegio 13, tel. 0577-286-811).

$ Osteria il Grattacielo is a funky hole-in-the-wall with a tight and homey interior and three tables under a tunnel-like arch outside, perfect for a cheap, hearty, memorable-yet-no-frills meal. Luca has no menu and just one solid house wine. You'll eat what he's cooking and pay €10-15 for dinner—look for a list of pastas posted outside or select dishes from the case on the counter (daily 12:00-15:00 & 19:30-21:30, Via dei Pontani 8, mobile 334-631-1458).

ON IL CAMPO

If you choose to eat on perhaps the finest town square in Italy, you'll pay a premium, meet waiters who don't need to hustle, and get mediocre food. And yet I highly recommend it. The clamshell-shaped Il Campo is lined with venerable cafés, bars, restaurants, and pizzerias. Consider surveying the scene during your sightseeing day and reserving a table of your choice at the place that feels best to you.

To experience Il Campo without paying for a full meal, do as the locals do and have drinks or breakfast on the square. For me, the best €6 you can spend in Siena is on a cocktail at Bar Il Palio, overlooking Il Campo. If your hotel doesn't include breakfast or if you'd like something more memorable, Il Campo has plenty of options. A cappuccino and a *cornetto* (croissant) run about €5-6. Frugal eaters gather a picnic and join the crowds sitting on the bricks.

Dining and Drinks on the Square

$$$ Ristorante Alla Speranza has primo views and is a decent option for dining on the square (daily 9:00-late, Piazza Il Campo 32, tel. 0577-280-190, www.allasperanza.it).

$$$ Il Bandierino is another option for drinks or food, with an angled view of City Hall (no cover but a 20 percent service charge, daily 11:00-23:00, Piazza Il Campo 64, tel. 0577-275-894).

$$$ Bar Il Palio is the best bar on Il Campo for a before- or after-dinner drink: It has straightforward prices, no cover, and a

Nightlife in Siena

Evenings are a wonderful time to be out and about in Siena, after the tour groups have left for the day. Join the evening *passeggiata* (peak strolling time is 19:00) along Banchi di Sopra with **gelato** in hand. The gourmet chain Venchi is reliably tasty (daily until 22:00, Via di Citta 28). A good locally owned option is La Vecchia Latteria (daily until at least 20:00, a 5-minute walk towards the Duomo at Via di San Pietro 10).

As elsewhere in Italy, you'll find bars all over town attracting an early evening crowd by offering an *aperitivo*—a free buffet of food that's included with the purchase of a drink. For many, this can make a light dinner. Or consider ending a meal or the day with a drink or dessert on Il Campo.

fantastic perspective out over the square (daily 8:30-late, Piazza Il Campo 47, tel. 0577-282-055).

$$$ Osteria Liberamente, a dynamic little bar with a trendy vibe, is popular with young locals. Drinks come with a small plate of snacks, and they also serve light meals (fine wines by the glass and €7 cocktails, daily 9:00-late, Piazza Il Campo 27, tel. 0577-274-733, Pino).

Drinks or Snacks Overlooking Il Campo

These places have skinny balconies with benches overlooking the main square for their customers. Sipping a coffee or nibbling a pastry here while marveling at the Il Campo scene is one of Europe's great experiences. And it's cheap. Survey these three places from Il Campo (with your back to the tower, they are at 10 o'clock, high noon, and 3 o'clock, respectively).

$ Gelateria Costarella, on the corner of Via di Città and Costarella dei Barbieri, has drinks, pastries, sandwiches, and light meals (I'd skip their gelato). The real attraction is the view from upstairs—the simple benches perched over Il Campo. To enjoy these, order your drink or snack from the menu rather than the cheaper bar (daily 8:00-late, Via di Città 33).

$ Bar Paninoteca San Paolo has a youthful English-pub ambience and a row of stools overlooking the square. They have 50 kinds of hearty sandwiches, big salads, and several beers on tap—it's not traditional Italian, but it's quick, filling, and available all day (order and pay at the counter, food served daily 12:00-late, under the arch on Vicolo di San Paolo, tel. 0577-226-622).

$ Key Largo Bar has a nondescript interior, but two long, upper-story benches in the corner offer a wonderful secret perch. Buy your drink or snack at the bar, climb upstairs, and slide the ancient bar to open the door (no cover and no extra charge to sit on the balcony). Enjoy stretching out, and try to imagine how, during the Palio, three layers of spectators cram into this space—notice the iron railing used to plaster the top row of sardines up against the wall. Suddenly you're picturing Palio ponies zipping wildly around the square's notoriously dangerous corner (Mon-Fri 7:30-late, Sat-Sun 9:00-late, on the corner of Via Rinaldini, tel. 0577-236-339).

DINING WITH LOCALS, AWAY FROM THE CENTER

A pleasant 10-minute stroll north of Il Campo, Via Camollia—a continuation of the chic Banchi di Sopra and Via dei Montanini shopping streets—offers a variety of good eating options. This more residential part of town has become popular with locals seeking to get away from the tourist crowds. Do as they do and peruse the street before making a choice, but consider the following reliable options.

$$ Trattoria Fonte Giusta, at #102, is a traditional eatery known for its meat dishes (daily 12:00-23:00, tel. 0577-40506). Further on at #167 is **$$ Osteria il Vinaio,** an informal place offering simple dishes at good prices (Mon-Sat 10:00-22:00, closed Sun, tel. 0577-49615). Beyond that, at #193, is **$$ Osteria Titti,** where friendly Duccio creates a lively atmosphere, serving Sienese classics in an eclectic and funky setting (Mon-Sat 12:00-15:00 & 17:00-23:00, closed Sun, tel. 0577-285-813).

At the end of the street is a good look at the city walls and the imposing Porta Camollia. Step outside the walls and notice the Medici coat of arms, under which you'll see the Latin inscription *"Cor magis tibi sena pandit"* ("Siena opens her heart to you more widely than this gate")—a sarcastic jab at longtime rival Florence, who had recently subjugated the city.

EATING CHEAPLY IN THE CENTER

$$ Antica Pizzicheria al Palazzo della Chigiana (a.k.a. *Pizzicheria de Miccoli*) may be the official name, but I bet locals just call it Antonio's. For most of his life, frenzied Antonio has carved salami and cheese for the neighborhood. Locals line up here for their sandwiches—meat and cheese sold by weight—with a good bottle of Chianti (Italian law dictates that he can't sell *vino* by the glass, only bottles, but he's got a number to choose from and will lend you the glasses). Antonio sells an enticing cheese and meat platter (starting at €15 per person)—but be careful...your costs can add up quickly (Mon-Sat 8:00-20:00, Sun 10:00-18:00, standing room only, Via di Città 95, tel. 0577-289-164).

Pizza: Budget eaters look for *pizza al taglio* shops, scattered throughout Siena, selling pizza by the slice. Here are a couple of good bets: **$ San Martino,** a couple of blocks behind Il Campo, is a local-feeling spot with slices and sandwiches to take away or eat in at one of their few tables (Mon-Sat 10:00-21:00, closed Sun, Via del Porrione 64). **$ Pizzeria Poppi,** a block off the Campo, is a simple, old-fashioned shop filled with locals. With very few menu options, the choice is easy. Grab a *ciaccino ripieno* (stuffed "white" pizza—no tomatoes) and use Il Campo as a dining room (Mon-Fri 10:00-15:00 & 16:30-20:30, Sat until 21:00, closed Sun, Banchi di Sotto 25—look for white-and-blue *Pizzeria* sign at the corner of Via di Calzoleria).

Gourmet Tuscan Supermarkets/Tavola Calda: Consorzio Agrario di Siena is a great place to browse, buy edible gifts, or assemble a cheap yet top-quality local meal. Wander through the entire place (salad and smoothie bar at the front, bakery/pizzeria at the back) and enjoy a parade of artisanal Tuscan foods. While office workers pack the excellent pizzeria in the rear, I create the ultimate salad, choose a smoothie, and enjoy it on the big comfy stone bench across the way on Piazza Salimbeni (Mon-Sat 8:00-20:30, Sun 9:30-20:00, just off Piazza Matteotti, facing Piazza Salimbeni at Via Pianigiani 9).

Morbidi is a modern upscale take on the same artisanal grocery idea, but with more focus on prepared food. It's a good choice for breakfast, a quick lunch, or an *aperitivo*—a before-dinner, light buffet is included with the price of a drink (Mon-Thu 8:00-20:00, Fri-Sat until 22:00, closed Sun, Banchi di Sopra 75, tel. 0577-280-268).

Sapori & Dintorni Conad, at the bottom of Il Campo next to the City Tower, is a classy bakery/supermarket/*rosticceria* serving fresh food to-go or at its bar. This is a good spot to put together a picnic to enjoy on the square (daily 8:30-20:00, Piazza Il Campo 80).

DESSERTS AND TREATS

Siena's claim to caloric fame is its panforte, a rich, chewy concoction of nuts, honey, and candied fruits that impresses even fruitcake haters. There are a few varieties: *Margherita*, dusted in powdered sugar, is fruitier, while *panpepato* has a spicy, peppery crust. Locals prefer a chewy, white macaroon-and-almond cookie called *ricciarelli*.

Nannini—ideally located in the center of the evening strolling scene a few blocks off the Campo—is Siena's venerable, top-end pastry shop/café. For a special dessert or a sweet treat any time of day, stop by. The local specialties are around back at the far end of the bar (Mon-Fri 7:30-21:30, Sat-Sun 8:00-23:00, *aperitivo* happy hour 18:00 until closing, Banchi di Sopra 24).

SIENA

Siena Connections

Siena has sparse train connections but is a great hub for buses to the hill towns, though frequency drops on Sundays and holidays. For most, Florence is the gateway to Siena. Even if you're a rail-pass user, connect these two cities by bus—it's faster than the train, and Siena's bus station is more convenient and central than its train station.

BY TRAIN

Siena's train station is at the edge of town. For details on getting between the town center and the station, see page 347.

From Siena by Train to: Florence (direct trains hourly, 1.5-2 hours; bus is better), **Pisa** (2/hour, 2 hours, change at Empoli), **Assisi** (10/day, about 4 hours, most involve 2 changes, bus is faster), **Rome** (1-2/hour, 3-4 hours, change in Florence or Chiusi), **Orvieto** (12/day, 2.5 hours, change in Chiusi). For more information, visit www.trenitalia.com.

BY BUS

The main bus companies are **Tiemme/Siena Mobilità** (mostly regional destinations, tel. 0577-204-111, www.sienamobilita.it) and **Sena/Baltour** (long-distance connections, tel. 0861-199-1900, www.baltour.it). On schedules, the fastest buses are marked *rapida*. Most buses depart Siena from Piazza Gramsci; others leave from the train station (confirm when you buy your ticket).

Tiemme/Siena Mobilità Buses to: Florence (roughly 2/hour, 1.5-hour *rapida/via superstrada* buses are faster than the train, avoid the 2-hour *ordinaria* buses unless you have time to enjoy the beautiful scenery en route; tickets also available at tobacco shops/*tabacchi*; generally leaves from Piazza Gramsci as well as train station), **San Gimignano** (8/day direct, on Sun must change in Poggibonsi, 1.5 hours, from Piazza Gramsci), **Volterra** (4/day Mon-Sat, no buses on Sun, 2 hours, change in Colle di Val d'Elsa, leaves from Piazza Gramsci), **Montepulciano** (6-8/day, none on Sun, 1.5 hours, from train station), **Pienza** (6/day, none on Sun, 1.5 hours, from train station), **Montalcino** (6/day Mon-Sat, 4/day Sun, 1.5 hours, from train station or Piazza del Sale), **Pisa's Galileo Galilei Airport** (3/day, 2 hours, one direct, two via Poggibonsi), **Rome's Fiumicino Airport** (3/day, 3.5 hours, from Piazza Gramsci).

Sena/Baltour Buses to: Rome (9/day, 3 hours, from Piazza Gramsci, arrives at Rome's Tiburtina station on Metro line B with easy connections to the central Termini train station), **Naples** (2/day, 6.5 hours, one at 17:00 and an overnight bus that departs at 00:20), **Milan** (2/day direct, 4.5 hours, more with change in Bologna, departs from Piazza Gramsci, arrives at Milan's Cadorna

Station with Metro access and direct trains to Malpensa Airport), **Assisi** (daily at 17:30, 2 hours, departs from Siena train station, arrives at Assisi Santa Maria degli Angeli; from there it's a 10-minute taxi/bus ride uphill to city center). To reach the town center of **Pisa,** the train is better (described earlier).

Tickets and Information: You can buy tickets in the underground passageway (called Sottopassaggio la Lizza) beneath Piazza Gramsci—look for stairwells in front of NH Excelsior Hotel. The larger office handles Tiemme/Siena Mobilità buses (Mon-Fri 6:30-19:30, Sat-Sun 7:00-19:30). The smaller one is for Sena/Baltour buses (Mon-Fri 7:30-20:00, Sat 7:30-12:30 & 13:45-16:15, Sun 10:15-13:15 & 14:00-18:45; Sena/Baltour office also has a desk selling *Eurolines* tickets for bus connections to other countries). Tiemme/Siena Mobilità is cash-only; Sena/Baltour accepts credit cards. You can also get tickets for both Tiemme/Siena Mobilità buses and Sena/Baltour buses at the train station (look for bus-ticket kiosk just inside main door), as well as on online (www.baltour.it, www.sena.it). If necessary, you can buy tickets from the driver, but it costs €3-5 extra.

Services: Sottopassaggio la Lizza also has luggage storage, posted bus schedules, and pay WCs.

ROUTE TIPS FOR DRIVERS

Drivers heading south from Siena can follow a scenic back-roads route into the heart of Tuscany by modifying my "Crete Senesi Drive," next (see options listed under "Heading South from Buonconvento").

Crete Senesi Drive

Between Siena and the Tuscan heartland is the hilly Crete Senesi area—the "Sienese Clay Hills." The Crete Senesi (KRAY-teh seh-NAY-zee) begins at Siena's doorstep and tumbles south through eye-pleasing scenery. You'll see an endless parade of classic Tuscan scenes: rolling hills topped with medieval towns, olive groves, rustic stone farmhouses, and a skyline punctuated with cypress trees.

During the spring, the fields are painted in yellow and green with fava beans and broom, dotted by red poppies on the fringes. Sunflowers decorate the area during June and July, and expanses of windblown grass fill the landscape for much of the early spring and summer.

For rural accommodations in the Crete Senesi, see page 528.

◉ SELF-GUIDED DRIVING TOUR

This driving route is designed for someone home-basing in Siena and seeking an accessible look at the Crete Senesi's dramatic landscape. Besides visits to some less-trampled hill towns, the tour includes the Abbey of Monte Oliveto Maggiore, the undisputed artistic treasure of this part of Tuscany. This back-roads loop takes you south from Siena to Buonconvento, where you'll track back to Siena on an even more remote—but visually stunning—road. The entire loop, without stops, takes about an hour and a half.

If you'd rather continue south toward Montepulciano and Montalcino (covered in my Heart of Tuscany chapter, later in this book), break the loop at Buonconvento, where you'll meet the main SR-2 highway—see under "Heading South from Buonconvento," below.

For a primer on this area's geology, see the sidebar on page 538.

Siena to Buonconvento

Begin by leaving Siena, heading east on E-78 (following green *Roma/A1* signs toward the expressway). After just three kilometers, take the Taverne d'Arbia exit (marked for *Presciano, Vico d'Arbia, Arba, Asciano,* and a brown sign for *Crete Senesi*). Once off the expressway, carefully track *Asciano* signs, which will put you on road S-438—also called the **Via Lauretana.** Just sit back and enjoy the drive; it's about 18 kilometers to Asciano, through a stunning and very desolate-feeling landscape. You'll come across plenty of turn-outs for panoramic photo opportunities on this road. Eventually you'll drop down into the village of **Asciano,** with a humble but historic townscape and a good lunch restaurant (for details, see page 408).

At Asciano's main roundabout, follow signs for *Chiusure* and *Monte Oliveto Maggiore.* This puts you on S-451, which winds through beautiful hills for about eight kilometers to our next two stops. What you do next depends on the time: If it's open, press on to the **Abbey of Monte Oliveto Maggiore,** with a remarkable inlaid-wood choir and a fascinating fresco cycle of the life of St. Benedict, painted by Renaissance masters Il Sodoma and Luca Signorelli (for a self-guided tour, see page 411). The abbey is just a few kilometers beyond Chiusure.

If the abbey is closed for its midday break, you might as well first drop into the pleasant village of **Chiusure**—a charming, steep, relatively untouristy town that's a fun place to explore or grab lunch (for details, see page 410; at the roundabout just before Monte

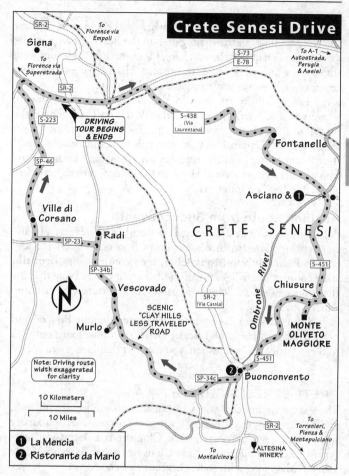

Crete Senesi Drive

To Florence via Empoli

Siena

To Florence via Superstrada

SR-2

SR-2

S-223

DRIVING TOUR BEGINS & ENDS

SP-46

Ville di Corsano

SP-23

Radi

SP-34b

N

Vescovado

Murlo

SCENIC "CLAY HILLS LESS TRAVELED" ROAD

Note: Driving route width exaggerated for clarity

10 Kilometers

10 Miles

① La Mencia
② Ristorante da Mario

S-73
E-78

To A-1 Autostrada, Perugia & Assisi

S-438 (Via Laurentana)

Fontanelle

Asciano & ①

CRETE SENESI

Ombrone River

S-451

Chiusure

SR-2 (Via Cassia)

MONTE OLIVETO MAGGIORE

S-451

② Buonconvento

SP-34c

SR-2

To Torrenieri, Pienza & Montepulciano

To Montalcino

ALTESINA WINERY

SIENA

Oliveto Maggiore, take the left turn, marked for *S. Giovanni d'Asso, Pienza,* and—in brown—*Chiusure*).

Carry on past the abbey on S-451, following *Buonconvento* and *Roma* signs. This takes you (in about 9 kilometers) to **Buonconvento,** a workaday town with some good eating options (see page 409).

Scenic "Clay Hills Less Traveled" Return Route, Buonconvento to Siena

This remote route (partly on gravel roads) culminates with a gorgeous approach to Siena. From the main parking lot next to Buonconvento's old town, head just a few short blocks south (toward *Roma*), and watch for the easy-to-miss turnoff on the right to *Murlo*. Drive 12 kilometers through beautiful countryside until you reach the sleepy hamlet of **Murlo,** where you could park your car and hike up through the main gate into the heart of town. While the Etruscans had a settlement here, the current fortifications were added by a bishop in the 13th century. His palace—at the very center of town—now hosts an Etruscan Museum.

Leaving Murlo, continue to Vescovado (the adjacent town), where you'll follow signs to *Grosetto.* Watch on the right for the turnoff to *Radi*—on a gravel road—and then on the left for *Ville di Corsano.* As you approach and go through **Ville di Corsano,** you'll start to notice sumptuous country-estate villas, built by aristocrats who wanted a grand view of Siena. In the village, turn right toward *Siena,* and head on into town.

Heading South from Buonconvento

All of these options are covered in detail in the Heart of Tuscany chapter, later in this book: From Buonconvento, wine lovers can head south to **Montalcino,** then continue into **Brunello wine country** following my self-guided driving tour. Note that the Buonconvento-Montalcino road passes the recommended Altesino winery.

If you'd instead like to head for **Montepulciano, Pienza,** and my self-guided "Heart of Tuscany Drive," continue south on SR-2 to San Quirico d'Orcia, where you can join that loop drive at Leg #3.

CRETE SENESI SIGHTS

These stops are linked by the Crete Senesi self-guided driving tour, earlier. Asciano and Buonconvento are no-nonsense, untouristy towns with a workaday feel, while Chiusure is a sleepy, well-preserved medieval hill town. Near Chiusure is the Abbey of Monte Oliveto Maggiore, with some gorgeous church art.

Asciano

This quaint but not-quite-charming town offers a medieval core, a smattering of churches and museums, and a rare look at everyday Tuscan living. Asciano is known as a center for white truffles, pecorino cheese, and olive oil. There's not much to see here other than a normal Tuscan town going about its work and play. That's why I like it. Stroll Asciano's wide, traffic-free main road, which boasts a relaxed and real passeggiata scene. **Bar Gelateria da Piero** is a popular hangout for gelato or coffee. On the main street, **$$ La Mencia** is an inviting restaurant with a charming garden terrace out back and not a tourist in sight (closed Mon, Corso Matteotti 85).

Buonconvento

This valley-crossroads town—an important refueling stop for weary pilgrims on the Via Francigena—has a name that literally means "happy meeting place." Today it's

humble but handy, with a large chunk of surviving town wall and some fine restaurants. Its economy has little to do with tourism, and it's an easy and accessible fortified town to explore.

Park in the big lot between the main road and the town wall (which hosts a farmers market every Saturday). As you face that wall, loop around the right side, passing the humble but endearing Sienese Sharecropping Museum (Museo della Mezzadria Senese, open Fri-Sun) to reach the 13th-century **main gate** of

Buonconvento, called Porta Senese. Buonconvento is 20 kilometers south of Siena—one day's trek for a pilgrim on the Via Francigena. Approaching this gate, they'd look up and be comforted to see two coats of arms, indicating that this town was sponsored and protected by the republic and the army of Siena.

Step inside the 17th-century doors (weathered by four centuries of thumbtacks) and venture to the right down a tight lane. This was the double-decker **guard path,** allowing town defenders to keep a close watch on approaching enemies. (Originally there was another gallery overhead.) Old houses lean up against the wall, like flying buttresses. Notice the slits—wide on the inside, but tapering to a very narrow opening—which allowed archers maximum range of motion but minimum exposure to enemy fire.

Head back to the main gate, then continue straight ahead down the main drag (Via Soccini) toward the courthouse and town hall (on the left). The **courthouse**'s facade is embedded with coats of arms—some dating from the 15th century—of the various regional aristocrats who served two-year terms here as the town judge. Next door is the Sacred Art Museum (Museo d'Arte Sacra, with pieces from the 14th-19th century) and a sleepy TI (tel. 0577-807-181). The **town hall** still sports a plaque celebrating the vote in 1860, when the people of Tuscany voted 388,571 to 14,923 to join the newly united country of Italy.

Farther along the street, you'll pass the outdoor tables at the recommended **$$ Ristorante da Mario** (closed Sat, Via Soccini 60), after which the lane opens up into the town's main square. Turning left, you're back to the parking lot where you started.

SIENA

Chiusure

The charming, neatly preserved clay village of Chiusure (kyew-ZOO-reh), with a population of just 89, is a fine stop for those seeking "untouristy Tuscany." (Notice that, as this is clay country, the dominant building material is brick.) This steep town offers no sights other than its grand views and real-world village atmosphere.

Park at the entrance to town, then follow signs as you walk up a steep driveway to the *casa di riposo* (the castle-turned-nursing home) and *Gesù Redentore*. Greet the old folks (a good percentage of the town's entire population) sitting in the shade. Then belly up to the railing to enjoy a fine viewpoint over the Crete Senesi, including jagged *calanchi* cliffs and the Abbey of Monte Oliveto Maggiore. On a clear day, you can see all the way to Siena.

Now follow the lone, twisty street steeply downhill into the village, enjoying the solitude. As this town is famed for its artichokes (and hosts an artichoke festival in late April), you'll notice artichoke-themed flowerpots decorating the walls. You'll arrive at Chiusure's general store/*tabacchi*/sometimes-restaurant, the local hangout—where Ilio can make you a hearty sandwich to munch back up at the viewpoint. Continuing to loop around (and bearing right after the square), you'll wind up back at the main road and parking lot.

▲▲▲Abbey of Monte Oliveto Maggiore

This Benedictine abbey features perhaps the best in-situ art you'll find in rural Tuscany. The order spared no expense in decorating their main church, importing the great artists of the day: Fra Giovanni da Verona, one of the most talented inlaid-wood artists who ever lived, and the skilled fresco artists Luca Signorelli and Il Sodoma. What you see today is very close to what a pilgrim would have seen during a 16th-century visit. It stars an astonishingly  detailed inlaid choir, and a cloister frescoed with vivid, detail-and-symbolism-packed, sometimes outlandish scenes by Renaissance masters Il Sodoma and Luca Signorelli.

Cost and Hours: Free, modest dress required, daily 9:15-12:00 & 15:15-18:00, Nov-March until 17:00; Gregorian chanting Mon-Fri at 15:30, Sun at 11:00—call to confirm; tel. 0577-707-611, www.monteolivetomaggiore.it.

Getting There: The abbey is well-signed both from the SR-2 highway (turn off at Buonconvento) and from the scenic S-451 road through the Crete Senesi. Park at the "La Torre" lot across from the fortress at the top of the monastery complex (pick up parking ticket and pay at meter near restaurant before returning to car). From the parking lot, it's a pleasant 10-minute wooded walk downhill to the monastery: Head across the drawbridge and through the fortress (fortified in the 14th century to protect against bandits; notice the fine ceramic Della Robbia sculptures over the doors of Mary and St. Benedict), pass the restaurant, and continue down the hill. (The big, artificial fish pond on the left made sure there was fish on Friday.) At the courtyard before the church, the shop and WCs are to the left; to reach the church entrance, circle around the right side.

Background: In the 14th century, Bernardo Tolomei (1272-1348), the middle son of a wealthy Sienese silver-mining family, moved to the hillsides south of Siena to become a hermit-monk. (That's his statue in the courtyard, holding the books of rules for this notoriously strict order.) One day he had a vision of a glorious staircase leading dramatically up into the heavens. He took this as a sign to build a church on that very spot, and founded the Olivetan order (a branch of the Benedictines, named for the Holy Mount of Olives). His original, humble church has since been turned into a brick monastery complex with a beautiful Baroque church interior and a Renaissance-frescoed cloister. (Tolomei was made a saint in 2009, and this complex is the now-global order's mother abbey.)

● Self-Guided Tour

Your visit has two parts: The church interior, with its amazing choir, and the adjacent, fresco-slathered cloister.

• *From the entrance, head into the cloister (ignoring the frescoes for now): Jog left and loop around the corridor, following* church *signs. Turn left at the end of the hall into the church. You'll enter near the right transept; once inside, head for the main nave, filled with...*

Fra Giovanni da Verona's Choir

This spectacularly detailed masterpiece is made entirely of inlaid wood—no paint or other foreign flourishes were used to enhance the remarkable detail and optical illusions. Fra Giovanni (1457-1525), from the city of Verona, used this painstaking method to achieve a mastery of three dimensions that eluded many of his contemporaries working in far more forgiving media. Even more astonishing, this was completed in just two years (1503-1505). Fra Giovanni is deservedly called the "Michelangelo of Wood." Have several €1 coins ready to illuminate the work, allowing you to linger on the details.

Start with the **left panel** (with your back to the main altar) and work clockwise. First you'll see a self-portrait of Fra Giovanni, then 3-D shutters that are left partway open, revealing olive branches, the symbol of the Olivetan order. The 3-D utopian city (showing off Fra Giovanni's mastery of perspective) is followed by a set of not two, but four shutters—as if upping the technical complexity of the first set. The fifth panel, showing Siena's City Hall and Il Campo, recalls that Olivetan monks—including their founder, Bernardo Tolomei—lost their lives helping plague victims in Siena in 1348. The next panel shows more shutters, decorated with a wafer for the Eucharist (symbolizing the sacrifice of Jesus—and suggesting Tolomei's own self-sacrifice). The seventh panel depicts a woodpecker, with this monastery on the right side. The terrain is accurate—showing the jagged *calanchi* (cliffs)—but is missing the now-familiar roads lined with cypresses planted in the 18th century to combat erosion. The next panel is another four-shutter composition. Examine the potted flower (representing fertility), where each petal is different. The ninth panel shows a utopian, geometrically flawless depiction of the artist's hometown of Verona. Finally, in the tenth panel, get lost in the perfectly executed, three-dimensional details of four shutters and two guitars. Notice the individual strings of the guitar, and the crumpled piece of sheet music with actual words.

Cross over to the **right side** and work your way back toward the front of the church, starting with the panel showing the skull—a common symbol for Adam, often shown at the base of Jesus' cross (reminding us that Jesus died to atone for the original sin of Adam). Next is Verona's arena (evoking the classical period that provided a foundation for the Renaissance), then tambourines that allow Fra Giovanni to experiment with the play of light and foreshortening. Next is another view of this monastery, followed by another four-shutter composition. In the top part, the universe rests on the Old and New Testaments; below that are the guild symbols of the monks (axe, compass, and so on) wrapped in a ribbon. This side finishes with another idealized Verona townscape; symbols of pharmacists and alchemists; another perfect town; the entire universe revolving around the earth (remember, this was a century before Galileo); and another self-portrait. Before moving on, pause and say *grazie* to Fra Giovanni.

• *Now check out a few more features worthy of note.*

The Rest of the Church

In the side chapel to the left of the main altar, find the medieval **crucifix** that clashes with its Baroque surroundings. Supposedly, this crucifix would periodically—and miraculously—speak to Bernardo Tolomei. Behind the crucifix is a painting of Tolomei talking to Jesus (added in 1701). In the sacristy to the right of the altar, examine the huge **stand** created by Fra Raffaele, a student of Fra Giovanni. This originally sat in the center of the choir to display huge music pages so that all the assembled monks could read and chant together.

• *Now head into the...*

Great Cloister

Big personalities—and clashes between them—influenced the art you're about to see. In 1419, the abbot of this monastery commis-

sioned the famous artist Luca Signorelli to decorate the cloister with scenes from the life of St. Benedict. But Signorelli completed only a third of the frescoes before he got an even better gig in Orvieto. After Signorelli left, the abbot commissioned another artist: Il Sodoma. To test him before entrusting the cloister to

him, the abbot had him paint the **panel** to the immediate left of the door as you leave the church, showing Benedict giving books to the Olivetan monks. It was a hit, and Sodoma was hired.

A temperamental artist, Sodoma liked to work at his own pace. But after his frustrating experience with Signorelli, the abbot was short on patience, and nudged Sodoma to work faster and faster (while not always paying him on time). To get back at the abbot, Sodoma included painted digs here and there in the panels (which I'll point out). We'll head clockwise around the cloister. The primary story traces events from the life of St. Benedict (based on the sixth-century accounts of St. Gregory). But the fresco series also offers insight into both monastic and pilgrim life at the cusp of the Renaissance...as well as some fun peeks at the personality of the artist. Gothic art was for the glory of God. Renaissance art—including these frescoes—is designed for a viewer: in this case, pilgrims walking the Via Francigena. This art tells a story and serves a propagandistic agenda: recruitment of pilgrims to join the Olivetan order and become monks.

• *Head into the cloister and begin with the first panel, on your left. The panels are titled in Italian, and aren't numbered—but to help you keep your place, I've numbered the descriptions below and organized them into sections: east, south, west, and north.*

East Wall (panels 1-11)

1. During the fifth century, Benedict (in blue tunic and orange sash) leaves his hometown and heads for Rome. He leans back on his horse toward his mother, suggesting his reluctance to set out on this journey. In the little townscape on the far-right horizon, notice the body of a man hanging on the gallows—suggesting the barbarism of the time. The servant in red leggings points ahead to Rome (the next panel, identified by the Tiber River and Castel Sant'Angelo). Just above and to the right, in the middle ground, notice the two donkeys that share six legs. According to Sodoma's

Il Sodoma (1477-1549)

Giovanni Antonio Bazzi was as irreverent as he was talented, a free spirit in every sense: He filled his house with exotic animals, he dressed in garish colors, and he was known to sing dirty little ditties to himself while he worked. During the time that he painted this cloister, the monks gave him the nickname Il Mattaccio ("the Madman").

A few years later, his contemporary Giorgio Vasari—an artist, academic, and vocal critic—gave him a different nickname, which stuck: Il Sodoma. Vasari wasn't a fan of Bazzi, and in those very primitive times, a homophobic slur ("The Sodomite") was one of the most withering insults possible. Ever iconoclastic, the artist embraced the nickname, and today it's how history remembers him.

But was Sodoma actually gay? Scholars are divided. Some art critics point to details in the frescoes that suggest a proclivity for the male form, or even suggestions of gay relationships between his figures. Others suggest that Sodoma was just being his usual, provocative self, adhering to an artistic style and documenting events he observed. As with other were-they-or-weren't-they greats throughout history—from Michelangelo to Shakespeare to Abraham Lincoln—it's impossible to know for sure.

diary, this intentional error was a message to the impatient abbot: "Working too fast causes mistakes."

2. Benedict (on the right) leaves the theology school in Rome (filled with fancy hedonists), which he has concluded is corrupt.

3. Angelic-looking Benedict (on the left) performs his first miracle: fixing a broken tray (shown before and after, on the ground in front of him). Sodoma has included a self-portrait in this scene, dead-center, with his pet badger and sarcastic smirk.

4. In the rounded panel, Benedict seeks a mentor (the hermit-monk Romano). He leaves his civilian clothes on the ground, taking on the white robe and beard of the monastic lifestyle, where individuality is irrelevant. By covering their bodies, monks are symbolically returning to the Garden of Eden.

5. A shaved-headed Benedict, now a hermit, goes into the wilderness to meditate. As he can't be seen by other people during this time, Romano must lower food to him with a basket on a rope. The devil spins in—Tasmanian-style—to throw a rock and break the bell on the food basket, so Benedict won't know it's chow time. The small snake peeking out to the right represents temptation.

6. After 40 days of isolation, it's Easter—the lamb is on the table (left of window). Inspired by a vision of Christ (far right, looking up toward a mysterious voice), a local priest brings some of the feast to Benedict, who realizes that it will be through community with others—not as a hermit—that he will find his calling.

7. Benedict begins his mission to convert shepherds, enumerating the points he's making on his fingers. (Notice the sheepdog at the far right. Why do dogs wear spiked collars? Because wolves would go after the sheepdogs first—clamping down on their necks—before attacking the sheep.) The two men whispering and giggling in the middle are interpreted by some as flirtatious, suggesting Sodoma's sexual orientation.

8. After being tempted by fantasies of a woman (at the top, with horns and a see-through negligee, being chased away by the Archangel Michael), Benedict tries to regain his self-control by stripping and throwing himself into a patch of poison ivy.

9. Impressed by his devotion, other brothers come to Benedict and ask him to become their leader.

10. Benedict accepts their offer and presents them with an extremely strict set of rules. The regretful monks try to kill him with poisoned wine (left side). But miraculously, the glass shatters in the poisoner's hand. (The man with the long nose, holding the glass, is an unflattering caricature of the abbot.) On the right, the watchful little cat is a symbol of vigilance against sin and temptation.

11. The last panel shows that Benedict was also an architect, building 12 monasteries in his life.

South Wall (panels 12-19)

12. The first panel on the next wall is one of Sodoma's masterpieces. Benedict meets the two young boys Placido and Mauro, who will

carry on his mission after his death. Sodoma has sprinkled some portraits of his contemporaries throughout this fresco, including Leonardo, Michelangelo, Raphael, and Lorenzo the Magnificent. Growing weary of hearing praise for Signorelli, Sodoma also included a portrait of his predecessor (immediately to the right of Benedict)...with a sarcastic halo.

13. The devil possesses a monk, leading him away from the monastery. Benedict catches up to him and beats the hell out of him—literally (right)—while the devil escapes (top).

14. Eight monks who live on a mountain are tired of hauling up their own water, so Benedict instructs them where to find a spring. The ghostly outlines of a tree and birds showing through

are a mistake: Sodoma painted over some frescoes he didn't like before they had dried—causing them to bleed through as a double exposure.

15. A monk loses the head of his shovel in a lake, but Benedict sticks the handle in to miraculously reattach it. The distant scene on the right, with the naked men wrestling, is quite unusual for church art (and has been taken as a speculation of Sodoma's sexuality).

16. Benedict's disciples Placido and Mauro are now teenagers. Placido is drowning, and Benedict—inspired by a divine vision—sends Mauro to walk across the water and save him.

17. This fresco has had a door unceremoniously cut into the middle of it. But that's OK—it's time for a break anyway.

• *Phew. That's a lot of frescoes. We're about halfway through. Let's take a break by ducking into the little side courtyard.*

Entering this **courtyard,** turn left and look to the far end of the hall to see a ghostly monk walking this way. Oops, it's not a monk—it's another Sodoma fresco, this one a well-executed practical joke.

Head into the **refectory,** the grand dining hall where monks gathered for meals (as they still do to this day). Monks ringed the outside of the long table, eating in silence, without distraction. Above the tables, notice the pulpit where holy words are read while the brothers dine. In the hall just outside the refectory, notice the big, yellow marble trough, where monks washed their hands before eating.

• *Head back out into the main cloister to resume our tour.*

18. The monastery's custodian, Florenzo (top left), is overcome with jealousy—and the devil—so he gives poisoned bread to a servant to bring to Benedict. On the right, Benedict throws the bread on the ground for a crow.

19. In this racy-for-church scene, Florenzo (still under the devil's influence) opens the monastery gate to let prostitutes in. Sodoma's salacious sensibilities come through boldly here. Notice the two ladies dancing, with their fingers intertwined (on the right)—one of them sticking her index finger into a hole formed by the other's hand. Subtle. In the lower right is another scandalously charged detail: A prostitute with a dark-skinned son. Even the animals are symbolic: The fluffy dog is a prostitute, while the hardworking donkey is a monk.

West Wall (panels 20-29)

20. The first fresco in the next wing is the only one in the cloister *not* by Sodoma or Signorelli. It shows Placido and Mauro (wearing cowboy boots and spurs) receiving their mission from Benedict.

Now begins the stretch of frescoes by **Signorelli.** Pay attention to the differences between the two artists: Signorelli is more of an anatomist (like Michelangelo), while Sodoma is less literal, gravitating to a figurative lyricism—like Botticelli. For example, compare the hands of Sodoma's prostitutes with the veiny, muscled monk's hand in Signorelli's first fresco.

21. Fed up with his failure to do in Benedict, the frenzied devil decides to kill Florenzo by collapsing the room he's in. In the upper right, cartoonish devils carry off Florenzo's screaming soul while they beat him.

22. Benedict goes to Monte Cassino—then deep in the pagan and barbarian wilds—on an important mission. On arrival, his monks pull graven images down from the temple (right), while the faint and ghostly devil escapes at the top. On the left, monks convert pagan worshippers. The hourglass hits you over the head with its message: It's time to convert.

23. The devil is busy tormenting the monks: In the center, he sits on a rock, making it impossible to move—until Benedict (far left) makes the sign of the cross. In the upper right, the devil sets a fire that the monks must scramble to extinguish.

24. The devil kills a monk who's building a church (upper left)—but other monks bring him to Benedict (lower left), who revives him (lower right). Notice the devil's fiery flatulence.

25. Two monks disobey the rules and eat in a restaurant in the company of fair maidens (left side). Returning to the monastery (tiny scene on right side), they lie about where they've been—so Benedict shames them by telling them exactly what they ordered. Like Sodoma earlier, Signorelli uses the fluffy dog (lower right) to suggest prostitution. Position yourself close to the wall and walk back and forth, noticing that the table moves with you—an impressive optical illusion.

26. A youth (in blue) aspiring to become a monk—who's supposed to be fasting—bumps into a friend on the road (on the right, horns and legless pants), and they decide to eat after all (upper left). In the main scene (lower left), the monk returns home and is admonished by Benedict.

27. The Ostrogoths' leader sends a stand-in (center, in armor) to pretend he wants to be converted. The monks sense the trick, and go to find the real guy (the half-moon at the top represents the "mysterious East").

28. In Signorelli's final scene, Benedict meets and converts the real Ostrogoth leader. Notice the fine details on the faces of the soldiers.

29. Sodoma returns, with bright colors and exacting details (see the horse's face). In the upper right, the monastery in Monte Cassino is destroyed—just as Benedict had prophesied.

North Wall (panels 30-35)

30. In the first panel on the final wall of the cloister, the monks have dinner. One sneaky fellow (far right) steals his neighbor's bread. This thief looks suspiciously like the accountant who was responsible for paying Sodoma. Sodoma got tired of hearing how amazing Signorelli's moving-table illusion was (back in #25)—so he topped it. You can actually see the objects on Sodoma's table more clearly the farther away you stand: Head back up the hallway you just came down, then walk slowly toward the table. When you reach it, turn right with the hall...and just keep your eyes on that table. The table stretches and shimmies, highlighting different details with each step.

31. Two monks dream of Benedict showing off a new monastery (left)—so they build it (right). The monk holding the plumb line is Fra Giovanni da Verona, who created the inlaid choir inside the church.

32. In this funeral memorial scene, two dead nuns who were excommunicated are on the left; in the center, the family makes a deal to get the Church to intervene; and in the tiny scene on the far right, Benedict forgives the nuns posthumously.

33. The corpse of a deceased monk surfaces from its grave each night because he had sinned by lying to Benedict. They place a communion host on top of the body, symbolizing the hope for rebirth, and his remains find peace.

• *Next, skip over two open arches.*

34. A monk (on the right) leaves the monastery and finds the devil. But he returns and begs forgiveness from Benedict (scene on the left). The monk's face radiates devotion—Sodoma has brilliantly captured his emotion. The message: The world outside the monastery is a dangerous place, where the devil will hijack your faith.

35. A farmer is captured by soldiers (right, middle ground). They demand his money, and he says Benedict has it. They bring him to Benedict (left), and miraculously, the rope binding him becomes untied.

The right side of this final scene is Sodoma's final kiss-off to the abbot: A horse's rear end is very prominent (symbolism obvious). Look at the house up above the horse, to the tiny upper-floor window where a shirt hangs in the breeze. During this era, a typical person owned seven shirts: six for workdays, and a seventh for Sunday, when they could rest (and do laundry). With this detail, Sodoma is saying to the abbot: "You made me work on Sunday—made me sweat through my seventh shirt. You horse's ass!"

• *With this, you've enjoyed all that's open to the public in this holy place. Go in peace.*

PISA

Famous for its tipsy Tower, Pisa ("PEE-zah") is much more than its iconic landmark. This thriving midsize city has a wealth of history and architectural treasures, an unexpectedly fun-to-explore arcaded core, and a prestigious university. The tower and its companion buildings at the Field of Miracles are undoubtedly a must-see. But beyond that tourist-clogged zone, Pisa feels like a real-world antidote to all that Tuscan cutesiness...a humbler Florence.

Centuries ago, Pisa was a major power—rivaling Venice and Genoa for control of the seas. City leaders erected a passel of Pisan Romanesque landmarks—the Duomo, Baptistery, and Tower—that float regally on the best lawn in Italy. Even as the church was being built, Piazza del Duomo was nicknamed the "Campo dei Miracoli," or Field of Miracles, for the grandness of the undertaking. After its port silted up, Pisa was left high and dry, and eventually entered a period of steady decline...leaving those grand landmarks as reminders of its past glory.

While Pisa is rewarding even on a short visit, lingering here helps you round out your Tuscan experience.

PLANNING YOUR TIME

For most visitors, Pisa is a touristy quickie—seeing the Tower, visiting the square, and wandering through the Duomo are 90 percent of their Pisan thrills. But it's a shame to skip the rest of the city. Considering Pisa's historic importance and the ambience created by its rich architectural heritage and vibrant student population, the city deserves a half-day visit. For many, the lack of tourists outside the Field of Miracles is both a surprise and a relief.

The Tower recently underwent a decade of restoration and topple-prevention. To ascend, you must get your ticket and book a time at in advance online (no sooner than 20 days but at least one day beforehand) at www.opapisa.it. Otherwise, go straight to the ticket office upon arrival to snag an appointment—usually for a couple of hours later, especially in summer (for directions to the Field of Miracles, see "Arrival in Pisa," later). If you'll be seeing both the town and the Field of Miracles, plan on a six-hour stop. If just blitzing the Field of Miracles, three hours is the minimum. Spending the night lets you savor a youthful Italian city scene.

If you're connecting Pisa and Lucca, note that a train runs at least hourly between Pisa's San Rossore train station near the Field of Miracles and Lucca, and buses leave frequently from Piazza Manin at the Field of Miracles gate (see page 453). This is so quick and easy that if you're just planning on seeing the Field of Miracles sights, Pisa makes a good half-day side-trip from Lucca.

Note that even the fastest trains stop in Pisa, so you might change trains here whether you plan to visit the sights or not.

Orientation to Pisa

The city of Pisa is manageable, with just 100,000 people, but its 45,000 students keep it lively, especially at night. The city is

framed on the north by the Field of Miracles (Leaning Tower) and on the south by Pisa Centrale train station. The Arno River flows east to west, bisecting the city. Walking from Pisa Centrale directly to the Tower

takes about 30 minutes (allow an hour if you take my self-guided walk). The two main streets for tourists and shoppers are Via Santa Maria (running south from the Tower) and Corso Italia/Borgo Stretto (running north from the station). A thousand years ago the city was a fortified burg on the north side of the river between those two main streets.

TOURIST INFORMATION

The main TI is located on the Field of Miracles, next to the Duomo's ticket office (daily 9:30-17:30, until 15:30 off-season, Piazza Duomo 7, tel. 050-550-100, www.turismo.pisa.it). It sells LAM bus tickets and offers videoguide walking tours of the main sights and the city center (€5-8), as well as guided tours on weekends (Sat-

A Brief History of Pisa

Pisa sits near the mouth of the Arno River (six miles from the coast—when the wind blows in a certain direction, you can still smell the sea). This easy access to the Mediterranean, with the added protection of sitting a bit upstream, made it a highly strategic settlement. The Romans established a naval base here, and Pisa's 150-foot galleys cruised the Mediterranean—gaining control of the sea, establishing outposts on the islands of Corsica, Sardinia, and Sicily, and trading with other Europeans, Muslims, and Byzantine Christians as far south as North Africa and as far east as Syria. European Crusaders hired Pisan boats to carry them and their supplies as they headed off to crusade against the Muslims ruling the Holy Land.

The Pisan "Republic" prided itself on its independence from both popes and emperors. For nearly three centuries (1000-1300), Pisa was a sea-trading power on par with Venice and Genoa, and by medieval times the city was a major player. The Pisans fancied themselves the natural heirs of the Roman Empire.

In 1200, Pisa's power peaked. The city used its sea-trading wealth to build the grand monuments of the Field of Miracles, including the iconic Tower. The Pisans peppered Roman engineering—and actual ancient fragments—into their distinct architectural style: Pisan Romanesque. In many of Pisa's buildings and decoration from these glory days, you can see the earliest inklings of the coming Renaissance—centuries before it took hold in earnest in Florence.

But the Pisan fleet was routed in battle by Genoa (1284, at Meloria, off Livorno), and their overseas outposts were taken away. After the port silted up, only the Field of Miracles and the university kept Pisa on the map. In 1406, it fell under the control of its former rival, the Medici family of Florence. Cosimo de' Medici favored Pisa for its mild climate (thanks to that sea breeze) and distance from his enemies. He built palaces here and raised a mighty army. But—as a subordinate to Florence—Pisa lacked the opportunities to flourish in its own right.

The city never regained its former glory, though its famous architectural sights give modern-day Pisa outsized name recognition and a thriving tourist economy.

Sun at 11:15, €10 and up). For those doing Pisa as a stopover, the TI offers baggage storage (€3-4). There's another TI at the airport, in the arrivals hall.

ARRIVAL IN PISA
By Train

Most trains (and visitors) arrive at Pisa Centrale station, about a mile south of the Tower and Field of Miracles. A few trains, particularly those from Lucca or La Spezia, stop at the smaller Pisa

San Rossore Station, an easy five-minute walk from the Tower (not all trains stop here, but if yours does, hop off).

Pisa Centrale Station: This station has a baggage-check desk—look for *deposito bagagli* (daily 6:00-21:00). With the tracks to your back, it's to the right at the far end of platform 1, just after the police station.

To get to the Field of Miracles, you can **walk** (30 minutes direct, one hour if you follow my self-guided walk), take a **taxi** (€10, tel. 050-541-600, taxi stand at station), or go by **bus**. At all bus stops in Pisa, be cautious of pickpockets, who take advantage of crowds to operate.

Bus **LAM Rossa** ("Red," also marked *L/R*) stops across the street from the train station, in front of the NH Cavalieri Hotel.

Buy a €1.20 bus ticket from the tobacco/magazine kiosk in the train station's main hall or at any tobacco shop (€2 on board; bus usually departs every 10 minutes, less frequent off-season, runs until 23:00, 15-minute trip). The bus lets you off at Piazza Manin, in front of the gate to the Field of Miracles (stop: Torre).

To return to the train station from the Tower, catch bus LAM Rossa in front of the BNL bank, across the street from where you got off. You'll also find a taxi stand 30 yards from the Tower (at Bar Duomo).

Pisa San Rossore Station: From this dreary little suburban station, it's just a five-minute walk to the tower. Exit the underpass at platform 2L, and follow the exit signs to *Torre Pendente*. Once out of the station area, turn left and follow brown *Torre Pendente* sights—you'll see the tower soon, straight ahead.

By Car

Driving in the city center is stressful, time-consuming, and risky, as Pisa has several restricted areas that are monitored by camera and marked by *"ZTL"* signs (you could get a ticket by mail).

For a quick visit, try the **Parcheggio di Piazza dei Miracoli** lot, just northwest of the tower (€2/hour, enter from Via Giovanni Battista Niccolini). From here, the Tower is practically across the street.

For a longer visit—or if the Parcheggio lot is full—it's best to leave your car at the big **Pietrasantina parking lot,** designed for tour buses (which pay to park) and tourists with cars (who park for free). From there, you can walk to the Field of Miracles or hop on a shuttle bus. To reach this parking lot, exit the autostrada at *Pisa Nord* and follow signs to *Pisa* (on the left), then *Bus Parking*.

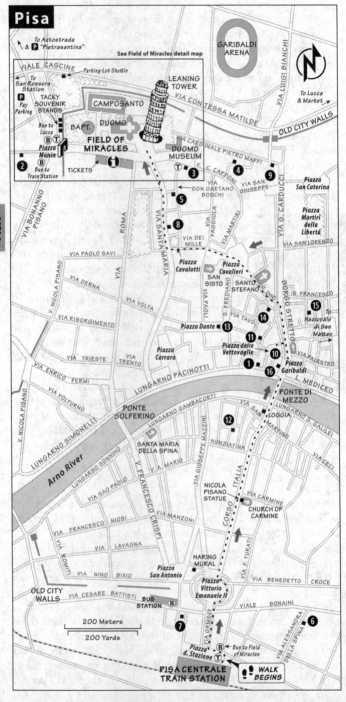

Pisa

To Autostrada
& P "Pietrasantina"

See Field of Miracles detail map

VIALE CASCINE — Parking-Lot Shuttle

To San Rossore Station

P Pay Parking

TACKY SOUVENIR STANDS

Bus to Lucca B T

BAPT.

Piazza Mahin ❶

❷ Bus to Train Station

TICKETS

FIELD OF MIRACLES

CAMPOSANTO

DUOMO

LEANING TOWER

GARIBALDI ARENA

VIA LUIGI BIANCHI

VIA CONTESSA MATILDE

OLD CITY WALLS

To Lucca & Market

DUOMO MUSEUM

VIA CARDINALE PIETRO MAFFI

VIA G. CAPPONI

❸ T ❹

VIA DON GAETANO BOSCHI

VIA SAN GIUSEPPE

❾

Piazza San Caterina

Piazza Martiri della Libertà

VIA SAN LORENZO

VIA G. CARDUCCI

❺

❽

VIA SANTA MARIA

VIA ROMA

VIA FAGGIOLA

VIA DEI MILLE

VIA MARTIRI

VIA PAOLO SAVI

Piazza Cavalotti

Piazza Cavalieri

SAN SISTO

SANTO STEFANO

BORGO STRETTO

S. FRANCESCO

❶❺ To Nazionale di San Matteo

VIA V. BONANNO PISANO

V. NICOLA PISANO

VIA DERNA

VIA VOLTA

S. FREDIANO

VIA TAVO

❶❹

VIA RISORGIMENTO

Piazza Dante ❶❸

❶❶

VIA PALESTRO

VIA TRIESTE

VIA TRENTO

Piazza Carrara

Piazza delle Vettovaglie

❶❶

❶❶

Piazza Garibaldi

VIA ENRICO FERMI

LUNGARNO PACINOTTI

L. MEDICEO

VIA VOLTURNO

PONTE DI MEZZO

LUNGARNO G. GALILEI

V. NICOLA PISANO

LUNGARNO SIMONELLI

PONTE SOLFERINO

LUNGARNO GAMBACORTI

SANTA MARIA DELLA SPINA

V. A. MARIO

❶❷

VIA SAN MARTINO

LOGGIA

VIA CECI

Arno River

LUNGARNO SONNINO

VIA SAO PAOLO

V. FRANCESCO CRISPI

VIA GIUSEPPE MAZZINI

NUNZIATINA

VIA FRANCESCO NIOSI

VIA MANZONI

CORSO ITALIA

NICOLA PISANO STATUE

VIA CARMINE

CHURCH OF CARMINE

VIA LAVAGNA

VIA NINO BIXIO

V. ROMITI

HARING MURAL

Piazza San Antonio

VIA F. TURATI

VIA BENEDETTO CROCE

OLD CITY WALLS

VIA CESARE BATTISTI

BUS STATION B

Piazza Vittorio Emanuele II

VIALE BONAINI

200 Meters

200 Yards

❼

Piazza d. Stazione

B T Bus to Field of Miracles

VIA ALESSANDRA DELLA SPINA

❻

VIA GIUSTI

PISA CENTRALE TRAIN STATION

WALK BEGINS

Pisa Key

1. Hotel Royal Victoria, Caffè dell'Ussero & De' Coltelli Gelato
2. Hotel Pisa Tower
3. Hotel Villa Kinzica
4. Casa San Tommaso
5. Pensione Helvetia
6. Hotel Alessandro della Spina
7. Hotel Milano
8. Via Santa Maria Eateries
9. Pizzeria al Bagno di Nerone
10. La Vineria di Piazza & Produce Market
11. Antica Trattoria il Campano
12. Il Vegusto
13. Caffetteria BetsaBea & Pizzeria l'Arancio
14. Il Montino Pizzeria
15. Orzo Bruno Brewpub
16. La Bottega del Gelato

The parking lot has a cafeteria and WC. At the center of the lot is a high-roofed bus stop where you can catch the LAM Rossa bus to Piazza Manin at the gate of the Field of Miracles (€1.20 at the parking lot's cafeteria, €2 on board, continues to central Pisa).

If you'd rather not wait for the bus, the **walk to the Tower** takes about 10 minutes: From the newspaper/souvenir kiosk at the east end of the lot, turn right onto the curving road. Follow the blue signs indicating a pedestrian path and brown signs pointing to the Leaning Tower. Or, to follow my self-guided walk through Pisa back to the Field of Miracles, take bus LAM Rossa to Pisa Centrale station.

By Plane

For details on Pisa's Galileo Galilei Airport, see page 453.

HELPFUL HINTS

Markets: An open-air produce market attracts picnickers to Piazza delle Vettovaglie, one block north of the Arno River near Ponte di Mezzo, and nearby Piazza Sant'Uomobuono (Mon-Sat 8:00-18:00, main section closes at 13:00, closed Sun). A street market—with more practical goods than food—bustles on Wednesday and Saturday mornings between Via del Brennero and Via Paparrelli (8:00-13:00, just outside of wall, about 6 blocks east of the Tower).

Festivals: Noon on March 25 (also the Feast of the Annunciation of the Virgin Mary) is the *Capodanno Pisano,* the end of the year according to the Pisan calendar used in the Middle Ages. In a tradition carried on from medieval times, the city hosts New Year's festivities for several days.

June is a big month in Pisa, when some hotels raise their rates. The first half of June has many events, culminating in a celebration for Pisa's patron saint (June 16-17). The last week in June is the *Gioco del Ponte* ("Game of the Bridge") festival, where burly residents of the city's four districts meet on the bridge for a game of tug-of-war with a big carriage.

Local Guides: Dottore Vincenzo Riolo is a great guide for Pisa and the surrounding area (€145/3 hours, mobile 338-211-2939, www.pisatour.it, info@pisatour.it). **Martina Manfredi** happily guides visitors through the Field of Miracles, but her real passion is helping them discover Pisa's other charms, from hidden gardens and piazzas to cuisine to artisans (3 hours-€140, 6 hours-€250, mobile 328-898-2927, www.tuscanyatheart.it, artemarty@libero.it).

Pisa Walk

A leisurely one-hour self-guided stroll from Pisa Centrale train station to the Tower is a great way to get acquainted with the more subtle virtues of this fine city. Because the hordes who descend daily on the Tower rarely bother with the rest of the town, you'll find most of Pisa to be delightfully untouristy—a student-filled, classy, Old World town with an Arno-scape much like its upstream rival, Florence.

• *From Pisa Centrale, walk north (under the fascist marble arcade) up Viale Antonio Gramsci to the circular square called...*

Piazza Vittorio Emanuele II

The Allies considered Pisa to be strategically important in World War II, and both the train station and its main bridge were targeted for bombing. Forty percent of this district was destroyed. The piazza has been rebuilt, and now this generous public space with grass and benches is actually a lid for an underground parking lot. The circular pink building in the middle of the square, on the right, is La Bottega del Parco, a shop that sells Tuscan products and light meals.

At the top of the square, on the left (by the Credito Artigiano bank), find the little piazza with a colorful bar/café that faces a mural, called *Tuttomondo (Whole Wide World)*, painted by American artist **Keith Haring** in 1989. Haring (who died of AIDS in 1990) brought New York City graffiti into the mainstream. This painting is a celebration of diversity, chaos, and the liveliness of our world, vibrating with energy.

• *Head back to the middle of the big square and take the first left. This is Pisa's main drag.*

Corso Italia

As you leave Piazza Vittorio Emanuele II, look to the right (on the wall of the bar on the corner, under the gallery) to see the circa-1960 wall map of Pisa with a steam train. Then follow the pedestrianized Corso Italia straight north for several blocks, toward the river. This is Pisa's main shopping street for locals, not tourists. This is where the midrange department stores are and where students hang out and stroll—you'll see plenty of youthful fashions.

A few blocks up, in front of the Church of Santa Maria del Carmine (#88), meet **Nicola Pisano.** He and his son, Giovanni (who worked in the 13th century) represented the pinnacle of Gothic art and inspired Michelangelo. Although they were from the south, their work in their adopted town earned them the name "Pisano" (from Pisa).

Continuing down Corso Italia, you'll run into a gorgeous **loggia.** Like much of the city, this was built under Medici (Florentine) rule—and it resembles the markets you'll still find in Florence. But remember that before Florence ruled Pisa, this city was an independent and strong maritime republic.

This area (south of the river) was a marshland until the 11th century, and in the Middle Ages it was a crossroads of merchants from faraway lands: smelly, polluted, and a commotion of activity. Like the Oltrarno neighborhood in Florence and Trastevere neighborhood in Rome (and the "wrong side of the tracks" in many American towns), this was the most characteristic part of the city. Now we cross to the "high town."

• *At the Arno River, cross to the middle of the bridge.*

Ponte di Mezzo

This modern bridge, the site of Pisa's first bridge and therefore its birthplace, marks the center of Pisa. In the Middle Ages, Ponte di Mezzo (like Florence's Ponte Vecchio) was lined with shops. It's been destroyed several times by floods...and in 1943 by British and American bombers. Enjoy the view from the center of the bridge of the elegant mansions that line the riverbank, recalling Pisa's days of trading glory—the cityscape feels a bit like Venice's Grand Canal. Back when the loggia area was stinky and crowded, nobles preferred to live in stately residences along the river.

Looking downstream on the right, notice the red-brick building (the former silk merchants' quarters) that looks like it's about to slide into the river. Pisa sits on shifting delta sand, making construction tricky. The entire town leans. Using innovative arches aboveground and below, architects didn't stop the leaning—but they have made buildings that wobble without being threatened.

• *Cross the bridge to...*

Piazza Garibaldi

This square is named for the charismatic leader of the Risorgimento, the unification movement that led to Italian independence in 1860. Knowing Pisa was strongly nationalist (and gave many of its sons to the national struggle), a wounded Garibaldi came here to be nursed back to health. Study the bronze relief at the base of the statue and see him docking in Pisa and receiving a warm and caring welcome.

For a gelato break, stop by **La Bottega del Gelato,** right on this square and most Pisans' sentimental favorite. Or, for a fresh take on the same old gelato, head about 100 yards downstream (to the left on Lungarno Pacinotti as you come off the bridge) to **De' Coltelli** (at #23), which scoops up organic, artisanal gelato with unusual and vibrant flavors...some of the best I've had. Just beyond that, in the slouching red building (at #28), step into **Caffè dell'Ussero.** This venerable café has long been a hangout of both politicians...and the students bent on overthrowing them. Greet the proprietor and then browse its time-warp interior all the way to its back room—it's lined with portraits and documents from the struggle for Italian independence.

• *Back on Piazza Garibaldi, continue north up the elegantly arcaded street called...*

Borgo Stretto

Welcome to Pisa's other main shopping street—this one higher-end. On the right, the Church of St. Michael, with its fine Pisan Romanesque facade, was likely built upon a Roman temple.

From here, look farther up the street and notice how it undulates like a flowing river. In the sixth century B.C., Pisa was born when two parallel rivers were connected by canals. This street echoes the flow of one of those canals. An 11th-century landslide rerouted the second river, destroying ancient Pisa, and the entire city had to rebuild.

• *Just past the church, pause to appreciate the Renaissance arcades (loggias) in every direction. Then detour left onto Via delle Colonne, and walk one block down to...*

Piazza delle Vettovaglie

Pisa's historic market square, Piazza delle Vettovaglie, is lively by day and sketchy by night. Its Renaissance loggia has hosted the fish-and-vegetable market for generations (closed Sun). Stalls are set up in this piazza in the morning and stay open later in the neighboring piazza to the west (Piazza Sant'Uomobuono). You could cobble together a picnic from the sandwich shops and fruit-and-veggie stalls ringing these squares, or enjoy lunch at the recommended **La Vineria di Piazza** trattoria (under the arcades of Piazza delle Vettovaglie).

• *Return to Borgo Stretto and continue north another 100 yards, passing an ugly bomb site on the right, with its horrible 1960s reconstruction (Largo Ciro Menotti). You'll pass Pasticceria Salza—while no place for fine food or snappy service, it has been an elegant place for a coffee and a central perch from which to observe the scene since 1898.*

Take the second left on nondescript Via Ulisse Dini (immediately at the arcade's end, just before the pharmacy). This leads to Pisa's historic core, the square called...

Piazza dei Cavalieri (Knights' Square)

With its old clock and colorfully decorated palace, this piazza was once the seat of the independent Republic of Pisa's government.

Around 1500, Florence conquered Pisa and made this square the training place for the knights of its navy. The statue of Cosimo I de' Medici shows the Florentine who ruled Pisa in the 16th century. With a foot on a dolphin, he reminded all who passed that the Florentine navy controlled the sea—at least a little of it. The frescoes on the exterior of the square's buildings, though damaged by salty sea air and years of neglect, reflect Pisa's fading glory under the Medici.

With Napoleon, this complex of grand buildings became part of the University of Pisa. The university is one of Europe's oldest, with roots in a law school that dates back as far as the 11th century. In the mid-16th century, the city was a hotbed of controversy, as spacey professors like Galileo Galilei studied the solar system—with results that challenged the Church's powerful doctrine. Galileo's legacy lives on, as the U of P is most highly regarded for its scientific faculties, especially engineering and medicine. The blind tenor Andrea Bocelli attended law school in Pisa before embarking on his well-known musical career.

From here, take Via Corsica (to the left of the clock). The humble 11th-century **Church of San Sisto,** ahead on the left (side entrance on Via Corsica), is worth a quick look. This was the typical Romanesque style that predated the more lavish Pisan Romanesque style of the Field of Miracles structures: simple bricks, assorted reused columns—some of them ancient Roman, a delightful assortment of capitals, heavy walls, and tiny windows.

PISA

• Follow Via Corsica as it turns into Via dei Mille, then turn right on Via Santa Maria, which leads north, becoming a touristy can-can of eateries, and finally ends at the Field of Miracles and the Tower.

Sights in Pisa

THE BEST OF THE FIELD OF MIRACLES

Imagine arriving in Pisa as a sailor in the 12th century, when the Arno River came to just outside the walls surrounding this square, the church here was one of the biggest in the world, and this ensemble in gleaming white marble was the most impressive space in Christendom. Calling it the Field of Miracles (Campo dei Miracoli) would not have been hyperbole.

Scattered across a golf-course-green lawn are five grand buildings: the cathedral (or Duomo), its bell tower (the Leaning Tower), the Baptistery, the hospital (today's Museum of the Sinopias), and the Camposanto Cemetery. The buildings are constructed from similar materials—bright white marble—and have comparable decoration. Each has a simple ground floor and rows of delicate columns and arches that form open-air arcades, giving the Campo a pleasant visual unity.

The style is called Pisan Romanesque. Unlike traditional Romanesque, with its heavy fortress-like feel—thick walls, barrel arches, few windows—Pisan Romanesque is light and elegant. At ground level, most of the structures have simple half-columns and arches. On the upper levels, you'll see a little of everything—tight rows of thin columns; pointed Gothic gables and prickly spires; Byzantine mosaics and horseshoe arches; and geometric designs (such as diamonds) and striped, colored marbles inspired by mosques in Muslim lands.

Architecturally, the Campo is unique and exotic, so I've rated it ▲▲▲. Traditionally, the Campo's buildings marked the main events of every Pisan's life: christened in the Baptistery, married in the Duomo, honored in ceremonies at the Tower, healed in the hospital, and buried in the Camposanto Cemetery.

Lining this field of artistic pearls are dozens of people who have simultaneously had the same bright idea: posing for a photo as though they're propping up the Leaning Tower. Although the smooth green carpet looks like the ideal picnic spot—and many people are doing just that—officially, lounging on this lawn can result in a €25 fine.

If your time is limited, focus on the best of the Campo—the Tower and the Duomo. For a longer visit, also see "The Rest of the Field of Miracles," later in this chapter, for details on the Baptistery, the Museum of the Sinopias, the Camposanto Cemetery, and the Duomo Museum (if open).

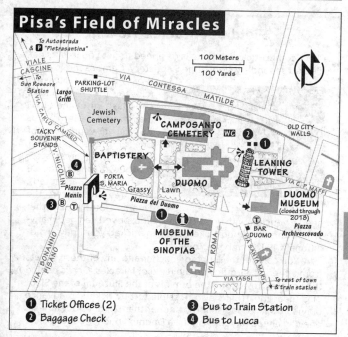

Pisa's Field of Miracles

❶ Ticket Offices (2)   ❸ Bus to Train Station
❷ Baggage Check   ❹ Bus to Lucca

▲▲▲Leaning Tower

You've seen it in TV ads, in movies, and on posters, key chains, and souvenir dishes—now it's time to see the actual tower. A 15-foot lean from the vertical makes the Leaning Tower one of Europe's most recognizable images. You can see it for free—it's always viewable—or you can pay to climb nearly 300 stairs to the top.

The off-kilter Tower parallels Pisa's history. It was started in the late 12th century, when Pisa was at its peak: one of the world's richest, most powerful, and most sophisticated cities. Pisans had built their huge cathedral to reflect their city's superpower status, and the cathedral's bell tower—the Leaning Tower—was the perfect complement. But as Pisa's power declined, the Tower reclined, and ever since, both have required a great deal of effort to prop up. However, after a 10-year renovation, the Tower's been stabilized. You can admire it in all its cockeyed glory and even climb up for a commanding view.

Cost and Hours: €18, kids under age 8 not allowed, daily April-Sept 8:00-20:00 (until 22:00 mid-June-Aug), Oct 9:00-19:00, Nov-Feb 10:00-17:00, March 9:00-18:00, ticket office opens 30 minutes early, reservations necessary if you value your time, www.opapisa.it.

Reservations: Entry to the tower is by a timed ticket good for a 30-minute visit. Every 15 minutes, 45 people can clamber up the

Field of Miracles Tickets

Pisa's combo-ticket scheme is designed to get you into its neglected secondary sights: the Baptistery, Camposanto Cemetery, Duomo Museum (closed for renovation), and Museum of the Sinopias (fresco patterns). For €5, you get your choice of one of these sights; for two sights, the cost is €7; for the works, you pay €8 (credit cards accepted). It's free to enter the Duomo, but you either need a voucher with an appointed time, or you can get in anytime with any combo-ticket. With any ticket, you'll pay an additional €18 to climb the Tower.

You can get the Duomo voucher and any of these tickets from either ticket office on the Field of Miracles: One is behind the Leaning Tower and the other is at the Museum of the Sinopias (near the TI). It's also possible to buy tickets in advance online at www.opapisa.it (no sooner than 20 days but at least one day ahead of your visit; free Duomo voucher not available online).

So, which ticket to buy? This depends on your time and level of interest. The shortest visit doesn't cost a dime: Ogle the Tower and other buildings, and enter the Duomo (with the best interior). If you're in a hurry, buy a €5 ticket to enter the Duomo right away. With more time, the interiors of the Baptistery and Camposanto Cemetery are well worth paying for and easy to appreciate. The two museums—Duomo Museum and Museum of the Sinopias—are "extra credit" for those fascinated by the artistic details of the other sights; for most travelers, they're skippable.

And what about entering the Tower? Is it worth that hefty price tag—and a likely wait to enter? It's a minor thrill to clomp up those twisty stairs, and the view from the top is enjoyable. But Pisa isn't particularly scenic, and it's a lot of expense and hassle for a view. Unless climbing the Tower is what you came to do, I consider ascending it optional. The real thrill comes from seeing it from the outside.

As you consider your itinerary, remember that until the "cult of the Leaning Tower" was born around 1900, people came to Pisa not to see the tower but to visit the historic Camposanto Cemetery.

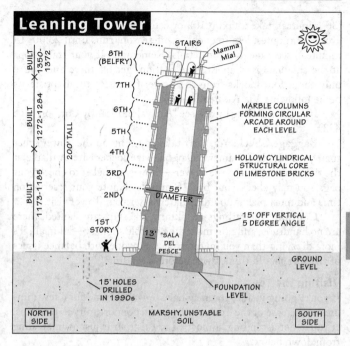

Leaning Tower

STAIRS

8TH (BELFRY)

Mamma Mia!

7TH

6TH

MARBLE COLUMNS FORMING CIRCULAR ARCADE AROUND EACH LEVEL

5TH

4TH

HOLLOW CYLINDRICAL STRUCTURAL CORE OF LIMESTONE BRICKS

3RD

2ND

55' DIAMETER

1ST STORY

13' "SALA DEL PESCE"

15' OFF VERTICAL 5 DEGREE ANGLE

GROUND LEVEL

15' HOLES DRILLED IN 1990s

FOUNDATION LEVEL

NORTH SIDE

MARSHY, UNSTABLE SOIL

SOUTH SIDE

BUILT 1350-1372

BUILT 1272-1284

BUILT 1173-1185

200' TALL

PISA

294 tilting steps to the top. Children ages 8-18 must be accompanied by—and stay at all times with—an adult.

Reserve your timed entry online or in person at either ticket office. **Online bookings** are accepted no earlier than 20 days and no later than one day in advance. Choose your entry time and buy your ticket at www.opapisa.it. Print out the voucher and bring it to the Tower no less than 15 minutes before your entry time.

To reserve in person, go to the **ticket office,** behind the Tower on the left (in the yellow building), or to the Museum of the Sinopias ticket office.

Planning Your Time: In summer, for same-day entry, you'll likely wait 2-3 hours before going up (see the rest of the monuments and grab lunch while waiting). It's busiest between 12:00 and 15:00; the wait is usually much shorter at the beginning or end of the day. Mondays, when museums in Florence are closed, are always the busiest.

Arrive at least 15 minutes ahead of your reservation or you may not be allowed in. Even though this is technically a guided visit, the "guide" is a museum guard who makes sure you don't stay past your scheduled time. For your 30-minute time slot, figure about 10 minutes to climb, and 10 to descend. This leaves about 10 minutes for vertigo at the top.

Getting There: From Pisa Centrale train station, you can walk

(30 minutes), take a taxi (€10), or catch bus LAM Rossa (usually every 10 minutes, less frequent in off-season, runs until 23:00, 15 minutes); see page 422 for details. Remember, if your train stops at the smaller Pisa San Rossore Station, get off there and you're only about four blocks from the Tower (head for the Baptistery's dome following Via Andrea Pisano).

If you're traveling by car, see "Arrival in Pisa: By Car," on page 423.

Baggage Check: You can't take anything up the Tower other than your phone or camera. Day-bag-size lockers are available at the ticket office next to the Tower—show your ticket to check your bag. You may check your bag 15 minutes before your reservation time and must pick it up immediately after your Tower visit.

Caution: The railings are skinny, the steps are slanted, there are no handrails, and rain makes the marble slippery—all in all, it's more dizzying than you might expect. Anyone with balance issues of any sort should think twice before ascending.

Visiting the Tower

If you're going inside, you may have to wait around for a few minutes at the base of the Tower—the perfect opportunity to read this. If you're not ascending, almost all of this tour is just as interesting from down below.

Yep, There It Is: Rising up alongside the cathedral, the Tower is nearly 200 feet tall and 55 feet wide, weighing 14,000 tons and currently leaning at a five-degree angle (15 feet off the vertical axis). It started to lean almost immediately after construction began (it would take two centuries to finish the structure). Count the eight stories—a simple base, six stories of columns (forming arcades), and a belfry on top. The inner structural core is a hollow cylinder built of limestone bricks, faced with  white marble brought here by barge from San Giuliano, northeast of the city. The thin columns of the open-air arcades make the heavy Tower seem light and graceful.

The Building of the Tower: The Tower was built over two centuries by at least three different architects. You can see how each successive architect tried to correct the leaning problem—once halfway up (after the fourth story), once at the belfry on the top.

The first stones were laid in 1173, probably under the direction of the architect Bonanno Pisano (who also designed the Duomo's

Galileo and Gravity

The Leaning Tower figures prominently in scientific lore. Legend has it that the scientific pioneer Galileo Galilei dropped objects off the Tower in an attempt to understand gravity. Galileo (1564-1642) was born in Pisa, grew up here on Via Giuseppe Giusti (where the family home still stands, adorned with a humble plaque), and taught math at the university. Galileo is said to have climbed the Tower and dropped two balls: one heavy and metal, the other a lighter wooden ball. Which object hit the ground first? The heavier object, of course—but through further reasoning and experimentation, Galileo figured out that the lighter object fell more slowly only because of air resistance. In doing so, he shattered the conventional wisdom, established by Aristotle, that heavier objects accelerate faster. We don't know whether Galileo actually dropped those orbs from this Tower, but we do know he tested this theory of gravity by rolling balls of different weights down ramps, which would have been easier to time (see page 258). These experiments led to Isaac Newton's formulation of the laws of gravity. Moreover, by forging theories through rigorous testing rather than through reasoning alone (as Aristotle had), Galileo helped reenvision science itself.

bronze back door). Five years later, just as the base and the first arcade were finished, someone said, "Is it just me, or does that look crooked?" The heavy Tower—resting on a very shallow 13-foot foundation—was sinking on the south side into the marshy, multilayered, unstable soil. (Actually, all of the Campo's buildings tilt somewhat.) The builders carried on anyway, until they'd finished four stories (the base, plus three arcade floors). Then, construction suddenly halted—no one knows why—and for a century the Tower sat half-finished and visibly leaning.

Around 1272, the next architect continued, trying to correct the problem by angling the next three stories backward, in the opposite direction of the lean. The project then again sat mysteriously idle for nearly another century. Finally, Tommaso Pisano put the belfry on the top (c. 1350-1372), also kinking it to overcome the leaning.

Man Versus Gravity: After the Tower's completion, several attempts were made to stop its slow-motion fall. The architect/artist/writer Giorgio Vasari reinforced the base in 1550, and it actually worked. But in 1838, well-intentioned engineers pumped out groundwater, destabilizing the Tower and causing it to increase its lean at a rate of a millimeter per year.

It got so bad that in 1990 the Tower was closed for repairs, and $30 million was spent trying to stabilize it. Engineers dried the soil with pipes containing liquid nitrogen, anchored the Tower to the ground with steel cables, and buried 600 tons of lead on the north side as a counterweight (not visible)—all with little success. The breakthrough came when they drilled 15-foot-long holes in the ground on the north side and sucked out 60 tons of soil, allowing the Tower to sink on the north side and straighten out its lean by about six inches.

As well as gravity, erosion threatens the Tower. Since its construction, 135 of the Tower's 180 marble columns have had to be replaced. Stone decay, deposits of lime and calcium phosphate, accumulations of dirt and moss, cracking from the stress of the lean—all of these are factors in its decline.

Thanks to the Tower's lean, there are special trouble spots. The lower south side (which is protected from cleansing rain and wind) is a magnet for dirty airborne particles, while the stone on the upper areas has more decay (from eroding rain and wind). The Tower, now stabilized, has been cleaned. Cracks have been filled, and accumulations removed with carefully formulated atomized water sprays and poultices of various solvents.

All the work to shore up, straighten, and clean the Tower has probably turned the clock back a few centuries. In fact, art historians figure the Tower leans today as much as it did when Galileo reputedly conducted his gravity experiment here 400 years ago.

• *Wait's over? Great. It's time to head inside.*

Climbing the Tower: First, you'll enter the room at the bottom of the tower known as the *Sala del Pesce* (for the Christian fish symbol on the wall). Gape up through the hollow Tower to the oculus at the top, and marvel at the acoustics. Also check out the heavy metal braces stretching up to the top.

Then you'll wind your way up the outside along a spiraling ramp to the first level, where you can stroll the colonnaded arcade. Then, finding the tiny spiral staircase next to where you entered the first level, head to the belfry on the top, climbing a total of 294 stairs. At the top, you'll have fine views over the Duomo and the rest of the Field of Miracles, as well as over the rooftops of Pisa (admittedly, not the most striking city).

▲▲Duomo (Cathedral)

The huge Pisan Romanesque cathedral, with its carved pulpit by Giovanni Pisano, is artistically more important than its more famous bell tower. Budget some sight-seeing time for the church's artistic and historic treasures.

Cost and Hours: Free, pick up a voucher with an entry time at either ticket office (every 30 minutes, voucher not available in advance online) or show your combo-ticket (see sidebar on page 432); daily April-Sept 10:00-20:00, Oct 10:00-19:00, Nov-Feb 10:00-13:00 & 14:00-17:00, March 10:00-18:00.

Crowd-Beating Tips: Because the Duomo is the only free interior at the Field of Miracles, it's on every tour itinerary and can be busy. Ideally, try to see the Duomo before 12:00 or after 15:00. Any combo-ticket or Tower ticket will let you in without an entry time.

Dress Code: Shorts are OK as long as they're not too short, and shoulders should be covered (although it's not really enforced).

Baggage: Big backpacks are not allowed, but you can leave your bags at the TI across the square.

❍ Self-Guided Tour

The Duomo is the centerpiece of the Field of Miracles' complex of religious buildings. Begun in 1063, it was financed by a galley-load of booty ransacked that year from the Muslim-held capital of Palermo, Sicily. The architect Buschetto created the frilly Pisan Romanesque style that set the tone for the Baptistery and Tower. In the 1150s, the architect Rainaldo added the impressive main-entrance facade.

❶ Exterior: The lower half of the church is simple Roman-esque, with blind arches. The upper half has four rows of columns

that form arcades. Stripes of black-and-white marble, mo-saics, stone inlay, and even re-cycled Roman tombstones com-plete the decoration.

• *Enter the church at the facade, opposite the Baptistery.*

❷ Nave: The 320-foot nave was the longest in Christendom when it was built. It's modeled on a traditional Roman basilica, with 68 Corinthian columns of granite (most shipped from Elba and Corsica in 1063) dividing the space into five aisles. But the striped marble and arches-on-columns give the nave an exotic, almost mosque-like feel. Dim

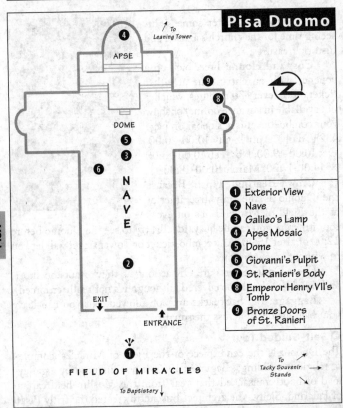

Pisa Duomo

→ To Leaning Tower

APSE

4

9

8

DOME

7

5

3

6

N A V E

2

EXIT ←

ENTRANCE ↑

1

FIELD OF MIRACLES

To Baptistery ↓

To Tacky Souvenir Stands

1 Exterior View
2 Nave
3 Galileo's Lamp
4 Apse Mosaic
5 Dome
6 Giovanni's Pulpit
7 St. Ranieri's Body
8 Emperor Henry VII's Tomb
9 Bronze Doors of St. Ranieri

PISA

light filters in from the small upper windows of the galleries. At the center of the gilded coffered ceiling is the shield of Florence's Medici family, with its round balls. With the arrival of the Florentine Renaissance, this powerful merchant and banking family took over Pisa after its glory days had passed.

• *Hanging from the ceiling of the central nave is...*

3 **Galileo's Lamp:** The bronze incense burner is said to be the one (actually, this is a replacement of the original) that caught the teenage Galileo's attention one day in church. According to legend, someone left a church door open, and a gust of wind set the lamp swinging. Galileo timed the swings and realized that the burner swung back and forth in the same amount of time regardless of how wide the arc. (This pendulum motion was a constant that allowed Galileo to measure our ever-changing universe.)

Galileo Galilei (1564-1642) was born in Pisa, grew up here on Via Giuseppe Giusti, and taught math at the university (1584-1591). Legend says he dropped things off the Tower to time their falls, fascinated by gravity (see sidebar on page 435).

• *The upper and front part of the church will be covered by scaffolding through at least 2018. But you can still pick out most of the following details. High up in the apse (behind the altar) is the...*

❹ Apse Mosaic: The mosaic (c. 1300, partly done by the great artist Cimabue) shows Christ as the Ruler of All (Pantocrator) between Mary and St. John the Evangelist. The Pantocrator image of Christ is standard fare among Eastern Orthodox Christians—that is, the "Byzantine" people who were Pisa's partners in trade.

As King of the Universe, Christ sits on a throne, facing directly out, with penetrating eyes. Only Christ can wear this style of halo, divided with a cross. In his left hand is a Bible open to the verse *"Ego Lux Sum Mundi"*—"I am the light of the world." While his feet crush the devil in serpent form, Christ blesses us with his right hand. His fingers form the Greek letters *chi* and *rho*, the first two letters of "Christos." The thumb (almost) touches the fingers, symbolizing how Christ unites both his divinity and his humanity.

❺ Dome: Look up into the dome. Because this church is dedicated to Mary—the patron and protector of the city—you'll see the Assumption of Mary. As the heavens open, and rings of saints and angels spiral upward, a hazy God greets Mary (in red). Beneath the dome is an inlaid-marble, Cosmati-style mosaic floor. The modern (and therefore controversial) marble altar and pulpit were carved by a Florentine artist in 2002.

• *Next to Galileo's Lamp, you'll find...*

❻ Giovanni Pisano's Pulpit (1301-1311): The 15-foot-tall, octagonal pulpit by Giovanni Pisano (c. 1240-1319) is the last, big-

gest, and most complex of the four pulpits created by the Pisano father-and-son team. Giovanni's father, Nicola, started the family tradition four decades earlier, carving the pulpit in the Baptistery. Giovanni grew up working side-by-side with his dad on numerous projects. Now on his own, he crams everything he's learned into his crowning achievement.

Giovanni left no stone uncarved in his pursuit of beauty. Four hundred intricately sculpted figures smother the pulpit, blurring the architectural outlines. In addition, the relief panels are actually curved, making it look less like an octagon than a circle. The creamy-white Carrara marble has the look and feel of carved French ivories, which the

Pisanos loved. Originally, this and the other pulpits were frosted with paint, gilding, and colored pastes.

At the base, lions roar and crouch over their prey, symbolizing how Christ (the lion) triumphs over Satan (the horse, as in the Four Horsemen of the Apocalypse).

Four of the pulpit's support "columns" are statues. The central "column" features three graceful ladies representing Faith, Hope, and Charity, the three pillars of Christianity. They in turn stand on the sturdy base of knowledge, representing the liberal arts taught at the University of Pisa. Another column is the pagan hero, Hercules, standing *contrapposto*, nude, holding his club and lion skin. To his right, Lady Church suckles the babies of the Old and New Testaments, while at her feet are the Four Virtues: Justice (with her scales), Moderation (modestly covering her nakedness), Courage (holding a lion), and Wisdom (with a horn of plenty).

Around the top of the pulpit, Christ's life unfolds in a series of panels saturated with carvings. The panels tilt out, so the viewer below has a better look, and they're bordered on top with a heavy cornice as a backdrop. Since the panels are curved and unframed, you "read" Christ's life less like a nine-frame comic strip and more like a continuous scroll.

The story unfolds from left to right, beginning at the back near the stairs:

1. Story of the Virgin Mary: Featuring Mary's birth, the Annunciation, and Mary meeting Elizabeth (John the Baptist's mother), among other events.

2. Nativity: Mary lounges across a bed, unfazed by labor and delivery. Her pose is clearly inspired by carved Roman sarcophagi (which you can see in the Camposanto Cemetery), showing the dearly departed relaxing for eternity atop their coffins. Mary and the babe are surrounded by angels (above) and shepherds (right).

3. Adoration of the Magi: The Wise Men ride in with horses and camels.

4. Presentation in the Temple: On the left side, Joseph and Mary hold Baby Jesus between them. On the right side of the panel, Giovanni adds the next scene in the story, when the nuclear family gets on a donkey and escapes into Egypt.

5. Massacre of the Innocents: Herod (at the top) turns and gestures dramatically, ordering the slaughter of all babies. A mother (bottom left corner) grabs her head in despair. Giovanni uses thick lips and big noses to let the faces speak the full range of human emotions. The soldiers in the tangled chaos are almost freestanding.

6. Kiss of Judas: Jesus is betrayed by a kiss (left side).

7. Crucifixion: An emaciated Christ is mourned by his followers, who turn every which way. A Roman horseman (bottom right corner) rides directly away from us—an example of Renaissance "foreshortening" a century before its time.

8. and 9. Last Judgment: Christ sits in the center, the dead rise from their graves, and he sends the good to heaven (left) and the bad to hell (right).

Giovanni was a better pure sculptor than his father. Armed with more sophisticated chisels, he could cut even deeper into the marble, freeing heads from the stone backdrop, creating almost freestanding, 3-D figures. Where Nicola showed figures either facing forward or in profile, Giovanni mastered the difficult three-quarters angle.

If the pulpit seems a bit cluttered and asymmetrical, blame Mussolini. Originally, Giovanni built the pulpit standing on the right side of the altar (the traditional location). But after a massive fire in 1595 (when the roof burned), the pulpit was disassembled and stored away for three centuries. In 1926, they pulled it out of storage, reassembled it on this spot...and ended up with pieces left over (now in other museums), leading scholars to debate the authenticity of the current look.

• *Find the following two sights in the right (south) transept. First, in an ornate, colonnaded, Baroque side-chapel at the end of the transept, you'll see...*

❼ **St. Ranieri's Body:** In a glass-lined casket on the altar, Pisa's patron saint lies mummified, encased in silver at his head, with his hair shirt covering his body. The silver, mask-like face dates from the year 2000 and is as realistic as possible—derived from an FBI-style computer scan of Ranieri's skull.

Ranieri Scucceri (1117-1161) was born into the city of Pisa at its peak, when the Field of Miracles was a construction zone. The son of a rich sea-trader, Ranieri chose the life of a partyer and musician. One day, he met a friar who inspired him to go seek deeper meaning in Jerusalem. Leaving his riches and the easy life, he joined a monastery and put on a hair shirt. When he finally returned to Pisa, he preached and performed miracles.

Ranieri, honored in grand style on June 16 and 17, is cause for Pisa's biggest local event—the Luminara—celebrated along the Arno with tens of thousands of candles lining the buildings and floating on the river. The next day, rowing teams play a game of capture-the-flag, racing to a boat in the Arno and shimmying up a long rope to claim the prize.

• *Look on the wall to the left to find...*

❽ **Emperor Henry VII's Tomb:** Pause at the tomb of Holy Roman Emperor Henry VII, whose untimely death plunged Pisa into its centuries-long decline. Henry lies sleeping, arms folded, his head turned to the side, resting on a soft pillow. This German king (c. 1275-1313) invaded Italy and was welcomed by Pisans as a nonpartisan leader who could bring peace to Italy's warring Guelphs and Ghibellines. In 1312, he was crowned emperor by the pope in Rome. He was preparing to polish off the last opposition when he caught a fever and died. No longer enjoying its connection with the Holy Roman Empire, Pisa declined.

• *Exit the church, turn left, and walk around to its back end (facing the Tower), where you'll find (under a canopy) the...*

❾ **Bronze Doors of St. Ranieri** (Porta San Ranieri): Designed by Bonanno Pisano (c. 1186)—who is thought by some historians to have been the Tower's first architect—the doors have 24 different panels that show Christ's story using the same simple, skinny figures found in Byzantine icons. (The doors are actually copies; the originals are housed—but not always on display—in the Duomo Museum.) Cast using the lost-wax technique, these doors were an inspiration for Lorenzo Ghiberti's bronze doors in Florence.

The story begins in the lower right panel ("Magis"), as the three Wise Men ride up a hill, heading toward...the panel to the left, where tiny Baby Jesus lies in a manger while angels and shepherds look down from above. Above the manger scene, King Herod ("Erodi") sits under a canopy (in Pisan Romanesque style) and orders a soldier to raise his sword to kill all potential Messiahs. The terrified mother pulls her hair out. In the panel to the right, John the Baptist stands under a swaying palm and baptizes the adult

Jesus, who wears the rippling River Jordan like a blanket. There are twenty more scenes which, if you were here as a medieval pilgrim, you wouldn't need this book to interpret.

THE REST OF THE FIELD OF MIRACLES

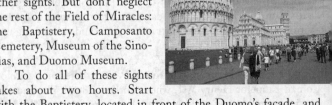

The Leaning Tower nearly steals the show from the massive cathedral, which muscles out the other sights. But don't neglect the rest of the Field of Miracles: the Baptistery, Camposanto Cemetery, Museum of the Sinopias, and Duomo Museum.

To do all of these sights takes about two hours. Start with the Baptistery, located in front of the Duomo's facade, and then head for Camposanto Cemetery, behind the church on the north side of the Field of Miracles. Next visit the Museum of the

Sinopias, across the street from the Baptistery entrance. If it has reopened, end your day at the Duomo Museum, housed behind the Tower.

Cost and Hours: €5 for one sight, €7 for two sights, €8 includes all the sights (see sidebar on page 432 for the rundown on various combo-tickets). All four sights share the same schedule: daily April-Sept 8:00-20:00, Oct 9:00-19:00, Nov-Feb 10:00-17:00, March 9:00-18:00. Note that the Duomo Museum will likely be closed for renovation through 2018.

Baptistery

Pisa's Baptistery is Italy's biggest. It's interesting for its pulpit and interior ambience, and especially great for its acoustics (which are demonstrated twice an hour).

Visiting the Baptistery: The building is 180 feet tall—John the Baptist on top is almost eye-to-eye with the tourists looking

out from the nearly 200-foot Leaning Tower. Notice that the Baptistery leans nearly six feet to the north (the Tower leans 15 feet to the south). The building (begun in 1153) is modeled on the circular-domed Church of the Holy Sepulchre in Jerusalem, seen by Pisan Crusaders who occupied Jerusalem in 1099.

From the outside, you see three distinct sections, which reflect the changing tastes of the years spent building it: simple Romanesque blind arches at the base (1153), ornate Gothic spires and pointed arches in the middle (1250), and a Renaissance dome (15th century). The roofing looks mismatched, but was intentionally designed with red clay tiles on the seaward side and lead tiles (more prestigious but prone to corrosion) on the sheltered east side. The statues of the midsection are by Nicola Pisano (c. 1220-1278, Giovanni's father), who sculpted the pulpit inside.

Interior: Inside, it's simple, spacious, and baptized with light. Tall arches atop thin columns once again echo the Campo's architectural theme of arches above

blank spaces. The columns encircle just a few pieces of religious furniture.

In the center sits the beautiful marble **octagonal font** (1246). A statue of the first Baptist, John the Baptist, stretches out his hand and says, "Welcome to my Baptistery."

PISA

The font contains plenty of space for baptizing adults by immersion (the medieval custom), plus four wells for dunking babies.

Baptismal fonts—where sinners symbolically die and are reborn—are traditionally octagons. The shape suggests a cross (symbolizing Christ's death), and the eight sides represent the eighth day of Christ's ordeal, when he was resurrected. The font's sides, carved with inlaid multicolored marble, feature circle-in-a-square patterns, indicating the interlocking of heaven and earth. The circles are studded with interesting faces, both human and animal. Behind the font, the altar features similar inlaid-marble work.

Nicola Pisano's Pulpit: On your left is the pulpit created by Niocola Pisano. Is this the world's first Renaissance sculpture? It's the first authenticated (signed) work by the "Giotto of sculpture," working in what came to be called the Renaissance style. The freestanding sculpture has classical columns, realistic people and animals, and 3-D effects in the carved panels.

The 15-foot-tall, hexagonal pulpit is the earliest (1260) and simplest of the four pulpits by the Pisano father-and-son team.

Nicola, born in southern Italy, settled in Pisa, where he found steady work. Ten-year-old Giovanni learned the art of pulpit-making here at the feet of his father.

The speaker's platform stands on columns that rest on the backs of animals, representing Christianity's triumph over paganism. The white Carrara-marble panels are framed by dark rose-colored marble, making a pleasant contrast. Originally, this and the other pulpits were touched up with paint, gilding, and colored pastes.

The relief panels, with scenes from the life of Christ, are more readable than the Duomo pulpit. They show bigger, simpler figures in dark marble "frames." Read left to right, starting from the back:

1. Nativity: Mary reclines across a bed like a Roman matron, a pose inspired by Roman sarcophagi, which had been found around Pisa in Nicola's day (on display in the Camposanto Cemetery, described later).

2. Adoration of the Magi: The Three Kings kneel before Baby Jesus in simple profile; but notice the strong 3-D of the horses' heads coming straight out of the panel. Just below and to the left of this relief, note the small statue of Hercules. Some art historians consider this the first Renaissance carving. Sculpted in 1260—200 years before Michelangelo—it's a nude depiction of a pagan character, with a realistic body standing in a believable *contrapposto* pose. This was clearly inspired by carvings found on ancient sarcophagi.

3. *Presentation in the Temple:* It lacks the star of the scene, the Christ Child, who got broken off, but on the panel's right side, a powerful, bearded man in a voluminous robe epitomizes Nicola's solemn classical style.

4. *Crucifixion:* Everyone faces either straight out or in profile; the Roman in front actually has to look back over his shoulder to taunt Jesus.

5. *Last Judgment:* Christ reigns over crowded, barely controlled chaos. The pulpit's lectern is an eagle clutching its prey, echoing the "triumph of Christianity" theme of the base.

Acoustics: Make a sound in here and it echoes for a good 10 seconds. A priest standing at the baptismal font (or a security guard today) can sing three tones within those 10 seconds—"Ave Maria"—and make a chord, singing haunting harmonies with himself. This medieval form of digital delay is due to the 250-foot-wide dome. Recent computer analysis suggests that the 15th-century architects who built the dome intended this building to function not just as a Baptistery, but also as a musical instrument. A security guard sings every 30 minutes (on the hour and half-hour), starting when the doors open in the morning.

Gallery: You can climb 75 steps to the interior gallery (midway up) for an impressive view back down on the baptismal font.

Camposanto Cemetery

Until people started getting excited about the Leaning Tower just a century ago, the big attraction in Pisa was its dreamy and exquisite cemetery, the Camposanto. Lined with faint frescoes, this centuries-old cemetery on the north side of the Campo is famous for its "Holy Land" dirt, reputedly brought here from the Middle East in the 12th century. Until 1278, tombs littered the ground around the ca-

thedral. Then things were cleaned up and the tombs were gathered into the Camposanto (built from 1278-1465). Highlights are the building's cloistered interior courtyard, some ancient sarcophagi, and the large 14th-century fresco, *The Triumph of Death*.

❷ **Self-Guided Tour:** Even though the Camposanto was bombed in World War II, it remains a powerful (if currently underappreciated) visit.

PISA

• *Past the ticket-taker, head straight out the walkway to the middle of the grassy...*

Courtyard: The delightful open-air courtyard is surrounded by an arcade with intricately carved tracery in the arches. The courtyard's grass grows on special dirt (said to turn a body into bones in a single day) shipped here by returning Crusaders from Jerusalem's Mount Calvary, where Christ was crucified.

• *Now head back into the...*

Arcade: The arcade floor is paved with the **coats of arms** of some 600 dearly departed Pisans. In death all are equal—the most humble peasant (or tourist) can walk upon these VIP tombstones. Today much of the marble flooring is scarred, the result of lead melting from the roof during WWII bombing.

Displayed in the arcade are dozens of ancient Roman **sarcophagi.** These coffins, which originally held dead Romans, were reused by medieval big shots. In anticipation of death, a wealthy Pisan would shop around, choose a good sarcophagus, and chip his message into it. When he died, his marble box was placed with the others around the exterior of the cathedral. Great sculptors such as Nicola and Giovanni Pisano passed them daily, gaining inspiration.

Circle the courtyard clockwise, noticing **traces of fresco** on the bare-brick walls. (We'll see some reconstructed frescoes later.)

As you round the corner, the huge **chains** you see hanging on the west wall once stretched across the mouth of Pisa's harbor as a defense. Then Genoa attacked, broke the chains, carried them off as a war trophy, and gave them to Pisa's archrival Florence. After unification (1860), they were returned to Pisa as a token of friendship.

Straight ahead is the cemetery's oldest object, an ochre-colored Greek tombstone. This **stele,** dating from the time of Alexander the Great (fourth century B.C.), shows a woman (seated) who's just given birth. A maid (standing) shows the baby while the mother gazes on adoringly.

In the floor 10 yards away, by the corner of the courtyard, is a **pavement slab** dedicated to an American artist, Deane Keller. After serving in Italy during World War II as one of the "Monuments Men," he helped rebuild the Camposanto Cemetery and restore its frescoes.

On the wall in the corner, what looks like a big, faded **bull's-eye** is the politically correct 14th-century view of the universe—everything held by Christ, with the earth clearly in the center.

• *Heading along the long north wall, you'll begin to see some...*

Restored Frescoes: After decorating these corridors for 600 years, the frescoes of Camposanto Cemetery were badly damaged in World War II. By the summer of 1944, Allied troops had secured much of southern Italy and pushed Nazi forces to the north bank of the Arno. German Field Marshal Kesselring dug in at Pisa, surrounded by the US Army's 91st Infantry. Germans and Americans lobbed artillery shells at each other. (The Americans even considered blowing up the Leaning Tower—the "Tiltin' Hilton" was suspected to be the German lookout point.) Most of the Field of Miracles was miraculously unscathed, but the Camposanto took a direct hit from a Yankee incendiary grenade. It melted the lead-covered arcade roof and peeled historic frescoes from the walls—one of the many tragic art losses of World War II. The Americans liberated the city on September 2 and rebuilt the Camposanto.

The frescoes have been under restoration ever since. Along these walls, you'll see the ones that have been returned to their original position.

• *At the far end of this corridor, you may see the (newly reinstalled) masterpiece fresco called...*

The Triumph of Death: This 1,000-square-foot fresco (c. 1340, by a 14th-century master) captures late-medieval Europe's concern with death—predating but still accurately depicting Pisa's mood in the wake of the bubonic plague (1348), which killed one in three Pisans. Well-dressed ladies and gents (left half of the painting) are riding gaily through the countryside when they come across three coffins with corpses (bottom left). Confronted with death, they each react differently—a woman puts her hand thoughtfully to her chin, a man holds his nose against the stench, while a horse leans in for a better whiff. Above them, a monk scours the Bible for the meaning of death.

In the right half of the painting, young people gather in a garden (bottom right) to play music (symbolizing earthly pleasure), oblivious to the death around them. Winged demons swoop down from above to pluck souls (shown as babies) from a pile of corpses, while winged angels fight them for the souls.

• *Having completed your circle, head back outside.*

Piazza: Stepping into the piazza, consider how this richly artistic but utilitarian square fit into the big picture of life. The

ensemble around you includes the Baptistery, the cathedral, the bell tower, the hospital (present-day Museum of the Sinopias), and the Christian cemetery you just visited. The Jewish cemetery is adjacent but just outside the walls. Pisa, a pragmatic port town, needed the money and business connections of the Jews and treated them relatively well for the age. Unlike in Rome or Venice, there was no Jewish ghetto here in the Middle Ages.

Museum of the Sinopias (Museo delle Sinopie)

Housed in a 13th-century hospital, this museum features the original preliminary sketches (sinopias) for the Camposanto's World War II-damaged frescoes. If you loved *The Triumph of Death* and others in the Camposanto, or if you're interested in fresco technique, this museum is worthwhile. If not, you'll wonder why you're here.

Visiting the Museum: Whether or not you pay to go in, you can watch two free videos in the entry lobby that serve to orient you to the square: a seven-minute, 3-D computer tour of the complex and a 15-minute story of the Tower, its tilt, and its fix. Good students might want to come here first for this orientation.

Once inside the turnstile, the stars of this museum are the sinopias: sketches made in red paint directly on the wall, designed to guide the making of the final colored fresco. The master always did the sinopia himself. It was a way for him (and for those who paid for the work) to see exactly how the scene would look in its designated spot. If it wasn't quite right, the master changed a detail here and there. Next, assistants made a "cartoon" by tracing the sinopia onto large sheets of paper *(cartone)*. Then the sinopia was plastered over. To put the drawing back on the wall, assistants perforated the drawing on the cartoon, hung the cartoon over the wall, and dabbed it with a powdered bag of charcoal. This process printed dotted lines onto the newly plastered wall, re-creating the cartoon. While the plaster was still wet, the master and his team quickly filled in the color and details, producing the final frescoes (now on display at the Camposanto). These sinopias—never meant to be seen—were uncovered by the bombing and restoration of the Camposanto and brought here.

The museum presents several sinopias in a one-way route. Just past the ticket-taker, you'll see the multiringed, earth-centric, Ptolemaic universe of the *Theological Cosmography*. Continue to your right to find a faint *Crucifixion* and scenes from the Old Testament. At the end of the long hall, climb the stairs to the next floor to find more red-tinted sinopias: *The Triumph of Death*, *The Last Judgment*, and *Hell*.

Duomo Museum (Museo dell'Opera del Duomo)

Near the Tower is the entrance to the Duomo Museum, which houses many of the original statues and much of the artwork that once adorned the Campo's buildings (where copies stand today), notably the statues by Nicola and Giovanni Pisano. It's big on Pisan art, displaying treasures of the cathedral, paintings, silverware, and sculptures (from the 12th to 14th century), as well as ancient Egyptian, Etruscan, and Roman artifacts. The museum will likely be closed for restoration through sometime in 2018. But if it's open, here's some of what you may see.

The museum has several large-scale wooden models of the Duomo, Baptistery, and Tower, as well as the Duomo's original 12th-century bronze doors of St. Ranieri, with scenes from the life of Jesus, done by Bonanno Pisano. Farther in, you can stand face-to-face with the Pisanos' very human busts, which once ringed the outside of the Baptistery. Giovanni Pisano's stone *Madonna del Colloquio* solemnly exchanges gazes with Baby Jesus in her arms. The most charming piece is Giovanni's small, carved-ivory *Madonna and Child*. Mary leans back gracefully to admire Baby Jesus, her pose matching the original shape of what she's carved from—an elephant's tusk.

You'll see a mythical sculpted hippogriff (a medieval jackalope) and other oddities brought back from the Holy Land by Pisan Crusaders. The church treasury is here as well, with vestments, chalices, and bishops' staves.

On the next floor up, you'll see the fine inlaid woodwork that once graced the choir stalls of the sacristy, as well as illuminated manuscripts. The collection of antiquities includes Etruscan funerary urns with reclining people—the inspiration for the Roman sarcophagi that inspired the Pisanos. Beyond the ancient sculptures are beautiful small-scale copies of the Camposanto frescoes, painted in the 1830s. There's also a scene that shows the building's appearance before it was bombed.

The museum's grassy interior courtyard has a two-story, tourist-free view of the Tower, Duomo, and Baptistery.

OTHER SIGHTS IN PISA
City Walls
The city is experimenting with opening the city walls that run behind the Field of Miracles to visitors, but details are constantly in flux. If you see people up on the walls, ask around about how to do it: The view from atop the walls offers a different angle on the great buildings.

Museo Nazionale di San Matteo
In a former convent on the river, this art museum displays early medieval to 15th-century works, including sculptures, illuminated manuscripts, and paintings on wood by pre- and early-Renaissance masters Martini, Masaccio, and others. It's a fine collection—especially its painted wood crucifixes—and gives you a chance to see Pisan innovation in 11th- to 13th-century art, before Florence took the lead.

Cost and Hours: €5, Tue-Sat 8:30-19:00, Sun until 13:00, closed Mon, near Piazza San Paolo at Lungarno Mediceo, a 5-minute walk upriver (east) from the main bridge, tel. 050-541-865.

Sleeping in Pisa

Pisa is an easy side-trip from Florence or Lucca, either of which is a more all-around pleasant place to stay. But there's more to Pisa than the Tower, and if you want time to experience it, consider a night here. To locate these hotels, see the map on page 424.

NORTH OF THE RIVER, NEAR THE TOWER

$$ Hotel Royal Victoria, a classy place along the Arno River, has been run by the Piegaja family since 1837 (though it was a hotel for more than 400 years before that and is likely the oldest hotel in Italy). Its tiled hallways and 38 creaky, historical rooms filled with antiques and chipped plaster may not be for everybody. But with the elegant ambience of a bygone era, it's ideal for romantics who missed out on the Grand Tour. The location—midway between the Tower and Pisa Centrale train station—is the most atmospheric of my listings (RS%, family rooms, air-con in most rooms, elevator, pay parking garage, bike rental, lush communal terrace, Lungarno Pacinotti 12, tel. 050-940-111, www.royalvictoria.it, post@royalvictoria.it, proud owner Nicola Piegaja).

$$ Hotel Pisa Tower provides a yesteryear elegance in a stately mansion with 14 rooms thoughtfully decorated with clean lines and graceful warmth. In good weather, enjoy the garden for breakfast or an *aperitivo*. The annex, with 12 similar rooms, overlooks the noisy, tacky-souvenir-stand square just outside the gate to the Field of Miracles, along a busy street. Three more rooms are in a nondescript apartment block across the street from the main building (family rooms, air-con, pay parking; a long block west of Piazza Manin at Via Andrea Pisano 23, tel. 050-520-0700, www.hotelpisatower.com, info@hotelpisatower.com).

$$ Hotel Villa Kinzica, a last resort, has 30 tired, worn rooms with high ceilings—and a prime location just steps from the Field of Miracles; ask for a room with a view of the Tower, ideally #75 (family rooms, air-con, elevator, Piazza Arcivescovado 2, tel. 050-560-419, www.hotelvillakinzica.com, info@hotelvillakinzica.com).

$ Casa San Tommaso has 22 classic-feeling, homey, reverent rooms on a quiet back lane about a five-minute walk from the Tower (air-con, Via San Tommaso 13, tel. 050-830-782, www.casasantommaso.it, santommaso@paimturismo.it).

$ Pensione Helvetia, a friendly, no-frills, clean, and quiet inn just 100 yards from the Tower, rents 29 economical rooms over four floors. Ask them to show you the "biggest cactus in Tuscany" in their garden courtyard...it really is (cheaper rooms with shared bath, family suites, no breakfast, ceiling fans, no elevator, Via Don G. Boschi 31, tel. 050-553-084, www.pensionehelvetiapisa.com, helvetiapisatower@gmail.com, Micaele and Sandra).

SOUTH OF THE RIVER, NEAR THE TRAIN STATION

This zone is far less atmospheric than the zone near the Tower— with a lot of concrete, congestion, and loitering. Stay here only if you value the convenience of proximity to the station.

$$$ Hotel Alessandro della Spina, run by Pio and family, has 16 elegant and colorful rooms, each named after a flower (RS%—use code "NEW GUEST," air-con, elevator, pay parking; leaving the station, go right on Via Filippo Corridoni, take the third left on Via Alessandro della Spina, then find #5; tel. 050-502-777, www.hoteldellaspina.it, info@hoteldellaspina.it, Louisa).

$ Hotel Milano has 10 stale, no-frills rooms in a humdrum area close to the train station (RS%, cheaper rooms with shared bath, family rooms, no breakfast, air-con, Via Mascagni 14, tel. 050-23-162, www.hotelmilano.pisa.it, hotelmilano.pisa@gmail.com, Giada).

Eating in Pisa

A QUICK LUNCH CLOSE TO THE TOWER

The **Via Santa Maria** tourist strip is pedestrianized and lined with touristy eateries. They seem competitive, and you can get a quick sandwich, pizza, or salad at any number of places along this street.

$$ Pizzeria al Bagno di Nerone, a five-minute walk from the Tower, is particularly popular with students. Belly up to the bar and grab a slice to go, or sit in their small dining room for a whole pie. Try the *cecina*, a crêpe-like garbanzo-bean flatbread (Wed-Mon 12:00-14:30 & 17:45-22:30, closed Tue, Largo Carlo Fedeli 26, tel. 050-551-085).

REAL MEALS DEEPER IN THE TOWN CENTER

Make no mistake: Pisa is in Tuscany. And if you want to sample some famously delicious Tuscan cuisine, these restaurants make it easy. All are within about a 10- to 15-minute walk from the Tower, near the river, and several are within a few steps of the old Renaissance-style market loggia, Piazza delle Vettovaglie (described on page 428).

$$ La Vineria di Piazza is a quintessential little Tuscan trattoria tucked under the arcades of Piazza delle Vettovaglie. The chalkboard menu lists today's seasonal choices: a few *antipasti*, a few *primi* (homemade pastas and soups), and a few *secondi*. Ask for a *bis* or even a *tris* to get a tasty sampling of two or three homemade pastas. English-fluent Claudia welcomes you to share dishes family-ly-style, and she and her family make this place feel sophisticated, but without pretense. Sit in the elegantly simple interior or out at long tables facing the market. They typically serve lunch only, as the square can be a bit sketchy after dark (daily 12:30-15:00, Piazza delle Vettovaglie 14, tel. 050-382-0433).

$$ Antica Trattoria il Campano, just off the market square, has a typically Tuscan menu and a candlelit, stay-awhile atmosphere. The ground floor, surrounded by wine bottles, is cozier, while the upstairs—with high wood-beam ceilings—is classier (Thu-Tue 19:30-22:45, closed Wed, open Sat-Sun for lunch in high season, Via Cavalca 19, tel. 050-580-585, Giovanna).

$$ Il Vegusto is a reasonably priced, quality, vegan restaurant with elegant modern ambience. It sits all by its lonesome on a gloomy square a block off the river (Mon-Fri 12:30-14:30 & 19:30-22:00, Sat 19:30-22:00 only, closed Sun, Piazza dei Facchini 13, tel. 050-520-0667).

SMART, MOSTLY-LOCALS OPTIONS IN THE TOWN CENTER

Piazza Dante is a characteristic square popular with university students and fun-loving locals, and graced with several good and economical eateries. I'd survey the five or six options on or near the square before sitting down.

$ Caffetteria BetsaBea is handy for takeaway meals, has good seating on the square, whips up hearty and creative salads—which you design with their interactive menu, and is popular for its *aperitivo* happy hour (Mon-Sat 8:00-24:00, closed Sun, Piazza San Frediano 6).

Just a few steps down Via l'Arancio is **$ Pizzeria l'Arancio,** where for decades Beppe and Papa Filippo have been serving pizza, *antipasti,* focaccia, and the delightful crêpe-like garbanzo-bean flatbread known as *cecina* (daily 12:00-15:30 & 19:00-22:00, Via l'Arancio 1, tel. 050-500-729).

$ Il Montino is a rambunctious favorite for tasty, no-frills pizza. Tucked behind a church in a grubby corner deep in the old center, it has a loyal following—particularly among students. Enjoy full pies in the *nuovo rustico* interior or out on the alley, or get a slice to go (Mon-Sat 11:30-15:00 & 17:30-22:30, closed Sun, Vicolo del Monte 1, tel. 050-598-695).

$$ Orzo Bruno—*il birrificio artigiano* ("the artisan brew-pub")—is a lively, rollicking brew hall filled with Pisans of all ages enjoying rock, jazz, and blues, with seven different microbrews (including a rotating tap) and a simple menu of sandwiches and salads (nightly 19:00-late, a block off Borgo Stretto at Via Case Dipinte 6, tel. 050-578-802).

Pisa Connections

Pisa has good connections by train, bus, or car. The busy airport (popular with discount airlines) is practically downtown. Note that the Pisa Centrale train station area is a maze of tunnels; leave yourself enough time to find the ticket machines and make it to the platform.

Side-Tripping to Lucca: Pisa and Lucca are well-connected by train and by bus (both options are about €3), making a half-day side-trip from one town to the other particularly easy. The **train** takes about half as long as the bus (about 25 minutes compared with 50 minutes)—but getting to the Centrale train station is more time-consuming. Perhaps the best option: If you're heading to Lucca from the Leaning Tower, you can catch the train at Pisa San Rossore Station, about a five-minute walk from the Field of Miracles: From the tacky souvenir zone just outside the gate, cross the busy street and continue straight ahead along Via Andrea Pisano. After two blocks, you'll see the gray gateway to the train station on your right.

A handy **bus** connects the Field of Miracles with Lucca's Piazzale Giuseppe Verdi in about 50 minutes (€3, Mon-Sat hourly, fewer on Sun, buy ticket on bus; in Pisa, wait at the Vaibus signpost off of Piazza Manin, immediately outside the wall behind the Baptistery on the right). You can also catch this bus at Pisa's airport, or at Pisa Centrale train station.

From Pisa Centrale Station by Train to: Florence (2-3/hour, 45-75 minutes), **Livorno** (2-3/hour, 20 minutes), **Rome** (2/hour, many change in Florence, 3-4 hours), **La Spezia**, gateway to the Cinque Terre (about hourly, 1.5 hours), **Siena** (2/hour, 2 hours, change at Empoli), **Lucca** (1-2/hour, 30 minutes, also stops at Pisa San Rossore Station).

By Car: The drive between Pisa and Florence is that rare case where the regular highway (free, more direct, and at least as fast) is a better deal than the autostrada.

By Plane: Pisa's handy **Galileo Galilei Airport**—just two miles from the train station ("So close you can walk," locals brag)—handles both international and domestic flights and tends to have more departures with lower fares than the Florence airport (airport code: PSA, tel. 050-849-300, www.pisa-airport.com). The new "Pisa Mover" train offers an easy connection to Pisa Centrale train station (€2.70, daily 6:00-24:00, every 5 minutes, 5-minute trip, www.pisa-mover.com). The airport is also on the line for public bus LAM Rossa, which stops first at the station and then continues to

the Leaning Tower (usually every 10 minutes, less frequent off-season, €1.20 ticket at kiosk, €2 on board). A taxi into town costs €10.

Pisa's airport is handy for other towns as well: The bus to **Lucca** (described above) originates at the airport. To reach **Florence,** the **Cinque Terre,** or other destinations in Italy, take the shuttle bus or Pisa Mover to Pisa Centrale train station and connect from there (allow about 1.5 hours total). Two companies also run buses from the airport directly to Florence's Santa Maria Novella train station in about 1.5 hours (about €5 for either one): Terravision (about hourly, www.terravision.eu) and Autostradale (typically coordinated with Ryanair flights, www.autostradale.it).

LUCCA

Surrounded by well-preserved ramparts, layered with history, alternately quaint and urbane, Lucca charms its visitors. The city is a paradox. Though it hasn't been involved in a war since 1430, it is Italy's most impressive fortress city, encircled by a perfectly intact wall. Most cities tear down their walls to make way for modern traffic, but Lucca's effectively keeps out both traffic and, it seems, the stress of the modern world. Locals are very protective of their wall, which they enjoy like a community roof garden.

Lucca has no single monumental sight to attract tourists—it's simply a uniquely human and undamaged, never-bombed city.

Romanesque churches seem to be around every corner, as do fun-loving and shady piazzas filled with soccer-playing children. Perhaps it's a blessing that Lucca has no Uffizi or Leaning Tower—that lack of big-league sights keeps away the most obnoxious slice of tourism: People who just want to tick an item off their "to do" list. Instead, refreshingly untrampled Lucca seems to attract travelers who want to melt into the local lifestyle for a few days.

Lucca is charming and well-preserved, and even its touristic center—the mostly traffic-free old town—feels more local than touristy (aside from a few cruise excursions from nearby Livorno that pass through each day). Refreshingly, the city lacks dodgy vendors selling junk on every corner. While many cities throughout Tuscany are tagged by Florentine lions and Medici balls, Lucca is proudly free of those symbols of conquest. The city is big enough to have its own heritage and pride, yet small enough that it seems like the Lucchesi (loo-KAY-zee) all went to school together. Simply put, Lucca has elegance and plenty of reasons to be proud.

PLANNING YOUR TIME

Lucca is easy to enjoy. With a day in town, start with my self-guided Lucca Walk and spend the afternoon biking (or strolling) atop the wall, popping in on whatever other sights interest you, and browsing. Music lovers enjoy the Puccini concert in the evening. The busy sightseer can consider visiting Pisa's Field of Miracles (with the Leaning Tower), an easy half-day side-trip away by train (to Pisa San Rossore Station in less than 30 minutes) or bus (from downtown Lucca to the Leaning Tower in 50 minutes).

Orientation to Lucca

Lucca (population 87,000, with roughly 10,000 living within the town walls) is big enough to be engaging but small enough to be manageable. Everything of interest to a visitor is within the 2.5-mile-long city wall; it takes just 20 minutes to walk from one end of the old town to the other. The train station sits south of the wall (just beyond the cathedral), and the bus to and from Pisa stops just inside the western tip. My self-guided walk traces the main thoroughfares through town; venturing beyond these streets, you realize Lucca is bigger than it first seems, but its back streets are very sleepy. While the core of the town is based on an old Roman grid street plan, the surrounding areas—especially near the circular footprint of the amphitheater—are more confusing. This, combined with tall houses and a lack of consistent signage, makes Lucca easy to get lost in. Pick up the town map at your hotel and use it.

TOURIST INFORMATION

Lucca's helpful TI is on Piazzale Giuseppe Verdi (daily 9:00-19:00, Oct-March until 17:00, futuristic WC, baggage storage—€1.50/hour for 2 bags, tel. 0583-583-150, www.turismo.lucca.it).

ARRIVAL IN LUCCA

By Train: See "Helpful Hints" for specifics on checking your bags. To reach the city center from the train station, walk toward the walls and head left, to the entry at Porta San Pietro. Or, if you don't mind steps, go straight ahead and follow the path through the moat-like park to go up and over the wall. Taxis may be waiting out front; otherwise, try calling 025-353 (ignore any recorded message—just wait for a live operator); a ride from the station to Piazza dell'Anfiteatro costs about €10.

By Bus: Buses from Pisa, Viareggio, and nearby villages arrive inside the walls at Piazzale Giuseppe Verdi (near the TI).

By Car: Don't try to drive within the walls. Much of the center of Lucca is designated a "ZTL" (limited traffic zone), which could cost you a €90 fine. The old town is ringed by convenient parking lots.

Parking is always free in Piazzale Don Franco, a five-minute walk north of the city walls. If you must park inside the city walls, try just inside Porta Santa Maria, at the northern edge of town (€1.50/hour). Or park outside the gates near the train station or on the boulevard surrounding the city (meter rates vary; about €1/hour). Overnight parking (20:00-8:00) on city streets and in city lots is usually free. Check with your hotelier to be sure.

HELPFUL HINTS

Shops and Museums Alert: City-run museums are closed Sunday and Monday. Shops close most of Sunday and Monday mornings.

Markets: Lucca's atmospheric markets are worth visiting. On the weekend of the third Sunday of the month, one of the largest **antique markets** in Italy sprawls in the blocks between Piazza Antelminelli and Piazza San Giovanni (8:00-19:00). The last weekend of the month, local artisans sell **arts and crafts** around town, mainly near the cathedral (also 8:00-19:00). At the **general market,** held Wednesdays and Saturdays on Piazza Don Franco Baroni, you'll find produce and household goods (8:30-13:00).

Concerts: San Giovanni Church hosts one-hour concerts featuring a pianist and singers performing works by hometown composer Giacomo Puccini (€20 at the door, €18 in advance—buy tickets at the venue, the TI, or possibly your hotel; daily April-Oct at 19:00, www.puccinielasualucca.com).

Festivals: On September 13 and 14, the city celebrates Volto Santo ("Holy Face"), with a procession of the treasured local crucifix and a fair in Piazza Antelminelli. Music lovers enjoy the annual Puccini Days festival in November.

Baggage Storage: For train travelers, there are two good options for paid baggage storage: **Cicli Primo,** in the train station at track 1 (€5/day, daily 8:00-20:00, shorter hours off-season, tel. 347-632-4315), and **Tourist Center Lucca,** on the left side of the square as you exit the train station (at #203; daily 9:00-19:00, Nov-March until 18:00). If you're arriving by bus, the **TI** on Piazzale Giuseppe Verdi also stores bags (see earlier).

Laundry: Lavanderia Self-Service Niagara is just off Piazza

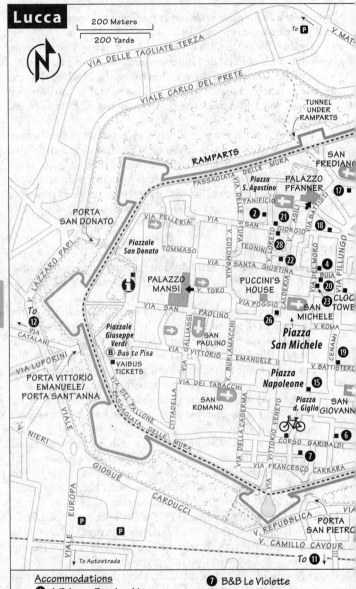

Lucca

200 Meters
200 Yards

N

VIA DELLE TAGLIATE TERZA

VIALE CARLO DEL PRETE

To P

V. MAT

TUNNEL
UNDER
RAMPARTS

RAMPARTS

SAN
FREDIANO

PASSAGGIATA DELLE MURA

PORTA
SAN DONATO

Piazza
S. Agostino

PALAZZO
PFANNER

17

VIA PELLERIA

VIA

PANIFICIO

2

21

VIA BATTISTI

18

VIA DELLE STUFA

V. SAN

VIA ASILI

GIORGIO

Piazzale
San Donato

TOMMASO

VIA COLOMBAIA

VIA LORETO

28

VIA DEL MORO

V. LAZZARO PAPI

PALAZZO
MANSI

VIA TOR O

SANTA GIUSTINA

22

VIA TEGNINI

PUCCINI'S
HOUSE

4

VIA FILLUNGO

BUIA

20

i

VIA SAN

PAOLINO

VIA POGGIO

CALDERIA

23

CLOC
TOWE

VIA GALLIASSI

SAN
PAULINO

SAN
MICHELE

To

12

VIA
CATALANI

Piazzale
Giuseppe
Verdi

B Bus to Pisa

VAIBUS
TICKETS

26

Piazza
San Michele

V. ROMA

V. LUPORINI

VIA SAN VITTORIO

VIA BURLAMACCHI

EMANUELE II

CENAMI

19

PORTA VITTORIO
EMANUELE/
PORTA SANT'ANNA

V. NIERI

CITTADELLA

VIA DELLA CASERMA

VIA DEI TABACCHI

Piazza
Napoleone

V. BATTISTERO

15

SAN
ROMANO

SAN
GIOVANN

VIA DEL PALLONE

VIALE

PASSAGGIATA DELLE MURA

Piazza
d. Giglio

VIA VITTORIO VENETO

6

V. EUROPA

GIOSUÈ

CARDUCCI

CORSO GARIBALDI

VIA FRANCESCO CARRARA

7

P

P

To Autostrada

V. REPUBBLICA

PORTA
SAN PIETRO

VIA

V. CAMILLO CAVOUR

To 11

PORTA
SAN DONATO

LUCCA

Accommodations

1 A Palazzo Busdraghi
2 La Locanda Sant'Agostino
3 La Romea B&B
4 La Bohème B&B
5 Hotel la Luna
6 Albergo San Martino &
   Hotel Diana Reception
7 B&B Le Violette
8 Ostello San Frediano
9 To Hotel San Marco
10 Hotel Rex
11 To Hotel Moderno
12 La Mimosa B&B
13 Sogni d'Oro Guesthouse

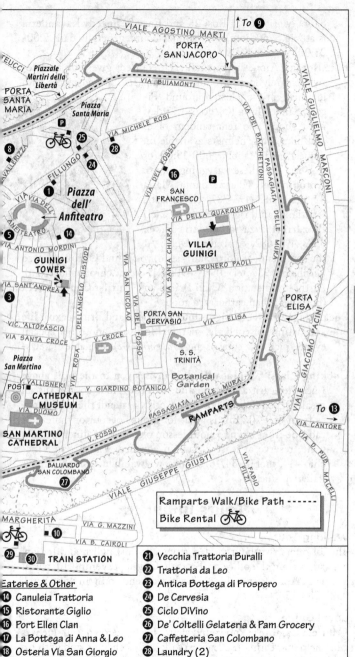

Ramparts Walk/Bike Path -----
Bike Rental 🚲

Eateries & Other
14 Canuleia Trattoria
15 Ristorante Giglio
16 Port Ellen Clan
17 La Bottega di Anna & Leo
18 Osteria Via San Giorgio
19 Il Cuore Enogastronomia
20 Pizzeria da Felice

21 Vecchia Trattoria Buralli
22 Trattoria da Leo
23 Antica Bottega di Prospero
24 De Cervesia
25 Ciclo DiVino
26 De' Coltelli Gelateria & Pam Grocery
27 Caffetteria San Colombano
28 Laundry (2)
29 Tourist Center Lucca (Bag Storage, Bikes)
30 Cicli Primo Bike (Bag Storage, Bikes)

LUCCA

Santa Maria at Via Rosi 26 and **Easy & Speedy Lavanderia** is at Via San Giorgio 45 (similar hours, generally daily 7:00-23:00).

Bike Rental: A one-hour rental (ID required) gives you time for two leisurely loops around the ramparts. Several places with identical prices cluster around Piazza Santa Maria (€3/hour, €15/day, most shops also rent tandem bikes and bike carts, helmets available on request, daily about 9:00-19:00 or sunset). Try these easygoing shops: **Antonio Poli** (Piazza Santa Maria 42, tel. 0583-493-787, enthusiastic Cristiana) and, right next to it, **Cicli Bizzarri** (Piazza Santa Maria 32, tel. 0583-496-682, Australian Dely). At the south end, at Porta San Pietro, you'll find **Chronò** (Corso Garibaldi 93, tel. 0583-490-591, www.chronobikes.com). At the train station, **Cicli Primo** and **Tourist Center Lucca** (both described earlier) are good.

Local Magazine: For insights into American and British expat life and listings of concerts, markets, festivals, and other special events, pick up a copy of the *Grapevine* (€2), available at newsstands.

Cooking Class: Gianluca Pardini invites you to the hills above Lucca to learn to prepare and then eat a four-course Tuscan meal. Depending on how many others attend, the price ranges from €50-70. This is great for groups of four or more (€14 cab ride from town, 3-hour lesson plus time to dine, includes wine, reserve at least 2 days in advance, Via di San Viticchio 414, mobile 347-678-7447, www.italiancuisine.it, info@italiancuisine.it).

Tours in Lucca

Walking Tours

The TI offers two-hour guided city walks in English and Italian, departing from the office on Piazzale Giuseppe Verdi (€10, pay at TI, daily April-Oct at 14:00, likely weekends only in winter, tel. 0583-583-150).

Local Guide

Gabriele Calabrese knows and shares his hometown well. He was a big help in creating the Lucca Walk in this chapter, and with his guidance you'll go even deeper into the city (€130/3 hours, by foot or bike, tel. 0583-342-404, mobile 347-788-0667, www.turislucca.com, turislucca@turislucca.com).

Lucca Walk

This hour-long self-guided walk (not counting time at the sights) connects Lucca's main points of interest by way of its most entertaining streets. A visit to Lucca has no single, logical starting point (since the bus stop, train station, and parking lots are in different corners of town), so I've started this walk right in the heart of things, at Lucca's main square. For the classic view of the circular square, stand at the east end of the oval at #29.

❶ Piazza dell'Anfiteatro

The architectural ghost of a Roman amphitheater can be felt in the delightful Piazza dell'Anfiteatro. With the fall of Rome, the the-

ater (which seated 10,000 and sat just outside the rectangular city walls) was gradually cannibalized for its stones and inhabited by people living in a mishmash of huts. The huts were cleared away at the end of the 19th century to better show off the town's illustrious past and make one purely secular square (every other square is dominated by a church) for the town market. The modern street level is nine feet above the original arena floor.

Today, the square is a circle of touristy shops, galleries (the art at #34 shows traditional folk scenes in Lucca), mediocre restaurants, and inviting al fresco cafés.

For a cheap seat on the square, buy a gelato at **Gelateria Anfiteatro**—it's made by Antonio and his son Fabrizio under an ancient arch at #18. You're welcome to nurse it for the takeout price at one of their tables.

Leave the amphitheater through the arch at #42, turn left, and begin circling it counterclockwise along Via Anfiteatro. At #89-95—right where you enter the street—is the butcher's shop (Carni Val Serchio) where Felicino prepares meat and special dishes for appreciative locals. Farther along, on the right at #75, "The Loom of Penelope" is an innovative and caring place that helps young people with mental problems and depression deal with their troubles through weaving therapy. Across from #61, look up and study the exterior of the Roman amphitheater and how medieval scavengers transformed it. Barbarians didn't know how to make bricks. But they could recycle building material and stack stones in order

Lucca Walk

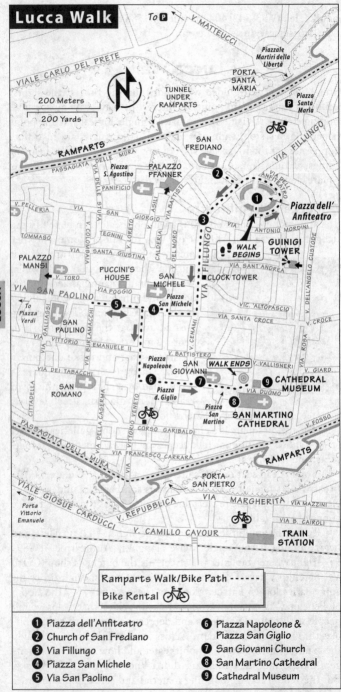

To P V. MATTEUCCI

VIALE CARLO DEL PRETE

200 Meters
200 Yards

N

Piazzale Martiri della Libertà

PORTA SANTA MARIA

Piazza Santa Maria

RAMPARTS

PASSAGGIATA DELLE MURA

TUNNEL UNDER RAMPARTS

VIA FILLUNGO

Piazza S. Agostino

PALAZZO PFANNER

SAN FREDIANO

2

VIA DELL' ANFITEATRO

PANIFICIO

V. PELLERIA

VIA

VIA DELLE STUFA

SAN GIORGIO

VIA ASILI

VIA BATTISTI

CALDERIA

VIA DEL MORO

3

1 Piazza dell' Anfiteatro

VIA

ANTONIO MORDINI

VIA COLOMBIA

SANTA GIUSTINA

V. TOMMASO

VIA TEGNINI

WALK BEGINS

GUINIGI TOWER

V. DELL'ANGELO CUSTODE

PALAZZO MANSI

V. TORO

PUCCINI'S HOUSE

VIA POGGIO

SAN MICHELE

Piazza San Michele

4

VIA SANT'ANDREA

CLOCK TOWER

VIA FILLUNGO

VIA SAN PAOLINO

To Piazza Verdi

SAN PAOLINO

VIA BURLAMACCHI

5

VIC. 'ALTOPASCIO

VIA SANTA CROCE

V. CROCE

VIA GALLIASSI

VIA VITTORIO EMANUELE II

V. CENAMI

V. BATTISTERO

V. ROSA

VIA DEI TABACCHI

Piazza Napoleone

SAN GIOVANNI

6

7

WALK ENDS

V. VALLISNERI

V. GIARD.

9 CATHEDRAL MUSEUM

SAN ROMANO

CITTADELLA

VIA DELLA CASERMA

VITTORIO VENETO

Piazza d. Giglio

Piazza San Martino

8

VIA DUOMO

SAN MARTINO CATHEDRAL

V. FOSSO

PASSAGGIATA DELLA MURA

CORSO GARIBALDI

VIA FRANCESCO CARRARA

VIALE GIOSUÈ CARDUCCI

To Porta Vittorio Emanuele

V. REPUBBLICA

PORTA SAN PIETRO

VIA MARGHERITA

RAMPARTS

VIA MAZZINI

V. B. CAIROLI

V. CAMILLO CAVOUR

TRAIN STATION

LUCCA

Ramparts Walk/Bike Path ------
Bike Rental 🚲

1 Piazza dell'Anfiteatro
2 Church of San Frediano
3 Via Fillungo
4 Piazza San Michele
5 Via San Paolino

6 Piazza Napoleone & Piazza San Giglio
7 San Giovanni Church
8 San Martino Cathedral
9 Cathedral Museum

to camp out in Roman ruins. As you circle for the next 100 yards or so, study the stonework and see how medieval buildings filled the ancient arches. At #18 (on the left), you may see Antonio and Fabrizio busy making their gelato. Next you'll pass the tempting Pizzicheria la Grotta *salumi* shop (on the left at #2) with lots of gifty edibles—worth popping into for a peek at local specialties. Then you reach the busy shopping street, Via Fillungo.

• *Turn left and walk a block down Via Fillungo, then go right and cross a little square to the big church with a fine mosaic.*

❷ Church of San Frediano

This impressive church was built in 1112 by the pope to one-up Lucca's bishop and his spiffy cathedral (which we'll see later on this

walk). Lucca was the first Mediterranean stop on the pilgrim route from northern Europe, and the pope wanted to remind pilgrims that the action, the glory, and the papacy awaited them in Rome. Therefore, he had the church made "Roman-esque." The pure marble facade frames an early Christian Roman-style mosaic of Christ with his 12 apostles.

Cost and Hours: €3, daily 9:00-18:00, Piazza San Frediano.

Visiting the Church: Inside, stand at the back (under a fine 16th-century pipe organ) and survey the classic basilica plan. The arches lope rhythmically to the altar (reminding me of the victory action when you win a solitaire game on your computer). The 40 powerful columns and lacy capitals (many of them recycled and ancient Roman) reminded pilgrims that, though this church may be impressive, the finale of their pilgrimage—in Rome—was worth the hike.

From here, circle the church interior counterclockwise to see the baptistery, Zita chapel, a painting of the Assumption, and a gorgeous statue of Mary.

Near where you enter, look for the 12th-century **baptistery.** Walk around it and follow the Old Testament stories about Moses (with the evil Pharaoh played by Lucca's contemporary arch enemy—the Holy Roman Emperor).

A few steps away is the **Chapel of St. Zita,** where St. Zita's actual body has been since 1278. Zita was a local Cinderella figure (abandoned by her parents when they were unable to care for her, she became a servant to a rich family and helped the poor). A painting on the left wall shows the famous episode: Her angry master thought he'd caught her disobediently distributing bread hidden in her apron to the poor—but when he opened up the apron, the bread

The History of Lucca

Lucca began as a Roman settlement. In fact, the grid layout of the streets (and the shadow of an amphitheater) survives from Roman times. Trace the rectangular Roman wall—indicated by today's streets—on the map. As in typical Roman towns, two main roads quartered the fortified town, crossing at what was the forum (main market and religious/political center)—today's Piazza San Michele. The amphitheater sat just outside the original Roman walls.

Christianity came here early; it's said that the first bishop of Lucca was a disciple of St. Peter. While churches were built here as early as the fourth century, the majority of Lucca's elegant Romanesque churches date from about the 12th century.

Feisty Lucca, though never a real power, enjoyed a long period of independence (maintained by clever diplomacy). Aside from 30 years of being ruled from Pisa in the 14th century, Lucca was basically an independent city-state until Napoleon came to town.

In the Middle Ages, wealthy Lucca's economy was built on the silk industry, dominated by the Guinigi (gwee-NEE-jee) family. Paolo Guinigi (1372-1432)—whose name you'll see everywhere around town—was the Lord of Lucca for the first three decades of the 15th century, during which time he spurred the town's growth and development. Without silk, Lucca would have been just another sleepy Italian town. By 1500, the town had 3,000 silk looms employing 25,000 workers. Banking was also big. Many pilgrims stopped here on their way to the Holy Land, deposited their money for safety...and never returned to pick it up.

In its heyday, Lucca packed 160 towers—one on nearly every corner—and 70 churches within its walls. Each tower was the home of a wealthy merchant family. Towers were many stories tall, with single rooms stacked atop each other: ground-floor shop, upstairs living room, and top-floor fire-safe kitchen, all connected by exterior wooden staircases. The rooftop was generally a vegetable garden, with trees providing shade. Later, the wealthy city folk moved into the countryside, trading away life in their city palazzos to establish farm estates complete with fancy villas. (You can visit some of these villas today—the TI has a brochure—but they're convenient only for drivers.)

In 1799, Napoleon stormed into Italy and took a liking to Lucca. He liked it so much that he gave it to his sister (who ruled 1805-1814). After Napoleon was toppled, Europe's ruling powers gave Lucca to Maria Luisa, the daughter of the king of Spain. Duchess Maria Luisa (who ruled 1817-1824) was partially responsible for turning the city's imposing (but no longer particularly useful) fortified wall into a fine city park that is much enjoyed today. Her statue stands on Piazza Napoleone, near Palazzo Ducale.

LUCCA

turned into flowers. (Hungary's St. Margaret has exactly the same story. Hmmm...)

Farther along (tucked along the back wall of a chapel on the right side, facing the main altar) is a painting of the *Assumption of the Virgin* (c. 1510). Admire the paint-ing on wood, with Doubting Thomas receiving Mary's red belt as she ascends so he'll doubt no more. The pinball-machine composition serves as a virtual catalog of the fine silk material produced in Lucca—a major industry in the 16th century.

Finally, across the nave, you'll find a **carved Virgin Mary.** It's in the corre-sponding chapel opposite the *Assumption* (high on the back wall, facing the stone-carved altar). This particularly serene Virgin Mary is depicted at the moment she gets the news that she'll bring the Messiah into the world (carved and painted by Lucchese artist Matteo Civitali, c. 1460).

• *Leaving the church, head straight back through the little square, and turn right onto...*

❸ Via Fillungo

Lucca's best street to stroll and main pedestrian drag connects the town's two busiest squares: Piazza dell'Anfiteatro (which we just left) and Piazza San Michele. Along the way, you'll get a taste of Lucca's rich past, including several elegant, century-old storefronts.

Head down the street. At #116 (left) is a truffle shop where you can often sample little treats with truffle oil. Just beyond, also on the left, you'll pass Piazza degli Scapellini, with market stalls and another entrance into Piazza dell'Anfiteatro.

Near #104 (on the left) notice the snazzy Old World **shopping gallery,** with glass canopies in the Liberty Style (Italy's version of Art Nouveau, from around 1900).

As you stroll, notice how many of the original storefront paintings, reliefs, and mosaics survive—even if today's shopkeeper sells something entirely different. Observe the warm and convivial small-town vibe on the street. Notice also the powerful heritage of shops named for the families that have run them for many genera-tions, the creative new energy brought by small entrepreneurs, and the aggressive inroads big chain stores are making in this tender urban econo-system.

At #92 (left) is a shop selling an array of beers from nearby microbreweries. Since 2007, vino-centric Italy has enjoyed a trendy and youthful microbrew industry. There are four breweries just in Lucca.

At #97 (right) is the classic old **Carli Jewelry Store.** Signore Carli is the 12th generation of jewelers from his family to work on this spot. (He still has a once-state-of-the-art 17th-century safe in the back.) The Carli storefront has kept its T-shaped arrangement, which lets it close up tight as a canned ham. After hours, all you see from the street is a wooden T in the wall, and during opening hours it unfolds with a fine old-time display. This design dates from when the merchant sold his goods in front, did his work in the back, and lived upstairs.

At #67 is a surviving five-story **tower house** (at the corner with Via Buia). At one time, nearly every corner in Lucca sported its own tower. The stubby stones that still stick out once supported wooden staircases (there were no interior connections between floors). So many towers cast shadows over this part of town that this cross-street is called "Dark Street" (Via Buia). Look left down Via Sant'Andrea for a peek at the town's tallest tower, Guinigi, in the distance—capped by its characteristic mini oak-tree forest. You can pay to climb up for the view (see "More Sights in Lucca," later).

The shop at #65 (right) sports a beautiful, Liberty Style *Profumaria Venus* sign. For over a century, its sexy reliefs (dating from the time of Puccini) have stirred Lucchesi menfolk to buy their woman a fragrant gift. Today the storefront is protected as a historic landmark—and, fittingly, a new perfume shop recently took up residence here.

At #45, you'll see two more good examples of tower houses. On the left is the 14th-century **Clock Tower** (Torre delle Ore), which has a hand-wound Swiss clock that clanged four times an hour since 1754...until it died for good a few years back (€4 to climb the 207 wooden steps for the view and to see the nonfunctioning mechanism, €9 combo-ticket includes Guinigi Tower, daily 9:30-18:30, Oct and March until 17:30, closed Nov-Feb, corner of Via Fillungo and Via del'Arancio).

A bit farther along, on the left, is the striking 13th-century facade of a **Pisan Romanesque church,** now filled with a tacky Leonardo da Vinci exhibition. (Note that the Leonardo exhibits and torture "museums"—which you see all over Europe these days—are often just deceptive business ventures with no artifacts. Avoid them like thumbscrews.)

The intersection of Via Fillungo and Via Roma/Via Santa Croce marks the center of town, where the two original Roman roads crossed. The big old palace you're facing (on the right)—with the heavy grates on the windows and the benches built into its stony

facade—is the **In Mondadori bookstore.** While the interior is worth a peek (for its speckled mosaic floors, columns, and stained-glass skylight), the benches out front are even more interesting: They're the town hangout, where old-timers sit to swap gossip.

• *Turn right down Via Roma, studying the people warming those stone benches along the way. You'll pop out at...*

❹ Piazza San Michele

This square has been the center of town since Roman times, when it was the forum. It's dominated by the **Church of San Michele.** Circle around to the church's main door. Towering above the fancy Pisan Romanesque facade, the archangel Michael stands ready to flap his wings (which he actually did on special occasions with the help of crude but awe-inspiring-in-its-day mechanical assistance from behind).

The square is surrounded by an architectural hodgepodge. The circa-1495 loggia (to the right as you face the church) was the first Renaissance building in town. There's a late 19th-century interior in Buccellato Taddeucci, a 130-year-old pastry shop (#34, behind the church, next to its tower). The left section of the BNL bank (#5, facing the church facade) sports an Art Nouveau facade that celebrates both Amerigo Vespucci and Cristoforo Colombo. This was the original facade of the Bertolli shipping company—famed among Italian-Americans as the shipping company their grandfathers sailed with to reach America. Bertolli is even better known as the first big-time Italian olive oil exporter. ("Bertolli" was even the generic term for olive oil coined by early Italian-Americans.)

Perhaps you've noticed that those statues of big shots that decorate many an Italian piazza are mostly absent from Lucca's squares. That's because unlike Venice, Florence, and Milan—which were dominated by a few powerful dynasties—Lucca was traditionally run by an oligarchy of a hundred leading families, with no one central figure to commemorate in stone. But after Italian unification—when leaders were fond of saying, "We have created Italy...now we need to create Italians"—stirring statues of national heroes popped up everywhere... even in Lucca. The statue on Piazza San Michele is a two-bit local guy, dredged up centuries after his death because he favored strong central government.

Look back at the church facade, which also has an element of patriotism—designed to give roots and legitimacy to Italian statehood. Perched above many of the columns are the faces of a dozen or so heroes in the Italian independence and unification movement: Victor Emmanuel II (with a crown, above the short red column on the right, second level up), the Count of Cavour (next to Victor, above the column with black zigzags), and—hey, look—there's Giuseppe Mazzini.

If the church is open, pop in. A fine 12th-century wooden crucifix hangs above the high altar. Immediately to its right is an exquisite painting, *The Four Saints,* by Filippino Lippi (a student of the Florentine master Sandro Botticelli). Painted in 1495, you can feel the spirit of the Renaissance (and the influence of Botticelli) in the idealized beauty of the faces and the detailed glorification of nature all around. You may notice visitors shining their iPhone flashlights on the pillars. They're squinting at curious little doodles scratched into the marble back in the 12th century.

• *From here, continue out of the square (opposite from where you entered) to take a little detour down...*

❺ Via San Paolino

This bustling street—which eventually goes all the way to Piazzale Guiseppe Verdi (with the TI and bus to Pisa)—is another fine shopping drag. Along here, a wide variety of storefronts cater not just to tourists but also to locals. Appliance and electronics stores are mixed in with gifty Tuscan specialty boutiques. You'll also pass—after just a half-block, on the right—my vote for the best gelato in town (De' Coltelli, Sicilian-style gelato, at #10; described under "Eating in Lucca").

One block down this street, in the little square called **Piazza Citadella** (on the right), a statue of Giacomo Puccini (1858-1924) sits genteelly on a chair, holding court. The great composer of operas was born in the house down the little alley over his left shoulder (now the well-presented Puccini's House museum, worth a visit for music lovers—see "More Sights in Lucca," later). The ticket office for the museum—on the left side of the square, in front of Puccini—is also a well-stocked gift shop with all manner of Puccini-bilia. (If you'd like to hear some Puccini while you're in town, soon we'll be passing a church that hosts nightly concerts of his music—see page 457).

Puccini had deep roots in Lucca. His musical family had served as choirmasters for the San Martino Cathedral for five generations. As a young man, Giacomo sang in the cathedral choir, served as the substitute organist, and attended the church school. Even when he left for Milan to pursue his opera career, he kept a villa near Lucca. The citizens of Lucca

LUCCA

can be rightfully proud of their native son: Puccini is easily the most popular opera composer today, and his *La Boheme, Madame Butterfly, Tosca,* and a half-dozen other works are regularly performed across the globe. His style, known as *verismo* (realism), is highly accessible and dramatic, making his works seem more like sung plays than merely a string of arias.

• *Feel free to browse your way as far down this street as you like, but eventually return to Piazza San Michele to continue the walk to Lucca's cathedral. Facing the church facade, turn right and go down Via Vittorio Veneto (with the loggia on your left) to the vast, café-lined pair of squares...*

❻ Piazza Napoleone and Piazza del Giglio

The first of these two squares is named for the French despot who was the first outsider to take over Lucca. The dominant building on the right was the seat of government for the independent Republic of Lucca from 1369 to 1799—the year Napoleon came and messed everything up. Caffè Ninci, on the left (with some nice tables for people-watching), has been caffeinating locals since 1925 and serves what's considered to be the best coffee in town.

Cross diagonally through this square into the smaller **Piazza del Giglio,** dominated by the Giglio Theater. Like a mini La Scala, this has long been the number-one theater (of seven) in the highly cultured city of Puccini.

• *Continue to the left, along the big orange building, up Via del Duomo. After a block, you'll see...*

❼ San Giovanni Church

This first cathedral of Lucca is interesting only for its archaeological finds. The entire floor of the 12th-century church has been excavated in recent decades, revealing layers of Roman houses, ancient hot tubs that date back to the time of Christ, early churches, and theological graffiti. Sporadic English translations help you understand what you're looking at. As you climb under the church's present-day floor and wander the lanes of Roman Lucca, remember that the entire city sits on similar ruins. Climb the 190 steps of the church's campanile (bell tower) for a panoramic view (but not quite as good as the one you'll enjoy if you climb the Guinigi Tower).

Cost and Hours: €4, €9 combo-ticket includes cathedral and Cathedral Museum, admission includes tower climb; mid-March-

Oct daily 10:00-18:00; Nov-March Mon-Fri until 14:00, Sat-Sun until 18:00; audioguide-€2, concert info on page 457.

• *Continuing past San Giovanni, you'll be face-to-face with...*

❽ San Martino Cathedral

This cathedral—the main church of the Republic of Lucca and worth ▲—begun in the 11th century, is an entertaining mix of ar-

chitectural and artistic styles. It's also home to the exquisite 15th-century tomb of Ilaria del Carretto, who married into the wealthy Guinigi family.

Cost and Hours: €3, €9 combo-ticket includes Cathedral Museum and San Giovanni Church, tower climb-€3; Mon-Fri 9:30-18:00, Sat until 19:00, Sun from 12:00; Nov-March daily 9:30-17:00; Piazza San Martino, www.cattedralelucca.it.

Visiting the Cathedral: The cathedral's elaborate Pisan Romanesque **facade** features Christian teaching scenes, animals, and candy-cane-striped columns.

The horseback figure (over the two right arches) is St. Martin, a Roman military officer from Hungary who, by offering his cloak to a beggar, came to more fully understand the beauty of Christian compassion. (The impressive original, a fine example of Romanesque sculpture, hides from pollution just inside, to the right of the main entrance.) Each of the columns on the facade is unique. Notice how the facade is asymmetrical: The 11th-century bell tower was already in place when the rest of the cathedral was built, so the builders fudged a bit while attempting to make it fit. Over the right portal (as if leaning against the older tower), the architect Guideo from Como holds a document declaring that he finished the facade in 1204.

Head under the arcade to see a few more details. On the right (at eye level on the pilaster), a labyrinth is set into the wall. The maze relates the struggle and challenge our souls face in finding

salvation. (French pilgrims on their way to Rome could relate to this, as it's the same pattern they knew from the floor of the church at Chartres.) The Latin plaque just left of the main door is where moneychangers and spice traders met to seal deals (on the doorstep of the church—

to underscore the reliability of their promises). Find the date: *An Dni MCXI* (A.D. 1111, second line from bottom, lower right).

The **interior**—bigger than it seems from outside—features brightly frescoed Gothic arches, Renaissance paintings, and stained glass from the 19th century.

On the left side of the nave, a small, elaborate, birdcage-like temple contains the wooden crucifix—much revered by locals— called **Volto Santo.** It's said to have been sculpted by Nicodemus in Jerusalem and set afloat in an unmanned boat that landed on the coast of Tuscany, from where wild oxen miraculously carried it to Lucca in 782. The sculpture (which is actually 12th-century Byzantine-style) had quite a jewelry collection, which you can see in the Cathedral Museum (described next).

When locals look at Volto Santo they recall how, in 1096, the Christian forces of England and France met Pope Urban II right here in front of this crucifix. Those inglorious bastards were blessed and sent by the pope east on the First Crusade. As an example of Lucca's stature in 12th-century Europe, rather than say "I swear on a stack of bibles," people would say "I swear in front of the holy face of Christ of Lucca."

Circle around the birdcage. On the back side stands a sculpture of St. Sebastian (without his arrows) by Matteo Civitali. Carved in the late 1400s, this was the epitome of early Renaissance beauty before the muscularity of Michelangelo's *David* came into vogue. Delicate and S-shaped, it's just as sensuous (though St. Sebastian is dressed in cute underpants in contrast to *David*'s powerful nudity).

On the right side of the nave, the sacristy houses the enchantingly beautiful **memorial tomb of Ilaria del Carretto** by Jacopo della Quercia (1407). Pick up a handy English description (on the right as you enter). This young bride of silk baron Paolo Guinigi is decked out in the latest, most expensive fashions, with the requisite little dog (symbolizing her loyalty) curled up at her feet in eternal sleep. She's so realistically realized that the statue was nicknamed "Sleeping Beauty." Her nose is partially worn off because of a long-standing tradition of lonely young ladies rubbing it for luck in finding a boyfriend.

As you head for the church's exit, stop by the third painting from the end (on the left)—*The Last Supper* by Jacopo Tintoretto. This is a typical Baroque spectacle, with the drama of the event emphasized as if it's theater. Notice the actors on the stage and how the mother, giving her child his "first supper" in the foreground, connects with us, inviting us to be present. Enjoy Tintoretto's perspective trick: As you walk by the painting, the foreshortened dinner table always faces you.

• *There's one more sight to consider, but it's extra credit—worthwhile only if you want to dig deeper into the history of the cathedral. As you face the cathedral facade, on the little square to the left is the entrance to the...*

❾ Cathedral Museum (Museo della Cattedrale)

This beautifully presented museum houses original paintings, sculptures, and vestments from the cathedral and other Lucca churches. Pass through a room with illuminated manuscripts on your way to the ticket desk, then follow the one-way route up and down through the collection. The first room displays jewelry made to dress up the Volto Santo crucifix (described earlier), including gigantic gilded silver shoes. Upstairs, notice the fine red brocaded silk—a reminder that this precious fabric is what brought riches and power to the city. You'll also see church paintings and sculptures, silver ecclesiastical gear, and a big cutaway model of the cathedral. The exhibits in this museum have basic labels and are meaningful only with the slow-talking €2 audioguide—if you're not in the mood to listen, skip the place altogether.

Cost and Hours: €4, €9 combo-ticket includes cathedral and San Giovanni Church; April-Oct daily 10:00-18:00; Nov-March Mon-Fri 10:00-14:00, Sat-Sun until 18:00; left of the cathedral on Piazza Antelminelli.

• *Our walk is finished. From here, it's just a short stroll south to the city wall—and a bike-rental office, if you want to take a spin. Otherwise, simply explore the city...lose yourself in Lucca.*

More Sights in Lucca

THE LUCCA RAMPARTS (AND BIKE RIDE)

Lucca's most remarkable feature, its Renaissance wall, is also its most enjoyable attraction, worth ▲▲—especially when circled on a rental bike. Stretching for 2.5 miles, this is an ideal place to come for an overview of the city by foot or bike.

Lucca has had a protective wall for 2,000 years. You can read three walls into today's map: the first rectangular Roman wall, the later medieval wall (nearly the size of today's), and the 16th-century Renaissance ramparts that still survive.

With the advent of cannons, thin medieval walls were suddenly vulnerable. A new design—the same one that stands today—was state-of-the-art when it was built (1550-1650). Much of the old medieval wall (look for the old stones) was incorporated into the Renaissance wall (with uniform bricks). The new wall was squat:

a 100-foot-wide mound of dirt faced with bricks, engineered to absorb a cannonball pummeling. The townspeople cleared a wide no-man's-land around the town, exposing any attackers from a distance. Eleven heart-shaped bastions (now inviting picnic areas) were designed to minimize exposure to cannonballs and to maximize defense capabilities. The ramparts were armed with 130 cannons.

The town invested a third of its income for more than a century to construct the wall, and—since it kept away the Florentines and nasty Pisans—it was considered a fine investment. In fact, nobody ever bothered to try to attack the wall. Locals say that the only time it actually defended the city was during an 1812 flood of the Serchio River, when the gates were sandbagged and the ramparts kept out the high water.

Today, the ramparts seem made-to-order for a leisurely bike ride (wonderfully smooth 20-30-minute pedal, depending on how

fast you go and how crowded the wall-top park is). You can rent bikes cheaply and easily from one of several bike-rental places in town (listed earlier, under "Helpful Hints"). There are also several handy places to get up on the wall. Note that the best people-watching—and slowest pedaling—is during *passeggiata* time,

just before dinner, when it seems that all of Lucca is doing slow laps around the wall.

OTHER MUSEUMS AND SIGHTS

Lucca has several small museums that stir local pride, but they're pretty dull on a pan-Italian scale (The Cathedral Museum is described earlier, on my "Lucca Walk"). Visit the following sights only if you have time to burn and/or a special interest.

Guinigi Tower (Torre Guinigi)

Many Tuscan towns have towers, but none is quite like the Guinigi

family's. Up 227 steps is a small garden with fragrant trees, surrounded by fine views over the city's rooftops. You'll head up wide stone stairs, then huff up twisty metal ones through the hollow brick tower. From the top, orient yourself to the town. Lucca sits in a flat valley ringed by protective hills, so it's easy to see how the town managed to stay independent through so much of its history, despite its lack of a strategic hilltop position. From up here, pick out landmarks: the circular form of Piazza dell'Anfiteatro to the north, with the mosaic facade of the Church of San Frediano nearby; to the left (east), the open top of the Clock Tower, marking the Roman grid-planned streets of the oldest part of town; and to the south, the big, marble facade of San Martino Cathedral.

Cost and Hours: €4, €6 combo-ticket includes Clock Tower, erratic hours but likely daily 9:30-18:30—maybe later in summer, shorter hours Nov-March, Via Sant'Andrea 41.

Puccini's House

This modern, well-presented museum fills the home where Giacomo Puccini grew up. It's well worth a visit for opera enthusiasts... but mostly lost on anybody else. Buy your ticket at the shop/office on the square, then buzz the door to be let in. You'll tour the composer's birthplace—including the room where he was born—and see lots of artifacts (including the Steinway piano where he did much of his composing, his personal belongings, and pull-out drawers with original compositions and manuscripts). An elaborate costume from one of his works is on display, and if you ask, the attendant can accompany you for a peek in the garret (storage room up above the house), where a stage set from *La Bohème* evokes the composer's greatest work.

Cost and Hours: €7; daily 9:30-19:30; April and Oct Wed-Mon until 18:30, closed Tue; Nov-March shorter hours and closed Tue; Corte San Lorenzo 9, tel. 0583-584-028, www.puccinimuseum.it.

Palazzo Pfanner

Garden enthusiasts (and anyone needing a break from churches) will enjoy this 18th-century palace built for a rich Austrian expat who came to Lucca to open a brewery. A visit has two parts: the residence and the garden. Up the stairs is the palace's lived-in interior, with Baroque furniture, elaborate frescoes, and a centuries-old kitchen. Those in the medical profession may be interested in the display of early-20th-century medical equipment and books. (Pfanner's son became a renowned doctor, and treated everyone from vagrants to Giacomo Puccini on the building's ground floor.) The second part is the restful garden, with manicured lawns, rows of dynamic statues, potted citrus trees, and gurgling fountains, tucked up against Lucca's imposing wall. While far from the finest garden in Italy, it's a nice escape from the crowds and heat of the city.

Cost and Hours: €6 for garden and residence, daily 10:00-18:00, closed Nov-March, Via degli Asili 33, tel. 0583-952-155, www.palazzopfanner.it.

Villa Guinigi

Built by Paolo Guinigi in 1413, the family villa is now a well-presented museum displaying a lot of art and artifacts that are meaningful to the Lucchesi. The exhibit starts with an archaeological section—Etruscan, Ligurian (a local pagan tribe), Roman. Upstairs, you proceed chronologically through the Middle Ages, with lots of church art and altars, and the Renaissance. Highlights include a precious crucifix by Berlinghiero Berlinghieri (who also created the fine mosaic facade at the Church of San Frediano), two terra-cotta *Madonna-and-Bambino* sculptures attributed to Donatello, fine inlaid-wood panels from San Martino Cathedral, several works by the locally famous Lucchese sculptor Matteo Civitali, a *Sacra Conversazione* by Fra Bartolomeo, and a fine triptych by the multitalented Giorgio Vasari. In Vasari's vibrant altar painting, Adam and Eve clutch the tree of knowledge, while the devil (a snake with a woman's head) twists up the trunk toward the sky, flanked by biblical big shots (David, Solomon, Moses, and John the Baptist). But Mary floats triumphant on top, with one foot keeping down the devil's head. The collection wraps up with the Counter-Reformation and Neoclassicism (with works by more locally beloved artists, Paolo Guidotti and Pompeo Batoni).

Cost and Hours: €4, €6.50 combo-ticket includes Palazzo Mansi, Tue-Sat 8:30-19:30, closed Sun-Mon, Via della Quarquonia, tel. 0583-496-033, www.luccamuseinazionali.it.

Palazzo Mansi

For a glimpse at a noble palace from centuries past, this is your best bet. Minor paintings by Tintoretto, Pontormo, Veronese, and others vie for attention, but the palace itself steals the show. This sumptuously furnished and decorated 17th-century confection gives you a chance to appreciate the wealth of Lucca's silk merchants. Exploring rooms on one magnificent floor, you'll gape through several grand halls of both public and private apartments. Notice the emphasis on crests, portraits, and family trees—reminders of how important it was to marry smartly if you wanted to create a powerful family. In one wing, every surface is slathered in bubbly Baroque scenes; in another, each room is completely draped in tapestries, leading to one of the most impressive two-story canopy beds I've seen.

Cost and Hours: €4, €6.50 combo-ticket includes Villa Guinigi, generally Tue-Sat 8:30-19:30, closed Sun-Mon, English info posted in each room, Via Galli Tassi 43, tel. 0583-55-570, www.luccamuseinazionali.it.

Sleeping in Lucca

FANCY LITTLE BOUTIQUE B&BS WITHIN THE WALLS

$$$ A Palazzo Busdraghi has eight comfortable, pastel-colored rooms with modern baths (some with Jacuzzi-style tubs) in a tastefully converted 13th-century palace tucked inside a creaky old courtyard. Sweet Marta hustles to keep guests happy, and bakes tasty cakes for breakfast. It's conveniently located on busy Via Fillungo, but can be noisy on weekends (family room, air-con, pay parking, Via Fillungo 170, tel. 0583-950-856, www.apalazzobusdraghi.it, info@apalazzobusdraghi.it).

$$$ La Locanda Sant'Agostino has three romantic, bright, and palatial rooms. The oasis-like setting—with a vine-draped terrace, beautiful breakfast spread, and quaint garden views—invites you to relax (family rooms, air-con, Piazza Sant'Agostino 3, tel. 0583-443-100, mobile 346-717-7762, www.locandasantagostino.it, info@locandasantagostino.it, Silvia and gruff Giacomo).

$$ La Romea B&B, in an air-conditioned, restored, 14th-century palazzo near Guinigi Tower, feels like a royal splurge. Its five rooms are lavishly decorated in handsome colors and surround a big, plush lounge with stately Venetian-style mosaic-linoleum floors (RS%, family rooms, Vicolo delle Ventaglie 2, tel. 0583-464-175, www.laromea.com, info@laromea.com, Giulio and wife Gaia). Giulio also offers excursions into the countryside.

$$ La Bohème B&B has a cozy yet elegant ambience, offering six large rooms, each named for a Puccini opera. Chandeliers, 1920s-vintage tile floors, and tasteful antiques add to the charm (RS%, air-con, Via del Moro 2, tel. 0583-462-404, www.boheme.it, info@boheme.it, Laura).

SLEEPING MORE FORGETTABLY WITHIN THE WALLS

$$$ Hotel la Luna, pricey but well-run by the Barbieri family, has 29 rooms in a great location in the heart of the city. Rooms are split between two adjacent buildings just off the main shopping street. Rooms in the main, historical building are larger and classier, with old wood-beam ceilings (and, in some, original frescoes), while the modern building feels newer and has an elevator but less personality (RS%, family rooms, air-con, pay parking, Via Fillungo at Corte Compagni 12, tel. 0583-493-634, www.hotellaluna.it, info@hotellaluna.it).

$$ Albergo San Martino is friendly and conveniently located for train travelers, with rooms in three different buildings. The 12 art-adorned rooms in the main hotel—with a nice lounge and curb-side breakfast terrace—are cozy, while the six rooms in the **annex**

are newer and slightly cheaper. And the nine budget rooms in their sister **$ Hotel Diana** are fresh, minimalist, and retro-style at an affordable price (breakfast extra at Hotel Diana; family rooms, air-con, pay parking, reception at Via della Dogana 9, tel. 0583-469-181, www.albergosanmartino.it, info@albergosanmartino.it, Andrea).

$ At **B&B Le Violette,** cheerful American Elisabeth will settle you into one of her six homey rooms near the train station inside Porta San Pietro (cheaper rooms with shared bath, air-con in one room, communal kitchen, self-service laundry, Via della Polveriera 6, tel. 0583-493-594, mobile 333-588-0982, www.bbleviolettelucca.com, bbleviolette@gmail.com).

¢ Ostello San Frediano, in a central, sprawling ex-convent, comes with huge public spaces and a peaceful garden facing the busy town wall. Its 29 rooms are bright and modern, and some have fun lofts (dorms and private rooms, nice two-story family rooms, includes breakfast, no curfew, elevator, restaurant, pay parking, Via della Cavallerizza 12, tel. 0583-348-477, www.ostellolucca.it, info@ostellolucca.it).

OUTSIDE THE WALLS

$$$ Hotel San Marco, a 10-minute walk outside the Porta Santa Maria, is a postmodern place decorated à la Stanley Kubrick. Its 42 rooms are sleek, with all the comforts (air-con, elevator, pool, bike rental, free parking, taxi from station-€13, Via San Marco 368, tel. 0583-495-010, www.hotelsanmarcolucca.com, info@hotelsanmarcolucca.com).

$$ Hotel Rex rents 25 rooms in a practical contemporary building on the train station square. While in the modern world, you're just 200 yards away from the old town and get more space for your money. Ask for a slightly quieter room at the back (family rooms, children's play area and toys, air-con, elevator, free loaner bikes, free parking, a few steps from the train station at Piazza Ricasoli 19, tel. 0583-955-443, www.hotelrexlucca.com, info@hotelrexlucca.com, Elisabetta).

$ Hotel Moderno is indeed modern, with 12 rooms tastefully decorated in shades of white. Although it backs up to the train tracks, the rooms are quiet, and it offers class unusual for this price range (RS%, air-con, Via Vincenzo Civitali 38—turn left out of train station and go over stair-heavy bridge across tracks, tel. 0583-55-840, www.albergomodernolucca.com, info@albergomodernolucca.com).

$ La Mimosa B&B has five cozy, if musty, rooms a 10-minute walk west of Porta Sant'Anna. Most practical if you're arriving or leaving Lucca by bus, this funky little house is run by the Zichi cousins, Giuseppe and Stefano, and decorated with modern paintings. It's on a main road, but double-paned windows reduce traffic noise (air-con, free loaner bikes, free street parking nearby, Via Pisana 66; leave Piazzale Giuseppe Verdi through Porta Sant'Anna, swing right, then cross road, walk straight down Via Catalani, and take second road on the left; tel. 0583-583-121, www.bblamimosa. it, info@bblamimosa.it).

$ Sogni d'Oro Guesthouse ("Dreams of Gold"), run by Davide, is a handy budget option for drivers, with five basic rooms and a cheery communal kitchen (grocery store next door). It's a 10-minute walk from the train station and a five-minute walk from the city walls (cheaper rooms with shared bath, free parking, free ride to and from station with advance notice—then call when your train arrives in Lucca; from the station, head straight out to Viale Regina Margherita and turn right, follow the main boulevard as it turns into Viale Giuseppe Giusti, at the curve turn right onto Via Antonio Cantore to #169; tel. 0583-467-768, mobile 329-582-5062, www.bbsognidoro.com, info@bbsognidoro.com).

Eating in Lucca

FINE AND ROMANTIC DINING

$$ Canuleia Trattoria is run by enthusiastic Matteo (the chef) and Eleonora (head waiter), who make everything fresh in their small kitchen. You can eat tasty Tuscan cuisine in a tight, dressy, and romantic little dining room or outside on the garden courtyard. As this place is justifiably popular, reserve for dinner (Tue-Sun 12:00-14:30 & 19:00-22:00, closed Mon, shorter hours in winter, Via Canuleia 14, tel. 0583-467-470, www.canuleiatrattoria.it).

$$$ Ristorante Giglio is a venerable old dining hall where waiters are formal, but not stuffy, and the spirit of Puccini lives on. This is where local families enjoy special occasions under a big chandelier. They also have simple tables outside facing a tranquil square and the old theater. The short but thoughtful menu—with both traditional and creative Tuscan dishes concocted by three young chefs—makes you want to return. It's only slightly pricier than most of my listings, but is a big step up in dining experience (impressive wine list, Wed-Mon 12:15-15:00 & 19:15-22:30, closed Tue, Piazza del Giglio 2, tel. 0583-494-058).

$$ Port Ellen Clan, unusual in traditional Lucca, is a combination restaurant, wine bar, and whisky bar in a trendy modern setting. Though the cuisine is purely Italian with a modern twist, the theme is creative and original, with a Scottish flair (Wed-Mon 19:30-24:00, closed Tue; Via del Fosso 120, tel. 0583-493-952, mobile 329-245-2762, www.portellenclan.com, Alessandro).

Specialties in Lucca

Lucca has some tasty specialties worth seeking out. *Ceci* (CHEH-chee), also called *cecina* (cheh-CHEE-nah), makes an ideal cheap snack any time of day. This crêpe-like garbanzo-bean flatbread is sold in pizza shops and is best accompanied by a nip of red wine. *Farro,* a grain (spelt) dating back to ancient Roman cuisine, shows up in restaurants in soups or as a creamy rice-like dish *(risotto di farro). Tordelli,* the Lucchesi version of *tortelli,* is homemade ravioli. It's traditionally stuffed with meat and served with more meat sauce, but chefs creatively pair cheeses and vegetables, too. *Lardo di Colonnata* is *salumi* made with cured lard and rosemary, sliced thin, and served as an antipasto.

Meat, not fish, is the star at most restaurants, especially steak, which is listed on menus as *filetto di manzo* (filet), *tagliata di manzo* (thin slices of grilled tenderloin), or the king of steaks, *bistecca alla fiorentina.* Order *al sangue* (rare), *medio* (medium rare), *cotto* (medium), or *ben cotto* (well). Anything more than *al sangue* is considered a travesty for steak connoisseurs. *Ravellino* is a thin cut of beef that's deep-fried, then pan-fried again later to heat it up.

Note that steaks (as well as fish) are often sold by weight, noted on menus as *s.q.* (according to quantity ordered) or *l'etto* (cost per 100 grams—250 grams is about an 8-ounce steak).

For something sweet, bakeries sell *buccellato,* bread dotted with raisins, lightly flavored with anise, and often shaped like a wreath. It's sold only in large quantities, but luckily it stays good for a few days (and it also pairs well with vin santo—fortified Tuscan dessert wine). An old proverb says, "Coming to Lucca without eating the *buccellato* is like not having come at all." *Buon appetito!*

LUCCA

CHARMING AND RUSTIC DINING

$$ La Bottega di Anna & Leo, run by Claudio and Lidia (and named for their children), is a pastel and lovable little eatery with a simple menu and a passion for quality. They have tight seating inside and a few charming tables facing the side of the Church of San Frediano (Tue-Sun 12:00-15:00 & 19:00-22:30, closed Mon, reservations smart, Via San Frediano 16, mobile 393-577-9910 or 393-530-2512, www.labottegadiannaeleo.it).

$$ Osteria Via San Giorgio, where Daniela cooks and her brother Piero serves, is a cheery family eatery that satisfies both fish and meat lovers. The seating is tight and convivial, and the house wine is high quality (daily 12:00-16:00 & 19:00-23:00, Via San Giorgio 26, tel. 0583-953-233).

$$ Il Cuore Enogastronomia is a cozy blend of deli and restaurant. Browse their cases of prepared dishes and order food to take away, or sit in the dining room for homemade pasta, meats, and desserts (daily 8:00-22:30, shorter hours off-season, closed Jan-Feb, Via del Battistero 4, tel. 0583-490-689).

$ Pizzeria da Felice is a little mom-and-pop hole-in-the-wall serving *cecina* (garbanzo-bean crêpes) and slices of freshly baked pizza to throngs of snackers. Grab an *etto* of *cecina* and a short glass of wine. From September through April, they're known for their *castagnaccio*, a cake made with roasted chestnuts and ricotta (daily 10:00-20:30 except closed Sun Jan-Aug and closed 2 weeks in Aug, Via Buia 12, tel. 0583-494-986).

Basic Trattorias: For an affordable, fill-the-tank meal in a lively traditional environment, consider these two options, run by relatives. They're a block apart in a quiet part of town, a short walk from the main sights: **$$ Vecchia Trattoria Buralli,** on quiet Piazza Sant'Agostino, has bright-pastel indoor and piazza seating. It's fun to order a *bis* (2 different half-portion pastas) and watch your *tordelli* being handmade at the pasta bar (Thu-Tue 12:00-15:00 & 18:30-22:30, closed Wed, Piazza Sant'Agostino 10, tel. 0583-950-611). **$$ Trattoria da Leo** packs in chatty locals for typical, cheap home-cooking in a high-energy, Mel's-diner atmosphere. Sit in the rollicking interior, or out on a tight, atmospheric lane (Mon-Sat 12:00-14:45 & 19:30-22:30, Sun 12:00-14:45, cash only, Via Tegrimi 1, tel. 0583-492-236, www.trattoriadaleo.it).

Fancy Deli: $ Antica Bottega di Prospero, proudly run by the Marcucci family, is an artisanal deli shop that feels more like a museum. Peruse their great selection of local meats and cheeses that are perfect for a picnic. You can satisfy your sweet tooth with cookies like *cantuccini* and *befanini*, or pick up dried pasta, spices, and beans for a tasty souvenir (daily 9:00-19:30, a block behind the Church of San Michele at Via Santa Lucia 13).

Après-Bike Drinks: In the little piazza just south of where Piazza Santa Maria (the bike rental hub) meets the end of Via Fillungo, young people gather each evening to socialize and drink. This is a perfect spot to unwind after a late-afternoon cycle on the city wall, before you head to dinner. **De Cervesia** is a craft beer pub, with three microbrews on rotating taps (and one English-style pull) and dozens by the bottle (Tue-Sun 17:00-22:00, closed Mon, Via Michele Rosi 20, tel. 0583-492-620, Matteo). **Ciclo DiVino,** across the street, is a wine bar with a bike-shop theme and enticing snacks (Mon-Fri 10:00-22:00, Sat-Sun 18:00-22:00, Via Michele Rosi 7, tel. 0583-471-869). As this is a fast-emerging scene, scope out the area for other hip new bars before you choose.

Gelato: Just off Piazza San Michele, **De' Coltelli** has some of my favorite gelato in Italy. It's proudly Sicilian-style (with Arab roots) and many of their flavors rotate with the season. The coffee gelato is serious (and not served to children), and their granita takes the slushy to new heights (Sun-Thu 11:00-20:00, Fri-Sat until 21:00, Via San Paolino 10, 0583-050-667).

Refreshments on the Wall: Caffetteria San Colombano is a handy pit stop for bikers and walkers on the city wall. This place is slick with cheap bite-sized snacks and cappuccinos, perfect for a takeaway meal on top of the wall (overpriced at the table). If you're not feeling too wobbly already from biking, try a *caffè corretto* (espresso with your choice of Sambuca, rum, or grappa) or a *Biadina,* a bittersweet liqueur served with pine nuts. The fancier sit-down restaurant serves pasta and big salads with a view (daily 9:00-late, near the top of ramp at Baluardo San Colombano, tel. 0583-464-641).

Groceries: Pam is a small, central market just off of Piazza San Michele (Mon-Sat 7:30-20:30, Via San Paolino 12).

Lucca Connections

Even if you have a car, I'd opt for the much faster and cheaper train or bus to reach the Leaning Tower. For more on day-tripping to Pisa, see page 453.

From Lucca by Train to: Florence (2/hour, 1.5 hours), **Pisa** (roughly 1-2/hour, 30 minutes; if going directly to Leaning Tower, hop off at Pisa San Rossore Station), **Livorno** (about hourly, 1-1.5 hours, transfer at Pisa Centrale), **Milan** (2/hour except Sun, 4-5 hours, transfer in Florence), **Rome** (1/hour except Sun, 3-4 hours, change in Florence), **Cinque Terre** (hourly, about 2 hours, transfer in Viareggio and La Spezia).

From Lucca by Bus: Vaibus has handy, direct routes from Lucca's Piazzale Giuseppe Verdi to **Florence** and its **airport** (bus #DD, Mon-Sat nearly hourly, less on Sun, 1.25 hours to airport, 1.5 hours total to downtown Florence), and to **Pisa** and its **airport** (drops you right at the Leaning Tower or at the station, Mon-Sat hourly, fewer on Sun, 50 minutes). Before boarding, buy tickets at the bus ticket office on Piazzale Giuseppe Verdi (Mon-Sat 6:00-20:00, Sun 8:00-19:30)—or you can buy them from the driver for a small surcharge.

VOLTERRA & SAN GIMIGNANO

This fine duo of hill towns—perhaps Italy's most underrated and most overrated, respectively—sits just a half-hour drive apart in the middle of the triangle formed by three major destinations: Florence, Siena, and Pisa. San Gimignano is the region's glamour girl, getting all the fawning attention from passing tour buses. And a quick stroll through its core, in the shadows of its 14 surviving medieval towers, is a delight. But once you've seen it, you've seen it...and that's when you head for Volterra. Volterra isn't as eye-catching as San Gimignano, but it has unmistakable authenticity and surprising depth, richly rewarding travelers adventurous enough to break out of the San Gimignano rut. With its many engaging museums, Volterra offers the best sightseeing of all of Italy's small hill towns.

To round things out with a look at a well-preserved hilltop fort, consider stopping off for a quick visit to Monteriggioni, perched above the highway south to Siena.

GETTING THERE

These towns work best for drivers, who can easily reach both in one go. Volterra is farther off the main Florence-Siena road, but it's near the main coastal highway connecting the north (Pisa, Lucca, and Cinque Terre) and south (Montalcino/Montepulciano and Rome).

If you're relying on public transportation, both towns are reachable—to a point. Visiting either one by bus from Florence or Siena requires a longer-than-it-should-be trek, often with a change (in Colle di Val d'Elsa for Volterra, in Poggibonsi for San Gimignano). Volterra can also be reached by a train-and-bus combination from La Spezia, Pisa, or Florence (transfer to a bus in Pontedera). See each town's "Connections" section for details.

San Gimignano is better connected, but Volterra merits the

Volterra & San Gimignano Area

additional effort. Note that while these towns are only about a 30-minute drive apart, they're poorly connected to each other by public transit (requiring an infrequent two-hour connection).

PLANNING YOUR TIME

Volterra and San Gimignano are a handy yin-and-yang duo. Ideally, you'll overnight in one town and visit the other either as a side-trip or en route. Sleeping in Volterra lets you really settle into a charming, real-feeling burg with good restaurants, but it forces you to visit San Gimignano during the day, when it's busiest. Sleeping in San Gimignano lets you enjoy that gorgeous town when it's relatively quiet, but some visitors find it *too* quiet—less interesting to linger in than Volterra. Ultimately I'd aim to sleep in Volterra, and try to visit San Gimignano as early or late in the day as is practical (to avoid crowds).

Volterra

Encircled by impressive walls and topped with a grand fortress, Volterra perches high above the rich farmland surrounding it. More than 2,000 years ago, Volterra was one of the most important Etruscan cities, and much larger than we see today. Greek-trained Etruscan artists worked here, leaving a significant stash

VOLTERRA & SAN GIMIGNANO

of art, particularly funerary urns. Eventually Volterra was absorbed into the Roman Empire, and for centuries it was an independent city-state. Volterra fought bitterly against the Florentines, but like many Tuscan towns, it lost in the end and was given a Medici fortress atop the city to "protect" its citizens.

Unlike other famous towns in Tuscany, Volterra feels neither cutesy nor touristy...but real, vibrant, and almost oblivious to the allure of the tourist dollar. Millennia past its prime, Volterra seems to have settled into a well-worn groove; locals are resistant to change. At a town meeting about whether to run high-speed Internet cable to the town, a local grumbled, "The Etruscans didn't need it—why do we?" This stubbornness helps make Volterra a refreshing change of pace from its more aggressively commercial neighbors. Volterra also boasts some interesting sights for a small town, from an ancient Roman theater, to a finely decorated Pisan Romanesque cathedral, to an excellent museum of Etruscan artifacts. And most evenings, charming Annie and Claudia give a delightful, one-hour guided town walk sure to help you appreciate their city (see "Tours in Volterra," later). All in all, Volterra is my favorite small town in Tuscany.

Orientation to Volterra

Compact and walkable, Volterra (pop. 11,000—6,000 inside the old wall) stretches out from the pleasant Piazza dei Priori to the old city gates and beyond. Be ready for some steep walking: While the spine of the city from the main square to the Etruscan Museum is fairly level, nearly everything else involves a climb.

TOURIST INFORMATION

The helpful TI is on the main square, at Piazza dei Priori 19 (daily 9:30-13:00 & 14:00-18:00, tel. 0588-87257, www.volterratur.it). The TI's excellent €5 audioguide narrates 20 stops (2-for-1 discount with this book). Their free *Handicraft in Volterra* booklet is useful for understanding the town's traditional artisans. Check the TI website for details on frequent summer festivals and concerts.

ARRIVAL IN VOLTERRA

By Public Transport: Buses stop at Piazza Martiri della Libertà in the town center. Train travelers can reach the town with a short bus ride (see "Volterra Connections," later).

By Car: Don't drive into the town center; it's prohibited except for locals (and you'll get a huge fine). It's easiest to simply wind to the top where the road ends at Piazza Martiri della Libertà. (Halfway up the hill, there's a confusing hard right—don't take it; keep going straight uphill under the wall.) Immediately before the

Piazza Martiri bus roundabout is the entry to an **underground garage** (€2/hour, €15/day, keep ticket and pay as you leave). It's safe, and you pop out within a few blocks of nearly all my recommended hotels and sights.

Parking lots ring the town walls (around €2/hour; try the handy-but-small lot facing the Roman Theater and Porta Fiorentina gate). Behind town, a lot named Docciola is free, but it requires a steep climb from the Porta di Docciola gate up into town.

Wherever you park, be sure it's permitted—stick to parking lots and pay street parking (indicated with blue lines). If you're staying in town, check with your hotel about the best parking options.

HELPFUL HINTS

Volterra Card: This €14 card covers all the main sights—except for the Palazzo Viti (valid 72 hours, buy at any covered sight). Without the card, the Etruscan Museum and Pinacoteca are €8 each, and the Palazzo Priori and Archaeological Park are €5 each. If traveling with kids, ask about the family card, an especially good deal (€22 for 1-2 adults and up to 3 kids under 16).

Market Day: The market is on Saturday morning near the Roman Theater (8:00-13:00, Nov-March it moves to Piazza dei Priori). The TI hands out a list of other market days in the area.

Festivals: Volterra's Medieval Festival takes place on the third and fourth Sundays of August. Fall is a popular time for food festivals. Notte Rossa, on the second Saturday in September, fills the town with music all night.

Laundry: The handy self-service **Lavanderia Azzurra** is just off the main square (change machine, daily 7:00-23:00, Via Roma 7, tel. 0588-80030). Their next-door dry-cleaning shop also provides wash-and-dry services that usually take about 24 hours (Mon-Fri 8:30-13:00 & 15:30-20:00, Sat 8:30-13:00, closed Sun).

Tours in Volterra

▲▲Guided Volterra Walk

Annie Adair (also listed individually, next) and her colleague Claudia Meucci offer a great one-hour, English-only introductory walking tour of Volterra for €10. The walk touches on Volterra's Etruscan, Roman, and medieval history, as well as the contemporary cultural scene (daily April-Oct, rain or shine—Mon and Wed at 12:30, other days at 18:00; meet in front of alabaster shop on Piazza Martiri della Libertà, no need to reserve, tours run with a minimum of 3 people or €30; www.volterrawalkingtour.com or www.tuscantour.com, info@volterrawalkingtour.com). There's no better way to spend €10 and one hour in this city. I mean it. Don't miss this beautiful experience.

Local Guides

American **Annie Adair** is an excellent guide for private, in-depth tours of Volterra (€60/hour, minimum 2 hours). Her husband **Francesco,** an easygoing sommelier and wine critic, leads a "Wine Tasting 101" crash course in sampling Tuscan wines (€50/hour per group, plus cost of wine). For more in-depth experiences, Annie and Francesco offer excursions to a nearby honey farm, alabaster quarry, and winery, or a more wine-focused trip to Montalcino or the heart of Chianti (about €450/day for 2-3 people) and can even organize Tuscan weddings (mobile 347-143-5004, www.tuscantour.com, info@tuscantour.com).

Sights in Volterra

I've linked these sights with handy walking directions.
· *Begin at the Etruscan Arch at the bottom of Via Porta all'Arco (about 4 blocks below the main square, Piazza dei Priori).*

▲Etruscan Arch (Porta all'Arco)

Volterra's renowned Etruscan arch was built of massive stones in the fourth century B.C. Volterra's original wall was four miles around—twice the size of the wall that encircles it today. Imagine: This city had 20,000 people four centuries before Christ. Volterra was a key trading center and one of 12 leading towns in the confederation of *Etruria Propria.* The three seriously eroded heads, dating from the first century B.C., show what happens when you leave something outside for 2,000  years. The newer stones are part of the 13th-century city wall, which incorporated parts of the much older Etruscan wall.

A plaque just outside remembers June 30, 1944. That night, Nazi forces were planning to blow up the arch to slow the Allied advance. To save their treasured landmark, Volterrans ripped up the stones that pave Via Porta all'Arco, plugged up the gate, and managed to convince the Nazi commander that there was no need to blow up the arch. Today, all the paving stones are back in their places, and like silent heroes, they welcome you through the oldest standing gate into Volterra. Locals claim this as the oldest surviving round arch of the Etruscan age; some experts believe this is where the Romans got the idea for using a keystone in their arches.

• *Go through the arch and head up Via Porta all'Arco, which I like to call...*

"Artisan Lane" (Via Porta all'Arco)

This steep and atmospheric lane is lined with interesting shops featuring the work of artisans and producers. Because of its alabaster heritage, Volterra developed a tradition of craftsmanship and artistry, and today you'll find a rich variety of handiwork (shops generally open Mon-Sat 10:00-13:00 & 16:00-19:00, closed Sun).

From the Etruscan Arch, browse your way up the hill, checking out these shops and items (listed from bottom to top): alabaster shops (#57 and #45); book bindery and papery (#26); jewelry (#25); etchings (#23); and bronze work (#6).

• *Reaching the top of Via Porta all'Arco, turn left and walk a few steps into Volterra's main square, Piazza dei Priori. It's dominated by the...*

Palazzo dei Priori

Volterra's City Hall, built about 1200, claims to be the oldest of any Tuscan city-state. It clearly inspired the more famous Pala-

zzo Vecchio in Florence. Town halls like this are emblematic of an era when city-states were powerful. They were architectural exclamation points declaring that, around here, no pope or emperor called the shots. Towns such as Volterra were truly city-states—proudly independent and relatively democratic. They had their own armies, taxes, and even weights and measures. Notice the horizontal "cane" cut into the City Hall wall (10 yards to the right of the door). For a thousand years, this square hosted a market, and the "cane" was the local yardstick. You can pay to see the council chambers, and to climb to the top of the bell tower.

Cost and Hours: €5, includes council chambers and tower climb, covered by Volterra Card, daily 10:30-17:30, Nov-mid-March until 16:30, tower closed in bad weather.

Visiting the Palazzo: When not in use for meetings or weddings, the building's historic **High Council Hall**—fine arches lavishly frescoed and lit with fun dragon lamps, as they have been for centuries of town meetings—is open to visitors. The adjacent Sala

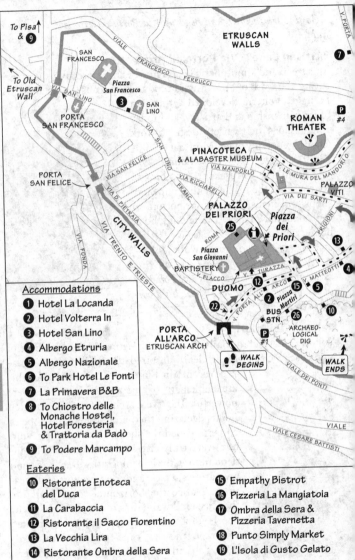

Accommodations

1. Hotel La Locanda
2. Hotel Volterra In
3. Hotel San Lino
4. Albergo Etruria
5. Albergo Nazionale
6. To Park Hotel Le Fonti
7. La Primavera B&B
8. To Chiostro delle Monache Hostel, Hotel Foresteria & Trattoria da Badò
9. To Podere Marcampo

Eateries

10. Ristorante Enoteca del Duca
11. La Carabaccia
12. Ristorante il Sacco Fiorentino
13. La Vecchia Lira
14. Ristorante Ombra della Sera
15. Empathy Bistrot
16. Pizzeria La Mangiatoia
17. Ombra della Sera & Pizzeria Tavernetta
18. Punto Simply Market
19. L'Isola di Gusto Gelato

della Giunta is a simpler, smaller meeting room with bare stone walls.

Climbing the 159 steps (they get pretty tight at the top) to the **tower** will earn you a fine view. Midway up is a modest exhibit about the history of the town, including a model of Volterra in the late 13th century (looking much as it does today) and a wooden cutaway model of the tower itself.

• *Facing the City Hall, notice the black-and-white-striped wall to the*

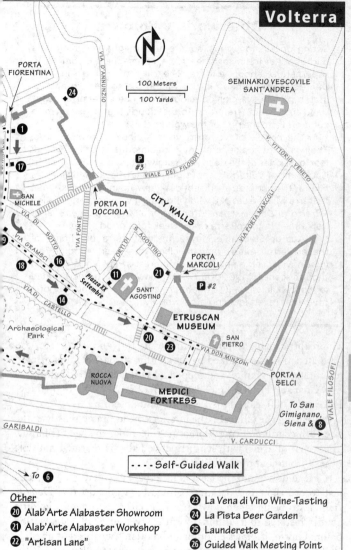

Volterra

Other

20 Alab'Arte Alabaster Showroom

21 Alab'Arte Alabaster Workshop

22 "Artisan Lane"

23 La Vena di Vino Wine-Tasting

24 La Pista Beer Garden

25 Launderette

26 Guided Walk Meeting Point

right (set back from the square). The little back door in that wall leads into Volterra's cathedral. (For a thousand years the bishop has lived next door, conveniently right above the TI.)

Duomo

This church, which may be closed for renovation until 2020, is not as elaborate as its cousin in Pisa, but it is a beautiful example of the Pisan Romanesque style. The simple 13th-century facade conceals

Otherworldly Volterra

Sitting on its stony main square at midnight, watching bats dart about as if they own the place, I sense there is something supernatural about Volterra. The cliffs of Volterra inspired Dante's "cliffs of hell." In the winter, the town's vibrancy is muted by a heavy cloak of clouds. The name Volterra means "land that floats"—referring to the clouds that often seem to cut it off from the rest of the world below.

The people of Volterra live in a cloud of mystery, too. Their favorite cookie, crunchy with almonds, is called Ossi di Morto ("bones of the dead"). The town's first disco was named Catacombs. Volterra's top sight—the Etruscan Museum—is filled with hundreds of ancient caskets. And in the 1970s, when Volterra was the set of a wildly popular TV horror series called *Ritratto di Donna Velata (Portrait of a Veiled Woman)*, all of Italy tuned in to Volterra every week for a good scare.

Author Stephanie Meyer made Volterra the home of the powerful Volturi vampire clan in her teen-vampire *Twilight* novels, and a new wave of interest swept Volterra (even though scenes in the 2009 *Twilight* film *New Moon* were filmed in Montepulciano)—just one more chapter in a long tale of a town that revels in being otherworldly.

a more intricate interior (rebuilt in the late 16th and 19th centuries), with a central nave flanked by monolithic stucco columns painted to imitate pink granite, and topped by a gilded, coffered ceiling.

Cost and Hours: Free, daily 8:00-12:30 & 15:00-18:00, Nov-Feb until 17:00, closed Fri 12:30-16:00 for cleaning.

Visiting the Church: The interior was decorated mostly in the late 16th century, during Florentine rule under the Medici family. Their coat of arms, with its distinctive balls, is repeated multiple times throughout the building.

Head down into the nave to face the main altar. Up the stairs just to the right is a dreamy, painted, and gilded-wood *Deposition* (Jesus being taken down from the cross, Nicodemus holding a nail), restored to its original form. Carved in 1228, a generation before Giotto, it shows emotion and motion way ahead of its time. Pop a euro into the box to buy some light and stand here as a 13th-century pilgrim would have (their eyes were better in the dark).

The glowing **windows** just to the left (in the transept and behind the altar) are sheets of alabaster. These, along with the recorded Gregorian chants, add to the church's worshipful ambience.

The 12th-century marble **pulpit**, partway down the nave, is also beautifully carved. In the relief panel of the Last Supper, all the apostles are together except Judas, who's under the table with the evil dragon (his name is the only one not carved into the relief). As with most medieval art, the artist remains anonymous.

Just past the pulpit on the right (at the Rosary Chapel), check out the *Annunciation,* painted in 1497 by Mariotto Albertinelli and Fra Bartolomeo (both were students of Fra Angelico). The two, friends since childhood, delicately give worshippers a way to see Mary "conceived by the Holy Spirit." Note the vibrant colors, exaggerated perspective, and Mary's *contrapposto* pose—all attributes of the Renaissance.

At the end of the nave, the large **chapel** to the right of the doors has painted terra-cotta statue groups of the Nativity and the Adoration of the Magi. One is by an anonymous local artist, the other is thought to be the work of master ceramist Andrea della Robbia. Remarkably, no one is certain who did which one—a testament to the skill of local craftsmen. Della Robbia's uncle, Luca, is credited with devising the glazing formula that makes Della Robbia's inventive sculptures shine even in poorly lit interiors. At the end of the chapel, ponder a statue with an unusual but poignant theme: Mary, *Mater Dolorosa* ("mother in pain"), literally pierced by swords as she suffers the agony of seeing her crucified son's dead body.

Step outside the door into Piazza San Giovanni. A common arrangement in the Middle Ages was for the church to face the baptistery (you couldn't enter the church until you were baptized)... and for the hospital to face the cemetery (now the site of an ambulance corps or misericordia). These buildings all overlooked a single square. That's how it is in Pisa's famous Field of Miracles (with its Leaning Tower), and that's how it is here. Step into the baptistery and look up into the vast, empty space—plenty of room for the Holy Spirit.

• *Facing the cathedral, circle to the left (passing a 1960 carving of St. Linus, the second pope and friend of St. Peter, who was born here) and go back into the main square, Piazza dei Priori. Face the City Hall, and go down the street to the left; after one short block, turn left on...*

▲Via Matteotti

The town's main drag, named after the popular Socialist leader Giacomo Matteotti (killed by the fascists in 1924), provides a good cultural scavenger hunt.

At #1, on the left, is a typical **Italian bank security door.** (Step in and say, "Beam me up, Scotty.") Back outside, stand at the corner and look up and all around. Find the medieval griffin torch-holder—symbol of Volterra, looking down Via Matteotti—and imagine it holding a flaming torch. The pharmacy sports the symbol of its medieval guild. Across the street from the bank, #2 is the base of what was a San Gimignano-style **fortified Tuscan**

tower. Look up and imagine heavy beams cantilevered out, supporting extra wooden rooms and balconies crowding out over the street. Throughout Tuscany, today's stark and stony old building fronts once supported a tangle of wooden extensions.

As you head down Via Matteotti, notice how the doors show centuries of refitting work. Doors that once led to these extra rooms are now partially bricked up to make windows. Contemplate urban density in the 14th century, before the plague thinned out the population. Be careful: A **wild boar** (a local delicacy) awaits you at #10.

At #12, on the right, notice the line of doorbells: This typical **palace,** once the home of a single rich family, is now occupied by many middle-class families. After the social revolution in the 18th century and the rise of the middle class, former palaces were condominium-ized. Even so, like in *Dr. Zhivago*, the original family still lives here. Apartment #1 is the home of Count Guidi.

On the right at #16, pop in to the **alabaster showroom.** Alabaster, mined nearby, has long been a big industry here. Volterra alabaster—softer and more translucent than marble—was sliced thin to serve as windows for Italy's medieval churches.

At #19, the recommended **La Vecchia Lira** is a lively cafeteria and restaurant. The **Bar L'Incontro** across the street is a favorite for breakfast and pastries; in the summer, they sell homemade gelato, while in the winter they make chocolates. In the evening, it's a bustling local spot for a drink.

Across the way, side-trip 10 steps up Vicolo delle Prigioni to the fun **Panificio Rosetti** bakery. They're happy to sell small quantities if you want to try the local *cantuccini* (almond biscotti) or another treat.

Continue on Via Matteotti to the end of the block. At #51, on the left, a bit of **Etruscan wall** is artfully used to display more alabaster art. And #56A is the alabaster **art gallery** of Paolo Sabatini, who specializes in unique, contemporary sculptures.

By the way, you can only buy a package of cigarettes at the machine in the wall just to the right—labeled *"Vietato ai Minori"* (forbidden to minors)—by inserting an Italian national health care card to prove you're over 18.

Locals gather early each evening at **Osteria dei Poeti** (at #57) for some of the best cocktails in town—served with free munchies. The cinema is across the street. Movies in Italy are rarely in *versione originale;* Italians are used to getting their movies dubbed into Italian. To bring some culture to this little town, they also show live broadcasts of operas and concerts (advertised in the window).

On the corner, at #66, another **Tuscan tower** marks the end of the street. This noble house had a ground floor with no interior access to the safe upper floors. Rope ladders were used to get upstairs. The tiny door was wide enough to let in your skinny friends... but definitely not anyone wearing armor and carrying big weapons.

Across the little square stands the ancient **Church of St. Michael.** After long years of barbarian chaos, the Langobards moved in from the north and asserted law and order in places like Volterra. That generally included building a Christian church on the old Roman forum to symbolically claim and tame the center of town. The church standing here today is Romanesque, dating from the 12th century.

Around the right side, find the crude little guy and the smiling octopus under its eaves—they've been making faces at the passing crowds for 800 years.

• *From here you have options. Three more sights—Palazzo Viti (fancy old palace), the **Pinacoteca** (Volterra's main painting gallery), and the **Alabaster Museum** (within the Pinacoteca building)—are a short stroll down Via dei Sarti: From the end of Via Matteotti, turn left. If you want to skip straight down to the Roman Theater, just head straight from the end of Via Matteotti onto Via Guarnacci, then turn left when you get to the Porta Fiorentina (Florence Gate). To head directly to Volterra's top sight, the Etruscan Museum, just turn around, walk a block back up Via Matteotti, turn left on Via Gramsci, and follow it all the way through Piazza XX Settembre up Via Don Minzoni to the museum.*

*Or linger a bit while making your decision over a glass of wine at **Enoteca Scali**, just across the street at Via Guarnacci 3. Friendly Massimo and Patrizia sell a vast selection of wines and local delicacies in an inviting atmosphere.*

▲Palazzo Viti

Palazzo Viti takes you behind the rustic, heavy stone walls of the city to see how the wealthy lived—in this case, rich from the 19th-century alabaster trade. This time warp is popular with Italian movie directors. With 12 rooms on one floor open to the public, Palazzo Viti feels remarkably lived in—because it is. Behind the ropes you'll see intimate family photos. You'll often find Signora Viti herself selling admission tickets. Your visit ends in the cellar with a short wine tasting.

Cost and Hours: €5, daily 10:00-13:00 & 14:30-18:30, by appointment only Nov-March, Via dei Sarti 41, tel. 0588-84047, www.palazzoviti.it, info@palazzoviti.it.

Visiting the Palazzo: The elegant interior is compact and well-described. You'll climb up a stately staircase, buy your ticket, and head into the grand ballroom. From here, you'll tour the blue-hued dining room (with slice-of-life Chinese scenes painted on rice paper); the salon of battles (with warfare paintings on the walls); and the long hall of temporary exhibits. Looping back, you'll see the porcelain hall (decorated with priceless plates) and the inviting library (notice the delicate lamp with a finely carved alabaster lampshade).

The Brachettone Salon is named for the local artist responsible for the small sketch of near-nudes hanging just left of the door into the next room. Brachettone (from *brache*, "pants") is the artistic nickname for Volterra-born Daniele Ricciarelli, who owns the dubious distinction of having painted all those wispy loincloths over the genitalia of Michelangelo's figures in the Sistine Chapel. (In this drawing, notice a similar aversion to showing the full monty... though everything-but is fair game.) On the table, notice the family wedding photo with Pope John Paul II presiding. In the red room, a portrait of Giuseppe Viti (looking like Pavarotti) hangs next to the exit door. He's the man who purchased the place in 1850. Your visit ends with bedrooms and a dressing room, making it easy to imagine how the other half lived.

Your Palazzo Viti ticket also gets you a fine little cheese, salami, and wine tasting. As you leave the palace, climb down into the cool cellar (used as a disco on some weekends), where you can pop into a Roman cistern, marvel at an Etruscan well, and enjoy a friendly sit-down snack. Take full advantage of this tasty extra.

• *A block past Palazzo Viti, also on Via dei Sarti, is the...*

Pinacoteca and Alabaster Museum

The Pinacoteca fills a 15th-century palace with fine paintings that feel more Florentine than Sienese—a reminder of whose domain this town was in. You'll see a stunning altarpiece by Taddeo di Bartolo, once displayed in the original residence. You'll also find roomfuls of gilded altarpieces and saintly statues, as well as a trio of striking High Renaissance altar paintings by Signorelli, Fiorentino, and Ghirlandaio.

Cost and Hours: €8, covered by Volterra Card, daily 9:00-19:00, Nov-mid-March 10:00-16:30, Via dei Sarti 1, tel. 0588-87580.

Visiting the Museum: Begin with the **Pinacoteca** and head upstairs to the first floor. Turn right at the landing and go directly into Room #11, with Luca Signorelli's beautifully lit *Annunciation* (1491), an example of classic High Renaissance from the town cathedral. To the right, find *Descent from the Cross* (a.k.a. *Deposition*, 1521), the groundbreaking Mannerist work by Rosso Fiorentino (note the elongated bodies and harsh emotional lighting and colors). In the adjacent room (#10), see Ghirlandaio's *Christ in Glory* (1492). The two devout-looking kneeling women are actually pagan, pre-Christian Etruscan demi-goddesses, Attinea and Greciniana. Rather than attempt to get locals to stop venerating them (as their images were all over town), the church simply sainted them. Upstairs, the second floor has three more rooms of similar art—huge frescoes and oil-on-wood paintings.

Back on the main floor, head through the fine, tranquil, cloister-like courtyard—with the remains of its original well—and enter the **Alabaster Museum.** With alabaster sculptures spread over three floors, this fun and easy little museum contains examples from Etruscan times until the present (no English descriptions—ask for an English brochure at the ticket office). Take the elevator to the top and work your way down. The top floor displays stone-working tools and offers fine views. Etruscan pieces are on the middle floor, and modern sculptures—including an intriguing alabaster fried egg—are on the lower floor.

• *Exiting the museum, circle right along the side of the museum building into the tunnel-like Passo del Gualduccio passage (which leads to the parking-lot square); turn right and walk along the wall, with fine views of the...*

Roman Theater

Built in the first century A.D., this well-preserved theater has good acoustics. With this fine aerial view from the city wall promenade,

there's no reason to pay to enter (although it is covered by the Volterra Card). The 13th-century wall that you're standing on divided the theater from the town center...so, naturally, the theater became the town dump. Over time, the theater was forgotten—covered in the garbage of Volterra. It was rediscovered in the 1950s and excavated.

The stage wall (immediately in front of the theater seats) was standard Roman design—with three levels from which actors would appear: one level for mortals, one for heroes, and the top one for gods. Parts of two levels still stand. Gods leaped out onto the third level for the last time around the third century A.D., which is when the town began to use the theater stones to build fancy baths instead. You can see the scant remains of the baths behind the theater, including the little round sauna in the far corner with brick supports that raise the heated floor.

From this vantage point, you can trace Volterra's vast Etruscan wall. Find the church in the distance, on the left, and notice the stones just below. They are from the Etruscan wall that followed the ridge into the valley and defined Volterra in the fourth century B.C.

• *From the Roman Theater viewpoint, continue along the wall downhill to the T-intersection (the old gate, Porta Fiorentina, with fine wooden medieval doors, is on your left) and turn right, making your way uphill on Via Guarnacci back to Via Matteotti. A block up Via Matteotti, you can't miss the wide, pedestrianized shopping street called Via Gramsci. Follow this up to Piazza XX Settembre, walk through that leafy square, and continue uphill on Via Don Minzoni. Watch on your left for the...*

▲▲Etruscan Museum (Museo Etrusco Guarnacci)

Filled top to bottom with rare Etruscan artifacts, this museum—even with few English explanations and its dusty, old-school style—makes it easy to appreciate how advanced this pre-Roman culture was.

Cost and Hours: €8, covered by Volterra Card, daily 9:00-19:00, Nov-mid-March 10:00-16:30, audioguide-€3, Via Don Minzoni 15, tel. 0588-86347, www.comune.volterra.pi.it/english.

Visiting the Museum: The museum's three floors feel dusty and disorganized. As there are scarcely any English explanations, consider the serious but interesting audioguide; the information below hits the highlights. There's an inviting public garden out back.

The collection starts on the **ground floor** with a small gathering of pre-Etruscan Villanovian artifacts (c. 1500 B.C.), with the oldest items to the left as you enter. To the right are an impressive warrior's hat and a remarkable, richly decorated, double-spouted military flask (for wine and water). Look down to see Etruscan foundations and a road (the discovery of which foiled the museum's attempt to build an elevator here). It's mind-boggling to think that 20,000 people lived within the town's Etruscan walls in 400 B.C.

Filling the rest of the ground floor is a vast collection of Etruscan **funerary urns** (dating from the seventh to the first century B.C.). Designed to contain the ashes of cremated loved ones, each urn is tenderly carved with a unique scene, offering a peek into the still-mysterious Etruscan society. Etruscan urns have two parts: The casket on the bottom contained the remains (with elaborately carved panels), while the lid was decorated with a sculpture of the departed.

First pay attention to the people on top. While contemporaries of the Greeks, the Etruscans were more libertine. Their religion was less demanding, and their women were a respected part of both the social and public spheres. Women and men alike are depicted lounging on Etruscan urns. While they seem to be just hanging out, the lounging dead were actually offering the gods a banquet—in order to gain the Etruscan equivalent of salvation. Etruscans really did lounge like this in front of a table, but this banquet had eternal consequences. The dearly departed are often depicted holding blank wax tablets (symbolizing blank new lives in the next world). Men hold containers that would generally be used at banquets, including libation cups for offering wine to the gods. The women are finely dressed, sometimes holding a pomegranate (symbolizing fertility) or a mirror. Look at the faces, and imagine the lives they lived and the loved ones they left behind.

Now tune into the reliefs carved into the fronts of the caskets. The motifs vary widely, from floral patterns to mystical animals (such as a Starbucks-like mermaid) to parades of magistrates. Most show journeys on horseback—appropriate for someone leaving this world and entering the next. Some show the fabled horseback-and-carriage ride to the underworld, where the dead are greeted by Charon, an underworld demon, with his hammer and pointy ears.

While the finer urns are carved of alabaster, most are made of limestone. Originally they were colorfully painted. Many lids are mismatched—casualties of reckless 18th- and 19th-century archaeological digs.

Head upstairs to the **first floor.** You'll enter a room with a circular mosaic in the floor (a Roman original, found in Volterra and transplanted here). Explore more treasures in a series of urn-filled rooms.

Fans of Alberto Giacometti will be amazed at how the tall, skinny figure called *The Evening Shadow* (*L'Ombra della Sera*, third century B.C.) looks just like the modern Swiss sculptor's work—but 2,500 years older. This is an example of the *ex-voto* bronze statues that the Etruscans created in thanks to the gods. With his supremely lanky frame, distinctive wavy hairdo, and inscrutable Mona Lisa smirk, this Etruscan lad captures the illusion of a shadow stretching long, late in the day. Admire the sheer artistry of the statue; with its right foot shifted slightly forward, it even hints at the *contrapposto* pose that would become common in this same region during the Renais-

sance, two millennia later.

The museum's other top piece is the **Urn of the Spouses** (*Urna degli Sposi*, first century B.C.). It's unique for various reasons, including its material (it's in terra-cotta—a relatively rare material for these funerary urns) and its depiction of two people rather than one. Looking at this elderly couple, it's easy to imagine the long life they spent together and their desire to pass eternity lounging with each other at a banquet for the gods.

Other highlights include alabaster urns with more Greek myths, *ex-voto* water-bearer statues, kraters (vases with handles used for mixing water and wine), bronze hand mirrors, exquisite golden jewelry that would still be fashionable today, a battle helmet ominously dented at the left temple, black glazed pottery, and hundreds of ancient coins.

The **top floor** features a re-created gravesite, with several neatly aligned urns and artifacts that would have been buried with the deceased. Some of these were funeral dowries that the dead would pack along—including mirrors, coins, hardware for vases, votive statues, pots, pans, and jewelry.

• *After your visit, duck across the street to the alabaster showroom and the wine bar (both described next).*

▲Alabaster Workshop

Across from the Etruscan Museum, Alab'Arte offers a fun peek into the art of alabaster. Their powdery workshop is directly op-

posite the shop, a block down a narrow lane, Via Porta Marcoli (near the wall). Here you can watch Roberto Chiti and Giorgio Finazzo at work. (Everything—including Roberto and Giorgio—is covered in a fine white dust.) Lighting shows off the translucent quality of the stone and the expertise of these artists, who are delighted to share their art with visitors. This is not a touristy guided visit, but something far more special: the chance to see busy artisans practicing their craft. For more such artisans in action, visit "Artisan Lane" (Via Porta all'Arco), described on page 487, or ask the TI for their list of the town's many workshops open to the public.

Cost and Hours: Free, showroom—daily 10:00-13:00 & 15:00-19:00, closed Nov-Feb, Via Don Minzoni 18; workshop—Mon-Sat 10:00-12:30 & 15:00-19:00, closed Sun, Via Orti Sant'Agostino 28, tel. 340-718-7189, www.alabarte.com.

▲La Vena di Vino (Wine Tasting with Bruno and Lucio)

La Vena di Vino, also just across from the Etruscan Museum, is a fun *enoteca* where two guys who have devoted themselves to the wonders of wine share it with a fun-loving passion. Each day Bruno and Lucio open six or eight bottles, serve your choice by the glass,

pair it with characteristic munchies, and offer fine music (guitars available for patrons) and an unusual decor (the place is strewn with bras). Hang out here with the local characters. This is your chance to try the Super Tuscan wine—a creative mix of international grapes grown in Tuscany. According to Bruno, the Brunello (€7/glass) is just right with wild boar, and the Super Tuscan (€6-7/glass) is perfect for meditation. Although Volterra is famously quiet late at night, this place is full of action.

Cost and Hours: Pay per glass, open Wed-Mon 11:30-24:00, closed Tue, Nov-Feb open Sat-Sun only, Via Don Minzoni 30, tel. 0588-81491, www. lavenadivino.com.

• *Volterra's final sight is perched atop the hill just above the wine bar. Climb up one of the lanes nearby, then walk (to the right) along the formidable wall to find the park.*

Medici Fortress and Archaeological Park

The Parco Archeologico marks what was the acropolis of Volterra from 1500 B.C. until A.D. 1472, when Florence conquered the pesky city. The Florentines burned Volterra's political and historic center, turning it into a grassy commons and building the adjacent Medici Fortezza. The old fortress—a symbol of Florentine dominance—now keeps people in rather than out. It's a maximum-security prison housing only about 150 special prisoners. Authorities prefer to keep organized crime figures locked up far away from their Sicilian family ties. (If you drive from Volterra to San Gimignano, you'll pass another big, modern prison—almost surreal in the midst of all the Tuscan wonder.)

The park sprawling next to the fortress (toward the town center) is a rare, grassy meadow at the top of a rustic hill town—a favorite place for locals to relax and picnic on a sunny day. Nearby are the scant remains of the acropolis, which can be viewed through the fence for free, or entered for a fee. Of more interest to antiquities enthusiasts is the acropolis' first-century A.D. Roman cistern. You can descend 40 tight spiral steps to stand in a chamber that once held about 250,000 gallons of water, enough to provide for more than a thousand people. While not huge, it provides a good look at Roman engineering and reminds you just how important a supply of water was to the survival of a hill town.

Cost and Hours: Park—free, open until 20:00 in peak of summer, shorter hours off-season; acropolis and cistern—€5, covered by Volterra Card, daily 10:30-17:30, closes at 16:30 off-season.

Under the Etruscan Sun
(c. 900 B.C.-A.D. 1)

Around 550 B.C.—just before the Golden Age of Greece—the Etruscan people of central Italy had their own Golden Age. Though their origins are mysterious, their mix of Greek-style art with Roman-style customs helped lay a civilized foundation for the rise of the Roman Empire. As you travel through Italy—particularly in Tuscany (from "Etruscan")—you'll find traces of this long-lost people.

Etruscan tombs and artifacts are still being discovered, often by farmers in the countryside. Museums in Volterra and Cortona house fine collections of urns, pottery, and devotional figures. You can visit several domed tombs outside Cortona.

The Etruscans first appeared in the ninth century B.C., when a number of cities sprouted up in sparsely populated Tuscany and Umbria, including today's hill towns of Cortona, Chiusi, and Volterra. Possibly immigrants from Turkey, but more likely local farmers who moved to the city, they became sailors, traders, and craftsmen, and welcomed new ideas from Greece.

More technologically advanced than their neighbors, the Etruscans mined metal, exporting it around the Mediterranean, both as crude ingots and as some of the finest-crafted jewelry in the known world. They drained and irrigated large tracts of land, creating the fertile farmland of central Italy's breadbasket. With their disciplined army, warships, merchant vessels, and (from the Greek perspective) pirate galleys, they ruled central Italy and the major ports along the Tyrrhenian Sea. For nearly two centuries (c. 700-500 B.C.), much of Italy lived a Golden Age of peace and prosperity under the Etruscan sun.

Judging from the frescoes and many luxury items that have survived, the Etruscans enjoyed the good life: They look healthy and vibrant as they play flutes, dance with birds, or play party games. Etruscan artists celebrated individual people, showing their wrinkles, crooked noses, silly smiles, and funny haircuts.

Thousands of surviving ceramic plates and cups attest to the importance of food and banqueting. Men and women celebrated together, propped on their elbows on dining couches, surrounded by colorful decor. The banqueters were entertained with music and dancing, and served by elegant and well-treated slaves. According to contemporary accounts, the Etruscans—even their slaves—were Europe's best-dressed people.

Scholars today have deciphered the Etruscans' Greek-style alphabet and some individual words, but they have yet to fully understand their language, which is unlike any other in Europe. Much of what we know of the Etruscans comes from their tombs. The tomb was a home in the hereafter, complete with the deceased's belongings. The funerary urn might have a statue on the lid of the deceased at a banquet—lying across a dining couch, spooning with

The Etruscan Empire

Bologna ■
Ravenna ●
*A d r i a t i c
S e a*

A p p e n i n e   M o u n t a i n s

La Spezia ●

Florence ● Fiesole ■
Arno R.
Pisa ●

*L i g u r i a n
S e a*

ITALY
100 Miles

E T R U S C A N

Volterra ■
(M)
Siena ●
Murlo ■
(M)

Cortona ■
(M)
Chiusi ■
(M)
*Lake
Trasimeno*
Perugia ●

E M P I R E
Populonia ●
Vetulonia ■
Roselle ■

Orvieto ■
(M)
Bolsena ■
*Lake
Bolsena*
Tiber R.

Elba

*T y r r h e n i a n
S e a*

Vulci ■
Tarquinia ■

Veio ■
Cerveteri ■
Rome ●
(M)

- ■ Etruscan Cities
- ● Modern Cities
- (M) Etruscan Museum
- – – – Border of Tuscany

VOLTERRA & SAN GIMIGNANO

his wife, smiles on their faces, living the good life for all eternity.

Seven decades of wars with the Greeks (545-474 B.C.) disrupted their trade routes and drained the Etruscan League, just as a new Mediterranean power was emerging: Rome. In 509 B.C., the Romans overthrew their Etruscan king, and Rome expanded, capturing Etruscan cities one by one (the last in 264 B.C.). Etruscan resisters were killed, the survivors intermarried with Romans, and their kids grew up speaking Latin. By Julius Caesar's time, the only remnants of Etruscan culture were its priests, who became Rome's professional soothsayers. Interestingly, the Etruscan prophets had foreseen their own demise, having predicted that Etruscan civilization would last 10 centuries.

But Etruscan culture lived on in Roman religion (pantheon of gods, household gods, and divination rituals), art (realism), lifestyle (the banquet), and in a taste for Greek styles—the mix that became our "Western civilization."

Countryside Strolls

All the sights listed above are in a tight little zone of the old town, about a 10-minute walk from each other. But if you have time for a stroll, Volterra—perched on a ridge overlooking pristine Tuscan hills—has countryside galore to explore. Get advice from the TI.

One popular walk is to head to the west end of town, out Porta San Francesco, into a workaday area (dubbed "Borghi," literally "neighborhoods") that sees few tourists. Continuing downhill from the gate, notice the bars and playgrounds filled with locals, before the imposing Church of San Giusto dramatically appears on your right. Soon after, you'll come to a cliff with a stretch of the original fourth-century B.C. Etruscan wall. Peering over the cliff from here, you can see that Volterra sits upon orange sandy topsoil packed onto clay cliffs, called Le Balze. At various points in its history, the town has been threatened by landslides, and parts of its hilltop have simply disappeared. The big church you see in the distance was abandoned in the late 1800s for fear that it would be swallowed up by the land. The distinctive ridged hills surrounding Volterra are called *calanchi* (similar to the French *calanques* that slash the Mediterranean coast).

Evening Scene

La Pista: Volterra is pretty quiet at night. For a little action during summer evenings you can venture just outside the wall to La Pista, a Tuscan family-friendly neighborhood beer-garden kind of hangout (DJ on weekends, snacks and drinks sold, playground, closed off-season). It's outside the Porta Fiorentina (100 yards to the right in the shadow of the wall).

Passeggiata: As they have for generations, Volterrans young and old stroll during the cool of the early evening. The main cruising is along Via Gramsci and Via Matteotti to the main square, Piazza dei Priori.

Aperitivo: Each evening several bars put out little buffet spreads free with a drink to attract a crowd. Bars popular for their *aperitivo* include VolaTerra (Via Turazza 5, next to City Hall), L'Incontro (Via Matteotti 19), and Bar dei Poeti (across from the cinema, Via Matteotti 57). And the gang at La Vena di Vino (described earlier, under "Sights in Volterra") always seems ready for a good time.

Sleeping in Volterra

Volterra has plenty of places offering a good night's sleep at a fair price. Lodgings outside the old town are generally a bit cheaper (and easier for drivers). But keep in mind that these places involve not just walking, but steep walking.

INSIDE VOLTERRA'S OLD TOWN

$$ Hotel La Locanda feels stately and old-fashioned. This well-located place (just inside Porta Fiorentina, near the Roman Theater and parking lot) rents 18 rooms with flowery decor and modern comforts (RS%, family rooms, air-con, elevator, Via Guarnacci 24, tel. 0588-81547, www.hotel-lalocanda.com, staff@hotel-lalocanda.com, Irina).

$$ Hotel Volterra In, opened in 2015, is fresh, tasteful, and in a central-yet-quiet location. Marco rents 12 bright and spacious rooms with thoughtful, upscale touches and a hearty buffet breakfast (RS%, air-con, elevator, Via Porta all'Arco 37, tel. 0588-86820, www.hotelvolterrain.it, info@hotelvolterrain.it).

$$ Hotel San Lino fills a former convent with 42 modern, nondescript rooms at the sleepy lower end of town—close to the Porta San Francesco gate, and about a five-minute uphill walk to the main drag. Although it's within the town walls, it doesn't feel like it: The hotel has a fine swimming pool and view terrace and is the only in-town option that's convenient for drivers, who can pay to park at the on-site garage (pricey "superior" rooms include parking—worthwhile only for drivers, air-con, elevator, closed Nov-Feb, Via San Lino 26, tel. 0588-85250, www.hotelsanlino.com, info@hotelsanlino.com).

$ Albergo Etruria is on Volterra's main drag. They offer a good location, a peaceful rooftop garden, and 18 frilly rooms (RS%, family rooms, fans but no air-con, Via Matteotti 32, tel. 0588-87377, www.albergoetruria.it, info@albergoetruria.it, Paola, Daniele, and Sveva).

$ Albergo Nazionale, with 38 big and aging rooms, is simple, a little musty, popular with school groups, and steps from the bus stop. It's a nicely located last resort if you have your heart set on sleeping in the old town (RS%, family rooms, elevator, Via dei Marchesi 11, tel. 0588-86284, www.hotelnazionale-volterra.it, info@hotelnazionale-volterra.it).

JUST OUTSIDE THE OLD TOWN

These accommodations are within a 5- to 20-minute walk of the city walls.

$$$ Park Hotel Le Fonti, a dull and steep 10-minute walk downhill from Porta all'Arco, can't decide whether it's a business hotel or a resort. The spacious, imposing building feels old and stately and has 64 modern, comfortable rooms, many with views. While generally overpriced, it can be a good value if you manage to snag a deal. In addition to the swimming pool, guests can use its small spa (pay more for a view or a balcony, air-con, elevator, on-site restaurant, wine bar, free parking, Via di Fontecorrenti 2, tel.

0588-85219, www.parkhotellefonti.com, info@parkhotellefonti.com).

$ La Primavera B&B feels like a British B&B transplanted to Tuscany. It's a great value just a few minutes' walk outside Porta Fiorentina (near the Roman Theater). Silvia rents five charming, neat-as-a-pin rooms that share a cutesy-country lounge. The house is set back from the road in a pleasant courtyard and garden to lounge in. With free parking and the shortest walk to the old town among my out-of-town listings, this is a handy option for drivers (RS%, fans but no air-con, Via Porta Diana 15, tel. 0588-87295, mobile 328-865-0390, www.affittacamere-laprimavera.com, info@affittacamere-laprimavera.com).

¢ Chiostro delle Monache, Volterra's youth hostel, fills a wing of the restored Convent of San Girolamo with 68 beds in 23 rooms. It's modern, spacious, and very institutional, with lots of services and a tranquil cloister. Unfortunately, it's about a 20-minute hike out of town, in a boring area near deserted hospital buildings (private rooms available and include breakfast, family rooms, reception closed 13:00-15:00 and after 20:00, elevator, free parking, kids' playroom; Via dell Teatro 4, look for hospital sign from main Volterra-San Gimignano road; tel. 0588-86613, www.ostellovolterra.it, info@ostellovolterra.it).

$ Hotel Foresteria, near Chiostro delle Monache and run by the same organization, has 35 big, utilitarian, new-feeling rooms with decent prices but the same location woes as the hostel; it's worth considering for a family with a car and a tight budget (family rooms, air-con, elevator, restaurant, free parking, Borgo San Lazzaro, tel. 0588-80050, www.foresteriavolterra.it, info@foresteriavolterra.it).

NEAR VOLTERRA

$$ Podere Marcampo is an *agriturismo* set in the dramatic scenery of the *calanche* (cliffs) about two miles north of Volterra on the road to Pisa. Run by Genuino (owner of the recommended Ristorante Enoteca del Duca), his wife Ivana, and their English-speaking daughter Claudia, this peaceful spot has three dark but well-appointed rooms and three apartments, plus a swimming pool with panoramic views. Genuino produces his Sangiovese and award-winning Merlot on site and offers €20 wine-tastings with five types of wine, cheese, homemade *salumi*, and grappa. Cooking classes at their restaurant in town are also available (apartments, breakfast included for Rick Steves readers, air-con, free self-service laundry, free parking, tel. 0588-85393, Claudia's mobile 328-174-4605, www.agriturismo-marcampo.com, info@agriturismo-marcampo.com).

Eating in Volterra

Menus feature a Volterran take on regional dishes. *Zuppa alla Volterrana* is a fresh vegetable-and-bread soup, similar to *ribollita*. *Torta di ceci*, also known as *cecina*, is a savory crêpe-like garbanzo-bean flatbread that's served at *pizzerie*. Those with more adventurous palates dive into *trippa* (tripe stew, the traditional breakfast of the alabaster carvers). *Fegatelli* are meatballs made with liver.

$$$$ Ristorante Enoteca del Duca, serving well-presented and creative Tuscan cuisine, offers the best elegant meal in town. You can dine under a medieval arch with walls lined with wine bottles, in a sedate, high-ceilinged dining room (with an Etruscan statuette at each table), in their little *enoteca* (wine cellar), or in their terraced garden in summer. Chef Genuino, daughter Claudia, and the friendly staff take good care of diners. The fine wine list includes Genuino's own highly regarded Merlot and Sangiovese. The spacious seating, dressy clientele, and calm atmosphere make this a good choice for a romantic splurge. Their €55 food-sampler fixed-price meal comes with a free glass of wine for diners with this book (Wed-Mon 12:30-15:00 & 19:30-22:00, closed Tue, near City Hall at Via di Castello 2, tel. 0588-81510, www.enotecadelduca-ristorante.it).

$$ La Carabaccia is unique: It feels like a local family invited you over for a dinner of classic Tuscan comfort food that's rarely seen on restaurant menus. They serve only two pastas and two *secondi* on any given day (listed on the chalkboard by the door), in addition to quality cheese-and-cold-cut plates. Committed to tradition, on Fridays they serve only fish. They also have fun, family-friendly outdoor seating on a traffic-free piazza (Tue-Sat 12:30-14:30 & 19:30-22:00, Sun 12:30-14:30, closed Mon, reservations smart, Piazza XX Settembre 4, tel. 0588-86239, Patrizia and her daughters Sara and Ilaria).

$$ Ristorante il Sacco Fiorentino is a family-run local favorite for traditional cuisine and seasonal specials. While mostly indoors, the restaurant has a few nice tables on a peaceful street (Thu-Tue 12:00-15:00 & 19:00-22:00, closed Wed, Via Giusto Turazza 13, tel. 0588-88537).

$$ Trattoria da Badò, a 10-minute hike out of town (along the main road toward San Gimignano, near the turnoff for the old hospital), is popular with a local crowd for its *cucina tipica Volterrana*. Giacomo and family offer a rustic atmosphere and serve food with no pretense—"the way you wish your mamma cooks." Reserve before you go, as it's often full, especially on weekends (Thu-Tue 12:30-14:30 & 19:30-22:00, closed Wed, Borgo San Lazzero 9, tel. 0588-80402).

$$ La Vecchia Lira, bright and cheery, is a classy self-serve eatery that's a hit with locals as a quick and cheap lunch spot by day and a fancier restaurant at night (Fri-Wed 11:30-14:30 & 19:00-22:30, closed Thu, Via Matteotti 19, tel. 0588-86180, Lamberto and Massimo).

$$ Ristorante Ombra della Sera is another good fine-dining option. While they have a dressy interior, I'd eat here to be on the street and part of the *passegiata* action (Tue-Sun 12:00-15:00 & 19:00-22:00, closed Mon and mid-Nov-mid-March, Via Gramsci 70, tel. 0588-86663, Massimo and Cinzia).

$$ Empathy Bistrot is a good bet for organic and vegetarian dishes. They also make creative cocktails and don't close in the afternoon, making this an option at any hour. Choose between charming streetside tables or the modern, stony interior, where the glass floor hovers over an excavated Etruscan archaeological site (Fri-Wed 11:30-21:00, closed Thu, Via Porta All'Arco 11, tel. 0588-81531).

$$ Pizzeria La Mangiatoia is a fun and convivial place with a Tuscan-cowboy interior and picnic tables outside amid a family-friendly street scene. Enjoy pizzas, huge salads, and kebabs at a table or to go (Thu-Tue 12:00-23:00, closed Wed, Via Gramsci 35, tel. 0588-85695).

Side-by-Side Pizzerias: $ Ombra della Sera dishes out what local kids consider the best pizza in town (Tue-Sun 12:00-15:00 & 19:00-22:00, closed Mon and mid-Nov-mid-March, Via Guarnacci 16, tel. 0588-85274). **$ Pizzeria Tavernetta,** next door, has a romantically frescoed dining room upstairs for classier pizza eating (Wed-Mon 12:00-15:00 & 18:30-22:30, closed Tue, Via Guarnacci 14, tel. 0588-88155).

Picnic: You can assemble a picnic at the few *alimentari* around town and eat in the breezy archaeological park. The most convenient supermarket is Punto Simply at Via Gramsci 12 (Mon-Sat 7:30-13:00 & 16:00-20:00, Sun 8:30-13:00).

Gelato: Of the many ice-cream shops in the center, I've found **L'Isola di Gusto** to be reliably high-quality, with flavors limited to what's in season (daily 11:00-late, closed Nov-Feb, Via Gramsci 3, cheery Giorgia will make you feel happy).

Volterra Connections

By Bus: In Volterra, buses come and go from Piazza Martiri della Libertà (buy tickets at the tobacco shop right on the piazza or on board for small extra charge). Most connections are with the C.T.T.

bus company (www.pisa.cttnord.it) through Colle di Val d'Elsa ("koh-leh" for short), a workaday town in the valley (4/day Mon-Sat, 1/day Sun, 50 minutes); for Pisa, you'll change in Pontedera or Saline di Volterra.

From Volterra, you can ride the bus to these destinations: **Florence** (4/day Mon-Sat, 1/day Sun, 2 hours, change in Colle di Val d'Elsa), **Siena** (4/day Mon-Sat, no buses on Sun, 2 hours, change in Colle di Val d'Elsa), **San Gimignano** (4/day Mon-Sat, 1/day Sun, 2 hours, change in Colle di Val d'Elsa, one connection also requires change in Poggibonsi), **Pisa** (9/day, 2 hours, change in Pontedera or Saline di Volterra).

By Train: The nearest train station is in Saline di Volterra, a 15-minute bus ride away (7/day, 2/day Sun); however, trains from Saline run only to the coast, not to the major bus destinations listed here. It's better to take a bus from Volterra to Pontedera (CTT bus #500, 7/day, fewer on Sun, 1.5 hours), where you can catch a train to **Florence, Pisa,** or **La Spezia** (convenient for the Cinque Terre).

Private Transfer: For those with more money than time, or for travel on tricky Sundays and holidays, a private transfer to or from Volterra is the most efficient option. **Roberto Bechi** and his drivers can take up to eight people in their comfortable vans (€130 to Siena, €180 to Florence, for reservations call mobile 320-147-6590, Roberto's mobile 328-425-5648, www.toursbyroberto.com, toursbyroberto@gmail.com).

San Gimignano

The epitome of a Tuscan hill town, with 14 medieval towers still standing (out of an original 72), San Gimignano (sahn jee-meen-YAH-noh) is a perfectly preserved tourist trap. There are no important interiors to sightsee, and the town  feels greedy and packed with crass commercialism. The locals seem spoiled by the easy money of tourism, and most of the rustic is faux. But San Gimignano is so easy to reach and so visually striking that it remains a good stop, especially if you can sidestep some of the hordes. The town is an ideal place to go against the touristic flow—arrive late in the day, enjoy it at twilight, then take off in the morning before the deluge begins. (Or day-trip here from Volterra—a 30-minute drive away—and visit early or late.)

In the 13th century—back in the days of Romeo and Juliet—

feuding noble families ran the hill towns. They'd periodically battle things out from the protection of their respective family towers. Pointy skylines like San Gimignano's were the norm in medieval Tuscany.

San Gimignano's cuisine is mostly what you might find in Siena—typical Tuscan home cooking. *Cinghiale* (cheeng-GAH-lay, boar) is served in almost every way: stews, soups, cutlets, and, my favorite, salami. The area is well-known for producing some of the best saffron in Italy; you'll find the spice for sale in shops (fairly expensive) and as a flavoring in meals at finer restaurants. Although Tuscany is normally a red-wine region, the most famous Tuscan white wine comes from here: the inexpensive, light, and fruity Vernaccia di San Gimignano.

Orientation to San Gimignano

While the basic ▲▲▲ sight here is the town of San Gimignano itself (pop. 7,000, just 2,000 of whom live within the walls), there are a few worthwhile stops. The wall circles an amazingly preserved stony town, once on the Via Francigena pilgrimage route to Rome. The road, which cuts through the middle of San Gimignano, is named for St. Matthew in the north of town (Via San Matteo) and St. John in the south (Via San Giovanni). The town is centered on two delightful squares—Piazza del Duomo and Piazza della Cisterna—where you find the town well, City Hall, and cathedral (along with most of the tourists).

TOURIST INFORMATION

The helpful TI is in the old center on Piazza del Duomo (daily March-Oct 10:00-13:00 & 15:00-19:00, Nov-Feb 10:00-13:00 & 14:00-18:00, sells bus tickets to Siena and Florence, tel. 0577-940-008, www.sangimignano.com). They offer a two-hour minibus tour to a countryside winery (€30, April-Oct Tue and Thu at 17:00, book one day in advance).

ARRIVAL IN SAN GIMIGNANO

The **bus** stops at the main town gate, Porta San Giovanni. There's no baggage storage in town.

You can't **drive** within the walled town; drive past the *"ZTL"* red circle and you'll get socked with a big fine. Three numbered pay lots are a short walk outside the walls: The handiest is Parcheggio Montemaggio (P2), at the bottom of town near the bus stop, just outside Porta San Giovanni (€2/hour, €20/day). Least expensive is the lot below the roundabout and Coop supermarket, called Parcheggio Giubileo (P1; €1.50/hour, €6/day), a steeper hike into town. And at the north end of town, by Porta San Jacopo,

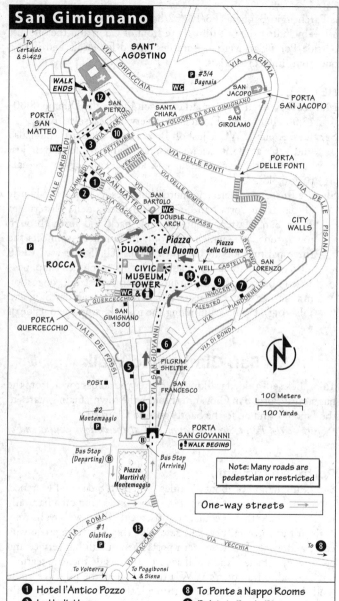

San Gimignano

1. Hotel l'Antico Pozzo
2. Le Undici Lune
3. Locanda il Pino
4. Hotel la Cisterna
5. Palazzo al Torrione
6. Tobacco Shop (Torrione Keys)
7. Le Vecchie Mura Camere & Ristorante
8. To Ponte a Nappo Rooms
9. Dulcis in Fundo Ristorante
10. Cum Quibus Ristorante
11. Trattoria Chiribiri
12. Locanda di Sant'Agostino
13. Coop Supermarket
14. Gelateria Dondoli

VOLTERRA & SAN GIMIGNANO

is Parcheggio Bagnaia (P3/P4, €2/hour, €15/day). Note that some lots—including the one directly in front of Coop and the one just outside Porta San Matteo—are designated for locals and have a one-hour limit for tourists.

HELPFUL HINTS

Market Day: Thursday is market day on Piazza del Duomo (8:00-13:00), but for local merchants, every day is a sales frenzy.

Services: A public WC is just off Piazza della Cisterna; you'll also find WCs at the Rocca fortress, near San Bartolo church, just outside Porta San Matteo, and at the Parcheggio Bagnaia parking lot.

Shuttle Bus: A little electric shuttle bus does its laps about hourly all day from Porta San Giovanni to Piazza della Cisterna to Porta San Matteo. Route #1 runs back and forth through town; route #2—which runs only in summer—connects the three parking lots to the town center (€0.75 one-way, €1.50 all-day pass, buy ticket in advance at TI or tobacco shop, possible to buy all-day pass on bus). When pedestrian congestion in the town center is greatest (Sat afternoons, all day Sun, and July-Aug), the bus runs along the road skirting the outside of town.

San Gimignano Walk

This quick self-guided walking tour takes you across town, from the bus stop at Porta San Giovanni through the town's main squares to the Duomo, and on to the Sant'Agostino Church.

• *Start at the Porta San Giovanni gate at the bottom (south) end of town.*

Porta San Giovanni

San Gimignano lies about 25 miles from both Siena and Florence, a day's trek for pilgrims en route to those cities, and on a naturally fortified hilltop that encouraged settlement. The town's walls were built in the 13th century, and gates like this helped regulate who came and went. Today, modern posts keep out all but service and emergency vehicles. The small square just outside the gate features a memorial to the town's WWII dead. Follow the pilgrims' route (and flood of modern tourists) through the gate and up the main drag.

About 100 yards up, where the street widens, look right to see a pilgrims' shelter (12th-century, Pisan Romanesque). The eight-pointed Maltese cross on the facade of the church indicates that it was built by the Knights of Malta, whose early mission (before they became a military unit) was to provide hospitality for pilgrims.

It was one of 11 such shelters in town. Today, only the wall of the shelter remains, and the surviving interior of the church houses yet one more shop selling gifty edibles.

• *Carry on past all manner of shops, up to the top of Via San Giovanni. Look up at the formidable inner wall, built 200 years before today's outer wall. Just beyond that is the central Piazza della Cisterna. Sit on the steps of the well.*

Piazza della Cisterna

The piazza is named for the cistern that is served by the old well standing in the center of this square. A clever system of pipes drained rainwater from the nearby rooftops into the underground cistern. This square has been the center of the town since the ninth century. Turn in a slow circle and observe the commotion of rustic-yet-proud facades crowding in a tight huddle around the well. Imag-

ine this square in pilgrimage times, lined by inns and taverns for the town's guests. Now finger the grooves in the lip of the well and imagine generations of maids and children fetching water. Each Thursday morning, the square fills with a market—as it has for more than a thousand years.

• *Notice San Gimignano's famous towers.*

The Towers

Of the original 72 towers, only 14 survive (and one can be climbed—at the City Hall). Some of the original towers were just

empty, chimney-like structures built to boost noble egos, while others were actually the forts of wealthy families.

Before effective city walls were developed, rich people needed to fortify their own homes. These towers provided a handy refuge when ruffians and rival city-states were sacking the town. If under attack, tower owners would set fire to the external wooden staircase, leaving the sole entrance unreachable a story up; inside, fleeing nobles pulled up behind them the ladders that connected each level, leaving invaders no way to reach the stronghold at the tower's top. These towers became a standard part of medieval skylines. Even after town walls were built, the towers continued to rise—now to fortify noble families feuding within a town (Montague and Capulet-style).

In the 14th century, San Gimignano's good times turned very bad. In the year 1300, about 13,000 people lived within the walls. Then, in 1348, a six-month plague decimated the population, leaving the once-mighty town with barely 4,000 survivors. Once fiercely independent, now crushed and demoralized, San Gimignano came under Florence's control and was forced to tear down most of its towers. (The Banca CR Firenze building occupies the remains of one such toppled tower.) And, to add insult to injury, Florence redirected the vital trade route away from San Gimignano. The town never recovered, and poverty left it in a 14th-century architectural time warp. That well-preserved cityscape, ironically, is responsible for the town's prosperity today.

• *From the well, walk 30 yards uphill to the adjoining square with the cathedral.*

Piazza del Duomo

Stand at the base of the stairs in front of the church. Since before there was gelato, people have lounged on these steps. Take a 360-degree spin clockwise: The cathedral's 12th-century facade is plain-Jane Romanesque—finished even though it doesn't look it. To the right, the two Salvucci Towers (a.k.a. the "Twin Towers") date from the 13th century. Locals like to brag that the architect who designed New York City's Twin Towers was inspired

by these. The towers are empty shells, built by the wealthy Salvucci family simply to show off. At that time, no one was allowed a vanity tower higher than the City Hall's 170 feet. So the Salvuccis built two 130-foot towers—totaling 260 feet of stony ego trip.

The stubby tower next to the Salvucci Towers is the Merchant's Tower. Imagine this in use: ground-floor shop, warehouse upstairs (see the functional shipping door), living quarters, and finally the kitchen on the top (for fire-safety reasons). The holes in the walls held beams that supported wooden balconies and exterior staircases. The tower has heavy stone on the first floor, then cheaper and lighter brick for the upper stories.

Opposite the church stands the first City Hall, with its 170-foot tower, nicknamed "the bad news tower." While the church got to ring its bells in good times, these bells were for wars and fires. The tower's arched public space hosted a textile market back when cloth was the foundation of San Gimignano's booming economy.

Next is the super-sized "new" City Hall with its 200-foot tower (the only one in town open to the public; for visiting info, see the Civic Museum and Tower listing, later). The climbing lion is the symbol of the city. The coats of arms of the city's leading families have been ripped down or disfigured. In medieval times locals would have blamed witches or ghosts. For the last two centuries, they've blamed Napoleon instead.

Between the City Hall and the cathedral, a statue of St. Gimignano presides over all the hubbub. The fourth-century bishop protected the village from rampaging barbarians—and is now the city's patron saint. (To enter the cathedral, walk under that statue.)
• *You'll also see the...*

Duomo (Collegiata)

Inside San Gimignano's Romanesque cathedral, Sienese Gothic art (14th century) lines the nave with parallel themes—Old Testament on the left and New Testament on the right. (For example, from back to front: Creation facing the Annunciation, the birth of Adam facing the Nativity, and—farther forward—the suffering of Job opposite the suffering of Jesus.) This is a classic use of art to teach. Study the fine Creation series (along the left side). Many scenes are portrayed with a 14th-century "slice of life" setting to help lay townspeople relate to Jesus—in the same way that many white Christians are more comfortable thinking of Jesus as Caucasian.

To the right of the altar, the St. Fina Chapel honors the devout, 13th-century local girl who brought forth many miracles on her death. Her tomb is beautifully frescoed with scenes from her life by Domenico Ghirlandaio (famed as Michelangelo's teacher). The altar sits atop Fina's skeleton, and its centerpiece is a reliquary that contains her skull (€4, includes dry audioguide; April-Oct Mon-Fri 10:00-19:30, Sat until 17:30, Sun 12:30-19:30; shorter hours off-season; buy ticket and enter from courtyard around left side).
• *From the church, hike uphill (passing the church on your left) following signs to* Rocca e Parco di Montestaffoli. *Keep walking until you enter a peaceful hilltop park and olive grove, set within the shell of a 14th-century fortress the Medici of Florence built to protect this town from Siena.*

Hilltop Views at the Rocca

On the far side, 33 steps take you to the top of a little tower (free) for the best views of San Gimignano's skyline; the far end of town and the Sant'Agostino Church (where this walk ends); and a commanding 360-degree view of the Tuscan countryside. San Gimignano is surrounded by olives, grapes, cypress trees, and—in the

Middle Ages—lots of wild dangers. Back then, farmers lived inside the walls and were thankful for the protection.

• *Return to the bottom of Piazza del Duomo, turn left, and continue your walk, cutting under the double arch (from the town's first wall). In around 1200, this defined the end of town. The* **Church of San Bartolo** *stood just outside the wall (on the right). The Maltese cross over the door indicates that it likely served as a hostel for pilgrims. As you continue down Via San Matteo, notice that the crowds have dropped by at least half. Enjoy the breathing room as you pass a fascinating array of stone facades from the 13th and 14th centuries—now a happy cancan of wine shops and galleries. Reaching the gateway at the end of town, follow signs to the right to reach...*

Sant'Agostino Church

This tranquil church, at the far end of town (built by the Augustinians who arrived in 1260), has fewer crowds and more soul. Behind the altar, a lovely fresco cycle by Benozzo Gozzoli (who painted the exquisite Chapel of the Magi in the Medici-Riccardi Palace in Florence) tells of the life of St. Augustine, a North African monk who preached simplicity (pay a few coins for light). The kind, English-speaking friars (often from Britain and the US) are happy to tell you about the frescoes and their way of life. Pace the peaceful cloister before heading back into the tourist mobs (free, April-Oct daily 9:00-12:00 & 15:00-17:00, shorter hours off-season; Sunday Mass in English at 11:00).

Sights in San Gimignano

▲Civic Museum and Tower (Musei Civici and Torre Grossa)

This small, entertaining museum, consisting of three unfurnished rooms, is inside the City Hall (Palazzo Comunale). The main reason to visit is to scale the tower, which offers sweeping views over San Gimignano and the countryside.

Cost and Hours: €9 includes museum and tower; daily 10:00-19:30, Oct-March 11:00-17:30, audioguide-€2, Piazza del Duomo, tel. 0577-990-312, www.sangimignanomusei.it.

Visiting the Museum: You'll enter the complex through a delightful stony courtyard (to the left as you face the Duomo). Climb up to the loggia to buy your ticket.

The main room (across from the ticket desk), called the **Sala di Consiglio** (a.k.a. Dante Hall, recalling his visit in 1300), is covered in festive frescoes, including the *Maestà* by Lippo Memmi (from 1317). This virtual copy of Simone Martini's *Maestà* in Siena proves that Memmi didn't have quite the same talent as his famous brother-in-law. The art gives you a peek at how people dressed, lived, worked, and warred back in the 14th century.

Upstairs, the **Pinacoteca** displays a classy little painting collection of mostly altarpieces. The highlight is a 1422 altarpiece by Taddeo di Bartolo honoring St. Gimignano (far end of last room). You can see the saint, with the town—bristling with towers—in his hands, surrounded by events from his life.

Before going back downstairs, be sure to stop by the **Mayor's Room** (Camera del Podestà, across the stairwell from the Pinacoteca). Frescoed in 1310, it offers an intimate and candid peek into the 14th century. As you enter, look right up in the corner to find a young man ready to experience the world. He hits his parents up for a bag of money and is on his way. Suddenly (above the window), he's in trouble, entrapped by two prostitutes, who lead him into a tent where he loses his money, is turned out, and is beaten. Above the door, from left to right, you see a parade of better choices: marriage, the cradle of love, the bride led to the groom's house, and newlyweds bathing together and retiring happily to their bed.

The highlight for most visitors is a chance to climb the **Tower** (Torre Grossa, entrance halfway down the stairs from the Pinacoteca). The city's tallest tower, 200 feet and 218 steps up, rewards those who climb it with a commanding view. See if you can count the town's 14 towers. It's a sturdy, modern staircase most of the way, but the last stretch is a steep, ladder-like climb.

San Gimignano 1300

Artists and brothers Michelangelo and Raffaello Rubino share an interesting attraction in their workshop: a painstakingly rendered 1:100 scale clay model of San Gimignano at the turn of the 14th century. Step through a shop selling their art to enjoy the model. You can see the 72 original "tower houses," and marvel at how unchanged the street plan remains today. You'll peek into cross-sections of buildings, view scenes of medieval life both within and outside the city walls, and watch a video about the making of the model.

Cost and Hours: Free, daily 10:00-18:00, Dec-April until 17:00, on a quiet street a block over from the main square at Via Costarella 3, mobile 327-439-5165, www.sangimignano1300.com.

VOLTERRA & SAN GIMIGNANO

Sleeping in San Gimignano

Although the town is a zoo during the daytime, locals outnumber tourists when evening comes, and San Gimignano becomes mellow and enjoyable.

NEAR PORTA SAN MATTEO, AT THE QUIET END OF TOWN

If arriving by bus, save yourself a crosstown walk to these accommodations by asking for the Porta San Matteo stop (rather than the main stop near Porta San Giovanni). Drivers can park at the less-crowded Bagnaia lots (P3 and P4), and walk around to Porta San Matteo.

$$$ Hotel l'Antico Pozzo is an elegantly restored, 15th-century townhouse with 18 tranquil, comfortable rooms, a peaceful interior courtyard terrace, and an elite air (RS%—use code "RICK," air-con, elevator, Via San Matteo 87, tel. 0577-942-014, www. anticopozzo.com, info@anticopozzo.com; Emanuele, Elisabetta, and Mariangela).

$$ Le Undici Lune ("The 11 Moons") is situated in a tight but characteristic circa-1300 townhouse with steep stairs at the tranquil end of town. Its three rooms and one apartment have been tastefully decorated with modern flair by Gabriele (RS%, air-con, Via Mainardi 9, mobile 389-236-8174, www.leundicilune.com, leundicilune@gmail.com).

$ Locanda il Pino has just seven rooms and a big living room. It's dank but clean and quiet. Run by English-speaking Elena and her family, it sits above their elegant restaurant at the quiet end of town, just inside Porta San Matteo (breakfast extra, fans, Via Cellolese 4, tel. 0577-940-218, www.locandailpino.it, locandailpino@gmail.com).

NEAR THE MAIN SQUARE, AT THE BUSY END OF TOWN

$$ Hotel la Cisterna, right on Piazza della Cisterna, feels old and stately. Its 48 rooms range from old-fashioned to contemporary, and some have panoramic view terraces—one of which served as the viewpoint for a scene in the film *Tea with Mussolini* (RS%, air-con, elevator, good restaurant with great view, closed Jan-Feb, Piazza della Cisterna 23, tel. 0577-940-328, www.hotelcisterna.it, info@hotelcisterna.it, Alessio and Paola).

$$ Palazzo al Torrione, on an untrampled side street just inside Porta San Giovanni, is quiet and handy. Despite the smoky reception area, this place is generally better than most local hotels. Their 10 modern rooms, some with countryside views, are spacious and tastefully appointed (RS%, family rooms, breakfast extra, air-con, pay parking, inside and left of gate at Via Berignano 76; operated from tobacco shop 2 blocks away, on the main drag at Via San Giovanni 59; tel. 0577-940-480, mobile 338-938-1656, www.palazzoaltorrione.com, palazzoaltorrione@palazzoaltorrione.com, Vanna and Francesco).

$ Le Vecchie Mura Camere offers three good rooms above their recommended restaurant along a rustic lane, clinging just below the main square (no breakfast, air-con, Via Piandornella 15, tel. 0577-940-270, www.vecchiemura.it, info@vecchiemura.it, Bagnai family).

IN THE COUNTRYSIDE, WITH A STUNNING VIEW OF SAN GIMIGNANO

$$ Ponte a Nappo, run by enterprising Carla Rossi and her English-speaking sons Francesco and Andrea, has six basic rooms and two apartments in a kid-friendly farmhouse boasting fine San Gimignano views. Located a mile below town, it can be reached by foot in about 20 minutes if you don't have a car. A picnic dinner lounging on their comfy garden furniture next to the big swimming pool as the sun sets is good Tuscan living (RS%—use code "RickSteves," air-con, free parking, tel. 0577-907-282, mobile 349-882-1565, www.accommodation-sangimignano.com, info@rossicarla.it). About 100 yards below the monument square at Porta San Giovanni, find tiny Via Baccanella/Via Vecchia and drive downhill. They also rent a dozen rooms and apartments in town.

Eating in San Gimignano

My first two listings cling to quiet, rustic lanes overlooking the Tuscan hills (yet just a few steps off the main street); the rest are buried deep in the old center.

$$$ Dulcis in Fundo Ristorante, small and family-run, proudly serves modest portions of "revisited" Tuscan cuisine (with a modern twist and gourmet presentation) in a jazzy ambience. This enlightened place uses top-quality ingredients, many of which come from their own farm. They also offer vegetarian and gluten-free options (Thu-Tue 12:30-14:30 & 19:15-21:45, closed Wed and Nov-Feb, Vicolo degli Innocenti 21, tel. 0577-941-919, Roberto and Cristina).

$$ Le Vecchie Mura Ristorante is welcoming, with good service, great prices, tasty if unexceptional home cooking, and the ultimate view. It's romantic indoors or out. They have a dressy, modern interior where you can dine with a view of the busy stainless-steel kitchen under rustic vaults, but the main reason to come is for the incredible, cliff-side garden terrace. Cliff-side tables are worth reserving in advance by calling or dropping by: Ask for "front view" (open only for dinner 18:00-22:00, closed Tue, Via Piandornella 15, tel. 0577-940-270, Bagnai family).

$$$ Cum Quibus ("In Company"), tucked away near Porta San Matteo, has a small dining room with soft music, beamed ceilings, modern touches, and a sophisticated vibe; it also offers al fresco tables in its interior patio. Lorenzo and Simona produce tasty and creative Tuscan cuisine (Wed-Mon 12:30-14:30 & 19:00-22:00, closed Tue, reservations advised, Via San Martino 17, tel. 0577-943-199).

$ Trattoria Chiribiri, just inside Porta San Giovanni on the left, serves homemade pastas and desserts at good prices. While its petite size and tight seating make it hot in the summer, it's a good budget option—and as such, it's in all the guidebooks (daily 11:00-23:00, Piazza della Madonna 1, tel. 0577-941-948, Roberto and Maurizio).

$$ Locanda di Sant'Agostino spills out onto the peaceful square, facing Sant'Agostino Church. It's homey and cheerful, serving lunch and dinner daily—big portions of basic food in a restful setting. Dripping with wheat stalks and atmosphere on the inside, it has shady on-the-square seating outside (daily 11:00-23:00, closed Wed off-season, closed Jan-Feb, Piazza Sant'Agostino 15, tel. 0577-943-141, Genziana and sons).

Near Porto San Matteo: Just inside Porta San Matteo are a variety of handy and inviting good-value restaurants, bars, cafés, and *gelaterie*. Eateries need to work harder here at the nontouristy end of town.

Picnics: The big, modern **Coop supermarket** sells all you need for a nice spread (Mon-Sat 8:30-20:00, closed Sun, at parking lot below Porta San Giovanni). Or browse the little shops guarded by boar heads within the town walls; they sell pricey boar meat *(cinghiale)*. Pick up 100 grams (about a quarter pound) of boar, cheese, bread, and wine and enjoy a picnic in the garden at the Rocca or the park outside Porta San Giovanni.

Gelato: To cap the evening and sweeten your late-night city stroll, stop by **Gelateria Dondoli** on Piazza della Cisterna (at #4). Gelatomaker Sergio was a member of the Italian team that won the official Gelato World Cup—and his gelato really is a cut above. He's usually near the front door greeting customers—ask what new flavors he's invented recently (tel. 0577-942-244, www.gelateriadondoli.com, sergio@gelateriadondoli.com, Dondoli family). Charismatic Sergio also offers hands-on gelato making classes in his kitchen down the street.

San Gimignano Connections

Bus tickets are sold at the bar just inside the town gate or at the TI. Many connections require a change at Poggibonsi (poh-jee-BOHN-see), which is also the nearest train station.

From San Gimignano by Bus to: Florence (hourly, fewer on Sun, 1.5-2 hours, change in Poggibonsi), **Siena** (8/day direct, on Sun must change in Poggibonsi, 1.5 hours), **Volterra** (4/day Mon-Sat; 1/day Sun—in the late afternoon and usually crowded—with no return to San Gimignano; 2 hours, change in Colle di Val d'Elsa, one connection also requires change in Poggibonsi). Note that the bus connection to Volterra is four times as long as the drive; if you're desperate to get there faster, you can pay about €70 for a taxi.

By Car: San Gimignano is an easy 45-minute drive from Florence (take the A-1 exit marked *Firenze Impruneta*, then a right past tollbooth following *Siena per 4 corsie* sign; exit the freeway at *Poggibonsi Nord*). From San Gimignano, it's a scenic and windy half-hour drive to Volterra.

Near San Gimignano: Monteriggioni

The perfectly preserved ring fort of Monteriggioni (mohn-teh-rih-jee-OH-nee) proudly caps its hill high above the main highway, running from the Volterra/San Gimignano area south to Siena. Although it's a mostly empty shell today—and a tourist-bus magnet on par with San Gimignano—it's worth a quick stop if you're ready for a stretch-your-legs break. Visitors enjoy strolling its tidy square and climbing parts of its walls. Unless you linger over a meal, Monteriggioni works best as a half-hour to hour-long stop.

Getting There: Monteriggioni is well-signed and only a mile off the main SR-2 highway, just north of Siena. Try parking in the lot at the top of the hill, below the main gate. If that's full, head to the large gravel lot closer to the base of the hill.

Visiting the Town: Monteriggioni's stout fortifications vividly illustrate two major historical trends in medieval Tuscany: Siena built the fortress around 1213 to protect its lands from the threatening expansion of its rival city-state, Florence. But Monteriggioni also protected religious pilgrims treading the Via Francigena route from northern Europe to Rome (who were, not coincidentally, a major source of Sienese wealth). Dante wrote poetically

about Monteriggioni's might in his *Divine Comedy*. It finally surrendered to the Medici in 1554, becoming part of Florence and remaining in remarkably good repair.

Today, Monteriggioni feels like a historical theme park. English information plaques posted around the village explain its history. Entering its main gate (Porta Romana), you emerge onto its pleasant piazza, ringed with souvenir shops and al fresco eateries. On the right side of the square, tucked back in a little courtyard, is the **TI** and **Armor Museum,** with historical exhibits and models of the fortress, an explanation of siege warfare, and modern re-creations of weapons and armor that you can try on (€3 combo-ticket with walls, TI/museum open daily 9:30-13:30 & 14:00-19:30, shorter hours mid-Sept-March, audioguide-€1.50, Piazza Roma 23, tel. 0577-304-834, www.monteriggioniturismo.it).

If you poke into the little courtyard beyond the TI, you'll find a **pilgrim's *ospitalità*,** a rustic refuge offering basic accommodations for present-day pilgrims following the Via Francigena. Like the more famous Camino de Santiago across northern Spain, this medieval pilgrim route is again in vogue—as, for the first time in centuries, people are walking its entire length, through Tuscan splendor to Rome. (For more on the Via Francigena, see page 569.)

The other main sight in Monteriggioni is the town's impressively intact **walls.** The blocky, angular towers—designed to shed incoming arrows—indicate the walls were built before the advent of cannons (when round towers became the norm). From Roman times through the Middle Ages, towers like these were built 50 yards apart—the distance an arrow could fly with accuracy. While the walls are about a third of a mile around, you can ascend them only for a stroll on two short stretches: above the town's main Porta Romana entrance gate, and at the opposite end, near the Porta Fiorentina gate. The same ticket—sold at the entry points or the TI—covers both sections (€3 combo-ticket with Armor Museum, same hours). Once up top, appreciate the strategic location, with 360-degree views over Tuscan hills. The busy highway below follows the route of the Via Cassia, the Roman-built road that connects Rome to Florence and points north, making it popular among ancient traders, medieval pilgrims...and contemporary tourists.

THE HEART OF TUSCANY

Montepulciano • Pienza • Montalcino • Heart of Tuscany Drive • Brunello Wine Country Drive

If your Tuscan dreams feature vibrant neon-green fields rolling to infinity, punctuated by snaking, cypress-lined driveways; humble but beautiful (and steep) hill towns; and world-class wines to make a connoisseur weep, set your sights on the heart of this region.

An hour south of Siena, this slice of splendor—which specializes in views and wine—is a highlight, particularly for drivers. With an astonishing diversity of towns, villages, abbeys, wineries, countryside restaurants, and accommodations—all set within jaw-dropping scenery, this subregion of Tuscany is a fine place to abandon your itinerary and just slow down.

Even though the area's towns sometimes seem little more than a rack upon which to hang the vine-draped hills, each one has its own endearing personality. The biggest and most interesting, Montepulciano, boasts a medieval cityscape wearing a Renaissance coat, wine cellars that plunge deep down into the cliffs it sits upon, and a classic town square. Pienza is a sure-of-itself, planned Renaissance town that gave the world a pope. And mellow Montalcino is (even more than most towns around here) all about its wine: the famous Brunello di Montalcino.

Outside these three centers are some low-key sights: the pleasant spa town of Bagno Vignoni, the perfectly manicured gardens of La Foce, and the historic Sant'Antimo Abbey. (Just to the north, closer to Siena, is the Abbey of Monte Oliveto Maggiore, one of Tuscany's top art treasures—see page 410.) And at the core of this region is the stunning landscape of the Val d'Orcia, with its famous tree-lined lanes and hill-capping farmhouses.

This area also enjoys a rich history: During the Middle Ages, the Via Francigena pilgrimage route ran from northern Italy—and northern Europe—right through here to Rome, blessing it with a series of stout fortresses (including the one at Rocca d'Orcia) and

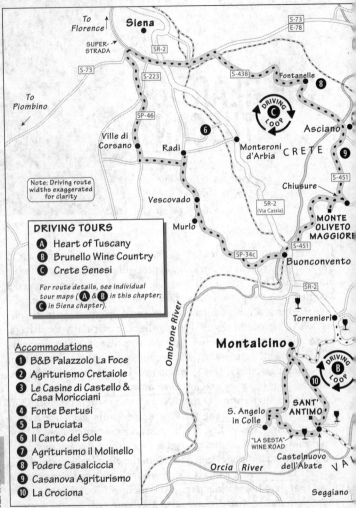

To Florence

Siena

S-73
E-78

SUPER-STRADA

SR-2

S-73

S-223

S-438

Fontanelle

8

To Piombino

SP-46

6

Monteroni d'Arbia

C R E T E

Asciano

9

Ville di Corsano

Radi

Chiusure

S-451

Note: Driving route widths exaggerated for clarity

Vescovado

SR-2 (Via Cassia)

MONTE OLIVETO MAGGIORE

Murlo

S-451

DRIVING TOURS

A Heart of Tuscany
B Brunello Wine Country
C Crete Senesi

*For route details, see individual tour maps (**A** & **B** in this chapter; **C** in Siena chapter).*

SP-34c

Buonconvento

SR-2

Torrenieri

Ombrone River

Montalcino

DRIVING LOOP B

10

Accommodations

1 B&B Palazzolo La Foce
2 Agriturismo Cretaiole
3 Le Casine di Castello & Casa Moricciani
4 Fonte Bertusi
5 La Bruciata
6 Il Canto del Sole
7 Agriturismo il Molinello
8 Podere Casalciccia
9 Casanova Agriturismo
10 La Crociona

S. Angelo in Colle

SANT' ANTIMO

"LA SESTA" WINE ROAD

Castelnuovo dell'Abate

Orcia River

VAL

Seggiano

welcoming pilgrim churches (including Sant'Antimo Abbey, where monks still worship God with a Gregorian chant).

Don't be overly focused on ticking off a list of sights here. This region's attractions—while substantial—are best seen as an excuse for a countryside drive. I've narrated two ideal routes in this chapter (and a third in the Siena chapter). As you explore, every few minutes you'll want to pull over and marvel at the plush mix of man-made and natural beauty. And each time you frame a photograph—filling your screen with rolling fields, wispy lines of cypress trees, and stony hill towns, all reaching up toward a wide azure sky—you can only think one word: Tuscany.

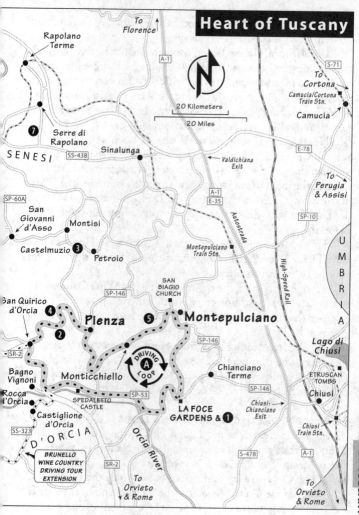

PLANNING YOUR TIME

This region richly rewards whatever time you're willing to give it. At a minimum, splice this area into your drive between destinations to the north (Siena, Florence) and to the south (Orvieto, Rome). As this compact region is hemmed in by Italy's two main north-south thoroughfares—the A-1 expressway and SR-2 highway—even those with a few hours to spare can get an enticing taste. But ideally, spend two nights and three full days (see my three-day plan on the next page). Many travelers enjoy home-basing here for up to a week, appreciating not only the area's many attractions, but also its strategic position for day trips to Siena and Cortona (each less than an hour away), or even to Volterra, San Gimignano, Florence, and Orvieto (each about 1.5 hours away).

Choosing a Home Base: Montepulciano is the most all-around engaging town; it's the best choice for those without a car (though connections can still be tricky). With easy access to the vineyards, Montalcino makes sense for wine pilgrims. For drivers who'd like to home-base in the countryside, I've listed several *agriturismi* and other rural accommodations below.

Navigating This Region: With so much to see scattered across a wide area, this region can be challenging to organize from a touring point of view. Many travelers just lace together two or three of the main towns, with a few stopovers en route. The "Heart of Tuscany at a Glance" sidebar will help you narrow down your options. But with more time, consider one of my self-guided driving tours:

From Montepulciano or Pienza, my circular **Heart of Tuscany Drive** laces together a scenic string of minor sights, giving you the essence of the area.

From Montalcino, the capital of **Brunello Wine Country,** I've recommended several fine countryside wineries, as well as a driving tour that ties some of them together, along with Sant'Antimo Abbey.

If you're connecting to or from Siena, the prettiest back-roads route takes you through the **Crete Senesi,** with one major sight: the Abbey of Monte Oliveto Maggiore (drive and abbey covered at the end of the Siena chapter, earlier in this book).

The Heart of Tuscany in Three Days

Three days is enough to get a good look at the area's many highlights. Here's a smart plan, assuming you're coming from Siena. (If coming from the south, do it in reverse.)

Day One: On your way south from Siena, enjoy the rugged landscape of the Crete Senesi (see the Siena chapter), then make a winery stop north of Montalcino before settling into Montepulciano (or your countryside accommodation).

Day Two: Follow my Heart of Tuscany Drive, including a sightseeing-and-gelato stop in Pienza. Have dinner back in Montepulciano, or in the nearby countryside.

Day Three: Your day is free to enjoy and sightsee Montepulciano, or drive to countryside attractions (reserve ahead to visit La Foce Gardens). You could head to your next destination this afternoon, or spend a third night.

GETTING AROUND THE HEART OF TUSCANY

By Car: This area is ideal by car, and I've designed this chapter primarily with drivers in mind, including two self-guided driving tours that link the best stops with the most picturesque routes. Distances are short, and it's easy to mix-and-match sights, but these routes offer the best combination of scenery and interesting stops.

Navigate by town names and use a good map (local hotels and TIs hand out a fine free one) or—better yet—a mapping app with GPS to keep you on track. Look at the routes it suggests before choosing one, and try to stay on paved roads. Some attractions are on tiny back lanes, marked only with easy-to-miss, low-profile signs. I've given distances in kilometers to match up with your rental car's odometer.

Many of the small towns in this area are designated as "ZTL" (limited-traffic zone)—off-limits to nonlocal traffic. While village ZTLs aren't monitored by cameras (as in big cities), you can still be ticketed if you're found crossing that line. In small hill towns, make it a habit to park at the lot just outside town and walk in. White lines indicate free parking; blue lines indicate paid parking (pay at the station, then display the ticket on your windshield); and yellow lines are only for locals. Parking machines typically don't accept bills or give change; have plenty of coins on hand.

By Public Transportation: While you can reach many of this chapter's sights by public buses, connections are slow, infrequent, and often require a transfer. Taxis can help connect the dots more efficiently. Montepulciano is the best home base for those without a car (though it's still not entirely convenient). See the map on page 651 for an overview.

TOURS IN TUSCANY

A good local guide can help you take full advantage of everything this area has to offer. One with a car can save you lots of time and stress.

Antonella Piredda, who lives in the village of Montisi (just north of Pienza), is smart, well-organized, and enjoyably opinionated (€60/hour, 3-hour minimum, €350/all day, she can join you in your car or hire a driver for extra, mobile 347-456-5150, www. antonellapiredda.com, antonella.piredda@live.it). Antonella also offers a beautiful apartment for rent in Montisi (www.casaparva. com).

Roberto Bechi, a great guide who lives in the Crete Senesi, runs all-day minibus tours with a passion for local culture, hands-on experiences, and offbeat sights. The price is reasonable, since he assembles groups of up to eight people to share the experience...and

Heart of Tuscany at a Glance

▲▲▲**Montepulciano** Hill town with grand vistas, wonderful wine cellars, and a medieval soul that corrals the essence of Tuscany within its walls. See page 530.

▲▲▲**Heart of Tuscany Drive** An unforgettable day lacing together the views, villages, and rural attractions of this region (including both Montepulciano and Pienza). See page 565.

▲▲**Pienza** Unique, pint-sized planned Renaissance town that's amazingly well-preserved, very touristy, and relatively unhilly. See page 546.

▲▲**Montalcino** Touristy "Brunello-ville" wine capital that still exudes a stony charm; aside from the wine, it feels like a second-rate repeat of Montepulciano. See page 554.

▲▲**Brunello Wine Country Drive** My favorite countryside places to sample the famous Brunello di Montalcino, all gorgeously situated among hills and vineyards. **Hours:** Call ahead to schedule a tour and tasting. See page 576.

▲▲**Crete Senesi** Beautiful scenery—the stuff of coffee-table photo books—and the ▲▲▲ Abbey of Monte Oliveto Maggiore, best seen on a driving tour between Siena and the "Heart of Tuscany." See the Siena chapter.

the cost (see website for tour options, special Rick Steves discount price: full-day minibus tours–€90/person, mobile 320-147-6590, www.toursbyroberto.com, toursbyroberto@gmail.com). For more on Roberto's tours, see page 354.

Giovanni Adreani, an energetic Cortona-based guide, is a good choice if you're home-basing in Cortona and want to efficiently hit Montepulciano, Pienza, and Montalcino in one day (€220 for up to 5 people, €10-15/person extra for wine-tasting stop—must reserve in advance, tel. 0575-630-665, mobile 347-176-2830, www.adreanigiovanni.com, adreanigiovanni@libero.it). For more on Giovanni, see page 584.

COUNTRYSIDE ACCOMMODATIONS

While I've listed fine accommodations in Siena, Montepulciano, and Montalcino, a beautiful way to more fully experience this area is to sleep in a farmhouse B&B. Here I list favorites near Pienza, in the Crete Senesi (closer to Siena), near Montalcino, and at La Foce Gardens (near Montepulciano). For locations, see the map on page 523. Many of these are working farms (a prerequisite to be of-

▲▲**Sleeping at an *Agriturismo* or Countryside B&B** The best way to experience rural Tuscany: rustic, rural accommodations ranging from fragrant working farms to luxurious retreats. Most are run by families dedicated to making sure their cows and their guests are both well-fed. See page 526.

▲**La Foce Gardens** Delightful, unique gardens with gorgeous plantings, engaging history, and fine panoramas. **Hours:** Visit by 50-minute tour only; April-Oct Wed at 15:00, 16:00, 17:00, and 18:00; Sat-Sun at 11:30, 15:00, and 16:30; no tours in winter. Reserve in advance. See page 530.

▲**Bagno Vignoni** Quirky little spa town that's simply fun to check out, whether you take a dip or not. See page 571.

▲**Sant'Antimo Abbey** Historic church—stranded, holy and pristine, in the thick of wine country— and worth a quick, easy visit for those touring the wineries. **Hours:** Mon-Sat 10:00-13:00 & 15:00-18:00, Sun 9:15-10:45 & 15:00-18:00. See page 579.

▲**Stony Hill Towns (Rocca d'Orcia, Monticchiello)** Two fortified hilltop hamlets that come with cozy restaurants, comatose economies, rocky lanes, and vast vistas. See page 573.

ficially called an *agriturismo*) and give a great sense of rural family life. Others are just lovely homes in the countryside. The beautiful common denominator about these listings is the wonderful people you'll meet as your hosts. (A few additional countryside accommodations closer to Siena are listed on page 397.)

Near Pienza

$$$ Agriturismo Cretaiole, ideally situated in pristine farmland just outside Pienza, is perfect for settling in and fully experiencing Tuscany. They offer a full slate of activities, and those with a car

can use this as a springboard for exploring virtually all of Tuscany. This family-friendly farm welcomes visitors for weeklong stays (Sat-Sat) in six comfortable apartments. One of my favorite *agriturismo* experiences in Italy, Cretaiole is warmly run by reformed city-slicker Isabella, who came here on vacation and fell in love with country-boy Carlo. Now Carlo and his father, Luciano, tend to the farm, while Isabella and her helper Carlotta assist guests in finding the Tuscan experience they're dreaming of—including thoughtfully planned optional activities such as pasta-making and olive-oil tasting classes, winery tours, and artisan studio visits (RS%, weeklong stays preferred but shorter stays sometimes possible; fewer activities and lower prices mid-Nov–mid-March, no air-con or swimming pool, loaner bikes, Isabella's mobile 338-740-9245, Carlotta's mobile 338-835-1614, tel. 0578-748-083, www.cretaiole.it, info@cretaiole.it). The same family runs two properties in the atmospheric medieval village of Castelmuzio, five miles north of Pienza (both with access to activities at the main *agriturismo*): **$$$ Le Casine di Castello,** a townhouse with two units, and **$$$$ Casa Moricciani,** a swanky villa with dreamy views, a garden terrace, and loads of extras. For special offers, short stays, and discounted rates for all three properties, check their umbrella website (www.theisabellaexperience.com).

$$$ Fonte Bertusi, a classy and artistic guesthouse between Pienza and Cretaiole, is nicely run by young couple Manuela and Andrea, Andrea's artist-father Edoardo, and their attention-starved cats. They have a cozy library/lounge/art gallery that hosts installations and occasional music events, and the eight apartments mix rustic decor with avant-garde creations. It's a bit pricey, but the setting is sublime (laundry service, swimming pool, grand sunset-view terrace, communal BBQ and outdoor kitchen, just outside Pienza toward San Quirico d'Orcia on the right—just after the turnoff for "Il Fonte," tel. 0578-748-077, Manuela's mobile 339-655-5648, www.fontebertusi.it, info@fontebertusi.it).

$$ La Bruciata is a family-friendly *agriturismo* charmingly tucked in the countryside a five-minute drive outside Montepulciano (on the way to Pienza). Can-do Laura and her family produce wine and olive oil and rent seven tasteful, modern rooms split among four apartments that share a peaceful yard with swimming pool. In the summer (June-Aug), they prefer one-week stays (air-con for extra charge, farm-fresh meals and cooking classes, Via del Termine 9, tel. 0578-757-704, mobile 339-781-5106, www.agriturismolabruciata.it, info@agriturismolabruciata.it). Leaving Montepulciano toward Pienza, turn off on the left for *Poggiano,* then carefully track red *La Bruciata* signs (using gravel roads).

In the Crete Senesi

If pastoral landscapes are your goal, you can't do much better than sleeping in the Crete Senesi. These countryside options line up on (or just off) the scenic roads (S-438 and S-451) south of Siena.

$$ Il Canto del Sole is a restored 18th-century farmhouse turned family-friendly B&B located just six miles outside Siena's

Porta Romana city gate. The Lorenzetti family (Laura, Luciano, and son Marco) enjoy engaging with their guests. They have 10 bright and airy rooms, a plush lawn surrounding a saltwater swimming pool, a game room, a piano, and bike rentals. Their two apartments with original antique furnishings fit six to eight people (RS%, air-con, free parking, free town shuttle service and pickup/drop-off from train/bus station, dinner available some nights, Val di Villa Canina 1292, 53014 Loc. Cuna, tel. 0577-375-127, www. ilcantodelsole.com, info@ilcantodelsole.com).

$$ Agriturismo il Molinello ("Little Mill") rents three rooms and six apartments (two built over a medieval mill) on the grounds of a working farm with organic produce, olives, and a truffle patch. Hardworking Alessandro and Elisa share their organic produce and offer wine and olive-oil tastings as well as bike and wine tours. More rustic than romantic, and lacking dramatic views, this is a family-friendly farm—complete with children, dogs, toys, and a relaxing swimming pool (breakfast extra, one-week Sat-Sat stay required July-Aug, discounts and no minimum stay off-season, bike rentals, between Asciano and Serre di Rapolano—on the road toward Rapolano, tel. 0577-704-791, mobile 335-692-5720, www. molinello.com, info@molinello.com).

$ Podere Casalciccia, run by recommended local guide Roberto Bechi and his American wife Patti, is a spacious, modern home perched on a remote ridge immersed in 360 degrees of gorgeous Crete Senesi scenery. All four rooms offer stunning Tuscan countryside vistas. They've designed their entirely "green" house to be self-sufficient, with a zero-carbon footprint (RS%, includes self-service breakfast, communal kitchen, 2-night minimum, Patti's mobile 328-727-3186, Roberto's mobile 328-425-5648, www. casalciccia.com, poderecasalciccia@gmail.com). It's just off road S-438: Turn down the rough gravel road next to the sign for *Fontanelle,* and follow it straight ahead for about five minutes.

$ Casanova Agriturismo is for people who *really* want to stay on an authentic working farm surrounded by spectacular scenery. This rustic place comes with tractors, plenty of farm noises, and a barn full of priceless Chianina cows. If the five simple rooms and two apartments take a backseat to the farm workings, the lodgings are accordingly inexpensive, and you'll appreciate the results of their hard work when you dig into one of their excellent farm-fresh dinners in the former barn (€25/person, available by request). Wiebke (from Germany, who speaks great English and runs the accommodations), her Tuscan husband Bartolo (who works the fields), his mama Paola (who cooks), and the rest of the Conte clan make this a true *agriturismo* experience (breakfast extra, air-con, swimming pool with a view, just outside Asciano on road S-451 toward Chiusure, tel. 0577-718-324, mobile 346-792-0859, www.agriturismo-casanova.it, info@agriturismo-casanova.it).

Near Montalcino

$$ La Crociona, an *agriturismo* farm and working vineyard, rents seven fully equipped apartments with dated furnishings. Fiorella Vannoni and Roberto and Barbara Nannetti offer cooking classes and tastes of the Brunello wine grown and bottled on the premises (reception open 9:00-13:00 & 14:30-19:30, laundry service, covered pool, hot tub, fitness room, La Croce 15, tel. 0577-847-133, www.lacrociona.com, info@lacrociona.com). The farm is about two miles south of Montalcino on the road to the Sant'Antimo Abbey; don't turn off at the first entrance to the village of La Croce—wait for the second one, following signs to *Tenuta Crocedimezzo e Crociona*. A good restaurant is next door.

At La Foce Gardens, near Montepulciano

$$$ B&B Palazzolo La Foce lets you sleep aristocratically in a small villa just below the La Foce Gardens. Its four colorful rooms share a welcoming kitchen/lounge with a giant fireplace, and an outdoor swimming pool with glorious Tuscan views. All the rooms bask in fine panoramas, and two rooms share a bathroom (no aircon but breezy, Strada della Vittoria 61—but check in at gardens' main entrance to get specific directions to your room, villas also available, tel. 0578-69101, www.lafoce.com, info@lafoce.com).

Montepulciano

Curving its way along a ridge, Montepulciano (mohn-teh-pull-chee-AH-noh) delights visitors with *vino,* views, and—perhaps more than any other large town in this area—a sense of being a real, bustling community rather than just a tourist depot.

Alternately under Sienese and Florentine rule, the city still retains its medieval *contrade* (districts), each with a mascot and flag. The neighborhoods compete the last Sunday of August in the Bravio delle Botti, where teams of men push large wine casks uphill from Piazza Marzocco to Piazza Grande, all hoping to win a banner and bragging rights. The entire last week of August is a festival: Each *contrada* arranges musical entertainment and serves food at outdoor eateries, along with generous tastings of the local *vino*.

The city is a collage of architectural styles, but the elegant San Biagio Church, just outside the city walls at the base of the hill, is its best Renaissance building. Most visitors ignore the architecture and focus more on the city's other creative accomplishment, the tasty Vino Nobile di Montepulciano red wine.

Montepulciano is a great starting and ending point for my scenic loop drive through the Heart of Tuscany (see page 565).

Orientation to Montepulciano

Commercial action in Montepulciano centers in the lower town, mostly along Via di Gracciano nel Corso (nicknamed "Corso"). This stretch begins at the town gate called Porta al Prato (near the TI, bus station, and some parking) and winds slowly up, up, up through town—narrated by my self-guided walk. Strolling here, you'll find eateries, gift shops, and tourist traps. The back streets are worth exploring. The main square, at the top of town (up a steep switchback lane from the Corso), is Piazza Grande. Standing proudly above all the touristy sales energy, the square has a noble, Florentine feel.

TOURIST INFORMATION

The helpful TI is just outside the Porta al Prato city gate, in the small P1 parking lot (Mon-Sat 9:00-13:00 & 15:00-19:00, Sun 9:00-13:00, daily until 20:00 in July-Aug, books rooms for no fee, sells bus and train tickets, Piazza Don Minzoni, tel. 0578-757-341, www.prolocomontepulciano.it).

The office on the main square that looks like a TI is actually a privately run "Strada del Vino" (Wine Road) agency. They provide wine-road maps, wine tours in the city, minibus winery tours farther afield, and cooking classes and other culinary experiences (Mon-Fri 10:00-13:00 & 15:00-18:00, Piazza Grande 7, tel. 0578-717-484, www.stradavinonobile.it).

ARRIVAL IN MONTEPULCIANO

Whether you arrive by car or bus, ease your climb to the top of town by riding up on the shuttle bus. For details, see "Helpful Hints," later.

By Car: Well-signed pay-and-display parking lots ring the city center (marked with blue lines). Some free spaces are mixed in (marked with white lines)—look around before you park and keep an eye out for time limits.

To start your visit by following my self-guided walk (up the length of the Corso to the main square), park at the north end of town, near the Porta al Prato gate, where you will find the easiest parking options. Around here, the handiest lots are P1 (in front of the TI, with some free spaces) and the unnumbered lot just above, directly in front of the stone gate. If these are full, try lots P2 or P4, or Lot P5 near the bus station (ride up to the gate on the elevator described under "By Bus," next).

There are also parking lots at the top end of town: Approaching Montepulciano, follow signs for *centro storico, duomo,* and *Piazza Grande,* and use the Fortezza or San Donato lots (flanking the fortress).

Avoid the "ZTL" no-traffic zone (signs marked with a red circle). If you're sleeping in town, your hotelier can give you a permit to park within the walls; be sure to get very specific instructions before you arrive.

By Bus: Buses leave passengers at the bus station on Piazza Nenni, downhill from the Porta al Prato gate. From the station, cross the street and head inside the modern orange-brick structure burrowed into the hillside, where there's an elevator. Ride to level 1, walk straight down the corridor (following signs for *centro storico*), and ride a second elevator (to a different level 1 and the Poggiofanti Gardens); walk to the end of this park and hook left to find the Porta al Prato gate. This is the starting point for my self-guided walk up the Corso to the main square.

HELPFUL HINTS

Market Day: It's on Thursday morning (8:00-13:00), near the bus station.

Services: There's no official **baggage storage,** but the TI might let you leave bags with them if they have space. Public **WCs** are located at the TI, to the left of Palazzo Comunale, and at the Sant'Agostino Church.

Shuttle Bus to the Top of Town: To avoid the hike up through town to Piazza Grande, hop on the orange shuttle bus. It departs twice hourly from the parking lot near the bus station and from the lane leading to the Porta al Prato gate, just above the TI (€1.10, buy tickets at bars, tobacco shops, or the TI).

Laundry: An elegant self-service launderette is at Via del Paolino 2, just around the corner from the recommended Camere Bellavista (daily 8:00-22:00, tel. 0578-717-544).

Taxis: Two taxi drivers operate in Montepulciano. Call 330-732-723 for short trips within town (€10 for rides up or down hill); to reach other towns, call 348-702-4124 (www.strollingintuscany.com).

Montepulciano

1. La Locanda di San Francesco Rooms & E Lucevan le Stelle Wine Bar
2. Mueblè il Riccio
3. Albergo Duomo
4. Vicolo dell'Oste B&B
5. Camere Bellavista
6. Ost. dell'Acquacheta
7. Osteria del Conte
8. Le Pentolaccia
9. Ai Quattro Venti
10. Caffè Poliziano
11. Mazzetti Copper Shop
12. Ramaio Cesare Copper Workshop
13. Contucci Cantina
14. De' Ricci Cantine
15. Cantina della Talosa
16. Launderette

- - - - Self-Guided Walk
Ⓑ Local Shuttle Bus

HEART OF TUSCANY

Montepulciano Walk

This two-part self-guided walk traces the spine of the town from its main entrance up to its hilltop seat of power. Part 1 begins at the big gate at the bottom of town, Porta al Prato (near the TI and several parking lots); Part 2 focuses on the square at the very top of town and the nearby streets. Part 1 is steeply uphill; to skip straight to the more level part of town (and Part 2), ride the twice-hourly shuttle bus up, or park at one of the lots near the Fortezza. (When you're done, you can still do Part 1—backwards—on the way back down.)

PART 1: UP THE CORSO

This guided stroll takes you up through Montepulciano's commercial (and touristy) gamut from the bottom of town to the top. While the street is lined mostly with gift shops, you'll pass a few relics of an earlier age.

Begin in front of the imposing Porta al Prato, one of the many stout city gates that once fortified this highly strategic town. Facing the gate, find the sign for the Porta di Bacco *"passaggio segreto"* on the left. While Montepulciano did have secret passages tunneled through the rock beneath it (handy during times of siege), this particular passage—right next to the city's front door—was probably no *segreto*...though it works great for selling salami.

Walk directly through the **Porta al Prato,** looking up to see the slot where the portcullis (heavily fortified gate) could slide down to seal things off. Notice that there are two gates, enabling defenders to trap would-be invaders in a no-man's-land where they could be doused with hot tar. Besides having a drop-down portcullis, each gate also had a hinged door—effectively putting four barriers between the town and its enemies.

Pass through the gate and head a block uphill to reach the **Colonna del Marzocco.** This column, topped with a lion holding the Medici shield, is a reminder that Montepulciano existed under the auspices of Florence—but only for part of its history. Originally the column was crowned by a she-wolf suckling human twins, the civic symbol of Siena. At a strategic crossroads of mighty regional powers (Florence, Siena, and the Papal States), Montepulciano often switched allegiances—and this column became a flagpole where the overlords du jour could tout their influence.

The column is also the starting point for Montepulciano's masochistic tradition, the **Bravio delle Botti,** held on the last Sunday of August, in which each local *contrada* (neighborhood) selects its two stoutest young men to roll a 180-pound barrel up the hill through town. If the vertical climb through town wears you out, be glad you're only toting a daypack.

A few steps up, on the right (at #91, with stylized lion heads), is one of the many fine noble palaces that front Montepulciano's main strip. The town is fortunate to be graced with so many bold and noble *palazzi*—Florentine nobility favored Montepulciano as a breezy and relaxed place for a secondary residence. Grand as this palace is, it's small potatoes—the higher you go in Montepulciano, the closer you are to the town center...and the fancier the mansions.

Farther up on the right, at #73 (Palazzo Bucelli), take a moment to examine the **Etruscan and Roman fragments** embedded

in the wall, left here by a 19th-century antiques dealer. You can quickly distinguish which pieces came from the Romans and those belonging to the earlier Etruscans by their alphabets: The "backwards" Etruscan letters (they read from right to left) resemble Greek. Many of the fragments show a circle flanked by a pair of inward-facing semicircular designs. This symbol represents the libation cup used for drinking at an Etruscan banquet.

At the top of the block on the right is the **Church of Sant'Agostino.** Its late-Gothic facade features a terra-cotta sculpture group by the architect Michelozzo, a favorite of the Medicis in Florence. Throughout Montepulciano, Florentine touches like this underline that city's influence.

Hike up a few more steps, then take a breather to look back and see the **clock tower** in the middle of the street. The bell ringer at the top takes the form of the character Pulcinella, one of the wild and carefree revelers familiar from Italy's commedia dell'arte theatrical tradition.

Continuing up, at the *alimentari* on the right (at #23), notice the classic old sign advertising milk, butter, margarine, and olive and canola oil. Keep on going (imagine pushing a barrel now), and bear right with the street under another sturdy **gateway**—indicating that this city grew in concentric circles. Passing through the gate and facing the loggia (with the Florentine Medici seal—a shield with balls), turn left and keep on going.

As you huff and puff, notice (on your right, and later on both sides) the steep, narrow, often-covered lanes called *vicolo* ("little street"). You're getting a peek at the higgledy-piggledy medieval Montepulciano. Only when the rationality of Renaissance aesthetics took hold was the main street realigned, becoming symmetrical and pretty. Beneath its fancy suit, though, Montepulciano remains a rugged Gothic city.

Again, notice the fine and ever-bulkier palaces. On the left, a tiny courtyard makes it easier to appreciate the grandiosity of the next palace, now home to **Banca Etruria.** "Etruria"—a name you'll see everywhere around here—is a term for the Etruscan territory of today's Tuscany. By the way, the stone scrolls under the window are a design element called a "kneeling window"—created by Michelangelo and a popular decorative element in High Renaissance and Mannerist architecture. You'll see kneeling windows all over town.

Just after is a fine spot for a coffee break (on the left, at #27): **Caffè Poliziano,** the town's most venerable watering hole (from 1868). Step inside to soak in the genteel atmosphere, with a busy espresso machine, loaner newspapers on long sticks, and a little terrace with spectacular views. It's named for a famous Montepulciano-born 15th-century poet who was a protégé of Lorenzo the Magnificent de Medici and tutored his two sons. So important is he to civic pride that townspeople are nicknamed *poliziani.*

A bit farther up, on the right, notice the precipitous **Vicolo dello Sdrucciolo**—literally "slippery lane." Any *vicolo* on the right can be used as a steep shortcut to the upper part of town, while those on the left generally lead to fine vistas. Many of these side lanes are spanned by brick arches, allowing centuries-old buildings to lean on each other for support rather than toppling over—a fitting metaphor for the tight-knit communities that vitalize small Italian towns.

The next church on the left, the Jesuit **Church of Gesù,** is worth a look. Its interior is elliptical in shape and full of 3-D illusions (don't miss the side chapels and the cupola—all painted on flat surfaces). Soon the street levels out—enjoy this nice, lazy, easy stretch, with interesting shops and artisan workshops (such as the mosaics studio at #14). Across from #64, a lane leads to a charming terrace with a commanding view of the Tuscan countryside.

The **Mazzetti** copper shop (#64) is crammed full of decorative and practical items. Because of copper's unmatched heat conductivity, it's a favored material in premium kitchens. The production of hand-hammered copper vessels like these is a dying art; in this shop, you can see works by Cesare, who makes them in his workshop just up the street. To reach the workshop, go up the tiny covered lane just after the copper shop (Vicolo Benci, on the right). When you emerge, turn right and head uphill steeply; #4 (on the left), marked *Ramaio,* is Cesare's workshop and museum (for details, see page 541). Continuing steeply uphill will take you to the main square. At the bend just before the square, Cesare's buddy Adamo loves to introduce travelers to Montepulciano's fine wines at the Contucci Cantina (see page 540). Visit Cesare and Adamo now, or head up to the square for Part 2 of this walk.

Either way, Montepulciano's main square is just ahead. You made it!

PART 2: PIAZZA GRANDE AND NEARBY

This pleasant, lively piazza is surrounded by a grab bag of architectural sights. The medieval **Palazzo Comunale,** or town hall, resembles Florence's Palazzo Vecchio—yet another reminder that Florence dominated Montepulciano in the 15th and 16th centuries. The crenellations along the roof were never intended to hide soldiers—they just symbolize power. The big, square central tower makes it clear that the city is keeping an eye out in all directions. It's made of locally quarried travertine stone, the same material ancient Romans used for their great buildings.

Take a moment to survey the square, where the town's four great powers stare each other down. Face the Palazzo Comunale,

and keep turning to the right. You'll see the one-time building of the courts, behind the well (Palazzo del Capitano); the noble Palazzo Tarugi, a Renaissance-arcaded confection (with a public loggia at ground level and a private loggia—now enclosed—directly above); and the aristocratic Palazzo Contucci, with its 16th-century Renaissance facade. (The Contucci family still lives in their palace, producing and selling their own wine.) Continuing your spin, you see the unfinished Duomo looking glumly on, wishing the city hadn't run out of money for its facade.

A cistern system fed by rainwater draining from the roofs of surrounding palaces supplied the fine **well** in the corner. Check out its 19th-century pulleys, the grilles to keep animals from contaminating the water supply, and its decorative top: the Medici coat of arms flanked by lions (representing Florence) dwarfing griffins (representing Montepulciano).

Climbing the town hall's **tower** rewards you with a windblown but commanding panorama from the terrace below the clock. Go into the Palazzo Comunale, head up the stairs to your left, and pay on the second floor. You can pay to go just as far as the terrace, at the base of the tower (€2.50, 71 stairs, or ride the elevator halfway up); or pay more to go all the way to the top, twisting up extremely narrow brick steps past the antiquated bell-ringing mechanism (€5, 76 additional stairs). If you don't mind the claustrophobic climb, it's worth paying extra to reach the very top, from where you can see

The Beauty of Tuscany's Geology (and Vice Versa)

While tourists have romanticized notions of the "Tuscan" landscape, there are a surprisingly wide variety of land forms in the region. Never having been crushed by a glacier, Tuscany is anything but flat. Its hills and mountains are made up of different substances, each suited to very different types of cultivation.

The Chianti region (between Florence and Siena) is rough and rocky, with an inhospitable soil that challenges grape vines to survive while coaxing them to produce excellent wine grapes.

Farther south, the soil switches from rock to clay, silt, and sand. The region called the Crete Senesi is the perfectly described "Sienese Clay Hills." Looking out from a breezy viewpoint, you can easily visualize how these clay hills were once at the bottom of the sea floor. The soil here is perfect for truffles and for vast fields of wheat, sun-yellow rapeseed (for canola oil), and periodically fava beans (to add nitrogen to the soil). In the spring and summer, the Crete Senesi is blanketed with brightly colorful crops and flowers in spring and summer, but by the fall, after the harvest, it's brown, dusty, and desolate. Within the Crete Senesi, you can distinguish two types of hills shaped by erosion: smooth, rounded *biancane* and pointy, jagged *calanchi*.

The sharecropping system—an almost feudal economic model, where a few super-elite aristocrats owned all the arable farmland and rented it out to peasant farmers—flourished here until soon after the birth of the Italian Republic in 1948. This prompted a population shift, as many Tuscans moved north to

all the way to Pienza (look just to the right of San Biagio Church; tower open daily May-Oct 10:00-18:00, closed in winter).

The street to the left as you face the tower leads to the **Fortezza.** While you might expect the town to be huddled protectively around its fortress, in Montepulciano's case, it's built on a distant ledge at the very edge of town. That's because this fort wasn't meant to protect the townspeople, but to safeguard the rulers keeping an eye on their townspeople.

To the Church of San Francesco and Views: From the main square, a short, mostly level walk leads to a fine viewpoint. You could head 200 yards straight down the wide street to the right as you face the tower. But for a more interesting look at Montepulciano behind its pretty Renaissance facades, go down **Via Talosa,** the narrow lane between the two palaces in the corner of the square. Within just a few steps, you'll be surrounded not by tidy columns and triangles, but by a mishmash of brick and stone. Pause at the recommended Mueblè il Riccio B&B (with a fine courtyard—peek inside) and look high up across the street to see how centuries

more lucrative industrial jobs in cities. The land they vacated became dirt-cheap, and investors moved in, including many Sardinians—who brought their sheep and recipes for the pecorino cheese that now abounds here. (Many Sardinians—with names typically ending in "u"—still live here.)

The area around Montepulciano and Montalcino is more varied, with rocky protuberances that break up the undulating clay

hills and provide a suitable home for wine grapes. Even farther south is the Val d'Orcia. This valley of the Orcia River is similar to the Crete Senesi, but has fewer rocks and jagged *calanchi*. Montepulciano sits in a unique position between the Val d'Orcia and the much flatter Val di Chiana (through which Italy's main north-south expressway runs).

You'll see many hot springs in this part of Tuscany, as well as town names with the word Terme (for "spa" or "hot spring") or Bagno ("bath"). These generally occur where clay meets rock: Water moving through the clay encounters a barrier and gets trapped. A byproduct of these mineral springs is the limestone called travertine, explaining the quarries you may see around spa towns.

of structures have been stitched together, sometimes gracelessly. Across the street is the recommended Cantina della Talosa wine cellar—imagine the wine caves below your feet.

Follow this lane as it bends left, and eventually you'll pop out just below the main square, a few doors from the recommended De' Ricci Cantine wine cellar. Turn right and head down toward the church. Just before #21 (on the left), look for a red-and-gold **shield** over a door with the name *Talosa*. This marks the home of one of Montepulciano's *contrade*, or neighborhoods; birth and death announcements for the *contrada* are posted on the board next to the door.

Across the street and a few steps farther (on the right), you hit a **viewpoint**. From here, it's easy to appreciate Montepulciano's highly strategic position. The ancient town sitting on this high ridge was surrounded by powerful forces—everything you see in this direction was part of the Papal States, ruled from Rome. In the distance is Lake Trasimeno, once a notorious swampland that made it even harder to invade this town.

Continue a few steps downhill, then uphill, into the big parking lot in front of the **Church of San Francesco.** Head out to the overlook for a totally different view: the rolling hills that belonged to Siena. And keep in mind that Montepulciano itself belonged to Florence. For the first half of the 16th century, those three formidable powers—Florence, Siena, and Rome (the papacy)—vied to control this small area. You can also see Montepulciano's most impressive church, San Biagio—well worth a visit for drivers or hikers (described later).

From here, you can head back up to the main square, or drop into one of my recommended cantinas to spelunk their wine cellars.

Sights and Experiences in Montepulciano

For me, Montepulciano's best "experiences" are personal: dropping in on Adamo, the winemaker at Contucci Cantina, and Cesare, the coppersmith at Ramaio Cesare. Both will greet you with a torrent of cheerful Italian; just smile and nod, pick up what you can from gestures, and appreciate this rare opportunity to meet a true local character. If you're visiting one of the wine cellars, study up on the local Vino Nobile di Montepulciano by reading the sidebar on page 560.

▲▲Contucci Cantina

Montepulciano's most popular attraction isn't made of stone—it's the famous wine, Vino Nobile. This robust red can be tasted in any of the cantinas lining Via Ricci and Via di Gracciano nel Corso, but the cantina in the basement of Palazzo Contucci is both historic and fun. Skip the palace's formal wine-tasting showroom facing the square, and instead head down the lane on the right to the actual cellars, where you'll meet lively Adamo (ah-DAH-moh), who has been making wine here since 1961 and welcomes tourists into the cellar. While at the palace, you may meet Andrea or Ginevra Contucci, whose family has lived here since the 11th century. They love to share their family's products with the public. Adamo and the Contuccis usually have a half-dozen bottles open, and at busy times, other members of their staff are likely to speak English.

After sipping a little wine with Adamo, explore the palace basement, with its 13th-century vaults. Originally part of the town's wall, these chambers have been filled since the 1500s with huge barrels of wine. Dozens of barrels of Croatian and

French oak (1,000-2,500 liters each) cradle the wine through a two-year in-the-barrel aging process, during which the wine picks up the personality of the wood. After about 35 years, an exhausted barrel has nothing left to offer its wine, so it's retired. Adamo explains that the French oak gives the wine "pure elegance," and the Croatian is more masculine. Each barrel is labeled with the size in liters, the year the wine was barreled, and the percentage of alcohol (determined by how much sun shone in that year). To be "Nobile," wine needs a minimum of 13 percent alcohol.

Cost and Hours: Free drop-in tasting, free cellar tour upon request, daily 9:30-19:00, Piazza Grande 13, tel. 0578-757-006, www.contucci.it.

▲Ramaio Cesare

Cesare the coppersmith is an institution in Montepulciano, carrying on his father's and grandfather's trade by hammering into

existence an immense selection of copper objects in his cavernous workshop. Though his English is limited, Cesare (CHEH-zah-ray) is happy to show you photos of his work—including the copper top of the Duomo in Siena and the piece he designed and personally delivered to Pope Benedict. Peruse his tools: a giant Road Runner-style anvil, wooden hammers, and stencils dating from 1857 that have been passed down from his grandfather and father. Next door, he has assembled a fine museum with items he and his relatives have made, as well as pieces from his personal collection. Cesare is evangelical about copper, and if he's not too busy, he'll create personalized mementoes for visitors—he loves meeting people from around the world who appreciate his handiwork (as his brimming photo album demonstrates). Cesare's justifiable pride in his vocation evokes the hardworking, highly skilled craft guilds that once dominated small-town Italy's commercial and civic life.

Cost and Hours: Demonstration and museum are free, Cesare is generally in his workshop Mon-Sat 8:00-12:30 & 14:30-18:30, closed Sun, 50 yards steeply downhill from the Contucci Cantina at Via del Teatro 4, tel. 0578-758-753, www.rameria.com. Cesare's delightful shop is on the main drag, a block below, at Corso #64—look for *Rameria Mazzetti*, open long hours daily.

Duomo

This church's unfinished facade—rough stonework left waiting for the final marble veneer—is not that unusual. Many Tuscan churches were built just to the point where they had a functional interior, and then, for various practical reasons, the facades were left unfinished. But step inside and you'll be rewarded with some fine art. A beautiful blue-and-white, glazed-terra-cotta *Altar of the Lilies* by Andrea della Robbia is behind the baptismal font (on the left as you enter). The high altar, with a top like a pine forest, features a luminous, late-Gothic Assumption triptych by the Sienese artist Taddeo di Bartolo. Showing Mary in her dreamy eternal sleep as she ascends to be crowned by Jesus, it illustrates how Siena clung to the Gothic aesthetic—elaborate gold leaf and lacy pointed arches—to show heavenly grandeur.

Cost and Hours: Free, daily 8:30-18:30.

▲De' Ricci Cantine

The most impressive wine cellars in Montepulciano sit below the Palazzo Ricci, just a few steps off the main square (toward the Church of San Francesco). Enter through the unassuming door and find your way down, down, down a spiral staircase—with rounded steps designed to go easy on fragile noble feet, and lined with rings held in place by tiny, finely crafted wrought-iron goat heads. You'll wind up in the dramatic cellars, with gigantic barrels under even more gigantic vaults—several stories high. As you go deeper and deeper into the cellars, high up, natural stone seems to take over the brick. At the deepest point, you can peer into the atmospheric Etruscan cave, where a warren of corridors spins off from a filled-in well. Finally you wind up in the shop, where you're welcome to taste a few wines (with some local cheese). Don't miss their delightful dessert wine, vin santo.

Cost and Hours: €3 tasting is free with this book; €12-20 bottles, affordable shipping, daily 11:00-19:00; enter Palazzo Ricci at Via Ricci 11, look for signs for *Cantine de' Ricci*; tel. 0578-757-166, www.cantinadericci.it, Enrico.

Cantina della Talosa

This historic cellar, which goes down and down to an Etruscan tomb at the bottom, ages a well-respected wine. With a passion and love of their craft, Cristian Pepi and Andrea give enthusiastic tours and tastings. While you can drop by for a free tasting, I'd call ahead to book a tour—€10, including five wines to taste.

Cost and Hours: Free tasting, daily March-Oct 10:00-19:30, shorter hours off-season, a block off Piazza Grande at Via Talosa 8, tel. 0578-757-929, www.talosa.it.

ON THE OUTSKIRTS
▲San Biagio Church (Chiesa de San Biagio)

Often called the "Temple of San Biagio" because of its Greek-cross style, this church—designed by Antonio da Sangallo the Elder and built of locally quarried travertine—feels like Renaissance perfection.

Cost and Hours: €3.50, includes audioguide, daily 9:30-17:30.

Getting There: The church is just west of town, at the base of Montepulciano's hill, down a picturesque cypress-lined driveway.

Visiting the Church: Before entering, appreciate the **exterior** (the original front door is on the right side of today's entrance).

The lone tower was supposed to have a twin, but it was never built. Walk around the building to study the freestanding towers—made that way so as not to interrupt the Greek cross.

Then step **inside.** The soaring interior, with a high dome and lantern, creates a quintessential Renaissance space. The proportions of the Greek-cross floor plan give the building a pleasing rhythmic quality. Stand on the center stone and do a slow 360-degree spin, enjoying the harmony and mathematical perfection in the design (and ignoring the bit of 18th-century, late-Baroque decor above the altar—which seems as appropriate as putting whipped cream on a nice steak). If the church is empty, experiment worshipfully with the marvelous acoustics.

Consider a picnic or snooze on the grass in back, with fine vistas over the Chiana Valley. The restaurant across the street from the church is a local favorite.

Sleeping in Montepulciano

$$$$ La Locanda di San Francesco is overpriced but luxurious, with four stylish view rooms over a classy wine bar on a quiet square at Montepulciano's summit (closed Nov-Easter, air-con, free parking nearby, Piazza San Francesco 5, tel. 0578-758-725, www.locandasanfrancesco.it, info@locandasanfrancesco.it, Cinzia and Luca).

$$ Mueblè il Riccio ("The Hedgehog") is medieval-elegant, with 10 modern and spotless rooms, an awesome roof terrace, and friendly owners. Five are new "superior" rooms with grand views across the Tuscan valleys (family rooms, breakfast extra, air-con, limited free parking—request when you reserve, a block below the

HEART OF TUSCANY

main square at Via Talosa 21, tel. 0578-757-713, www.ilriccio.net, info@ilriccio.net, Gió and Ivana speak English). Charming Gió and his son Iacopo give tours of the countryside (€50/hour) in one of their classic Italian cars; for details, see their website. Ivana makes wonderful breakfast tarts.

$$ Albergo Duomo is big, modern, and nondescript, with 13 decent rooms (with small bathrooms) and a comfortable lounge downstairs. With a handy location just a few steps from the main square, it's at the very top of town, with free private parking nearby (RS%—use code "Steves," family rooms, elevator, air-con in some rooms—extra charge, Via di San Donato 14, tel. 0578-757-473, www.albergoduomo.it, albergoduomo@libero.it, Elisa and Saverio).

$$ Vicolo dell'Oste B&B, just off the main drag halfway up through town, has five family-friendly modern rooms. Some are like tiny apartments (RS%, includes breakfast at nearby café, on Via dell'Oste 1—an alley leading right off the main drag just after Caffè Poliziano and opposite the *farmacia* at #47, tel. 0578-758-393, www.vicolodelloste.it, info@vicolodelloste.it, Luisa and Giuseppe).

$ Camere Bellavista has 10 tidy rooms. True to its name, each room has a fine view—though some are better than others. Room 6 has a view terrace worth reserving (cash only, no breakfast, lots of stairs with no elevator, reception not always staffed—call before arriving or ring bell, Via Ricci 25, mobile 347-823-2314, www.camerebellavista.it, bellavista@bccmp.com, Gabriella speaks just enough English).

Eating in Montepulciano

These places are all open for lunch (about 12:30-14:30) and again for dinner (about 19:30-22:00).

$$$ Osteria dell'Acquacheta is a carnivore's dream come true, beloved among locals for its beef steaks. Its long, narrow room is jammed with shared tables and tight, family-style seating, with an open fire in back and a big hunk of red beef lying on the counter like a corpse on a gurney. Giulio and his wife, Chiara, run a fun-loving but tight ship—posing with slabs of red meat yet embracing decades of trattoria tradition (you'll get one glass to use alternately for wine and water). Giulio—think George Carlin with a meat cleaver and a pen tucked into his ponytail—whacks off slabs of beef, confirms the weight and price with the diner, and tosses the

meat on the grill, seven minutes per side. (You won't be asked how you like your steak.) Steaks are sold by weight (€32/kilo). Typically, two people split a 1.6-kilo steak (that's 3.5 pounds; the smallest they'll cook is 1.2 kilos). They also serve hearty pastas and salads, other meaty plates, and a fine house wine (possible to bring your own wine for a tiny corkage fee, reservations required; seatings at 12:30, 14:30, 19:30, and 21:30 only; closed Tue, Via del Teatro 22, tel. 0578-717-086, www.acquacheta.eu).

$$ Osteria del Conte, an attractive but humble family-run bistro, offers a €30 *menù del Conte*—a four-course dinner of local specialties including wine—as well as à la carte options and cooking like your Italian mom's. While the interior is very simple, they also have outdoor tables on a stony street at the top of the historic center (closed Wed, Via San Donato 19, tel. 0578-756-062).

$$ Le Pentolaccia is a small, family-run restaurant at the upper, relatively untouristy end of the main drag. With both indoor and outdoor seating, they make tasty traditional Tuscan dishes as well as daily fish specials. Cristiana serves, and husband-and-wife team Jacobo and Alessia stir up a storm in the kitchen (closed Thu, Corso 86, tel. 0578-757-582).

$$ Ai Quattro Venti is right on Piazza Grande, with a simple dining room and outdoor tables on the square. It offers reasonable portions of unfussy Tuscan food in an unpretentious setting. Try their very own organic olive oil and wine (closed Thu, next to City Hall on Piazza Grande, tel. 0578-717-231, Chiara).

Wine Bar/Bistro: With a terrace on a tranquil square in front of the Church of San Francesco, **$ E Lucevan le Stelle** (part of La Locanda di San Francesco) is a fine place to nurse a glass of local wine (also pastas, salads, and soups; daily 12:00-24:00, closed Nov-Easter, Piazza San Francesco 5, tel. 0578-758-725, Luca).

Near Montepulciano, in Monticchiello: If you'd enjoy getting out of town for dinner—but not *too* far—consider the 20-minute drive to the picturesque hill town of Monticchiello, where you can dine at the excellent **Osteria La Porta** with its fine view terrace, or at the modern-feeling **La Cantina della Porta** (both described on page 576). To get there, follow signs to Pienza; then, shortly after passing the road to San Biagio Church (on the right), watch on the left for the Albergo San Biagio. Turn off, take the rough little road that runs up past the left side of this big hotel, and follow it to Monticchiello.

Montepulciano Connections

Get bus schedules at the TI or the bus station on Piazza Pietro Nenni, which seems to double as the town hangout, with a lively bar and locals chatting inside. In fact, there's no real ticket window—buy your tickets at the bar. Check www.sienamobilita.it or www.tiemmespa.it for schedules.

By Bus to: Florence (1-2/day, 2 hours, change in Bettolle, LFI bus, www.lfi.it; or take a bus to Chiusi to catch a train—see below), **Siena** (6-8/day, none on Sun, 1.5 hours, also possible to change here for Florence express bus), **Pienza** (8/day, 30 minutes), **Montalcino** (3-4/day, none Sun, change in Torrenieri, 1 hour; or consider a taxi—see below).

By Train: Trains are impractical here; the Montepulciano train station, five miles from town and connected by an infrequent bus, has only milk-run trains (but could be useful for reaching Siena on a Sunday—get details at the TI). More convenient, consider riding the hourly bus 50 minutes to the town of **Chiusi,** which is on the main Florence-Rome rail line.

Taxi Alternatives: As the **Montalcino** bus connection is infrequent and complicated, consider hiring a taxi (about €70; see contact info under "Helpful Hints," earlier). **Cortona** is another awkward public-transit connection, involving a bus to Chiusi, then a 30-minute train ride to the Camuccia-Cortona train station, four miles below town with poorly timed bus connections to Cortona itself. Consider taking a taxi instead (about €60).

Pienza

Set on a crest and surrounded by green, rolling hills, the small town of Pienza packs a lot of Renaissance punch. In the 1400s, locally born Pope Pius II of the Piccolomini family decided to remodel his birthplace into a city fit for a pope, in the style that was all the rage: Renaissance. Propelled by papal clout, the town of Corsignano was transformed—in only five years' time—into a jewel of Renaissance architecture. It was renamed Pienza,

after Pope Pius. The plan was to remodel the entire town, but work ended in 1464 when both the pope and his architect, Bernardo Rossellino, died. Their vision—what you see today—was completed a century later.

Pienza's architectural focal point is its main square, Piazza Pio II, surrounded by the Duomo and the pope's family residence, Palazzo Piccolomini. While Piazza Pio II is Pienza's pride and joy, the entire town—a mix of old stonework, potted plants, and grand views—is fun to explore, especially with a camera or sketchpad in hand. You can walk every lane in the tiny town in well under an hour. Pienza is situated on a relatively flat plateau rather than the steep pinnacle of more dramatic towns like Montepulciano and Montalcino. (This is a plus for visitors with limited mobility, who find basically-level Pienza easy to explore.)

Tidy, tranquil, and tame, Pienza feels like the idealized Renaissance burg it was designed to be. But along with that civic pride comes more than its share of pretense. (I guess constantly being reminded of your "Renaissance perfection" tends to stoke the ego.) And, cute as the town is, it's far from undiscovered; tourists flood Pienza on weekends and in peak season, and boutiques selling gifty packages of pecorino cheese and local wine greatly outnumber authentic local shops. Restaurants here tend to be more expensive and less reliable than alternatives in the nearby countryside. For these reasons, Pienza is made to order as a stretch-your-legs break to enjoy the townscape and panoramas, but it's not ideal for lingering overnight (though for some excellent countryside options just outside town, see page 527). For the best experience, visit late in the day, after the day-trippers have dispersed.

Nearly every shop sells the town's specialty: pecorino, a pungent sheep's cheese (you'll smell it before you see it) that's sometimes infused with other ingredients, such as truffles or cayenne pepper. Look on menus for warm pecorino *(al forno* or *alla griglia)*, often topped with honey and pine nuts or pears and served with bread. Along with a glass of local wine, this just might lead you to a new understanding of *la dolce vita*.

Orientation to Pienza

Tourist Information: The TI is 10 yards up the street from Piazza Pio II, inside the skippable Diocesan Museum (Wed-Mon 10:30-13:30 & 14:30-18:00 except Sat-Sun 10:00-16:00 off-season, closed Tue year-round, Corso il Rossellino 30, tel. 0578-749-905). Ignore the *Informaturista* kiosk just outside the gate—it's a private travel agency.

Arrival in Pienza: If **driving,** read signs carefully—some parking spots are reserved for locals, others require the use of a cardboard clock, and others are pay-and-display. Parking is tight, so if you don't see anything quickly, head for the large pay lot at Piazza del Mercato near Largo Roma outside the old town: As you approach town and reach the "ZTL" cul-de-sac (marked with a red circle) in front of the town gate, head up the left side of town and look for the parking turnoff on the left (closed Fri morning during market). **Buses** drop you just a couple of blocks from the town's main entrance.

Helpful Hints: On Friday mornings, a **market** fills Piazza del Mercato, the main parking lot just outside the town walls. A public

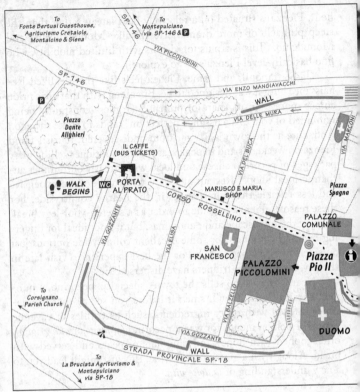

WC, marked *gabinetti pubblici,* is on the right as you face the town gate from outside on Piazza Dante Alighieri (down the lane next to the faux TI).

Sights in Pienza

I've connected Pienza's main sights with walking directions, which can serve as a handy little orientation to the town. You could do this stroll in 30 minutes, but entering some of the sights could extend your visit to a few hours.

• *Begin in the little park just in front of the town (near the main roundabout and bus stop), called Piazza Dante Alighieri. Facing the town, go through the big, ornamental gateway on the right (which was destroyed in World War II, and rebuilt in 1955) and head up the main street...*

Corso il Rossellino

This main drag—named for Bernardo Rossellino (1409-1464), the Renaissance architect who redesigned Pienza according to Pius' orders—is jammed with touristy boutiques. While you won't find great values, these shops are (like Pienza) cute and convenient.

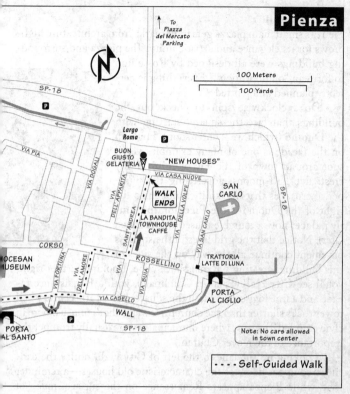

At the end of the second block on the left, at #21, step into the **Marusco e Maria** cheese-and-salami shop. Take a deep whiff and survey the racks of pecorino cheese, made from sheep's milk. Fabio or his staff can give you a quick taste of three types of pecorino: *fresco* (young, soft, and mild), *medio* (medium), and *stagionato* (hard, crumbly, and pungent). Consider stocking up at one of these shops for a pricey but memorable picnic. *Finocchiona* is salami with fennel seeds. This was first popularized by wine traders, because fennel seeds make wine taste better. To this day, Italians use the word *infinocchiare* ("fennel-ize") to mean "to trick."

Farther along, watch for the **Church of San Francesco** on the right. It's the only important building in town that dates from before the Pius II extreme makeover. Its humble facade, simple nave, wood-beamed ceiling, bits of 14th-century frescoes, and tranquil adjacent cloister have a charm that's particularly peaceful in the 21st century. But this gloomy medieval style was exactly what Pius wanted to get away from.

• *Continuing one more block, you'll pop out at Pienza's showcase square...*

▲Piazza Pio II

Pienza's small main piazza gets high marks from architecture high-brows for its elegance and artistic unity. The piazza and surrounding buildings were all designed by Rossellino to form an "outdoor room." Everything is perfectly planned and plotted.

Do a clockwise spin to check out the buildings that face the square, starting with the **Duomo** (which we'll enter soon). High up on the facade is one of many examples you'll spot around town of the Piccolomini family crest: five half-moons, advertising the number of crusades that his family funded. To the right of the Duomo is the **Piccolomini family palace,** now a tourable museum (described later). Notice that the grid lines in the square's pavement continue all the way up the sides of this building, creating a Renaissance cube. Looking farther right, you'll see **City Hall** (Palazzo Comunale), with a Renaissance facade and a fine loggia (to match the square) but a 13th-century bell tower that's shorter than the church's tower. (That's unusual here in civic-minded Tuscany, where municipal towers usually trumpet the importance of town over Church.)

Looking up the lane to the left of City Hall, notice the cantilevered upper floors of the characteristic old houses—a reminder that, while Pienza appears Renaissance on the surface, much of that sheen was added later to fit Pius' vision. Turning right again, see the **Bishop's Palace,** also called the Borgia Palace (now housing the TI and the skippable Diocesan Museum). Pius invited prominent cardinals to occupy the real estate in his custom-built town. The Borgia clan, who built this palace, produced one of the most controversial popes of that age, Alexander VI, who ascended to the papacy a few decades after Pius II. The Borgia were notorious for their shrewd manipulation of power politics. Our word "nepotism"—which comes from the Italian *nipote* (nephew)—dates from this era, when a pope would pull strings to ensure his relatives would succeed him.

Finally, between the Bishop's Palace and the Duomo, a lane leads to the best **view terrace** in town.

• *Now take the time to tour whichever of the square's sights interest you:*

Duomo

The cathedral's classic, symmetrical Renaissance facade (1462) dominates Piazza Pio II. The interior, bathed in light, is an illuminating encapsulation of Pius II's architectural philosophy.

Pope Pius II

Pope Pius II (Enea Silvio Bartolomeo Piccolomini, 1405-1464) was born into one of the most powerful families in Siena. He had an illustrious career as a diplomat, traveled far and wide (fathering two illegitimate children, in Switzerland and Scotland), and gained a reputation for his erotic writings *(The Tale of Two Lovers)*. Upon donning the frock, Piccolomini went from ordination to the papacy in just 11 years—a stunning pace spurred, no doubt, by his esteemed lineage. Owing to his educated and worldly upbringing, upon ascending to the papacy Piccolomini chose a name that was not religious, but literary: the ancient poet Virgil first used the term "pious" to describe his hero, Aeneus. One of the most enlightened popes of his time, Pius embraced the burgeoning Renaissance and set out to remake his hometown in pure Renaissance style. Pius was also the first prominent figure known to have suggested the notion of a united Europe, with a common heritage and shared goals (at that time, facing off against the invading Ottomans).

Cost and Hours: Free, generally daily 7:00-13:00 & 14:30-19:00.

Visiting the Church: Step inside...and into the light. Pius envisioned this church as an antidote to dark, claustrophobic medieval churches, like the Church of San Francesco we saw earlier. Instead, this was to be a "house of glass," representing the cultural enlightenment that came with the Renaissance. This concept clashed with the architect's plans for the building, but Pius insisted on his way—creating this unusual (and unstable) space. Although an east-west footprint would have better suited this location, Pius demanded that the nave's tall Gothic windows face south to capture maximum light. Atop the columns, notice the short extenders. Pius was into astronomy: He had the cathedral made tall enough so that on the spring equinox, the shadow cast by the facade would just reach the pavement grid line defining the far end of the square.

All of this caused structural problems. As you walk to the end of the church, notice the cracks in the apse walls and floor, and get seasick behind the main altar. The church's cliff-hanging position bathes the interior in light, but the building also feels as though it could break in half if you jumped up and down.

The church decoration is also a bit unusual. Rather than Jesus and Mary, the emphasis is on the pope and his family (like the crescent-moon crest of Pius II on the windows). Instead of the colorful frescoes you'd expect, the church has clean, white walls to reflect the light. And with this "modern" interior, the Sienese Gothic altarpieces and painted arches with gold leaf seem out of place.

▲Palazzo Piccolomini

This palace, the home of Pius II and the Piccolomini family (until 1962), is not quite the interesting slice of 15th-century aristocratic life that it could be (I'd like to know more about the pope's toilet). But this is still the best small-town palace experience I've found in Tuscany. (It famously starred as the Capulets' home in Franco Zeffirelli's 1968 Academy Award-winning *Romeo and Juliet*.) You can peek inside the door for free to check out the well-preserved courtyard. In Renaissance times, most buildings were covered with elaborate paintings like those you'll see here.

Cost and Hours: €7, includes dry audioguide, Tue-Sun 10:00-18:30, until 16:30 off-season, closed Mon, Piazza Pio II 2, tel. 0578-748-392, www.palazzopiccolominipienza.it.

Visiting the Palazzo: You'll see six rooms (dining room, armory, bedroom, library, and so on), three art-strewn galleries, and a panoramic loggia before being allowed to linger in the beautiful hanging gardens. The palace's drab interiors, faded paintings, coffered ceilings, and scuffed furniture have a mothballed elegance that makes historians wish they'd seen it in its heyday, when this small-town palace hosted a big-name player in European politics.

View Terrace

As you face the church, the upper lane leading left brings you to a panoramic promenade. Views from the terrace include the Tuscan countryside and, in the distance, Monte Amiata, the largest mountain in southern Tuscany. You can exit the viewpoint down the first alley, Via del'Amore—the original Lover's Lane—which leads back to the main drag.

The Rest of the Town

Explore your choice of flower-lined back lanes. Work your way to the back-left corner of town, where—along **Via delle Case Nuove**—you'll find a charming row of homes with staggered doorways. These "new houses" (as the street's name means) were built by the pope to house the poor.

Just to the left (as you face these houses) is Pienza's "destination" *gelateria:* **Buon Gusto** is run by Nicola and chef Giuseppe, who focus on quality ingredients and intense, original flavors, like carrot-ginger. They make just a few batches each morning (typically ready by around 13:30—just in time for after lunch), and once they're gone, they're gone. They also do fresh-pressed juices, smoothies, and jams designed to complement local cheeses and other flavors (Tue-Sun 11:00-20:00, until 22:00 in summer, closed Mon and in winter, Via delle Case Nuove 26, mobile 335-704-9165).

JUST OUTSIDE PIENZA

A short drive or a longish walk from Pienza, you can step into one of this region's many well-preserved Romanesque churches.

Corsignano Parish Church (Pieve di Corsignano)

This classic Romanesque parish church *(pieve)*, hugging the slope just below Pienza, is a reminder of a much earlier, rougher, simpler time (before Pope Pius II). This was one of the medieval pilgrimage stops on the Via Francigena (see sidebar on page 569).

Getting There: On foot from Pienza, it's a steep 10-minute downhill walk (as you exit Pienza into the main park, look to your left for *pieve di Corsignano* signs). Similar signs direct drivers to the turn-off just below the old town.

Visiting the Church: The round, eighth-century watchtower guards the squat, 11th-century church, whose unusual exterior

iconography is from an age when the pagan roots of early Christianity were vivid and unmistakable—especially here, deep in the countryside. The church is decorated not with saints and angels, but with geometric and flowery motifs as well as mysterious creatures. In the stone lintel immediately above the front door, find the mermaid-like creature holding the two halves of her split tail—a warm and fertile invitation to enter and find life. Locals enjoy the (quite plausible) idea that Starbucks appropriated its logo from this common pagan symbol. She's flanked by other figures fighting off demons, including (on the left) a snake that represents the sins of humanity. The mermaid tails and wavy water-like lines suggest the springs that spout near here. The figure high above seems like both a Greek and an Etruscan fertility goddess.

For more mysterious medieval art, walk around the right side of the church and study the 13th-century carving above the doorway, showing the three kings journeying to Bethlehem, where the Baby Jesus lies under a star and an angel.

If the church is open, step inside and let your eyes adjust to the very low light. This gloomy, cave-like interior—with just slits for windows—is a far cry from later, brighter architectural styles. Near the entrance on the right, look for the font that was used to baptize the infant who would grow up to be Pope Pius II.

HEART OF TUSCANY

Eating in Pienza

$$$ La Bandita Townhouse Caffè offers a break from Tuscan rusticity, focusing instead on tempting modern Italian cuisine (such as spring pea soup or peppered Chianina beef carpaccio). Diners watch the chef work in his open kitchen (lunch served Tue-Sun and dinner nightly, indoor/outdoor seating, Corso il Rossellino 111, easier to enter around the corner on Via Sant'Andrea, tel. 0578-749-005).

$$ Trattoria Latte di Luna, with outdoor tables filling a delightful little square, is the more traditional choice. Run by friendly Roberto with Delfina in the kitchen, the dining room features an ancient well and sits on top of Etruscan tunnels (closed Tue, near the end of Corso il Rossellino at Via San Carlo 2, tel. 0578-748-606).

Quick Lunch: For something cheap, characteristic, and fast, just grab a tasty *porchetta* sandwich (€3.50) at the little shop 30 yards off the main square (at Corso il Rossellino 81) and munch it under the loggia or at the viewpoint.

Pienza Connections

Bus tickets are sold at the bar/café (marked *Il Caffè*, closed Tue) just outside Pienza's town gate (or pay a little extra and buy tickets from the driver). Buses leave from a few blocks up the street, directly in front of the town entrance. Montepulciano is the nearest transportation hub.

From Pienza by Bus to: Siena (6/day, none on Sun, 1.5 hours), **Montepulciano** (8/day, 30 minutes), **Montalcino** (3-4/day Mon-Sat, none Sun, change in Torrenieri, 45-60 minutes). Bus info: www.tiemmespa.it.

Montalcino

On a hill overlooking vineyards and valleys, Montalcino is famous for its delicious and pricey Brunello di Montalcino red wines. It's a pleasant, low-impact town crawling with wine-loving tourists, a smattering of classy shops, but little sightseeing. Everyone touring this area seems to be relaxed and in an easy groove...as if enjoying a little wine buzz.

In the Middle Ages, Montalcino (mohn-tahl-CHEE-noh) was considered Siena's big-

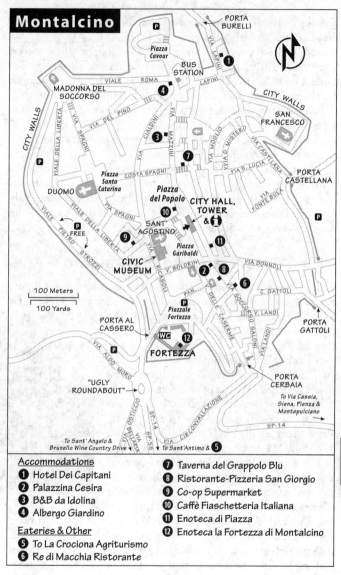

Montalcino

Accommodations
1 Hotel Dei Capitani
2 Palazzina Cesira
3 B&B da Idolina
4 Albergo Giardino

Eateries & Other
5 To La Crociona Agriturismo
6 Re di Macchia Ristorante

7 Taverna del Grappolo Blu
8 Ristorante-Pizzeria San Giorgio
9 Co-op Supermarket
10 Caffè Fiaschetteria Italiana
11 Enoteca di Piazza
12 Enoteca la Fortezza di Montalcino

gest ally. Originally aligned with Florence, the town switched sides after the Sienese beat up Florence in the Battle of Montaperti in 1260. The Sienese persuaded the Montalcinesi to join their side by forcing them to collect corpses and sleep one night in the bloody, Florentine-strewn battlefield. Later, the Montalcinesi took in Sienese refugees. To this day, in gratitude for their support, the

Sienese invite the Montalcinesi to lead the parade that kicks off Siena's Palio celebrations.

Montalcino prospered under Siena, but like its ally, it waned after the Medici family took control of the region. The village became a humble place. Then, in the late 19th century, the Biondi Santi family created a fine, dark red wine, calling it "the brunette" (Brunello). Today's affluence is due to the town's much-sought-after wine. (For more on this wine, see the "Wines in the Region" sidebar, page 560). If you're not a wine lover, you may find Montalcino (a.k.a. Brunello-ville) to be too touristy.

Montalcino provides a handy springboard for exploring the surrounding wine region. "Montalcino" literally means "Mountain of Oaks"—and sure enough, its surrounding hills are generously forested. For a self-guided driving tour connecting some of the most enjoyable wineries and views, see page 576.

Orientation to Montalcino

Sitting atop a hill amidst a sea of vineyards, Montalcino is surrounded by walls and dominated by the Fortezza (a.k.a. "La Rocca"). From here, roads lead down into the two main squares: Piazza Garibaldi and Piazza del Popolo.

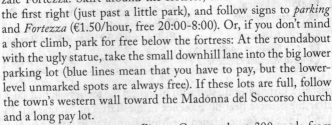

Tourist Information: The helpful TI, just off Piazza Garibaldi in City Hall, sells bus tickets; can call ahead to book a visit at a countryside winery (small fee); and has information on taxis to nearby towns, abbeys, and monasteries (daily 10:00-13:00 & 14:00-17:50, tel. 0577-849-331, www.prolocomontalcino.com).

Arrival in Montalcino: Drivers here for a short visit should head to the pay lot in Piazzale Fortezza: Skirt around the fortress, take the first right (just past a little park), and follow signs to *parking* and *Fortezza* (€1.50/hour, free 20:00-8:00). Or, if you don't mind a short climb, park for free below the fortress: At the roundabout with the ugly statue, take the small downhill lane into the big lower parking lot (blue lines mean that you have to pay, but the lower-level unmarked spots are always free). If these lots are full, follow the town's western wall toward the Madonna del Soccorso church and a long pay lot.

The **bus** station is on Piazza Cavour, about 300 yards from the town center. From here, simply follow Via Mazzini straight up into town. While Montalcino has no official baggage storage, a few shops are willing to hold on to one or two bags on a short-term basis; ask at the TI.

Helpful Hints: Market day is Friday (7:00-13:00) on Viale della Libertà, near the Fortezza.

Sights in Montalcino

Fortezza

This 14th-century fort, built under Sienese rule, is now little more than an empty shell. You're welcome to enter the big, open courtyard (with WCs out the far end), or just enjoy a picnic in the park surrounding the fort, but if you want to climb the ramparts for a panoramic view, you'll have to pay (€4, enter though wine bar, daily 9:00-20:00, shorter hours off-season). Most people visit the fortress for its recommended wine bar.

Piazza del Popolo

All roads in tiny Montalcino lead to the main square, Piazza del Popolo ("People's Square").

Since 1888, the **Caffè Fiaschetteria Italiana** has been *the* elegant place to enjoy a drink. Its founder, inspired by Caffè Florian in Venice, brought fine coffee to this humble town of woodcutters.

City Hall was the fortified seat of government. It's decorated by the coats of arms of judges who, in the interest of fairness, were from outside of town. Like Siena, Montalcino was a republic in the Middle Ages. When Florentines took Siena in 1555, Siena's ruling class retreated here and held out for four more years. The Medici coat of arms (with the six balls, or pills) dominates the others. This, and the much-reviled statue of Cosimo de' Medici in the loggia, are reminders that Florence finally took Montalcino in 1559.

The one-handed **clock** was the norm until 200 years ago. For five centuries, the arcaded **loggia** hosted the town market. And, of course, it's fun to simply observe the passeggiata—these days mostly a parade of tourists here for the wine.

For some wine-centric whimsy, go around the right side of the City Hall and find a series of plaques (each designed by a different artist), which show off the annual rating of the Brunello harvest from two to five stars—important, as wine is the lifeblood of the local economy.

HEART OF TUSCANY

Montalcino Museums (Musei di Montalcino)

While technically three museums in one (archaeology, medieval art, and modern art), and surprisingly big and modern for this little town, Montalcino's lone museum ranks only as a decent bad-weather activity. The cellar is filled with interesting artifacts dating back as far as—gulp—200,000 B.C. The ground, first, and second floors hold the medieval and modern art collections, with an emphasis on Gothic sacred art (with works from Montalcino's heyday, the 13th to 16th century). The ground floor is best, with a large collection of crucifixes and the museum's highlights, a glazed terracotta altarpiece and a statue of St. Sebastian, both by Andrea della Robbia.

Cost and Hours: €4.50, Tue-Sun 10:00-13:00 & 14:00-17:50, closed Mon, Via Ricasoli 31, to the right of Sant'Agostino Church, tel. 0577-846-014.

Wineries near Montalcino

The countryside around Montalcino is littered with wineries, some of which offer tastings. As Brunello is the poshest of Italian wines, these wineries feel a bit upscale, and most require an advance reservation. It's a simple process (just call and arrange a time), and they'll delight in showing you around. Tours generally last 45-60 minutes, cost €10-15 per person, and conclude with a tasting of three or four wines. The Montalcino TI can give you a list of more than 150 regional wineries and will call ahead for you. Or check with the vintners' consortium (tel. 0577-848-246, www.consorziobrunellodimontalcino.it). Many wineries are closed on Sunday, so check before heading out.

If you lack a car (or don't want to drive), you can take a tour on the **Brunello Wine Bus,** which laces together visits to four wineries, with a lunch break in the middle, either on your own in Montalcino or at a farmhouse for an extra fee (€90, May-Oct Tue and Thu-Sat, departs at 10:00, returns at 19:00, tours leave from their office, or they will pick you up within 3 miles—5 km—of Montalcino, half-day tours available, Viale della Liberta 12, tel. 0577-846-021, www.winetravelsforyou.com, info@winetravelsforyou.com).

If you're paying for a wine tasting, you aren't obligated to buy. But if a winery is doing a small tasting just for you, they're hoping you'll buy a bottle or two. Italian vintners understand that North Americans can't take much wine with them, and they don't expect to make a big sale, but they do hope you'll look for their wines in the US. Some shops and wineries can arrange shipping.

South of Montalcino

These options are linked by my Brunello Wine Country Drive, later in this chapter. For locations, see the map on page 577).

Mastrojanni

Perched high above the Sant'Antimo Abbey, overlooking sprawling vineyards, this winery (owned by the Illy coffee company) is big and glitzy—yet doesn't feel as corporate or soulless as some of the bigger players (€17-36 bottles, reserve ahead, Podere Loreto e San Pio, tel. 0577-835-681, www.mastrojanni.com, Andrea). To reach it, head up into the town of Castelnuovo dell'Abate (just above Sant'Antimo Abbey), bear left at the Bassomondo restaurant, and continue up along the gravel road (enjoying vineyard and abbey views).

Ciacci Piccolomini d'Aragona

Easier to remember by just its first name (pronounced like Chachi in *Happy Days*), this well-respected, family-run vineyard has a classy tasting room/*enoteca* and an outdoor view terrace. If you're just dropping in, belly up to the wine bar for two or three free tastes. Or reserve ahead for a more formal tasting of top-quality wines for €10-25, which includes a tour of the cellar (open Mon-Fri 9:00-19:00, Sat 10:30-18:30, closed Sun, down a back lane near Sant'Antimo Abbey—for directions, see page 576, tel. 0577-835-616, www.ciaccipiccolomini.com, visite@ciaccipiccolomini.com). They have a special passion for bikers, with a gallery of historic bikes and a shower for anyone who cycles in.

Castello Banfi-Poggio alle Mura

Much bigger and glossier than the other recommended wineries, Banfi is one of the largest producers in the area. Despite its size, the estate is charming, set in a castle located in a picturesque corner southwest of Sant'Antimo. This is a great option for Sundays, when other places are closed, or for a spontaneous drop-in tasting at the winery's *enoteca* (tastings start at €12, daily 10:00-19:30, until 18:00 Nov-March, tours available on request, tel. 055-877-500, www.castellobanfiilborgo.com, enoteca@banfi.it). You'll find Banfi about 20 minutes south of Montalcino; follow SP-14 to Borgo Santa Rita and cut back north, following signs to *Poggio alle Mura*.

North of Montalcino

These more remote wineries are most convenient if you're linking Montalcino to the Siena area. But either one is also worth a special trip—Altesino feels like a classy California winery, with stunning views, while Santa Giulia feels like you're dropping in on friends who run a cool farm. For locations, see the map on page 577.

Wines in the Region

This region has two well-respected red wines, each centered on a specific town: Montepulciano is known for its Vino Nobile, while Montalcino is famous for its Brunello. In each wine, the predominant grape is a clone of sangiovese (Tuscany's main red wine grape).

Vino Nobile di Montepulciano ("noble wine of Montepulciano") is a high-quality, dry ruby red, made mostly with the Prugnolo Gentile variety of sangiovese (70 percent), plus other varieties including Mammolo (30 percent). Aged two years (or three for a *riserva*)—one year of which must be in oak casks—it's more full-bodied than a typical Chianti and less tannic than a Brunello. It pairs well with meat, especially roasted lamb with rosemary, rabbit or boar ragu over pasta, grilled portobello mushrooms, and local cheeses like pecorino. Several large wineries

produce and age their Vino Nobile in the sprawling cellars beneath the town of Montepulciano. Two of these—Contucci Cantina and De' Ricci Cantine—are fun and easy to tour (see "Sights and Experiences in Montepulciano" on page 540). The oldest red wine in Tuscany, Vino Nobile has been produced since the late 1500s. (Don't mistake this wine for lesser-quality wines from the Le Marche or Abruzzo regions that use a grape confusingly named Montepulciano.)

Brunello di Montalcino ("the little brown one of Montalcino"—named for the color of the grapes before harvest) is even more highly regarded and ranks among Italy's finest and most expensive wines. Made from 100 percent Sangiovese Grosso (a.k.a. Brunello) grapes, it's smooth, dry, and aged for a minimum of two years in wood casks, plus an additional four months in the bottle. *Riserva* wines are aged an additional year. Brunello is designed to cellar for 10 years or longer—but who can wait? It pairs well with the local cuisine, but the perfect match is the fine Chianina beef. *Buon appetito!*

First created by the Biondi Santi clan in the late 19th century, this wine quickly achieved a sterling reputation. Today, there are around 240 mostly small producers of Brunello in the Montalcino region; I've recommended just a few, which I find fun and accessible (see listings on page 576). A simpler option (that avoids having the taster be behind the wheel) is to sample a few different wines at one of the good wine bars in Montalcino (see page 563).

You'll also see Rosso di Montalcino (a younger version of Brunello), which is aged for one year. This "poor man's Brunello" is very good, at half the price. Note that in lesser-quality harvest years, only Rosso di Montalcino is produced.

Montalcino's climate is drier and warmer than Chianti or Montepulciano. Diverse soils and slopes create many microclimates that affect the wine. Locals explain that, due to overall temperature increases resulting from climate change, wineries on the higher ground reap benefits from slightly cooler temperatures (grapes love hot days and cool nights). Elevation is a bonus for wine-loving tourists, who enjoy stellar views while sampling the best wines.

Touring a winery, you'll see that many winemakers age Brunello in giant oak casks. This means that less liquid is in con-

tact with the wood surface, so the wine picks up less of the harsh wood (tannic) taste and vanilla-like flavors, while still absorbing the desired leathery and peppery notes.

You'll also notice glass jars poking up from the tops of those casks, which allow expansion of the liquid during fermentation, and—by providing a small overflow reservoir—ensure that the wine reaches the very top of the cask. Before placing the wine in casks, modern wineries ferment it in temperature-controlled cement or stainless-steel tanks, which are easier to maintain than wood and preserve a more fruity bouquet.

Strolling through vineyards, you may notice "sentinel" roses at the ends of some of the rows of vines. These aren't just decorative; because disease affects roses before grapes, historically the flowers acted as a kind of canary in a coal mine, giving vintners advance notice if a phylloxera epidemic was imminent. Today the roses can warn of mildew.

But disease isn't the only pest: Locals say that wild boars make the best winemakers—they wait to raid the vineyards until the grapes are perfectly sweet. At that magic moment, it becomes a race between the boars and the human harvesters. But humans have the last laugh (or bite)—boar is found on many Tuscan menus and is considered the perfect accompaniment to the local wines.

Altesino

Elegant and stately, Altesino owns perhaps the most stunning location of all, just off the back road connecting Montalcino north to Buonconvento. You'll twist up on cypress-lined gravel lanes to this perch, which looks out over an expanse of vineyards with Montalcino hovering on the horizon (€15 for tour and basic tasting, daily, reserve ahead, Loc. Altesino 54, tel. 0577-806-208, www.altesino.it, info@altesino.it). You'll find the turnoff for Altesino along the back road (SP-45) between Montalcino and Buonconvento.

Santa Giulia

On the outskirts of Torrenieri, this is a quintessential family-run winery, with an emphasis on quality over quantity (only 20,000 bottles a year). They also produce excellent olive oil, prosciutto, and salami. Less picturesque and much more rustic than the other wineries listed here, a tour at Santa Giulia is a Back Door experience. The son, Gianluca, and his wife, Kae, enjoy showing off their entire working farm—ham hocks, cheese, and winery—before giving you a chance to taste their produce. Call to find a time that fits their schedule; around lunchtime, you can arrange a "Zero Kilometer" tasting, with everything farm-made (€15 tasting and tour, 2-person minimum, €13-30 bottles, Loc. Santa Giulia 48, closed Sun, tel. 0577-834-270, www.santagiuliamontalcino.it, info@santagiuliamontalcino.it). From Torrenieri's main intersection, follow the brown *Via Francigena* signs. After crossing the train tracks and a bridge, watch on the left to follow signs for *Sasso di Sole*, then *Sta. Giulia;* you'll take gravel roads through farm fields to the winery.

Sleeping in Montalcino

$$$ Hotel Dei Capitani, at the end of town near the bus station, has plush public spaces, an inviting pool, and a cliffside terrace offering plenty of reasons for lounging. About half the 29 rooms come with vast Tuscan views for the same price (request a view room when you reserve), the nonview rooms are bigger, and everyone has access to the terrace (RS%, air-con, elevator, limited free parking—first come, first served, Via Lapini 6, tel. 0577-847-227, www.deicapitani.it, info@deicapitani.it).

$$ Palazzina Cesira, right in the heart of the old town, is a gem, renting five spacious and tastefully decorated rooms in a fine 13th-century residence with a palatial lounge and a pleasant garden. You'll enjoy a refined and tranquil ambience, a nice breakfast (with eggs), and the chance to get to know Lucilla and her American husband Roberto, who are generous with local advice

(RS%, 2-night minimum, 3-night minimum on holiday weekends, air-con, free off-street parking, Via Soccorso Saloni 2, tel. 0577-846-055, www.montalcinoitaly.com, info@montalcinoitaly.com).

$$ B&B da Idolina has four good, midrange rooms above a wine shop on the main street (includes basic breakfast in shared kitchen, check-in 14:00-20:00—call if arriving later, parking available, Via Mazzini 65, tel. 0577-849-212, www.bebdaidolina. com, fulvia.soda@gmail.com, Fulvia).

$ Albergo Giardino, a great value, has nine big rooms done in a modern-minimalist style, no public spaces, and a convenient location near the bus station (RS%, no breakfast, Piazza Cavour 4, tel. 0577-848-257, mobile 320-404-4655, www.albergoilgiardino. it, info@albergoilgiardino.it, Roberto and dad Mario).

Eating in Montalcino

RESTAURANTS

$$$ Re di Macchia is an invitingly intimate restaurant where Antonio serves up the Tuscan fare Roberta cooks. Look for their seasonal menu and a fine Montalcino wine list (Fri-Wed 12:00-14:00 & 19:00-21:00, closed Thu, reservations strongly recommended, Via Soccorso Saloni 21, tel. 0577-846-116).

$$ Taverna del Grappolo Blu is bright and fresh; it's unpretentious, friendly, and serious about its wine, game, homemade pasta, and vegetarian options (Sat-Thu 12:00-15:00 & 19:00-22:00, closed Fri, reservations smart, a few steps off Via Mazzini at Scale di Via Moglio 1, tel. 0577-847-150, Luciano, www.grappoloblu.it).

$$ Ristorante-Pizzeria San Giorgio is a homey trattoria/pizzeria with traditional decor and reasonable prices. It's great for families and a reliable choice for a simple meal (daily 12:00-15:00 & 19:00-22:30, closed Tue off-season, Via Soccorso Saloni 10, tel. 0577-848-507, Mara).

Picnic: Gather ingredients at the **Co-op supermarket** on Via Sant'Agostino (Mon-Sat 8:30-13:00 & 16:00-20:00, closed Sun, just off Via Ricasoli in front of Sant'Agostino Church), then enjoy your feast up at the Madonna del Soccorso Church, with vast territorial views.

WINE BARS

There are two basic approaches for sampling Montalcino's wines: at an *enoteca* in town or at a countryside winery. Serious wine connoisseurs will enjoy a day of winery-hopping, sipping wines right where they were created; see the good options listed earlier. But if you're short on time (or don't have a designated driver—penalties here are harsh for driving under the influence), simply visit a wine bar in town, where you can comfortably taste a variety of vintages

HEART OF TUSCANY

before stumbling safely back to your hotel. This is also a great strategy for Sundays, when many wineries are closed. These places also serve light food.

Caffè Fiaschetteria Italiana, a classic café/wine bar, was founded by Ferruccio Biondi Santi, the creator of the famous Brunello wine. The wine library in the back of the café boasts many local choices. A meeting place since 1888, this grand café also serves light lunches and espresso to tourists and locals alike (Brunellos by the glass, light snacks and plates; same prices inside, outside, or in back room; daily 7:30-23:00, Piazza del Popolo 6, tel. 0577-849-043). And if it's coffee you need, this place—with its classic 1961 espresso machine—is considered the best in town.

Enoteca di Piazza is one of a chain of wine shops with a system of mechanical dispensers. A "drink card" (like a debit card) keeps track of the samples you take, for which you'll pay from €1 to €9 for each 60-milliliter taste of 100 different wines, including some whites—rare in this town. They hope you'll buy a bottle of the samples you like, and are happy to educate you in English. (Rule of thumb: A bottle costs about 10 times the price of the sample. If you buy a bottle, the sample of that wine is free.) While the place feels a little formulaic, it can be fun—the wine is great, and the staff is casual and helpful. Their small restaurant lets you enjoy your drink card with local dishes (daily 9:00-20:00, near Piazza del Popolo at Via Matteotti 43, tel. 0577-848-104, www.enotecadipiazza.com).

Enoteca la Fortezza di Montalcino offers a chance to taste top-end wines by the glass, each with an English explanation. While the prices are a bit higher than other *enoteche* in town, the medieval setting inside Montalcino's fort is a hit for most visitors. Spoil yourself with Brunello in the cozy *enoteca* or at an outdoor table in the fortress courtyard (tastings start at €13 for 3 wines and go up from there; sampler plates of cheeses, *salumi*, honeys, and olive oil; daily 9:00-20:00, until 18:00 Nov-March, inside the Fortezza, tel. 0577-849-211).

Montalcino Connections

Montalcino is well-connected to Siena; other bus connections are inconvenient but generally workable. Montalcino's bus station is on Piazza Cavour, within the town walls. Bus tickets are sold at the bar on Piazza Cavour, at the TI, and at some tobacco shops, but not on board (except for the bus to Sant'Antimo). Check schedules at the TI, at the bus station, or online (at www.sienamobilita.it or www.tiemmespa.it). The nearest train station is a 30-minute bus ride away, in Buonconvento.

From Montalcino by Bus: The handiest direct bus is to **Siena** (6/day Mon-Sat, 4/day Sun, 1.5 hours). To reach **Pienza** or **Mon-**

tepulciano, ride bus #114 to Torrenieri (3-4/day Mon-Sat, none on Sun, 20 minutes), where you'll switch to line #112 for the rest of the way (from Torrenieri: 25 minutes to Pienza, 45 minutes to Montepulciano). Since the Montepulciano bus connection is sporadic, consider hiring a taxi (about €70 one-way). A local bus runs to **Sant'Antimo** (3/day Mon-Fri, 2/day Sat, none on Sun, 15 minutes, buy tickets on board). Anyone going to **Florence** by bus changes in Siena; since the bus arrives at Siena's train station, it's handier to go the rest of the way to Florence by train. Alternatively, you could take the bus to **Buonconvento** (8/day, fewer on Sun, 30 minutes), and catch the train from there to Florence. The transit website www.tiemmespa.it has a good map of the bus lines, which may clarify your options—click the link "Mappa extraurbano Siena."

Heart of Tuscany Drive

If you have just one day to connect the ultimate Tuscan towns and views, this is the loop I'd stitch together with a driving tour. Most of this journey is through velvety, gentle, rolling hillsides generously draped with vivid-green crops in the springtime, and a parched moonscape in the late summer and fall. This almost otherworldly smoothness constitutes many travelers' notions of Tuscan perfection.

❷ SELF-GUIDED DRIVING TOUR

In addition to larger towns (Montepulciano, Pienza) and smaller ones (Bagno Vignoni, Rocca d'Orcia), this self-guided loop drive, worth ▲▲▲, gives you a good look at the area called the Val d'Orcia (val DOR-chah), boasting some of the best scenery in Italy.

If you're in a rush and don't linger in any of the towns, you could do this drive in a couple of hours. To hit the sights, explore the towns, and linger over a meal or a glass of wine, spread it out over an entire day. (You could even splice in a side-trip to a Brunello winery for a tasting, if you like.) I've started and ended the clockwise loop in Montepulciano, but you could just as easily start and end in Pienza. If gardens are your thing, do this loop when La Foce Gardens are open (see page 570).

Leg #1: Montepulciano to La Foce to Bagno Vignoni

Before leaving Montepulciano, consider dropping by the showpiece Renaissance **San Biagio Church,** which sits at the base of the town (watch for its long, level, tree-lined driveway exactly where you leave Montepulciano on the road toward Pienza—see page 543).

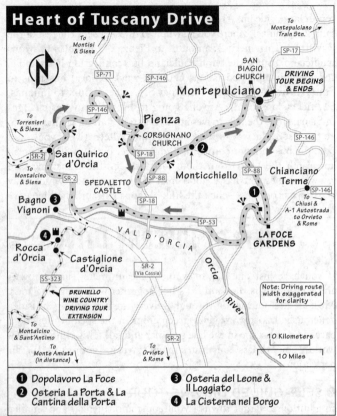

Heart of Tuscany Drive

To Montisi & Siena

To Montepulciano Train Stn.

SP-17

SP-71 · SP-146

SAN BIAGIO CHURCH

DRIVING TOUR BEGINS & ENDS

SP-146

Montepulciano

To Torrenieri & Siena

Pienza

CORSIGNANO CHURCH

SP-146

San Quirico d'Orcia

SR-2

❷

SP-18

Monticchiello

SP-88

Chianciano Terme

SP-146

To Montalcino & Siena

SR-2

SP-88

To Chiusi & A-1 Autostrada to Orvieto & Rome

SPEDALETTO CASTLE

SP-18

❶

Bagno Vignoni ❸

SP-53

LA FOCE GARDENS

❹

Rocca d'Orcia

Castiglione d'Orcia

V A L   D' O R C I A

SR-2 (Via Cassia)

Orcia River

SS-323

BRUNELLO WINE COUNTRY DRIVING TOUR EXTENSION

Note: Driving route width exaggerated for clarity

To Montalcino & Sant'Antimo

To Monte Amiata (in distance) ↓

To Orvieto & Rome

SR-2

10 Kilometers

10 Miles

❶ Dopolavoro La Foce
❷ Osteria La Porta & La Cantina della Porta
❸ Osteria del Leone & Il Loggiato
❹ La Cisterna nel Borgo

To begin our loop, drive south, at first following signs to *Chianciano Terme* and *Chiusi*. Just 1 kilometer south of Montepulciano, watch on the right for the turnoff to *Castelluccio* and *Monticchiello*. Turn off here and zip along a pastoral back road for 5 kilometers. Pass the turnoff for Monticchiello on your right, and carry on straight ahead, as the road continues uphill and becomes gravel. Grinding your way up, watch on your right for the jagged Tuscan cliffs called *calanchi*. You'll pop out at the T-intersection in front of the entrance to the **La Foce Gardens** (from this intersection, parking and reception are 50 yards to the left—look for *Loc. La Foce;* for details on the gardens, see page 570).

From La Foce, head downhill toward *Siena* and *Roma*. After a few hundred yards, watch on the left for the big gravel parking lot of the recommended **Dopolavoro La Foce** restaurant (across the street). From this lot, you have a fine view of one of the iconic cypress-lined driveways of Tuscany (see the "Top Tuscan Views" sidebar on page 574).

Continue downhill along this road for about 5 kilometers, through pristine farm fields, until you reach a major intersection, where you'll turn right toward *Pienza* and *Siena* (on SP-53). Immersed in spectacular scenery, you'll twist between giant cypresses for about 10 kilometers. This road parallels the region's namesake Orcia River ("Val d'Orcia" means "Orcia River Valley").

Take a moment to simply appreciate your surroundings. The famous Chianti region to the north (right) and the Brunello region to the west (straight ahead) are each a short drive away; in those places, the rocky soil is perfect for grapes. But here, instead of rocks, you're surrounded by clay hills—once the floor of a prehistoric sea—that are ideal for cereal crops. Grains alternate every few years with a crop of fava beans, which help reintroduce nitrogen to the soil. It seems that every grassy hilltop is capped with a family farmhouse. Partway along this road, you'll pass a turnoff (on the right) offering a speedy shortcut to Pienza, just 8 stunning kilometers away. But there's so much more to see; I'd rather carry on with our loop.

The tower looming on the hill ahead of you is **Rocca d'Orcia**'s Tentennano Castle (see page 573). Nearing the end of the road, you'll pass (on the left) the front door of an old farmhouse with oddly formidable crenellated towers, like a little castle in the field. This is **Spedaletto Castle,** built during the 12th century as a hospice for pilgrims walking the Via Francigena to Rome. Today it serves a similar purpose, as an *agriturismo* called La Grancia ("The Granary"), housing wayfarers like you.

When you reach a T-intersection with the main SR-2 highway, turn left (toward *Roma*), then immediately take the exit for **Bagno Vignoni.** To explore this fascinating medieval spa town—with its main square filled with a thermal-spring-fed pool—see page 571. To see the empty fortress at **Rocca d'Orcia,** stay on the SR-2 highway just 1 kilometer past Bagno Vignoni, then watch for the next turnoff (see page 573).

Leg #2: Bagno Vignoni to Pienza (with Detours to Brunello Wineries and Tuscan Views)

From Bagno Vignoni, head north on SR-2 (toward *San Quirico d'Orcia* and *Siena*). After just 4 kilometers, in San Quirico d'Orcia, turn off onto the SP-146 road to Pienza, also marked for *Chiusi*, *Chianciano Terme*, and *Montepulciano*.

But before heading down that road, consider a few potential detours: First, if you won't have time to delve deeply into Brunello wine country, now is a good time to side-trip to your choice of **Brunello wineries;** those I've recommended on page 576 are all within about a 20- to 25-minute drive of San Quirico. Read the descriptions, take your pick, and ideally call ahead to reserve a tour and tasting. Another option is to zip into the town of **Montalcino** itself—an easy and well-signed 15-minute drive from San Quirico—and taste some local vintages at a wine bar there (see page 558). And if you're collecting **views,** you could continue straight on SR-2 past San Quirico—toward *Siena*—for four kilometers and pull over next to the circle of cypress trees in a field called the Rondò (see the "Top Tuscan Views" sidebar).

Back on the SP-146 road from San Quirico to Pienza, you enjoy one of the region's most postcard-worthy stretches—with grand panoramas in both directions, including two more quintessential Tuscan scenes: the **Chapel of Madonna di Vitaleta** (after 2 kilometers, on the right); and a classic **farmhouse with trees,** just before Pienza (about 9 kilometers after San Quirico, on the left (also described in the "Top Tuscan Views" sidebar).

Finally you'll pull into **Pienza,** where you can park and tour the town using the information earlier in this chapter.

Leg #3: Pienza to Montepulciano (via Monticchiello)

If you're in a hurry or losing sunlight, just hop back on the main SP-146 road for the 12-kilometer straight-shot back to Montepulciano (enjoying some pullouts on the left with fine views of the town). But I prefer this longer, even more dramatic route, via the fortified village of Monticchiello.

From the traffic circle at the entry to Pienza's town center, instead of heading for Montepulciano, follow the road that runs along the left side of town (marked *Amiata* and *Monticchiello*—as you face Pienza, you'll continue straight when the main road bends left). This road loops around behind and below the far end of the village, where you can consider a brief detour to see Pienza's oldest church: Turn off on the right at the brown sign for *Pieve di Corsigiano* and drive a few hundred yards to **Corsignano Parish Church** (described on page 553).

Continuing on the main road past that turnoff, you'll drop steeply down into the valley, feeling as if you're sinking into a lavish painting. Dead ahead is **Monte Amiata,** the tallest mountain in Tuscany. This looming behemoth blocks bad weather, creating a mild microclimate that makes the Val d'Orcia a particularly pleasant place to farm...or to vacation. Meanwhile, don't forget to savor the similarly stellar views of Pienza in your rearview mirror. After 5 kilometers, look on the left for the turnoff to Monticchiello (brown sign). From here, carry on for 4 kilometers—watching on the left for fine vistas of Pienza and for another classic twisty cypress-lined road—to the pleasant town of **Monticchiello.** This town, with an excellent recommended restaurant (Osteria La Porta) and a com-

The Via Francigena

Many of the sights in this region—and others in this book (including Siena, Lucca, and San Gimignano)—line up along the route of the Via Francigena (VEE-ah frahn-CHEE-jeh-nah). During the Middle Ages, when devout Christians undertook a once-in-a-lifetime pilgrimage to Rome, this route was heavily trod by the footsore faithful flowing in from northern Europe (hence the name, "Road of the Franks"—referring to the Germanic tribes who lived in present-day Germany and France). The main Via Francigena followed more or less the route of today's SR-2 highway, from Florence to Siena, then through the Val d'Orcia south to Rome. Without even realizing it, many modern-day tourists follow this millennium-old route as they travel through this part of Italy.

The first documented pilgrimages along here took place around A.D. 725, and the trend continued for many centuries. In 990, Archbishop Sigeric of Canterbury undertook the entire 1,100-mile round-trip from England. Upon his return, he documented tips for fellow pilgrims about where to sleep, where to eat, what to see, and how to pack light in a carry-on-the-plane-size rucksack...arguably the world's first travel guidebook.

The history of Tuscany is inextricably tied to the Via Francigena. Pilgrim traffic represented an injection of wealth into communities along the Via Francigena, and fortresses popped up—or were repurposed—to keep the route safe. Abbeys and churches were built to cater to the masses. And many shrewd communities leveraged the passing pilgrim trade into enormous prosperity; for example, Siena boomed both as a financial center and a trading outpost for Via Francigena pilgrims.

Like the Camino de Santiago in northern Spain, this medieval pilgrim route—forgotten for centuries—has recently enjoyed renewed interest. Though the numbers are still small—and the path lacks the well-orchestrated conveniences of the Camino de Santiago—a handful of modern-day pilgrims are, once again, walking through Tuscany south to Rome.

HEART OF TUSCANY

pact, fortified townscape worth exploring, is a good place to stretch your legs (described on page 573).

From Monticchiello, there are two routes back to Montepulciano: For the shorter route (6 kilometers), partly on gravel roads, drive all the way to the base of the Monticchiello old town, then turn right. For the longer route (10 kilometers), which stays on paved roads but circles back the way our loop started, turn off for Montepulciano at the main intersection, in the flat part of town that's lower down.

HEART OF TUSCANY SIGHTS

Below are the main sights you'll pass on my Heart of Tuscany driving route. Two of the main stops—the towns of Montepulciano and Pienza—are covered earlier in this chapter.

▲La Foce Gardens

One of the finest gardens in Tuscany, La Foce (lah FOH-cheh) caps a hill with geometrical Italian gardens and rugged English gardens that flow seamlessly into the Tuscan countryside. The gardens were a labor of love for Iris Origo, an English-born, Italian-bred aristocrat who left her mark on this area and wrote evocatively about her time here. The gardens—which are worth a pilgrimage for garden lovers—can be visited only with a guided tour, and only three days a week (Wed, Sat, Sun) and some holidays.

Cost and Hours: €10; 50-minute tours offered April-Oct Wed at 15:00, 16:00, 17:00, and 18:00, Sat-Sun and holidays at 11:30, 15:00, and 16:30; private tours available, no tours in winter, confirm tour time and reserve in advance, ticket office opens 15 minutes before tour time, tel. 0578-69101, www.lafoce.com.

Getting There: La Foce sits in the hills above the busy town of Chianciano Terme. You can avoid SP-146 from Montepulciano through Chianciano (heavy traffic, poor signage) by following a more scenic route through the countryside (described at the start of my Heart of Tuscany Drive on page 565).

Background: In 1924, the British aristocrat Iris Cutting—who had grown up amidst wealth and privilege in Fiesole, overlooking Florence—married Antonio Origo, the son of the marquis of the Val d'Orcia. They took over a dilapidated country home high in the hills above Chianciano Terme and set about converting it into a luxurious estate of manor homes and gardens, importing British landscape architect Cecil Pinsent to bring their vision to life. The Origo clan also revived the Renaissance ideal of landowners supporting the local peasants, and built a school and other institutions for the public good. During World War II, the Origos took in refugee children and hid partisans—all recounted in Iris Origo's memoir, *War in Val d'Orcia*. Iris' daughters, Benedetta ("blessed") and Donata ("given"), still own and manage the property today.

Visiting the Gardens: From the entrance, your tour guide leads you first into the tidy Renaissance garden nearest the main house, with angular hedges, wisteria-draped walls, and potted citrus trees on pedestals. As you move away from the house, the garden's style changes to a more rugged, English-style design that bridges the tidy villa and the pristine Tuscan wilderness all around. From the garden, you'll have a perfect view of a classic Tuscan road—a cypress-lined lane zigzagging up an adjacent hill. If this road seems a little too perfect, that's because it is: It was built by the grandfather of Antonio Origo, who had a similar appreciation for aesthetics, and made sure even this utilitarian road was beautiful. He based the road's design on scenes in Renaissance-era frescoes in Florence's Medici-Riccardi Palace.

Eating and Sleeping near La Foce: Near the gardens, the Origo family runs a remote, restful B&B (described on page 530) and a memorably charming roadside restaurant, **$$ Dopolavoro La Foce** ("After Work"). Once the quitting-time hangout for local farmers, today its interior is country-chic. The menu offers basic sandwiches or pasta and meat (featuring elegant hamburgers). The garden terrace out back is a chirpy delight, and the parking lot across the busy road offers one of the best vantage points on that perfect Tuscan road (Tue-Sun 9:00-22:00, closed Mon and Nov-March, Strada della Vittoria 90, tel. 0578-754-025, run with flair by Azia).

▲Bagno Vignoni

Thanks to the unique geology of this part of Tuscany (see sidebar on page 538), several natural hot springs bubble up between

the wineries and hill towns. And the town of Bagno Vignoni (BAHN-yoh veen-YOH-nee)—with a quirky history, a pleasant-to-stroll street plan punctuated with steamy canals, and various places to take a dip—is the most accessible and enjoyable to explore. If you'd like to recuperate from your sightseeing and wine tasting by soaking in the thermal baths, bring your swimsuit.

Getting There: Bagno Vignoni is well-signed, just off the main SR-2 highway linking Siena to Rome (5 kilometers south of San Quirico d'Orcia). Park in the pay lot (coins only) by the big roundabout and walk into town, taking the left fork (in front of Hotel Le Terme).

Bagno Vignoni Town Walk: Emerging into the main square, walk under the covered loggia and look out over the aptly named **Piazza delle Sorgenti** ("Square of the Sources"), filled with a vast pool. Natural spring water bubbles up at the far end at temperatures around 125 degrees Fahrenheit. Known since Roman times, these hot springs were harnessed for their medicinal properties in the Middle Ages, when footsore pilgrims could stop for a soothing soak midway through their long walk from northern Europe to Rome along the Via Francigena. St. Catherine of Siena also came here to convalesce, but—in true ascetic style—threw herself into the hottest part of the spring as a form of self-flagellation. (Under the loggia, notice the little chapel to St. Catherine, with pottery vases decorated with her symbolic goose.) Other Tuscan big shots—from Lorenzo the Magnificent (the Medici paterfamilias) to Pope Pius II (who remade Pienza in his own image)—also came here seeking cures for arthritis and other ailments.

You're not allowed to wade or swim in this main pool today, but an easy stroll through town shows you other facets of these healing waters. Facing the pool, turn left, walk to the end of the loggia, then turn left again down Via delle Sorgenti (passing the recommended Il Loggiato restaurant, then Piazza del Moretto and the recommended Osteria del Leone restaurant). Listen for the water that gushes under your feet, as it leaves the pool and heads for its big plunge over the cliff. Continuing straight, notice the stairs (on your right) down to Hotel Posta Marcucci, with the Piscina Val di Sole—the most accessible place in town for a dip (details later).

But continuing straight ahead for now, you'll emerge at an open zone with the cliff-capping **ruins** of medieval mills and cisterns that once made full use of Bagno Vignoni's main resource. Here you'll also have a chance to dip your toes or fingers into streams of now-tepid water. At the canals' end, the water plunges down into the gorge carved by the Orcia River. Looking deep into the valley, notice the pond with white mud, where locals enjoy going for a free soak. Then peek into the giant basin at the edge of the cliff, where thick, pillar-like mineral deposits indicate where natural showers once poured—back when this was a bathing complex. On the adjacent hillside is the castle-crowned **Rocca d'Orcia,** a heavily fortified near-ghost-town that's just a short drive away.

Taking the Waters: The modern **Piscina Val di Sole** bath complex, inside Hotel Posta Marcucci, is simple but sophisticated. It's a serene spot to soak (in water ranging from 90 to 109 degrees Fahrenheit) while taking in soaring views of Rocca d'Orcia across the valley (€27, €5 towel rental with €10 deposit, Fri-Wed 9:30-18:00, shorter hours off-season, closed Thu year-round, tel. 0577-887-112, www.piscinavaldisole.it).

Eating in Bagno Vignoni: $$$ Osteria del Leone, on the cheery little *piazzetta* just behind the loggia, is the town's class act, with charming tables out on the square. Inside it's dull and modern, with a fine interior garden (closed Mon, Via dei Mulini 3, tel. 0577-887-300, www.osteriadelleone.it). For something a bit more affordable and casual, drop by the nearby **$$ Il Loggiato,** with stony indoor seating or outdoor tables (closed Thu, Via delle Sorgenti 36, tel. 0577-888-973).

Rocca d'Orcia

The fortress looming over Rocca d'Orcia (ROH-kah DOR-chah) perches high above the main SR-2 highway. Likely inhabited and

fortified since Etruscan times, this strategic hilltop was a seat of great regional power in the 12th century. During this time, Rocca d'Orcia was one of a chain of forts that watched over pilgrims walking the Via Francigena to Rome. Supposedly, St. Catherine of Siena miraculously learned to read and write overnight while staying here.

Today the **Rocca di Tentennano** fortress—an empty shell of a castle with modern steel stairs and a grand 360-degree panorama at its top—looks stark and abandoned. It seems to dare you to pay €3 to take the very steep hike up from the parking lots below (June-Sept daily 10:00-13:00 & 16:00-19:00; Fri-Sun only in May; shorter hours off-season, mobile 333-986-0788).

The pleasant village of Rocca d'Orcia, just below the castle, is a sleepy community for a stroll, but there's not much to see. The village focuses on its stone cistern, in the aptly named Piazza della Cisterna. The bigger town just behind Rocca, Castiglione d'Orcia, also has a fortified hilltop town center.

Eating in Rocca d'Orcia: $$ La Cisterna nel Borgo sits on Rocca's main square, facing the town's namesake cistern. Marta and Fede serve up deliciously executed dishes in a classic setting (Mon-Fri 12:00-14:00 and 19:00-22:00, Sat-Sun dinner only, Borgo Mestro 37, tel. 0577-887-280).

▲Monticchiello

This 200-person fortified village clings to the high ground in the countryside just south of Pienza and Montepulciano. As it's not along a main road, it feels more remote (for route tips on getting there from Pienza, see page 568; from Montepulciano, see page 545). While not quite "undiscovered," Monticchiello is relatively untrampled, and feels like a real place where you can get in touch with authentic Tuscan village life. It's also a fine place for a meal.

Ignore the flat, modern lower town, and head up to the circular, fortified upper town huddled against the hillside. Park for free at the base of the village and hike up through the main gate (passing the recommended La Porta restaurant on your left), and just explore. The town is dominated by the late-13th-century Church of Sts. Leonardo and Christopher, with a Gothic exterior and Renaissance interior along with a few surviving 14th-century frescoes. Tucked in a square nearby is the TI (with gifty local products) and

Top Tuscan Views

Tuscany is a land of splendid vistas, and many of the best—and most famous—viewpoints are in or near the Val d'Orcia. Shutterbugs who want to make their own custom calendar of iconic Tuscan scenes (rolling fields, cypress trees, serpentine driveways) should prioritize fitting these stops into their itineraries.

Cypress-Lined Driveways: You'll find dozens upon dozens of these in your Tuscan travels. But two in this area are classics. The first is the perfectly twisty road near La Foce gardens; the most accessible and unobstructed angle on this is from the parking lot across the street from the recommended Dopolavoro La Foce restaurant (see page 571)—but if you're touring the gardens, the views from inside are even better. Another postcard-ready driveway crests a hill adjacent to Monticchiello (you'll spot it on the main road from Pienza).

Circle of Cypresses (Rondò): This ring of cypress trees stands dramatically alone on a gently sloping hillside of brilliant-green-in-springtime crops. Planted as a shelter for shepherds caught out in the elements, today it's one of Tuscany's top photo ops. You'll find it along the main SR-2 road north of San Quirico d'Orcia (about 4 kilometers north of the main San Quirico exit; it's just 1 kilometer south of the Montalcino exit, and 2 kilometers south of the Torrenieri exit). Pullouts on both sides of the road—next to a long bridge—can get crowded. Avid photographers walk partway across the bridge for fine views back on the Rondò.

Chapel and Trees: The super-scenic road between San Quirico d'Orcia and Pienza (SP-146) has several fine viewpoints, but the best-known is the tidy little chapel (Cappella della Madonna di

Piazza del Teatro, where townspeople periodically enact a summer al fresco theatrical show—called Teatro Povero ("Theater of the Poor")—about the town's past and present (www.teatropovero.it). Continuing up through town, you'll find a large park sprawling at the base of a leaning tower, which keeps watch over valley views.

Eating in Monticchiello: $$$ **Osteria La Porta** is just inside the town's gate, where warm and classy Daria pleases diners either

Vitaleta) on a ridge, flanked by pudgy cypress trees. Keep an eye out for this (distant) church on the south side of the road, about 2 kilometers north of San Quirico d'Orcia (near Agriturismo Poderino). On the same road, closer to Pienza, is a classic "farmhouse with trees" scene (north side of road, a kilometer from Pienza).

Farmhouse with Twisty Driveway: Another timeless tableau is easy to spot if you're visiting Pienza: From anywhere along the

panoramic terrace, just gaze off to the south, to the rolling hills of the Val d'Orcia. In the foreground, you'll see a perfect little farmhouse with a meandering driveway (Agriturismo Podere Terrapille). If this looks familiar, you may remember it as Russell Crowe's dreamy home-sweet-home in *Gladiator*.

Abbey in Pasture and Olive Grove: The Sant'Antimo Abbey, which is well worth a visit and described on page 579, sits in a

picturesque meadow. An adjacent cypress tree towers toward the heavens, seemingly in a contest with the church's bell tower to see who will get there first. Views of the abbey from the road above, or from the abbey to the surrounding landscape, are equally thrilling.

Honorable Mention—Winery Views: Several wineries—clinging to the high ground to pull the maximum sweetness out of their vines—have spectacular territorial vistas overlooking rolling vineyards, with other landmarks lingering on the horizon. Two of the best are Altesino (10 kilometers north of Montalcino, on the road to Buonconvento; see page 562) and Mastrojanni (11 kilometers south of Montalcino, on a ridge high above Sant'Antimo Abbey; see page 559).

indoors or out with traditional Tuscan dishes presented with flair. La Porta is particularly enjoyable for its idyllic little terrace, which comes with grand Tuscan vistas. This is a destination restaurant, and reservations are a must (fixed price lunch *menu*, dinner à la carte; seatings at 12:30, 14:00, 19:30, and 21:30—but they'll seat you at other times if they have room; closed Thu, Via del Piano 1, tel. 0578-755-163, www.osterialaporta.it).

$$ La Cantina della Porta, 50 yards up the hill and to the right, is run by the same family, but feels more utilitarian and modern. It's a good bet if you're looking to eat rather than dine (closed Wed, Via San Luigi 3, tel. 0578-755-170).

Brunello Wine Country Drive

The rocky hillsides immediately surrounding Montalcino produce some of the best wine in Italy: Brunello di Montalcino (and the less pricey, nearly-as-good Rosso di Montalcino). This route takes you through a wooded and jagged terrain, where sangiovese grapes struggle for survival on their way to becoming fine wine. Ideal for wine lovers, the Brunello wine country features remote rural wineries where you have the opportunity to sample the prized local wine. And tucked between the wineries, you'll also find time-passed villages and an evocative abbey in a secluded valley (Sant'Antimo). For a primer on this area's wines, see page 560.

❍SELF-GUIDED DRIVING TOUR

This self-guided loop drive, worth ▲▲, starts in Montalcino and heads southwest through the hills before cutting the corner on a dramatic but challenging gravel road called "La Sesta." You'll be rewarded with the chance to visit three wineries and a fine old Romanesque abbey before either returning to Montalcino (on easier roads) or twisting over the hills to the Heart of Tuscany zone.

Easier Alternative: To skip the gravel La Sesta stretch, you can simply drive from Montalcino down to Castelnuovo dell'Abate on easier roads. After visiting the abbey, you're about a five-minute drive from two scenic wineries (in opposite directions): Ciacci Piccolomini d'Aragona and Mastrojanni.

Montalcino to Sant'Antimo Abbey and Back

At the south end of Montalcino, when you reach the roundabout circling a famously ugly statue, head for *Grosetto* and *S. Angelo*. This road will take you all the way to Sant'Angelo in Colle (9 kilometers south).

Back to the main road, continue south toward *Grosseto*. Just 1 kilometer before the town of **Sant'Angelo in Colle** (worth visiting only for its restaurants—see page 579), watch carefully on the left for *Strada Sesta* signs, indicating the small turn-off onto the gravel road **La Sesta** ("The Sixth"). This dramatic road—7 gravelly kilometers—comes with spectacular views. Near the end of La Sesta, on the right, watch carefully for the snazzy **Ciacci Piccolomini d'Aragona** winery. This is effectively the only one in the area with a

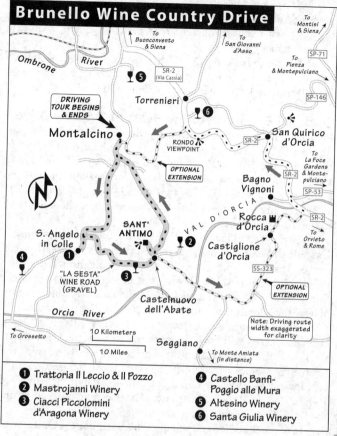

Brunello Wine Country Drive

Ombrone River

To Buonconvento & Siena

To San Giovanni d'Asso

To Montisi & Siena

SP-71

To Pienza & Montepulciano

SR-2 (Via Cassia)

5

Torrenieri

SP-146

DRIVING TOUR BEGINS & ENDS

Montalcino

RONDÒ VIEWPOINT

6

San Quirico d'Orcia

SR-2

OPTIONAL EXTENSION

Bagno Vignoni

VAL D'ORCIA

To La Foce Gardens & Montepulciano

SR-2

SP-53

Rocca d'Orcia

SR-2

S. Angelo in Colle

SANT' ANTIMO

Castiglione d'Orcia

To Orvieto & Rome

4

1

"LA SESTA" WINE ROAD (GRAVEL)

3

2

SS-323

OPTIONAL EXTENSION

Castelnuovo dell'Abate

Orcia River

To Grosseto

10 Kilometers

Seggiano

Note: Driving route width exaggerated for clarity

10 Miles

To Monte Amiata (in distance)

1 Trattoria Il Leccio & Il Pozzo
2 Mastrojanni Winery
3 Ciacci Piccolomini d'Aragona Winery

4 Castello Banfi-Poggio alle Mura
5 Altesino Winery
6 Santa Giulia Winery

Napa Valley-style "drop in anytime you like for a taste" approach... just head to the wine bar inside and ask for a pour (for details, see page 559).

From Ciacci, it's 2 kilometers to the **Sant'Antimo Abbey:** Curl up a gravel road around the bottom of the town of Castelnuovo dell'Abate ("New Castle of the Abbot"), watching for the abbey below you in a field. Drive down toward the abbey, park in the large lot, and head inside to step back to the Romanesque period (abbey described on page 579).

After visiting Sant'Antimo Abbey, consider driving up into the hills above Castelnuovo dell'Abate to the **Mastrojanni** winery, worth a visit for its vintages and views (see page 559). To get there, coming up the hill from the abbey, take the road around the left side of the Bassomondo restaurant. The road turns to gravel and climbs up, up, and up along the ridge. You'll enjoy spectacular panoramas back down over the pasture and olive groves surrounding Sant'Antimo. After 2.5 stunning kilometers, you'll reach Mastrojanni. Don't continue on the road past the winery; it quickly becomes a rocky trail.

Now head back down to the main road at Castelnuovo dell'Abate. It's easy to cut this loop short by taking the main (paved) road back up to Montalcino. Or consider an...

Optional Extension to the Heart of Tuscany Drive

For a back-roads route from Brunello wine country to the Heart of Tuscany Drive described earlier (about a 35-minute drive away), do this: From the main road in front of Castelnuovo dell'Abate, head south on the uphill road, following signs for *Seggiano* (brown) and *Castiglione d'Orcia* (blue). This twisty road—with few worthwhile stops, but ample vistas—twists 19 kilometers over the mountains to the main valley road.

Leaving Castelnuovo, you'll crest a hill, then pass the dramatic **Castello di Velona,** a medieval castle-turned-luxury hotel. Locals explain that Silvio Berlusconi (Italy's repeatedly disgraced former prime minister) considered buying this property a few years back. But when he came to Montalcino—in the famously liberal region of Tuscany—locals threw rocks at the conservative politician.

The road drops down steeply to the valley village of Monte Amiata, where you'll cross the train tracks, then the Orcia River, then wind your way back up the other side. From here, enjoy the remote farmscapes as you follow signs: At the T-intersection, turn left, toward *Castiglione d'Orcia.* You'll pass through the hamlet of Poggio Rosa, and then, at the next T-intersection, bear left again, for *Siena, San Quirico d'Orcia,* and *Castiglione d'Orcia.*

In about 4 kilometers, you'll reach **Castiglione d'Orcia,** with a fortified hilltop old town; just past that, you'll see the dramatic hill-capping Tentennano Castle, with the village of **Rocca d'Orcia** at its base (described on page 573). The easiest way to reach the top of Rocca is to drive through the town of Castiglione, and then—on the twisty road past Castiglione heading down toward the main valley road—watch for the turnoff on the left for *Rocca d'Orcia.* Drive up that road, park in the free lot at the base of the rock, and hike the rest of the way up into town and to the castle.

About 3 kilometers farther along, you'll reach the intersection with the main SR-2 Siena-to-Rome highway. Head north (toward Siena), then immediately turn off (on the left) for **Bagno Vignoni,** a fascinating old thermal spa town (to explore this town, see page 571).

Back on SR-2, head north (toward Siena) to reach the crossroads at San Quirico d'Orcia. From here you can turn off for **Pienza** (10 kilometers away) and **Montepulciano** (24 kilometers). Or you can continue straight, to pass the dramatic **Rondò** viewpoint.

Soon after the Rondò, you can turn off on the left to return to **Montalcino.** Or stay on SR-2 northbound a bit farther to reach the two recommended wineries north of Montalcino: For **Santa Giulia,** turn off to the right soon after the Rondò toward San Giovanni d'Asso (and follow the directions on page 562); for **Altesino,** stay on SR-2 all the way to Buonconvento, then turn off on the back road (SP-45) to Montalcino, and watch for the Altesino turn-off (see page 562).

BRUNELLO WINE COUNTRY SIGHTS

These sights are linked by my driving tour, above.

Sant'Angelo in Colle

This nondescript hill town, about 9 kilometers south of Montalcino, is worth visiting only if you'd like a lunch break with some high-altitude views. Twist up to the top of the hill and park by the square; both restaurants are just steps away. **$$$ Trattoria Il Leccio** is the pricier option, with a cozy stone interior and seating out on the square (fried vegetables and beef are fortés, closed Wed off-season, Costa Castellare 1, tel. 0577-844-175, www.trattoriailleccio.it). **$$ Il Pozzo** sits just a few steps below the square, serving affordable homemade pasta dishes in a pleasant interior with big windows overlooking the hillsides (free glass of vin santo for dessert with this book, closed Tue, tel. 0577-844-015, www.trattoriailpozzo. com, Binerelli family).

▲Sant'Antimo Abbey

Set amidst postcard-perfect olive groves and pastures ringed by cypress-prickled hills, this Romanesque abbey—adorned with mysterious, pagan-seeming carvings—is one of the region's most rewarding to visit.

Cost and Hours: Free, open to tourists Mon-Sat 10:00-13:00 & 15:00-18:00, Sun 9:15-10:45 & 15:00-18:00, open to worshippers daily 7:00-19:00, tel. 0577-835-659, www.antimo.it.

Getting There: From Montalcino, **drivers** should head south toward Castelnuovo dell'Abate. Keep an eye out for the abbey—below you in the fields—as you approach. Large parking lots are in the field near the abbey. A **bus** runs from Montalcino (see "Montalcino Connections," earlier).

Background: Legends suggest that Sant'Antimo was founded by

Charlemagne, who passed through here around the year 781, following the Via Francigena on his way back north from Rome (for more on this route, see page 569). His army, suffering from illness, convalesced near here, and in appreciation Charlemagne presented the local religious community with relics of St. Anthimus (Sant'Antimo). Most of the abbey's current structure dates from the 11th and 12th centuries, when Sant'Antimo became a highly important center both for local aristocrats and for pilgrims walking the Via Francigena. But after Pope Pius II moved the diocese from Montalcino to Pienza in 1462, the abbey sat neglected for centuries, even becoming a stable for a time. Finally, starting in the late 19th century, it was restored, and in 1992 a small number of Augustinian monks moved in, reconnecting Sant'Antimo with its medieval importance. And today, once again, Sant'Antimo is a functioning abbey.

Visiting the Abbey: Before going inside, circle the building to see its faded but evocative decorations. At the back end of the church is the Charlemagne-era round apse (dwarfed by the Romanesque apse). Examine the varied carvings at the tops of the pillars under the roofline: geometrical patterns, heads of monsters, and pagan symbols. The stout rectangular bell tower is echoed by a strategically planted cypress tree. On the back side of the tower (next to the big tree), look up to find the sphinx, the small Madonna and Bambino, and the four evangelists.

Head back around to the main entrance. Ignore the modern doors and pick out the faint outline of the four original arches; at its peak, this church had two doors—an entrance and an exit—to handle the massive number of Via Francigena pilgrims who passed through. Just to the right, peek into the tranquil garden that fills the ruins of the original cloister.

Step inside the church and let your eyes adjust to the low light. Being Romanesque, this was as bright and as high as a church could be. (Gothic would soon come along, allowing churches to be brighter and loftier.) Looking up, see the windows of a gallery that once kept the female worshippers separate from the men. The carved capital of each pillar lining the nave is different. The second one on the right side—Daniel and the lions—is a favorite. On one side, a fearless Daniel prays despite being surrounded by lions; on the other side, those lions attack his enemies.

In the apse, notice that part of the altar platform is made of giant chunks of prized translucent alabaster. The many small chapels around the apse are a French architectural feature that made its way to Sant'Antimo. These chapels—and the overall height of the building—suggest a French influence...which seems fitting, here along the Via Francigena.

CORTONA

Cortona blankets a 1,700-foot hill surrounded by dramatic Tuscan and Umbrian views. Frances Mayes' book *Under the Tuscan Sun* placed this town in the touristic limelight, just as Peter Mayle's books popularized the Luberon region in France. But long before Mayes ever published a book, Cortona was popular with 19th-century Romantics and considered one of the classic Tuscan hill towns. Although it's unquestionably touristy and has long welcomed expatriates besotted by Tuscan charm, Cortona, unlike San Gimignano, maintains a rustic and gritty personality.

The city began as one of the largest Etruscan settlements, the remains of which can be seen at the base of the city walls, as well as in nearby tomb sites. It grew to its present size from the 13th to 16th century, when it was a colorful and crowded city, eventually allied with (or dominated by) Florence. The farmland that fills almost every view from the city was marshy and uninhabitable until about 200 years ago, when it was drained and turned into some of Tuscany's most fertile land.

Art lovers know little Cortona as the home of Renaissance painter Luca Signorelli, Baroque master Pietro da Cortona (Berretini), and the 20th-century Futurist artist Gino Severini. The city's museums and churches reveal many of the works of these native sons.

Orientation to Cortona

Most of the main sights, shops, and restaurants cluster around the level streets on the Piazza Garibaldi-Piazza del Duomo axis, but Cortona will have you huffing and puffing up some steep hills. From Piazza Garibaldi, it's a level five-minute walk down bustling shop-lined Via Nazionale to Piazza della Repubblica, the heart of

the town, which is dominated by City Hall (Palazzo del Comune). From this square, a two-minute stroll leads you past the TI, the interesting Etruscan Museum, and the theater to Piazza del Duomo, where you'll find the recommended Diocesan Museum. These sights are along the more-or-less level spine that runs through the bottom of town; from here, Cortona sprawls upward. Steep streets, many of them stepped, go from Piazza della Repubblica up to the San Niccolò and Santa Margherita churches and the Medici Fortress (a 30-minute climb from Piazza della Repubblica). In this residential area, you'll see fewer tourists and get a better sense of the "real" Cortona.

In the flat valley below Cortona sprawls the modern, workaday town of Camucia (kah-MOO-cha), with the train station and other services (such as launderettes) that you won't find in the hill town itself.

TOURIST INFORMATION

The TI, just off Piazza Signorelli, is in the courtyard of the Etruscan Museum (generally Mon-Fri 9:00-13:00 & 12:00-18:00, Sat 9:30-13:00, closed Sun, tel. 0575-637-223, www.comunedicortona.it).

ARRIVAL IN CORTONA

Cortona is challenging to reach by public transportation. Your best bet is by train (connecting by bus or taxi) or by car. Schedules for Cortona-area buses are available at www.etruriamobilita.it.

By Train: Most trains arrive at the unstaffed Camucia station, in the valley four miles below Cortona. A shuttle **minibus** connects the train station and Piazza Garibaldi in Cortona in about 10 minutes (bus stop to left of station, schedule posted—not coordinated with train arrival, about hourly but only twice on Sun, buy €1.30 ticket from driver or from Bar Stazione, to the right as you exit the train station; departures marked *S* don't run during school vacations, and those marked with *N* run *only* during school vacations). Regular city buses also connect the station with the less convenient Piazza del Mercato (just outside the city walls near Porta Santa Maria, departures about hourly), requiring a 10-minute uphill walk to Piazza Signorelli. For about €12, you can hop a **taxi** from the station (or call for Dejan and his 8-seater cab, mobile 348-402-3501; see listing under "Tours in Cortona," later).

To return to the train station from Cortona, take a taxi or hop on the shuttle or a city bus (buy tickets at a newsstand or tobacco shop, or from driver). Confirm the schedule with the TI or your hotel.

The high-speed trains that link Rome, Florence, and Assisi nearly hourly arrive 10 miles away at **Terontola,** where you can catch a bus to Cortona (see "Cortona Connections" for details).

By Car: Piazza Garibaldi is the convenient entry to the city. While there's no parking here, it's a handy place to drop people. You'll find parking along streets and in lots outside the walls; some are free (no lines or white lines), others require payment (blue lines), and still others are for local residents only (yellow lines). The best option is to find something on the street a couple of blocks below Piazza Garibaldi or use the large, free Santo Spirito lot on Viale Cesare Battisti, just after the big Santo Spirito Church. From here, a series of stairs and escalators take you steeply up to Piazza Garibaldi. The small town is actually very long, and it can be smart to drive to the top for sightseeing up there (free parking and WC at Santa Margherita Basilica).

HELPFUL HINTS

Market Day: The market is on Saturday on Piazza Signorelli (early morning until about 14:00). The most colorful produce section stretches to the cathedral square.

Services: The town has no baggage storage. The public WC is located in Piazza del Duomo, under Santa Margherita's statue.

Tuscan Cooking Classes: Romano (of Ristorante La Bucaccia) and **Magi** offer hands-on cooking and cheesemaking classes, as well as wine, cheese, and oil tastings (RS%, €100/person for 5-hour class/meal, includes wine, reserve at least 30 days in advance; offered daily at 9:30 at Ristorante La Bucaccia, Vicolo Cattani 1, tel. 0575-606-039, mobile 335-536-9535, www.labucaccia.it, info@labucaccia.it).

Tours in Cortona

Tuscan Day Trips with Driver/Guide Giovanni Adreani

Giovanni can be a great resource for anyone home-basing in Cortona with limited time and an interest in the highlights of Tuscany. For €220, high-energy Giovanni takes up to five people in his car to Montepulciano, Pienza, Montalcino, and a winery for a tour and tasting (winery visit optional and €10-15/person extra; must reserve in advance). He also offers tours in and around Cortona (€110/half-day, €220/day with his car, tel. 0575-630-665, mobile 347-176-2830, www.adreanigiovanni.com, adreanigiovanni@libero.it).

Tuscan Day Trips and Transfers with Driver Dejan Pruvlovic

Reliable, English-speaking taxi driver Dejan (DAY-zhan) and his brother Miky can take you on full-day tours from Cortona (€280 for up to 5 people). Most popular are Montepulciano, Pienza, Montalcino, and a winery tour. They also do Siena/San Gimignano day tours and airport transfers (up to 8 people, to or from Florence's airport-€170, Rome-€280, mobile 348-402-3501, dejanprvi70@yahoo.it).

Cortona Walk

This introductory self-guided walk takes you from Piazza Garibaldi up the main strip to the town center, its piazzas, and the Duomo. (If your bus drops you at Piazzale del Mercato, use the map on page 586 to locate Piazza Garibaldi.)

• Start at the bus stop in...

Piazza Garibaldi

Many visits start and finish in this square, thanks to its bus stop. While the piazza, bulging out from the town fortifications like a big turret, looks like part of an old rampart, it's really a souvenir of those early French and English Romantics—the ones who first created the notion of a dreamy, idyllic Tuscany in the early 19th century. During the Napoleonic Age, the occupying French built this balcony (and the scenic little park behind the adjacent San Domenico Church) simply to enjoy a commanding view of the Tuscan countryside.

With Umbria about a mile away, Cortona marks the end of Tuscany. This is a major cultural divide, as Cortona was the last town in Charlemagne's empire and the last under Medici rule. Umbria, just to the south, was papal territory for centuries. These deep-seated cultural disparities were a great challenge for the visionaries who unified the fractured region to create the modern nation of Italy during the 1860s. An obelisk in the center of this square honors one of the heroes of the struggle for Italian unification—the brilliant revolutionary general, Giuseppe Garibaldi.

Enjoy the impressive view from here. Assisi is just over the ridge on the left. Lake Trasimeno peeks from behind the hill, looking quite normal today. But, according to legend, it was blood-red after Hannibal defeated the Romans here in 217 B.C., when 15,000 died in the battle. The only sizable town you can see (just to the right of the volcanic mountain) is Montepulciano. Cortona is still defined by its Etruscan walls—remnants of these walls, with stones laid 2,500 years ago, stretch from here in both directions.

Frances Mayes put Cortona on the map for many Americans with her book (and later movie) *Under the Tuscan Sun*. The book

describes her real-life experience buying, fixing up, and living in a run-down villa in Cortona with her husband, Ed. Mayes' villa isn't "under the Tuscan sun" very often; it's named "Bramasole"—literally, "craving sun." On the wrong side of the hill, it's in the shade after 15:00. She and her husband still live in their adopted community for part of each year (Bramasole is outside the walls, behind the hill on the left—a 20-minute walk away; ask at the TI for directions if you'd like to see it up close). By the way, if you are moved to sing, Signor Franco Migliacci—who wrote the lyrics to the popular Italian song "Che sarà"—claims the words came to him as he stood right here and enjoyed this view.

• *From this square, head into town along...*

Via Nazionale

The only level road in town, locals have nicknamed Via Nazionale the *ruga piana* (flat wrinkle). This is the main commercial street in this town of 2,500, and it's been that way for a long time. Every shop seems to have a medieval cellar or an Etruscan well. Notice the crumbling sandstone door frames. The entire town is constructed from this grainy, eroding rock.

• *Via Nazionale leads to...*

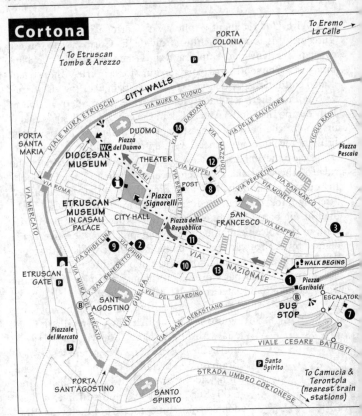

Cortona

CORTONA

Piazza della Repubblica

City Hall faces Cortona's main square. The building is a clever hodgepodge: twin medieval towers with a bell tower added to connect them, and a grand staircase to lend some gravitas. Notice the fine wood balcony on the left. In the Middle Ages, wooden extensions like this (this one was rebuilt in the 19th century) were common features on the region's stone buildings, adding a pleasant outdoor living space to the dark, cold *palazzo*.

This spot has been the town center since Etruscan times. Four centuries before Christ, an important street led from here up to the hill-capping temple. Later, the square became the Roman forum. Opposite City Hall is the handy, recommended Molesini market, good for cheap sandwiches and grocery staples. Above that is the loggia—once a fish market, now the recommended Ristorante La Loggetta. Most of the buildings lining this square originally stood atop similar arched arcades, of which you can still see traces.

• *Walk down the lane to the right of City Hall to reach...*

1. Hotel San Luca
2. Dolce Maria B&B & Locanda al Pozzo Antico
3. San Marco Hostel
4. Hotel Villa Marsili
5. Casa Betania
6. Villa Santa Margherita
7. Casa Kita
8. Osteria del Teatro
9. Ristorante La Bucaccia
10. Trattoria la Grotta
11. Ristorante La Loggetta & Molesini Market
12. Fiaschetteria Fett'Unta
13. Caffè la Saletta
14. Via Dardano Eateries

Piazza Signorelli

Dominated by Casali Palace, this square was the headquarters of the Florentine captains who used to control the city. Peek into the palace entrance (under the *MAEC* sign) for a look at the coats of arms. Every six months, Florence would send a new captain to Cortona, who would help establish his rule by inserting his family coat of arms into the palace's wall. These date from the 15th to the 17th century and were once painted with bright colors. Cortona's fine Etruscan Museum (described on the next page) is in the Casali Palace courtyard, which is lined with many more of these family coats of arms. To the left of the palace, in the side wall of the City Hall, you can see a door leading to a long-gone wooden balcony—all that's left is the holes for the beams. On the right side of the Casali Palace, the inviting Caffè del Teatro fills the loggia of the theater that is named for the town's most famous artist, Luca Signorelli. The charming 19th-century theater is *the* place in town for a movie or concert. Its café offers a delightful all-weather perch.

• Head down the street, just to the right of the museum, to...

Piazza del Duomo

Here you'll find the Diocesan Museum (described later), the cathedral, a fine view, and (closer to the top of the square) a statue of Santa Margherita (above a public WC). The cathedral's facade, though recently renovated, still seems a little underwhelming and tucked away. Cortona so loves its hometown saint, Margherita, that it put the energy it would otherwise have invested in its cathedral into the Santa Margherita Basilica, at the top of the hill. Margherita was a 13th-century rich girl who took good care of the poor and was an early follower of St. Francis and St. Clare. Many locals believe that Margherita protected Cortona from WWII bombs.

The Piazza del Duomo terrace comes with a commanding view of the Tuscan countryside. Notice Cortona's cemetery in the foreground. If you were standing here before the time of Napoleon, you'd be surrounded by tombstones. But Cortona's graveyards—like other urban graveyards throughout Napoleon's realm—were cleaned out in the early 1800s to reclaim land and improve hygiene.

Ready for a melody switch? The parents of Dino Paul Crocetti were born in this valley. Their son made a number of smaltzy Italiano songs popular in the US...as Dean Martin.

• *Next, everybody loves a cathedral sometime, so* Mambo Italiano *to your left and enter the...*

Duomo

The Cortona cathedral is not, strictly speaking, a cathedral, because it no longer has a bishop. The clean and elegant arches and

columns defining its nave are pure Renaissance, inspired by the Basilica of San Lorenzo in Florence. While the once-pristine interior has been mucked up with lots of Baroque chapels filling the side niches, the cathedral still has the same heating system it had during the Renaissance (daily in summer 7:30-18:30).

• *From here, you can visit the nearby Diocesan Museum, or head back toward Piazza della Repubblica, where you can visit the Etruscan Museum in Piazza Signorelli or get a bite to eat.*

Sights in Cortona

▲Etruscan Museum
(Museo dell'Accademia Etrusca e della Città di Cortona)

Located in the 13th-century Casali Palace and called MAEC for short, this fine gallery (established in 1727) is one of the first dedicated to artifacts from the Etruscan civilization. (In the logo, notice the E is backwards—in homage to the Etruscan alphabet.) This sprawling collection is nicely installed on four big floors.

Cost and Hours: €10; April-Oct daily 10:00-19:00; Nov-March Tue-Sun 10:00-17:00, closed Mon; Casali Palace on Piazza Signorelli, tel. 0575-637-235, www.cortonamaec.org.

Visiting the Museum: The bottom two floors (underground) are officially the "Museum of the Etruscan and Roman City of Cortona." You'll see an exhibit on the Roman settlement and take a virtual tour of the Etruscan "Il Sodo" tombs (in the nearby countryside, possible to visit—see "Etruscan Tombs" listing below). The Cortona Tablet (*Tabula Cortonensis*, second century B.C.), a 200-word contract inscribed in bronze, contains dozens of Etruscan words archaeologists had never seen before its discovery in 1992. Along with lots of gold and jewelry, you'll find a seventh-century B.C. grater (for some *very* aged Parmesan cheese). The top two floors, called the "Accademia," display an even more eclectic collection, including more Etruscania, Egyptian artifacts, fine Roman mosaics, and a room dedicated to 20th-century abstract works by Severini, all lovingly described in English. A highlight is the magnificent fourth-century B.C. bronze oil lamp chandelier with 16 spouts. On the top floor, peek into the classic old library of the Etruscan Academy, founded in 1727 to promote an understanding of the city through the study of archaeology.

▲Diocesan Museum (Museo Diocesano)

This small collection contains some very choice artworks from the town's many churches, including works by Fra Angelico and Pietro Lorenzetti, and masterpieces by hometown hero and Renaissance master Luca Signorelli.

Cost and Hours: €5; daily 10:00-19:00; Nov-March Tue-Sun 10:00-17:00, closed Mon; audioguide-€3, Piazza del Duomo 1, tel. 057-562-830.

Visiting the Museum: The L-shaped first room contains masterpieces by **Luca Signorelli,** Cortona's most famous son. Signorelli worked during the height of the Renaissance, around 1500, often painting in fresco. A generation ahead of Michelangelo, Signorelli's passion for new painting ideas, his techniques of foreshortening and perspective, and his jewel-like colors strongly influenced the younger artist. Signorelli's San Brizio Chapel in Orvieto inspired Michelangelo's Sistine Chapel frescoes (to see more Signorelli works, visit the San Niccolò Church near the top of town). Take a slow stroll past his very colorful canvases, mostly relocated here from local churches. Among the most striking is *Lamentation over the Dead Christ* (1502). Everything in Signorelli's painting has a meaning: The skull of Adam sits under the sacrifice of Jesus; the hammer represents the Passion (the *Crucifix*ion leading to the Resurrection); the lake is blood; and so on.

Across the top of the stairwell, the next room was the nave when this was the Gesù Church (look up at the beautiful wood-

carved ceiling). Above a sweet 14th-century carved marble baptismal font is an early Renaissance masterpiece: In **Fra Angelico**'s sumptuous *Annunciation* (c. 1430), Mary says "Yes," consenting to bear God's son. The angel's words are top and bottom, while Mary's answer is upside down (logically, since it's directed to God, who would be reading while looking down from heaven). Mary's house sits on a pillow of flowers...the new Eden. The old Eden, featuring the expulsion of Adam and Eve from Paradise, is in the upper left. On the bottom edge, comic strip-like scenes narrate Mary's life. Compare the style in Fra Angelico's work to the Signorelli you just saw. Where Fra Angelico's figures are light and often out of scale—like paper dolls—Signorelli's are more realistic, with heft, and show his understanding of human anatomy. In only a few decades, the skills of painters had made huge leaps.

On the wall to the right, the crucifix (by Pietro Lorenzetti, c. 1325) is striking in its severity. Notice the gripping realism—even the tendons in Jesus' arms are pulled tight. (Speaking of realism, as this church is now deconsecrated, notice how the relic has been taken from the altar table below this painting and replaced by a wooden plug.)

Now head back to the stairwell, which is lined with colorful Stations of the Cross scenes by another local but much later artist, the 20th-century's **Gino Severini.** These are actually "cartoons," models used to create permanent mosaics that line the approach up to the Santa Margherita Basilica today.

Downstairs, the lower refectory has a vault with dramatic frescoes (1545) by the workshop of **Giorgio Vasari,** the architect and painter who designed the Uffizi in Florence (he did the ceiling here). Take a close look at the exquisitely painted circa-1500 terracotta pietà decorating the altar.

Back up near the entrance, another staircase leads down to a collection of vestments and ecclesiastical gear.

San Francesco Church

Established by St. Francis' best friend, Brother Elias, this church dates from the 13th century. The wooden beams of the ceiling are original. While the place was redecorated in the Baroque age, some of its original frescoes peek through the whitewash in the second chapel on the left. Francis fans visit for its precious Franciscan relics. To the left of the altar, you'll find one of Francis' tunics, his pillow (inside a fancy cover), and his gospel book. Notice how the entire high altar seems designed to frame its precious relic—a piece of the cross Elias brought back from his visit to the patriarch in Constantinople. You're welcome to climb the altar for a close-up look. In the humble choir area behind the main altar is Elias' very simple tomb (see the *Frate Elia da Cortona* plaque).

Cost and Hours: Free, daily 9:00-17:30, often until 19:00 in summer; Mass on Sun at 10:00, Mon-Sat at 17:30.

Santa Margherita Basilica

High above Cortona, capping the hill, is the basilica, which houses the remains of Margherita, the town's favorite saint (her actual mummy is behind glass at the altar). The red-and-white-striped interior boasts some colorfully painted vaults. Santa Margherita, an unwed mother from Montepulciano, found her calling in the mid-1200s with the new Franciscan order in Cortona, tending to the sick and poor. The well-preserved and remarkably emotional 13th-century crucifix (made in Germany, painted on wood) on the right is the cross that, according to legend, talked to Margherita.

Cost and Hours: Free, daily 6:50-19:30 except closed Mon morning, tel. 0575-603-116, fine WC outside.

Nearby: Need more altitude and expansive views? Continuing uphill five more minutes takes you to the 13th-century **Medici Fortezza Girifalco,** today a parklike shell with a café, viewpoint, and special exhibits (confirm hours at TI). When Cosimo I de' Medici made a tour of all his fortresses in 1540 to assess their strategic value, he decided this one should be strengthened and modernized (and that Cortona's citizens should pay for it). **San Niccolò Church,** a few streets below, is a humble church with impressive views that houses a few paintings from Luca Signorelli and his workshop, the most famous being *The Deposition of Christ*.

NEAR CORTONA

▲Eremo Le Celle

Hiding out in the fold of the neighboring hills, above a little river and buried in a forest, is an evocative hermitage founded in the early 1200s by St. Francis' best friend, Brother Elias. Even today, 800 years later, you can feel the calm of this retreat. Francis visited three times (you can visit his cell—*celle* means cells). Today, the monastery is still alive, run by the Cappucin order, an offshoot of the Franciscans that focuses on living with nature in solitude. The friars are on call—to meet one, just pull the cord outside the main chapel. Visitors are welcome to wander through two chapels and a couple of stark pilgrim's rooms, as well as the beautiful grounds. It's a five-minute drive from the top of Cortona (free, always open, follow signs to *Le Celle*, easy parking, Strada dei Cappuccini 1).

Etruscan Tombs (Tumuli del Sodo)

The area around Cortona is rich with Etruscan tombs (dating to the sixth century B.C.). Visitors are welcome to enter this active archaeological site, and bits of the ruins can be seen even from outside the fence. The two main tombs, called the Tumuli del Sodo, are connected by a footpath (free; Tumulus II usually Tue-Sun 8:30-13:30, closed Mon; Tumulus I open by reservation; tel. 0575-637-235, www.cortonamaec.org, prenotazioni@cortonamaec.org). The tombs are in Sodo, just off the Arezzo road—R-71—at the foot of the Cortona hill (ask anyone for "Il Sodo," parking available at entrance and at Tumulus I).

Sleeping in Cortona

WITHIN OLD TOWN

$$$ Hotel San Luca, perched on the side of a cliff, has 54 impersonal business-class rooms, half with stunning views of Lago Trasimeno. While the hotel feels tired and the rooms have seen better days, it's friendly and conveniently located, right on Piazza Garibaldi at the entrance to the old town (request a view room when you reserve, family rooms, popular with Americans and groups, air-con, elevator, Piazza Garibaldi 2, tel. 0575-630-460, www. sanlucacortona.com, info@sanlucacortona.com). If driving, you can unload bags in front of the hotel in Piazza Garibaldi, then park at the big, free Santo Spirito lot below and ride the escalator up.

$ Dolce Maria B&B is centrally located in a 16th-century building with high-beamed ceilings. The six rooms are a good value, luminous, and spacious, with tasteful period furnishings and modern bathrooms. The B&B is efficiently run by Paola, who also runs the Antico Pozzo restaurant next door—the two businesses share a patio (family rooms, air-con, Via Ghini 12, tel. 0575-601-577, www.cortonastorica.com, info@cortonastorica.com).

$ San Marco Hostel, at the top of town, is housed in a remodeled 13th-century palace (family rooms available, midday closure; from Piazza Garibaldi head up steep Via Santa Margherita, then turn left to find Via Maffei 57; tel. 0575-601-392, mobile 335-315-9587, www.cortonahostel.com, ostellocortona@libero.it, Sergio).

OUTSIDE THE OLD TOWN

These accommodations line up along the road that angles downhill from Piazza Garibaldi, with easy parking on the street or at the large lot on Viale Battisti. All are just a five-minute uphill walk from the entrance to the old town.

$$$$ Hotel Villa Marsili, a comfortable splurge, pampers its visitors with thoughtful service. Originally a 15th-century church, and then an elegant 18th-century home, the hotel has 25 artfully decorated, romantic rooms and inviting public areas. They offer an evening aperitif with free snacks on the panoramic terrace (19:00-20:00) and a sweet goodnight treat after dinner (air-con, elevator, free street parking nearby—first come, first served, otherwise pay garage parking, Viale Cesare Battisti 13, tel. 0575-605-252, www.villamarsili.net, info@villamarsili.net, Marina).

$ Casa Betania, a big, wistful former convent with an inviting view terrace, rents 28 basic rooms for the best price in town. Anyone looking for a peaceful place to call home will feel welcome in this funky pilgrims' resort. Marco, a big-city lawyer escaping from the rat race, has turned it into a retreat facility of sorts, with conference rooms, a chapel, wine cellar, cooking classes, and more (family rooms, breakfast extra, free parking, through iron gates and down a long driveway on the right at Via Gino Severini 50, tel. 0575-630-423, www.casaperferiebetania.com, info@casaperferiebetania.com).

$ Villa Santa Margherita, run by the Serve di Maria Riparatrici sisters, rents 22 nicely renovated rooms in a smaller, more professional and hotel-like convent just across the street from Casa Betania (family rooms, elevator, free parking, Viale Cesare Battisti 17, tel. 0575-630-336, fax 0575-630-549, www.santamargherita.smr.it, info@villasm.it or comunitacortona@smr.it).

$ Casa Kita, renting five quirky, boldly decorated rooms at great prices, is a homey place with fine views from its terrace. It's a good option for budget travelers with lots of luggage, just 100 yards from the bus stop in Piazza Garibaldi. You'll really feel like you're staying in someone's home (below the piazza at Vicolo degli Orti 7, tel. 389-557-9893, www.casakita.com, casakita@gmail.com, Lorenzini family).

Eating in Cortona

FINER DINING

$$$ Osteria del Teatro tries hard to create a romantic Old World atmosphere, and does it well. The dining rooms, each decorated differently, are part of an old palace, and there's good outdoor seating, too. Chef/owner Emiliano serves nicely presented and tasty local cuisine that changes to match the season. They are known for their homemade chocolate—it's served spread on a cutting board with a big knife. (Thu-Tue 12:30-14:30 & 19:30-22:00, closed

Wed, 2 blocks uphill from the main square at Via Maffei 2, tel. 0575-630-556, www.osteria-del-teatro.it).

$$$ Ristorante La Bucaccia, dressy and romantic, is a family-run eatery set in a rustic medieval wine cellar. Husband and wife Romano and Agostina take an evangelical pride in their Chianina beef dishes and homemade pastas. Agostina cooks while frisky Romano presides over the dining room with humor and charm—he will sit down at your table to advise you on your meal choices. Their *pici in crosta di pecorino* (homemade pasta in the crust of a cheese wheel, for two only) is a favorite. Reservations are required for dinner (daily 12:30-15:00 & 19:00-22:30; show this book for a welcome snack; Via Ghibellina 17, tel. 0575-606-039, mobile 335-536-7535, www.labucaccia.it). Romano also runs Tuscan cooking classes (see "Helpful Hints," earlier).

TRADITIONAL RESTAURANTS, TRATTORIA, AND OTHER EATERIES

$$ Trattoria la Grotta, just off Piazza della Repubblica, is a traditional family place, with Giancarlo and his daughters serving daily specials to an enthusiastic clientele under grotto-like vaults. The family owns the *enoteca* across the lane and will let you bring wine from their shop into the restaurant (good wine by the glass, Wed-Mon 12:00-14:30 & 19:00-22:00, closed Tue, Piazza Baldelli 3, tel. 0575-630-271).

$$ Locanda al Pozzo Antico offers an affordable menu of traditional Cortona fare (like *pici al fumo,* pasta with a creamy bacon sauce), with a focus on fresh, quality produce and local olive oil. Eat in a homey dining room or tucked away in a tranquil secret courtyard. Paola is a charming hostess (Fri-Wed 12:30-14:30 & 19:30-22:00, closed Thu, Via Ghini 12, tel. 057-562-091 or 0575-601-577; Paola, husband Franco, and son Gianni).

$$ Ristorante La Loggetta serves up big portions of well-presented Tuscan cuisine on the loggia overlooking Piazza della Repubblica. While they have fine indoor seating under clamorous stone vaults, I'd eat on their loggia for the chance to gaze at the square while dining (Thu-Tue 12:30-15:00 & 19:30-23:00, closed Wed, Piazza Pescheria 3, tel. 0575-630-575).

$ Fiaschetteria Fett'Unta, which employs the same kitchen as chef Emiliano's recommended Osteria del Teatro, is small and rustic. It serves traditional plates driven by the season—*bruschette,* soups, pastas, sandwiches, and good wine by the glass (closed Mon evening and Tue, across from Osteria del Teatro at Via Maffei 5, tel. 0575-630-582).

$ Caffè la Saletta, a dark and classy coffee bar with a nice, mellow vibe, is good for fine wine and a light meal. You can sit inside surrounded by wine bottles or outside to people-watch on

CORTONA

the town's main drag (daily 7:30-24:00, meals served 11:00-22:00, Wi-Fi, Via Nazionale 26, tel. 0575-603-366).

$ Restaurants along Via Dardano: A handful of eateries line this street. **Pizzeria Croce del Travaglio** is good for pizza and **Trattoria Dardano** is a favorite for game. **Taverna Pane e Vino** offers good-value dishes and a great setting on Piazza Signorelli.

Picnic: On the main square, the chic little **Molesini** market makes tasty sandwiches, served with a smile (see list on counter and order by number, or invent your own), and sells whatever else you might want for a picnic (daily 7:00-13:30 & 16:30-20:00, shorter hours off-season, Piazza della Repubblica 3). Munch your picnic across the square on the steps of City Hall or just past Piazza Garibaldi in the public gardens behind San Domenico Church.

Cortona Connections

Cortona has decent train connections with the rest of Italy through its Camucia-Cortona station at the foot of the hill. It's usually unstaffed, but has two ticket machines (one in front of the station, and one on platform 1; both take credit cards and cash). Bar Stazione, the café to the right as you exit the station, also sells tickets.

From Camucia-Cortona by Train to: Rome (7/day direct, 2.5 hours), **Florence** (hourly, 1.5 hours), **Assisi** (hourly, 1.5 hours), **Montepulciano** (9/day, 1-2 hours, change in Chiusi; because few buses serve Montepulciano's town center from its distant train station, it's better to go by train to Chiusi, then by hourly 40-minute bus to Montepulciano, or easier still to take a taxi for about €60), **Chiusi** (hourly, 25 minutes).

From Terontola by Train: Nearly hourly high-speed trains to/from **Rome, Florence,** and **Assisi** stop at Terontola, 10 miles away (linked to Cortona's Piazza del Mercato or Camucia station by hourly buses, 20-30 minutes, check schedule at bus stop or at www.etruriamobilita.it).

CORTONA

FLORENTINE & TUSCAN HISTORY

This chapter presents Florence and Tuscany's history in a nutshell, divided into major historical periods. For each era, I've given a list of sights you can see during your travels that bring that period to life.

ETRUSCANS, ROMANS, AND "BARBARIANS" (550 B.C.-A.D. 1000)

In prehistoric times, much of what we today call "Tuscany" was part of the Etruscan Empire. This mysterious early civilization built hilltop forts (such as at Fiesole), traded metals with other Mediterranean peoples (including the Golden Age Greeks), established agriculture in central Italy, and buried their dead in distinctive caskets that show the deceased lounging at an eternal banquet. Having lived their day in the sun, the Etruscans faded as Rome rose. (For more on the Etruscans, see page 500.)

In 59 B.C., Julius Caesar founded Florentia (meaning "flowering" or "flourishing") at an easy-to-cross point on the Arno River. By A.D. 200, it had become a thriving provincial capital (population 10,000). The rectangular-grid street plan—aligned by compass points, rather than the river—is still evident in today's layout.

When the Empire converted to Christianity, Bishop (and Saint) Zenobius built a church where the Duomo stands today. Even as Rome fell and Italy was overrun by barbarians, Florence never really fell. Proud medieval Florentines traced their roots back to civilized Rome, and the city remained a Tuscan commercial center during the Dark Ages.

Many of Tuscany's medieval hill towns date from this era. Some were founded by the Etruscans, who appreciated a safe, sky-high location. Others date from after the fall of Rome, when terrified locals fled to hilltop forts. Some of those forts were constructed to protect the Via Francigena, the pilgrimage route from northern Europe to Rome, which passed through the heart of today's Tuscany (for more on the Via Francigena, see page 569).

Sights

- Roman and Etruscan fragments in Florence's Duomo Museum
- Etruscan wall in cellar of Church of San Francesco and artifacts in Archaeological Area, Fiesole
- Etruscan gate, museum, and other artifacts in Volterra
- Etruscan museums in Cortona, Chiusi, and many other towns
- Florence's Piazza della Repubblica—the old Roman Forum

FLORENCE'S FLOURISHING, PISA'S PEAK, AND SIENA'S SUMMIT (1000-1400)

Through the Middle Ages, Tuscany remained (relative to the rest of Europe) prosperous. Florence hummed along on trade. It became a regional capital in Charlemagne's Europe-wide empire

(c. 800-1100). In 990, Archbishop Sigeric of Canterbury passed through Florence along the Via Francigena and was impressed enough to write it up in history's first travel guidebook. ("Verily," he supposedly wrote, "makest thou Uffizi reservations.") Around 1050, the Baptistery was built, likely on the site of an ancient Roman temple. Around 1100 (under Countess Matilda of Tuscany), Florence broke from its German-based Holy Roman Empire, gaining its independence. Florence was growing rich making wool cloth and trading it abroad. Traders became bankers, moneylenders, and investors. The merchant class, organized into guilds, was growing more powerful than the rural, feudal nobles. Florence emerged as Europe's first urban-based, capitalist economy.

Meanwhile, the maritime republic of Pisa (at the mouth of the Arno River) was also prospering, through sea trade with the Far East. They funneled their wealth into a glorious ensemble of buildings in the "Pisan Romanesque" style: a church, a baptistery, and a curious bell tower that began to lean before it had even been completed.

Siena, Florence's archrival, was also on the rise. Unlike Florence, Siena sat right along the bustling Via Francigena, which

Guelphs vs. Ghibellines

In medieval times, Italy was divided between two competing political factions, the Guelphs and the Ghibellines. Their conflict had more to do with power than ideology. (It wasn't what you believed, but who your allies were.) The faction names could mean something different depending on the particular place and time.

Guelphs	Ghibellines
Supported Pope	Supported Emperor
Middle-class merchants and craftsmen	Aristocrats of feudal order
Favored urban, new economy	Favored rural, traditional economy
Wanted independent city-states under local Italian leaders	Wanted unified small states under traditional dukes and kings

kept it wealthy. In all of these thriving merchant towns, aristocratic families erected tall, fortified tower houses, showing off their wealth and might (San Gimignano had 72).

By the 1200s, Florence was beginning to surpass its neighbors through shrewd diplomacy, military conquest, and sheer economic might. The Florentine currency, the gold florin, became Europe's strongest. There was a budding democracy. In 1266, the city's nobles were ousted, establishing the *primo popolo*, or "rule by the people." (This was part of a larger ongoing power struggle between merchant-class Guelphs and noble-class Ghibellines—see the sidebar.) Bursting with civic pride, Florence's guilds financed major construction projects: the Duomo (begun in 1296), Santa Croce, and Santa Maria Novella. Giotto was pioneering realistic painting, and the poet Dante (a prominent Guelph) wrote his epic poem, *The Divine Comedy*. By 1347, Florence (population 90,000) had become one of Europe's biggest cities, and the Renaissance seemed right around the corner. But then...

The Black Death (bubonic plague) arrived in 1348. Suddenly, Florence's population was cut nearly in half. Recovery was slowed by more plagues, bank failures, and political rivalries. But eventually a new leading family emerged: the Medici.

Sights

- Baptistery and interior mosaics
- Pisa's Field of Miracles (Duomo, Baptistery, Cemetery, and Leaning Tower)
- San Gimignano's 14 surviving tower houses
- Bargello (Florence's first City Hall)

- Palazzo Vecchio (the next City Hall)
- Orsanmichele Church (originally a bustling granary)
- Duomo and Campanile (and original decorations in Duomo Museum)
- Santa Croce, Santa Maria Novella, and Giotto's bell-tower design (Campanile) and his paintings in the Uffizi

THE QUATTROCENTO: A RENAISSANCE CITY UNDER MEDICI PRINCES (1400s)

There was just something dynamic about the Florentines. Pope Boniface VIII said there were five elements: earth, air, fire, water... and Florentines. For 200 years, starting in the early 1300s, their city was a cultural hub.

While 1500 marks Europe's Renaissance, in Florence—where the whole revival of classical culture got its start—the Renaissance began and ended in the 1400s (the Quattrocento). In fact, some say the Renaissance "began" precisely in the year 1401. That's when a competition to create new Baptistery doors caught the public's imagination, energizing the city. That was followed by a plan to top the medieval Duomo with Brunelleschi's Renaissance dome (dedicated in 1436).

The city was rich—from the wool trade, silk factories, and banking. There was a large middle class and strong guilds (trade associations for skilled craftsmen). Success was a matter of civic pride, and Florentines showed that pride by beautifying the city.

Florence's Golden Age coincided with the rise of the Medici family, whose wealth gave them political leverage around Europe. The Medici had grown wealthy as textile traders, then became bankers. The Medici bank had branches in 10 European cities, in-

cluding London, Geneva, Bruges, and Lyon. The pope kept his checking account in the Rome branch. With money came power. In 1434, Cosimo the Elder took control of Florence. Although outwardly he honored the Florentine tradition of popular rule, in reality he used his great wealth to rule as a tyrant, buying popularity with lavish patronage of public art. Cosimo was succeeded by his son Piero the Gouty, who ruled stiffly but ably. It was under the next Medici ruler that Florence reached its peak.

Lorenzo de' Medici (1449-1492)—inheritor of the family's wealth and power, and his grandfather Cosimo's love of art—was young (20 when he took power), athletic, and intelligent, in addition to being a poet, horseman, musician, and leader. He wrote love songs and humorous ditties to be performed loudly and badly at carnival time. His marathon drinking bouts and illicit love affairs were legendary. He learned Greek and Latin and read the classics, yet his great passion was hunting. He was the original Renaissance Man—a man of knowledge and action, a patron of the arts, a scholar and a man of the world. He was Lorenzo the Magnificent.

Lorenzo epitomized the Florentine spirit of optimism. Born on New Year's Day and raised in the lap of luxury (Donatello's

David stood in the family courtyard) by loving parents, he grew up feeling that there was nothing he couldn't do. Florentines saw themselves as part of a "new age," a great undertaking of discovery and progress in man's history. They boasted that within the city walls, there were more "nobly gifted souls than the world has seen in the entire thousand years before." These people invented the term "Dark Ages" for the era that preceded theirs.

Lorenzo surrounded himself with Florence's best and brightest. They created an informal "Platonic Academy," based on that of ancient Greece, to meet over a glass of wine under the stars at the Medici villa and discuss literature, art, music, and politics—witty conversation was considered an art in itself.

Their neo-Platonic philosophy stressed the goodness of man and the created world; they believed in a common truth behind all religion. The Academy was more than just an excuse to go out with the guys: The members were convinced that their discussions were changing the world and improving their souls.

Sandro Botticelli (1445-1510) was a member of the Platonic Academy. He painted scenes from the classical myths that the group read, weaving contemporary figures and events into the ancient subjects. He gloried in the nude body, which he considered God's greatest creation.

Artists such as Botticelli thrived on the patronage of wealthy individuals, the government, the Church, and guilds. Botticelli commanded as much as 100 florins for one work, enough to live on for a year in high style, which he did for many years. In Botticelli's art we see the lightness, gaiety, and optimism of Lorenzo's court.

Another of Lorenzo's protégés was the young **Michelangelo Buonarroti** (1475-1564). Impressed with his work, Lorenzo took the poor, unlearned 13-year-old boy into the Medici household and treated him like a son.

Michelangelo's playmates were the Medici children, later to become Popes Leo X and Clement VII, who would give him important commissions. For all the encouragement, education, and contacts Michelangelo received, his most important gift from Lorenzo was simply a place at the dinner table, where he could absorb the words of the great men of the time and their love of art for art's sake.

But there was another side to Florence. Even with all the art and philosophy of the Renaissance, violence, disease, and warfare were still present in medieval proportions. For the lower classes, life was as harsh as ever. Florence's streets were filled with tough-talking, hardened, illiterate merchants who strode about singing verses from Dante's *Divine Comedy*. Though Florence was technically a republic with some upward mobility, most power was in the hands of a few wealthy banking families. This was the time of the ruthless tactics of the Borgias (known for murdering their political enemies) as they battled for power. Lorenzo himself barely escaped assassination in the Duomo during Easter Mass; his brother died in the attack. Many artists and scholars wore swords and daggers as part of everyday dress.

Florence's contributions to Western culture are immense: the revival of the arts, humanism, and science after centuries of medieval superstition and oppression; the seeds of democracy; the modern Italian language (which grew out of the popular Florentine dialect); the art of Botticelli, Leonardo, and Michelangelo; the writings of Machiavelli, Boccaccio, and Dante; and the explorations of Amerigo Vespucci, who gave his name to a newly discovered continent.

Florence dominated Italy economically and culturally. Meanwhile, 1400s Rome was a dirty, decaying, crime-infested place. Italy itself was a gaggle of squabbling city-states. (When someone suggested to the Renaissance Florentine Niccolò Machiavelli that the Italian city-states might unite against their common enemy, France, he wrote back, "Don't make me laugh.")

In 1492, Lorenzo the Magnificent died suddenly, many Medici

banks went bankrupt, France invaded, and Florentine politics were thrown into disarray. In this political vacuum, the monk Girolamo Savonarola appeared on the scene as a voice of moral authority. He reestablished the Florentine constitution, sent the Medici into exile, and ruled with stern dictates. Condemning Renaissance excesses, he organized bonfires on Piazza della Signoria, where citizens burned their "vanities"—rich clothes, secular books, and paintings. In 1498, Savonarola was arrested, hanged, and burned by political enemies and a citizenry tired of his morally strict rule.

After a decade of chaos, Florence would never fully recover, and the Florentine Renaissance headed south.

Sights
- Brunelleschi's Duomo dome and Pazzi Chapel
- Donatello's statues (Bargello, Duomo Museum, and Orsanmichele)
- Ghiberti's bronze Baptistery doors (originals in Duomo Museum)
- Botticelli's paintings in Uffizi
- Uffizi (painting's history from medieval to Michelangelo)
- Bargello (sculpture's history)
- Masaccio frescoes in Santa Maria Novella and Brancacci Chapel
- Fra Angelico paintings (and Savonarola history) in Museum of San Marco

DECLINE, MEDICI DUKES, RENAISSANCE GOES SOUTH (1500-1800)

The center of the Renaissance gradually shifted to Rome, but its artists were mostly Florentine. When Rome began a beautification campaign (under popes that included Lorenzo's son and nephew), they hired Michelangelo, Raphael, and others. When the King of France wanted Renaissance culture, he hired Florence's Leonardo da Vinci to move north. The Florentine Renaissance was over, but Florentine culture lived on.

After Savonarola, the Medici returned. They'd spent their exile in Rome, where they married into royalty, and they returned as even less democratic nobles. Florence's long tradition as a self-governing republic ended for good in 1530, when—after a long siege—their last-gasp rebellion was snuffed out by a Medici pope backed by foreign powers. In succeeding centuries, the Medici dukes ruled an economically and politically declining city.

HISTORY

Typical Church Architecture

History comes to life when you visit a centuries-old church. Even if you wouldn't know your apse from a hole in the ground, learning a few simple terms will enrich your experience. Note that not every church has every feature, and that a "cathedral" isn't a type of church architecture, but rather a designation for a church that's a governing center for a local bishop.

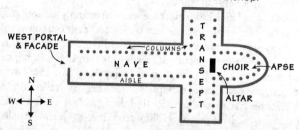

Aisles: The long, generally low-ceilinged arcades that flank the nave.

Altar: The raised area with a ceremonial table (often adorned with candles or a crucifix), where the priest prepares and serves the bread and wine for Communion.

Apse: The space beyond the altar, generally bordered with small chapels.

Barrel Vault: A continuous round-arched ceiling that resembles an extended upside-down U.

Choir: A cozy area, often screened off, located within the church nave and near the high altar, where services are sung in a more intimate setting.

Cloister: Covered hallways bordering a square or rectangular open-air courtyard, traditionally where monks and nuns got fresh air.

Facade: The exterior surface of the church's main (west) entrance, generally highly decorated.

Groin Vault: An arched ceiling formed where two equal barrel vaults meet at right angles. Less common usage: term for a medieval jock strap.

Narthex: The area (portico or foyer) between the main entry and the nave.

Nave: The long, central section of the church (running west to east, from the entrance to the altar) where the congregation sits or stands through the service.

Transept: In a traditional cross-shaped floor plan, the transept is one of the two parts forming the "arms" of the cross. The transepts run north-south, perpendicularly crossing the east-west nave.

West Portal: The main entry to the church (on the west end, opposite the main altar).

But as a city of culture, Florence still had that certain cachet that all of Europe wanted. The Medici married off their refined daughters (Catherine de' Medici, and later, Marie de' Medici) to the kings of Europe's new superpower, France. In Florence, Cosimo I and his sophisticated wife, Eleonora of Toledo, ruled as enlightened despots, beautifying the city with the Uffizi, a renovated Palazzo Vecchio, and a rebuilt Pitti Palace. The Medici supported Galileo in his scientific studies.

But by the late 1500s, Florence was increasingly a minor player in world affairs—a small dukedom with a stagnant economy, ruled by a series of forgettable Francescos, Ferdinandos, and Cosimos. In 1587, the Duomo's medieval facade was torn down in hopes of being rebuilt in a glorious new style. It remained bare brick for the next 200 years, a fitting metaphor for Florence's stalled dreams. In 1737, the last of the Medici line died, and in 1799 Florence was conquered by French revolutionary forces under Napoleon, who briefly installed his sister as duchess. With Napoleon's fall, the once-proud city-state of Florence came under the rule of Austrian Habsburg nobles.

Sights

- Michelangelo's Florentine works—*David*, Medici Chapels, and Laurentian Medici Library
- Pitti Palace and Boboli Gardens (the later Medici palace)
- Later paintings (Uffizi) and statues (Bargello)
- Destruction of the original Duomo facade (Duomo Museum)
- Medici Chapels—pompous tombs of (mostly) later Medici
- Ponte Vecchio cleaned up for jewelry shops
- Baroque interiors of many older churches
- Galileo's fingers, telescopes, and experiments in the Galileo Science Museum

ITALIAN UNIFICATION, URBANIZATION, AND URBAN RENEWAL (1800s TO TODAY)

After years of rule by Austrian nobles, Florence peacefully booted out the *Ausländer*s and joined the Italian unification movement. The city even served briefly as modern Italy's capital (1865-1870). It enjoyed an artistic revival of both medieval (Neo-Gothic) and Renaissance (Neoclassical) styles. The Duomo finally got its long-wished-for facade.

The 20th century was turbulent, with rapid population growth and rapid industrialization. During World War II, Florence was under Nazi occupation. As the Allies closed in, all the Arno bridges except Ponte Vecchio were blown up. In 1966, a disastrous flood, up to nearly 20 feet high, covered the city's buildings and artistic treasures in mud. The city was a cultural, economic, and touristic mess. An international effort of volunteer "mud angels" slowly brought the city's cultural heritage back into view.

More recently, the city's traffic-choked streets have been gradually pedestrianized. And in 2014, Florence's idealistic and visionary mayor, Matteo Renzi, became prime minister of Italy (and remained in office until December 2016). Today, the city of Florence—with a thriving university, plentiful cafés, and revamped museums, has become a model cultural destination. Now if they could just do something about those Vespas...

Sights

- Duomo's current Neo-Gothic facade
- Piazza della Repubblica (commemorating unification), with fine 19th-century cafés
- Upscale designer boutiques on Via de' Calzaiuoli, Via degli Strozzi, and Via de' Tornabuoni
- Ever-growing pedestrian zones in the city center

For more on Florentine and Tuscan history, consider Europe 101: History and Art for the Traveler, *written by Rick Steves and Gene Openshaw (available at www.ricksteves.com).*

PRACTICALITIES

This chapter covers the practical skills of European travel: how to get tourist information, pay for things, sightsee efficiently, find good-value accommodations, eat affordably but well, use technology wisely, and get between destinations smoothly. To round out your knowledge, check out "Resources from Rick Steves." For more information on these topics, see www.ricksteves.com/travel-tips.

Tourist Information

Before your trip, scan the website of the Italian national tourist office (www.italia.it) for a wealth of travel information. If you have a specific question, try contacting one of their US offices (New York: Tel. 212/245-5618, newyork@enit.it; Chicago: Tel. 312/644-9335, chicago@enit.it; Los Angeles: Tel. 310/820-1898, losangeles@enit.it).

In Italy, a good first stop in every town is generally the tourist information office (abbreviated **TI** in this book). Be aware that TIs are in business to help you enjoy spending money in their town. While this corrupts much of their advice—and you can get plenty of information online—I still make a point to swing by to confirm sightseeing plans, pick up a city map, and get information on public transit, walking tours, special events, and nightlife. Prepare a list of questions and a proposed plan to double-check. While Italian TIs are about half as helpful as those in other countries, their information is twice as important.

For TIs in Florence, see page 16 (www.firenzeturismo.it). Some TIs have information on the entire country or at least the region, so pick up maps and printed information for destinations you'll be visiting later in your trip.

Travel Tips

Emergency and Medical Help: In Italy, dial 113 for English-speaking police help. To summon an ambulance, call 118. If you get sick, do as the locals do and go to a pharmacist for advice. Or ask at your hotel for help—they'll know the nearest medical and emergency services. For English-speaking doctors in Florence, see page 17.

Theft or Loss: To replace a passport, you'll need to go in person to an embassy (see page 673). If your credit and debit cards disappear, cancel and replace them (see "Damage Control for Lost Cards" on page 612). File a police report, either on the spot or within a day or two; you'll need it to submit an insurance claim for lost or stolen rail passes or travel gear, and it can help with replacing your passport or credit and debit cards. For more information, see www.ricksteves.com/help.

Time Zones: Italy, like most of continental Europe, is generally six/nine hours ahead of the East/West Coasts of the US. The exceptions are the beginning and end of Daylight Saving Time: Europe "springs forward" the last Sunday in March (two weeks after most of North America), and "falls back" the last Sunday in October (one week before North America). For a handy online time converter, see www.timeanddate.com/worldclock.

Business Hours: Traditionally, Italy used the siesta plan, with people generally working from about 9:00 to 13:00 and from 15:30 or 16:00 to 19:00 or 19:30, Monday through Saturday. But siesta hours are no longer required by the law, so many shops stay open through lunch or later into the evening, especially larger stores in tourist areas. Shops in small towns and villages are more likely to close during lunch. Stores are usually closed on Sunday, and often on Monday. Many Florence shops close for a couple of weeks around August 15. Banking hours are generally Monday through Friday 8:30 to 13:30 and 15:30 to 16:30, but can vary wildly.

Saturdays are virtually weekdays, with earlier closing hours. Sundays have the same pros and cons as they do for travelers in the

US: Sightseeing attractions are generally open, while banks and many shops are closed, public transportation options are fewer (for example, no bus service to or from the smaller towns), and there's no rush hour. Friday and Saturday evenings are lively; Sunday evenings are quiet.

Watt's Up? Europe's electrical system is 220 volts, instead of North America's 110 volts. Most newer electronics (such as laptops, battery chargers, and hair dryers) convert automatically, so you won't need a converter, but you will need an adapter plug with two round prongs, sold inexpensively at travel stores in the US. Sockets in Italy (and Switzerland) only accept plugs with slimmer prongs: Don't buy an adapter with the thicker ("Schuko" style) prongs—it won't work. Avoid bringing older appliances that don't automatically convert voltage; instead, buy a cheap replacement in Europe.

Discounts: Discounts for sights are generally not listed in this book. However, many sights offer discounts or free admission for youths (up to age 18), students (with proper identification cards, www.isic.org), families, seniors (loosely defined as retirees or those willing to call themselves a senior), and groups of 10 or more. Always ask. Italy's national museums generally offer free admission to children under 18, but some discounts are available only for citizens of the European Union (EU).

Online Translation Tips: Google's Chrome browser instantly translates websites. You can also paste text or the URL of a foreign website into the translation window at Translate.google.com. The Google Translate app converts spoken English into most European languages (and vice versa) and can also translate text it "reads" with your smartphone's camera.

Money

Here's my basic strategy for using money in Europe:
- Upon arrival, head for a cash machine (ATM) at the airport and load up on local currency, using a debit card with low international transaction fees.
- Withdraw large amounts at each transaction (to limit fees) and keep your cash safe in a money belt.
- Pay for most items with cash.
- Pay for larger purchases with a credit card with low (or no) international fees.

PLASTIC VERSUS CASH

Although credit cards are widely accepted in Europe, day-to-day spending is generally more cash-based than in the US. I find cash is the easiest—and sometimes only—way to pay for cheap food, bus fare, taxis, tips, and local guides. Some businesses (especially

> ## Exchange Rate
>
> ### 1 euro (€) = about $1.10
>
> To convert prices in euros to dollars, add about 10 percent: €20=about $22, €50=about $55. (Check www.oanda.com for the latest exchange rates.) Just like the dollar, one euro is broken down into 100 cents. Coins range from €0.01 to €2, and bills from €5 to €200 (bills over €50 are rarely used; €500 bills are being phased out).

smaller ones, such as B&Bs and mom-and-pop cafés and shops) may charge you extra for using a credit card—or might not accept credit cards at all. Having cash on hand helps you out of a jam if your card randomly doesn't work.

I use my credit card to book hotel reservations, to buy advance tickets for events or sights, and to cover major expenses (such as car rentals or plane tickets). It can also be smart to use plastic near the end of your trip, to avoid another visit to the ATM.

WHAT TO BRING

I pack the following and keep it all safe in my money belt.

Debit Card: Use this at ATMs to withdraw local cash.

Credit Card: Use this to pay for larger items (at hotels, larger shops and restaurants, travel agencies, car-rental agencies, and so on).

Backup Card: Some travelers carry a third card (debit or credit; ideally from a different bank), in case one gets lost, demagnetized, eaten by a temperamental machine, or simply doesn't work.

US Dollars: I carry $100-200 US as a backup. While you won't use it for day-to-day purchases, American cash in your money belt comes in handy for emergencies, such as if your ATM card stops working.

What NOT to Bring: Resist the urge to buy **euros** before your trip or you'll pay the price in bad stateside exchange rates. Wait until you arrive to withdraw money. I've yet to see a European airport that didn't have plenty of ATMs.

BEFORE YOU GO

Use this pretrip checklist.

Know your cards. Debit cards from any major US bank will work in any standard European bank's ATM (ideally, use a debit card with a Visa or MasterCard logo). As for credit cards, Visa and MasterCard are universal, American Express is less common, and Discover is unknown in Europe.

Newer credit and debit cards have chips that authenticate and secure transactions. In Europe, the cardholder inserts the chip card into the payment machine slot, then enters a PIN. (In the US, you provide a signature to verify your identity.)

Any American card, whether with a chip or an old-fashioned magnetic stripe, will work at Europe's hotels, restaurants, and shops. I've been inconvenienced a few times by self-service payment machines in Europe that wouldn't accept my card, but it's never caused me serious trouble.

If you're concerned, ask if your bank offers a true chip-and-PIN card. Cards with low fees and chip-and-PIN technology include those from Andrews Federal Credit Union (www.andrewsfcu.org) and the State Department Federal Credit Union (www.sdfcu.org).

Report your travel dates. Let your bank know that you'll be using your debit and credit cards in Europe, and when and where you're headed.

Know your PIN. Make sure you know the numeric, four-digit PIN for all of your cards, both debit and credit. Request it if you don't have one and allow time to receive the information by mail.

Adjust your ATM withdrawal limit. Find out how much you can take out daily and ask for a higher daily withdrawal limit if you want to get more cash at once. Note that European ATMs will withdraw funds only from checking accounts; you're unlikely to have access to your savings account.

Ask about fees. For any purchase or withdrawal made with a card, you may be charged a currency conversion fee (1-3 percent), a Visa or MasterCard international transaction fee (1 percent), and—for debit cards—a $2-5 transaction fee each time you use a foreign ATM (some US banks partner with European banks, allowing you to use those ATMs with no fees—ask).

If you're getting a bad deal, consider getting a new debit or credit card. Reputable no-fee cards include those from Capital One, as well as Charles Schwab debit cards. Most credit unions and some airline loyalty cards have low-to-no international transaction fees.

IN EUROPE
Using Cash Machines
European cash machines have English-language instructions and work just like they do at home—except they spit out local currency instead of dollars, calculated at the day's standard bank-to-bank rate.

In most places, ATMs are easy to locate—in Italy ask for a *bancomat* When possible, withdraw cash from a bank-run ATM located just outside that bank. Ideally use it during the bank's opening hours; if your card is munched by the machine, you can go inside for help.

If your debit card doesn't work, try a lower amount—your

request may have exceeded your withdrawal limit or the ATM's limit. If you still have a problem, try a different ATM or come back later—your bank's network may be temporarily down.

Avoid "independent" ATMs, such as Travelex, Euronet, Moneybox, Cardpoint, and Cashzone. These have high fees, can be less secure than a bank ATM, and may try to trick users with "dynamic currency conversion" (see below).

Exchanging Cash

Avoid exchanging money in Europe; it's a big rip-off. In a pinch, you can always find exchange desks at major train stations or airports—convenient but with crummy rates. Banks in some countries may not exchange money unless you have an account with them.

Using Credit Cards

European cards use chip-and-PIN technology, while most cards issued in the US use a chip-and-signature system. But most European card readers can automatically generate a receipt for you to sign, just as you would at home. If a cashier is present, you should have no problems. Some card readers will instead prompt you to enter your PIN (so it's important to know the code for each of your cards).

At self-service payment machines (transit-ticket kiosks, parking, etc.), results are mixed, as US chip-and-signature cards aren't configured for unattended transactions. If your card won't work, look for a cashier who can process your card manually—or pay in cash.

Drivers Beware: Be aware of potential problems using a credit card to fill up at an unattended gas station, enter a parking garage, or exit a toll road. Carry cash and be prepared to move on to the next gas station if necessary. When approaching a toll plaza, use the "cash" lane.

Dynamic Currency Conversion

Some European merchants and hoteliers cheerfully charge you for converting your purchase price into dollars. If it's offered, refuse this "service" (called dynamic currency conversion, or DCC). You'll pay extra for the expensive convenience of seeing your charge in dollars. Some ATMs also offer DCC, often in confusing or misleading terms. If an ATM offers to "lock in" or "guarantee" your conversion rate, choose "proceed without conversion." Other prompts might state, "You can be charged in dollars: Press YES for dollars, NO for euros." Always choose the local currency.

Security Tips

Pickpockets target tourists. To safeguard your cash, wear a money belt—a pouch with a strap that you buckle around your waist like a belt and tuck under your clothes. Keep your cash, credit cards, and passport secure in your money belt, and carry only a day's spending money in your front pocket or wallet.

Before inserting your card into an ATM, inspect the front. If anything looks crooked, loose, or damaged, it could be a sign of a card-skimming device. When entering your PIN, carefully block other people's view of the keypad.

Don't use a debit card for purchases. Because a debit card pulls funds directly from your bank account, potential charges incurred by a thief will stay on your account while the fraudulent use is investigated by your bank.

To access your accounts online while traveling, be sure to use a secure connection (see page 649).

Damage Control for Lost Cards

If you lose your credit or debit card, report the loss immediately to the respective global customer-assistance centers. Call these 24-hour US numbers collect: Visa (tel. 303/967-1096), MasterCard In Italy, to make a collect call to the US, dial 800-172-170 and stay on the line for an English-speaking operator. European toll-free numbers (listed by country) can be found at the websites for Visa and MasterCard.

You'll need to provide the primary cardholder's identification-verification details (such as birth date, mother's maiden name, or Social Security number). You can generally receive a temporary card within two or three business days in Europe (see www.ricksteves.com/help for more).

If you report your loss within two days, you typically won't be responsible for unauthorized transactions on your account, although many banks charge a liability fee of $50.

TIPPING

Tipping in Italy isn't as automatic and generous as it is in the US. For special service, tips are appreciated, but not expected. As in the US, the proper amount depends on your resources, tipping philosophy, and the circumstances, but some general guidelines apply.

Restaurants: In Italy, a service charge *(servizio)* is usually built into your bill, so the total you pay already includes a basic tip. It's up to you whether to tip beyond this. For more details on restaurant tipping, see page 629.

Taxis: For a typical ride, round up your fare a bit (for instance, if the fare is €4.50, pay €5). If the cabbie hauls your bags and zips you to the airport to help you catch your flight, you might want to toss in a little more. But if you feel like you're being driven in circles or otherwise ripped off, skip the tip.

Services: In general, if someone in the tourism or service industry does a super job for you, a small tip of a euro or two is appropriate...but not required. If you're not sure whether (or how much) to tip, ask a local for advice.

GETTING A VAT REFUND

Wrapped into the purchase price of your Italian souvenirs is a Value-Added Tax (VAT) of about 22 percent. You're entitled to get most of that tax back if you purchase more than €155 (about $170) worth of goods at a store that participates in the VAT-refund scheme. Typically, you must ring up the minimum at a single retailer—you can't add up your purchases from various shops to reach the required amount. (If the store ships the goods to your US home, VAT is not assessed on your purchase.)

Getting your refund is straightforward...and worthwhile if you spend a significant amount on souvenirs.

Get the paperwork. Have the merchant completely fill out the necessary refund document. You'll have to present your passport. Get the paperwork done before you leave the store to ensure you'll have everything you need (including your original sales receipt).

Get your stamp at the border or airport. Process your VAT document at your last stop in the European Union (such as at the airport) with the customs agent who deals with VAT refunds. Arrive an additional hour early before you need to check in to allow time to find the customs office—and to stand in line. Some customs desks are positioned before airport security; confirm the location before going through security.

It's best to keep your purchases in your carry-on. If they're too large or dangerous to carry on (such as knives), pack them in your checked bags and alert the check-in agent. You'll be sent (with your tagged bag) to a customs desk outside security; someone will examine your bag, stamp your paperwork, and put your bag on the belt. You're not supposed to use your purchased goods before you leave. If you show up at customs wearing your new Italian leather shoes, officials might look the other way—or deny you a refund.

Collect your refund. Many merchants work with services—such as Global Blue or Premier Tax Free—that have offices at major airports, ports, or border crossings (either before or after security, probably strategically located near a duty-free shop). These services, which extract a 4 percent fee, can refund your money immediately in cash or credit your card (within two billing cycles). Other refund services may require you to mail the documents from home, or more quickly, from your point of departure (using an envelope you've prepared in advance or one that's been provided by the merchant). You'll then have to wait—it can take months.

CUSTOMS FOR AMERICAN SHOPPERS

You can take home $800 worth of items per person duty-free, once every 31 days. Many processed and packaged foods are allowed, including: vacuum-packed cheeses, dried herbs, jams, baked goods, candy, chocolate, oil, vinegar, mustard, and honey. Fresh fruits and vegetables and most meats are not allowed, with exceptions for some canned items. As for alcohol, you can bring home one liter duty-free (it can be packed securely in your checked luggage, along with any other liquid-containing items).

To bring alcohol (or liquid-packed foods) in your carry-on bag on your flight home, buy it at a duty-free shop at the airport. You'll increase your odds of getting it onto a connecting flight if it's packaged in a "STEB"—a secure, tamper-evident bag. But stay away from liquids in opaque, ceramic, or metallic containers, which usually cannot be successfully screened (STEB or no STEB).

For details on allowable goods, customs rules, and duty rates, visit http://help.cbp.gov.

Sightseeing

Sightseeing can be hard work. Use these tips to make your visits to Florence and Tuscany's finest sights meaningful, fun, efficient, and painless.

MAPS AND NAVIGATION TOOLS

A good map is essential for efficient navigation while sightseeing. The black-and-white maps in this book are concise and simple, designed to help you locate recommended destinations, sights, and local TIs, where you can pick up more in-depth maps. Maps with even more detail are sold at newsstands and bookstores.

You can also use a mapping app on your mobile device. Be aware that pulling up maps or looking up turn-by-turn walking directions on the fly usually requires an Internet connection: To use this feature, it's smart to get an international data plan (see page 644). With Google Maps or City Maps 2Go, it's possible to download a map while online, then go offline and navigate without incurring data-roaming charges, though you can't search for an address or get real-time walking directions. A handful of other apps—including Apple Maps, OffMaps, and Navfree—also allow you to use maps offline.

PLAN AHEAD

Set up an itinerary that allows you to fit in all your must-see sights. For a one-stop look at opening hours, see "Florence at a Glance" on page 32 (also see the "Daily Reminder" on page 22). You'll find "Siena at a Glance" on page 355. Most sights keep stable hours, but you can easily confirm the latest by checking with the TI or visiting museum websites.

For Florence, it's smart to get a Firenze Card (see page 30) or make reservations for the Uffizi and Accademia (see page 34).

Don't put off visiting a must-see sight—you never know when a place will close unexpectedly for a holiday, strike, or restoration. Given how precious your vacation time is, I recommend getting reservations for any must-see sight that offers them (see page 7). Many museums are closed or have reduced hours at least a few days a year, especially on holidays such as Labor Day (May 1), Christmas, and New Year's. A list of holidays is on page 673; check online for possible museum closures during your trip. In summer, some sights may stay open late. Off-season, many museums have shorter hours.

Going at the right time helps avoid crowds. This book offers tips on specific sights. Try visiting popular sights very early or very late. Evening visits (when possible) are usually peaceful, with fewer crowds.

If you plan to hire a local guide, reserve ahead by email. Popular guides can get booked up.

Study up. To get the most out of the self-guided tours and sight descriptions in this book, read them before you visit.

AT SIGHTS

Here's what you can typically expect:

Entering: Be warned that you may not be allowed to enter if you arrive less than 30 to 60 minutes before closing time. And guards start ushering people out well before the actual closing time, so don't save the best for last.

Some important sights have a security check, where you must open your bag or send it through a metal detector. Some sights require you to check daypacks and coats. (If you'd rather not check your daypack, try carrying it tucked under your arm like a purse as you enter.)

Photography: If the museum's photo policy isn't clearly posted, ask a guard. Generally, taking photos without a flash or tripod is allowed. Some sights ban selfie sticks; others ban photos altogether.

Temporary Exhibits: Museums may show special exhibits in addition to their permanent collection. Some exhibits are included in the entry price, while others come at an extra cost (which you may have to pay even if you don't want to see the exhibit).

Expect Changes: Artwork can be on tour, on loan, out sick, or shifted at the whim of the curator. Pick up a floor plan as you enter, and ask the museum staff if you can't find a particular item. Say the title or artist's name, or point to the photograph in this book and ask, *"Dov'è?"* (doh-VEH, meaning "Where is?").

Audioguides and Apps: Many sights rent audioguides, which generally offer excellent recorded descriptions in English. If you bring your own earbuds, you can enjoy better sound. To save money, bring a Y-jack and share one audioguide with your travel partner. Museums and sights often offer free apps that you can download to your mobile device (check their websites). And, I've produced free, downloadable audio tours for my Florence Renaissance and Siena City walks, as well as my tours of Florence's Accademia, Uffizi, Bargello, and Museum of San Marco; look for the 🎧 in this book. For more on my audio tours, see page 8.

Dates for Artwork: It helps to know the terms. Art historians and Italians refer to the great Florentine centuries by dropping a thousand years. The Trecento (300s), Quattrocento (400s), and Cinquecento (500s) were the 1300s, 1400s, and 1500s. The Novecento (900s) means modern art (the 1900s). In Italian museums, art is dated with *sec* for *secolo* (century, often indicated with Roman numerals), A.C. (*avanti Cristo*, or B.C.), and D.C. (*dopo Cristo*, or A.D.). OK?

Services: Important sights may have an on-site café or cafeteria (usually a handy place to rejuvenate during a long visit). The WCs at sights are free and generally clean.

Before Leaving: At the gift shop, scan the postcard rack or thumb through a guidebook to be sure you haven't overlooked something that you'd like to see.

Every sight or museum offers more than what is covered in this book. Use the information in this book as an introduction—not the final word.

FIND RELIGION

Churches offer some amazing art (usually free), a cool respite from heat, and a welcome seat.

A modest dress code—no bare shoulders or shorts for anyone, even kids—is enforced at larger churches, such as the Duomo in both Florence and Siena, but is often overlooked elsewhere. If you're caught by surprise, you can improvise, using maps to cover your shoulders and a jacket for your knees. A few major churches let you borrow or buy disposable ponchos to cover up in a pinch. (I wear a super-lightweight pair of long pants rather than shorts for my hot and muggy big-city Italian sightseeing.)

Some churches have coin-operated audioboxes that describe the art and history; just set the dial on English, put in your coins, and listen. Coin boxes near a piece of art illuminate the art (and present a better photo opportunity). I pop in a coin whenever I can. It improves my experience, is a favor to other visitors trying to appreciate a great piece of art in the dark, and is a little contribution to that church and its work. Whenever possible, let there be light.

Sleeping

I favor hotels and restaurants that are handy to your sightseeing activities. Rather than list hotels scattered throughout a city, I choose hotels in my favorite neighborhoods. My recommendations run the gamut, from dorm beds to fancy rooms with all of the comforts. To stay in the countryside, try *agriturismo* farmhouses—I've listed several.

Extensive and opinionated listings of good-value rooms are a major feature of this book's Sleeping sections. I like places that are clean, central, relatively quiet at night, reasonably priced, friendly, small enough to have a hands-on owner and stable staff, and run with a respect for Italian traditions. I'm more impressed by a convenient location and a fun-loving philosophy than flat-screen TVs and a fancy gym. Most places I recommend fall short of perfection. But if I can find a place with most of these features, it's a keeper.

Book your accommodations as soon as your itinerary is set, especially if you want to stay at one of my top listings or if you'll be traveling during busy times. See page 673 for a list of major holidays and festivals in Italy; for tips on making reservations, see page 622.

Some people make reservations as they travel, calling hotels a few days to a week before their arrival. If you anticipate crowds (worst weekdays at business destinations and weekends at tourist locales) on the day you want to check in, call hotels at about 9:00 or 10:00, when the receptionist knows who'll be checking out and which rooms will be available. Some apps—such as HotelTonight. com—specialize in last-minute rooms, often at business-class hotels in big cities. If you encounter a language barrier, ask the fluent receptionist at your current hotel to call for you.

RATES AND DEALS

I've categorized my recommended accommodations based on price, indicated with a dollar-sign rating (see sidebar). The price ranges suggest an estimated cost for a one-night stay in a standard double room with a private toilet and shower in high season, include breakfast, and assume you're booking directly with the hotel (not through a booking site, which extracts a commission). Room prices can fluctuate significantly with demand and amenities (size, views, room class, and so on), but relative price categories remain constant. Taxes vary from place to place (in Florence, figure between €2-5 per person, per night).

Room rates are especially volatile at larger hotels that use

Sleep Code

Hotels are classified based on the average price of a standard double room with breakfast in high season.

$$$$	**Splurge:**	Most rooms over €170
$$$	**Pricier:**	€130-170
$$	**Moderate:**	€90-130
$	**Budget:**	€50-90
¢	**Backpacker:**	Under €50
RS%	**Rick Steves discount**	

Unless otherwise noted, credit cards are accepted, hotel staff speak basic English, and free Wi-Fi is available. Comparison-shop by checking prices at several hotels (on each hotel's own website, on a booking site, or by email). For the best deal, *book directly with the hotel.* Ask for a discount if paying in cash; if the listing includes **RS%,** request a Rick Steves discount.

"dynamic pricing" to set rates. Prices can skyrocket during festivals and conventions, while business hotels can have deep discounts on weekends when demand plummets. Of the many hotels I recommend, it's difficult to say which will be the best value on a given day—until you do your homework.

Once your dates are set, check the specific price for your preferred stay at several hotels. You can do this either by comparing prices online on the hotels' own websites, or by emailing several hotels directly and asking for their best rate. Even if you start your search on a booking site such as TripAdvisor or Booking.com, you'll usually find the best deal through a hotel's own website. (While many hotels are contractually obligated not to undercut booking-site prices, when you go direct, the hotel avoids the 15-20 percent commission, giving them wiggle room to treat you better—offering perhaps a nicer room or free breakfast.)

Some hotels offer a discount to those who pay cash or stay longer than three nights. To cut costs further, try asking for a cheaper room (for example, with a shared bathroom or no window) or offer to skip breakfast.

Additionally, some accommodations offer a special discount for Rick Steves readers, indicated in this guidebook by the abbreviation **"RS%."** Discounts vary: Ask for details when you reserve. Generally, to qualify you must book directly (that is, not through a booking site), mention this book when you reserve, show this book upon arrival, and sometimes pay cash or stay a certain number of nights. In some cases, you may need to enter a discount code (which I've provided in the listing) in the booking form on the hotel's website. Rick Steves discounts apply to readers with ebooks as well as

The Good and Bad of Online Reviews

User-generated review sites and apps such as Yelp, Booking. com, and TripAdvisor can give you a consensus of opinions about everything from hotels and restaurants to sights and nightlife. If you scan reviews of a hotel and see several complaints about noise or a rotten location, it tells you something important that you'd never learn from the hotel's own website.

But as a guidebook writer, my sense is that there is a big difference between the uncurated information on a review site and a guidebook. A user-generated review is based on the experience of one person, who likely stayed at one hotel in a given city and ate at a few restaurants there (and who doesn't have much of a basis for comparison). A guidebook is the work of a trained researcher who, year after year, visits many alternatives to assess their relative value. I recently checked out some top-rated user-reviewed hotel and restaurant listings in various towns; when stacked up against their competitors, some were gems, while just as many were duds.

Both types of information have their place, and in many ways, they're complementary. If something is well-reviewed in a guidebook, and also gets good ratings on one of these sites, it's likely a winner.

printed books. Understandably, discounts do not apply to promotional rates.

TYPES OF ACCOMMODATIONS
Hotels

In Florence, you can snare a spartan, clean, and comfortable double with breakfast and a private bath for about €100. You get near-elegance in peak season for €170. Most hotels offer single rooms, and some offer larger rooms for four or more people (I call these "family rooms" in the listings). Some hotels can add an extra bed to a double room to make a triple for a small charge. If there's space for an extra cot, they'll cram it in for you. In general, a triple room is cheaper than the cost of a double and a single. Three or four people can economize by requesting one big room. Florence hoteliers are eager to fill their rooms in the off-season. Consider prices negotiable.

Arrival and Check-In: Hotels and B&Bs are sometimes located on the higher floors of a multipurpose building with a secured door. In that case, look for your hotel's name on the buttons by the main entrance. When you ring the bell, you'll be buzzed in. (The hotelier doesn't control the building's common areas, so try not to let a slightly dingy entryway color your opinion of the hotel.)

Hotel elevators are becoming more common, though some

older buildings still lack an elevator, or you may have to climb a flight of stairs to reach it (if so, you can ask the front desk for help carrying your bags up). Also, elevators are often very small—pack light, or you may need to send your bags up without you.

When you check in, the receptionist will normally ask for your passport and keep it for anywhere from a couple of minutes to a couple of hours. Hotels are legally required to register each guest with the police. Relax. Americans are notorious for making this chore more difficult than it needs to be.

If you're arriving in the morning, your room probably won't be ready. Check your bag safely at the hotel and dive right into sightseeing.

In Your Room: More pillows and blankets are usually in the closet or available on request. Towels and linens aren't always replaced every day. Hang your towel up to dry. Some hotels use lightweight "waffle," or very thin, tablecloth-type towels; these take less water and electricity to launder and are preferred by many Italians.

Nearly all places offer private bathrooms. You'll save by booking a room with a shared bathroom down the hall. Generally rooms with a private bathroom have a bath or shower, a toilet, and a bidet (which Italians use for quick sponge baths). The cord over the tub or shower is not a clothesline. You pull it when you've fallen and can't get up.

Most hotel rooms have a TV, telephone, and free Wi-Fi (although in old buildings with thick walls, the Wi-Fi signal doesn't always make it to the rooms; sometimes it's only available in the lobby). Sometimes there's a guest computer with Internet access in the lobby. Simpler places rarely have a room phone, but often have free Wi-Fi. Pricier hotels usually come with a small fridge stocked with beverages called a *frigo bar* (FREE-goh bar; pay for what you use).

Double beds are called *matrimoniale,* even though hotels aren't interested in your marital status. Twins are *due letti singoli.* Convents offer cheap accommodation but have more *letti singoli* than *matrimoniali.*

Breakfast and Meals: Italian hotels typically include breakfast in their room prices. If breakfast is optional, you may want to skip it. While convenient, it's usually pricey for what you get: a simple continental buffet with (at its most generous) bread, ham, cheese, yogurt, and unlimited *caffè latte.* A picnic in your room followed by a coffee at the corner café can be lots cheaper.

Checking Out: While it's customary to pay for your room upon departure, it can be a good idea to settle your bill the day before, when you're not in a hurry and while the manager's in. That way you'll have time to discuss and address any points of contention.

Keep Cool

If you're visiting Italy in the summer, the extra expense of an air-conditioned room can be money well spent, particularly in the south. Most hotel rooms with air-conditioners come with a control stick (like a TV remote; the hotel may require a deposit) that generally has similar symbols and features: fan icon (click to toggle through wind power, from light to gale); louver icon (choose steady airflow or waves); snowflake and sunshine icons (cold air or heat); clock ("O" setting: run X hours before turning off; "I" setting: wait X hours to start); and the temperature control (20 degrees Celsius is comfortable; also see the thermometer diagram on page 680). When you leave your room for the day, turning off the air-conditioning is good form.

Hotelier Help: Hoteliers can be a good source of advice. Most know their city well, and can assist you with everything from public transit and airport connections to finding a good restaurant, the nearest launderette, or a late-night pharmacy. English works in all but the cheapest places.

Hotel Hassles: Even at the best places, mechanical breakdowns occur: Sinks leak, hot water turns cold, toilets may gurgle or smell, the Wi-Fi goes out, or the air-conditioning dies when you need it most. Report your concerns clearly and calmly at the front desk. For more complicated problems, don't expect instant results. Above all, keep a positive attitude. Remember, you're on vacation. If your hotel is a disappointment, spend more time out enjoying the place you came to see.

If you find that night noise is a problem (if, for instance, your room is over a nightclub), ask for a quieter room in the back or on an upper floor. To guard against theft in your room, keep valuables out of sight. Some rooms come with a safe, and some hotels have safes at the front desk. I've never bothered using one and, in a lifetime of travel, I've never had anything stolen out of my room.

Short-Term Rentals

A short-term rental—whether an apartment, house, or room in a local's home—is an increasingly popular alternative, especially if you plan to settle in one location for several nights. For stays longer than a few days, you can usually find a rental that's comparable to—and even cheaper than—a hotel room with similar amenities. Plus, you'll get a behind-the-scenes peek into how locals live.

Many places require a minimum-night stay, and compared to hotels, rentals usually have less-flexible cancellation policies. And you're generally on your own: There's no hotel reception desk, breakfast, or daily cleaning service.

Making Hotel Reservations

Reserve your rooms as soon as you've pinned down your travel dates. For busy national holidays, it's wise to reserve far in advance (see 673).

Requesting a Reservation: It's easiest—and generally cheaper—to book your room through the hotel's official website (not a booking agency's site). If there's no reservation form, or for complicated requests, send an email. Most recommended hotels take reservations in English.

Here's what the hotelier wants to know:

- type(s) of rooms you need and size of your party
- number of nights you'll stay
- your arrival and departure dates, written European-style as day/month/year (for example, 18/06/19 or 18 June 2019);
- special requests (such as en suite bathroom vs. down the hall, cheapest room, twin beds vs. double bed, quiet room)
- applicable discounts (such as a Rick Steves reader discount, cash discount, or promotional rate)

Confirming a Reservation: Most places will request a credit-card number to hold your room. If they don't have a secure online reservation form—look for the *https*—you can email it (I do), but it's safer to share that confidential info via a phone call or fax.

Canceling a Reservation: If you must cancel, it's courteous—and smart—to do so with as much notice as possible, especially for smaller family-run places. Cancellation policies can be strict; read the fine print or ask about these before you book. Many dis-

Finding Accommodations: Aggregator websites such as Airbnb, FlipKey, Roomorama, Booking.com, and the Home-Away family of sites (HomeAway, VRBO, and VacationRentals) let you browse properties and correspond directly with European property owners or managers. If you prefer to work from a curated list of accommodations, consider using a rental agency such as InterhomeUSA.com or RentaVilla.com. Agency-represented apartments typically cost more, but this method often offers more help and safeguards than booking directly. Or try Steve and Linda of Cross-Pollinate, a booking service for private rooms and apartments in the old centers of Rome, Florence, and Venice; rates start at €30 per person (www.cross-pollinate.com).

Before you commit, be clear on the details, location, and amenities. I like to virtually "explore" the neighborhood using the Street View feature on Google Maps. Also consider the proximity to public transportation, and how well connected the property is with the rest of the city. Ask about amenities (elevator, laundry, coffee maker, Wi-Fi, parking, etc.). Reviews from previous guests can help identify trouble spots.

From:	rick@ricksteves.com
Sent:	Today
To:	info@hotelcentral.com
Subject:	Reservation request for 19-22 July

Dear Hotel Central,

I would like to stay at your hotel. Please let me know if you have a room available and the price for:
• 2 people
• Double bed and en suite bathroom in a quiet room
• Arriving 19 July, departing 22 July (3 nights)

Thank you!
Rick Steves

count deals require prepayment, with no cancellation refunds.

Reconfirming a Reservation: Always call or email to reconfirm your room reservation a few days in advance. For B&Bs or very small hotels, I call again on my day of arrival to tell my host what time to expect me (especially important if arriving late—after 17:00).

Phoning: For tips on calling hotels overseas, see page 646.

Think about the kind of experience you want: Just a key and an affordable bed...or a chance to get to know a local? There are typically two kinds of hosts: those who want minimal interaction with their guests, and those who are friendly and may want to interact with you. Read the promotional text and online reviews to help shape your decision.

Apartments and Rental Houses: If you're staying somewhere for four nights or longer, it's worth considering an apartment or rental house (shorter stays aren't worth the hassle of arranging key pickup, buying groceries, etc.). Apartment and house rentals can be especially cost-effective for groups and families. European apartments, like hotel rooms, tend to be small by US standards. But they often come with laundry machines and small, equipped kitchens *(cucinetta)*, making it easier and cheaper to dine in. If you make good use of the kitchen (and Europe's great produce markets), you'll save on your meal budget.

Private and Shared Rooms: In small towns, there are often few hotels or apartments to choose from, but an abundance of *affittacamere*, or rental rooms. This can be anything from a set of keys and a basic bed to a cozy B&B with your own Tuscan grandmother. Renting a room in someone's home is a good option for those traveling alone, as you're more likely to find true single rooms—with just one single bed, and a price to match. Beds range from air-mattress-in-living-room basic to plush-B&B-suite posh. Some places allow you to book for a single night; if staying for several nights, you can buy groceries just as you would in a rental house. While you can't expect your host to also be your tour guide—or even to provide you with much info—some may be interested in getting to know the travelers who come through their home.

In Italy, even luxury B&Bs can suffer from absentee management—the proprietors often live off-site (or even in another town) and may be around only when they are expecting guests, so clearly communicate your arrival time. After checking in, be sure you have your host's telephone number in case you need to reach them.

Local TIs can give you a list of possibilities (or try the free Ciao Italia Bed & Breakfast, which books B&Bs and hostels in Rome, Florence, and Venice; www.ciaoitalia-bb.com). These rooms are usually a good budget option, but since they vary in quality, shop around to find the best value. It's always OK to ask to see the room before you commit.

Other Options: Swapping homes with a local works for people with an appealing place to offer, and who can live with the idea of having strangers in their home (don't assume where you live is not interesting to Europeans). A good place to start is HomeExchange. To sleep for free, Couchsurfing.com is a vagabond's alternative to Airbnb. It lists millions of outgoing members, who host fellow "surfers" in their homes.

Confirming and Paying: Many places require you to pay the entire balance before your trip. It's easiest and safest to pay through the site where you found the listing. Be wary of owners who want to take your transaction offline to avoid fees; this gives you no recourse if things go awry. Never agree to wire money (a key indicator of a fraudulent transaction).

Hostels

A hostel provides cheap beds in dorms where you sleep alongside strangers for about €20-30 per night. Travelers of any age are welcome if they don't mind dorm-style accommodations and meeting other travelers. Most hostels offer kitchen facilities, guest computers, Wi-Fi, and a self-service laundry. Hostels almost always provide bedding, but the towel's up to you (though you can usually rent one for a small fee). Family and private rooms are often available.

Independent hostels tend to be easygoing, colorful, and informal (no membership required; www.hostelworld.com). You may pay slightly less by booking directly with the hostel. **Official**

hostels are part of Hostelling International (HI) and share a booking site (www.hihostels.com). HI hostels typically require that you be a member or pay extra per night.

Agriturismi

Agriturismi—working farms that double as countryside B&Bs—began cropping up in the 1980s to allow small family farms to survive (as in the US, many have been squeezed out by giant agribusinesses). By renting rooms to travelers, farmers receive generous tax breaks that allow them to remain on their land and continue to grow food crops. These B&Bs make a peaceful home base for

those exploring rural Italy, and are ideal for those traveling by car—especially families.

It's wise to book several months in advance for high season (late May-mid-Oct). July and August are jammed with Italians and other European vacationers; in spring and fall, it's mostly Americans. Weeklong stays (typically Saturday to Saturday) are preferred at busy times, but shorter stays are possible off-season. To sleep cheaper, try early spring and late fall. Many places are closed in winter.

As the name implies, *agriturismi* are in the countryside, although some are located on the outskirts of a large town or city. Most are family-run. *Agriturismi* vary dramatically in quality—some properties are rustic, while others are downright luxurious, offering amenities such as swimming pools and riding stables. The rooms are usually clean and comfortable. Breakfast is often included, and *mezza pensione* (half-pension, which in this case means a home-cooked dinner) might be built into the price whether you want it or not. Most places serve tasty homegrown food; some are vegetarian or organic, others are gourmet. Kitchenettes are often available to cook up your own feast.

To qualify officially as an *agriturismo*, the farm must still generate more money from its farm activities, thereby ensuring that the land is worked and preserved. Some farmhouse B&Bs aren't working farms, but are still fine places to stay. Some travelers who are enticed by romanticized dreams of *agriturismi* are turned off when they arrive to actual farm smells and sounds. These folks would be more comfortable with a countryside B&B or villa that offers a bit more upscale comfort. In this book, I've listed both types of rural

PRACTICALITIES

Tips for Enjoying an *Agriturismo* Farmhouse Stay

- To sleep cheap, avoid peak season. Rental prices follow the old rule of supply and demand. Prices that are sky-high in summer can drop dramatically in early spring and late fall.
- Make sure your trip fits their requirements. Many properties rent on a traditional Saturday-to-Saturday time period. You might be unable to rent for a different or shorter time, especially during peak season.
- If you want amenities, be willing to pay more. A swimming pool can add substantially to the cost, but at the height of summer, could be worth every extra euro, particularly if you're bringing kids.
- Consider renting a rural apartment rather than an entire villa or farmhouse. Often the owners have renovated an original rambling farmhouse or medieval estate into a series of well-constructed apartments with private kitchens, bathrooms, living areas, and outdoor terraces. They usually share a common pool.
- You will need a rental car to fully enjoy—or even reach—your accommodations.
- To make the most of your time, ask an expert—the owner—for suggestions on restaurants, sights, and activities. Make sure you know how to operate the appliances.
- Slow down. One of the joys of staying for at least a week in one location is you can develop a true *dolce far niente* (sweetness of doing nothing) attitude. If it rains, grab a book from the in-house library and curl up on the sofa.
- While your time in the countryside may not be action-packed, staying put in one spot leaves you open to the unexpected pleasures that come when you just let the days unwind without a plan.

accommodations; if you want the real thing, make sure the owners call their place an *agriturismo*.

In addition to my listings, local TIs can give you a list of places in their area. For a sampling, visit www.agriturismoitaly.it or search online for *agriturismo*. One booking agency among many is Farm Holidays in Tuscany (closed Sat-Sun, tel. 0564-417-418, www.byfarmholidays.com, info@byfarmholidays.com).

Eating

The Italians are masters of the art of fine living. That means eating long and well. Lengthy, multicourse meals and endless hours sitting in outdoor cafés are the norm. Americans eat on their way to an evening event and complain if the check is slow in coming. For Italians, the meal is an end in itself, and only rude waiters rush you.

A highlight of your Italian adventure will be this country's cafés, cuisine, and wines. Trust me: This is sightseeing for your palate. Even if you liked dorm food and are sleeping in cheap hotels, your taste buds will relish an occasional first-class splurge. You can eat well without going broke. But be careful: You're just as likely to blow a small fortune on a disappointing meal as you are to dine wonderfully for €25. Your euros typically will go much further, and will net you far better food, in smaller Tuscan towns than in Florence. Rely on my recommendations in the Eating in Florence chapter and under the "Eating" sections in other destinations.

In general, Italians eat meals a bit later than we do. At 7:00 or 8:00, they have a light breakfast (coffee—usually cappuccino or espresso—and a pastry, often standing up at a café). Lunch (between 13:00 and 15:00) is traditionally the largest meal of the day. Then they eat a late, light dinner (around 20:00-21:30, or maybe earlier in winter). To bridge the gap, people drop into a bar in the late afternoon for a *spuntino* (snack) and aperitif.

RESTAURANT PRICING

I've categorized my recommended eateries based on price, indicated with a dollar-sign rating (see sidebar). The price ranges suggest the average price of a typical main course—but not necessarily a complete meal. Sticking to pastas will save you plenty over ordering meat-and-fish *secondi*. Obviously, expensive items (steak, seafood, truffles), fine wine, appetizers, and dessert can significantly increase your final bill.

The categories also indicate a place's personality:

Budget eateries include street food, takeaway, order-at-the-counter shops, basic cafeterias, and bakeries selling sandwiches.

Moderate eateries are nice (but not fancy) sit-down restaurants, ideal for a straightforward, fill-the-tank meal. Most of my listings fall in this category—great for a good taste of local cuisine on a budget.

Pricier eateries are a notch up, with more attention paid to the setting, service, and cuisine. These are ideal for a memorable meal that doesn't break the bank. This category often includes affordable "destination" or "foodie" restaurants. And **splurge** eateries are dress-up-for-a-special-occasion-swanky—typically with an

---

Restaurant Price Code

I've assigned each eatery a price category, based on the average cost of a typical main course (pasta or *secondi*). Drinks, desserts, and splurge items (steak and seafood) can raise the price considerably.

$$$$	**Splurge:** Most main courses over €20
$$$	**Pricier:** €15-20
$$	**Moderate:** €10-15
$	**Budget:** Under €10

In Italy, pizza by the slice and other takeaway food is **$**; a basic trattoria or sit-down pizzeria is **$$**; a casual but more upscale restaurant is **$$$**; and a swanky splurge is **$$$$**.

---

elegant setting, polished service, pricey and intricate cuisine, and an expansive (and expensive) wine list.

To assign price ranges for restaurants in Italy, these price points were my rule of thumb: **$$$$**—most pastas over €13, *secondi* over €20; **$$$**—most pizzas/pastas €11-12, *secondi* €15-20; **$$**—most pizzas/pastas under €11, *secondi* under €15; **$**—meals under €10. I haven't categorized places where you might snack, graze, or assemble a picnic: supermarkets, delis, ice cream stands, cafés or bars specializing in drinks, chocolate shops, and so on.

BREAKFAST

Italian breakfasts, like Italian bath towels, are small: The basic, traditional version is coffee and a roll with butter and marmalade. These days, many places also have yogurt and juice (the delicious red orange juice—*spremuta d'arancia rossa*—is made from Sicilian blood oranges), and possibly also cereal, cold cuts and sliced cheese, and eggs (typically hard-boiled; scrambled or fried eggs are rare). Small budget hotels may leave a basic breakfast in your room (stale croissant, roll, jam, yogurt, coffee).

If you want to skip your hotel breakfast, consider browsing for a morning picnic at a local open-air market. Or do as the Italians do: Stop into a bar or café to drink a cappuccino and munch a *cornetto* (croissant) while standing at the bar. While the *cornetto* is the most common pastry, you'll find a range of *pasticcini* (pastries, sometimes called *dolci*—sweets). Look for *otto* (an 8-shaped pastry, often filled with custard, jam, or chocolate), *sfoglia* (can be fruit-filled, like a turnover), or *ciambella* (doughnut filled with custard or chocolate)—or ask about local specialties.

ITALIAN RESTAURANTS

While *ristorante* is self-explanatory, you'll also see other types of Italian eateries. A *trattoria* and an *osteria* (which can be more ca-

sual) are both generally family-owned places serving home-cooked meals, often at moderate prices. A *locanda* is an inn, a *cantina* is a wine cellar, and a *birreria* is a brewpub. *Pizzerie, rosticcerie* (delis), *enoteche* (wine bars), and other alternatives are explained later.

I look for restaurants that are convenient to your hotel and sightseeing. When restaurant-hunting, choose a spot filled with locals, not the place with the big neon signs boasting, "We speak English and accept credit cards." Restaurants parked on famous squares generally serve bad food at high prices to tourists. Venturing even a block or two off the main drag leads to higher-quality food for less than half the price of the tourist-oriented places. Locals eat better at lower-rent locales. Family-run places operate without hired help and can offer cheaper meals.

Most restaurant kitchens close between their lunch and dinner service. Good restaurants don't reopen for dinner before 19:00. Small restaurants with a full slate of reservations for 20:30 or 21:00 often will accommodate walk-in diners willing to eat a quick, early meal, but you aren't expected to linger.

When you want the bill, mime-scribble on your raised palm or request it: *"Il conto, per favore."* You may have to ask for it more than once. If you're in a hurry, request the check when you receive the last item you order.

Cover and Tipping

Before you sit down, look at a menu to see what extra charges a restaurant tacks on. Two different items are routinely factored into your bill: the *coperto* and the *servizio*.

The *coperto* (cover charge), sometimes called *pane e coperto* (bread and cover), is the fee for your table setting (including the typical basket of bread). It's not negotiable, even if you don't eat the bread. Think of it as covering the cost of using the table for as long as you like. (Italians like to linger.) Most restaurants add the *coperto* onto your bill as a flat fee (€1-3 per person; the amount should be clearly noted on the menu).

The *servizio* (service charge) of about 10 percent is similar to the mandatory gratuity that American restaurants often add for groups of six or more. Most eateries don't have a tacked-on service charge, but instead, include it in the menu prices. The words *servizio incluso* on the menu and/or the receipt indicate that you're not required to pay anything beyond the listed prices (the *servizio* is built in). You can add an additional tip, if you choose, by including €1-2 for each person in your party. While Italians don't think about tips in terms of percentages—and some don't tip at all—this extra amount usually comes out to about 5 percent (10 percent is excessive for all but the very best service).

Some touristy or trendy restaurants don't include the service in the menu prices—instead they tack a *servizio* charge onto your bill. In these cases you'll see something like *"servizio 10%"* on the menu, and the fee will be added onto your bill (so you don't need to calculate it yourself and pay it separately). Rarely, you'll see the words *servizio non incluso* on the menu or bill; here you are expected to add a tip of about 10 percent.

Most Italian restaurants have a cover charge and include service in the menu prices. A few have just a service charge. Places with *both* a cover and a tacked-on service charge are best avoided—that's a clue that a restaurant is counting on a nonlocal clientele who can't gauge value. Self-service restaurants never have a cover or service charge, and in recent years some (especially less formal) cafés and restaurants with table service have stopped charging these fees as well.

Courses: *Antipasto, Primo,* and *Secondo*

For a list of Italian cuisine staples, including some of the most common dishes, see page 636. A full Italian meal consists of several courses:

Antipasto: An appetizer such as bruschetta, grilled veggies, deep-fried tasties, thin-sliced meat (such as prosciutto or carpaccio), or a plate of olives, cold cuts, and cheeses. To get a sampler plate of cold cuts and cheeses in a restaurant, ask for *affettato misto* (mixed cold cuts), *antipasto misto* (cold cuts, cheeses, and marinated vegetables), or—in Tuscany—*tagliere* (a sampler "board"). This could make a light meal in itself.

Primo piatto: A "first dish" generally consisting of pasta, rice, or soup. If you think of pasta when you think of Italy, you can dine well here without ever going beyond the *primo*.

Secondo piatto: A "second dish," equivalent to our main course, of meat or fish/seafood. Italians freely admit the *secondo* is the least interesting part of their cuisine. A vegetable side dish *(contorno)* may come with the *secondo* but more often must be ordered separately.

For most travelers, a meal with all three courses (plus *contorni*, dessert, and wine) is simply too much food—and euros can add up in a hurry. To avoid overeating (and to stretch your budget), share dishes. A good rule of thumb is for each person to order any two courses. For example, a couple can order and share one antipasto, one *primo*, one *secondo*, and one dessert; or two *antipasti* and two *primi;* or whatever combination appeals.

Another good option is sharing an array of *antipasti*—either by ordering several specific dishes or, at restaurants that offer self-serve buffets, by choosing a variety of cold and cooked appetizers from an *antipasti* buffet spread out like a salad bar. At buffets, you pay per plate; a typical serving costs about €8 (generally Italians don't treat buffets as all-you-can-eat, but take a one-time moderate serving; watch others and imitate).

To maximize the experience and flavors, small groups can mix *antipasti* and *primi* family-style (skipping *secondi*). If you do this right, you can eat well in better places for less than the cost of a tourist *menù* in a cheap place.

A few restaurants serve a *piatto unico*, with smaller portions of each course on one dish (for instance, a meat, starch, and vegetable).

Ordering Tips

Seafood and steak may be sold by weight (priced by the kilo—1,000 grams, or just over two pounds; or by the *etto*—100 grams. The abbreviation *s.q. (secondo quantità)* means an item is priced "according to quantity." Unless the menu indicates a fillet *(filetto)*, fish is usually served whole with the head and tail. However, you can always ask your waiter to select a small fish for you. Sometimes, especially for steak, restaurants require a minimum order of four or five *etti* (which diners can share). Make sure you're clear on the price before ordering.

Some special dishes come in larger quantities meant to be shared by two people. The shorthand way of showing this on a menu is "X2" (for two), but the price listed generally indicates the cost per person.

In a traditional restaurant, if you order a pasta dish and a side salad—but no main course—the waiter will bring the salad after the pasta (Italians prefer it this way, believing that it enhances digestion). If you want the salad with your pasta, specify *insieme* (een-see-YEH-meh; together). At eateries more accustomed to tourists, you may be asked when you want the salad.

Because pasta and bread are both starches, Italians consider them redundant. If you order only a pasta dish, bread may not come with it; you can request it, but you may be charged extra. On the other hand, if you order a vegetable antipasto or a meat *secondo*, bread is often provided to balance the ingredients.

At places with counter service—such as at a bar or a freeway rest-stop diner—you'll order and pay at the *cassa* (cashier). Take your receipt to the counter to claim your food.

Fixed-Price Meals and Ordering à la Carte

You can save by getting a fixed-priced meal, which is frequently exempt from cover and service charges. Avoid the cheapest ones

MENU € 19,00
TURISTICO

ANTIPASTO di MARE

PRIMI PIATTI

RISOTTO alla PESCATORA
SPAGHETTI alla MARINARA
SPAGHETTI allo SCOGLIO
TRENETTE al PESTO

SECONDI PIATTI

PESCE ai FERRI
FRITTO MISTO
GRIGLIATA di CARNE

CONTORNI

PATATE FRITTE o INSALATA

(often called a *menù turistico*), which tend to be bland and heavy, pairing a very basic pasta with reheated schnitzel and roast meats. Look instead for a genuine *menù del giorno* (menu of the day), which offers diners a choice of appetizer, main course, and dessert. It's worth paying a little more for an inventive fixed-price meal that shows off the chef's creativity.

While fixed-price meals can be easy and convenient, galloping gourmets prefer to order à la carte with the help of a menu translator (see "Italian Cuisine Staples," later). When going to an especially good restaurant with an approachable staff, I like to find out what they're eager to serve. Sometimes I'll simply say, *"Mi faccia felice"* (Make me happy) and set a price limit.

BUDGET EATING

Italy offers many budget options for hungry travelers, but beware of cheap eateries that sport big color photos of pizza and piles of different pastas. They often have no kitchens and simply microwave disgusting prepackaged food.

Self-service cafeterias offer the basics without add-on charges. Travelers on a hard-core budget equip their room with a pantry stocked at the market (fruits and veggies are remarkably cheap), or pick up a sandwich or *döner kebab*, then dine in at picnic prices. Bars and cafés are also good places to grab a meal on the go.

Pizzerias

Pizza is cheap and readily available. Stop by a pizza shop for stand-up or takeout (*pizza al taglio* means "by the slice"). Supermarkets usually have a pizza counter too. Some shops sell individual slices of round, Naples-style pizza, while others feature *pizza rustica*—thick pizza baked in a large rectangular pan and sold by weight. If you simply ask for a piece, you may wind up with a gigantic slab and be charged top euro. In-stead, clearly indicate how much you

want: 100 grams, or *un etto*, is a hot and cheap snack; 200 grams, or *due etti*, makes a light meal. Or show the size with your hands— *tanto così* (TAHN-toh koh-ZEE; this much). They'll often helpfully cut it up into smaller pieces. If you want your pizza warm, say *"sì"* when they ask if you want it heated up (*scaldare*; skahl-DAH-ray). For a rundown of common types of pizza, see page 636. Pizzerias also sell *cecina*, a savory crêpe-like garbanzo-bean flatbread—a cheap snack that pairs well with a glass of red wine.

Bars/Cafés

Italian "bars" are not taverns, but inexpensive cafés. These neighborhood hangouts serve coffee, mini pizzas, sandwiches, and drinks from the cooler. Many dish up plates of fried cheese and vegetables from under the glass counter, ready to reheat. This budget choice is the Italian equivalent of English pub grub.

Many bars are small—if you can't find a table, you'll need to stand or find a ledge to sit on outside. Most charge extra for table service. To get food to go, say, *"da portar via"* (for the road). All bars have a WC *(toilette, bagno)* in the back, and customers—and the discreet public—can use it.

Food: For quick meals, bars usually have trays of cheap, premade sandwiches (*panini*, on a baguette; *piadini*, on flatbread; or *tramezzini*, on crustless white bread)—some are delightful grilled. (Others have too much mayo.) To save time for sightseeing and room for dinner, stop by a bar for a light lunch, such as a ham-and-cheese sandwich (called *toast*); have it grilled twice if you want it really hot.

Prices and Paying: You'll notice a two- or three-tiered pricing system. Drinking a cup of coffee while standing at the bar is cheaper than drinking it at an indoor table (you'll pay still more at an outdoor table). Many places have a *lista dei prezzi* (price list) with two columns—*al bar* and *al tavolo* (table)—posted somewhere by the bar or cash register. If you're on a budget, don't sit down without first checking out the financial consequences. Ask, "Same price if I sit or stand?" by saying, *"Costa uguale al tavolo o al banco?"* (KOH-stah oo-GWAH-lay ahl TAH-voh-loh oh ahl BAHN-koh). Throughout Italy, you can get cheap coffee at the bar of any establishment, no matter how fancy, and pay the same low, government-regulated price (generally less than a euro if you stand).

If the bar isn't busy, you can probably just order and pay when you leave. Otherwise: 1) Decide what you want; 2) find out the price by checking the price list on the wall, the prices posted near the food, or by asking the barista; 3) pay the cashier; and 4) give the receipt to the barista (whose clean fingers handle no dirty euros) and tell him or her what you want.

For more on drinking, see "Beverages," later.

Ethnic Food

A good bet for a cheap, hot meal is a *döner kebab* (Middle Eastern-style rotisserie meat wrapped in pita bread). Look for little hole-in-the-wall kebab shops, where you can get a hearty take-away dinner—either as a sandwich or a wrap—for about €3. Asian restaurants, although not as common as in northern Europe, usually serve only Chinese dishes and can also be a good value.

Rosticcerie

For a fast and cheap lunch, find an Italian variation on the corner deli: a *rosticceria* (specializing in roasted meats and accompanying *antipasti*). For a healthy light meal, ask for a mixed plate of vegetables with a hunk of mozzarella (*piatto misto di verdure con mozzarella*; pee-AH-toh MEE-stoh dee vehr-DOO-ray). Don't be limited by what's displayed. If you'd like a salad with a slice of cantaloupe and a hunk of cheese, they'll whip that up for you in a snap. Belly up to the bar; with a pointing finger, you can assemble a fine meal. If something's a mystery, ask for *un assaggio* (oon ah-SAH-joh) to get a little taste. To have your choices warmed up, ask for them to be heated (*scaldare;* skahl-DAH-ray).

Wine Bars

Wine bars *(enoteche)* are a popular, fast, and inexpensive option for lunch. Surrounded by the office crowd, you can get a salad, a plate of meats (cold cuts) and cheeses, and a glass of good wine (see blackboards for the day's selection and price per glass). A good *enoteca* aims to impress visitors with its wine, and will generally feature excellent-quality ingredients for the simple dishes it offers with the wine (though the prices add up—be careful with your ordering to keep this a budget choice). For more on Italian cocktails and wines, see page 642.

Aperitivo Buffets

The Italian term *aperitivo* means a predinner drink, but it's also used to describe their version of what we might call happy hour: a light buffet that many bars serve to customers during the predinner hours (typically around 18:00 or 19:00 until 21:00). The drink itself may not be cheap (typically around €8-12), but bars lay out an enticing array of meats, cheeses, grilled vegetables, and other *antipasti*-type dishes, and you're welcome to nibble to your heart's content while you nurse your drink. While it's intended as an appetizer course before heading out for a full dinner, light eaters could discreetly turn this into a small meal. Bars advertising *"apericena"* (*cena* means dinner) tend to have buffets hearty enough to pass as dinner. Drop by a few bars around this time to scope out their buffets before choosing.

Groceries and Delis

Another budget option is to visit a supermarket, *alimentari* (neighborhood grocery), or *salumeria* (delicatessen) to pick up some cold cuts, cheeses, and other supplies for a picnic. Some *salumerie,* and any *paninoteca* or *focacceria* (sandwich shop), can make a sandwich to order. Just point to what you want, and they'll stuff it into a *panino;* if you want it heated, remember the word *scaldare* (skahl-DAH-ray). If ordering an assortment of cold cuts and cheeses, some unscrupulous shops may try to pad the bill by pushing their most expensive ingredients. Be clear on what you want: *"un tagliere* (tahl-YEH-ray) *da __ euro, per favore."* For more on *salumi* and cheeses, see page 638.

Picnics

Picnicking saves lots of euros and is a great way to sample regional specialties. A typical picnic for two might be fresh rolls,

100 grams—or about a quarter pound—of cheese (*un etto,* EH-toh, plural *etti,* EH-tee), and 100 grams of meat, sometimes ordered by the slice *(fetta)* or piece *(pezzi).* For two people, I might get *un etto* of prosciutto and *due pezzi* of bread. Add two tomatoes, three carrots, two apples, yogurt, and a liter box of juice. Total cost: about €10.

In the process of assembling your meal, you get to deal with Italians in the market scene. For a colorful experience, gather your ingredients in the morning at a produce market; you'll probably need to hit several market stalls to put together a complete meal (note that many stalls close in the early afternoon).

While it's fun to visit small specialty shops, an *alimentari* is your one-stop corner grocery store (most will slice and stuff your sandwich for you if you buy the ingredients there). A rare *supermercato* (look for the Conad, Despar, and Co-op chains) gives you more efficiency with less color for less cost. At busier supermarkets, you'll need to take a number for deli service. And *rosticcerie* sell cheap food to go—you'll find options such as lasagna, rotisserie chicken, and sides like roasted potatoes and spinach.

Picnics can be an adventure in high cuisine. Be daring. Try the fresh mozzarella, *presto* pesto, shriveled olives, and any regional specialties the locals are excited about. If ordering *antipasti* (such as grilled or marinated veggies) at a deli counter, you can ask for *una porzione* in a takeaway container *(contenitore).* Use gestures to show exactly how much you want. The word *basta* (BAH-stah; enough) works as a question or as a statement.

Shopkeepers are happy to sell small quantities of produce, but it's customary to let the merchant choose for you. Say *"per oggi"* (pehr OH-jee; for today) and he or she will grab you something ready to eat. To avoid being overcharged, know the cost per kilo, study the weighing procedure, and do the arithmetic.

ITALIAN CUISINE STAPLES

Much of your Italian eating experience will likely involve the big five: pizza, pasta, *salumi*, cheese, and gelato. For a look at cuisine specific to Florence and Tuscany, see the sidebar on page 290. For more food help, try a menu translator, such as the *Rick Steves Italian Phrase Book & Dictionary*, which has a menu decoder and plenty of useful phrases for navigating the culinary scene.

Pizza

Here are some of the pizzas you might see at restaurants or at a pizzeria. Note that if you ask for pepperoni on your pizza, you'll get *peperoni* (green or red peppers, not sausage); request *diavola*, *salsiccia piccante*, or *salame piccante* instead (the closest thing in Italy to American pepperoni).

Bianca: White pizza with no tomatoes (also called *ciaccina*).

Capricciosa: Prosciutto, mushrooms, olives, and artichokes—literally the chef's "caprice."

Funghi: Mushrooms.

Margherita: Tomato sauce, mozzarella, and basil—the red, white, and green of the Italian flag.

Marinara: Tomato sauce, oregano, garlic, no cheese.

Napoletana: Mozzarella, anchovies, and tomato sauce.

Ortolana: "Greengrocer-style," with vegetables (also called *vegetariana*).

Quattro formaggi: Four different cheeses.

Quattro stagioni: Different toppings on each of the four quarters.

Pasta

While we think of pasta as a main dish, in Italy it's considered a *primo piatto*—first course. There are more than 600 varieties of Italian pasta, and each is specifically used to highlight a certain sauce, meat, or regional ingredient. Italian pasta falls into two broad categories: *pasta lunga* (long pasta) and *pasta corta* (short pasta).

Pasta lunga can be round, such as *capellini* (thin "little hairs"), *vermicelli* (slightly thicker "little worms"), and *bucatini* (long and hollow), or it can be flat, such as *linguine* (narrow "little tongues"), *fettuccine* (wider "small ribbons"), *tagliatelle* (even wider), and *pappardelle* (very wide, best with meat sauces).

The most common *pasta corta* are tubes, such as *penne, rigatoni, ziti, manicotti,* and *cannelloni;* they come either *lisce* (smooth) or *rigate* (grooved—better to catch and cling to sauce). Many short pastas are named for their shapes, such as *conchiglie* (shells), *farfalle* (butterflies), *cavatappi* (corkscrews), *ditali* (thimbles), *gomiti*

Eating with the Seasons

Italian cooks love to serve you fresh produce and seafood at its tastiest. If you must have porcini mushrooms outside of fall,

they'll be dried. Each region in Italy has its specialties, which you'll see displayed in open-air markets. To get a plate of the freshest veggies at a fine restaurant, request *"Un piatto di verdure della stagione, per favore"* (A plate of seasonal vegetables, please). Italians take fresh, seasonal ingredients so seriously that a restaurant cooking with frozen ingredients must note it on the menu—look for *congelato.*

Here are a few examples of what's fresh when:

April-May: Green beans and artichokes
April-May and Sept-Oct: Black truffles
April-June: Asparagus, zucchini flowers, and zucchini
May-June: Mussels, cantaloupe, loquats, and strawberries
May-Aug: Eggplant, clams
July-Sept: Figs
Oct-Nov: Mushrooms, white truffles, persimmons, and chestnuts
Nov-Feb: Cardoon (wild artichoke)
Fresh year-round: Meats and cheese

("elbow" macaroni), *lumache* (snails), *marziani* (spirals resembling "Martian" antennae), and even *strozzapreti* (priest stranglers). Some are filled *(ripieni),* including *tortelli* (C-shaped, stuffed ravioli) and *angolotti* or *mezzelune* (shaped like "priest's hats" or "half-moons").

Most types of pasta come in slightly different variations: If it's a bit thicker, *-one* is added to the end; if it's a bit thinner, *-ine, -ette,* or *-elle* is added. For example, *tortellini* are smaller *tortelli,* while *tortelloni* are bigger.

Here's a list of common pasta toppings and sauces. On a menu, these terms are usually preceded by *alla* (in the style of) or *in* (in):
Aglio e olio: Garlic and olive oil.
Alfredo: Butter, cream, and parmesan.
Amatriciana: Pork cheek, *pecorino* cheese, and tomato.
Arrabbiata: "Angry," spicy tomato sauce with chili peppers.
Bolognese: Meat and tomato sauce.
Boscaiola: Mushrooms and sausage.

Burro e salvia: Butter and sage.

Cacio e pepe: *Parmigiano* cheese and ground pepper.

Carbonara: Bacon, egg, cheese, and pepper.

Carrettiera: Spicy and garlicky, with olive oil and little tomatoes.

Diavola: "Devil-style," spicy hot.

Frutti di mare: Seafood.

Genovese: Basil ground with *parmigiano* cheese, garlic, pine nuts, and olive oil; a.k.a. pesto.

Gricia: Cured pork and *pecorino romano* cheese.

Marinara: Usually tomato, often with garlic and onions, but can also be a seafood sauce ("sailor's style").

Norma: Tomato, eggplant, and ricotta cheese.

Pajata: Calf intestines (also called *pagliata*).

Pescatora: Seafood ("fisherman style").

Pomodoro: Tomato only.

Puttanesca: "Harlot-style" tomato sauce with anchovies, olives, and capers.

Ragù: Meaty tomato sauce.

Scoglio: Mussels, clams, and tomatoes.

Sorrentina: "Sorrento-style," with tomatoes, basil, and mozzarella (usually over gnocchi).

Sugo di lepre: Rich sauce made of wild hare.

Tartufi: Truffles (also called *tartufate*).

Umbria: Sauce of anchovies, garlic, tomatoes, and truffles.

Vongole: Clams and spices.

Salumi

Salumi ("salted" meats), also called *affettati* ("cut" meats), are an Italian staple. While most American cold cuts are cooked, in Italy they're far more commonly cured by air-drying, salting, and smoking. (Don't worry; these so-called "raw" meats are safe to eat, and you can really taste the difference.)

The two most familiar types of *salumi* are *salame* and *prosciutto*. *Salame* is an air-dried, sometimes spicy sausage that comes in many varieties. When Italians say *"prosciutto,"* they usually mean *prosciutto crudo*—the raw ham that air-cures on the hock and is then thinly sliced. Produced mainly in the north of Italy, *prosciutto* can be either *dolce* (sweet) or *salato* (salty). Purists say the best is *prosciutto di Parma*.

Other *salumi* may be less familiar:

Bresaola: Air-cured beef.

Capocollo: Peppery pork shoulder (also called *coppa*).

Culatello: Prosciutto made with only the finest cuts of meat.

Finocchiona: *Salame* with fennel seeds.

Lonzino: Cured pork loin.

Mortadella: A finely ground pork loaf, similar to our bologna.

Pancetta: Salt-cured, peppery pork belly meat, similar to bacon; can be eaten raw or added to cooked dishes.

Quanciale: Tender pork cheek.

Salame di Sant'Olcese: What we'd call "Genoa salami."

Salame piccante: Spicy hot, similar to pepperoni.

Speck: Smoked pork shoulder.

If you've got a weak stomach, avoid *testa in cassetta* (headcheese—organs in aspic), *lampredotto* (cow stomach), and *sopressata* (in other parts of Italy, this is a spicy *salame*—but in Tuscany, it's often headcheese).

Cheese

When it comes to cheese *(formaggio),* you're probably already familiar with most of these Italian favorites:

Asiago: Hard cow cheese that comes either *mezzano* (young, firm, and creamy) or *stravecchio* (aged, pungent, and granular).

Burrata: A creamy mozzarella.

Fontina: Semihard, nutty, Gruyère-style mountain cheese.

Gorgonzola: Pungent, blue-veined cheese, either *dolce* (creamy) or *stagionato* (aged and hard).

Mascarpone: Sweet, buttery, spreadable dessert cheese.

Mozzarella di bufala: Made from the milk of water buffaloes.

Parmigiano-reggiano: Hard, crumbly, sharp, aged cow cheese with more nuanced flavor than American parmesan; *grana padano* is a less expensive variation.

Pecorino: Either *fresco* (fresh, soft, and mild) or *stagionato* (aged and sharp, sometimes called *pecorino romano*).

Provolone: Rich, firm, aged cow cheese.

Ricotta: Soft, airy cheese made by "recooking" leftover whey.

Scamorza: Similar to mozzarella, but often smoked.

Gelato

While American ice cream is made with cream and has a high butterfat content, Italian gelato is made with milk. It's also churned more slowly, making it denser. Connoisseurs believe that because gelato has less air and less fat (which coats the mouth and blocks the taste buds), it's more flavorful than American-style ice cream.

A key to gelato appreciation is sampling liberally and choosing flavors that go well together. At a *gelateria,* ask, as Italians do, for a taste: *"Un assaggio, per favore?"* (oon ah-SAH-joh pehr fah-VOH-ray). You can also ask what flavors go well together: *"Quali gusti stanno bene insieme?"* (KWAH-lee GOO-stee STAH-noh BEH-nay een-see-EH-may).

Most *gelaterie* clearly display prices and sizes. But in the textbook *gelateria* scam, the tourist orders two or three flavors—and the clerk selects a fancy, expensive chocolate-coated waffle cone,

PRACTICALITIES

piles it high with huge scoops, and cheerfully charges the tourist €10. To avoid rip-offs, point to the price or say what you want—for instance, a €3 cup: *"Una coppetta da tre euro"* (OO-nah koh-PEH-tah dah tray eh-OO-roh).

The best *gelaterie* display signs reading *artiginale, nostra produzione,* or *produzione propia,* indicating that the gelato is made on the premises. Seasonal flavors are also a good sign, as are mellow hues (avoid colors that don't appear in nature). Gelato stored in covered metal tins (rather than white plastic) is more likely to be homemade. Gourmet gelato shops are popping up all over Italy, selling exotic flavors. Avoid a chain called Grom—it's the Starbucks of gelato in Italy. Classic gelato flavors include:

After Eight: Chocolate and mint.

Bacio: Chocolate hazelnut, named for Italy's popular "kiss" candies.

Cassata: With dried fruits.

Cioccolato: Chocolate.

Crema: Vanilla.

Croccantino: "Crunchy," with toasted peanut bits.

Fior di latte: Sweet milk.

Fragola: Strawberry.

Macedonia: Mixed fruits.

Malaga: Similar to rum raisin.

Riso: With actual bits of rice mixed in.

Stracciatella: Vanilla with chocolate shreds.

Tartufo: Super chocolate.

Zabaione: Named for the egg yolk and Marsala wine dessert.

Zuppa inglese: Sponge cake, custard, chocolate, and cream.

Gelato variations or alternatives include *sorbetto* (sorbet—made with fruit, but no milk or eggs); *granita* or *grattachecca* (a cup of slushy ice with flavored syrup); and *cremolata* (a gelato-*granita* float).

BEVERAGES

Italian bars serve great drinks—hot, cold, sweet, caffeinated, or alcoholic.

Water, Juice, and Cold Drinks

Italians are notorious water snobs. At restaurants, your server just can't understand why you wouldn't want good water to go with your good food. It's customary and never expensive to order a *litro* or *mezzo litro* (half-liter) of bottled water. *Acqua leggermente effervescente* (lightly carbonated water) is a meal-time favorite. Or simply ask for *con gas* if you want fizzy water and *senza gas* if you prefer still water. You can ask for *acqua del rubinetto* (tap water) in restaurants, but your server may give you a funny look. Chilled bottled water—still *(naturale)* or carbonated *(frizzante)*—is sold cheap in stores. Half-liter mineral-water bottles are available everywhere for about €1. (I refill my water bottle with tap water.)

Juice is *succo,* and *spremuta* means freshly squeezed. Order *una spremuta* (don't confuse it with *spumante,* sparkling wine)—it's usually orange juice *(arancia),* and from February through April it's almost always made from blood oranges *(arance rosse).*

In grocery stores, you can get a liter of O.J. for the price of a Coke or coffee. Look for *100% succo* or *senza zucchero* (without sugar) on the label—or be surprised by something diluted and sugary sweet. Hang on to your water bottles. Buy juice in cheap liter boxes, then drink some and store the extra in your water bottle.

Tè freddo (iced tea) is usually from a can—sweetened and flavored with lemon or peach. Lemonade is *limonata.*

Coffee and Other Hot Drinks

The espresso-based style of coffee so popular in the US was born in Italy. If you ask for *"un caffè,"* you'll get a shot of espresso in a little cup—the closest thing to American-style drip coffee is a *caffè americano.* Most Italian coffee drinks begin with espresso, to which they add varying amounts of hot water and/or steamed or foamed milk. Milky drinks, like cappuccino or *caffè latte,* are served to locals before noon and to tourists any time of day (to an Italian, cappuccino is a morning drink; they believe having milk after a big meal or anything with tomato sauce impairs digestion). If they add any milk after lunch, it's just a splash, in a *caffè macchiato.* Italians like their coffee only warm—to get it very hot, request *"Molto caldo, per favore"* (MOHL-toh KAHL-doh pehr fah-VOH-ray). Any coffee drink is available decaffeinated—ask for it *decaffeinato* (deh-kah-feh-NAH-toh). *Cioccolato* is hot chocolate. *Tè* is hot tea.

Experiment with a few of the options:

Cappuccino: Espresso with foamed milk on top (*cappuccino freddo* is iced cappuccino).

Caffè latte: Espresso mixed with hot milk, no foam, in a tall glass (ordering just a "latte" gets you only milk).

Caffè macchiato: Espresso "marked" with a splash of milk, in a small cup.

Latte macchiato: Layers of hot milk and foam, "marked" by an espresso shot, in a tall glass. Note that if you order simply a *"macchiato,"* you'll probably get a *caffè macchiato.*

Caffè corto/lungo: Concentrated espresso diluted with a tiny bit of hot water, in a small cup.

Caffè americano: Espresso diluted with even more hot water, in a larger cup.

Caffè corretto: Espresso "corrected" with a shot of liqueur (normally *grappa, amaro,* or *sambuca*).

Marocchino: "Moroccan" coffee with espresso, foamed milk, and cocoa powder; the similar *mocaccino* has chocolate instead of cocoa.

Caffè freddo: Sweet and iced espresso.

Caffè hag: Instant decaf.

Alcoholic Beverages

Beer: While Italy is traditionally considered wine country, in recent years there's been a huge and passionate growth in the production of craft beer *(birra artigianale)*. Even in small towns, you'll see microbreweries slinging their own brews. You'll also find local brews (Peroni and Moretti), as well as imports such as Heineken. Italians drink mainly lager beers. Beer on tap is *alla spina*. Get it *piccola* (33 cl, 11 oz), *media* (50 cl, about a pint), or *grande* (a liter). A *lattina* (lah-TEE-nah) is a can and a *bottiglia* (boh-TEEL-yah) is a bottle.

Cocktails and Spirits: Italians appreciate both *aperitivi* (palate-stimulating cocktails) and *digestivi* (after-dinner drinks designed to aid digestion). Popular *aperitivo* options include Campari (dark-colored bitters with herbs and orange peel), Americano (vermouth with bitters, brandy, and lemon peel), Cynar (bitters flavored with artichoke), and Punt e Mes (sweet red vermouth and red wine). Widely used vermouth brands include Cinzano and Martini.

Digestivo choices are usually either a strong herbal bitters or something sweet. Many restaurants have their own secret recipe for a bittersweet herbal brew called *amaro;* popular commercial brands are Fernet Branca and Montenegro. If your tastes run sweeter, try *amaretto* (almond-flavored liqueur), Frangelico (hazelnut liqueur), *limoncello* (lemon liqueur), *nocino* (dark, sweet walnut liqueur), and *sambuca* (syrupy, anise-flavored liqueur; *con moscha* adds "flies"— three coffee beans). *Grappa* is a brandy distilled from grape skins and stems; *stravecchio* is an aged, mellower variation.

Wine: The ancient Greeks who colonized Italy more than 2,000 years ago called it Oenotria—land of the grape. Centuries later, Galileo wrote, "Wine is light held together by water." Wine *(vino)* is certainly a part of the Italian culinary trinity—grape, olive, and wheat. (I'd add gelato.) Ideal conditions for grapes (warm climate, well-draining soil, and an abundance of hillsides) make the Italian peninsula a paradise for grape

growers, winemakers, and wine drinkers. For regional wines produced in Tuscany, see the sidebar on page 290.

Ordering Wine

To order a glass of red or white wine, say, *"Un bicchiere di vino rosso/bianco."* House wine comes in a carafe; choose from a quarter-liter pitcher (8.5 oz, *un quarto*), half-liter pitcher (17 oz, *un mezzo*), or one-liter pitcher (34 oz, *un litro*). When ordering, have some fun, gesture like a local, and you'll have no problems speaking the language of the *enoteca. Salute!*

English	Italian
wine	*vino* (VEE-noh)
house wine	*vino della casa* (VEE-noh DEH-lah KAH-zah)
glass	*bicchiere* (bee-kee-EH-ree)
bottle	*bottiglia* (boh-TEEL-yah)
carafe	*caraffa* (kah-RAH-fah)
red	*rosso* (ROH-soh)
white	*bianco* (bee-AHN-koh)
rosé	*rosato* (roh-ZAH-toh)
sparkling	*spumante/frizzante* (spoo-MAHN-tay/freed-ZAHN-tay)
dry	*secco* (SEH-koh)
earthy	*terroso* (teh-ROH-zoh)
elegant	*elegante* (eh-leh-GAHN-tay)
fruity	*fruttato* (froo-TAH-toh)
full-bodied	*corposo/pieno* (kor-POH-zoh/pee-EH-noh)
mature	*maturo* (mah-TOO-roh)
sweet	*dolce* (DOHL-chay)
tannic	*tannico* (TAH-nee-koh)
young	*giovane* (JOH-vah-nay)

Even if you're clueless about wine, the information on an Italian wine label can help you choose something decent. Terms you may see on the bottle include *classico* (from a defined, select area), *annata* (year of harvest), *vendemmia* (harvest), and *imbottigliato dal produttore all'origine* (bottled by producers). To figure out what you like—and what suits your pocketbook—visit an *enoteca* (wine bar) and sample wines side by side. For tips on ordering wine, see the sidebar.

In general, Italy designates its wines by one of four official categories:

Vino da Tavola (VDT) is table wine, the lowest grade, made from grapes grown anywhere in Italy. It's often inexpensive, but Italy's wines are so good that, for many people, a basic *vino da tavola* is just fine with a meal. Many restaurants, even modest ones, take pride in their house wine *(vino della casa)*, bottling their own or working with wineries.

Denominazione di Origine Controllata (DOC) meets national

standards for high-quality wine. Made from grapes grown in a defined area, it's usually quite affordable and can be surprisingly good. Hundreds of wines have earned the DOC designation. In Tuscany, for example, many such wines come from the Chianti region, located between Florence and Siena.

Denominazione di Origine Controllata e Guarantita (DOCG), the highest grade, meets national standards for the highest-quality wine (made with grapes from a defined area whose quality is "guaranteed"). These wines can be identified by the pink or green label on the neck...and the scary price tag on the shelf. Only a limited number of wines in Italy can be called DOCG. They're generally a good bet if you want a quality wine, but you don't know anything else about the winemaker. (*Riserva* indicates a DOC or DOCG wine matured for a longer, more specific time.)

Indicazione Geographica Tipica (IGT) is a broad group of wines that range from basic to some of Italy's best. These wines don't follow the strict "recipe" required for DOC or DOCG status, but give local vintners creative license. This category includes the Super Tuscans—wines made from a mix of international grapes (such as cabernet sauvignon) grown in Tuscany and aged in small oak barrels for only two years. The result is a lively full-bodied wine that dances all over your head...and is worth the steep price for aficionados.

Staying Connected

One of the most common questions I hear from travelers is, "How can I stay connected in Europe?" The short answer is: more easily and cheaply than you might think.

The simplest solution is to bring your own device—mobile phone, tablet, or laptop—and use it just as you would at home (following the tips below, such as connecting to free Wi-Fi whenever possible). Another option is to buy a European SIM card for your mobile phone—either your US phone or one you buy in Europe. Or you can use European landlines and computers to connect. Each of these options is described below; and more details at www.ricksteves.com/phoning. For a very practical one-hour talk covering tech issues for travelers, see www.ricksteves.com/travel-talks.

USING A MOBILE PHONE IN EUROPE

Here are some budget tips and options.

Sign up for an international plan. Using your cellular network in Europe on a pay-as-you-go basis can add up (about $1.70/minute for voice calls, 50 cents to send text messages, 5 cents to receive them, and $10 to download one megabyte of data). To stay connected at a lower cost, sign up for an international service plan

Hurdling the Language Barrier

Many Italians—especially those in the tourist trade and in big cities—speak English. Still, you'll get better treatment if you learn and use Italian pleasantries. In smaller, non-touristy towns, Italian is the norm. Italians have an endearing habit of talking to you even if they know you don't speak their language—and yet, thanks to gestures and thoughtfully simplified words, it somehow works. Don't stop them to tell them you don't understand every word—just go along for the ride. For a list of survival phrases, see the appendix.

Note that Italian is pronounced much like English, with a few exceptions, such as: *c* followed by *e* or *i* is pronounced ch (to ask, *"Per centro?"*—To the center?—you say, pehr CHEHN-troh). In Italian, *ch* is pronounced like the hard c in Chianti (*chiesa*—church—is pronounced kee-AY-zah). Adding a vowel to the English word often gets you close to the Italian one. Give it your best shot. Italians appreciate your efforts.

through your carrier. Most providers offer a simple bundle that includes calling, messaging, and data. Your normal plan may already include international coverage (T-Mobile's does).

Before your trip, call your provider or check online to confirm that your phone will work in Europe, and research your provider's international rates. Activate the plan a day or two before you leave, then remember to cancel it when your trip's over.

Use free Wi-Fi whenever possible. Unless you have an unlimited-data plan, you're best off saving most of your online tasks for Wi-Fi. You can access the Internet, send texts, and even make voice calls over Wi-Fi.

Most accommodations in Europe offer free Wi-Fi, but some—especially expensive hotels—charge a fee. Many cafés (including Starbucks and McDonald's) have free hotspots for customers; look for signs offering it and ask for the Wi-Fi password when you buy something. You'll also often find Wi-Fi at TIs, city squares, major museums, public-transit hubs, airports, highway rest stops (Autogrills), and aboard trains and buses.

You can access municipal hotspots throughout Italy, including in Rome, Florence, Venice, Pisa, and Livorno, by registering (once) for "Free ItaliaWiFi" at www.freeitaliawifi.it, which lists network names for each location. A credit-card number is required (but you won't be charged, and your card number will not be saved). After creating a user name and password, you'll get two hours of free access per day.

Minimize the use of your cellular network. Even with an international data plan, wait until you're on Wi-Fi to Skype, download apps, stream videos, or do other megabyte-greedy tasks. Using

How to Dial

International Calls

Whether phoning from a US landline or mobile phone, or from a number in another European country, here's how to make an international call. I've used one of my recommended Florence hotels as an example (tel. 055-213-154).

Initial Zero: Drop the initial zero from international phone numbers—except when calling Italy.

Mobile Tip: If using a mobile phone, the "+" sign can replace the international access code (for a "+" sign, press and hold "0").

US/Canada to Europe

Dial 011 (US/Canada international access code), country code (39 for Italy), and phone number.

▶ To call the Florence hotel from home, dial 011-39-055-213-154.

Country to Country Within Europe

Dial 00 (Europe international access code), country code, and phone number.

▶ To call the Florence hotel from Germany, dial 00-39-055-213-154.

Europe to the US/Canada

Dial 00, country code (1 for US/Canada), and phone number.

▶ To call from Europe to my office in Edmonds, Washington, dial 00-1-425-771-8303.

Domestic Calls

To call within Italy (from one Italian landline or mobile phone to another), simply dial the phone number, including the initial 0 if there is one.

▶ To call the Florence hotel from Rome, dial 055-213-154.

More Dialing Tips

Italian Phone Numbers: Italian phone numbers vary in length; a hotel can have, say, an eight-digit phone number and a nine-digit fax number. Italy's landlines start with 0; mobile lines start with 3 and cost substantially more to dial.

a navigation app such as Google Maps over a cellular network can take lots of data, so do this sparingly or use it offline.

Limit automatic updates. By default, your device constantly checks for a data connection and updates apps. It's smart to disable these features so your apps will only update when you're on Wi-Fi, and to change your device's email settings from "auto-retrieve" to "manual" (or from "push" to "fetch").

When you need to get online but can't find Wi-Fi, simply turn on your cellular network just long enough for the task at hand.

Toll and Toll-Free Calls: Italy's toll-free lines, called *numero verde* (green number), begin with 800 or 803. They can be dialed free from Italian phones without using a phone card but don't work from the US. Any Italian phone number that starts with 8 but isn't followed by a 0 is a toll call (generally costing €0.10-0.50/minute). International rates apply to US toll-free numbers dialed from Italy—they're not free.

More Phoning Help: See www.howtocallabroad.com.

European Country Codes		Ireland & N. Ireland	353 / 44
Austria	43	Italy	39
Belgium	32	Latvia	371
Bosnia-Herzegovina	387	Montenegro	382
Croatia	385	Morocco	212
Czech Republic	420	Netherlands	31
Denmark	45	Norway	47
Estonia	372	Poland	48
Finland	358	Portugal	351
France	33	Russia	7
Germany	49	Slovakia	421
Gibraltar	350	Slovenia	386
Great Britain	44	Spain	34
Greece	30	Sweden	46
Hungary	36	Switzerland	41
Iceland	354	Turkey	90

When you're done, avoid further charges by manually turning off data roaming or cellular data (either works) in your device's Settings menu. Another way to make sure you're not accidentally using data roaming is to put your device in "airplane" mode (which also disables phone calls and texts), and then turn your Wi-Fi back on as needed.

It's also a good idea to keep track of your data usage. On your device's menu, look for "cellular data usage" or "mobile data" and reset the counter at the start of your trip.

Use Wi-Fi calling and messaging apps. Skype, Viber, Face-Time, and Google+ Hangouts are great for making free or low-cost voice and video calls over Wi-Fi. With an app installed on your phone, tablet, or laptop, you can log on to a Wi-Fi network and contact friends or family members who use the same service. If you buy credit in advance, with some of these services you can call any mobile phone or landline worldwide for just pennies per minute.

Many of these apps also allow you to send messages over Wi-Fi to any other person using that app. Be aware that some apps, such as Apple's iMessage, will use the cellular network if Wi-Fi isn't available: To avoid this possibility, turn off the "Send as SMS" feature.

USING A EUROPEAN SIM CARD

With a European SIM card, you get a European mobile number and access to cheaper rates than you'll get through your US carrier. This option works well for those who want to make a lot of voice calls or need faster connection speeds than their US carrier provides. Fit the SIM card into a cheap phone you buy in Europe (about $40 from phone shops anywhere), or swap out the SIM card in an "unlocked" US phone (check with your carrier about unlocking it).

In Italy, tourists should buy SIM cards at mobile-phone shops. You'll be required to register the SIM card with your passport as an antiterrorism measure, which may mean you can't use the phone for the first hour or two. (You may see SIM cards sold at convenience stores and other shops, but these require an Italian Social Security number to activate.) Costing about $5-10, SIM cards usually include about that much prepaid calling credit, with no contract and no commitment. Expect to pay $20-40 more for a SIM card with a gigabyte of data. If you travel to other countries in the European Union, there are no extra roaming fees—your SIM card works just like it does in Italy.

The major mobile phone providers in Italy are Wind, TIM, Vodafone, and 3 ("Tre"). Certain SIM-card brands—including Lycamobile, which operates in multiple European countries and has an English version of its Italian website—are reliable and economical. Ask the clerk to help you insert your SIM card, set it up, and show you how to use it. Be sure to find out how to check your credit balance. When you run out of credit, you can top it up at newsstands, tobacco shops, mobile-phone stores, or many other businesses (look for your SIM card's logo in the window).

Tips on Internet Security

Make sure that your device is running the latest versions of its operating system, security software, and apps. Next, ensure that your device and key programs (like email) are password- or passcode-protected. On the road, use only secure, password-protected Wi-Fi hotspots. Ask the hotel or café staff for the specific name of their Wi-Fi network, and make sure you log on to that exact one.

If you must access your financial info online, use a banking app rather than accessing your account via a browser. A cellular connection is more secure than Wi-Fi. Avoid logging onto personal finance sites on a public computer.

Never share your credit-card number (or any other sensitive information) online unless you know that the site is secure. A secure site displays a little padlock icon, and the URL begins with *https* (instead of the usual *http*).

PUBLIC PHONES AND COMPUTERS

It's possible to travel in Europe without a mobile device. You can make calls from your hotel (or the increasingly rare public phone).

Most hotels charge a fee for placing calls—ask for rates before you dial. You can use a prepaid international phone card (*carta telefonica prepagata internazionale*, KAR-tah teh-leh-FOHN-ee-kah pray-pah-GAH-tah in-ter-naht-zee-oh-NAH-lay—available at post offices, newsstands, street kiosks, tobacco shops, and train stations) to call out from your hotel. Dial the toll-free access number, enter the card's PIN code, then dial the number.

You'll see **public pay phones** in a few Metro and train stations. The phones generally come with multilingual instructions and take coins and credit cards (as well as hard-to-find Telecom Italia phone cards, which may be sold at newsstands).

Most hotels have **public computers** in their lobbies for guests to use; otherwise you may find them at Internet cafés and public libraries (ask your hotelier or the TI for the nearest location). On a European keyboard, use the "Alt Gr" key to the right of the space bar to insert the extra symbol that appears on some keys. Italian keyboards are a little different from ours; to type an @ symbol, press the "Alt Gr" key and the key that shows the @ symbol. If you can't locate a special character, simply copy it from a Web page and paste it into your email message.

MAIL

You can mail one package per day to yourself worth up to $200 duty-free from Europe to the US (mark it "personal purchases"). If you're sending a gift to someone, mark it "unsolicited gift." For details, visit www.cbp.gov, select "Travel," and search for "Know Before You Go."

The Italian postal service works fine, but for quick transatlantic delivery (in either direction), consider services such as DHL (www.dhl.com).

Transportation

When deciding how to get between destinations in Europe, consider these factors: Cars are best for three or more traveling together (especially families with small kids), those packing heavy, and those delving into the countryside. Trains and buses are best for solo travelers, blitz tourists, city-to-city travelers, and those who don't want to drive in Europe. Intra-European flights are an increasingly inexpensive option. While a car gives you more freedom, trains and buses zip you effortlessly and scenically from city to city, usually dropping you in the center, often near a TI. Cars are an expensive headache in places like Florence, but if you want to stay in an out-of-the-way *agriturismo* and focus on isolated hill towns, having your own wheels will save you time and headaches.

If your itinerary mixes cities and countryside, arrange your car rental strategically: Wait to pick up your car until the last big city you visit, then use it for lacing together the hill towns and exploring the countryside. For more detailed information on transportation throughout Europe, including trains, buses, flying, renting a car, and driving, see www.ricksteves.com/transportation.

TRAINS

To travel by train affordably within Italy, you can simply buy tickets as you go, including online. For travelers ready to lock in dates and times weeks or months in advance, buying nonrefundable tickets online can cut costs in half. Note that the Italy rail pass is generally not a good value; but if your travel extends beyond Italy, there are various multicountry rail passes that might be worth checking into. For advice on figuring out the smartest train-ticket or rail-pass options for your trip, visit the Trains & Rail Passes section of my website at www.ricksteves.com/rail.

Types of Trains

Most trains in Italy are operated by the state-run **Trenitalia** company (www.trenitalia.com, a.k.a. Ferrovie dello Stato Italiane, abbreviated FS or FSI). Since ticket prices depend on the speed of the train, it helps to

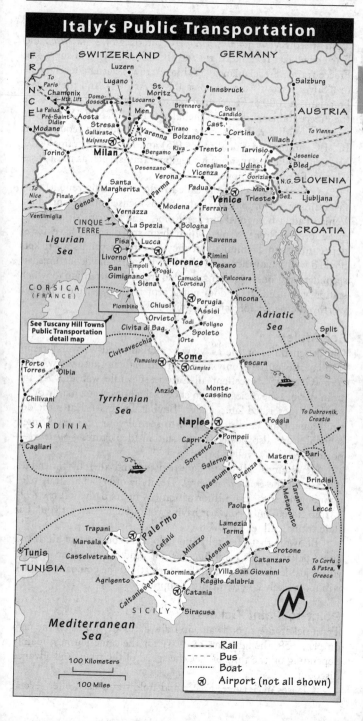

Italy's Public Transportation

SWITZERLAND GERMANY

FRANCE

Luzern
To Paris
Chamonix · Mtn. Lift
La Palud
Pré-Saint
Didier
Modane
Torino

Lugano
St. Moritz
Locarno
Domo- dossola
Men.
Stresa
Gallarate
Malpensa ⊗
Como
Bergamo
Santa Margherita
Desenzano
Finale
Genoa
Vernazza
La Spezia

Innsbruck
Salzburg
Brennero
San Candido
Cast.
Tirano
Bolzano
Riva
Trento
Conegliano
Vicenza
Padua
Ferrara
Bologna

AUSTRIA
To Vienna →
Villach
Jesenice
Bled
Tarvisio
Udine
Gorizia
Mon.
Trieste
Sez.
Ljubljana

N.G. SLOVENIA

CROATIA

Ligurian Sea

CINQUE TERRE →

Ventimiglia
To Nice

CORSICA (FRANCE)

See Tuscany Hill Towns Public Transportation detail map

Pisa
Lucca
Livorno ⊗
Florence ⊗
San Gimignano
Empoli
Pogg.
Siena
Chiusi
Piombino

Ravenna
Rimini
Pesaro
Falconara
Ancona

Adriatic Sea

Camucia (Cortona)
Perugia ⊗
Assisi
Todi
Foligno
Spoleto

Civita di Bag.
Orvieto
Orte

Split

Civitavecchia
Fiumicino ⊗
Rome
Ciampino ⊗
Pescara
To Dubrovnik, Croatia →

Anzio
Monte-cassino

PortoTorres
Olbia
Chilivani

Tyrrhenian Sea

SARDINIA

Cagliari

Naples ⊗
Capri
Pompeii
Sorrento
Salerno
Paestum
Potenza
Paola
Metaponto

Foggia
Matera
Bari
Brindisi
Lecce

To Corfu & Patra, Greece →

Tunis

TUNISIA

Trapani
Marsala
Castelvetrano
Agrigento
Caltanissetta

Palermo ⊗
Cefalù
Milazzo
Messina
Taormina
Villa San Giovanni
Reggio Calabria
Catania ⊗
Siracusa

Lamezia Terme
Crotone
Catanzaro

Mediterranean Sea

SICILY

Legend:
— · — Rail
- - - Bus
· · · · Boat
⊗ Airport (not all shown)

100 Kilometers
100 Miles

know the different types of trains: pokey R or REG *(regionali)*; medium-speed RV *(regionali veloce)*, IR (InterRegio), D *(diretto)*, and E *(espresso)*; fast IC (InterCity) and EC (EuroCity); and super-fast Frecce trains: Frecciabianca ("White Arrow"), faster Frecciargento ("Silver Arrow"), Frecciarossa ("Red Arrow"), and the newest Frecciarossa 1000 or Freccemille (up to 225 mph). You may also see the Frecce trains marked on schedules as ES, AV, or EAV. If you're traveling with a rail pass, note that reservations are required for IC, EC, and international trains (€5) and for Frecce trains (€10). You can't make reservations for regional trains, such as most Pisa-Cinque Terre connections.

A private train company called **Italo** (www.italotreno.it) runs fast trains on major routes in Italy. Italo is focused on two corridors: Venice-Padua-Bologna-Florence-Rome and Turin-Milan-Bologna-Florence-Rome-Naples. Their high-speed trains have fewer departures than Trenitalia, but they do offer discounts for tickets booked well in advance. In Milan and Rome, some departures use secondary stations—if taking an Italo train, pay attention to which station you need. Italo does not accept rail passes, but they're a worthy alternative for point-to-point tickets.

Schedules

Check schedules online at www.trenitalia.it and www.italotreno.it (domestic journeys only); for international trips, use www.bahn.com (Germany's excellent all-Europe schedule website). At the train station, the easiest way to check schedules is at a handy ticket machine (described later, under "Buying Tickets"). Enter the desired date, time, and destination to see all your options. Printed schedules are also posted at the station (departures—*partenze*—posters are always yellow).

Newsstands sell up-to-date regional and all-Italy timetables (€5, ask for the *orario ferroviaro*). Trenitalia offers an all-Italy telephone number for train information (24 hours daily, toll tel. 892-021, in Italian only, consider having your hotelier call for you). For Italo trains, call tel. 06-0708.

Be aware that Trenitalia and Italo don't cooperate at all. If you buy a ticket for one train line, it's not valid on the other. Even if you're just looking for schedule information, the company you ask will most likely ignore the other's options.

Point-to-Point Tickets

Train tickets are a good value in Italy. Fares are shown on the map on page 659, though fares can vary for the same journey, mainly depending on the time of day, the speed of the train, and advance discounts.

Classes of Service: Frecce and Italo trains each offer several

Deciphering Italian Train Schedules

At the station, look for the big yellow posters labeled *Parten-ze—Departures* (white posters show arrivals). Departures are

listed chronologically, hour by hour, showing the trains leaving the station throughout the day.

Reading from the left, the schedule lists the time of departure *(ora)*, the type of train *(treni)*, and service classes offered *(classi servizi)*—first- and second-class cars, dining car, *cuccetta* berths, and, more important, whether you need reservations (usually denoted by an R in a box). All Frecce trains, many EuroCity (EC) and InterCity (IC) trains, and most international trains require reservations.

The next column lists the train's destination *(principali fermate destinazioni)*, often showing intermediate stops (with arrival times in parentheses). Note that your destination may be listed in fine print as an intermediate stop. For example, if you're going from Florence to Cortona, scan the schedule and you'll notice that many trains that terminate in Rome stop in Cortona en route (and fast trains stop in Terontola, near Cortona). Travelers who read the fine print end up with a far greater choice of trains. You may also see pertinent notes about the train, such as "also stops in..." *(ferma anche a...)*, "doesn't stop in..." *(non ferma a...)*, "stops in every station" *(ferma in tutte le stazioni)*, "delayed..." *(ritardo...)*, and so on.

The last column gives the track *(binario)* the train departs from. Confirm the *binario* with a ticket seller or railway official, the electronic board that lists immediate departures, or monitors on the platform.

For any odd symbols on the poster, look at the key at the end. Some phrasing can be deciphered easily, such as *servizio periodico* (periodic service—doesn't always run). For the trickier ones, ask a local or railway official, or try your *Rick Steves Italian Phrase Book & Dictionary.*

You can also check schedules for trains anywhere in Italy at ticket machines. Enter the date and time of your departure (to or from any Italian station), and view all your options.

Open or Non-Reserved Ticket—Need to Validate

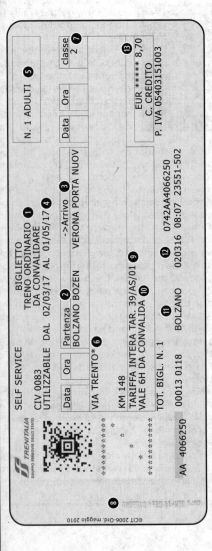

1 Open ticket for non-express train, must be validated

2 Point of departure

3 Destination

4 Period in which ticket is valid

5 Number of passengers

6 Route

7 Class of travel (1st or 2nd)

8 Validation stamp

9 Full fare for non-express train

10 Ticket good for 1 trip within 6 hours after validation

11 Location of ticket sale

12 Date of ticket purchase

13 Ticket cost

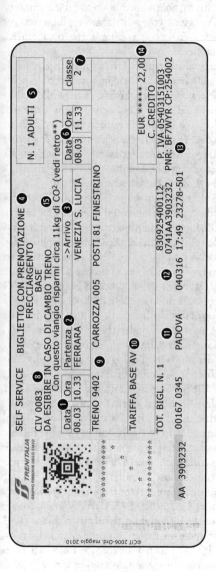

1. Departure date & time
2. Point of departure
3. Destination
4. "Ticket with reservation"
5. Number of passengers
6. Arrival date & time
7. Class of travel (1st or 2nd)
8. "Present to official if changing trains"
9. Train, car & seat numbers (finestrino=window seat)
10. Fast-train fare
11. Location of ticket sale
12. Date of ticket purchase
13. Booking ID
14. Ticket cost
15. Amount of CO_2 usage reduced by this train trip

classes of service where all seats are reserved: Standard, Premium, Business, or Executive on Frecciarossa; Smart, Comfort, Prima, or Club Executive on Italo. Other trains offer standard first- and second-class seating (with first class costing up to 50 percent more than second). Buying up gives you a little more elbow room, a snack, or perhaps a better chance at seating a group together, if you're buying on short notice.

Advance Discounts: Ticket price levels for both companies are Base (full fare, easily changeable or partly refundable before scheduled departure), Economy (one schedule change allowed before departure, for a fee), and Super Economy or Low Cost (sells out quickly, no refund or exchange). Discounted fares typically sell out several days before departure. Fares labeled *servizi abbonati* are available only for locals with monthly passes—not tourists. Regional trains don't offer advance discounts or seat assignments, so there's little need to buy those tickets in advance.

Speed vs. Savings: For point-to-point tickets, you'll pay more the faster you go. Spending a modest amount of extra time in transit can save money. On longer, mainline routes, fast trains save more time and provide most of the service. For example, speedy Florence-Rome trains run hourly, cost €47 in second class, and make the trip in 1.5 hours. To make the same trip, infrequent InterCity trains (only 1-2/day) cost €35 and take 3 hours, while Regionale Veloce trains cost €21 and take about 4 hours.

Age-Based Discounts: Families with young children can get price breaks—kids ages 4 and under travel free; ages 4-11 at half-price. When booking online, be sure to confirm the exact age ranges that qualify for discounts by clicking on the info links. With the "Offerta Familia" discount, families of three to five people with at least one kid (under 12) get 50 percent off the child fare and 20 percent off the adult fare. The deal doesn't apply to all trains at all times, but it's worth checking out. You may also see a "Bimbi Gratis" offer: One child age 5–15 free per adult paying the full base fare. If buying tickets at a counter, ask for the "Offerta Familia" deal (or, at a ticket machine, choose "Yes" at the "Do you want ticket issue?" prompt, then choose "Familia").

Discounts for youths and seniors require purchase of a separate card (Carta Verde for ages 12-26 costs €40; Carta Argento for ages 60 and over is €30), but the discount on tickets is so minor (10-15 percent respectively for domestic travel), it's not worth it for most.

Buying Tickets: It's easy to buy tickets for **domestic travel** online at www.trenitalia.com or www.italotreno.it. On either website, choose English and be sure to read the pricing info, as many of the cheaper tickets are not refundable or changeable. You can keep the ticket on your mobile device (either as a PDF or in a "ticketless" format with a booking code), or you can print it out.

If you instead go to the train station to buy your ticket, avoid ticket-office lines whenever possible by using the ticket machines in station halls. Pay all ticket costs in the station before you board, or you'll pay a penalty on the train. You'll be able to easily purchase tickets for travel within Italy, make seat reservations, and even book a *cuccetta* (koo-CHEH-tah; overnight berth). If you do use the ticket windows (e.g., to buy international tickets), be sure you're in the correct line. Key terms: *biglietti* (general tickets), *prenotazioni* (reservations), *nazionali* (domestic), and *internazionali*.

Trenitalia's ticket machines (new ones are red, old ones are green-and-white; marked *Trenitalia/Biglietti*) are user-friendly and found in all but the tiniest stations in Italy. You can pay with cash (change given when indicated) or by debit or credit card (even for small amounts, but you may need to enter your PIN). Select English, then your destination. If you don't immediately see the city you're traveling to, keep keying in the spelling until it's listed. You can choose from first- and second-class seats, request tickets for more than one traveler, and (on the high-speed Frecce trains) choose an aisle or window seat. Don't select a discount rate without being sure that you meet the criteria (for example, Americans are not eligible for certain EU or resident discounts). Rail-pass holders can use the machines to make seat reservations. If you need to validate your ticket, you can do it in the same machine if you're boarding your train right away.

For longer-haul runs, it can be cheaper to buy Trenitalia tickets in advance. Because most Italian trains run frequently and there's no deadline to buy tickets, you can keep your travel plans flexible by purchasing tickets as you go. (You can buy tickets for several trips at one station when you are ready to commit.) For busy weekend or holiday travel, however, it can be a good idea to buy tickets in advance.

To buy tickets at the station for **Italo** trains, look for a dedicated service counter (in most major stations) or a red ticket machine labeled *Italo*.

Most **international tickets** can't be bought online or from machines; for these tickets and anything else that requires a real person, you must go to a ticket window at the station. A good alternative, though, is to drop by a local travel agency. Agencies sell domestic and international tickets and make reservations. They charge a small fee, but the language barrier (and the lines) can be smaller than at the station's ticket windows.

Validating Tickets: If your ticket includes a seat reservation on a specific train *(biglietto con prenotazione)*, you're all set and can just get on board. An open ticket with no seat reservation (generally for a *regionali* train) must always be validated. Before you board, stamp your ticket (it may say *da convalidare* or *convalida*) in the machine near the platform (usually marked *convalida biglietti* or *vidimazione)*. Once you validate a ticket, you must complete your trip within the timeframe shown on the ticket. If you forget to validate your ticket, go right away to the train conductor—before he comes to you—or you'll pay a fine. Note that you don't need to validate a rail pass each time you board (after it's been activated at a ticket window, you write in each travel date as you go).

Tickets purchased online are prevalidated, meaning that they can be used only for the date and time that you select (or within a four-hour window for unreserved regional trains).

Rail Passes

The single-country Eurail Italy Pass may save you money if you take several long train rides or prefer first-class travel, but for most people it's not a good value. Most train travelers in Italy take relatively short rides on the Milan-Venice-Florence-Rome circuit. For these trips, it can be cheaper to buy point-to-point tickets instead. Remember that rail passes are valid only on the Italian state railway, not on Italo-brand trains.

Furthermore, a rail pass doesn't offer much hop-on convenience in Italy, since many trains, such as Le Frecce, EuroCity, and InterCity, require paid seat reservations (€5-10 each). Most regional trains (such as Florence-Pisa-Cinque Terre service) don't require (or offer) reservations. Reservations for berths on overnight trains cost extra and aren't covered by rail passes. All Eurail passes allow up to two kids (ages 4-11) to travel free with an adult.

The Eurail Select Pass allows you to travel in two to four adjacent countries directly connected by rail or ferry. For instance, you could choose a four-country pass for France-Switzerland-Italy-Greece or Benelux-Germany-Austria-Italy. A two-country version could cover France and Italy, Switzerland and Italy, Austria and Italy, Greece and Italy, or even Spain and Italy (assuming you fly or take a ferry in between).

For more detailed advice on figuring out the smartest rail-pass options for your train trip, visit www.ricksteves.com/rail.

Train Tips

Seat Reservations: Trains can fill up, even in first class. If you're on a tight schedule, you'll want to reserve a few days ahead for fast trains (see "Types of Trains," earlier). Purchasing tickets or passholder reservations onboard a train comes with a nasty penalty. Buying them at the station can be a time waster unless you use the ticket machines.

If you're taking an unreserved *regionali* train that originates at your departure point (e.g., you're catching the Florence-Pisa train

Rail Passes and Train Travel in Italy

A Eurail **Italy Pass** lets you travel by train in Italy for three to eight days (consecutively or not) within a one-month period. Discounted rates are offered for two or more people traveling together. Italy can also be included in a Eurail **Select Pass,** which allows travel in two to four neighboring countries over two months, and it's covered (along with most of Europe) by the classic Eurail **Global Pass.**

Rail passes are sold only outside Europe (through travel agents or Rick Steves' Europe). For more on the ins and outs of rail passes, including prices, download my **free guide to Eurail Passes** (www.ricksteves.com/rail-guide) or go to www.ricksteves.com/rail.

If you're taking just a couple of train rides, look into buying

individual **point-to-point tickets,** which may save you money over a pass. Use this map to add up approximate pay-as-you-go fares for your itinerary, and compare that to the price of a rail pass. Keep in mind that significant discounts on point-to-point tickets may be available with advance purchase.

Map shows approximate costs, in US$, for one-way, second-class tickets on faster trains

in Florence or a direct Rome-Assisi train in Assisi), arriving at least 15 minutes before the departure time will help you snare a seat.

On the platforms of some major stations, posters showing the train composition *(composizione principali treni)* indicate where first- and second-class cars will line up when the trains arrive (letters on the poster are supposed to correspond to letters posted over the platform—but they don't always). Other stations may post the order of the cars on video screens along the track shortly before the train arrives. Since most trains now allow you to make reservations up to the time of departure, conductors post a list of the reservable and nonreservable seat rows (sometimes in English) in each train car's vestibule. This means that if you board a crowded train and get one of the last seats, you may be ousted when the reservation holder comes along.

Baggage Storage: Many Italian stations have *deposito bagagli* where you can safely leave your bag for a standardized but rather steep price (€6/5 hours, €12/12 hours, €17/24 hours, payable when you pick up the bag, double-check closing hours; they may ask to photocopy your passport). Because of security concerns, no Italian stations have lockers.

Theft Concerns: In big cities, exercise caution and prudence at train stations to avoid thieves and con artists. Homeless and marginalized people lurk around the station trying to skim tips (or worse) from unsuspecting tourists. If someone helps you to find your train or carry your bags, be aware that they are not an official porter; they are simply hoping for some cash. And if someone other than a uniformed railway employee tries to help you use the ticket machines, politely refuse.

Italian trains are famous for their thieves. Never leave a bag unattended. Police do ride the trains, cutting down on theft. Still, for an overnight trip, I'd feel safe only in a *cuccetta* (a bunk in a special sleeping car with an attendant who keeps track of who comes and goes while you sleep—approximately €20 in a six-bed compartment, €25 in a less-cramped four-bed compartment, €50 in a more private, double compartment).

Strikes: Strikes, which are common, generally last a day (often a Friday). Train employees will simply explain, *"Sciopero"* (strike). But in actuality, a minimum amount of "essential" mainline service is maintained (by law) during strikes. When a strike is pending, travel agencies (and hoteliers) can check to see when the strike goes into effect and which trains will continue to run. Revised schedules may be posted online and in Italian at stations, and station personnel still working can often tell you what trains are expected to run. If I need to get somewhere and know a strike is imminent, I leave early (before the strike, which often begins at 9:00), or I just go to the station with extra patience in tow and hop on anything rolling in the direction I want to go. See www.trenitalia.com, choose English, then "Information and Contacts," and then "In Case of Strike."

BUSES

You can usually get anywhere you want to in Italy by bus, as long as you're not in a hurry and plan ahead using bus schedules (pick

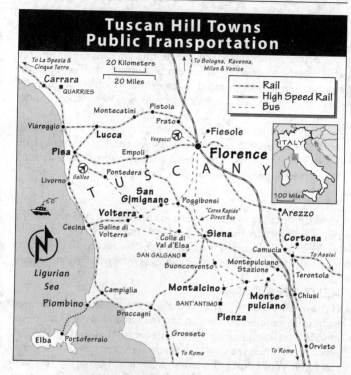

up at local TIs). For reaching small towns, buses are sometimes the only option if you don't have a car. In many hill towns, trains leave you at a station in the valley far below, while buses more likely drop you right into the thick of things. (If the bus stop or station is below town, sometimes an escalator or elevator helps get you up into town.)

Long-distance buses are catching on in Italy as an alternative to the train. They are usually cheaper, modern, and often (unlike trains) have free Wi-Fi. They're especially useful on routes poorly served by train. Some of the operators you'll see are Eurolines/Baltour (www.baltour.it), Megabus (www.megabus.com), Flixbus (www.flixbus.com), and Marozzi (www.marozzivt.it). In general, orange buses are local city buses, and blue buses are for long-distances.

Larger towns have a (usually chaotic) long-distance bus station *(stazione degli autobus)*, with ticket windows and several stalls (usually labeled *corsia, stallo,* or *binario)*—but to save time, buy your ticket at a travel agent or online, and print it out. Smaller towns—where buses are more useful—often have a central bus stop *(fermata),* likely along the main road or on the main square, and maybe several more scattered around town. In small towns, buy bus tickets at newsstands or tobacco shops (with the big *T* signs). When buying your ticket, confirm the departure point *("Dov'è la fermata?")*.

Before boarding, confirm the destination with the driver. You are expected to stow big backpacks underneath the bus (open the luggage compartment yourself if it's closed). Upon arrival, double-check that the posted schedule lists your next destination and departure time.

Sundays and holidays are problematic; even from large cities, schedules are sparse, departing buses are jam-packed, and ticket offices are often closed. Plan ahead and buy your ticket in advance. Most travel agencies book bus (and train) tickets for a small fee.

TAXIS

Most European taxis are reliable and cheap. In many cities, couples can travel short distances by cab for little more than two bus or subway tickets. Taxis can be your best option for getting to the airport for an early morning flight or to connect two far-flung destinations.

RENTING A CAR

If you're renting a car in Italy, bring your driver's license. You're also technically required to have an International Driving Permit—an official translation of your driver's license (sold at your local AAA office for $20 plus the cost of two passport-type photos; see www.aaa.com). While that's the letter of the law, I generally rent cars without having this permit. How this is enforced varies from country to country: Get advice from your car-rental company.

Rental companies require you to be at least 21 years old and to have held your license for one year. Drivers under age 25 may incur a young-driver surcharge, and some rental companies do not rent to anyone 75 or older. If you're considered too young or old, look into leasing (covered later), which has less-stringent age restrictions.

Research car rentals before you go. It's cheaper to arrange most car rentals from the US. Consider several companies to compare rates.

Most of the major US rental agencies (including Avis, Budget, Enterprise, Hertz, and Thrifty) have offices throughout Europe. Also consider the two major Europe-based agencies, Europcar and Sixt. It can be cheaper to use a consolidator, such as Auto Europe/Kemwel (www.autoeurope.com—or the often cheaper www.autoeurope.eu) or Europe by Car (www.europebycar.com), which compares rates at several companies to get you the best deal—but because you're working with a middleman, it's especially important to ask in advance about add-on fees and restrictions.

Always read the fine print or query the agent carefully for add-on charges—such as one-way drop-off fees, airport surcharges, or mandatory insurance policies—that aren't included in the "total price."

For the best deal, rent by the week with unlimited mileage. To save money on fuel, request a diesel car. I normally rent the smallest, least-expensive model with a stick shift (generally cheaper than an automatic). Almost all rentals are manual by default, so if you need an automatic, request one in advance; be aware that these cars are usually larger models (not as maneuverable when dealing with tight parking spaces and narrow, winding roads). You'll do yourself a favor by renting the smallest car that meets your needs.

Figure on paying roughly $250 for a one-week rental. Allow extra for supplemental insurance, fuel, tolls, and parking.

Picking Up Your Car: Compare pickup costs (downtown can be less expensive than the airport) and explore drop-off options. Always check the hours of the location you choose: Many rental offices close from midday Saturday until Monday morning and, in smaller towns, at lunchtime.

When selecting a location, don't trust the agency's description of "downtown" or "city center." In some cases, a "downtown" branch can be on the outskirts of the city—a long, costly taxi ride from the center. Before choosing, plug the addresses into a mapping website. You may find that the "train station" location is handier. Returning a car at a big-city train station or downtown agency can be tricky; get precise details on the car drop-off location and hours, and allow ample time to find it. And be aware that most Italian cities have a "ZTL" (limited traffic zone) that's carefully monitored by cameras. If your drop-off point is near this zone, get clear directions on how to get there without crossing the line and getting a big fine.

When you pick up the rental car, check it thoroughly and make sure any damage is noted on your rental agreement. Rental agencies in Europe tend to charge for even minor damage, so be sure to mark everything. Before driving off, find out how your car's gearshift, lights, turn signals, wipers, radio, and fuel cap function, and know what kind of fuel the car takes (diesel vs. unleaded). When you return the car, make sure the agent verifies its condition with you. Some drivers take pictures of the returned vehicle as proof of its condition.

Car Insurance Options

Accidents can happen anywhere, but when you're on vacation, the last thing you need is stress over car insurance. When you rent a car, you're liable for a very high deductible, sometimes equal to the entire value of the car. Limit your financial risk in case of an accident by choosing one of these two options: Buy Collision Damage Waiver (CDW) coverage from the car-rental company (figure roughly 30-40 percent extra), or get coverage through your credit card (free, but more complicated).

In Italy, most car-rental companies' rates automatically include CDW coverage. Even if you try to decline CDW when you reserve your Italian car, you may find when you show up at the counter that you must buy it after all.

While each rental company has its own variation, basic CDW costs $15-30 a day and reduces your liability, but does not eliminate it. When you pick up the car, you'll be offered the chance to "buy down" the deductible to zero (for an additional $10-30/day; this is sometimes called "super CDW" or "zero-deductible coverage").

If you opt for credit-card coverage, there's a catch. You'll technically have to decline all coverage offered by the car-rental company, which means they can place a hold on your card for up to the full value of the car. In case of damage, it can be time-consuming to resolve the charges with your credit-card company. Before you decide on this option, quiz your credit-card company about how it works.

For more on car-rental insurance, see www.ricksteves.com/cdw.

Theft Insurance: Note that theft insurance (separate from CDW insurance) is mandatory in Italy. The insurance usually costs about $15-20 a day, payable when you pick up the car.

Leasing

For trips of three weeks or more, consider leasing (which automatically includes zero-deductible collision and theft insurance). By technically buying and then selling back the car, you save lots of money on tax and insurance. Leasing provides you a brand-new car with unlimited mileage and a 24-hour emergency assistance program. You can lease for as little as 21 days to as long as five and a half months. Car leases must be arranged from the US. Two of many companies offering affordable lease packages are Europe by Car (www.europebycar.com) and Auto Europe (www.autoeurope.com).

Navigation Options

If you'll be navigating using your phone or a GPS unit from home, remember to bring a car charger and device mount.

Your Mobile Device: The mapping app on your mobile phone works fine for navigation in Europe, but for real-time turn-by-turn directions and traffic updates, you'll generally need Internet access. And driving all day while online can be very expensive. Helpful exceptions are Google Maps, Here WeGo, and Navmii, which provide turn-by-turn voice directions and recalibrate even when they're offline.

Download your map before you head out—it's smart to select a large region. Then turn off your cellular connection so you're not charged for data roaming. Call up the map, enter your destination, and you're on your way. View maps in standard view (not satellite view) to limit data demands.

GPS Devices: If you prefer the convenience of a dedicated GPS unit, consider renting one with your car ($10-30/day). These units offer real-time turn-by-turn directions and traffic without the data requirements of an app. Note that the unit may only come loaded with maps for its home country; if you need additional maps, ask. Also make sure your device's language is set to English before you drive off.

A less-expensive option is to bring a GPS device from home. Be aware that you'll need to buy and download European maps before your trip.

Maps and Atlases: Even when navigating primarily with a mobile app or GPS, I always make it a point to have a paper map. It's invaluable for getting the big picture, understanding alternate routes, and filling in when my phone runs out of juice. The free maps you get from your car-rental company usually don't have enough detail. It's smart to buy a better map before you go, or pick one up at a European gas station, bookshop, newsstand, or tourist shop.

DRIVING

Driving in Italy can be scary—a video game for keeps, and you only get one quarter. Italian drivers can be aggressive. They drive fast

and tailgate as if it were required. They pass where Americans are taught not to—on blind corners and just before tunnels. Roads have narrow shoulders or none at all. Driving in the countryside is less stressful than driving through urban areas or on busy highways, but stay alert. On one-lane roads, larger vehicles have the right-of-way. If you're on a truckers' route, stifle your Good Samaritan impulse when you see provocatively dressed women standing by camper-vans at the side of the road; they're not having car trouble. (For more on driving in Tuscany, see page 565.)

Road Rules: Stay out of restricted traffic zones or you'll risk huge fines. Car traffic is restricted in many city centers. Don't drive or park in any area that has a sign reading *Zona Traffico Limitato* (*ZTL*, often shown above a red circle—see image). If you do, your license plate will likely be photographed and a hefty (€80-plus)

PRACTICALITIES

Driving in Tuscany

To Venice

To Milan

EMILIA - ROMAGNA

ITALY

100 Miles

To Cinque Terre
(La Spezia)

50m · 1h

190m · 3.5h

160m · 3.5h

20 Kilometers

20 Miles

50m · 1h

50m · 1h

Lucca

20m · .5h

Pisa

70m · 1.25h
(via FiPiLi)

Florence

LE
MARCHE

70m · 1.5h

15m · .5h

60m · 1.25h

55m · 1.5h

40m · .75h
(via Superstrada)

45m · 1h

75m · 1.5h
(via A-1)

Livorno

San
Gimignano

45m · 2h
(via S-222)

T   U   S   C   A   N   Y

20m · .5h

30m · .75h

Cortona

Volterra

Siena

45m · 1h

40m · 1h

To
Assisi

25m · .75h

30m · .75h

50m · 1h

40m · 1.5h
(via S-438)

10m · .25h

20m · .75h

30m · .75h

40m · 1h

Chiusi

San Galgano
Monastery

55m · 1.5h

15m · .5h

Pienza

15m · .5h

Monte-
pulciano

UMBRIA

Montalcino

To Assisi

Mediterranean
Sea

210m · 4h

60m · 1.5h

35m · 1h

60m · 1.5h

Orvieto

m = miles   h = hours
Note: Your times may
vary based on traffic,
construction, and
road conditions.

Bagnoregio
(Civita)

15m · .5h

75m · 1.5h

To Rome

To
Rome

L A Z I O

ticket mailed to your home without your ever having met a cop. Bumbling in and out of these zones can net you multiple fines. If your hotel is within a restricted area, it's best to ask your hotelier to direct you to parking outside the zone. (Although your hotelier can register your car as an authorized vehicle permitted to enter the zone, this usually isn't worth the hassle.) If you get a ticket, it could take months to show up (for specifics relating to Tuscany, see www. bella-toscana.com/traffic_violations_italy.htm).

Be aware of typical European road rules; for example, many countries require headlights to be turned on at all times, and nearly all forbid talking on a mobile phone without a hands-free headset. Seatbelts are mandatory, and children under age 12 must ride in child-safety or booster seats. In Europe, you're not allowed to turn right on a red light, unless there is a sign or signal specifically authorizing it, and on expressways it's illegal to pass drivers on the right. Ask your car-rental company about these rules, or check the US State Department website (www.travel.state.gov, search for your country in the "Learn about your destination" box, then click on "Travel and Transportation").

Drive carefully: Italians are aggressive drivers. Even worse, motor scooters are very popular, and scooter drivers often see themselves as exempt from rules that apply to automobiles.

Tolls: Italy's freeway system, the autostrada, is as good as our interstate system, but you'll pay a toll (for costs, use the trip-planning tool at www.autostrade.it or search "European Tolls" on www.theaa.com). When approaching a tollbooth, skip lanes marked *Telepass;* for an attended booth, choose a lane with a sign that shows a hand.

While I favor the freeways because I feel they're safer and less nerve-racking than smaller roads, savvy local drivers know which toll-free *superstrada*s are actually faster and more direct than the autostrada (e.g., Florence to Pisa). In some cases, if you have some time to spare, scenic smaller roads can be worth the extra hassle—for example, the super-scenic S-222, which runs through the heart of the Chianti region (connecting Florence and Siena); or the SR2-south from Siena into the heart of Tuscany (en route to Montepulciano, Orvieto, and Rome).

Fuel: Fuel is expensive—often about $8.50 per gallon. Diesel cars are more common in Europe than back home, so be sure you know what type of fuel your car takes before you fill up. Diesel costs less, about $6 per gallon. Gas pumps are color-coded: green for unleaded *(senza piombo)*, black for diesel *(gasolio)*. Autostrada rest stops are self-service stations open daily without a siesta break. Many 24-hour stations are entirely automated. Small-town stations are usually cheaper and offer full service but shorter hours.

Maps and Signage: A big, detailed regional road map (buy one at a newsstand, gas station, or bookstore) and a semiskilled navigator are essential. Learn the universal road signs (see illustration). Although roads are numbered on maps, actual road signs give just a city name (for

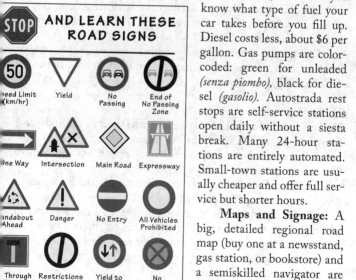

STOP AND LEARN THESE ROAD SIGNS

Speed Limit (km/hr) · Yield · No Passing · End of No Passing Zone

One Way · Intersection · Main Road · Expressway

Roundabout Ahead · Danger · No Entry · All Vehicles Prohibited

Through Road · Restrictions No Longer Apply · Yield to Oncoming Traffic · No Stopping

Parking · No Parking · Customs or Toll Road · Peace

PRACTICALITIES

example, if you were heading west out of Montepulciano, the map would be marked "route SP-146"—but you'd follow signs to Pienza, the next town along this road). The signs are inconsistent: They may direct you to the nearest big city or simply the next town along the route.

Theft: Cars are routinely vandalized and stolen. Thieves easily recognize rental cars and assume they are filled with a tourist's gear. Be sure all of your valuables are out of sight and locked in the trunk, or even better, with you or in your room.

Parking: White lines generally mean parking is free. Yellow lines mean that parking is reserved for residents only (who have permits). Blue lines mean you'll have to pay—usually around €1.50 per hour (use machine, leave time-stamped receipt on dashboard). You'll usually pay at a centrally located pay-and-display machine, then put the receipt in your windshield. Study the signs. Often the free zones have a 30- or 60-minute time limit. Signs showing a street cleaner and a day of the week indicate which day the street is cleaned; there's a €100 tow-fee incentive to learn the days of the week in Italian.

Zona disco has nothing to do with dancing. Italian cars come equipped with a time disc (a cardboard clock), which you can use in a *zona disco*—set the clock to your arrival time and leave it on the dashboard. (If your rental car doesn't come with a *disco*, pick one up at a tobacco shop or just write your arrival time on a piece of paper and place it on the dashboard.)

Garages are safe, save time, and help you avoid the stress of parking tickets. Take the parking voucher with you to pay the cashier before you leave.

FLIGHTS

The best comparison search engine for both international and intra-European flights is Kayak.com. An alternative is Google Flights, which has an easy-to-use system to track prices. For inexpensive flights within Europe, try Skyscanner.com.

Flying to Europe: Start looking for international flights about four to six months before your trip, especially for peak-season travel. Off-season tickets can usually be purchased a month or so in advance. Depending on your itinerary, it can be efficient to fly into one city and out of another. If your flight requires a connection in Europe, see my hints on navigating Europe's top hub airports at www.ricksteves.com/hub-airports.

Flying Within Europe: If you're considering a train ride that's more than five hours long, a flight may save you both time and money. When comparing your options, factor in the time it takes to get to the airport and how early you'll need to arrive to check in.

Well-known cheapo airlines include Easyjet and Ryanair.

Budget airlines out of Florence (airport code: FLR) include Belle Air (www.belleair.it), Darwin Airline (www.darwinairline.com), and Vueling (www.vueling.com). Cheaper airlines use Pisa (airport code: PSA). Airport websites may list small airlines that serve your destination.

Remember that Florence is well-connected by train to plenty of airports—giving you more options—including Parma, Perugia, Bologna, and Rimini (which all have budget flights available). Rome, Milan, and Venice are only a two-hour train ride away.

Be aware of the potential drawbacks of flying with a discount airline: nonrefundable and nonchangeable tickets, minimal or nonexistent customer service, pricey and time-consuming treks to secondary airports, and stingy baggage allowances with steep overage fees. If you're traveling with lots of luggage, a cheap flight can quickly become a bad deal. To avoid unpleasant surprises, read the small print before you book.

These days you can also fly within Europe on major airlines affordably—and without all the aggressive restrictions—for around $100 a flight.

Flying to the US and Canada: Because security is extra tight for flights to the US, be sure to give yourself plenty of time at the airport. It's also important to charge your electronic devices before you board because security checks may require you to turn them on (see www.tsa.gov for the latest rules).

Resources from Rick Steves

Begin your trip at www.ricksteves.com: My mobile-friendly **website** is *the* place to explore Europe. You'll find thousands of fun articles, videos, photos, and radio interviews organized by country; a wealth of money-saving tips for planning your dream trip; monthly travel news dispatches; a video library of my travel talks; my travel blog; and my latest guidebook updates (www.ricksteves.com/update).

Our **Travel Forum** is an immense yet well-groomed collection of message boards where our travel-savvy community answers questions and shares their personal travel experiences—and our well-traveled staff chimes in when they can be helpful (www.ricksteves.com/forums).

Our **online Travel Store** offers travel bags and accessories that I've designed specifically to help you travel smarter and lighter. These include my popular bags (rolling carry-on and backpack versions, which I helped design...and live out of four months a year), money belts, totes, toiletries kits, adapters, other accessories, and a wide selection of guidebooks and planning maps.

Choosing the right **rail pass** for your trip—amid hundreds of options—can drive you nutty. Our website will help you find the perfect fit for your itinerary and your budget: We offer easy, one-stop shopping for rail passes, seat reservations, and point-to-point tickets (www.ricksteves.com/rail).

Small Group Tours: Want to travel with greater efficiency and less stress? We offer more than 40 itineraries and have over 900 departures annually reaching the best destinations in this book... and beyond. Our Italy tours include "The Best of" in 17 days, Village Italy in 14 days, South Italy in 13 days, Sicily in 11 days, Venice-Florence-Rome in 10 days, the Heart of Italy in 9 days, a My Way: Italy "unguided" tour in 13 days, and a week-long Rome tour. You'll enjoy great guides, a fun bunch of travel partners (with small groups of 24 to 28 travelers), and plenty of room to spread out in a big, comfy bus when touring between towns. You'll find European adventures to fit every vacation length. For all the details, and to get our Tour Catalog, visit www.ricksteves.com/tour or call us at 425/608-4217.

Books: *Rick Steves Florence & Tuscany* is one of many books in my series on European travel, which includes country guidebooks, city guidebooks (Venice, Rome, Paris, London, etc.), Snapshot guidebooks (excerpted chapters from my country guides), Pocket guidebooks (full-color little books on big cities, including Florence), "Best Of" guidebooks (condensed country guides in a full-color, easy-to-scan format), and my budget-travel skills handbook, *Rick Steves Europe Through the Back Door*. Most of my titles are available as ebooks.

My phrase books—for Italian, French, German, Spanish, and Portuguese—are practical and budget-oriented. My other books include *Europe 101* (a crash course on art and history designed for travelers); *Mediterranean Cruise Ports* and *Northern European Cruise Ports* (how to make the most of your time in port); and *Travel as a Political Act* (a travelogue sprinkled with tips for bringing home a global perspective). A more complete list of my titles appears near the end of this book.

TV Shows: My public television series, *Rick Steves' Europe*, covers Europe from top to bottom with over 100 half-hour episodes, and we're working on new shows every year. We have 20 episodes on Italy—that's 10 hours of vivid video coverage of one of my favorite countries. To watch full episodes online for free, visit www.ricksteves.com/tv.

Travel Talks on Video: You can raise your travel I.Q. with video versions of our popular classes (including talks on travel skills, packing smart, cruising, tech for travelers, European art for travelers, travel as a political act, and individual talks covering most European countries). See www.ricksteves.com/travel-talks.

Radio: My weekly public radio show, *Travel with Rick Steves,* features interviews with travel experts from around the world. It airs on 400 public radio stations across the US, and you can also listen to it as a podcast on iTunes, iHeartRadio, Stitcher, Tune In, and other platforms. A complete archive of programs (over 400 in all) is available at www.soundcloud.com/rick-steves.

Audio Tours on My Free App: I've also produced dozens of free, self-guided audio tours of the top sights in Europe, including sights in Florence. My audio tours and other audio content are available for free through my **Rick Steves Audio Europe app,** an extensive online library organized into handy geographic playlists. For more on my app, see page 8.

APPENDIX

Useful Contacts

Emergency Needs
Police, Fire, and Ambulance (Europe-wide in English): 112
Police: 113
Ambulance: 118
Road Service: 116

Embassies and Consulates
US Embassy: 24-hour emergency line—tel. 06-46741, nonemergency—tel. 06-4674-2420 (by appointment only, Via Vittorio Veneto 121, Rome, http://italy.usembassy.gov)
US Consulate: Tel. 055-266-951 (Lungarno Vespucci 38, Florence, http://florence.usconsulate.gov)
Canadian Embassy: Tel. 06-854-442-911 (Via Zara 30, Rome, www.italy.gc.ca)

Holidays and Festivals

This list includes selected festivals in Florence, Siena, Pisa, and Lucca, plus national holidays observed throughout Italy. Many sights and banks close on national holidays—keep this in mind when planning your itinerary. Before planning a trip around a festival, verify the dates with the festival website, the tourist office, or my "Upcoming Holidays and Festivals in Italy" web page (www.ricksteves.com/europe/festivals).

In Florence, hotels get booked up on Easter weekend (from Good Friday through Monday), April 25 (Liberation Day), May 1 (Labor Day), May 25 (Ascension Day), June 24 (St. John the Baptist festival), November 1 (All Saints' Day), and on Fridays and Saturdays year-round. Some hotels require you to book the full three-day weekend around a holiday.

Jan	Florence fashion convention
Jan 1	New Year's Day
Jan 6	Epiphany
Early Feb	Carnival celebrations/Mardi Gras in Florence (costumed parades, street water fights, jousting competitions)
March/April	Easter weekend (Good Friday-Easter Monday): March 30-April 1, 2018; April 19-21, 2019. Explosion of the Cart (Scoppio del Carro) in Florence (fireworks, bonfire in wooden cart)
April 25	Italian Liberation Day
April or May	Gelato Festival, Florence
May	Ascension Day: May 10, 2018; May 30, 2019. Cricket Festival in Florence (music, entertainment, food, crickets sold in cages)
May 1	Labor Day
June	Florence fashion convention
June	Annual Flower Display in Florence (carpet of flowers on Piazza della Signoria)
June 2	Anniversary of the Republic
June 16-17	Festival of St. Ranieri in Pisa
June 24	Festival of St. John the Baptist in Florence (parades, dances, boat races, fireworks). Also Calcio Storico (costumed soccer game on Florence's Piazza Santa Croce)
June-July	Florence Dance Festival (www.florencedancefestival.org)
Late June-early Sept	Florence's annual outdoor cinema season (contemporary films)

July 2	Palio horse race in Siena
Aug 15	Assumption of Mary (Ferragosto)
Aug 16	Palio horse race in Siena
Early Sept	Festa della Rificolona in Florence (children's procession with lanterns, street performances, parade)
Sept 13-14	Volto Santo in Lucca (procession and fair)
Sept-Oct	Musica dei Popoli Festival in Florence (ethnic and folk music and dances)
Nov 1	All Saints' Day
Dec 8	Feast of the Immaculate Conception
Dec 25	Christmas
Dec 26	St. Stephen's Day

APPENDIX

Books and Films

To learn more about Italy past and present, and specifically Florence, check out a few of these books and films. For kids' recommendations, see page 306.

NONFICTION

The Architecture of the Italian Renaissance (Peter Murray, 1969). Heavily illustrated, this classic presents the architectural life of Italy from the 13th through the 16th century.

The City of Florence (R. W. B. Lewis, 1994). The author's 50-year love affair with Florence started in the chaos of World War II; this book is both a personal biography and an informal history of the city.

Dark Water (Robert Clark, 2008). Florentines race to save seven centuries of human achievement in the face of the city's destructive 1966 floods.

Fortune Is a River (Roger D. Masters, 1998). Two geniuses of the Renaissance—Niccolo Machiavelli and Leonardo da Vinci—conspire to reroute the Arno River (unsuccessfully, thankfully).

The Hills of Tuscany (Ferenc Máté, 1998). After traveling all over the globe, a writer and his wife try to settle down in the Tuscan countryside.

The House of Medici (Christopher Hibbert, 1974). Florence's first family of the Renaissance included power-hungry bankers, merchants, popes, art patrons—and two queens of France.

Italian Renaissance Art (Laurie Schneider Adams, 2001). In one of the definitive works on this pivotal period, Adams focuses on the most important and innovative artists and their best works.

The Lives of the Artists (Giorgio Vasari, 1550). The man who invented the term "Renaissance" offers anecdote-filled biographies of his era's greatest artists, some of whom he knew personally.

Looking at Painting in Florence, A Learner's Handbook (Richard Peterson, 2014). An illustrated interpretive guide to the city's art masterpieces.

The Prince (Niccolò Machiavelli, 1532). The original "how-to" for gaining and maintaining political power, still chillingly relevant after 500 years.

A Small Place in Italy (Eric Newby, 1994). A young American couple tries to renovate a Tuscan farmhouse in the late 1960s.

The Stones of Florence (Mary McCarthy, 1956). McCarthy applies wit and keen observation to produce a quirky, impressionistic investigation of Florence and its history.

A Tuscan Childhood (Kinta Beevor, 1993). The daughter of a bohemian painter reminisces about growing up in prewar Tuscany among writers like Aldous Huxley and D. H. Lawrence.

Under the Tuscan Sun (Frances Mayes, 1996). Mayes' best seller describes living la dolce vita in the Tuscan countryside (and is better than the movie of the same name).

FICTION

The Agony and the Ecstasy (Irving Stone, 1958). This fictional biography of Michelangelo brings to life the great artist's dramatic passions and furies (also a 1965 movie starring Charlton Heston).

Birth of Venus (Sarah Dunant, 2003). Dunant follows the life of a Florentine girl who develops feelings for the boy hired to paint the walls of the family's chapel.

Death in the Mountains: The True Story of a Tuscan Murder (Lisa Clifford, 2008). Clifford explores the region's humble roots as she re-creates life in the countryside before Tuscany became glamorous.

The Decameron (Giovanni Boccaccio, 1348). Boccaccio's collection of 100 hilarious, often bawdy tales is a masterpiece of Italian literature and inspired Chaucer, Keats, and Shakespeare.

Divine Comedy (Dante Alighieri, 1321). Dante's epic poem—a journey through hell, purgatory, and paradise—is one of the world's greatest works of literature.

Galileo's Daughter (Dava Sobel, 1999). Sobel's historical memoir centers on Galileo's correspondence with his oldest daughter and confidante.

The Light in the Piazza (Elizabeth Spencer, 1960). A mother and daughter are intoxicated by the beauty of 1950s Florence (also a 1962 movie and an award-winning Broadway musical).

Murder of a Medici Princess (Caroline P. Murphy, 2008). This historical novel recounts the life and death of Isabella de Medici, daughter of the duke who ruled Renaissance Florence and Tuscany.

Romola (George Eliot, 1863). In this historical novel set in Renaissance Florence, Eliot depicts the awakening of a young woman in the time of the Medicis and Savonarola.

A Room with a View (E. M. Forster, 1908). A young Englishwoman visiting Florence finds a socially unsuitable replacement for her snobby fiancé (also a 1985 movie starring Helena Bonham Carter).

The Sixteen Pleasures (Robert Hellenga, 1994). Set during the 1966 floods in Florence, a young student discovers an erotic manuscript banned by the pope and lost for centuries.

FILM AND TV

The Best of Youth (2003). Beginning in the turbulent 1960s, this award-winning miniseries follows the dramatic ups and downs in the lives of two brothers over four decades.

Brother Sun, Sister Moon (1972). Franco Zeffirelli presents a sensitive account of the life of St. Francis of Assisi, including his friendship with St. Clare.

Medici: Godfathers of the Renaissance (2004). This PBS miniseries reveals the good, the bad, and the ugly about Florence's first family.

Tea with Mussolini (1999). Franco Zeffirelli's look at prewar Florence involves proper English ladies, a rich American Jew, and the son of a local businessman—all caught in the rise of fascism.

Up at the Villa (2000). Based on a W. Somerset Maugham novella, the film follows a wealthy young Englishwoman in 1930s Florence who is brutally confronted by the consequences of her whimsy.

Where Angels Fear to Tread (1991). In this adaptation of an E. M. Forster novel, a rich Edwardian widow impulsively marries a poor Tuscan but dies in childbirth, prompting a custody battle.

Conversions and Climate

Numbers and Stumblers

- Europeans write a few of their numbers differently than we do. 1 = 1, 4 = 4, 7 = 7.
- In Europe, dates appear as day/month/year, so Christmas 2019 is 25/12/19.
- Commas are decimal points, and decimals are commas. A dollar and a half is $1,50, one thousand is 1.000, and there are 5.280 feet in a mile.
- When counting with fingers, start with your thumb. If you hold up your first finger to request one item, you'll probably get two.
- What Americans call the second floor of a building is the first floor in Europe.
- On escalators and moving sidewalks, Europeans keep the left "lane" open for passing. Keep to the right.

Metric Conversions

A **kilogram** equals 1,000 grams (about 2.2 pounds). One hundred **grams** (a common unit at markets) is about a quarter-pound. One **liter** is about a quart, or almost four to a gallon.

A **kilometer** is six-tenths of a mile. To convert kilometers to miles, cut the kilometers in half and add back 10 percent of the original (120 km: 60 + 12 = 72 miles). One **meter** is 39 inches—just over a yard.

1 foot = 0.3 meter	1 square yard = 0.8 square meter
1 yard = 0.9 meter	1 square mile = 2.6 square kilometers
1 mile = 1.6 kilometers	1 ounce = 28 grams
1 centimeter = 0.4 inch	1 quart = 0.95 liter
1 meter = 39.4 inches	1 kilogram = 2.2 pounds
1 kilometer = 0.62 mile	32°F = 0°C

Roman Numerals

In the US, you'll see Roman numerals—which originated in ancient Rome—used for copyright dates, clocks, and the Super Bowl. In Italy, you're likely to observe these numbers chiseled on statues and buildings. If you want to do some numeric detective work, here's how: In Roman numerals, as in ours, the highest numbers (thousands, hundreds) come first, followed by smaller numbers. Many numbers are made by combining numerals into sets: V=5, so VIII=8 (5 plus 3). Roman numerals follow a subtraction principle for multiples of four (4, 40, 400, etc.) and nine (9, 90, 900, etc.); the number four, for example, is written as IV (1 subtracted from 5), rather than IIII. The number nine is IX (1 subtracted from 10).

Big numbers such as dates can look daunting at first. The easiest way to handle them is to read the numbers in discrete chunks. For example, Michelangelo was born in MCDLXXV. Break it down: M (1,000) + CD (100 subtracted from 500, so 400) + LXX (50 + 10 + 10, or 70) + V (5)=1475. It was a very good year.

M = 1000	XL = 40
CM = 900	X = 10
D = 500	IX = 9
CD = 400	V = 5
C = 100	IV = 4
XC = 90	I = duh
L = 50	

Clothing Sizes

When shopping for clothing, use these US-to-European comparisons as general guidelines (but note that no conversion is perfect).

Women: For pants and dresses, add 36 in Italy (US 10 = Italian 46). For blouses and sweaters, add 8 for most of Europe (US 32 = European 40). For shoes, add 30-31 (US 7 = European 37/38).

Men: For shirts, multiply by 2 and add about 8 (US 15 = European 38). For jackets and suits, add 10. For shoes, add 32-34.

Children: Clothing is sized by height—in centimeters (2.5 inches = 1 cm), so a US size 8 roughly equates to 132-140. For shoes up to size 13, add 16-18, and for sizes 1 and up, add 30-32.

Florence's Climate

First line, average daily high; second line, average daily low; third line, average days without rain. For more detailed weather statistics for destinations in this book (as well as the rest of the world), check www.wunderground.com.

J	F	M	A	M	J	J	A	S	O	N	D
54°	54°	59°	66°	75°	82°	88°	88°	81°	70°	59°	52°
37°	39°	43°	48°	55°	63°	66°	64°	61°	54°	45°	39°
25	21	24	23	24	23	27	26	22	22	21	23

Fahrenheit and Celsius Conversion

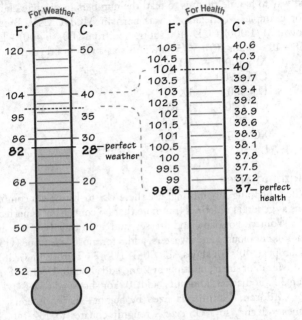

Europe takes its temperature using the Celsius scale, while we opt for Fahrenheit. For a rough conversion from Celsius to Fahrenheit, double the number and add 30. For weather, remember that 28°C is 82°F—perfect. For health, 37°C is just right. At a launderette, 30°C is cold, 40°C is warm (usually the default setting), 60°C is hot, and 95°C is boiling. Your air-conditioner should be set at about 20°C.

Packing Checklist

Whether you're traveling for five days or five weeks, you won't need more than this. Pack light to enjoy the sweet freedom of true mobility.

Clothing

- ❑ 5 shirts: long- & short-sleeve
- ❑ 2 pairs pants (or skirts/capris)
- ❑ 1 pair shorts
- ❑ 5 pairs underwear & socks
- ❑ 1 pair walking shoes
- ❑ Sweater or warm layer
- ❑ Rainproof jacket with hood
- ❑ Tie, scarf, belt, and/or hat
- ❑ Swimsuit
- ❑ Sleepwear/loungewear

Money

- ❑ Debit card(s)
- ❑ Credit card(s)
- ❑ Hard cash ($100-200 in US dollars)
- ❑ Money belt

Documents

- ❑ Passport
- ❑ Tickets & confirmations: flights, hotels, trains, rail pass, car rental, sight entries
- ❑ Driver's license
- ❑ Student ID, hostel card, etc.
- ❑ Photocopies of important documents
- ❑ Insurance details
- ❑ Guidebooks & maps
- ❑ Notepad & pen
- ❑ Journal

Toiletries Kit

- ❑ Basics: soap, shampoo, toothbrush, toothpaste, floss, deodorant, sunscreen, brush/comb, etc.
- ❑ Medicines & vitamins
- ❑ First-aid kit
- ❑ Glasses/contacts/sunglasses

- ❑ Sewing kit
- ❑ Packet of tissues (for WC)
- ❑ Earplugs

Electronics

- ❑ Mobile phone
- ❑ Camera & related gear
- ❑ Tablet/ebook reader/media player
- ❑ Laptop & flash drive
- ❑ Headphones
- ❑ Chargers & batteries
- ❑ Smartphone car charger & mount (or GPS device)
- ❑ Plug adapters

Miscellaneous

- ❑ Daypack
- ❑ Sealable plastic baggies
- ❑ Laundry supplies: soap, laundry bag, clothesline, spot remover
- ❑ Small umbrella
- ❑ Travel alarm/watch

Optional Extras

- ❑ Second pair of shoes (flip-flops, sandals, tennis shoes, boots)
- ❑ Travel hairdryer
- ❑ Picnic supplies
- ❑ Water bottle
- ❑ Fold-up tote bag
- ❑ Small flashlight
- ❑ Mini binoculars
- ❑ Small towel or washcloth
- ❑ Inflatable pillow/neck rest
- ❑ Tiny lock
- ❑ Address list (to mail postcards)
- ❑ Extra passport photos

Italian Survival Phrases

English	Italian	Pronunciation
Good day.	*Buon giorno.*	bwohn **jor**-noh
Do you speak English?	*Parla inglese?*	**par**-lah een-**gleh**-zay
Yes. / No.	*Sì. / No.*	see / noh
I (don't) understand.	*(Non) capisco.*	(nohn) kah-**pees**-koh
Please.	*Per favore.*	pehr fah-**voh**-ray
Thank you.	*Grazie.*	**graht**-see-ay
You're welcome.	*Prego.*	**preh**-go
I'm sorry.	*Mi dispiace.*	mee dee-spee-**ah**-chay
Excuse me.	*Mi scusi.*	mee **skoo**-zee
(No) problem.	*(Non) c'è un problema.*	(nohn) cheh oon proh-**bleh**-mah
Good.	*Va bene.*	vah **beh**-nay
Goodbye.	*Arrivederci.*	ah-ree-veh-**dehr**-chee
one / two	*uno / due*	**oo**-noh / **doo**-ay
three / four	*tre / quattro*	tray / **kwah**-troh
five / six	*cinque / sei*	**cheeng**-kway / **seh**-ee
seven / eight	*sette / otto*	**seh**-tay / **oh**-toh
nine / ten	*nove / dieci*	**noh**-vay / dee-**ay**-chee
How much is it?	*Quanto costa?*	**kwahn**-toh **koh**-stah
Write it?	*Me lo scrive?*	may loh **skree**-vay
Is it free?	*È gratis?*	eh **grah**-tees
Is it included?	*È incluso?*	eh een-**kloo**-zoh
Where can I buy / find...?	*Dove posso comprare / trovare...?*	**doh**-vay **poh**-soh kohm-**prah**-ray / troh-**vah**-ray
I'd like / We'd like...	*Vorrei / Vorremmo...*	voh-**reh**-ee / voh-**reh**-moh
...a room.	*...una camera.*	**oo**-nah **kah**-meh-rah
...a ticket to ____.	*...un biglietto per ____.*	oon beel-**yeh**-toh pehr ____
Is it possible?	*È possibile?*	eh poh-**see**-bee-lay
Where is...?	*Dov'è...?*	doh-**veh**
...the train station	*...la stazione*	lah staht-see-**oh**-nay
...the bus station	*...la stazione degli autobus*	lah staht-see-**oh**-nay **dehl**-yee ow-toh-boos
...tourist information	*...informazioni per turisti*	een-for-maht-see-**oh**-nee pehr too-**ree**-stee
...the toilet	*...la toilette*	lah twah-**leh**-tay
men	*uomini / signori*	**woh**-mee-nee / seen-**yoh**-ree
women	*donne / signore*	**doh**-nay / seen-**yoh**-ray
left / right	*sinistra / destra*	see-**nee**-strah / **deh**-strah
straight	*sempre dritto*	**sehm**-pray **dree**-toh
What time does this open / close?	*A che ora apre / chiude?*	ah kay **oh**-rah ah-**pray** / kee-**oo**-day
At what time?	*A che ora?*	ah kay **oh**-rah
Just a moment.	*Un momento.*	oon moh-**mehn**-toh
now / soon / later	*adesso / presto / tardi*	ah-**deh**-soh / **preh**-stoh / **tar**-dee
today / tomorrow	*oggi / domani*	**oh**-jee / doh-**mah**-nee

APPENDIX

In an Italian Restaurant

English	Italian	Pronunciation
I'd like...	Vorrei...	voh-**reh**-ee
We'd like...	Vorremmo...	vor-**reh**-moh
...to reserve...	...prenotare...	preh-noh-**tah**-ray
...a table for one / two.	...un tavolo per uno / due.	oon **tah**-voh-loh pehr **oo**-noh / **doo**-ay
Is this seat free?	È libero questo posto?	eh **lee**-beh-roh **kweh**-stoh **poh**-stoh
The menu (in English), please.	Il menù (in inglese), per favore.	eel meh-**noo** (een een-**gleh**-zay) pehr fah-**voh**-ray
service (not) included	servizio (non) incluso	sehr-**veet**-see-oh (nohn) een-**kloo**-zoh
cover charge	pane e coperto	**pah**-nay ay koh-**pehr**-toh
to go	da portar via	dah **por**-tar **vee**-ah
with / without	con / senza	kohn / **sehnt**-sah
and / or	e / o	ay / oh
menu (of the day)	menù (del giorno)	meh-**noo** (dehl **jor**-noh)
specialty of the house	specialità della casa	speh-chah-lee-**tah deh**-lah **kah**-zah
first course (pasta, soup)	primo piatto	**pree**-moh pee-**ah**-toh
main course (meat, fish)	secondo piatto	seh-**kohn**-doh pee-**ah**-toh
side dishes	contorni	kohn-**tor**-nee
bread	pane	**pah**-nay
cheese	formaggio	for-**mah**-joh
sandwich	panino	pah-**nee**-noh
soup	zuppa	**tsoo**-pah
salad	insalata	een-sah-**lah**-tah
meat	carne	**kar**-nay
chicken	pollo	**poh**-loh
fish	pesce	**peh**-shay
seafood	frutti di mare	**froo**-tee dee **mah**-ray
fruit / vegetables	frutta / legumi	**froo**-tah / lay-**goo**-mee
dessert	dolce	**dohl**-chay
tap water	acqua del rubinetto	**ah**-kwah dehl roo-bee-**neh**-toh
mineral water	acqua minerale	**ah**-kwah mee-neh-**rah**-lay
milk	latte	**lah**-tay
(orange) juice	succo (d'arancia)	**soo**-koh (dah-**rahn**-chah)
coffee / tea	caffè / tè	kah-**feh** / teh
wine	vino	**vee**-noh
red / white	rosso / bianco	**roh**-soh / bee-**ahn**-koh
glass / bottle	bicchiere / bottiglia	bee-kee-**eh**-ray / boh-**teel**-yah
beer	birra	**bee**-rah
Cheers!	Cin cin!	cheen cheen
More. / Another.	Di più. / Un altro.	dee pew / oon **ahl**-troh
The same.	Lo stesso.	loh **steh**-soh
The bill, please.	Il conto, per favore.	eel **kohn**-toh pehr fah-**voh**-ray
Do you accept credit cards?	Accettate carte di credito?	ah-cheh-**tah**-tay **kar**-tay dee **kreh**-dee-toh
tip	mancia	**mahn**-chah
Delicious!	Delizioso!	day-leet-see-**oh**-zoh

For more user-friendly Italian phrases, check out *Rick Steves' Italian Phrase Book & Dictionary* or *Rick Steves' French, Italian, & German Phrase Book*.

INDEX

A

Abbey of Monte Oliveto Maggiore: 391, 406, 410–419; background, 411; general info, 355, 410; self-guided tour, 411–419

Abbey of Sant'Antimo: 527, 577, 579–580

Abraham, Clet: 226, 303, 319–320

Accademia: 41–42, 93–103; *David*, 41, 94–97, 100–101; eating near, 94, 293–295; gelato near, 297; general info, 32, 42, 93–94; guided tours, 26; map, 95; reservations, 30, 34–35, 38, 93; self-guided tour, 94–103; sleeping near, 269, 272

Accademia Musicale Chigiana (Siena): 360

Accommodations: *See Agriturismo; Sleeping; and specific destinations*

Adam and Eve Banished from Eden (Masaccio): 230–231

Adam and Eve Tempted by the Serpent (Masalino): 231

Addresseses, locating in Florence: 20

Adoration of the Magi (Botticelli): 114

Adoration of the Magi (da Vinci): 116–117

Adoration of the Magi (Fabriano): 110–111

Agriturismo: 345, 625–626; Crete Senesi, 528–530; near Florence, 280–281; near Montalcino, 530; near Montepulciano, 530; near Pienza, 526–528; near San Gimignano, 517; near Siena, 397; near Volterra, 504

Airfares (airlines): 4, 668–669

Airports: Florence, 339; Pisa, 453–454

Alabaster Museum (Volterra): 493, 494–495

Alabaster Workshop (Volterra): 498

Allegory of Spring (Botticelli): 113–114

Almanac, Florence: 6

Altarpiece of the Linen-Drapers (Fra Angelico): 143

Altesino Winery: 562, 579

Ambulance: 607, 673

American Cemetery and Memorial: 69–70

Amerigo Vespucci Airport: 339

Ammanati, Bartolomeo: 89, 242

Annalena Altarpiece (Fra Angelico): 143–144

Annunciation (da Vinci): 116

Annunciation (Fra Angelico): 147

Annunciation (Martini): 110

Antipasti (appetizers): 290, 630. *See also* Eating

Apartment rentals: 621–624

Aperitivo buffets: 25, 289, 299, 331–332, 401, 502, 634

Apps: 7, 645–646; for children, 307; foodie, 283; maps and navigation, 614; messaging, 648; Rick Steves, 8; sightseeing, 616; sleeping, 617; transit, 22

Aquaflor: 210, 318, 326

Aquinas, Thomas: 145–146, 208

Archaeological museums: Fiesole, 71–72; Siena, 389; Volterra, 499

Archimedes Screw Model: 262

Argenti/Silverworks Museum (Pitti Palace): 252

Armor Museum (Monteriggioni): 520

Arnolfo di Cambio: 37–38, 159, 160, 165, 173, 175, 180; Florence Duomo Museum, 156–158, 163, 169; Santa Croce, 209, 210

Arno River: 12, 13, 91–92, 219, 220, 421, 427; floods, 217; views of, 119, 329

Art: books, 675–676; guided tours, in Florence, 26–27; Mannerism, about, 176; reproductions, shopping for, 320. *See also* Renaissance; *and specific artists and artworks*

Art classes: 26, 310

"Artisan Lane" (Volterra): 487

Art museums: with children, 306, 307–308; daily reminder, 22–23; Firenze Card, 4, 7, 17, 30–31, 34; free Sundays, 13–14, 22, 29; sightseeing tips, 29–31, 34–35, 38, 615–616. *See also specific museums*

Artviva: 26, 302, 310

INDEX

INDEX

MAP INDEX

Explore Europe

At ricksteves.com you can browse through thousands of articles, videos, photos and radio interviews, plus find a wealth of money-saving travel tips for planning your dream trip. And with our mobile-friendly website, you can easily access all this great travel information anywhere you go.

TV Shows

Preview the places you'll visit by watching entire half-hour episodes of Rick Steves' Europe (choose from all 100 shows) on-demand, for free.

your travel dreams into affordable reality

Radio Interviews

Enjoy ready access to Rick's vast library of radio interviews covering travel

tips and cultural insights that relate specifically to your Europe travel plans.

Travel Forums

Learn, ask, share! Our online community of savvy travelers is a great resource

for first-time travelers to Europe, as well as seasoned pros. You'll find forums on each country, plus travel tips and restaurant/hotel reviews. You can even ask one of our well-traveled staff to chime in with an opinion.

Travel News

Subscribe to our free Travel News e-newsletter, and get monthly updates from Rick on what's happening in Europe.

Rick's Free Travel App

Get your FREE **Rick Steves Audio Europe**™ app to enjoy…

- Dozens of self-guided tours of Europe's top museums, sights and historic walks
- Hundreds of tracks filled with cultural insights and sightseeing tips from Rick's radio interviews
- All organized into handy geographic playlists
- For Apple and Android

With Rick whispering in your ear, Europe gets even better.

Find out more at ricksteves.com

Save time and energy

This guidebook is your independent-travel toolkit. But for all it delivers, it's still up to you to devote the time and energy it takes to manage the preparation and logistics that are essential for a happy trip. If that's a hassle, there's a solution.

Rick Steves Tours

A Rick Steves tour takes you to Europe's most interesting places with great

great tours, too!

with minimum stress

guides and small groups of 28 or less. We follow Rick's favorite itineraries, ride in comfy buses, stay in family-run hotels, and bring you intimately close to the Europe you've traveled so far to see. Most importantly, we take away the logistical headaches so you can focus on the fun.

travelers—nearly half of them repeat customers—along with us on four dozen different itineraries, from Ireland to Italy to Athens. Is a Rick Steves tour the right fit for your travel dreams? Find out at ricksteves.com, where you can also request Rick's latest tour catalog. Europe is best experienced with happy travel partners. We hope you can join us.

Join the fun

This year we'll take thousands of free-spirited

See our itineraries at ricksteves.com

A Guide for Every Trip

BEST OF GUIDES

Full color easy-to-scan format, focusing on Europe's most popular destinations and sights.

Best of France
Best of Germany
Best of England
Best of Europe
Best of Ireland
Best of Italy
Best of Spain

COMPREHENSIVE GUIDES

City, country, and regional guide with detailed coverage for a multi-week trip exploring the most iconic sights and venturing off the beaten track.

Amsterdam & the Netherlands
Barcelona
Belgium: Bruges, Brussels, Antwerp & Ghent
Berlin
Budapest
Croatia & Slovenia
Eastern Europe
England
Florence & Tuscany
France
Germany
Great Britain
Greece: Athens & the Peloponn
Iceland
Ireland
Istanbul
Italy
London
Paris
Portugal
Prague & the Czech Republic
Provence & the French Riviera
Rome
Scandinavia
Scotland
Spain
Switzerland
Venice
Vienna, Salzburg & Tirol

THE BEST OF ROME

ome, Italy's capital, is studded with
oman remnants and floodlit-fountain
uares. From the Vatican to the Colos-
um, with crazy traffic in between, Rome
wonderful, huge, and exhausting. The
wds, the heat, and the weighty history

of the Eternal City where Caesars walked
can make tourists wilt. Recharge by taking siestas, gelato breaks, and after-dark
walks, strolling from one atmospheric
square to another in the refreshing evening air.

ired *Pantheon*—which
rgest dome until the
arly 2,000 years old
day over 1,500).

l of Athens in the Vat-
bodies the humanistic
ance.

s gladiators fought
another, entertaining
0.

his Rome *ristorante*.
rds at St. Peter's
rk seriously.
in, toss in a coin

Rick Steves guidebooks are published by Avalon Travel,
an imprint of Perseus Books, a Hachette Book Group co

KET GUIDES

pact, full color city guides with
ssentials for shorter trips.

terdam   Paris
ns   Prague
elona   Rome
nce   Venice
s Cinque Terre Vienna
lon
ch & Salzburg

PSHOT GUIDES

sed single-destination coverage.

que Country: Spain & France
enhagen & the Best of Denmark
in
ovnik
burgh
owns of Central Italy
ow, Warsaw & Gdansk
on
Valley
id & Toledo
n & the Italian Lakes District
es & the Amalfi Coast
hern Ireland
mandy
vay
javik
la, Granada & Southern Spain
etersburg, Helsinki & Tallinn
kholm

CRUISE PORTS GUIDES
Reference for cruise ports of call.

Mediterranean Cruise Ports
Northern European Cruise Ports

Complete your library with...

TRAVEL SKILLS & CULTURE
Study up on travel skills and gain
insight on history and culture.

Europe 101
European Christmas
European Easter
European Festivals
Europe Through the Back Door
Postcards from Europe
Travel as a Political Act

PHRASE BOOKS & DICTIONARIES

French
French, Italian & German
German
Italian
Portuguese
Spanish

PLANNING MAPS

Britain, Ireland & London
Europe
France & Paris
Germany, Austria & Switzerland
Ireland
Italy
Spain & Portugal

eves books are available from your favorite bookseller.
uides are available as ebooks.

Credits

Researcher
To update this book, Rick and Gene relied on research by Sarah Murdoch.

Sarah Murdoch

Sarah trained as an architect, then abandoned her drafting board in 2000 to lead tours and research guidebooks for Rick Steves' Europe. She blogs about her crazy life on adventureswithsarah.net and often writes about her passion for the perfectly packed bag. She lives in Seattle with her husband Patrick and sons Lucca and Nicola.

Avalon Travel
Hachette Book Group
1700 Fourth Street
Berkeley, CA 94710

Printed in Canada by Friesens.
First printing October 2017.

ISBN: 978-1-63121-665-7
17th Edition

For the latest on Rick's lectures, guidebooks, Europe tours, public television series, and public radio show, contact Rick Steves' Europe, 130 Fourth Avenue North, Edmonds, WA 98020, 425/771-8303, www.ricksteves.com, rick@ricksteves.com.

Rick Steves' Europe
Managing Editor: Jennifer Madison Davis
Special Publications Manager: Risa Laib
Assistant Managing Editor: Cathy Lu
Editors: Glenn Eriksen, Tom Griffin, Katherine Gustafson, Suzanne Kotz, Carrie Shepherd
Editorial & Production Assistant: Jessica Shaw
Editorial Intern: Alexandra Ivy
Researcher: Sarah Murdoch
Graphic Content Director: Sandra Hundacker
Maps & Graphics: David C. Hoerlein, Lauren Mills, Mary Rostad

Avalon Travel
Senior Editor and Series Manager: Madhu Prasher
Editor: Jamie Andrade
Associate Editor: Sierra Machado
Editorial Intern: Rachael Sablik
Copy Editor: Maggie Ryan
Proofreader: Jamie Real
Indexer: Stephen Callahan
Cover Design: Kimberly Glyder Design
Maps & Graphics: Kat Bennett

Photo Credits
Front Cover: Val d'Orcia © SOPA/estock Photo
Title Page: Florence couple © Dominic Arizona Bonuccelli
Additional Photography: Dominic Arizona Bonuccelli, Ben Cameron, Rich Earl, Jennifer Hauseman, Cameron Hewitt, David C. Hoerlein, Gene Openshaw, Michael Potter, Robyn Stencil, Rick Steves, Laura VanDeventer, Bruce VanDeventer, Wikimedia Commons (PD-Art/PD-US). Photos are used by permission and are the property of the original copyright owners.

Let's Keep on Travelin'

Your trip doesn't need to end.

Follow Rick on social media!